THE FARAWAY WAR

PERSONAL DIARIES OF THE SECOND WORLD WAR IN ASIA AND THE PACIFIC

RICHARD J. ALDRICH

CORGI BOOKS

THE FARAWAY WAR
A CORGI BOOK: 0552151092
9780552151092

Originally published in Great Britain by Doubleday,
a division of Transworld Publishers

PRINTING HISTORY
Doubleday edition published 2005
Corgi edition published 2006

1 3 5 7 9 10 8 6 4 2

Introduction, commentary and this selection
copyright © Richard J. Aldrich 2005

The right of Richard J. Aldrich to be identified as the author of
this work has been asserted in accordance with sections 77
and 78 of the Copyright Designs and Patents Act 1988.

Condition of Sale
This book is sold subject to the condition that it shall not,
by way of trade or otherwise, be lent, re-sold, hired out or
otherwise circulated in any form of binding or cover other
than that in which it is published and without a similar
condition including this condition being imposed on the
subsequent purchaser.

Set in 9.75/12pt Palatino by
Falcon Oast Graphic Art Ltd.

Corgi Books are published by Transworld Publishers,
61–63 Uxbridge Road, London W5 5SA,
a division of The Random House Group Ltd,
in Australia by Random House Australia (Pty) Ltd,
20 Alfred Street, Milsons Point, Sydney, NSW 2061, Australia,
in New Zealand by Random House New Zealand Ltd,
18 Poland Road, Glenfield, Auckland 10, New Zealand
and in South Africa by Random House (Pty) Ltd,
Isle of Houghton, Corner of Boundary Road & Carse O'Gowrie
Houghton 2198, South Africa.

Printed and bound in Great Britain by
CPI Antony Rowe, Chippenham and Eastbourne

Papers used by Transworld Publishers are natural, recyclable products
made from wood grown in sustainable forests. The manufacturing
processes conform to the environmental regulations of the
country of origin.

FSC
Mixed Sources
Product group from well-managed
forests and other controlled sources

Cert no. SGS-COC-2953
www.fsc.org
© 1996 Forest Stewardship Council

For Libby
(nightwork and overtime)

South Tyneside Libraries

EBO

0130175 6	
Askews & Holts	28-Mar-2011
940.542509	£9.99

CONTENTS

Maps

Acknowledgements

A number of individuals have done much to awaken and sustain a long-standing interest in the war in Asia and the Pacific. I would like to record my debt to Peter Lowe at the University of Manchester, Anthony Short at the University of Aberdeen, the late Ralph Smith at the School of Oriental and African Studies in London, and Anthony Low at the University of Cambridge and Australian National University, Canberra. Their patient guidance has often changed the way I have thought about this conflict. Most importantly, they have often reminded me, gently but persistently, of its complexities and paradoxes, underlining that this war was in fact several different wars, fought by different peoples for quite different reasons.

Many individuals and institutions have offered kind support or advice about obscure locations where diaries might be found. I would particularly like to thank Matthew Aid, Antony Best, Robert Bothwell, Frank Cain, Stephen Connor, Alex Danchev, Peter Dennis, Saki Dockrill, Jonathan Fenby, Irving Finkel, M. R. D. Foot, David and Joan Hamer, E. D. R. Harrison, Eva-Lotta Hedman, Rhodri Jeffreys-Jones, Matthew Jones, David Kahn, Saul Kelly, Sheila Kerr, Yoichi Kibata, Katrina Lee Koo, Scott Lucas, Philip Murphy, Ian Nish, David Painter, Gary Rawnsley, Ming-Yeh Rawnsley, E. Bruce Reynolds, Annie Rigdeon, Aviel Roschwald, Nicholas E. Sarantakes, Bradley F. Smith, Michael Smith, David Stafford, Joe Straczek, Takahiko Tanaka, Hans Van der Ven, Wesley K. Wark, Donald Cameron Watt, Neville Wylie and John W. Young. Responsibility for interpretation and errors, however, remains with the author.

Archivists, librarians and departmental record officers – tireless in their efforts – have been most kind and cannot all be named here. Roderick Suddaby, Stephen Walton and the staff at the Imperial War Museum, Patricia Methven and her team at the Liddell Hart Centre for Military Archives in London, and Piers Brendon and all those at the Churchill

Archives, Cambridge deserve a special mention – as indeed does John E. Taylor in Washington. Several experts, notably David Jolliffe and Matthew Thomson at the Australian War Memorial, offered excellent advice, and their institution should be singled out for special praise on account of its exceptional photographic archive. The staff of the India Office Collections at the British Library, the Special Collections at the School of Oriental and African Studies, and also the Rhodes House Library at the Bodleian in Oxford were most helpful; I would like to express particular gratitude to Lucy McCann at Rhodes House. Historians working at the US Military History Institute at Carlisle Barracks in Pennsylvania and also at the US Navy Yard in Washington saved many long-neglected captured Japanese diaries from obscurity. Librarians at the Library of Congress, the Lauinger Library at Georgetown University and the Hallwood Library at the University of Nottingham were also unfailingly helpful. Many other archives and libraries might be mentioned. Above all, it is the overworked but unfailingly courteous staff of the numerous repositories, often confronted with a slightly irascible researcher, who have facilitated this book.

Significant papers, journals and diaries have been lost to us down the years. Others are still being found, sometimes by friends and family of those who experienced the war. Protecting what now survives is of crucial importance. Specialist archives are always welcoming to those who might help them expand their collections, and readers of this anthology who might wish to consider depositing diaries and papers, or copies of them, can find details of how they might do this at the end of the book.

Permission to quote from books, manuscripts and private papers has been generously given by a great number of publishers, archives, libraries and individuals. These are acknowledged at the end of the book. Every effort has been made to contact copyright holders. In the case of a few manuscripts and diaries which are held in museums, this has not been possible. We would be grateful for any information that might help to trace those who are unknown. Attempting to contact these people has been an arduous task, and I would like to thank the Australian War Memorial, Churchill College Cambridge, the Liddell Hart Centre for Military Archives, the Imperial War Museum and the National Library of Australia for their efforts on my behalf.

An army of postgraduate research assistants and helpers have aided in putting this collection together, many in countries that I could not visit personally, and have greatly extended the reach of this project. They have investigated, selected, noted, translated and typed with tireless efficiency. I would like to offer my sincere thanks to Nadine Armiger, Mahar Aziz, Francisco Baretto, Corrie Burrow, Hannah Cameron, Jessica Darley, Carrie Deacon, Ingeborg Erikstad, Kathryn Hall, Chris Hawkins, David Hay, Geoff Heyes, Chris Hill, Naomi Hilliar, Michael Goodman, Sidharth Jiwnani, Sandanina Khan, David Layfield, Nick Mackie, Chiyako Matsumoto, Morjani Morisini, Laura Naylor, Amanda Rowley, Danny Scatola, Matthew Sharps, Darren Solomon, Tom Steiner, Lawrence Wong Cheuk Yin and Tom Wright. I would also like to thank the staff of King Visual Technology in Maryland and Foto Margo in Nottingham for their kind and enthusiastic assistance with images and photography.

There are a few individuals to whom I owe a particularly heavy debt of gratitude. Michèle Hutchison, Jo Micklem and Marianne Velmans at Transworld have been tremendously encouraging and have brought their vast expertise to bear on a project that presented some unusual problems. Andrew Lownie has offered continuous encouragement, inspiration and not a few substantive diary suggestions. C. W. Haigh kindly offered further refinements. I owe an enormous debt to all my family for their encouragement over the years. My brother James read the finished text with an expert eye. As ever, my wife Libby has offered fabulous support, extraordinary breadth of knowledge and, most importantly, boundless love during a project that has been in progress for some years. My children, Nicholas and Harriet, deserve special thanks for their forbearance during my many absences conducting far-flung research on a faraway war. They are pleased that, for a little while at least, the long journeys and late nights are over.

Introduction

RACE, BARBARITY AND EXPERIENCE
IN ASIA AND THE PACIFIC

A T FIRST SIGHT, Japan's visible resources, as compared
with those of Germany, appeared so meager that
the whole program suggested the dream of a madman.
But Hitler had shown that even a madman could
precipitate a world holocaust, and Japan's warrior-
statesmen had demonstrated that they were audacious,
but not mad; that, on the contrary, they were coolly
calculating strategists who prided themselves on their
realism.

D URING MID-FEBRUARY 1941 Otto Tolischus, the newly arrived
New York Times correspondent in Tokyo, recorded these
reflections in his diary. His words touch upon some important
questions. Having recently covered the European war from
Berlin, and having been harassed and then thrown out of the
country by Hitler's Gestapo, he was perfectly placed to reflect on
the similarities and contrasts between war-makers in Europe and
those presiding over a rising war in Asia and the Pacific.[1] How
might this war and its leaders be compared to the Second World
War in Europe and the Middle East? And were these two conflicts
largely separate or closely connected?

In the global conflict of the mid-twentieth century, the war in
Asia and the Pacific had the first and the last word. Arguably, the
first 'fighting' of the Second World War began in September 1931,
with Japan's invasion of Manchuria. By July 1937 the conflict had

---

[1] Otto D. Tolischus, *Tokyo Record* (New York: Reynal & Hitchcock, 1943), p. 22.

spilled out across the mainland of Asia as Japan occupied much of the eastern seaboard of China and perpetrated several unspeakable massacres at Nanking and elsewhere. Perhaps a third of a million civilians were put to the sword, often quite literally. Notoriously, it was at Nanking that two Japanese officers embarked on a friendly competition to see who could be the first to kill one hundred and fifty civilians with his sword. Japan claimed not to be 'at war' with China and an embarrassed international community attempted to draw a veil over the matter by referring to the ongoing fighting as the 'China Incident'; nevertheless, Japan's reputation for aggression and extreme brutality was already well established by 1937.

The war in Asia and the Pacific would also continue well beyond the defeat of Germany, with 'Victory over Japan Day' or 'VJ-Day' formally closing the conflict on 15 August 1945, some three months after peace in Europe. Even after this, the war in Asia and the Pacific proved to be more persistent than the European conflict, running onwards almost in spite of itself, its embers fanned by other emerging conflicts that had been smouldering within it. One of these was a struggle in China between nationalism and communism that would continue until the communist victory of 1949. Another was the struggle between empire and anti-colonialism. Accordingly, the arrival of VJ-Day did not mean the end of fighting everywhere in Asia and the Pacific.[2]

Notwithstanding the fact that fighting in Asia and the Pacific began before war erupted in Europe, Japan did not cause the Second World War. Although events in the region undeniably formed much of the prologue, they did not constitute the 'driver' of this global conflict. Indeed, during the 1930s many states, including Japan, devoted considerable energy to staying out of war with other major powers in Asia and the Pacific. Even in 1940, with the war widening to include much of Europe and the

---

[2] In 1942 Indians, Indonesians, Burmese and many others had joined Japan in fighting the western colonial powers, and this struggle continued beyond August 1945, with heavy fighting in Indochina and Indonesia from late 1945 into 1946. In Burma the Karen Hill tribes, armed and trained by the wartime British secret services, took exception to the post-war settlement and fought on for more than forty years in the hope of local independence.

Mediterranean, policy-makers in London, Washington, Moscow and even Tokyo were simultaneously seeking ways to avoid becoming further embroiled in an expanding conflict. The consequences of wider war, including the new phenomenon of city bombing, had been all too visible on the newsreels of the Spanish Civil War. Decision-makers worked strenuously to keep their states and their societies away from the horrors of modern warfare, which were still, for many of them, fresh in the memory.

Exactly what transforms a mundane local or regional war into a vast, sprawling, systemic conflict remains a hotly debated question. However, in the case of the Second World War there can be little doubt that the catalyst was Hitler's remarkable decision to launch Operation Barbarossa, the German attack on Russia begun just before dawn on 22 June 1941. This extraordinary moment, when 3 million Germans and their allies began their violent surge to the east, provides the fulcrum for the entire war, perhaps for the whole twentieth century.[3] This was certainly the experience of observers in Washington and Tokyo, the last two major world capitals then not yet at war – observers who felt increasingly trapped by a rising tide of global conflict. By August 1941 these policy-makers on opposite sides of the world recognized the near-inevitability of their involvement and were increasingly focused on when and how they would join the struggle. President Franklin D. Roosevelt in Washington and the unstable government of Prince Konoye in Tokyo were alike confronted with an international system that offered a rapidly darkening series of scenarios. War remained unattractive in mid-1941, but greater potential dangers now appeared to lurk for those who remained on the sidelines, in particular the looming possibility of a Nazi state stretching from the English Channel to Vladivostok, and so fear propelled them towards involvement. Japanese ultra-nationalists, perhaps more in tune with the spirit of the age than their leaders, offered the handy slogan: 'Don't miss the bus!' In the event Roosevelt, by applying economic pressure on Tokyo, probably triggered the entry of both the United States and Japan into war in December 1941. However,

[3] For an alternative argument suggesting 1940, rather than 1941, as fulcrum, see David Reynolds, '1940: Fulcrum of the Twentieth Century', *International Affairs*, vol. 66, no. 2 (1990): 325–50.

while Roosevelt may have effectively taken a decision for war, his own range of available options was perceived as rapidly diminishing. Arguably, in provoking Japan into action he was merely passing the buck.

The Second World War agitated the entire international system, inexorably drawing in more and more countries, even remote and somewhat improbable participants from South America. Argentina declared war on Germany on 28 March 1945, while Brazil declared war on Japan on 6 June 1945. The last significant declaration of war was probably made by Joseph Stalin, who declared war on Japan on 8 August 1945, permitting him to seize territory in Manchuria. Complex wars that involve many actors and cause substantive changes to the international system occur on average only once or twice in any century. The benchmarks for comparison are few, but they include the vast wars launched by Napoleon and Frederick the Great. In common with these other systemic conflicts in which everything was up for grabs, the Second World War was characterized by a twin sense of extreme danger and extreme opportunity. Each country was compelled to make critical power calculations as the conflict reverberated from region to region, remorselessly drawing in new participants.

Ideas, ideals and indeed ideology counted for little in this process, either in Europe or in Asia. Among the democracies, Britain had given Czechoslovakia a guarantee of its security in 1938, but notoriously found it convenient to stand aside when the German invasion began. This behaviour was unexceptional. During 1940, the United States wrung its hands and expressed idealistic sympathy for democracies in peril such as France and Britain, but was loath to step forward as a combatant. No less dysfunctional was the family of fascist nations, the Axis alliance. Although Germany, Italy and Japan were linked by an ideological pact against communism, signed as early as 1936 (the following year by Italy), they chose to act separately and in their own interests. In 1939 Berlin had decided that it was expedient to cut a deal with Moscow in order to carve up eastern Europe, taking its Axis partners by surprise. In spring 1940 Mussolini opted not to assist Hitler in his invasion of France and instead bided his time until June, when France was on its knees. Only then did Rome step in, shamelessly declaring war on France at the last minute to seize territory in southern France near the Italian border. Thereafter, Tokyo rejected the joint urgings of Berlin and Rome to enter a joint Axis struggle against the Allies. It too bided its time, pursuing an opportunist policy of 'watchful waiting'. Remarkably, between 1939 and December 1941 Japan's only new territorial encroachment was in fact made at the expense of another Axis state, Vichy France, when it seized bases in the French colony of Indochina. One of the unmistakable lessons of the Second World War is that alliance behaviour tends to be 'not a matter of principle but of expediency'. This was never more clearly demonstrated than in the dog-eat-dog world of the Axis alliance.[4]

The electric atmosphere of danger and opportunity created during the period 1937 to 1941 by the curious dynamics of power and coalition-making goes a long way towards explaining how two localized conflicts – one in Europe and one in Asia – gradually coalesced to become 'the war of the century'. However, while abstract ideas help us to describe the nature of the international system in the mid-twentieth century, in seeking a full picture of how the conflict developed and spread we also need to address the role of the individual. Inescapably, the Second World War, like most systemic wars, also owed something to 'world-historical figures' with quite distinctive characteristics. These individuals often have pronounced tendencies towards megalomania and an unshakeable belief in their own destiny, which in turn result in high risk-taking – often successful risk-taking – that is impervious to alternative arguments offered by more conventionally minded advisers and cautious counsellors. Such behaviour is usually allied to a 'realist' conviction that violence is the most effective way to bend the international system to their will and a supreme indifference to the value of human life. Such individuals are rare, but when they appear they have the capacity to leave a trace on the landscape of international history akin to that made by an indelible marker pen. Adolf Hitler was certainly one such individual.[5]

[4] Hans J. Morgenthau, 'Alliances in Theory and Practice', in Arnold Wolfers (ed.), *Alliance Policy in the Cold War* (Oxford: Johns Hopkins University Press, 1959), p. 185.
[5] On the failure of international relations theory to address the significance of the individual as decision-maker, see Daniel L. Byman and Kenneth M. Pollack, 'Now Let us Praise Great Men: Bringing the Statesman back In', *International Security*, vol. 25, no. 4 (Spring 2001), pp. 107–46.

Taken together, abstract ideas of power and an appreciation of the dangers presented by powerful and charismatic leaders take us a long way in explaining the origins of the Second World War. However, explaining war is not the same as understanding war. Understanding and contextualizing conflict is often thought to be the realm not so much of political science as of history, with its interest in the specific and the particular.[6] Nevertheless, even historians have found it hard to resist the temptation to generalize, abstract and interpret when confronted with events on such a grand scale. Almost unavoidably the practice of *academic* history, with its taste for long words and sweeping generalizations, quickly blurs any immediate sense of what war does to the individual. Most histories of the Second World War sketch out the dynamics of conflict, but struggle to give us a sense of the despair felt by baffled generals, the frustration created by mediocre political leaders, or the misery experienced by battered soldiers and bombed civilians. Postmodern approaches to history, with their self-regarding obsession with 'discourse' and 'text', are perhaps the worst example of how far history can stray from meaningful projects.[7]

Even the 'real' history conducted by those who still labour long hours in the archives – and in some university departments such people are an endangered species – must inevitably offer us the past viewed through the lens of the present. Historians were once defined, rather unkindly but not inaccurately, as those people who have raised hindsight to the level of a profession. Diarists and their diaries, by contrast, offer us an alternative route to the past: a close – almost physical – connection. They focus on the particular and catalogue the microcosmic. Moreover, they take history out of the hands of the academic historian, or government, and place the narrative in the hands of the subject. Diaries are not only interesting, they are also potentially subversive and certainly deserving of our attention. Most importantly, while they may not do much to explain, they help us

---

[6] Ngaire Woods (ed.), *Explaining and Understanding International Relations* (Oxford: Oxford University Press, 1996), pp. 3–66.

[7] For a thoughtful riposte to the postmodernists see Keith Windschuttle, *The Killing of History: How a Discipline is Being Murdered by Literary Critics and Social Theorists* (New York: Encounter Books, 2000).

to understand: especially, to understand what war does to the individual.

*

This is the second of a two-part study of diaries from the Second World War. Each volume attempts to capture war as it was experienced by specific individuals at the time. The first volume, *Witness to War*, drew on diaries from Europe and the Middle East. This volume focuses on the four main theatres of war that existed in Asia and the Pacific. By 1943 these had been designated as: South East Asia Command; China–Burma–India; the South West Pacific Area; and the Pacific Ocean Area. Why separate a conflict that was undeniably global in scope into two regionally focused volumes? Precisely because, while both academic historians and political scientists generally agree that by late 1941 the Second World War should be explained as a single systemic conflict, diaries nevertheless reveal that it needs to be understood as a distinct regional experience. The war in Asia and the Pacific was different from the war in Europe and the Middle East in many ways, partly because of the salience of racial issues, partly because of its widespread barbarity, and also because of the use of atomic weapons.

Diaries reveal aspects of conflict which differ from and challenge those preserved in mainstream history. This is perhaps even more true of the war in Asia and the Pacific than for accounts from the areas covered in the first volume. For example, Peter 'Johnno' Pinney, a soldier in an elite Australian commando unit, kept a journal during the bitter fighting on Papua New Guinea. He rationalized his diary-keeping as one man's attempt to capture 'a slender thread of truth' in a world in which the raw facts of war were so often shaded or even hidden. Rediscovering his diary after many years, he was initially surprised to find that he could hardly read it, written as it was in 'tiny cramped writing'. In many places it was starting to fade and discolour, while the binding had rotted away. However, he persevered and, reading it again after decades of travelling and deliberately trying to forget the war, he was pleasantly surprised by its tone and its contents. One of the reasons he found value in it was because it seemed to offer a view of war quite different from what he called the 'glorifying bull' written by patriotic war historians. As a serving soldier during the war, and later in retirement, he was never one to toe the line, or to follow convention.[8]

Diaries like those of 'Johnno' Pinney do not represent a 'higher form of truth'. However, unless they have been embellished at some later point, they do reflect immediate experience. They avoid the serious problems presented by other types of witness accounts – typically memoirs – because they are written without retrospect, hindsight or the reductive tendencies of memory.[9] Diaries, especially those written by those experiencing war 'at the sharp end', reveal many things that governments, newspapers and official historians fail to record. In part, this phenomenon reflects the extremely elaborate mechanisms of wartime press censorship. Newspaper reportage is so often the 'first draft of history'. However, in wartime, the men (and few women) of the press were tightly controlled and required to work within guidelines that were largely justified on grounds of operational security. Their writings were also filtered to ensure that they did not 'damage morale' or cause undue public alarm. On top of this, both the authorities and the newspapers themselves judged some aspects of the war to be unfit for public consumption on grounds of 'taste'. The overall result was a particular view of war that was uplifting, purposeful and patriotic.

Accidents and self-inflicted disasters were especially unlikely to reach the ears of the public. Mack Morriss, a US army journalist working on the army newspaper *The Yank*, was an excellent example of the diarist as frustrated reporter. He spent three years covering the war in the South Pacific, punctuated by occasional periods of leave in Auckland, and always accompanied by his inseparable friend 'Brodie'. Like many journalists he kept a diary to capture events that might not get past the censor. It was often the more curious and ironic incidents that seemed to him to symbolize the essential randomness of war, yet these were precisely the things that the authorities tended to declare 'off

[8] Peter Pinney, *The Barbarians: A Soldier's New Guinea Diary* (St Lucia: University of Queensland Press, 1988), p. 1.

[9] Mariska Heijmans-van Bruggen and Remco Raben, 'Source of Truth: Dutch Diaries from Japanese Internment Camps', in Remco Raben (ed.), *Representing the Japanese Occupation of Indonesia: Personal Testimonies and Public Images of Indonesia, Japan and the Netherlands* (Zwolle: Waanders Publishers/NIOD, 1999), p. 163.

limits'. On 23 December 1942 he recorded the fate of an American troop transport vessel, the *Coolidge*. This had sailed all the way across the Pacific from San Francisco without an escort, carrying 6,000 men to Guadalcanal in the Solomon Islands. During the voyage she was not attacked, but on reaching Guadalcanal she was sunk by an American minefield just outside the harbour where she was supposed to dock. Two brave men stayed in the bowels of the ship conducting damage control, ensuring the ship sank slowly so that everyone else could escape and make it to shore. Morriss recorded how all but these two men came out of the sea, some naked and covered in oil. Every item of equipment, including their food, had gone down with the ship. Local personnel literally gave them the shirts off their backs and everyone in the area went on short rations to ensure that they were fed. The benevolence of individual servicemen handing over their possessions to their fellows struck Morriss as 'one of the most beautiful examples of mass Americanism anyone has ever seen'. However, stories about such unnecessary disasters were seen differently by the high command and rarely got past the censors. Morriss's colleague Ralph Morse, who worked for *Life* magazine, had also tried to do a story about the sinking but could not get it cleared; he 'almost cried about the thing'. Such incidents, which were not infrequent, were poured out into private diaries and journals.

The majority of press stories written at the time, together with official histories written immediately after the war, suggested that Allied soldiers fought to defend their countries and for high-minded values. They did not dodge the draft, commit atrocities or use the war as a cover for large-scale organized crime. In this official version of history, soldiers were respectful to their officers, and officers did not run away or wet their trousers when they came under enemy fire. Received wisdom was not dissimilar in Japan, where all soldiers were portrayed as keen to volunteer, unquestioning in their obedience and ready, if necessary, to die for their Emperor.

Japanese soldiers' diaries tell a rather different story. They not only document fear, they also reveal widespread anger and resentment at senior commanders. Kiyoshi Yamamoto was an army lieutenant serving with the Yokosuka 5th Special Naval Landing Force in mid-1942. He had initially formed part of the task force despatched to conquer Midway Island, but his transport ship, the *Kinryu Maru*, had turned back when the Battle of Midway was lost in June 1942. His unit had then attempted to go to Guadalcanal, but their ship had been sunk by one of the two dozen American submarines patrolling this relatively small area of sea. After being rescued, he had ended up at the major Japanese base at Rabaul on New Britain. Yamamoto was already distinctly unimpressed with his own experience of Japanese military achievement. To add to his worries, in early September 1942 he then found that his battalion was being used as part of the reinforcement effort for a failing Japanese attack near Milne Bay in New Guinea. Some of his battalion had already been sent ahead. Indignantly, he noted in his diary that these men had been sent forward 'without proper recce' and with no proper orders as to their objective. The lead infantry companies had reported that they had been attacked by air during the day and then wandered about through heavy rain by night. They were now being 'bombed intensively by an invisible enemy from all sides, while their losses steadily grew'. In Yamamoto's opinion they were 'cornered', and he was not overly keen to join them. Yet he was now ordered forward to the same location. His reaction was certainly not stoical silence. On 4 September he noted in his diary:

> Our earlier move towards RABI [Milne Bay] had [now] been ordered, regardless of our chance of success, simply to patch up the failure of this op[eration]. I could not accept this and frankly expressed my indignation, to Capt.[ain] Yasuda in these words – 'I can't bear the idea of going to my death to save the face of the Marine Staff, trying to cover up the failure of an inept organisation. Staff officers are contemptible when they are satisfied they have done their duty by driving us to our deaths with a single order, knowing it is like 'having [pouring?] water on hot stones'. I absolutely can't accept dying in this way.

His commanding officer was inclined to agree, but offered a more traditional response, advising Yamamoto that he should 'try to endure'.

Yamamoto's intense dislike of staff officers was a sentiment with which many field soldiers, on all sides, would have sympathized during the war in Asia and the Pacific – or indeed, perhaps any war. However, this contempt resonates particularly strongly through the diaries kept by Japanese soldiers. Officers and men alike recorded how their military machine was hopelessly over-stretched and quite incapable of supplying its soldiers in the field. Moreover, from late 1942 onwards their personal stories are dominated by depression, fatigue and, above all, constant starvation.

Yamamoto's diary certainly records some reactions one would expect. 'I thought I might go into the sea, carrying a pistol to commit suicide.' However, many of his diary entries also confound expectation. On 5 September 1942, as his ship sailed forward from Rabaul, taking his unit towards the fighting near Milne Bay, he was struck by the beautiful mountains of New Britain in the early evening light – 'a slightly saffron colour as if gold were sprinkled on them'. As they moved a little further up the coast, he noticed a small settlement composed of modern, western-style buildings. Enquiring what these were, he learned that they were the homes of a local colony of German civilians 'who were living in such places aloof from the war'. He discussed this phenomenon with his fellow officers and they concluded that they felt sympathy – even envy – adding wistfully 'how we understood the feelings of people who forsook the world in the age of feudal war'.[10]

Yamamoto's diary reveals that, at a remarkably early stage in the conflict, Japanese soldiers on the front line knew that they were losing the war. Perhaps alarmed by this, the Japanese authorities worked hard to hide the scale of Axis strategic reverses for the purpose of sustaining morale, and especially to mask the defeats of the German and Italian allies. One of the reasons why the Japanese commandants of POW camps required regular searches for radios, illegal newspapers and diaries to be made was that Allied prisoners were often better informed about the progress of the war than their guards. Indeed, it was not unusual for prisoners and guards to trade information in the hope that by doing so they might begin to piece together a picture of what was really happening in the war.

[10] Lt Kiyoshi Yamamoto, diary entry for 4–5 Sept. 1942, 422/8/43, Australian War Memorial.

One of the pleasures of diaries, both for their writers and for later readers, is that they capture the war as it was really experienced, not as it was supposed to be. Accordingly, they can present a direct challenge to official orthodoxies. In the Japanese press, soldiers were portrayed as enthusiastic about the prospect of fulfilling Japan's wider destiny in Asia, which would at one and the same time confirm Japan's regional supremacy and also usher in a period of happy pan-Asian brotherhood. Every officer and NCO was a stickler for discipline. Outwardly, the constraints of military society ensured these values were displayed, but diaries reveal a softer side. A Japanese sergeant serving in the Solomon Islands in October 1942 recorded how much he hated imposing the traditional tough Japanese military discipline on his subordinates, noting in his diary for 27 October 1942:

> Last night's guard neglected his duty so I slapped his face in front of everyone this morning. I felt very sorry for him, but the military discipline must be maintained with great strictness and severity. He did not show any sign of resentment against me; so it is hard for me to face him . . . Please carry out your army activities justly! I didn't strike because I disliked you. How can I hate and strike my beloved men? Please understand me!![11]

Although the behaviour and attitude of Japanese soldiers were different from those of the Allied troops, particularly in terms of the notions of honour, discipline and national purpose, the personal content of Japanese diaries can often overturn the stereotype of the 'robot' warrior that still abounds in the historical literature. Few of those who wrote were genuinely at ease with war and its distorting effect on human relationships.

Japanese soldiers kept their diaries for much the same reason as Allied soldiers. Whether intended as private or public documents, all were driven by a very basic human need for comfort or self-expression when placed under pressure. Their

---

[11] Japanese sergeant's diary, captured at Guadalcanal, 18 Jan. 1943, translated by the Combat Intelligence Center South Pacific Force, Item #1195 (S-1444), 28 March 1944, Box 8, Records of Japanese Navy and Related Documents, NORPAC and SORPAC translations, US Naval Historical Center, Navy Yard, Washington DC.

wartime function was as a solace, substitute friend and counsellor. Shigenobu Matsubara, a lance-corporal from Shiga, had been a student at Doshisha University in Japan before being drafted into the army. He did not like the idea of military service and longed to be back with his books. He comforted himself by recording the events of each day. His opening sentence read: 'This is my diary. Thinly and faintly, in order to survive the many years of solitude – or the internal silence – I shall keep on writing as long as the sorrow keeps on.' Just like his western counterparts, his activity was secret, for 'a diary cannot be kept openly in the military', but he was determined to safeguard it by eventually sending it home. He hoped the censors would think it was merely a notebook filled with trivial matters, 'just a fool's words set down foolishly'. In reality the penalties for a Japanese soldier breaking such a regulation on active service were likely to be severe.[12]

Diaries also assist us in recovering a range of actors who are almost invisible in traditional accounts of the war in Asia and the Pacific, including women and children. At first glance women seem peculiarly absent from a conflict that seems to consist mostly of the business of man hunting man in the jungle. In fact, large numbers of women were interned as civilians and waited out more than four years to regain their freedom. Many of them kept excellent diaries. In 1941 Natalie Crouter and Elizabeth Vaughan were both American civilians living with their husbands and children in the Philippines, where, like many Europeans and Americans in Asia and the Pacific, they enjoyed a good lifestyle. This ended abruptly in early 1942 with the Japanese invasion. Civilians of all Allied nations were interned. Natalie Crouter and her family were confined in a small camp near Baguio; Elizabeth Vaughan, whose husband joined the US army at the outbreak of hostilities, spent the majority of the war with her two children, Beth and Clay, in a camp which made use of the campus of Santo Tomas University in Manila. Sheila Allan and Freddy Bloom, who had failed to escape in the flood of refugees out of Singapore during January and February 1942, found themselves in Changi gaol overlooking the Straits of Jahore. Laurie McNeill is one of the

---

[12] Kike Wadatsumi no Koe, *Listen to the Voices from the Sea* (Scranton: Scranton University Press, 2000), pp. 211–12.

few commentators on diaries of the war in Asia and the Pacific to reflect at length on the purpose of such journals. She asserts that for many, especially for women who were interned for long periods, diaries were important, indeed essential, to an exercise in recovering 'a sense of self'.

Western women under civilian internment were better equipped to keep diaries than POWs because they were afforded a quite different status by the Japanese and enjoyed superior conditions. Although denied mail privileges, they were usually supplied with pens and paper. Freddy Bloom even enjoyed access to a typewriter – 'an old Royal' – which she used daily and adored. Supplied with ample stationery, and with endless hours to fill, internees were in perfect diary-writing territory. Dislocated from their previous communities and cut off from the outside world, Allan, Bloom, Crouter and Vaughan all sought to fill this void by writing. Many diaries kept by those in captivity began as letters that could not be sent and, bizarrely, continued to address themselves to the desired recipient. On 5 December 1941 Natalie Crouter started writing to her mother, and she continued to do so even after the Japanese invasion made it unlikely she would be able to send her letter. Keeping a diary came to take the place of sharing experiences with family or visiting friends.[13]

Even for civilian women internees, however, diary-keeping was specifically forbidden, and possession of such personal writings punishable by death; nevertheless, all these women decided that having a record of this extraordinary experience was worth the risk. H. J. Kluit-Kleder, a Dutch woman interned in the Netherlands East Indies, recalls keeping her diary hidden in a basket of charcoal. One day the Japanese guards went right into the corridor – 'oh fright!' – alongside the house, where the basket holding her diary and drawings stood. Worst of all, if it were found, severe punishment would be meted out not only to the diarist, but also to everyone else in the house in which she was living. Fortunately, the guards did not look in the basket, but the shock of near-discovery had been too much. The writer noted, 'a few days later I destroyed and burned everything, because I

---

[13] Laurie McNeill, '"Somewhere Along the Line I Lost Myself": Recreating Self in the War Diaries of Natalie Crouter and Elizabeth Vaughan', *Legacy: A Journal of American Women Writers*, vol. 17, no. 1 (Jan. 2002), pp. 98–105.

could not take this risk regarding my housemates.' Later, however, she secretly resumed her writing, hiding it in suitcases, bedclothes and pillowcases.[14]

Natalie Crouter penned her diary on small pieces of paper, which were then sewn into pouches inside an old raincoat. A straw basket containing these diaries was one of the few items she took with her when she was liberated in 1945. Despite her success in keeping her diary safe from the Japanese, she was then forced to surrender it to the US army, who feared that it might contain sensitive military information. Because Crouter had been 'behind enemy lines for four years', woodenheaded bureaucrats in the military considered that her diary contained information that was potentially sensitive. It was eventually recovered from a huge army warehouse where the carefully sewn packets had never been opened.[15]

Diaries were even more dangerous items to have in POW camps. RAF officer Donald Hill kept his journal in secret, writing the entire text in a unique numerical substitution code. Donald survived almost four years in POW camps and brought the diary out with him at the end of the war; however, his experiences had been so traumatic that he did not like to talk about them, and the diary was never written out in plain text before his death in 1985. In 1996 Mrs Pamela Hill, Donald's widow, decided to try to have the diary decoded so that she could find out more about a closed chapter in his life. The code was finally cracked by Dr Philip J. Aston at the Department of Mathematics and Statistics at the University of Surrey, and so, more than half a century after the diary was written, it could once more be read.[16]

Among the most peculiar forms of wartime writing are the few diaries that were apparently never meant to be read by anyone other than the diarists themselves. At first glance, it seems a bizarre and irrational act to write many thousands of words

[14] Esther Captain, 'Written with an Eye on History: Wartime Diaries of Internees as Testimonies of Captivity Literature', *Tydskrif vir Nederlands en Afrikaans*, vol. 5, no. 1 (1998), pp. 1–20.

[15] Lynn Z. Bloom (ed.), *Natalie Crouter, Forbidden Diary: A Record of Wartime Internment, 1941–45* (New York: Burt Franklin, 1980), p. 524.

[16] Squadron Leader Donald Hill's diary for December 1941. More about this fascinating diary can be read at www.mcs.surrey.ac.uk/Personal/P.Aston/code.html.

intending them to be seen by no-one other than oneself.[17] Yet the sizeable number of diaries that have been found and brought to light by relatives, sometimes from among the personal effects of the deceased, suggests that a proportion of people kept diaries with no view to publication, or indeed perhaps any future reader-ship. Han de Meyier, who had been interned in Cimahi camp in the Netherlands East Indies as a boy, is one example. Some twenty-five or thirty years after the war his mother came to him with his camp diary, which she had found while clearing up. He had all but forgotten the existence of this diary and had put his time in the camp to the back of his mind, remarking that 'you never thought about it'. Clearly he was not especially keen to remember it or revisit his experiences, and now he found his diary a puzzle: 'What was I supposed to do with it? So I put it in the bottom of a closet with some other junk. There it stayed for several more years.' It was only when some friends found out about his past in the camp and finally the diary was mentioned to a local newspaper that he was prodded into doing something with it. Eventually he did publish his diaries, but even then only privately.[18] Very private diarists are a rare species, but they clearly exist. Archivists at one repository in Australia have explained that over the years they have been given several such manuscripts by aged veterans in sealed packets or boxes, along with strict instructions that they are never to be opened. The archive continues to preserve this material and also to respect the wishes of the donors. In accordance with this policy, no-one – not even an archivist – has yet been allowed to look at the material inside the packets, and perhaps no-one ever will.

It is certain, then, that some diaries of the war in Asia and the Pacific remain unread; and perhaps many are as yet un-discovered. Surprisingly, new diaries continue to surface almost daily more than half a century after the end of this conflict. Even

[17] Many commentators on diary literature would assert that all diaries are written with an audience in mind and hopes that some day they will be read. See e.g. Lynn Z. Bloom, '"I Write for Myself and Strangers:" Private Diaries as Public Documents', in Suzanne L. Bunkers and Cynthia A. Huff (eds), *Inscribing the Daily: Critical Essays on Women's Diaries* (Amherst: University of Massachusetts Press, 1996), pp. 23–37.

[18] Han de Meyier, quoted in Heijmans-van Bruggen and Raben, 'Sources of Truth', pp. 173–4.

the diary material that is currently available is capable of illuminating many 'hidden' issues in the war in Asia and the Pacific. Some of these issues were deliberately disguised at the time, but others were matters that 'history' had judged unimportant and had failed to deem worthy of record. Diaries, for example, illuminate not only the day-to-day experiences of the living but also the fate of the dead. Inevitably, world wars generate very large numbers of dead, in this case perhaps 50 million in all theatres between 1939 and 1945. However, in the history of wars the dead are curiously invisible, and the depressing issue of what happened to their remains, how they were recorded and commemorated, is rarely discussed.[19] Even in more recent wars, for example in the Middle East, some governments have been anxious to discourage media coverage of returning caskets, and the issue of what arrangements are made for the bodies of enemy soldiers has rarely been broached.

The fate of the remains of enemy dead – then as now – is a mysteriously elusive subject. Yet in diaries and journals of the war in Asia and the Pacific the dead are mentioned everywhere because, inevitably, they were almost omnipresent. Where they could not be seen they could be smelt. The fate of the dead was not particularly a hidden thing or a secret, since it was being confronted everywhere; but at the same time, not being considered very important, it was rarely mentioned publicly. The conceptual model for those back home was the First World War, and so the unspoken presumption was that most of the war dead were carefully tidied up and respectfully placed in neat cemeteries.[20]

The strong – almost unbreakable – grip exercised by this assumption of respectfulness is underlined by the diary of Rena Krasno. Rena was a teenager and a Russian Jew experiencing exile in Shanghai, which was under Japanese rule. After the Russian Revolution her family had fled to Shanghai's International Settlement, an extraterritorial area covering much of the city, which the Chinese had been forced to concede and in

[19] A specialist literature on war memorials and commemoration has begun to emerge, largely in the context of the study of the First World War.

[20] One of the first historical accounts to contradict this directly was William Manchester's autobiographical account of his time as a US marine, *Goodbye Darkness: A Memoir of the Pacific War* (Boston: Little, Brown, 1980).

which the major powers each controlled a section. In late 1941, with the Japanese in control of the city, she regarded herself as relatively safe. She enjoyed a protection and a status very different from those she would have found in her Ashkenazi homeland within the borders of the Soviet Union, now occupied by Nazi Germany. Although her movements were somewhat restricted, within the former International Settlement of Shanghai a degree of cosmopolitanism still prevailed, and she even enjoyed the benefits of attending the first year of medical school.

Rena Krasno was someone who enjoyed precision and accuracy, and it was perhaps this trait that first drew her towards medicine. The same instincts prompted her to note in her diary the extent of falsification and untruth that appeared daily in the Japanese-controlled press. As the war progressed, she enjoyed recording examples of especially improbable newspaper stories about the success of the Axis, showing how the Japanese were 'bringing to a crescendo their efforts at misinformation'. The Japanese had done everything they could to hide the defeat of the Italians in mid-1943 and to disguise the fact that Rome had then joined the side of the Allies. In July 1944 Rena quoted in her diary what she regarded as laughable reports from Japanese correspondents claiming that in the United States it was not uncommon for children to be found playing with the bones, even the skulls, of Japanese soldiers. These, the reporters said, were the remains of soldiers killed in action that American GIs had sent home as toys and souvenirs. There was even a photo, purporting to be reproduced from *Life* magazine and to show an American girl with the skull of a Japanese soldier that had been sent to her by her boyfriend at the front. She was about to write a letter of thanks for the unusual souvenir. Another improbable story in a Japanese newspaper insisted that a congressman had given Roosevelt a gift of a letter-opener made from the forearm bone of a Japanese soldier. Japanese editorials offered all this as 'evidence' of American barbarism, linking it together with their extermination of the native peoples of North America and the 'lynching of negroes'. Overtly, they said, the Americans were proclaiming freedom and the dignity of the common man, but lurking underneath was dollar oppression and a war driven by racial hatred. Rena could not understand how anyone could be taken in by such obvious propaganda.

All the examples offered by the Japanese editorials were in fact true. Rena discovered this long after the war was over. In preparing her diary for publication many years on, she noted that, '[to] my amazement, I later learned that this actually did happen'. Rena was especially shocked to discover that the photograph did come from *Life* magazine in 1944 and was indeed a genuine photograph of a girl in Phoenix, Arizona, sitting down to thank her boyfriend in the navy for the present of a Japanese skull. These sorts of story were not particularly uncommon in the American media during 1943 and 1944. However, the story in *Life* magazine, with its full-page photograph, was unusually high-profile. An obvious gift for Axis propagandists, it had somehow slipped past the censors, and its appearance in print horrified the authorities. As for Roosevelt's letter-opener, the President was forced to admit that he had been sent the offending gift, but claimed that he had refused to accept it.[21]

The great 'skull question' which surfaced in the summer of 1944 was a remarkable event. Here was a moment when the real face of the war in Asia and the Pacific momentarily showed itself to all. Bodily remains were in fact everywhere: they were floating in the waters off Tarawa, while on Okinawa dead marines had been piled in stacks like firewood. Frequently, gas masks were worn to try to fend off the stench of rotting flesh. Men even slept on corpses and used them to build barricades. Neither side took many prisoners, and respect for the remains of enemy dead was quickly eroded. However, all this was too grisly for the public to gaze upon. The authorities claimed that the skull episode was an aberration. Diaries, however, captured, and recorded, the reality.

By the autumn of 1944 the Allied authorities were vigorously enforcing a 'no skulls' policy and making efforts to discourage the defiling of enemy dead. Perhaps the most common practice was the kicking out of gold fillings, something which officers knew to be common on the battlefield but which had never been addressed. This was noted by John Gaitha Browning, a US soldier serving in New Guinea. On 3 October 1944 he was being relocated to yet another campsite, one in a long line of 'very unhappy places' he had been based, all of which were

---

[21] Rena Krasno, *Strangers Always: A Jewish Family in Wartime Shanghai* (Berkeley: Pacific View Press, 1992), pp. 132–3.

characterized by mud and impenetrable jungle. The mud was the worst aspect: described as a sticky, black 'mud-gumbo', it was ankle-deep and clung to shoes like glue. Here the fighting had been finished for some weeks. Their new camp had initially been defended by a number of machine-gun posts, but almost all the remaining Japanese were deemed to have been killed or to have fled into the hills. All that was visible now was the detritus of the former Japanese occupation – including their skulls. Browning picked up one skull and took it back to camp, noting that his comrades who took pictures of it were unlikely ever to get their prints back – the army having, as he put it, 'gotten the holy jitters about the skull question'. Browning also referred to the photo published in *Life* magazine and acknowledged that 'such publicity didn't help any. Even Tokyo Rose used the photo as an example of the "barbarous" Americans' attitude toward a "superior race".'[22]

The Japanese observations about Allied behaviour on the battlefield had found their mark because the criticism was in fact twofold. The Japanese not only made a specific charge of disrespectful attitudes towards the remains of soldiers who had made the ultimate sacrifice on the battlefield; they also used this issue to make the wider and more troubling charge of racism.

Hitherto, the Allies had enjoyed a monopoly on levelling charges of 'racism' against the enemy, mostly in the context of an ideological war against Nazi Germany. However, during the war in Asia and the Pacific, and indeed for some forty years afterwards, both official and unofficial history ignored the extent to which the war against Japan was, in many respects, a racial war. The Germans were a familiar enemy – not just neighbours but a nation against whom a world war had been fought within living memory. However, the Japanese were a people with whom most Americans and most Europeans had naturally had very little contact. The mythology of the exotic and savage Orient had been propounded by representation rather than direct experience.[23] Bizarre racial stereotypes about the 'diminutive Nipponese' had contributed to an Allied under-estimation of their enemy before

[22] Oleta Stewart Toliver (ed.), *An Artist at War: The Journal of John Gaitha Browning* (Denton, Tex.: University of North Texas Press, 1994), p. 241.
[23] Edward Said, *Orientalism: Western Conceptions of the Orient* (New York: Vintage, 1978) is still regarded as the most authoritative text on this subject.

1941. These stereotypes, including the idea that the 'slant-eyed' Japanese had difficulty seeing in the dark, underpinned the dramatic military reverses suffered by Britain and the United States in December 1941. Overtly racist terminology was used by officers and men in a conflict that was undoubtedly all the more savage because the enemy was often regarded as somewhat less than human. These attitudes were not deliberately hidden at the time and often surfaced in newspaper editorials. Nevertheless, it took historians more than forty years to recognize that this attitude was a central component of the war in Asia and the Pacific, and they began to address it in a concerted way only in the mid-1980s and the 1990s.[24]

Diaries are the perfect place to find racial stereotypes captured and preserved. They reveal that racist terminology was not the sole preserve of soldiers on the battlefield. Many of Winston Churchill's immediate circle were busy keeping diaries during the war and so captured the rich vocabulary that he employed to refer to Asian peoples. The Prime Minister, who had a low regard for the capabilities of the Japanese armed forces, described them as 'the Wops of the East', and always referred to the Chinese as 'pigtails'; but his greatest distaste was reserved for the Indians, whom he derided as 'baboos' and dismissed as 'gross, dirty and corrupt' on account of their inconvenient desire to seek independence under wartime conditions. At one point he expressed a wish to find a spare squadron of RAF bombers that he could use to wipe out 'the hindoos'. He repeatedly opposed plans to expand the Indian Army because of his racially motivated suspicions of their loyalty.[25] Whitehall deployed much the same language, with Alexander Cadogan, the most senior official at the Foreign Office, referring to the Japanese as 'savages', 'monkeys' and 'little yellow dwarf slaves'.[26]

[24] The issue of race was first raised in a coherent way by Christopher Thorne, *The Issue of War: States, Societies and the Far Eastern Conflict of 1941–1945* (London: Hamish Hamilton, 1985), pp. 177ff. It was brilliantly illuminated in John Dower's breakthrough book *War without Mercy: Race and Power in the Pacific War* (New York: Pantheon, 1986).

[25] Thorne, *Issue of War*, pp. 18–19, 27–32. See also Christopher Thorne, *Allies of a Kind: The United States, Britain and the War against Japan, 1941–1945* (London: Hamish Hamilton, 1978), pp. 3–19.

[26] See e.g. D. Dilks (ed.), *The Diaries of Sir Alexander Cadogan, 1938–1945* (London: Cassell, 1971), pp. 316–17, 416. The Italians were the 'dirty ice-creamers': see p. 333.

By the early twentieth century, modern ideas of eugenics had reinforced more traditional myths that indigenous peoples were somehow less human than supposedly more civilized Europeans, ensuring that racist ideas were not only commonplace but also widely accepted in western society during the 1930s and 1940s. It is not surprising to find such words used by Churchill, whose mindset was formed at the end of the nineteenth century. More shocking was the fact that Roosevelt, perhaps the most liberal American president of the twentieth century, also entertained such ideas. Diplomats at the British embassy in Washington were amazed to find that Roosevelt had encouraged a programme of scientific investigation into Asiatic racial types at the Smithsonian Institution. In 1942 these scientists reported to Roosevelt on their belief that the different skull shapes of various Asian peoples dictated particular types of behaviour. Roosevelt endorsed the view that the Japanese skull was 'some 2,000 years less developed than ours', and his entourage were even discussing 'racial crossing' in the hope of producing a 'breed' that was less aggressive. The 'skull question' was not restricted to the battlefield; it could also be found under active discussion in the Oval Office.[27]

Racial stereotypes undoubtedly contributed to a rapid barbarization of the war in Asia and the Pacific. Japan had a well-earned reputation for brutality on and off the battlefield, evidenced particularly by widely publicised incidents during its invasion of China, and this barbarity was explained in racial rather than cultural terms. However, the desire for revenge was the reason most commonly cited by soldiers for the high proportion of American and Australian units, especially in the US marines, that operated a 'no prisoners' policy. Gunner Stephen Brown was an Australian soldier taking part in the push towards Buna in New Guinea. In late 1942 he noted in his diary the sort of incident that typically changed the attitude of a unit to taking prisoners: 'Yesterday, while an MO was dressing a wounded Jap, the dirty swine pulled out a revolver and shot him dead. It's incidents like this that makes us all so mad with the Japs and accounts for little quarter being given.' He added that locally the Japanese were surrendering to some US army units but not to

---

[27] This widely discussed message is Campbell to Cadogan, 5 Aug. 1942, PREM 4, 42/9, PRO.

the Australians.[28] Many diaries record the widespread practice of refusing the surrender of Japanese soldiers. Moreover, they depict a vicious downward circle of distrust: once even a few surrendering Japanese soldiers had thrown hand grenades, taking surrenders was no longer an attractive occupation; so thereafter, Japanese officers were able to tell their own troops that they should fight to the finish because if they surrendered they would be slaughtered anyway. It is almost impossible to cast up a reliable estimate of the numbers of Japanese soldiers shot while attempting to surrender, or even after surrender. However, the anecdotal evidence provided by diaries – and the evidence is strong – suggests that a substantial number of Japanese who tried to surrender faced summary execution.

Charles Lindbergh's diaries of a year spent in the Pacific theatre capture this depressing downward spiral rather well. Lindbergh, who was in his early forties, was not serving in the military and instead worked as a consultant for the United Air Corporation. However, in 1944, as one of America's most experienced aviators, he was sent out to New Guinea to help the US air force with operational research and also to brief commanders on how to extend the range of their aircraft by skilful flying. Lindbergh was something of a maverick, being both a national hero and also a pre-war campaigner for isolationism. Moreover, as a civilian on the battlefield he was curiously half in and half out of the war. Keen to learn about the 'sharp end' problems of the pilots he was advising, he flew some fifty 'illegal' combat missions from air bases in New Guinea. Yet as a civilian he was suspicious of the groupthink of his military comrades. Flying over the jungles and primitive settlements of New Ireland, he was uncomfortable about the target instructions: 'The area is unlimited. Everything is a target. All natives are unfriendly.'[29] Even more disturbing to him were the frequent tales of the Allied killing of prisoners, often recounted to him with barely concealed glee by generals. When he objected he was regarded with an attitude of tolerant scorn and pity: 'The sons of bitches do

---

[28] Gunner Stephen Brown, diary entry for 20 Dec. 1942, PR 91/061, Australian War Memorial.
[29] Charles Lindbergh, *The Wartime Journals of Charles A. Lindbergh* (New York: Harcourt Brace Jovanovich, 1970), pp. 822–3.

it to us' was the reply: 'it's the only way to handle them'.[30]

Allied soldiers on the battlefield claimed that brutal Japanese behaviour towards Allied prisoners justified a suspension of the rules. Fascinatingly, diaries themselves played no small part in a developing culture of revenge. On Tuesday 23 November 1943, Jesse Gardner, an American pilot flying B-25 bombers, visited a forward intelligence unit on the island of Guadalcanal. Here intelligence officers, quite often Japanese Americans or 'Nisei' with the necessary language skills, were busy translating and analysing documents recently picked up by troops as they advanced through captured Japanese positions. 'Combat intelligence centers' in the Pacific circulated a remarkable quantity of translated Japanese material, and this became an important primary window through which Allied commanders viewed their enemy. These included some captured Japanese diaries. Gardner recorded in his own diary the experience of reading one of these documents:

> Read an excerpt from a Japanese diary reproduced in an Intelligence report today. Written by a Japanese officer, it described the execution of a captured American airman. The American was killed personally by the Japanese commanding officer with one stroke of his sword. Once it was decided to kill the pilot, they proceeded to 'take him for a ride' to a secluded spot where they cut off his head. The diary described the gory details with enthusiasm . . . It is true what they say about the Japs. Major Jones of the 6th NFS [Night Fighter Squadron] emphasised this in a talk to all crew members two days ago. They go to extremes in means of torture and killing. He admitted that our men who took Guadalcanal weren't sissies either. He warned that we should think twice before allowing ourselves to be captured by the Japs.[31]

Many similar instances of evidence of atrocities, taken from captured Japanese diaries, were posted on Allied bulletin boards

[30] Lindbergh, *Wartime Journals*, p. 854.
[31] Jesse Henry Gardner, *Beachheads and Black Widows: A South Pacific Diary* (privately published, 1995), p. 11.

or widely circulated. The result was the increasing reluctance of Allied troops 'to be bothered' with taking POWs. An additional factor was the greater logistical problems involved in transporting and maintaining large groups of prisoners in the Pacific as compared to Europe. By 1945 the United States was host to about a third of a million enemy POWs, and a breakdown of the number is interesting. That year, the POW population in the United States consisted of 305,873 Germans, 50,561 Italians and just 2,820 Japanese.

The tendency to shoot prisoners or survivors at sea, often in the context of the sinking of troop transports, was not entirely hidden from public view. In 1942 this matter was reported in the American press, including *Time* magazine.[32] Yet the extent of this practice was not widely mentioned and coverage was often discouraged. On Friday 9 April 1943 H. L. Mencken, an eminent Baltimore journalist and critic, attended a dinner at the Maryland Club in Baltimore given for William Haley, managing director of the *Manchester Guardian* and head of the British Press Association. Haley had recently been out to the Pacific to visit Admiral Chester Nimitz's headquarters. Mencken was interested to hear Haley speak to the gathering about press coverage of the naval war in the Pacific. Haley decided to recount a recent press conference he had attended at navy headquarters in Hawaii, where a number of newspaper correspondents were present to listen to the commander of an American submarine squadron. This commander reported that he had sunk three or four small transports and probably disposed of several thousand Japanese soldiers. 'One of the reporters asked him what he had done when those soldiers were thrown into the water. His answer was: "I machine-gunned the sons of bitches." The officer in charge of the conference thereupon said to the reporter: "Please remember, gentlemen, this is off the record." '[33]

Charles Lindbergh came across countless such 'incidents' in the Pacific, and they preyed on his mind. Like many in the United States during 1942 and 1943, he had been assured that the United States was fighting to take the torch of freedom to oppressed peoples and that right was on their side. Yet by 1944 he

[32] Dower, *War without Mercy*, pp. 67–8.
[33] Charles A. Fecher (ed.), *The Diary of H. L. Mencken* (New York: Knopf, 1989) pp. 245–6.

had been told that Americans had machine-gunned groups of Japanese prisoners on Hollandia airstrip and that Australians had pushed captured Japanese soldiers out of transport planes which were taking them south over the New Guinea mountains. The Australians reportedly claimed that their prisoners had 'committed suicide' or else had been 'resisting'. After serving in the Pacific in 1944, Lindbergh was then sent on to Germany towards the end of the European war to inspect new German aeronautical developments. In particular he visited the notorious V-2 rocket development site at Camp Dora, where Russian slave labour had been used cruelly and extensively. Lindbergh, never an enthusiast for conflict, was thus able to compare the practice of war in Europe and in Asia and the Pacific. Standing by a furnace where the bodies of the many dead Russian labourers had been incinerated, he concluded: 'It is not the Germans alone, or the Japanese, but the men of all nations to whom this war had brought shame.'[34]

Lindbergh's diary usefully illuminates comparisons between Europe and Asia that are also drawn out in the pages of this volume. In this book, the end-of-war settlements and the matter of war crime investigation after May 1945 in all theatres are drawn together. Mistreatment of POWs who reached captivity in both Europe and Asia was determined to a large degree by the urgent need of both the Germans and the Japanese for forced labour. Just as thousands of Russian slave labourers had died at Camp Dora in Germany, infamously, many Allied POWs worked alongside Asian slave labourers on the 'railway of death' in Burma and Thailand. Less well documented are the vast numbers of POWs transported to Japan, where they laboured in mines and on dockyards in equally appalling conditions. Some of their diaries appear in this volume. Throughout the Second World War, whether in the south-west Pacific or on the Eastern Front, there are many examples of appalling treatment of POWs. Although different in style, all involved needless cruelty and resulted in many deaths. Cruelty was most apparent where perceived racial differences were used to justify barbaric treatment, as the Holocaust confirms. The perplexing anomaly, then, is perhaps the Japanese treatment of civilians. This was markedly worse, by any standard, than that of the Allies in the war in Asia and the Pacific; indeed, it was almost medieval in its savagery, as some of the diary accounts of the war in China in this anthology testify. Oddly, it was often civilians in China and south-east Asia, whom the Japanese claimed to be liberating in the spirit of 'Asia for the Asiatics' and anti-colonialism, who were treated worst of all.

War crimes are often followed by war crimes trials. Disturbingly, diaries, atrocities and war crimes go hand in hand, as this volume underlines. Some of the diaries of the more senior figures, including those of Joseph Goebbels, Hitler's propaganda minister, and Marquis Koichi Kido, Emperor Hirohito's closest adviser, were translated with the specific purpose of being used as evidence in war crimes trials immediately after the cessation of conflict. The texts reproduced in these volumes are the same ones used there, which allowed some of the wartime Axis leaders to be condemned by the writings of their own circle. More importantly for those in the camps, in both Europe and Asia, keeping a diary was not only a way of affirming their own continued existence, it was also an act of resistance and, potentially, of vengeance. A. E. Field, an Australian soldier in the 2nd AIF, was captured in Java in April 1942. Suffering mistreatment in numerous camps, he kept a detailed diary hidden in the false bottom of a ration tin. His diary was subsequently employed in the Singapore war crimes trials that began in January of the following year.[35] Les Chater, a Canadian officer imprisoned in Java and then in Japan, recorded his experiences and observations in minute handwriting in four small diaries. These were presented as evidence at the Tokyo war crimes trials in 1947. However, while some of his material was used to convict, he and his fellow prisoners appealed successfully to the tribunal to lighten the sentences of guards who they thought had committed only minor offences. Chater also pointed out that some individuals arraigned had been decent and should not be on trial at all.[36] Several of the diaries reproduced here, then, were not mere passive receptacles of emotion and experience; they were also effective instruments in the hands of post-war investigators.

[35] A. E. Field, diary, 81/32/1, Imperial War Museum.
[36] Elizabeth Hamid (ed.), *Behind the Fence, Life as a POW in Japan: The Diaries of Les Chater* (St Catherine's, Ontario: Vanwell Publishing, 2001), pp. 271–4.

As well as dealing with the repercussions of wartime actions, the final sections of the book also herald the conflicts that were to bedevil the post-war world, east and west alike, as diarists ponder the complexities of the anti-colonial struggles now coming to the fore and the inter-Allied mistrust soon to slide downhill into Cold War. Nevertheless, while some diaries bear witness to terrible atrocities and some are full of fearful anxiety about the future, others give cause for optimism. Diaries remind us again and again that particular experiences often do not sit comfortably with accepted wisdom or broad generalizations made by historians about the behaviour of either the Allies or the Axis. Some diaries document moments of unexpected kindness by the Japanese towards their POWs. One of these is recorded by Squadron Leader Donald Hill, the British RAF officer referred to earlier in this introduction, who was taken prisoner on Boxing Day 1941, shortly after the fall of Hong Kong. Donald Hill already counted himself lucky to be alive since he had endured several near-misses during recent bombing. On 23 December he was just leaving his billet when a bomb landed literally on his bed, obliterating the place where he had been resting moments before. On Christmas Day a ceasefire was announced, although it was quickly followed by another heavy bombardment. Hill noted: 'Not my idea of a truce.' On the evening of Boxing Day he was taken prisoner and recorded the moment in his diary: 'Several [Japanese] officers started arguing and kept pointing at me and looking aggressive. Suddenly one of the officers whipped out his sword and I thought they had decided to bump me off but to my amazement he produced a bottle of beer, nipped the top off with his sword, and handed me the bottle.' The two officers then decided to move him back to general headquarters and invited him to join them in the comfort of their captured Ford Ten.[37]

---

[37] Squadron Leader Donald Hill's diary for 23–26 Dec. 1941.

1941

'IT LOOKS LIKE war with Japan. Planes have bombed Hawaii and the Philippines . . . Now Germany and Italy have declared war on the United States, according to a radio report. Air-raid alarms have sounded three times in New York, though only a third of the population hear them and only one third of these heed the warning . . . It's a strange thing, Diary. I started you when no wise man could foretell the future . . . What shall I do with you when the conflagration nears? Bury you deep in the ground, to be unearthed some day by the trunk of some sagacious elephant, or serve as food for the larvae of a fantastic insect? . . . The worst of it is that we, in our criminal lunacy, shall not only ruin the planet for ourselves, but for all the creatures who have made a better go of their lives than we have.'

Viola C. White, Vermont socialist and pacifist, diary entries for 7–13 December 1941

JULY 1940 – MARCH 1941

DURING THE 1930s militarism had been on the rise in Japan. This had manifested itself in a number of ways, most importantly through a progressive invasion of China. In 1931 Japan had annexed Manchuria – a region fought over and occupied variously by Russia, China and Japan in the early twentieth century – and on 7 July 1937 had begun a war against China proper following the 'Marco Polo Bridge incident'. This incident appears to have been manufactured by Japan's Kwantung Army, a semi-autonomous element in the Japanese armed forces, to provide a pretext for the invasion of central China. The Japanese insisted that one of their soldiers was missing and demanded that they be allowed to search in a suburb of Beijing; this demand was refused by the Chinese nationalists and fighting, which began on the bridge, gradually escalated. Bizarrely, neither of these mainland adventures had ever been ordered by the government in Tokyo: local commanders had taken the initiative and then the orders had been given retrospectively by the civilian government in Tokyo to avoid embarrassment.

One of the figures involved in this improvised war-making was General Tojo Hideki. Tojo, a rising star in the Imperial Japanese Army, reached the rank of major-general in 1933 and became head of the Kwantung Army's military police in the autumn of 1935. After further promotion he had attained the influential position of Chief of Staff to the Kwantung Army in March 1937, contemporaneously with the widening of Japan's war in China; and in 1938 he had returned to Japan to become Vice-Minister of War. Like many army officers, Tojo held extreme right-wing views and was a supporter of Nazi Germany, a stance closely connected to a fear of communism. Japan and Germany had signed an agreement to combat communism in 1936 (joined by Italy in 1937), the Anti-Comintern Pact. However, in 1939 Hitler had chosen to sign a treaty with Stalin, the Nazi–Soviet Pact, as a prelude to their joint attack on Poland. The Japanese regarded this as a major affront: in Tokyo the Nazi–Soviet Pact was regarded as a public humiliation and the Cabinet was forced to resign. Privately, Japan's senior policy-makers had learned that their fascist alliance partners had little loyalty to each other and would behave opportunistically, a trait which continued in evidence during 1940 and in 1941.

The extent to which decisions about China were taken by leaders of Japan's Kwantung Army in mainland China – the so-called 'Manchurian Gang' – rather than in Tokyo underlined the unhealthy nature of Japanese decision-making at this period. Within Japan, these decisions were nothing if not controversial. Between 1937 and 1941 the Japanese argued vigorously, even violently, among themselves over what future course their foreign policy should take. These internal tensions were of two fundamental kinds. The first was between conservatives, who wished to pursue Japan's ambitions in mainland Asia gradually, without provoking major war, and radicals, who embraced the idea that large-scale war was inevitable. The second was between an army faction who wished to push north against the Soviet Union and a navy faction who wished to push south into south-east Asia and the south-west Pacific. These tensions had a raw edge. The military used their intelligence services to watch liberal politicians (and, indeed, all foreigners) closely inside Japan, with an element of harassment gradually becoming palpable as the 1930s wore on. Meanwhile, the Imperial Japanese Army and the Imperial Japanese Navy could not co-operate, and when senior officers met to attempt planning conferences there were often fist-fights. In common with the United States, Japan had no third service or separate air force at this time.

Accordingly, the style of decision-making in Japan was the very opposite of that in Berlin. Although western commentators in the run-up to the Second World War were quick to apply the term 'fascist' to the increasingly militarist governments in Tokyo, the Japanese lacked a charismatic leader with a single vision. Indeed, the dominating characteristics of Japan's behaviour during 1940 and 1941 were division, confusion and uncertainty. All outside observers agreed that Japan claimed some ill-defined historic mission on the mainland of Asia, since this idea was to some degree 'culturally embedded' in the Japanese consciousness. Moreover, all were convinced that the increasingly turbulent international system presented a special opportunity for Japan to fulfil its perceived destiny. However, it was difficult to judge what shape this attempt might take. Japan's so-called 'ultra-nationalists' admired the gains that had been made by Germany and Italy in 1940, but at the same time feared that these revisionist powers might seize the Asian colonial territories that Japan had its own eye on. Italy certainly had ambitions to take over many of Britain's colonies and had even shown an interest in Burma in 1939. Ultra-nationalists in Tokyo – many of them young army officers – cried 'Don't delay!' – but the traditionally cautious civilians still hesitated. Arguably, waging war in May 1940 would have been a better option for Japan, since at that point Britain was preoccupied with the threat of cross-Channel invasion, while America had hardly begun to rearm. However, Japan found the major international events of 1939 and 1940, most of which were occurring in Europe, a bewildering faraway spectacle, and hesitated, unsure how to respond – and deterred from action also by wariness of Russia, against which it had fared badly in a significant border clash at Nomohan in 1939.

Hitler's foreign policy in Europe had initially looked like that of a traditional, albeit ambitious German statesman. Unsurprisingly, his initial focus had been on revising those elements of the Treaty of Versailles that Germans had found most odious. However, his personal writings, available to all since the 1920s, set out a much more far-reaching vision. He wished to unite all German-speaking peoples in one country and to secure new living space, or *Lebensraum*, to the east. Although Hitler's military staff had a good appreciation of the importance of conventional strategic issues such as logistics, armament technologies and manpower, his own vision was other-worldly and underpinned fundamentally by racist ideas: he envisaged the Germans as conquering and ruling the 'weak Slavs' as far eastwards as the Caucasus, Iran and Afghanistan. Several members of Hitler's entourage, including Himmler, entertained a bizarre notion that Tibet might be the original seat of the 'Aryan race'.

Nevertheless, during the 1930s Hitler had pursued limited

aims, which he justified by claims to be uniting or reuniting German people. Although there were pockets of Germans scattered across Europe as far as the Volga, the initial targets had been the Rhineland and Austria. In contrast to Japan, which had embarked on a long and exhausting war in China in 1937, Germany was willing to launch only short offensives at this time. Meanwhile it revived its economy through rearmament, bringing unemployment down from 6 million to 1.5 million and enhancing Hitler's popularity in the process. Observers in Tokyo found Hitler's achievements fascinating.

During 1940 the events which preoccupied observers in Tokyo most were the fall of France and the Netherlands, together with the impending invasion of Britain. This had direct implications for Asia, since a vast swathe of resource-rich colonies in south-east Asia now seemed to be 'up for grabs'. The attractions of these prizes were increased by the fact that Japan had so little by way of natural resources within its home islands.

Throughout 1940 and 1941 the militarists gradually extended their influence in Tokyo. In July 1940 Prince Fumimaro Konoye, a civilian, had become Prime Minister, replacing Mitsumasa Yonai. His Cabinet approved the idea that Japan should set out to build a 'New Order' in east Asia that would eclipse the imperial influence of the western powers. It was now recognized that this might mean war with Britain and America. Japan was already a member of the Anti-Comintern Pact; now, on 27 September 1940, it signed a military alliance called the Tripartite Pact with the other Axis powers, Germany and Italy. In the same month Japan occupied air bases in northern French Indochina, and the United States retaliated by placing an embargo on the export of iron and steel scrap to Japan.

In early 1941 Britain and the United States continued to deal with Japan reactively. Over the previous decade they had not worked closely together in their efforts to contain Japan's ambitions. Now British and American naval officers met secretly and with increasing frequency to generate joint war plans for the Pacific. Nevertheless, from early 1941 onwards London was preoccupied elsewhere and increasingly anxious to see Washington take a lead in negotiations dealing with Japan. Accordingly, Japan and the United States began bilateral negotiations in Washington to settle a range of disputes – a process that would continue through most of 1941, without substantial results.

Fundamentally, British and American policies in Asia were still at odds. Churchill's government would have preferred to see Japan completely deterred from further encroachments by American and Russian power. However, Britain was so gravely threatened by the fighting in Europe and the Middle East that it was willing ultimately to appease Japan if that would avoid war on a third front. In contrast, the United States would not accept Japan's aggression towards China and pressed Tokyo to withdraw. To some degree this stance reflected more than half a century of close Sino-American relations and the 'special' place that China had always occupied in American foreign policy. However, the level of sacrifice – in casualties, economic privation and honour – that the Japanese population had expended in China by 1941 ensured that no government in Tokyo would have been able to sell the idea of withdrawal from China to its people, and indeed any government that had attempted to do so would have fallen. In the long term this meant that Japanese–American diplomacy was almost bound to collapse.

Early 1941 saw a growing commitment to Britain on the part of the United States. During 1940 a number of voices, including that of the American ambassador in London, Joseph P. Kennedy, had warned that giving aid to Britain was merely loading goods onto a sinking ship. But by early 1941 Hitler's invasion of Britain – Operation Sealion – had been repeatedly postponed and his thoughts had turned instead towards the invasion of the Soviet Union. Willliam J. Donovan, emerging at this time as Roosevelt's intelligence chief, had visited Britain and assured the President that Britain was resilient. In early 1941 a new and more sympathetic American ambassador, John P. Winant, arrived in London. Roosevelt had already implemented the 'destroyers for bases' deal, which had given Britain a large number of destroyers in return for use of bases in the West Indies, and this was now followed by the Lend–Lease arrangement, which provided goods without immediate payment. In 1941 Roosevelt would portray America as a belligerent neutral, not at war with the Axis but serving as the 'arsenal of democracy'.

In foreign affairs Roosevelt and Churchill saw eye to eye on many things, including their implacable resistance to the fascist regimes in Europe and rising Japanese militarism in Asia. However, on many other matters, including domestic affairs, Churchill was a Tory, while Roosevelt and his close confidant Harry Hopkins were left liberals or 'New Dealers'. These ideological tensions emerged during Hopkins's visit to Britain in January 1941 as Roosevelt's special representative to discuss Lend–Lease. On a host of issues, including the future of British colonies such as India, Roosevelt and Hopkins were actually politically closer to Clement Attlee, leader of the Labour Party and Deputy Prime Minister in Churchill's coalition government, than they were to the premier himself. These tensions would emerge frequently during the war in Asia and the Pacific.

Early January 1941

Silvia Baker flees the war and spends time in a hospital in Calcutta

Silvia Baker was an itinerant artist and world traveller. She had spent the 1930s working as an illustrator and had undertaken a series of paintings of zoo animals for the Manchester Guardian. *In 1938 her husband, the art collector Athole Hay, died suddenly. Europe was already a troubled place and so she sold their house and moved to Tangier, thinking it 'would be a good place to live . . . if we should be at war'. But as the conflict spread its tentacles from Europe to the Mediterranean she was forced to travel further afield to escape its grasp. She headed west to Jamaica, then to Hollywood, and finally across the Pacific Ocean to Bali and Singapore in 1940. For this 'gentle ironic cast-away', south and south-east Asia were some of the last regions of the world not yet touched by the devastation of war. She continued to travel west, reaching Calcutta in early 1941. Here she was taken ill with acute appendicitis and found herself in a hospital with all the trappings of colonial India.*

'You are for operation,' said the Nurse brightly, about ten minutes after I had been admitted to the Hospital. They didn't even make me sign a paper to say I was willing to undergo the operation. Perhaps they were in a hurry.

'Please take care of my false tooth,' I said to Sister. 'I got it in Hollywood, and it was rather expensive.' The magic word Hollywood produced the usual effect. Nurses sprang up from nowhere, and crowded round my bed. 'She's been to Hollywood,' they told each other. I had achieved a social status.

While they wheeled me to the theatre, I tried to assume a lion-hearted expression, but with very poor success. It seems that the Hospital padre saw me, and thought: 'That poor woman, how frightened she looks,' so he got permission to go to the theatre, and say a prayer, while I was taking the ether. I was about to sniff the anæsthetic ('Now breathe slowly,' . . .) when I heard a voice behind me, intoning a prayer. After a minute or two it was comforting, but at first I naturally assumed there was no hope for me at all.

Some time after I recovered consciousness, the surgeon appeared. 'Because of you, I had to leave a dinner party,' he said.

'I hope it was a straightforward appendix,' I murmured, trying to placate him.

'Straightforward, ha!' he said in a voice charged with irony and derision.

(I then realized that I had two tubes stuck into me.) . . .

There is a new patient today. Mrs S. is built on a heroic scale, and has the appearance of a Brazilian opera-singer. Her speaking voice is deep and gorgeous, and one hears a lot of it in the night, when she shouts: 'Oh God, oh God,' at intervals. She is said to be dying of heart-trouble, and her sons and daughters are flitting about on the veranda behind her bed.

She is so heavy the nurses can't lift her, and coolies are called in to help. She is Eurasian by birth, and dark-skinned, but she calls out: 'I won't be touched by these niggers!'

A Roman Catholic Priest came today to give the Sacrament to Mrs S., who is dying. They hung a curtain round the bed, and between the curtain and the floor I could see the priest's black boots, two inches of black trousers, and then the spreading folds of white satin vestments. He walked round the bed many times, and after what seemed an eternity, he went away, and later in the day she died . . .

A girl came into the ward, who had made herself very ill, by taking slimming medicines. It was the third time she had done this and had been brought to hospital. She refused to answer any questions, so after three days they said: 'Patients who won't collaborate are no use to us,' and, followed by her family, the girl was removed on a stretcher, protesting vehemently . . .

The chief amusement I have is watching the sweeperesses, who are called mehtaranis – a word meaning Princesses. There is constant friction between them and the nurses, who call them 'These jungly dames'. The chief of them, Miriam, is short and fat, but moves majestically in her sari – so majestic she is, and so opulent are her charms, that one thinks of the goddess Juno. She wears a gold stud in her nose, and bangles on her ankles, and is sly, and thievish, and bold. (I'm certain she has pinched my eau-de-Cologne, but when I asked her where it was, she pointed to a cross at her throat, and said she was a Catholic, and a Mother.) She chucks me under the chin and calls me darling. This from a mehtarani to a memsahib! Truly the British Raj crumbles.

These servants are notoriously greedy for tips. An Englishman who was leaving the hospital last week, having been cured of an illness, was surrounded by the hospital orderlies and coolies, all wanting baksheesh. He gave out money to one, and then to another, and finally said to a third man: 'But I've never seen you before; what have you done for me?' – 'Sahib,' the man said, 'if you had died, I should have had to carry you out.'

'Oh well, I think that's worth a rupee,' the Englishman said.

Although Japan had invaded China in 1937 and many Indian troops were already serving in the Middle East, the war still seemed a world away to the residents of India with its vast cities and remote hill stations. Silvia Baker's diary nevertheless records an underlying struggle that was moving in parallel with the struggle between the Axis and the

Allies, namely the confrontation between imperialists and anti-colonialists in which Gandhi was already a key player. Respect for Europeans was being eroded, and after one military reverse she would note: 'There was a certain amount of back-chat from the Indians to be endured.'

During 1941 more and more soldiers made their appearance in Calcutta, and finally one morning over coffee Sylvia would be accosted by 'a tough Commando' claiming to be a friend. It proved to be Marcel, her 'elegant hairdresser' from London. Marcel pleaded with her: 'Don't call me Marcel now I'm in the army. You must call me Bill.' Concluding that the war was now coming to Asia and was about to catch up with her, Sylvia moved on, heading for the remote hinterland of Kashmir.

Sylvia Baker would return to London in late 1944, having travelled the world for seven years.

Friday 10 – Saturday 11 January 1941

John Colville joins Harry Hopkins, Roosevelt's special envoy, in a visit to Ditchley near Oxford to talk about Lend–Lease

John (Jock) Colville was born on 28 January 1915 and was educated at Harrow before going up to Trinity College, Cambridge. He became assistant private secretary to Neville Chamberlain in 1939, and then to Winston Churchill from 1940.

10 January

The President's envoy, Mr. Hopkins, was lunching with the P.M. and they were so impressed with each other that their tête-à-tête did not break up till nearly 4.00. Then we left for Ditchley, I travelling down with Brendan [Bracken]. Brendan said that Hopkins, the confidante of Roosevelt, was the most important American visitor to this country we had ever had. He had come to tell the President what we needed and to form an opinion of the country's morale. He could influence the President more than any living man. At Lisbon Ronnie Campbell had made a bad impression by saying that 'the morale of the lower classes was wonderful' – a remark which offended the liberal and democratic Hopkins. But apparently Hopkins had been much impressed by Halifax [Britain's ambassador in Washington], whose religious views and variety of interests would, he said, appeal to Roosevelt. While we were thus discoursing, an icy mist descended and we collided with a fish-and-chips wagon which burst into flames. Nobody was hurt and we arrived safely at Ditchley.

Besides the Trees, Venetia Montagu was there, Dinah Brand (with her Australian beau) and the Captain of the Guard, a former schoolmaster, who seemed very intelligent. Before dinner we drank and thawed while Winston pointed out, in reply to Mrs. Tree, that Wavell had done very well but that the Italians were the sort of enemy against whom any general should be only too happy to be matched.

Dinner was an exquisite meal at which I sat next to Mrs. Tree. Afterwards Winston smoked the biggest cigar in history and became very mellow. There was an interlude in which I talked to the exceptionally pleasant Dinah, after which Winston retired to bed with a very full box and in an excellent temper while I whiled away the time arranging the box in my beautiful working room below . . .

11 January

Very annoyed at being disturbed early by the P.M.

He is delighted by the new American bill which allows British warships the use of American ports and contains wide powers for the President in every sphere of assistance to us. He says this is tantamount to a declaration of war by the United States. At any rate it is an open challenge to Germany to declare war if she dares. In view of this bill it will be more difficult for us to resist the American tendency – which Kingsley Wood lamented to me yesterday – to strip us of everything we possess in payment for what we are about to receive.

During 1940 there had been growing concern that Chequers, the Prime Minister's country residence, was too visible from the air and presented a target of opportunity to the Luftwaffe. As an alternative, Ronald Tree

MP had offered the Prime Minister his house at Ditchley Park, near Oxford, which was then closely surrounded by mature woodland and much less conspicuous from the air. Churchill began to use it in November 1940. Tree and his wife were American by birth and so the venue proved ideal for hosting a visit by Harry Hopkins, Roosevelt's special envoy and, as Brendan Bracken had rightly observed, the single person with the greatest influence on Roosevelt. During this gathering the crucial Lend–Lease agreement was discussed. Among the reasons why Chamberlain's government had been slow to turn to America for help at the start of the Second World War were financial considerations. Many of Chamberlain's circle were Treasury men and, like Kingsley Wood, wondered whether the Second World War would leave Europe as indebted to America as the First World War had. SEE ALSO PP. 78–9.

Monday 27 January 1941

Samuel Grafton observes the impact of the war boom on the east coast town of Bridgeport

Samuel Grafton was a columnist on the New York Post and an essayist for the New Republic. His column was syndicated to twenty-five other papers across the United States. He was a committed left liberal and New Dealer and so followed the economic impact of rearmament on the east coast of the United States with avid interest.

Bridgeport: Twelve new families move into Bridgeport every day. Where they sleep is a mystery. One tours the town for two hours in a cab, looking for a room. It seems incredible that this sprawling city, of big, old-fashioned wooden houses, should not have sleeping space to spare. It is true.

A flyblown chamber in a dirty rooming house, with iron cot and wooden washstand, costs $7.00 per week. But you can't get it. Last year the rate was $2.00. Farther up the rich Naugatuck Valley, where the defense boom boils and bubbles, the rate for the rooms you cannot get is still $2.00. But that is rural Connecticut where they have not yet caught the bonanza spirit which is beginning to flare up in Bridgeport.

Bridgeport has not seen the like since World War days.

Read's, the big store, had to take an advertisement apologizing to its charge customers for its inability to mail bills on
time; a buying rush caught it short. A woman has been
elected an officer of the old Machinists' Union for the first
time; down at the ancient Moose Temple, where the union
meets, they have had to recognize the fact that women have
come into the defense factories.

The people piling into town come from everywhere:
Michigan, Virginia, Massachusetts, New York State. A hotel
clerk lets me flip through a pile of registration cards. 'It's a
funny thing,' he says. 'A lot of the people coming into town
to take rooms and live are just looking for jobs, and a lot of
the people who have jobs don't live here at all; they just
drive in every day.'

One gets to Mayor Jasper McLevy and finds him much
more anxious to talk about 'the good old stable industries' in
town, like Singer Sewing Machine and Jenkins Valve, than
about the quadrupled Bullard Company plant, which makes
machine tools, or Remington Arms, or Sikorsky, or General
Electric, all roaring night and day.

It is, therefore, not like the 1929 boom. That was the boom
men were proud of; this one scares them.

I talked to a group of boys outside the Trade School. Three
admitted that they had given up former hopes of professional careers for a quick shot at a trade-school course and
a job. The kids are placing the longest bets of all on the hope
that this thing will last.

*Samuel Grafton defined himself a 'diarist', but confessed that he was
rather alarmed at the thought that anything up to 10 million people read
his diary in a single day. He was an interventionist and so favoured
America's participation in the war as the 'arsenal of democracy'. Even
before the passage of the Lend–Lease Act in March 1941, the impact of
the war upon the American economy was remarkable. Vast new orders
for war equipment to supply Britain, and also for America's own, still
small, armed forces resulted in a boom. In May 1941 it would be
reported that, but for shortages of materials, another 4 million people
could be put to work. The demand for labour resulted in rapid social as
well as economic change, with many more women entering the workplace in America. SEE ALSO P. 70–1.*

Wednesday 5 – Friday 7 February 1941

Hugh Dalton watches a Japan war scare take hold in Whitehall

Hugh Dalton was born in Neath, Glamorgan in 1887 and was the son of the chaplain to Queen Victoria. Following an education at Eton and Cambridge, he fought in the First World War. In 1924 he was elected a Labour MP and in 1940 had joined Churchill's coalition government. His Cabinet post was Minister of Economic Warfare, presiding over a range of new bodies tasked with economic warfare, blockade and sabotage, including the Special Operations Executive.

5 February

Leith-Ross [Director-General of the Ministry of Economic Warfare, answering directly to Dalton] thinks that the Japs will make a move southward before the end of March, possibly against North Borneo and the Dutch East Indies. Only two things, he thinks, are likely to stop them, either the U.S. sending their fleet to the Western Pacific (and there are difficulties about this through lack of bases and Jap control of Marshall and neighbouring islands), or by Russians making threatening noises in the north. Of the latter, I say, there is no chance at all at present.

[R. A.] Butler [Under-Secretary of State for Foreign Affairs], whom I see later in the day, thinks that the Japs are more likely to attack Burma through Siam. There is nothing to stop them bombing Rangoon from Siamese bases . . .

7 February

Am summoned to Buckingham Palace by His Majesty this morning and have half an hour with him alone. He shows an interest in M.E.W. [Ministry of Economic Warfare] but has not, I think, heard very much, if anything, of the rest . . . We speak also of gas-masks, and he says he has been thinking that perhaps they ought to have a gas-mask drill in Buckingham Palace and he receive his visitors in his . . .

News today is that much evidence, coming through many

different channels, accumulates that Jap entry into the war is very imminent. 'Wait for *the* cable next week . . . cut off all social contacts and hold yourselves aloof' (I said I thought that this one was all wrong, according to the theory. They should get all they could as late as they could. But I was told that this was the Jap way. Much wooden pride.) They seem also to be settling down in Cam Ranh Bay and other points in Thailand.

Many people appreciated that significant opportunities awaited Japan in 1940 and early 1941. Much of south-east Asia consisted of colonial territories formerly owned by France or the Netherlands, countries which had now been defeated by the Germans. The colonial regimes running Indochina and the Netherlands East Indies were very weak, while Britain was over-stretched by home defence and by struggles against the Italians and Germans in the desert. The presumption was that if Japan could move into this area without provoking Russia or the United States it would 'clean up' – and this is what most expected it to do. Dalton was warned to cool off any social contacts with the Japanese embassy in London. Many high-ranking officials and politicians, including Churchill, had friends who were close to Tokyo's diplomats in London. SEE ALSO PP. 93–4, 603–4.

Thursday 6 – Saturday 15 February 1941

Sir Alexander Cadogan eavesdrops on the Japanese embassy in London during the February war scare

Alexander Cadogan had made his name as a diplomat in China and had been Britain's ambassador there in 1935–6. He was then brought back to London and served as the top official in the Foreign Office from 1938. Because of his proximity to the Foreign Secretary Anthony Eden and Churchill, his diaries are perhaps the most important personal record of Britain's inner governing circle in wartime.

6 February
Cabinet 12.15. Complete Italian rout in N. Africa, and Wavell expects to be at Benghazi 'in a day or 2'. Discussion of

undertaking to Dutch about E.[ast] Indies. Admiralty tiresome and it had to be adjourned for discussion between the two Departments ... Some more very bad-looking Jap telephone conversations, from which it appears they have decided to attack us. A.[nthony Eden] was seeing [Harry] Hopkins and I went in and guardedly gave them the news. We then went over to see P.M., about 6.50 ... Instructed H.[alifax, British ambassador in Washington] to pass on to U.S. government our information about the machinations of these beastly little monkeys. Home about 7.30.

7 February

A.[nthony Eden] saw Shigemitsu [Japanese ambassador in London] and told me after he was afraid he might have gone too far, as S. seemed surprised and shocked. I assured him it was all right: a little of that medicine was good for them ... 3.20 meeting with A. and Chiefs of Staff on F[ar] E[ast] – particularly in regard to our position vis-à-vis Dutch in E.[ast] Indies. We wanted to give Dutch a sort of guarantee, but Staffs against it – particularly Admiralty. Didn't reach any agreement. Benghazi fell today! ...

15 February

Showed R.A.B. [Rab Butler, Foreign Office minister] some telephone conversations which seem to show Japs are climbing down. If this is really so, how valuable this form of eavesdropping has been!

Alexander Cadogan's diary gives us a precise picture of the interaction between secret intelligence and diplomacy. For some months British intelligence officers had been tapping the phones of the Japanese embassy in London, and during February calls seemed to suggest that Tokyo was about to make a move. Anthony Eden decided to warn off the Japanese ambassador, Shigemitsu, despite the danger that this might alert the Japanese to the fact that the British had suspiciously good insights into their affairs. In fact the February war scare was probably exaggerated and action had not been imminent. Cadogan himself loathed the Japanese, a reflection of his time in China, where he had seen their behaviour at close hand, and his diary is full of disparaging terms for them. SEE ALSO PP. 761–2.

Sunday 9 February 1941

Otto Tolischus, a *New York Times* reporter, arrives in Tokyo
and discovers that Japan is a country already at war

*Otto D. Tolischus, born in Lithuania, had renounced his German
citizenship in 1907 to come to the United States. He graduated from the
Columbia School of Journalism in 1916, and later worked as a foreign
correspondent for the Universal Service in Berlin, then London. In 1931
he returned to Berlin as a* New York Times *correspondent. He had
gained experience as a war reporter when he accompanied the German
troops who invaded Poland in 1939. He was expelled by the Nazi regime
in 1940 and the same year won a Pulitzer Prize for his coverage of
events in Berlin. In February 1941 he was sent to Tokyo to cover events
for the* New York Times *and the London* Times.

Three days of looking and listening in Japan brought two
things home to me. The first – and I was surprised at my
own surprise at it – was the discovery that Japan was a
country already at war. I knew that, of course – at war with
China. But I learned what tricks mere juggling with words
can play, and what a difference there is between knowing a
thing and realising its significance. Japan called her war in
China the 'China Incident,' and we too, to save ourselves
embarrassment under our Neutrality Laws, had refused to
call the China war a war. As a result I, for one, had somehow
detached Japan from the 'China Incident,' and I began to
suspect that America as a whole, and even foreigners in
Japan, labored under the same optical illusion. Whenever
there was talk of war, it was not the 'China Incident' that was
meant, but a war between Japan, America, and Great Britain.
    The subconscious corollary drawn from this was that
Japan was still at peace, and could make decisions as a
country still at peace. But I knew from my own experience in
Europe that the psychology and dynamics of a country at
war are quite different from those of a country at peace, and
create quite different reactions and compulsions. Japan, I
realised, not only was at war, but felt herself at war, and

I began to wonder how far the rest of the world took this into account in dealing with Japan.

Having seen Germany at war, I recognised the symptoms. The material symptoms were obvious. Tokyo already had a dimout, and the bright lights which, I was told, once rivalled those of Broadway were gone. There were the same complaints about growing restrictions and declining standards of living – about shortages of all sorts of things, especially imported goods, about queues before food shops and the scarcity of taxicabs, about the poor quality of ersatz materials and native whisky – that I had heard in Germany. A still peaceful and well-supplied American public took them as a possible indication of Axis collapse, but I had learned to evaluate them as tokens of Axis determination to carry on according to the principle of 'guns before butter.'

Although the Sino-Japanese War is usually dated from the 'Marco Polo Bridge incident' on 7 July 1937, Japan had been fighting on the Asian mainland since 1931, when the Japanese army, acting largely independently of Tokyo, had occupied Manchuria and set up a puppet state called Manchukuo. Japan's military operations in China after 1937 were on a massive scale and involved at least a quarter of a million soldiers. By 1940 the fighting had reached a stalemate: while Japan held most of the eastern coastal areas of China, the Chinese nationalists and the Chinese communists held most of the hinterland. Guerrilla fighting continued even in the conquered areas since Japan did not have the capacity to conquer or administer all of China. SEE ALSO PP. 67–70, 80–1, 90–2.

Thursday 6 – Tuesday 25 February 1941

Captain Malcolm Kennedy, a Japanese-speaker and code-breaker at Bletchley Park, finds his services in demand as tensions rise in the Pacific

Malcolm Kennedy had joined the British army before the outbreak of the First World War. Wounded on the Western Front and unable to continue on active service, he had become a language officer and was sent to Tokyo to learn Japanese. Having gained a good understanding of both the

*language and the Japanese military, he followed the usual course of such
officers and served in the military intelligence section of the War Office
dealing with Asia. After leaving the army in the early 1920s he had put
his skills to use working in Japan for an oil company and then for
Reuters. On returning to Britain in 1934 he was hired by the
Government Code and Cipher School, the forerunner of GCHQ, to work
on breaking Japanese codes and ciphers. By 1941 this organization,
which was superintended by the Foreign Office, had moved to Bletchley
Park.*

6 February
Denniston [Head of G.C. & C.S.] rang me up to say that the
W.O. [War Office] have been pressing once more for my
transfer to MI.2.c but that the F.O. [Foreign Office] cannot
spare me, so I must stay put.

12 February
News from Japan reaching the F.O. [Foreign Office] increasingly disconcerting the last few days and, unless something
unexpected comes along to ease the present rapidly increasing tension between our countries, it looks as though we
shall be at war with Japan very shortly now. The next few
days are likely to be extremely critical – and we may even
find Japan entering into an unholy alliance or pact with the
Soviet, similar to the one into which Germany entered in
Aug. 39. As a result of the increasing tension and consequent
field of work, our section of the F.O. [Foreign Office] now has
to work from 9 a.m. to 6 p.m. without even a half-day off.

25 February
To Camberley in morning for two days, as I have not had a
day off for 3 weeks.

*During 1941 Malcolm Kennedy would find his language skills in ever-
greater demand, a sure sign of rising tensions in Asia. Japan had
significantly improved its communications security and British
intelligence had lost the ability to read high-grade Japanese ciphers that
it had enjoyed the previous year. With American assistance, Bletchley
Park regained the ability to read high-grade diplomatic material during
1941, although military material remained more elusive. Accordingly,*

Kennedy was able to follow the February war scare and also Tokyo's diplomatic overtures to Moscow, which would eventually lead to a neutrality pact later in the spring. SEE ALSO PP. 131–2.

Sunday 9 – Tuesday 25 March 1941

Viola C. White, a college librarian and pacifist in Vermont, bemoans the draft and the passage of the Lend–Lease Bill

Viola C. White was born in 1889. Graduating from Wellesley College in 1911, she took an MA at Columbia and completed her PhD at the University of North Carolina. She became a college librarian in Vermont.

9 March
A heavy fall of snow: flakes are still tumbling out of the white sky onto a white earth of Sunday . . . The Lend–Lease Bill passed the Senate 60–31, with no qualifying amendment against sending troops overseas. Now follow our entrance into the war, and our accelerated progress toward American fascism at home.

25 March
Across the expanse of snowfields the brilliant sun is almost overpowering, as in Bermuda's white coral islands. Otter Creek, literally flowing through snow on either side, is unique, even for March. We don't usually have a snow-covered landscape when the ice breaks up. The drip of water down the mossy cliff face of rocks, like the mesmeric passing of hands, very slow, very gentle, even and undisturbed in rhythm, seemed with magic power to be summoning up the life of spring on the glistening rocks below.

Mr. Whiston [preacher] spoke in the morning on America's responsibility for her Lend–Lease Bill decision and her intent to make herself the arsenal for Europe – that if this were against the will of God, she would be punished for it and, persisting in her error, would be destroyed. This is really prophetic, I think, prophetic in the line of Amos and Jeremiah, using the measure of God's righteousness to measure the nation. Colonel Lindbergh is a more secular witness, but he too says that if our nation persists in entering the European conflict, it will be defeated and humiliated.

Thanks to the National Federation for Constitutional Liberties, the action taken by federal authorities in Washington against protesters last fall has been declared a violation of the Bill of Rights. As the Burke–Wadsworth Bill approached final voting, thousands of anti-conscription lobbyists from organizations throughout the country descended on Washington. They were greeted with police violence and with every form of official intimidation. At the railroad station the protesters were ordered to remove badges and buttons expressing opposition to conscription. Drivers were stopped by police and 'Stop the Draft' signs torn from their cars. Police arrested leaflet distributors, confiscated anti-conscription literature and harassed picket lines. Clergymen who sought to hold a night-long worship service and vigil on the Capitol steps were arrested, their followers slugged and violently driven away. The courts at least have clarified the right of citizens to dissent . . .

This week, with the students absent, is wholly delightful. It fulfils Dr. Russell Booker's definition of happiness, 'A college campus with all its equipment and faculty, without the students.'

In 1940 the United States had been anxious about supplying food and weapons to countries in Europe that appeared to be about to fall into Axis hands. However, by 1941 it had become clear that Britain was holding out successfully against the possibility of German invasion and the American mood towards supplies became more benevolent. Congress enacted a draft for military service and Roosevelt signed the Lend–Lease Bill in March to permit aid to be given to nations at war with Germany and Italy. In Britain, the immediate impact was an improvement in rations and the appearance of new foods such as Spam and soya flour. Although Lend–Lease was relatively uncontroversial, the draft was less popular and there were protests all over the United States. Both anti-draft protesters and isolationist campaigners suffered harassment from the police and the FBI. SEE ALSO PP. 109–10.

Saturday 15 March 1941

Guy Heriot returns to Malaya after nine months' leave and notices some changes

Guy Heriot was a British colonial civil servant in inter-war Malaya. In June 1940 he had gone on a long period of leave from a relatively peaceful country untroubled by the threat of war. When he returned in 1941, he found the scene quite changed.

To a certain extent, Malaya had changed since I had left it in the preceding June. There were far more troops, British, Australian and Indian. Conscription for Europeans had been introduced; those under forty-one having to serve in the Federated Malay States Volunteer Forces; and those others who were fit, in the Local Defence Corps or some other Auxiliary Service. The Volunteer training, naturally, had been increased and, apart from normal parades during the week, each man had to serve in camp for a continuous training period of two months each year. In my case, the Local Defence Corps drew the short straw and I became a full private, which did not entail anything much more arduous than a couple of parades a week and an occasional field day on Sunday; and, of course, standing by for any internal trouble which might occur.

And there was trouble, oh yes; I arrived back in Klang to find half the Indian labour forces from the estates on strike. In some cases there were genuine grievances – which were easily and soon adjusted – but in most cases it was a case of agitators stirring up trouble. And, undoubtedly there was Japanese propaganda behind it all. The majority of the coolies had no wish to strike – I speak from experience: my own informed me they were only striking because they had been intimidated by neighbours. The trouble came to a head. There were one or two isolated riots: very regrettably, one or two deaths; a few minor injuries; and then the Police, aided by the L.D.C. [Local Defence Corps] were called out. Police raids were carried out on various estates and any agitator among the labour forces who could be identified by the Manager was taken off to Pudu Gaol in Kuala Lumpur, where he languished for some time until Government had set up a commission to enquire into his case. Incidentally, in my opinion Government might have stepped in much earlier and quashed the thing from the start, but they seemed to adopt rather a blind eye policy.

Apart from this, life went on much the same as it had done before the war. Twice a week there were L.D.C. parades and, in due course, I became a lance corporal; mainly I think because I and another man took some interest in carrying out the defences of the big railway bridge over the Klang River. The main piers had been chambered for mines, and a very rough guard house had been built – at the wrong end of the bridge, but this is a detail – and the powers that be ordained that this guard house must be sandbagged and barbed wire entanglement put all round it and the bridge. So Sam and I, with the aid of his conductor and a band of coolies from our respective estates, did the job.

I suppose very few of us really thought there was going to be trouble with the Japanese. We knew, of course, that there was a lot of talk going on between America and Japan regarding sanctions, and that ambassadors were rushing about hither and thither; but I don't think the idea of Japan actually attacking Malaya at this time . . . occurred to us.

During early 1941 there was continual vague talk of Japan advancing south, but most people thought that it would move only against countries such as Indochina or Thailand. Despite the acquisition of bases in Indochina, Japan was 3,000 miles away from Malaya. Indeed, some families were arriving from cities like London with a view to escaping from the bombing and the threat of war. Nevertheless, Japanese undercover organizations were already at work in Malaya.

Guy Heriot would later be interned as a civilian in camps at Changi and Sime Road at Singapore. He would survive the war and return to Britain in 1945.

Monday 17 – Tuesday 18 March 1941

Joseph Goebbels detects a change in Roosevelt's attitude

Joseph Goebbels was born on 29 October 1897 in Rheydt, Germany. An excellent student, he won scholarships and undertook a doctorate at Heidelberg University. In 1914 he failed to gain acceptance into the army because of medical problems, and also failed as a writer. He joined the Nazi Party in 1926 and was an ardent adherent of Hitler from the outset. The admiration was mutual, for Hitler recognized Goebbels' qualities as a propagandist. When Hitler became Chancellor in January 1933, he appointed Goebbels as Minister for Public Enlightenment and Propaganda. A feverish workaholic, Goebbels would often put in twenty-hour days, pausing only to capture events in his extensive diary.

17 March

Yesterday: Roosevelt has made a blustering, shameless speech attacking us. A lacky of the Jews! I have attacked him unmercifully by the press and radio. There is no point in holding back any longer. It only makes the Americans more insolent. In exchange for the temporary imprisonment of our *Transozean* correspondents in the USA, I have the representative of the United Press in Berlin arrested on suspicion of spying. So that the Yankees realise that they cannot do as they like with us. I am also taking steps against the brazen US radio reporters who are making disgraceful broadcasts from Berlin. The USA will have to be shown that our patience and forbearance are now exhausted.

Little air activity over England. Only some unimportant trouble in the West here. The weather was too bad. Good to be able to get a proper night's sleep . . .

18 March

At my suggestion, the Führer allows Roosevelt's speech to be released to the press for comment. We take a very hard line against it. England is making a big sensation out of the US aid. 'Turning-point of the war'. We must spare no effort to counter this claim. But what else has England to cling to?

One has to have some kind of a support when one intends to continue such a harsh struggle. The Führer's speech at the Zeughaus has resounded round the world. His phrase 'England will fail' sets the tone for the international debate. Very useful! . . .

Party Comrade Salzmann from Shanghai reports on the situation in the Far East. He sees things in very clear, simple terms. Japan has got herself stuck, she cannot hold down the huge areas she has already occupied. China is avoiding set-piece battles. Chiang Kai-Shek is the man so far as all Chinese are concerned. Time and human beings are unimportant when measured against all these huge expanses of territory. Both the nations involved would probably like to make peace, but neither wants to lose face. Japan is in no position to take large-scale action anywhere else. This view seems to me correct. I am presented with it in written form, and I intend to make it available to the Führer as well.

In March 1941 the nature of the Second World War was changing. Despite Goebbels' public confidence, privately he was forced to concede that Roosevelt was wheeling round to offer unqualified material support to Britain. He later noted that Hitler was confident of winning 'even against the USA'. With the United States offering increasing aid to Britain and Hitler planning an attack on the Soviet Union, the hitherto local war in Europe was set to expand rapidly. After a discussion with Hitler, Goebbels remarked in another diary entry that the Führer was 'no longer clear that this will be the last year of the war'.

APRIL – JUNE 1941

O N 13 APRIL 1941 two embittered enemies – Japan and the Soviet Union – signed a five-year neutrality agreement. The details were finalized by the Japanese foreign minister, Yosuke Matsuoka, returning to Japan via Moscow after a visit to Berlin. Ironically, although the government in Tokyo was pleased with the treaty, it was increasingly unhappy with

Matsuoka's brash and independent attitude. Matsuoka was seen as too pro-German and was removed from office shortly after his return. Nevertheless, his remarkable treaty would remain in place until the summer of 1945.

For Stalin this treaty provided significant advantages and offered reassurance that his Asian territories – the area around Vladivostok close to the North Pacific – would be safe while he faced the dangerous Nazi threat from Europe. Stalin certainly did not trust the Japanese and employed an extensive network of spies in Tokyo, including the famous Richard Sorge, positioned to offer him advance warning of possible Japanese aggression. Taken together, this covert NKVD (Soviet secret police) network and the overt neutrality agreement insured him against any surprise Japanese attack. It was also a diplomatic masterstroke that increased the turbulence within the Axis alliance, for Hitler was about to launch his attack on the Soviet Union and would have liked Japanese support.

For the Japanese, this neutrality agreement reflected and emphasized a current shift in policy. As we have already seen, during the 1930s Japan's expansion had been northward, into Manchuria, eventually resulting in serious border clashes with the Soviet Union. The most serious had been at Nomohan in 1939, almost a small undeclared war in which the Japanese were heavily defeated. Partly because of this serious reverse, many Japanese strategists now looked to the south as an alternative direction for expansion. This new trend was accelerated by American trade embargoes on commodities, imposed in retaliation for Japan's policy in China and its incursion into Indochina in September 1940. As a result, Japan was short of raw materials and this made south-east Asia, with its reserves of oil and coal, all the more attractive.

While Berlin and Tokyo grew apart, especially over the issue of Russia, London and Washington drew ever closer. May 1941 saw the continued emergence of a de facto Anglo-American alliance, even though the United States was officially neutral. The ships of the Royal Navy were now allowed to undergo repairs in American dockyards, and even to refuel there while on active operations. Roosevelt increasingly stretched the definition of neutrality. Also in May 1941, a small and secretive group of British scientists named the Maud Committee were coming to the conclusion that it would be possible to make an atomic bomb using uranium. At this moment their findings were largely theoretical, but the following month their views were reported to Churchill, leading to the creation of a research programme codenamed Tube Alloys. Before long, Britain and the United States would agree to pool their resources in this highly secret area. Roosevelt was now pursuing rapid American rearmament, and on 5 June 1941 Congress passed an appropriations bill approving an increase in spending on the US army to a new total of over $10 billion.

Early on the morning of 22 June 1941 Hitler launched his attack on the Soviet Union – Operation Barbarossa. Despite many accurate intelligence reports, warnings by allies and even obvious overt indications of impending attack, Moscow had been living in a state of denial. Accordingly, Soviet forces were unprepared and took very heavy losses in the first few days. Hitler's attack on the Soviet Union was an allied effort, involving twenty-one divisions of the Finnish army in the north. The Finns were anxious to repay the Russians for the Russo-Finnish 'Winter War' of 1940. In the south, the Germans were accompanied by divisions from Romania and Italy, and even a division of fascist volunteers contributed by 'neutral' Spain. However, the ally conspicuous by its absence in this assault on Soviet communism was Japan. Hitler informed Baron Oshima, the Japanese ambassador in Berlin, about the attack only two weeks before it occurred. Tokyo decided to continue to abide by its neutrality treaty with Moscow. The partners in the Axis alliance were now badly out of step.

Tuesday 22 April 1941

Otto Tolischus, *New York Times* reporter in Toyko, hears about the signing of the Russo-Japanese neutrality pact

Welcomed home like a victor entitled to the thanks of the nation, Matsuoka returned by air this afternoon and was given a rousing reception by the Government, the Army, the people, and the press. There was a formal military reception and ceremony at the airfield where he landed; the Government gave a banquet in his honor; the streets along which he rode were lined with crowds shouting 'Banzai!' ['Hooray!'/'We did it!']; and the press was unanimous in his praise. He first reported to the Emperor and then to a liaison conference between the Government and the Imperial Headquarters. In formal statements, radio speeches, and press interviews, he declared that Japan's foreign policy would continue in the spirit of Hakko Ichiu and under the double motto of 'Peace in the Pacific' and 'Construction of the Greater East Asia Co-prosperity Sphere.'

To the foreign press he gave a 'blitz interview' at his official residence, lasting five minutes. Again he walked on air and bore the mien of a conqueror; he was obviously living through the big moments of his life . . .

Perhaps the most interesting feature of the day, however, was revelations by Matsuoka's entourage about the signing of the Moscow pact. This took place in the Kremlin in scenes of great conviviality. Stalin himself arranged tables and chairs to toast the new friendship. Stalin, who does not use wine, drank a self-prepared red liquid, but much wine flowed. Raising his glass, Stalin shouted: 'Banzai for His Majesty, the Emperor!' and declared that a diplomatic relation, once pledged, is unchangeable, however much ideologies may differ. Matsuoka toasted Stalin, and said:

'The treaty has been made. I do not lie. If I lie, my head shall be yours. If you lie, be sure I will come for your head.'

Stalin seemed embarrassed. Then he replied:

'My head is important to my country. So is yours to your country. Let's take care to keep both our heads on our shoulders.'

Thereupon, Stalin toasted the Japanese delegation, including the military and naval members.

'Oh, these military and naval men have concluded the Neutrality Pact from the standpoint of the general situation, but they are always thinking of how to defeat the Soviet Union,' Matsuoka joked.

Stalin did not joke. 'The Japanese Army is very strong,' he said. 'The United States is probably building a large navy, but it will prove of no effect in the end as it does not have the spiritual strength of the Japanese Navy.' But Soviet Russia, he told the Japanese, was not the Russia of the Czars which Japan had defeated.

Finally, Stalin said to Matsuoka: 'You are an Asiatic. So am I.'

'We're all Asiatics,' Matsuoka exclaimed. 'Let us drink to the Asiatics!'

At the station, Stalin tapped Matsuoka on the shoulder and said: 'The European problem can be solved in a natural way if Japan and the Soviets co-operate.'

'Not only the European problem!' Matsuoka answered. 'Asia also can be solved!'

'The whole world can be settled!' said Stalin.

To Colonel Yatsuji Nagai, representing the Japanese Army, Stalin said: 'England's present plight is due to the fact that she views soldiers with little esteem.'

Nagai also told something about Matsuoka's meeting with Hitler: 'Hitler grew so heated in his conversation that it seemed he didn't know to whom he was talking. He raised his fist and, pounding the table, exclaimed, "England must be beaten!" . . .

'But,' said Nagai, 'Matsuoka is also a person who becomes heated in his conversation. I believe an interesting scene was revealed of the two men enthusiastically debating world affairs.'

'Debating' was scarcely the word. Nagai's words seemed to confirm Japanese press reports that Hitler had demanded that Japan move against Britain, instead of wasting time with China. And that Matsuoka had demurred. At the press conference, Ishii [Cabinet Office official] denied the *Nichi Nichi* report about a Six-Power Pact designed to encircle Japan, saying: 'It's just a newspaper story in which the Japanese Government puts no credence.'

Otto Tolischus was an experienced journalist and quickly developed good sources among the junior officials who formed the entourage of Japan's foreign minister, Matsuoka. His diary provides one of the few 'inside' accounts of the signing of the remarkable Neutrality Pact between two unlikely partners. Japan had never forgiven Germany for signing the Nazi–Soviet Pact of 1939. Now, in April 1941, precisely two months before Hitler launched his attack on Russia, Tokyo was able to pay its disloyal German 'ally' back in the same coin. This illuminates the nature of the Axis alliance between Berlin and Tokyo as a relationship in which each side was trying to trick the other, rather than one based on genuine sympathy or trust. SEE ALSO PP. 57–8, 80–1, 90–2.

Monday 28 April 1941

Samuel Grafton, *New York Times* journalist, on the isolationist campaign of Charles Lindbergh

If Colonel Lindbergh's speech had been delivered at the Berlin Sportspalast it would have evoked cheers at precisely the points marked by applause in New York.

The colonel said: 'It is now obvious that England is losing the war.' The crowd went wild. It slobbered over the tasty morsel. I submit that this is strange. An assemblage of genuine friends of democracy, ie, genuine haters of fascism, should have shed tears at this point.

One can perhaps visualize honest isolationists deciding we had better save our own skins because England, alas, alas, may fall. This was different. This had a lot of hurrah in it. This was *sieg heil.*

The colonel said: 'We cannot win this war for England,' and, again, the crowd was delighted. Not a groan went up at the unhappy prospect. This crowd reveled in our alleged American helplessness to save England; it doted upon its own proclamation of our weakness. It felt the national muscle and rejoiced greatly to find it thin.

Some who spoke and some who listened were undoubtedly sincere isolationists. These, like Mr John T Flynn, are the true strays and casuals of an incredible time.

Charles Lindbergh was a famous American aviation pioneer who had made numerous record long-distance journeys in the 1920s, either alone or with his wife Anne. Together they had done much to open up

inter-American air travel across the western hemisphere in the 1930s. Charles Lindbergh had also visited Germany during the 1930s and had received a decoration from the Nazi regime. By 1941 the Lindberghs had become committed isolationists and leading lights in an organization called America First, which urged that the United States ignore the conflicts of 'old Europe'. In contrast, Roosevelt's administration was increasingly intervention-minded and deliberately attempted to smear figures such as Lindbergh with accusations of pro-Nazi sympathy.

Samuel Grafton used his syndicated column to press for American intervention in the war against Germany; he also pressed for tougher embargoes on what could be sold to Japan. Later he would select some of his 'diary entries' to be published as a book. SEE ALSO PP. 52–3.

Wednesday 7 May 1941

Vera Brittain, pacifist and socialist, experiences the impact of war on Bristol and Bath

Vera Brittain was born in Staffordshire in 1893, the daughter of a wealthy paper manufacturer. Primarily a writer, she was probably best known for her autobiographical work Testament of Youth, *first published in 1933. This narrated Brittain's provincial, late Victorian upbringing and her struggle, as a woman, to secure a place in higher education against her parents' wishes. It also described her nursing career in the First World War and her subsequent work for the League of Nations Union. Above all, her inter-war writings were statements against war. By 1939 Vera Brittain was one of the leaders of the Peace Pledge Union, which reflected her views as a Christian, a socialist and a pacifist.*

Breakfast in bed kindly given me by Mrs Mottram. Dressed & went down to town (long pleasant walk downhill in cold sunshine). I learnt a good deal about Bath, which seems to be as typical as any spa could be of reception towns taking the war comfortably. It had about 60,000 inhabitants before war; now has between 80,000 & 90,000. Many people from Bristol here, & others still living there come over to do their shopping owing to Bristol's loss of shops. Bath dominated by Admiralty (Naval staff & civil service) who swank. Preface orders in shops or restaurants with remark: 'I'm Admiralty' – much to annoyance of normal residents, of whom many have left. Others were turned out of hotels in wh[ich]. they had lived for years when Admiralty took them over. Rest[auran]t. was crowded. Tables have to be reserved for lunch if any hope of service. Ample choice of food. Prices higher than London. Tables so crowded that 2 women shared ours. One, elderly, with saggy discontented face, complained because just what she wanted was not there. 'What, no lamb! You don't mean to say the lamb's finished! I can't stand these made-up dishes!'

Vera Brittain

After lunch took bus to Bristol; met there by a charming young P.P.U. [Peace Pledge Union] girl, Kathleen Tucker. Had tea with Kathleen & Eric Tucker at their house on the edge of a housing estate wh[ich]. got the force of the Good Friday Blitz. The taxi-driver who drove us lived there too; he acted as assistant to an undertaker in his spare time & did a good deal of digging people out – talked of one street where he found '27 bodies & 5 sackfulls of human remains'. Smokes a pipe while working. Both the taxi-driver & K.T. told me of Churchill's reception here. He did not really come bec[ause]. Bristol was bombed but to the Univ. to get an hon. degree with Winant the U.S. Ambassador. When they realised the Blitz was on, his train was stopped outside Bristol at 5 a.m. & he was taken in when the Blitz was over. Went straight to Grand Hotel & had a slap-up breakfast when many people in Bristol were homeless & hungry. Local paper made a good deal of this. When Churchill got to the housing estate where the bombs had just fallen, he was met by an angry procession with a placard: 'We're tired of Churchill & his cigar. Give us peace.' It had to be put down by police. Taxi-driver said you don't feel patriotic after being bombed.

The newly arrived American ambassador, John B. Winant, who accompanied Churchill to Bristol, had replaced Joseph Kennedy in February 1941. Unlike his predecessor, he was an advocate of American support for Britain against the Axis. At the end of May, he would return to Washington for discussions with Roosevelt about what further aid could be supplied.

Vera Brittain had been working with the Peace Pledge Union's main campaign for a negotiated peace and took comfort from the barracking that Churchill received in Bristol. Throughout the war she would be a vocal critic of the British policy of area bombing. However, as the war persisted the position of pacifists became more difficult as the scale of atrocities by the Axis powers became more evident. May 1941 was perhaps the last month in which the war still seemed to be confined largely to Europe and a negotiated peace still seemed conceivable. SEE ALSO PP. 217–18.

Wednesday 4 June 1941

General Raymond E. Lee talks with the British about the delicate problem of Allied codes and ciphers

General Raymond E. Lee took up his post as US military attaché in London in June 1940 just as France fell. He was witness to the dramatic period in which a war in Europe expanded to become a world war. An ardent advocate of US support for Britain, by the summer of 1941 he was assisting in directing increasing quantities of American aid to the British war effort. As military attaché, he was also a focal point for intelligence exchange between London and Washington, which drew him into the highly secretive world of codes and ciphers.

At half-past eleven I called on Davidson at the War Office and stayed an hour trying to straighten out him and Whiteford on the matter of Intelligence. The whole thing has been so tangled up.

The talk then turned again on the question of security. They wanted to know whether my despatches went by radio or cable and were relieved to hear that we have a direct wire straight into the War Department. However, I pointed out that this wire was subject to interception by their people here in England and I had no doubt they had taken our messages and attempted to decipher them. Saw a wonderful opportunity, too good to miss, and said, 'If you are worried about this, why don't you let me give you two or three messages in our cipher and you can put it up to your cryptographic crowd to crack it, and if you do succeed in cracking it, then you can let me know and also cease giving me vital information to transmit to Washington.' This has them where I want them. Under any other circumstances I might ask them to crack the cipher and if they succeeded in doing it, they might still say they had not done so, in order to take off the stuff I am sending. But it is now to their interest to assure me as to its security or not, because the stuff that is going over it is more vital to them than to us.

Raymond Lee's diary entry describes a fascinating conversation with General Davidson, the British Director of Military Intelligence. It records the beginnings of the most secret alliance between Britain and America – the signals intelligence alliance – which persists to this day. During the period before Pearl Harbor, British codebreakers had attacked the codes not only of Axis countries but also of neutral and friendly countries, because the secrets that this revealed assisted Britain in conducting its diplomacy. As Raymond Lee was aware, his nascent allies in London did not hesitate to 'take off' American enciphered messages sent from the US embassy in London back to the United States. However, Lee also recognized the most important principle of intelligence-sharing with allies, namely that there comes a point when an ally becomes so close and important that vital intelligence is being shared with it. Once this point is reached then the two allies have a greater interest in protecting that shared information from any third party than they have in reading each other's communications. As Lee realized, Britain and America reached this magical point in mid-1941. It was now more important for the British to ensure that American codes were unreadable than it was for them to read the coded material. Mutual co-operation to ensure good communications security would become the bedrock of several highly secret intelligence-sharing agreements between London and Washington during the war. SEE ALSO PP. 112–14.

Friday 6 – Saturday 21 June 1941

Marquis Kido worries about the coming German attack on Russia

Koichi Kido was born in 1889. He had been Secretary to the Lord Keeper of the Privy Seal in the mid-1930s and became Minister of Education in 1937. After further periods as Minister of Welfare and then Home Affairs, he was appointed Lord Keeper of the Privy Seal in 1940 and remained in this post throughout the war. He was Emperor Hirohito's closest adviser during the most critical periods of the wars with China and the Allies.

6 June

At nine in the morning Prince Konoye telephoned me to say that Ambassador Oshima [Japan's ambassador in Berlin] had had an interview with Fuehrer Hitler at Berchtesgaden. According to the report of the ambassador, it seems that Germany has at last decided to attack Russia, and Hitler has made an indirect demand for a joint front against Russia. Prince Konoye also said that a liaison conference was held to consider the report of the ambassador this morning, and he asked me to relay what he had said to me to the Throne.

From 10:20 to 11:05 A.M. I had my audience with the Emperor in order to do what I had been asked by Premier Konoye . . .

21 June

Mr Kakichi Imai came to my house to see me at 9:00 A.M. At 11:50 Foreign Minister Matsuoka telephoned me to say that the news concerning the interview with the Soviet ambassador in Tokyo was not correct. I was received in audience by the Emperor from 1:15 to 2:05 P.M. I heard State Minister Ogura's economic policy at 3:00 P.M. I attended the reception for Mr. Wang Ching-wei at the Imperial Hotel at five in the evening. At six-thirty I went to the residence of Prince Konoye at Mejiro to dine with him and Baron Hiranuma and to exchange opinions concerning current problems.

The gist of our talk was as follows: If war between Germany and the Soviets breaks out, it will prove a serious hindrance to our alliance with Germany, as was the case with the antiwar pact between Germany and Soviet Russia, signed when Baron Hiranuma was the premier. Prince Konoye said that it would be necessary for the Cabinet to bear the responsibility. I objected to his opinion, saying that, in the case of the Hiranuma Cabinet, Germany signed the antiwar treaty with Soviet Russia, which had long been our hypothetical enemy, before the members of the Cabinet had reached a complete agreement on the opening of war against the Soviets. The resignation of Baron Hiranuma from the post of premiership was therefore necessary in order to assume the responsibility for his own lack of sagacity, which was revealed as a result of an unexpected incident, for Baron Hiranuma had long emphasized to the Throne the necessity of attacking Russia. One of the very important objects of the alliance with Germany was to promote our diplomatic relations with the Soviets, a fact which Germany knew and completely understood. Moreover, Germany did not show any objection to the neutrality treaty between the Soviets and Japan. Also, the present pending war between Germany and the Soviets should come as no surprise. Ambassador Oshima had been informed, though informally, about the attitude of Germany toward the Soviets, thus leaving much time for the government to take measures to cope with the situation. Should the Konoye Cabinet resign, it would create an undesirable precedent.

Foreign Minister Matsuoka was not clear in his attitude. At a time when this country is facing a crisis, it was not desirable for us to incur a split in the Cabinet. We should do everything to avoid such a split, for it would disgrace the honor of this country to break up the Cabinet because of other countries' affairs. The premier is expected to assume his leadership powers if the following events occur:

(1) A war between Germany and Soviet Russia.
(2) The participation of America in the war.

Kido's diary notes the first concrete warning that Tokyo received from its allies in Berlin about the impending attack on the Soviet Union. Baron Oshima enjoyed close and cordial relations with Adolf Hitler and yet was told only in June about this dramatic new development. Both Berlin and Tokyo were unaware that the United States had succeeded in breaking the Japanese diplomatic codes, often referred to as 'Magic', and were reading the messages that Oshima sent. Indeed, at this early stage in the war Oshima's missives to Tokyo offered the Allies one of their best windows into the mind of Hitler and his entourage. Western strategists had found it hard to credit that Hitler would take such a gamble, but Oshima's messages helped to convince them that Hitler did indeed intend to launch Operation Barbarossa. Japan was initially confused and perplexed by the coming war between Germany and the Soviet Union. It could not help but recall the events of autumn 1939, when Germany had signed the Nazi–Soviet Pact, apparently betraying the anti-communist alliance that Germany and Japan had signed in 1936. Kido surmised – correctly – that Hitler's move against Russia would raise the stakes and make the chance of both American and Japanese involvement in the war more likely. SEE ALSO PP. 86–7, 123–5, 457–8, 586–7.

Saturday 21 – Sunday 22 June 1941

John Colville, Churchill's private secretary, visits
Chequers and listens to the Prime Minister, the Foreign
Secretary Anthony Eden, and John B. Winant, the
American ambassador, discussing the coming German
attack on Russia

21 June
The P.M. says a German attack on Russia is certain and
Russia will assuredly be defeated. He thinks that Hitler is
counting on enlisting capitalist and right-wing sympathies
in this country and the U.S. The P.M. says he is wrong:
he will go all out to help Russia. Winant asserts that the same
will be true in the U.S. After dinner, when I was walking on
the lawn with the P.M., he elaborated this and I said that for
him, the arch anti-Communist, this was bowing down in the
House of Rimmon. He replied that he had only one single
purpose – the destruction of Hitler – and his life was much
simplified thereby. If Hitler invaded Hell he would at least
make a favourable reference to the Devil!

During dinner there was much talk on the U.S. coming
into the war and also on Pétain's emissary, who has made it
clear that what was holding Frenchmen back from us was
their uncertainty about our victory and about the U.S.
coming in . . .

When I was alone in the garden with the P.M. he said to
me, 'You will live through many wars, but you will never
have such an interesting time as you are having now – and
you may get some fighting later on.' He then spoke of Wavell
and Auchinleck and said it had been very difficult. I
wondered if Wavell might not sulk and refuse India, but the
P.M. said he had been afraid of just putting him on the shelf
as that would excite much comment and attention. I
suggested (as the C.I.G.S. [Chief of the Imperial General
Staff] had) that Wavell would use his pen after the war; the
P.M. replied that he could use his too and would bet he sold
more copies.

There were various nocturnal prowls before we went to bed. During one of them Eden, while holding forth on some topic, took a step backwards and disappeared head over heels into the deep ha-ha and barbed-wire fence at the edge of the lawn.

22 June

Awoken by the telephone with the news that Germany had attacked Russia. I went on a round of the bedrooms breaking the news and produced a smile of satisfaction on the faces of the P.M., Eden and Winant . . .

Churchill was delighted at Hitler's decision to attack the Soviet Union because it took the pressure off Britain and offered it vital breathing space. Having failed to invade Britain the previous year, by early 1941 Hitler was distracted by events in the Balkans and then by his attack on the Soviet Union which took place in the early hours of 22 June. Hitler hoped that his move against Russia would be another brief Blitzkrieg campaign but instead it would prove to be a quagmire.

During this visit to Chequers Churchill also revealed to John Colville that he thought of India as a safe place to dump under-performing generals since he was sure there would be no war there for a long time. Wavell and then Auchinleck were both sent to India from the Middle East.

After the war John Colville would marry Lady Margaret Egerton, with whom he had two sons and one daughter. He served as private secretary to the then Princess Elizabeth (1947–9) and as joint principal private secretary to the Prime Minister, Sir Winston Churchill (1951–5). Colville took a leading role in raising funds for the establishment of Churchill College, Cambridge as a national memorial to Sir Winston Churchill and was made an honorary fellow in 1971. His diaries, together with others quoted in this collection, are kept in the Churchill Archive Centre at the college. SEE ALSO PP. 50–2.

Wednesday 25 – Friday 27 June 1941

Otto Tolischus, *New York Times* reporter, watches the
Japanese weigh their opportunities after the launch of
Operation Barbarossa

25 June

Recovering from the surprise of an actual war between
Germany and Russia, the Japanese Government got busy
today to consider the situation, and – weigh its opportunities. The Cabinet and Army and Navy authorities sat in
almost continuous conferences, climaxed by a liaison conference between the Government and the High Command and
an extraordinary Cabinet session. After that, Konoye saw the
Emperor, and then Marquis Koichi Kido, Keeper of the Privy
Seal. The *Japan Times Advertiser* said the topic of the
discussions was 'a question of supreme importance arising
from the outbreak of Russo-German hostilities.' But what
question? It was impossible to find out.

All Japanese lips were sealed. The police issued a special
warning against groundless rumors and threatened severe
punishment to all, including 'big men in all walks of life,
who, because of their special knowledge, are believed to be
the source of the rumors.' The only rumors afloat were those
of internal Government dissensions, and the conferences
suggested that the Government was still trying to make up
its mind. Moreover, as a rule, the Premier conferred with
Kido only when a Cabinet change was in the wind. Was the
conflict about Matsuoka coming to a head? . . .

27 June

The Government and the High Command held another
extraordinary liaison conference today. Ishii told the press
conference the situation was so delicate that there would be
no statement on government policy. But it began to
appear that there was no statement because there was no
policy.

Tolischus was quite right in his estimation of the Japanese position immediately after the launch of Operation Barbarossa. Tokyo had been given only limited warning of this event, and for a week after the attack there was complete confusion about how Japan might respond. However, as Hitler's legions drove deep into the Soviet Union, several trends were gradually emerging in Japanese thinking. First was the idea that this represented an opportunity and that some sort of action should be taken soon. Second, a continuing gradual shift among the divided policymakers of Tokyo could be seen in favour of the 'southern option' which they hoped might provide access to raw materials without provoking war with either Russia or the United States. On 2 July a major imperial conference would express a clear preference for an expedition into the resource-rich islands of south-east Asia, rather than an attack on the north. This was reflected in subsequent Cabinet changes during July which removed Japan's pro-Hitler foreign minister, Matsuoka. SEE ALSO PP. 57–8, 67–9, 90–2.

JULY – SEPTEMBER 1941

THE PERSON WHOSE 'war diary' historians would most like to read is probably that of President Franklin D. Roosevelt. To our everlasting regret, he did not keep one. Roosevelt was perhaps the most intelligent and sophisticated of the national leaders operating on an increasingly international stage in 1941. He was also the most enigmatic and paradoxical. He was strongly idealistic and liberal-minded, continually enunciating his foreign policy in terms of 'freedoms'; yet in the pursuit of those ideals he was pragmatic, instrumental and ruthless. Even within his own tight circle he operated a policy of divide and rule, rarely revealing his inner thoughts to his kitchen cabinet and often setting one protégé against another. Accordingly, historians continue to disagree about the real nature of Roosevelt's foreign policy. Was he fundamentally an isolationist who was seeking to avoid direct American involvement in the war by supplying the Allied cause? Was he actively seeking American intervention as a belligerent? Or was he an opportunist, simply responding on a day-to-day basis to a bewildering series of world events? Reading his remarks in retrospect, any of these conclusions is possible.

What is clear is that Hitler's attack on Russia in June 1941 fundamentally changed the nature of Roosevelt's dilemma. Many intelligence experts were predicting that the Soviet Union would hold out only for a matter of weeks. Stalin's regime had suffered self-inflicted wounds in the late 1930s, not least the infamous purges in which thousands of the Red Army's best officers had been executed. Although weakened, the Soviet Union had nevertheless been one of the main deterrents imposing restraint on the militarists in Japan. Roosevelt knew that the removal of this pressure through a German victory over Moscow was likely to trigger a Japanese adventure, either north against the remnants of Soviet Asia, or south against the vulnerable European colonies of south-east Asia. Japan's increasing restlessness had already been evident in its seizure of military bases in southern Indochina during July 1941. By the autumn of that year Roosevelt recognized that he might eventually be confronting a situation in which the Axis dominated the whole world apart from the western hemisphere. He realized that his policy of making America the 'arsenal of democracy' was no longer adequate to avert this; however, American public opinion was not yet ready for direct intervention in the war. Put simply, it was no longer in America's own interests to stand aside from war, but by the time the American public realized this it might well be too late.

In July Roosevelt responded to the Japanese seizure of bases in the south of Vichy French Indochina that month by increasing the levels of economic sanctions against Japan, especially on oil exports. In London, this was perceived as a welcome effort on the part of the United States to take up the slack and keep Japan in its place. In Washington, however, there was a growing realization that the continuing negotiations with Japan were unlikely to come to a successful conclusion. In the second week of August Churchill sailed on the battleship HMS *Prince of Wales* to meet Roosevelt at Placentia Bay off Newfoundland. Churchill clearly hoped that Roosevelt would join the war, but the President explained that American public opinion was not yet ready for such a move. Instead, on 14 August the two leaders made a joint declaration which became known as the 'Atlantic Charter', setting forth the Allies' basic postwar principles. These included the repudiation of all territorial aggrandizement, popular consent to all territorial changes, and the rights of peoples to self-determination. Publicly enthusiastic about the Charter, Churchill and many Cabinet members privately worried about what it meant for the future of the British Empire.

Wednesday 30 July – Saturday 2 August 1941

Cecil Brown flies from Cairo to Calcutta and Rangoon, then on to Singapore

Cecil Brown was a veteran US war correspondent who had worked with radio luminaries such as Edward R. Murrow, Eric Sevareid and William Shirer. Like William Shirer, he was a fanatical keeper of his journal. He had broadcast from Rome when Italy entered the war in June 1940. Thereafter he covered the war in the Middle East for CBS. Thriving on adventure, he reported on the war in Syria and experienced some of the fighting in the western desert as the CBS reporter officially attached to the British forces. He was already famous by the time he arrived in Singapore in August 1941, and some regarded his presence as a clear sign that war was coming to south-east Asia.

30 July
Early in the morning I was out on the seaplane base on the Nile for the take-off to Singapore. Since I carry so many papers I am always concerned by last minute difficulties in getting out of a country or into a country. But the Egyptian customs didn't even open my bags . . .

31 July
Before dawn we took off and flew the entire way to Bahrein Island over the Persian Gulf at ten to eleven thousand feet altitude . . .

1 August

All afternoon we've paralleled the Ganges River. My pen is leaking at this altitude. I am having great difficulty in making these notes . . .

2 August

We have three new passengers out of Calcutta, three American tobacco men who have been in Turkey buying the fillings for American cigarettes. We are over the Ganges Delta with its million mouths. Not until we were one hundred miles out of the Bay of Bengal did the water change from a muddy brown to a dull blue. The silt from the Ganges extends one hundred miles out to sea.

At Akyab, inside the Burma frontier, we came down in the inlet of very muddy water lined by forests and swamps filled with chattering monkeys and some crocodiles.

The resident agent of the Airways company has told me a local story about the owner of Akyab's single cinema. In every picture that comes to Akyab, he cuts out all the scenes showing girls kicking their legs and love episodes. Then, at the time of an important local marriage, the movie operator gives a showing of disjointed erotic shots from scores of films showing legs and love-making. It takes an hour to show the Hollywood cheesecake-and-oomph in this special presentation and the prices are special – three times the usual rate . . .

Rangoon is not a tourist spot. There isn't a tourist atmosphere about it. Women sit around smoking huge, fat cigars, drawing so hard on them that their cheeks cave in at each inhalation. Evidently the cigars were a bit strong. Every woman I've seen smoking reclines as though the cigars were too much for her. The faces of all the women are painted grotesquely with a white powder. They look like cigar-smoking death masks. This is my first contact with the Far East. It's like a movie . . .

It is impossible to conceive how any army could find its way down from Thailand to Singapore through this terrain. The jungle and disease would finish off any army which had to face even minor guerrilla operations. It won't be an invasion. It would be a jungle safari. I think the monkeys in the jungle down below are going to remain undisturbed by artillery fire.

After I made that note I fell asleep and the steward woke me for tea and to announce we would be in Singapore in twenty minutes. For five days of flying, from Suez to Singapore, at almost every stop we had touched on water under the protection of the British flag. It was a stunning reflection on Empire.

Over the island of Singapore the town looked aged and weather-beaten. The roofs were red and even near the town there seemed to be thick jungle.

At the customs office of Kalang Airport a huge customs official with dripping flesh and a big smile said: 'You're Cecil Brown, aren't you? We've been expecting you.'

'You said that pretty ominously.'

'It sounds bad,' he laughed, 'when all you journalist vultures start flocking here.'

'I came for war,' I remarked. 'Is it coming?'

'Of course not,' he retorted. 'We've had these Jap scares before. They are an old thing with us by now.' . . .

Representatives from the *Singapore Free Press* and the *Malaya Tribune* interviewed me. I thought it strange, but they explained that I was the first American war correspondent to come to Singapore and the general tone of their questions was: 'Will war come to the Far East?'

I had dinner tonight in the beautiful palm-lined courtyard of Raffles Hotel. Each table, set on the grass, had a pink-shaded lamp and a vase of orchids. The Argyll and Sutherland Highlanders band played for the smartly dressed officials and women in gay print dresses. The members of the band wore plaid hats and white coats and kilts, and the war seemed a million miles away.

Although action was expected in south-east Asia, the majority view was that Japan would move incrementally and cautiously. In August most observers predicted that it would use recently acquired bases in French Indochina to move into neutral Thailand, but go no further. Cecil Brown quickly discerned that the British had a secret plan to forestall the Japanese by moving some way into southern Thailand. After only a few days in Singapore, Brown concluded that the situation was hot.

Convinced that war would come sooner rather than later, he set about urging colleagues to improve broadcasting facilities so that they could cover developments when the time came. As a veteran correspondent, Brown was adept at dealing with censors and censorship. Restrictions on journalists were especially tight in Singapore, but like many other reporters he put the material that he could not broadcast into his diary.
SEE ALSO PP. 94–6, 152–6, 185–7.

Saturday 2 August 1941

Marquis Kido and Prime Minister Konoye worry about the growing strength of the 'intransigent elements' in the Japanese navy

I went to my office at 10:00 A.M. Prince Konoye visited me at eleven. He said he was annoyed to find that there was a noticeable tendency for the intransigent elements in the navy to gather strength, a tendency which would be a great hindrance to the maintenance of harmony between the supreme command and the government. If the U.S.A. adopts decisive measures, such as the cutting off of our supplies of oil, we will run out of oil. Under these circumstances, we will be threatened with an acute national crisis if we make a mistake in our diplomatic movements. Hence, an understanding with the war and navy ministers concerning our fundamental national policy should be secured as soon as possible, and if a complete agreement is not reached, there will be no alternative but for the government to resign en bloc. And it would be the army and the navy that would assume charge of the administration of the country. I talked with the chief secretary about the problem.

In July 1941 Japanese forces had seized bases in the south of Indochina (now Vietnam), although they left the Vichy French administration in charge of the country. This was a clear indication that Tokyo was contemplating an aggressive move to the south. Roosevelt had responded by increasing the constraints on the sale of commodities to Japan, especially oil, and freezing Japan's assets in the United States. The British government and the Dutch government-in-exile followed the lead of the United States in imposing economic sanctions on Japan. By August 1941 Japan faced an almost total embargo on the military-related imports it needed to continue its undeclared war on China, including oil and aviation fuel. These restrictions confronted the military with some stark choices, including whether to accept that their armed forces would be degraded, or to expand further to become autonomous. On the one hand, Japan was weaker than the western powers; but on the other hand, with oil stocks dwindling, it seemed likely that in a year's time the situation might be far worse. Kido understood that the imposition of sanctions by the United States would lead to pressure, especially from the Japanese navy, for action to improve the supply situation. SEE ALSO PP. 75–7, 123–5, 457–8, 586–7.

Friday 8 August 1941

Leo Amery watches planning for Siam and realizes that Britain is desperately weak in the Far East

Leopold Amery was born on 22 November 1873 in India. After going to school at Harrow and studying at Oxford he became a correspondent for The Times. *He spent several years covering the Boer War before becoming an MP in 1911. His career was always intertwined with the Empire: he was a junior minister for the colonies in the early 1920s and Secretary of State for the Colonies in the late 1920s. Like Churchill, he was a fierce critic of appeasement, and in 1940 had joined Churchill's new Cabinet as Secretary of State for India and Burma.*

Leo Amery

[Cabinet] Defence Committee at which we first decided a programme for the sequence of action against Persia . . .

Then we go on to Siam and the Chiefs of Staff report on Anthony[Eden]'s proposal to warn the Japanese that any invasion of Siam would lead to direct countermeasures . . . The report was a miserable woolly document suggesting that even if the Japanese occupied the Kra Isthmus [joining Thailand and Malaya] we should do nothing because we are so helpless at sea. I took a very vehement line on this and on Philip's [Admiral Tom Philips's] support of it, pointing out that this was sheer defeatism and that if our position at sea was desperately weak it would be even weaker if Singapore were under attack from aerodromes on the Isthmus and supporting the land attack on it. As for the Americans, they wouldn't give us assurances beforehand and would be much more likely to help us if we show courage than if we offered our throats to be cut like sheep. I added that no government could live here that sat down while the Japanese seized the Isthmus. We have got so used to sea supremacy and working with numbers on our side that some of our senior sailors simply cannot contemplate risks and lose all their nerve and judgement when faced with the possibility of working with the odds against them . . .

As a matter of fact this whole business of a Chief of Staffs Committee with no Chairman is hopeless. None of the three likes to interfere in the others' domain, still less to tell one of the others that he is lacking in courage; so the conclusion is always timid as well as platitudinous. What is needed is a single Chief of Staff, head of a planning department to make positive plans, which the Chiefs of Staff should be free to criticise before carrying them out; the alternative would be a deputy defence minister who should preside at every meeting of the Chiefs of Staff and direct it . . .

We then finally came on to India expansion. Three months ago India offered to work up to an extra four divisions plus an armoured division for overseas service. This involves besides certain equipment, a complement of British personnel amounting to 25,000 without counting l. of c. [line of communication] troops. For this the WO would get the use of 200,000 men. However tight the man power position here such an offer could not be refused, even if it involved breaking up a British division. But no, the WO simply could not make up its mind whether it would have the spare personnel next year, and therefore held up authorisation. Finally – having been much too patient I fear – I sent a very strong minute to Winston asking to be allowed to authorise India making its initial preparations now and trusting to the fact that the British complement would inevitably be forthcoming in the end. With a helpful Attlee in the Chair I got this through . . .

During August, London responded to Japan's seizure of bases in the south of Indochina by planning for an expected incursion into neutral Siam. The new military government in Bangkok had recently renamed its country 'Thailand', but the more traditional term 'Siam' still prevailed in most western circles. British planning was in line with the view that the Japanese would not dare attack the British colonies of Burma, Malaya and Singapore outright and would instead nibble their way forward, moving into neutral Thailand and perhaps the Netherlands East Indies. For decades, neutral Thailand had provided the British colonies with a cheap buffer state and planners now had to confront its possible occupation by Japan. Their answer was a plan to occupy southern Siam at the narrowest and most defensible point of the peninsula, but the Foreign Office feared American reactions. Amery was especially keen on the 'Siam Plan' because this annexation of southern Thailand would have linked up the British territories of Burma and Malaya, an ambition which colonialists had secretly nurtured for decades. At the end of the war the British would still hope to implement this plan.

Leo Amery was also seeking to expand the Indian Army during 1941 because the subcontinent was an excellent source of military manpower, but met resistance in Whitehall, partly from Churchill who doubted its loyalty. In the event Indian troops would prove to be some of the most effective forces during the war in Burma. SEE ALSO PP. 299–300, 431–3, 637–9.

Thursday 14 – Sunday 17 August 1941

Otto Tolischus, *New York Times* reporter, covers the
attempted assassination of Baron Hiranuma

14 August

The assassins struck today. I was eating lunch at the Tokyo
Club when Count Kabayama asked me whether I had heard
that Hiranuma had been shot.

'Good God, no!' I exclaimed.

'Yes,' he said, 'he was hit by four bullets in the jaw. But I
believe he is expected to live.'

That was all Kabayama would say. He had always assured
me that everything was moving in the right direction, and
that developments were in the wind which would soon
dispel the clouds. He did not look as if this was one of the
developments he had in mind.

Rushing home, I ran into Dooman, who had also heard
about the shooting but knew no further details. We agreed
that it was a bad sign and would undoubtedly complicate
the situation.

After getting some details from the Information Board,
and getting hold of the official bulletin issued in the meantime, I put in a telephone call for New York and was
fortunate to get the story there within half an hour.

What had happened was that a man bearing a letter of
introduction from Hiranuma's home prefecture had called at
Hiranuma's home at 8 A.M. and asked for a sample of the
Minister's calligraphy, which takes the place of autographs
in Japan. While talking with him, the assassin had whipped
out a pistol concealed in a roll of coloured papers, and had
fired at him point-blank. Hiranuma's bulletproof vest must
have saved him, though he was hit in the neck and jaw.
Despite his seventy-five years, Hiranuma gave chase, and
the assassin was captured by a guard at the porch.

The assassin gave his name as Naohiko Nishiyama, and
that is all the press or the police would say about him.

Ten Cabinet Ministers had been assassinated for political

reasons since the time of Meiji. But this was the first assassination attempt since the Army revolt of February 26, 1936,
when the 'younger officers' attempted to wipe out the entire
government of 'greybeards,' killing three Ministers and
injuring one. Judging from the circumstances, another
'February Incident' was in the making, and the Government
was apparently powerless to cope with it. The Emperor sent
to Hiranuma's home his court physician and a basket of
fruit, and Konoye, Home Minister Tanabe, in charge of the
police, and other Cabinet Ministers and prominent personalities called to express their sympathy. But that was all.
More unimportant persons were arrested and hundreds
hauled to the police stations for questioning. But Nakano,
Toyama, and others who gave hunting licenses to their gun-
men remained at liberty, and the police were making every
effort to hush up the whole affair.

16 August

Guests arriving at my house for a dinner and a poker party
were surprised to see an unusual number of policemen lurking in the neighborhood. It was no surprise to me. I had seen
them before, but had thought they might be watching the
Russian newspapermen and some Russian Embassy people
living in the adjacent compound, instead of me. Now there
was no doubt; the guard was for me, and it had been
increased for tonight, probably to identify the guests. That
meant the police knew about the party in advance,
which meant that they were in constant touch with my
servants.

However, the foreign colony was already completely
isolated, and there was little doubt that every foreigner was
under some kind of surveillance, if not perhaps as conspicuously as in my case. Except for a reception given by
Ambassador and Mrs. Grew at the Embassy at which some
Japanese guests were present, and a tea enlivened by
the clever tricks of Japanese jugglers given by the
America–Japan Society during the summer, contact between
foreigners and Japanese had become rare. I had been told by
a Japanese some time ago that my wastepaper basket was
being rifled by the police every day. But so was every other

foreign wastepaper basket. The office boy of Robert Bellaire, United Press correspondent, had conveyed to his boss a request by a policeman not to tear up matter thrown in the wastepaper basket, because it gave the policeman added trouble in putting it together again.

17 August

Hiranuma, strong man of the Konoye Cabinet, guardian of the constitution and the Imperial Prerogatives, and chief opponent of too close commitments to the Axis, was going to live, but was dead politically. The last conservative brakes were being removed. The radicals were triumphant. Nobody dare oppose them.

By August 1941 the radicals were taking increasing control in Japan. The attempted assassination of former Prime Minister Baron Kiichiri Hiranuma, a cautious conservative, underlined how serious the situation had become. More remarkably, three weeks later, a similar attempt would be made on the life of the serving Prime Minister, Prince Konoye. Four masked men, with daggers and short swords, jumped on the running board of his car as he was about to leave his private residence at Ogikubo. Fortunately the doors of the car were locked inside and the assassins were quickly repelled by secret police. As Otto Tolischus noticed, newspaper reporting was also an increasingly dangerous business in Tokyo. The secret police considered that simply being a foreign correspondent was grounds for suspicion and journalists were often arrested during 1940 and 1941. Melville Cox, the Tokyo Reuters correspondent, had already died in police custody.

Otto D. Tolischus would be arrested in November 1941, accused of espionage and tortured. Sentenced to eighteen months' hard labour, he was eventually extricated in 1942 as part of an exchange of diplomats and reporters and returned to the United States, where he remained with the New York Times *as a member of the editorial board and an editorial writer until 1964. SEE ALSO PP. 57–8, 67–70, 80–1.*

Tuesday 26 August 1941

Hugh Dalton, Minister for Economic Warfare, speaks with
Churchill about the Prime Minister's mid-Atlantic
meeting with Roosevelt and America's views on Japan

The P.M. still does not think that the Japs will go to war with
us. The Americans have been giving them very serious
warnings which they may well interpret as meaning that the
U.S. will make war on them if they advance any further, e.g.
into Thailand. He has said that, if the Americans get
involved in war in the Far East, we shall wholeheartedly go
in with them. He has been very rude to the Japs in his broadcast on Sunday – 'All this has got to stop' – and he thinks this
will have had the effect of checking them. The Russians also
have been very firm to them regarding supplies to
Vladivostok from the U.S.A.

Meanwhile, the President is gaining time by conducting
what is really rather a humbugging negotiation with the Japs
on the conditions on which there could be a general
guarantee of the neutrality of Indo-China and Thailand. This
might be guaranteed, not only by the U.S. and the Japs and
the British Commonwealth, but by France and China and
everybody else! The President first hoped to keep this
negotiation going for thirty days; he now hopes he can spin
it out to ninety. Long before then *we* shall be able to put a
really strong fleet in the Indian Ocean without denuding the
Mediterranean. One of our damaged battleships has nearly
completed its repair in the American yards, and a new one is
just coming off the stocks.

The P.M. thinks that the Russians are doing very well
indeed, and jeers at all the experts who began by saying it
would all be over in a few days or weeks. He is confident
that Russian resistance will continue through and beyond
the winter, though they may lose more ground. He thinks
that Leningrad may fall, but not Moscow. He says the
German losses have been prodigious. Never in any nine

weeks, either of this war or the last, have the Germans lost anything like these casualties. They are behaving with the most complete brutality towards the Russians, murdering them, soldiers and civilians alike, like rats by tens of thousands behind their advancing lines . . .

Returning to the Atlantic Conference, the P.M. says that there has been a slide back in U.S. opinion since May or June. (Several other people have told me that the President could have brought them right in then, but his health was not good and he could not decide, and so missed that tide, which has not yet returned.) There is a good deal of playing politics and this will only be remedied when they 'unfurl the flag'.

Churchill had been slightly disappointed by his mid-Atlantic meeting with Roosevelt on the Prince of Wales, *which had begun on 9 August 1941. Churchill had hoped that Roosevelt might promise to enter the war on Britain's side within a matter of weeks. He had also expected a British victory in the Middle East during July 1941 and hoped that the United States would keep Japan guessing until this longed-for success in the desert war freed up Empire forces to reinforce Britain's exposed Asian colonies. Roosevelt certainly succeeded in this regard – keeping Tokyo guessing for some months – but Britain's lacklustre performance in the desert would mean that few forces could be released for service in Asia. Roosevelt, typically, kept his cards close to his chest and did not reveal his thoughts to Churchill or indeed to anyone else. While Churchill thought that the United States was engaged in a game of deterrence, Roosevelt was increasingly bent on a course that was likely to lead to an eventual confrontation.* SEE ALSO PP. 54–5, 603–4.

Thursday 28 August 1941

Cecil Brown, CBS correspondent, patrols the jungle with British troops on the border between Malaya and Thailand

'We have the advantage,' Colonel Moorehead said, 'of know-ing all this territory well. That's a very great advantage. We are sure the Japs don't know it because it was only mapped three months ago, and none of these maps has fallen into Japanese hands as yet.'

Hunched over, I follow behind the corporal along the meager, cluttered, soggy path tunneled through the jungle bordering the frontier between Malaya and Thailand, territory only recently mapped.

It is twilight in here. An inextricable mass and jumble of palms, gum trees, bamboo, teak and intertwined vines and creepers shut out the midday sun and deny the sky itself.

Every now and then the corporal, grunting and muttering softly, swings his sharp-edged *parang* to slice a creeper vine yearning for a neck to choke. At every step our feet sink above the ankles into rotted branches and the muck of the jungle floor.

Colonel Moorehead is too far ahead. Now we can no longer even hear him thrashing his way over fallen trees or slapping away at the aerial vines blocking his path.

Dank and steaming – those are the clichés to describe the jungle. In this hodge-podge of nature gone slightly mad, where the British and Japanese will one day fight, it is dank and steaming, all right – nearly asphyxiating. Hardly a whisper of air, and there's the musty smell of wet places and the piercing scents of decaying matter, animal and vegetable. The sweat pours off our faces and streams down the middle of our backs as though we're in a downpour.

It is the frightening feeling of inability to find the next breath that's most alarming in here. That, and the hidden things poised to leap and bite, or claw and gore.

Ten minutes of this for an amateur is like running two miles. I call to the corporal and we sit on a fallen, slanting tree hemmed in by leaves and tree-trunks and utter silence. Even the birds have deserted us.

This is where claustrophobia takes on a new, neck-crawling, spine-itching meaning. Trees, leaves and creepers seem to be closing in. You can only see a few feet on all sides. The range of vision seems to be narrowing and constantly it gets darker.

You strain ears to listen for a python slithering across the earth or cracking a twig. Your eyes roll in all directions, overhead, left and right and you twist your head to look behind.

Brown's remarks about the terrain on the peninsula stretching south from Thailand to Singapore reflected a widely held public misconception that Malaya's best defence was its 'impassable' jungle. It struck him as inconceivable that any modern army could fight their way through such difficult territory. This was an illusion, for the production of tin and rubber, boosted by commodity price rises in the 1930s, had led to the rapid development of communications networks – but unfortunately out-of-date Allied military plans and old maps, plus a reluctance on the part of civilian developers to inform the military of projects they knew would be frowned on, had prevented this information getting through. Malaya was now criss-crossed with excellent roads and railways, of which the Japanese would eventually take full advantage.

The remote and narrow strip of land linking southern Thailand with northern Malaya – the Kra Isthmus – was subject to intense interest at this time. In the autumn of 1941 British intelligence officers travelled over the border from Malaya into southern Thailand, pretending to be on holiday, in order to reconnoitre this future battleground. They found Japanese officers there, also in civilian clothes and staying in the same hotels. SEE ALSO PP. 83–6, 152–6, 185–7.

Tuesday 2 – Tuesday 16 September 1941

Lord Reith complains about Churchill's 'entertainment of foreigners'

John Reith was a tall and striking Scot who had headed the BBC in the inter-war period. Born in 1889 as one of many children of a minister of the Free Church of Scotland, he had come up the hard way. His family were short of money and, although he was an academic success at Gresham's School, were unable to send him to university, something which would rankle with him throughout his life. Reith had served in the First World War in the front line and was wounded. He had drive and a talent for leadership, but also a propensity to develop grudges against his superiors.

John Reith

2 September
Dined with CIGS [Alan Brooke]. Scathing comment on Churchill's invariable habit of putting the blame on the chiefs of staff whenever he could but of giving them no credit when things went right and contrary to his expectations. CIGS said he had never known subordinates treated as Churchill treats them. Contemptible he said.

4 September
Went all over the Great George Street underground [the underground complex of Cabinet War rooms]. Churchill and his favourites will be safe from any bombing.

16 September
Lunched with Lord Bennett [former prime minister of Canada] at the Savoy and had quite an interesting talk – most damning it was. He said Beaverbrook [Minister for War Production] was as much a puppet in the hands of Churchill as anyone else. Churchill would have only yes-men about him. Of course I could do far better than most any of them. He said the war was a very secondary consideration with

lots of them. (It is No. 5 in my view: (1) their own interests personally; (2) their particular preconceptions, prejudices and partialities; (3) their political party; (4) friends and relatives; and (5) country.) He said that though power might be concentrated in the executive rather than in Parliament, it was an executive of twenty or thirty which is absolutely true. I can't get things done because of blasted departmental particularism.

I have been asked to approve £450 odd for wines etc. on the *Prince of Wales* for Churchill and Co., under guise of entertainment of foreigners. I wonder how much of it Roosevelt drank. Today I was asked to approve £1300 for a special train for Beaverbrook and Co. going to the north of Scotland en route for Moscow. I hope Beaverbrook gets killed en route. It would be a splendid release and escape for this country. And this also is under guise of entertainment of foreigners.

Reith's extraordinary diaries, which extend to almost 2 million words, capture his visceral emotions. One of his most pronounced sentiments was an intense dislike of Churchill and his circle, combined with a deep suspicion of their motives. Reith's splenetic outpourings reveal the bitter political and bureaucratic battles that were under way in Whitehall and Westminster during 1941. They also touch upon two vital meetings in the autumn of 1941. The first was the mid-Atlantic meeting between Churchill and Roosevelt on the ill-fated Prince of Wales. Shortly thereafter, Lord Beaverbrook, press baron and Minister of Production, headed north by train and then travelled by sea to meet with Britain's new allies in Moscow. London and Moscow had recently agreed on a joint occupation of Iran to facilitate a supply route from the western Allies to the Soviet Union.

After serving as Minister of Transport and then Minister of Works, John Reith would finally leave government for the Royal Navy in 1942. Between 1946 and 1950 he was chairman of the Commonwealth Telecommunications Board.

Thursday 11 September 1941

Charles Lindbergh, isolationist campaigner, addresses a
meeting of America First at Des Moines in Iowa

*Charles Lindbergh was born on 4 February 1902 in Detroit and raised
on a farm near Little Falls in Minnesota. His father had served as a
congressman for Minnesota from 1907 to 1917. After studying
engineering at university Lindbergh became fascinated by aviation and
was the first person to fly across the Atlantic, travelling from New York
to Paris in the* Spirit of St Louis *in 1927. He subsequently made
numerous record long-distance journeys, either alone or with his wife
Anne. Charles Lindbergh was also a committed isolationist and a
leading figure in the organization America First which opposed intervention by the United States in the war against Germany.*

Afternoon spent reading over my address, and in
conferences . . . All sorts of people came in during the afternoon. One, a preacher, said a prayer as he left. Another had
a religious prophecy he wanted to tell me about. One man
had a new economic plan. A fourth wanted to show me his
collection magazine and newspaper records of 'undercover
British dealings'. Several 'old friends' came to call, most of
whom I had apparently met *once* many years ago at a time
when I was meeting thousands of people every week. They
recalled the circumstances surrounding our meeting 'fourteen years ago,' and expected me to then remember all
details connected with it. The unfortunate part is that the
real friends you would like to see stay away because they are
afraid of intruding when you are busy, and you are left
surrounded by people who push themselves forward claiming to be friends. Then, the wildest and most absurd
newspaper stories appear about you, told by 'an old friend,'
who probably bases his lifetime acquaintanceship on two
meetings, more than ten years apart, of less than half an hour
each, and with several other people in the room at the time.
  Supper with several members of the America First
Committee at a nearby club. Then back to hotel, where our

party assembled, and from there to the meeting hall behind the usual police escort. I always ask the police to avoid using sirens if possible. I think people dislike them when their use is not essential. I know I do. We drove into the car entrance to the meeting hall and sat behind the curtain until the President finished his address . . .

Mrs Fairbank was the first speaker. She did a very good job under very difficult conditions. Before long we began to win over the crowd, and the clapping and cheering of our supporters overcame the cries of our opposition. [Hanford] MacNider made a strong address and was well received. (It was interesting to note that the least popular portion of his address consisted of a quotation from President Hoover.) I spoke for twenty-five minutes. It seemed that over eighty per cent of the crowd was with us by the time I finished; but the ice had been well broken before I started by the previous speakers. When I mentioned the three major groups agitating for war – the British, the Jewish and the Roosevelt Administration – the entire audience seemed to stand and cheer. At that moment whatever opposition existed was completely drowned out by our support.

Dozens of people came to our hotel rooms after the meeting – America First members and supporters and advisers, local officials, newspapermen, etc. Some were solid, stable citizens; some erratic, some intelligent; some stupid; all types are present at these meetings, but on the whole we have a much better than average cross section of the communities where we meet. Our opposition press, of course, picks out and emphasizes the radical and fanatical types who attend.

By September 1941 the strain of almost a year of non-stop campaigning was beginning to tell on Lindbergh, although his message was still highly popular. He was also the subject of increasingly orchestrated attacks by interventionists. Lobby groups pressing for intervention were being secretly funded by British intelligence, a matter that has only recently come to light. At many public meetings of America First, the organizers had to double-wire the lights and public address system because political opponents would resort to sabotage. However, at Des Moines it was his speech, rather than saboteurs, that caused problems.

His attacks on the interventionist activities of 'Jewish groups' soon got him branded an anti-semite. He also forecast defeat for America if the United States took on the armed might of Germany, and many now suspected him of harbouring pro-German sympathies. SEE ALSO PP. *573–4, 598–9, 611–12.*

OCTOBER 1941

DURING LATE SEPTEMBER and early October, Konoye and his government in Tokyo worked hard for a settlement with the United States, and initial hopes were high. They sought a major conference which they hoped would be attended by Roosevelt. Washington was uneasy about the idea of a conference and insisted that it should be preceded by a preliminary agreement. Time was running out for Konoye, whose political power was fast being eroded, and he lacked the flexibility to negotiate any preliminary agreement. He continued to request a meeting with Roosevelt as the last means for peace. Roosevelt replied that he would entertain the idea of a summit only if Japan withdrew from China first. By 2 October both sides accepted that the negotiations were going nowhere. In Tokyo, assassination attempts against Baron Hiranuma in August and Konoye himself in September had already signalled the wisdom of their moving aside to make way for more radical figures.

On 16 October 1941, having failed in his avowed objective to reach an agreement with the United States, Prime Minister Konoye resigned in Tokyo. Although Konoye had presided over a balanced Cabinet, he represented a personal impediment to militarism. A lawyer by training and a committed constitutionalist, he had entered Japan's parliament hoping to reduce the power of the army general staff over foreign policy decisions. However, few civilians were now willing to step forward and take his place, and so the War Minister, General Tojo Hideki, became Prime Minister. Tojo reappointed himself War Minister and also took on the home affairs ministry. Although this change marked the rapid ascendancy in Tokyo of the group in favour of going to war, the decision to do so had not yet been taken. Tojo's decision to appoint himself Home Affairs Minister in fact reflected his recognition that he would have to suppress violent opposition from the radicals if his government should come to a peaceful accommodation with the United States.

On 25 October the British battleship the *Prince of Wales*, which had carried Churchill to meet Roosevelt in August, left the Clyde for the Far East. On board was Admiral Tom Philips, who had been ordered to take command of a new Far East fleet to be built around this battleship and the cruiser the *Repulse*. London intended that they should be joined by the carrier *Indomitable* but this ship was damaged while training in the West Indies.

One of the noticeable changes in the United States during the autumn of 1941 was the increasing numbers of people under conscription. The fall of France in June 1940 had prompted Congress to adopt a conscription act as a general measure of preparedness. Because of vigorous opposition from pacifists, isolationists and others, those conscripted were required to serve for only one year, and could not be sent outside the western hemisphere. However, in August 1941 Congress decided, by a one-vote margin, to keep the one-year draftees in the army beyond their term. During the following five years some 10 million American men would be drafted through the selective service system.

Monday 6 – Tuesday 7 October 1941

Captain Hyman Samuelson worries about the plight of under-educated black conscripts drafted into the US army

Hyman Samuelson was born in Donaldsonville, Louisiana in 1919 and grew up in New Orleans. In 1940 he graduated in civil engineering from Louisiana State University and embarked on a master's degree while working as a university teaching fellow. In 1941 he was drafted into the 96th Engineers Battalion (Colored).

Captain Hyman Samuelson

6 October

Very much depressed this evening. Tired of these poor negroes, tired of punishing them, trying to reason with them. Such a shame for people with education to let such ignorance exist. If they were ignorant but happy, I would say nothing, but they are miserable. Superstitious, emotional! I never knew what it was before to see a 25 year old man come crying to me because so-and-so stole his cigarettes. What goes on in a man's mind who can't tell a seven from a two? Men who can hardly understand English – how can they be good soldiers? And citizens? Is it fair that we treat them as our equal when we go inducting them into the army and treat them as a domestic animal when it comes to education? What horrid creatures we whites are!

I messed up the courts martial case against Floyd this evening. My evidence in his defense was either irrelevant or it was laughed at. Poor negro got six months of hard labor with forfeiture of ⅔rds of his pay during the time. When I close my eyes at night, I see the fear-marked faces of these darkies. Their tears when you scold them for being unable to execute 'inspection arms' properly. Their dirty uniforms! Their scars. Their salutes – what a wild and nervous look in their eyes when they salute; fear that they will do it wrong. They salute horribly. I walk among them with a sick feeling. Hundreds of men sleeping on the ground. Most do not know the names of their tent mates. Some cannot write home; they don't know how. Some don't get mail; they couldn't read it anyway. Many don't know where they are. Some don't care where they are going. I wish there was something I could do. But I'm helpless. I saw that more than ever at tonight's courts martial.

No mail! I am unhappy this evening. Hardly feel like speaking, and writing is difficult with this frame of mind.

7 October

A letter from Dora today made me feel better, and my answer to her – pouring out all the things which were bothering me – made me feel still better. But I'm still pretty gloomy. Perhaps after awhile I'll get used to taking these negroes' problems as part of my work, but life is going to be pretty gloomy for me during the transition.

Captain Hyman Samuelson was a young, white, Jewish officer in command of African American troops. Initially he assisted with their training at Fort Bragg, but later he would be sent with them to New Guinea on active service. His remarkable diaries deal with conscription and racial segregation in the US army. They also illuminate the relationships between black troops and their white officers. Segregation was remarkably deep rooted and between 1920 and 1940 only one African American officer had served in the US army. Moreover, during the depression of the 1930s only whites had been allowed to join the army in any capacity. By 1941 the civil rights movement was already active, forcing Roosevelt to desegregate the defence industry, although he was able to defer desegregation of the armed forces until after the war. SEE ALSO PP. 282–4, 338–9.

Thursday 16 October 1941

Admiral Matome Ugaki hears that the Konoye government has collapsed and that General Tojo will form a new Cabinet

Matome Ugaki was born on 15 February 1890 at Seto-machio in the Okayama prefecture. He entered naval cadet school in 1909 and progressed rapidly, attending staff college at the remarkably young age of thirty-two. Having spent some time on attachment in Germany in the inter-war years, he was promoted to admiral in 1938. On 10 August 1941 he was appointed to the key position of Chief of Staff to Admiral Yamamoto, the commander of the Combined Fleet. As such he was in a superb position to witness Japan's naval policy during the six months prior to the outbreak of war, and recorded this in his excellent diary, which must count as one of the outstanding records of Tokyo's inner circle under pressure of war.

At 1830 the radio announced that the third Konoye Cabinet resigned en bloc. The main reason he gave up was broadcast as being that his cabinet colleagues cannot be of one mind in deciding important national policy. Of course, that means the problems with the United States. And no doubt it is due to the answer from the United States on the 2nd. I feel it rather too late to expect Konoye to succeed. Concessions have to be made in the adjustment of diplomatic relations. In this case, concessions would have to be beyond the minimum decided at the council in the imperial presence. If that were done, the result would be that the China Incident, which has cost 150,000 souls and more than fifteen billion yen in war costs, will be all for nothing, and the idea of establishing the Greater East Asia Co-prosperity Sphere must be given up as a fruitless dream. Konoye, who has been responsible for them from the beginning, will not be able to find it in his heart to do so. Will he then choose to open a war? This needs a prompt decision. Rather strenuous opposition can be expected among the cabinet ministers. It is a deadlock. I realize that the only alternative left for him was to abandon the cabinet.

Is no one else among our politicians but Konoye capable of being premier now? I think there should be, and is. But in fact a man of ability worthy of such an important responsibility usually turns up in some more remote position. After sticking in such mire as this, probably no one will be willing to wear his mantle.

Konoye is 'a lord who wears long sleeves at court' [someone who is excessively relaxed and leisurely]. He used to abandon anything once he lost interest in it. Of course, this time will be no exception. At the Diet session last year in the presence of His Imperial Majesty, he gave many assurances of his readiness which sounded soothing to our ears, but I wondered whether he had a sincere love for the state and sufficient patriotism to do his bit unselfishly. Still, today's crisis is too much for a dilettante. I would rather admire Konoye if he were to reform his cabinet with the purpose of purging the moderate faction. But I doubt if he can do this on his own responsibility. Then who will succeed him? A navy man? Or army? And can he win the war? Or will it come about after another political change? One way or another, we have no time to lose. After the cabinet is formed, much time will be required before our great plan can be framed. During that period, their [the western allies'] war preparations will climb hand over hand, while we shall fall into poverty by inches, expending the oil on hand. A day's delay costs us that much disadvantage. The conclusion is to place our state under a military administration, if need be, at one bound.

I ordered one of the staff to put down what was broadcast. Reportedly the Council of Chief Vassals who had served as premier was held at court in the morning. It came over the air at night that His Majesty asked [War Minister] Lieutenant [General] Tojo to form a new cabinet. The official residence of the war minister was fixed up for the Cabinet Organization headquarters. It went so far as to report the names of several visitors already. 'Tojo should be prime minister!' I felt a slight resistance, but he is a man of excellent caliber. He will do the job, I am sure.

Without hesitation, in spite of the shortage of talent, this same man was plucked out of the domain of the army, which has been urging war. He has a deep understanding of the present situation and has merely changed his post. If we don't go to war, this selection could be a way to put down the army. If we decide to open war, he will be the man to dare to do so.

On 16 October 1941 the government of Prince Fumimaro Konoye, Prime Minister of Japan, collapsed. Konoye's first Cabinet had fallen in 1933 after action in China by the military. In 1940 Konoye had been asked to form a second Cabinet. He attempted to contain the long-running war with China, but relations with the United States had deteriorated. Now he resigned again, because of confrontations with the army minister, Tojo Hideki. From mid-October Japan's foreign policy would be formally controlled by the military. However, they remained undecided about which course Japan should take. SEE ALSO PP. 394–5, 632–3, 740–1.

Thursday 16 – Friday 17 October 1941

Oliver Harvey, Anthony Eden's private secretary at the Foreign Office, hears of the collapse of the Konoye government in Japan

Oliver Harvey was born in Norwich on 26 November 1893. He was educated at Malvern College and studied at Cambridge before serving in the First World War. Between the wars he joined the Foreign Office and was posted to Paris and Rome. From 1936 he was private secretary to Foreign Secretaries Lord Halifax and Anthony Eden, and was continually close to the centre of power.

16 October

Bad news again this evening. Resignation of moderate Konoye Cabinet in Tokio, following on Russian difficulties, seems to portend a forward movement by Japanese extremists, who were never enamoured of Konoye's United States conversations ... But where? North against Vladivostok or South against Siam? No news yet of Konoye's successor. Cabinet Defence Committee are considering what we can do, obviously nothing without the

Americans. It is intended to put the case squarely to them and say we'll do whatever they'll do. We are also considering despatch of capital ships to the Far East. That would make a difference. Japs so hysterical a people, one can never be certain they may not rush themselves off their feet.

17 October

... Maisky [Soviet ambassador in London] yesterday very anxious about events in Russia, pleads for despatch of troops to Murmansk and to Caucasus. We have proposed to release Soviet troops in Persia by taking it over entirely (but Soviets are suspicious of that!) and possibly to send a token force to Caucasus. Cripps [British ambassador in Moscow] strongly urges latter too because of effect on Soviet morale. Maisky also worried at Japs and anxious to know what we think.

Oliver Harvey

Oliver Harvey's diary underlines the transformation effected by Hitler's invasion of Russia in how people thought about the war. In the course of a few short months during the summer of 1941 this conflict had ceased to be two separate regional wars, limited to Europe and China: it was now a global systemic conflict in which a political shift in Tokyo had alarming consequences for Washington, London and Moscow. Although the Japanese now seemed more likely to go to war, no-one knew in which direction they would move. General Tojo was an army man and the Japanese army had traditionally desired war with Russia – the 'go north' option that would involve a land campaign. Many, including Roosevelt, expected Japan to choose the northern option now, so it was not surprising that Ivan Maisky was nervous. SEE ALSO PP. 297–9.

Wednesday 29 October – Thursday 6 November 1941

Viola C. White, pacifist and librarian, watches tanks appear in the countryside around Middlebury College in Vermont

29 October

Miss MacKay, who is Business Manager Fritz's new secretary, says a military man has filled out the forms for permission to stage a tank drill on Bread Loaf Mountain. Instead of expressing horror at these mechanistic monsters crushing the life out of the mountain side, all the ladies at the Bartell dining room could think of was wanting to have a ride in one of the tanks. I am noticing in this war what I noticed in the last – a sort of juvenile play acting . . .

30 October

We now know that one of our vessels, the *Greer*, that peaceful emissary of a neutral nation, was helping a British bombing plane to attack a German U-boat, when torpedoed. What the destroyer *Kearny* was doing when torpedoed still remains in doubt, something probably as helpful and innocent as the *Greer*'s performance. And on the strength of these phony provocations, the President hollers that we are already in the shooting war – as we indeed shall be, if he can compass it.

As the chance of war and the tension mounts, I find myself

considering alternatives to the not too pleasant nor glorious role of passive dissenter in a war-minded community. Only two possibilities exist, and they are almost impossibilities for me: to join the Quakers – and it's most unlikely they would accept a woman of 51 with my unuseful training; take to the woods in one of these abandoned Vermont farmhouses, which can be bought for a song. But there again my unhelpful training and spoiled city habits make me hesitate. I, who have never prepared my own meals or even made my own bed – could I so much as keep alive in a farmhouse through the Vermont winter?

6 November

Indian Summer. Three army men rushed in under the guidance of Mr Fritz, who is showing them the campus . . . A poster adorns the library bulletin board – a jolly smiling marine . . . with 'Welcome Tanks' in large letters beneath.

By the second half of 1941 the US navy was increasingly engaged in escorting convoys carrying Lend–Lease goods to Britain as they moved through the western Atlantic. As a result, US destroyers and German U-boats were effectively engaged in open warfare off the American east coast. British and American naval operations were fully integrated, and in the western Atlantic Royal Navy ships operated under direction from Washington. There were several incidents in the autumn of 1941, including the sinking of the US destroyers Greer *and* Kearny *by German submarines. The* Kearny *was sunk by a German U-boat on 17 October after a convoy battle involving British, Canadian and American ships. Curiously, this loss of American life did not do much to alter American attitudes to intervention in the war and public opinion continued to favour a position where the United States would supply democracies but not enter the conflict itself. Everywhere there were signs of conscription and Viola White, a naturalist, resented the arrival of tank units, which went on exercise around Middlebury and churned up the local countryside.*

A poet and scholar of literature as well as a socialist and pacifist, Viola C. White eventually became Curator of the Abernethy Library of American Literature at Middlebury College. SEE ALSO PP. 60–1.

NOVEMBER 1941

DURING EARLY NOVEMBER the Tojo government decided on a last-ditch effort to secure agreement with the United States and despatched a special envoy to Washington: Saburo Kurusu, a career diplomat who had previously been ambassador in Berlin. Meanwhile ministers set themselves a deadline of late November for a substantive outcome from these talks if war were to be avoided. Accordingly, during November 1941 all eyes were fixed on the negotiations in Washington between Kurusu and Cordell Hull, the American Secretary of State. Initially talks focused on a short-term modus vivendi which would have involved a withdrawal of some Japanese forces from Indochina in return for the lessening of sanctions.

However, Hull was an ardent opponent of territorial change achieved through the use of force and was now caught in a dilemma. On the one hand, he wished to avert war and to emerge from his talks with a peaceful settlement. On the other hand, he knew that the Japanese would accept only limited withdrawals from their hard-won position on mainland Asia, perhaps at most the abandonment of their new bases in Indochina. Any viable peace deal would therefore mean condoning the extensive and violent gains Japan had made in China since 1937. Hull confronted the awkward but familiar choice between peace and justice. Partly under pressure from the Chinese, and after discussions involving Roosevelt and his Cabinet on 25 November, Washington decided to adopt a tough bargaining position. On 26 November Hull presented the Japanese with a ten-point document demanding withdrawal from China as well as Indochina, offering to drop trade sanctions if they did so. Saburo Kurusu and Admiral Nomura, the Japanese representatives in Washington, conveyed this to Tokyo – and at this point all parties were aware that the talks had effectively failed.

Roosevelt's own position remains obscure, but he cannot have believed that the Japanese would accept these terms. Indeed, he may have had no particular wish for an agreement.

During 1941 the widening war had put him in an increasingly difficult position, and now he may have hoped to pass the buck by placing the burden of decision on Tokyo. Some have argued that he may even have hoped to push Tokyo into making the first move, thus resolving the problem of how America might enter the war on the side of the democracies.

Many in London, however, hoped that Hull would find a successful diplomatic solution. Once this possibility evaporated, London planners convinced themselves that Japan would not dare attack Malaya and would advance only as far as Thailand. However, out in south-east Asia, British intelligence officers were reading local Japanese consular codes and were already aware of Japanese preparations for sabotage and subversion in Malaya in the coming weeks. Even the local populations had noticed that fifth columnists were out and about preparing for a dramatic campaign that would take the Japanese all the way to Singapore and beyond. By late November 1941, everyone seemed to know what was about to happen in south-east Asia – except the local Allied commanders.

Monday 17 November 1941

General Raymond E. Lee, US military attaché in London, enjoys a joke over lunch with his Japanese friends

Raymond Lee lunched with Japanese diplomats and dignitaries in the hope of learning more about the mission of Saburo Kurusu, Tokyo's special envoy who was negotiating in Washington in November and December 1941.

I lunched today as the guest of Major General Tatsumi, my Japanese Army colleague, and a very old friend. I sat on his right and next to me on the other side was Viscount Kano, the head of the Yokohama Specie Bank, a roly-poly man, with a very delicate brown skin and sparkling, intelligent eyes behind spectacles. The other guests were Greenwell, the Japanese Chargé d'affaires, Major General Piggott (Ret.) of the British Army, who has for many years been their Military Attaché in Tokyo and is a great Japanese sympathizer, together with one of the assistant attachés. It was evident that the party was staged to take place at a critical time and the Japs were all nervous, jumpy and preternaturally solemn. It reminded me of nothing more than the attitude of the Germans on the day they marched into the Rhineland. They displayed the same symptoms of anxiety. We know now that had the French or British shown any sign of determination at all, the Germans were prepared to back up and call the whole thing off. I could not help but feel this today and said so in a cable to G-2 [American Military Intelligence in Washington].

I asked Kano about Kurusu, whom he said he knew well. Kurusu has lived in the United States a good deal, speaks American fluently, and has an American wife. I asked what he went there for. Kano said solemnly that it was necessary to have something concrete come from the negotiations which have been dragging along interminably. I asked him how long he thought it would now be before some decision was reached. He said that it could be more than a week or ten days. It was necessary, he said, that something be done because the people in Japan were at a breaking point and could not stand any longer delay. Unless some decision was reached they might fly off the handle and do something foolish. After a little of this very serious conversation I tried to lighten it a bit by saying that I had my own solution of Kurusu's mission. Kano asked me, with great interest, what it was. I said I thought that Kurusu was following in the footsteps of a great many other national representatives who had come to Washington to see if their countries could not benefit under the Lend–Lease Bill. This was a little too fast for him and he blinked a bit and then began to explain that the Japanese could help quite a lot with it because they had a large merchant marine which could help carry weapons and munitions. I finally had to hammer the point home by asking him how many tanks, warships and airplanes he thought the Japanese would like the United States to furnish Japan. At this point he saw the joke and gave some evidence of enjoying it.

Raymond Lee's lunch was a notable success. The assertion that some-thing had to be done in the next week to ten days 'because the people in Japan were at a breaking point' and could not tolerate further delay summed up the situation in Tokyo perfectly. With this information Lee probably knew as much about the state of play in Tokyo as most members of the Japanese embassy in London. This was neither surpris-ing nor unusual. Links between British, Japanese and American military officers were in some cases remarkably close, especially when they had been on exchanges or served together as attachés in other locations. Joining in the discussions with Lee and the Japanese was Major-General F. S. G. Piggott, who had been a long-serving British military attaché in Tokyo and was probably closer to Japan than he was to Whitehall. Raymond Lee, a pro-fessional intelligence officer, read their faces like a book and knew instinctively that war was only weeks away. SEE ALSO PP. 73–5.

Saturday 22 – Friday 28 November 1941

Jack Woodward gets the word about the coming invasion from the locals at Fort Butterworth in Malaya

Jack Woodward was born in Cairns in Queensland, Australia, and attended Brisbane Grammar School. He later worked as a book-keeper and then an accountant during the difficult years of the depression. He married in November 1940, and had just completed his final account-ancy examinations in early 1941 when he was called up, joining the Royal Australian Air Force (RAAF). By November he was serving with a unit of Blenheim bombers near Fort Butterworth in Malaya.

22 November

This day, we went into Butterworth to play football, but the game was scrubbed when we arrived, as they could not field a team. We then decided to go in the ferry to Penang, and there met R.A.A.F. sergeant from Alor Star. In conversation he told me that during the previous Thursday, an aircraft they thought was a German M.E. 110 had flown over their airfield coming from the direction of Thailand. It circled the drome, and then returned in the direction of the border.

I went for a walk during the afternoon, and stopped to watch some Chinese playing badminton. After a while, I was invited in, and our conversation turned out most startling. They were very concerned and informed me that the Japanese would be invading Malaya within the next three weeks. I found that hard to believe, and asked them why they thought that this was the case. They told me that it was common knowledge amongst them. They had their own source of information, and had reported it to the British authorities, but nobody would take any notice of their concern.

They also informed me that there were several Japanese photography shops in Penang who would sell films, and develop and print them at only half the rate that we would pay at our station (where we already had a cut price). These shops would then take a copy of any photo they thought would give information of a military nature, and pass it on to the Japanese authorities. (This was what was known as fifth column espionage or spying for their country).

If any of our personnel took photographs on our station, which could possibly be considered to have information useful to the Japanese, the photographs would be confiscated and censored by the air force or other military commands. The Chinese informed me that there were three such photography shops in Penang, and advised where to find them. I was so concerned about this that I purposely visited two of these shops, and the prices quoted confirmed what my friends contended.

When I returned to the Station, I reported to intelligence, and although they passed it on to the higher authorities, it was more than a week before action was taken. By then it was too late, and the people connected with the shops had disappeared just the previous day. Perhaps they had been warned.

Another matter that the Chinese were concerned about was the coming invasion, which they maintained would be made from the North through Thailand. If they were issued with arms they considered they would be able to resist the Japanese invasion or at least do much to hinder their advance. This would also make it much easier for our army to hold them. As it was, they considered that even the Australian army would not be able to hold back the invasion. I ridiculed this idea and the thought that the Japanese assault was imminent . . .

26–28 November

The Squadron was carrying out exercises with the army, doing dive bombing and general reconnaissance. The news was not good, as relations with Japanese diplomats in the United States were grim. Consequently we were on standby alert. The following day, all leave was cancelled, and all crews placed on instant standby, ready to take off at any moment. Extra guards had been summoned at night, and the situation was very tense.

Jack Woodward's diary is one of many that confirm the widespread knowledge of Japanese intentions by the third week of November. Indeed, the overall pattern of Japan's plans for the invasion of Malaya had been common knowledge for some years. The large Japanese community in the colony had been openly reconnoitring bases, roads and bridges. Meanwhile to the north the Japanese had discussed their plans with the Thais and thereafter invasion plans circulated freely around the diplomatic community in Bangkok. However, complacent senior commanders in Singapore were reluctant to believe that the Japanese would move beyond Thailand. All were sceptical of Japan's military capabilities.

Jack Woodward would retreat south from Malaya to Singapore and then from Singapore to Java in early 1942. When the Japanese arrived in Java he was evacuated again, this time to Ceylon (Sri Lanka), and eventually transferred to Australia. There he would continue to serve in the RAAF on training and instructional duties until the end of the war.

Sunday 23 – Sunday 30 November 1941

Colonel Lewis Brereton, US Army Air Force, visits Australia and realizes that relations with Japan have 'become critical'

Colonel Lewis Brereton was born on 21 June 1890. He graduated from the US Naval Academy in 1911 and was one of America's first aviation officers, graduating from the Signal Corps Aviation School in 1913. During the First World War he had commanded the 12th Aero Squadron, one of the first American flying units on the front. In 1941 he was commander of the Far East Air Force in the Philippines.

Colonel Brereton

Melbourne, Australia, 23 and 24 November

With the finishing of our work, I declared a two-day holiday. Everyone was fagged. The crews were given passes and we spent the time sightseeing and resting. Sir Charles Burnett was very hospitable, as indeed was everyone with whom we came into contact, and Australian enthusiasm everywhere at the sight of an American aircraft was gratifying. My hardest

job was to prevent publicity regarding our visit. We wore
civilian clothes and no one used his military title. But we did
not succeed in fooling anybody. A Tokyo broadcast reported
my presence in Australia and most of the details of our
business. The Japs had their agents everywhere . . .

Manila, 28 November

During my trip to Australia, relations with Japan had
become critical. The conferences in Washington hit a snag
and Kurusu admitted to the press that there seemed no basis
for further negotiation. Tokyo's attitude became more
belligerent with Tojo demanding that the U.S. end the
military encirclement of Japan, lift the economic blockade,
and keep hands off the China–Japan conflict.

On 26 November, Secretary of State Hull gave Kurusu and
Nomura a document setting forth the position of the U.S.
Confidential information from Washington disclosed that
the parleys seemed doomed to failure.

I was sufficiently impressed with the gravity of the situation to recommend to General MacArthur that I put all the
Air Force immediately on a war footing. He concurred, and
it was done at once. Blackouts were established at all fields
and at the depot. A 24-hour alert was established for half the
Bombardment Force and Fighter Force. All air troops were
kept on their stations, except the 15 percent allowed away on
week ends. Permission to visit Manila was kept to a
minimum, and all personnel were required to hold themselves in readiness to return on three hours' notice . . .

Manila, 30 November

Two messages from the War Department alerted us to the
possibility of an attack by Japan at any hour. One from
General Marshall to General MacArthur on 27 November
stated that negotiations with Japan appeared to be
terminated and that there was only the barest possibility of
reopening of the negotiations. I did not see this message, but
General MacArthur told me that General Marshall directed
that if trouble came the first overt act must be committed by
Japan.

The US Army Air Force in the Philippines was notoriously caught napping by the Japanese at the outbreak of war and many of its aircraft were destroyed on the ground. Fearing sabotage by ever-present Japanese secret agents, they had been parked close together to make them easier to guard; but this also made them easier targets for bombardment from the air. Brereton's diary claims to be a contemporary account and much of it appears to be a spontaneous record. However, this section dealing with the approach of war appears to have been written with unusual care, perhaps a little while after the event. SEE ALSO PP. 247–9.

Tuesday 25 – Thursday 27 November 1941

Henry L. Stimson, US Secretary of War, discusses the Japan situation at the White House

Henry L. Stimson was born on 21 September 1867 in New York City. He served in the administrations of five American presidents from 1911 onwards. He was Secretary of War under President William Howard Taft, then served as a special emissary to Nicaragua in 1927 and as Governor-General of the Philippines in the late 1920s. Under President Herbert Hoover, Stimson was Secretary of State, and under Roosevelt, Secretary of War. He maintained a vast diary that ran to many volumes and records discussions with Roosevelt and Hull in detail.

Henry L. Stimson

25 November

At 9:30 Knox [Navy Secretary] and I met in Hull's office for our meeting of three. Hull showed us the proposal for a three months' truce which he was going to lay before the Japanese today or tomorrow. It adequately safeguarded all our interests, I thought, as we read it, but I don't think that there is any chance of the Japanese accepting it because it was so drastic . . . We were an hour and a half with Hull, and then I went back to the Department, and I got hold of Marshall. Then at twelve o'clock I went to the White House where we were until nearly half past one. At the meeting were Hull, Knox, Marshall, Stark, and myself. There the President brought up the relations with the Japanese. He brought up the event that we were likely to be attacked perhaps (as soon as) next Monday [December 1], for the Japanese are notorious for making an attack without warning, and the question was what we should do. The question was how we should maneuver them into the position of firing the first shot without allowing too much danger to ourselves. It was a difficult proposition . . . The others brought out the fact that any such expedition to the South as the Japanese were likely to take would be an encirclement of our interests in the Philippines and cutting into our vital supplies of rubber from Malaysia. I pointed out to the President that he had already taken the first steps toward an ultimatum in notifying Japan way back last summer that if she crossed the border into Thailand she was violating our safety and that therefore he had only to point out (to Japan) that to follow any such expedition was a violation of a warning we had already given.

27 November

The first thing in the morning, I called up Hull to find out what his final decision had been with the Japanese – whether he had handed them the new proposal which we passed on two or three days ago or whether, as he suggested yesterday, he had broken the whole matter off. He told me now he had broken the whole matter off. As he put it, 'I have washed my hands of it, and it is now in the hands of you and Knox, the Army and Navy'.

The entries in Stimson's diary for late November 1941 have perhaps generated more discussion than any other relating to the outbreak of war with Japan. Although the key section of the diary had been retyped at some stage, few doubt the substance of the content. Indeed, Stimson testified in much the same terms to a congressional committee shortly after the war. He explained that in spite of the risk involved in letting the Japanese 'fire the first shot', the Cabinet realized this was essential in order to have the full support of the American people for joining the war. Roosevelt's Cabinet wanted to be sure that there was no doubt in anyone's mind as to who were the aggressors. Perhaps even more compelling is an earlier reference in Stimson's diary, for 6 October: 'We face the delicate question of the diplomatic fencing to be done so as to be sure Japan is put into the wrong and makes the first bad move – overt move.' However, although it is clear that the hawks in Roosevelt's Cabinet expected to be attacked – perhaps even wished to be attacked – there is no indication that Stimson knew of the Japanese plan to attack Pearl Harbor. Most observers in Washington expected the Japanese to hit Thailand, the Netherlands East Indies and perhaps the Philippines. Roosevelt's discussions with his Cabinet on 25 November occurred shortly before Hull presented the Japanese with the demand for withdrawal from China. As Stimson observed, Hull knew this was unacceptable to Tokyo. SEE ALSO PP. 787–9, 809–10.

Wednesday 26 November – Friday 5 December 1941

Georges 'Blacky' Verreault, a Canadian soldier, arrives at Kowloon and experiences China and its customs

Georges Verreault was born on 14 April 1920 in the St Henri quarter of Montreal. He left school to work for the Bell telephone company in 1939. His background in communications ensured that when he joined up in the summer of 1941 he was assigned to the Canadian army signal corps. In November 1941 he formed part of the Canadian Brigade headquarters commanding a number of units despatched to reinforce Hong Kong, including the Winnipeg Grenadiers and the Royal Rifles of Canada. He had sailed from Vancouver on 27 October 1941 and began his diary two days later.

26 November

China! Here I am. It's already a week since we tied in Kowloon across from Hong Kong. What a country! But I'll tell you about it later. It's getting dark and my eyes hurt. There's a lot to tell about China and its customs. Good night!

27 November

Here it is winter and the heat is unbearable. Our camp is at the far end of Kowloon. A chain link fence separates us from the locals. The huts are low slung and made of concrete because of the typhoons that hit two or three times a year apparently. The 'Winnipeg Grenadeers' and the 'Royal Riffles' are housed in these huts. As for Brigade Headquarters, we occupy a magnificent five storey building that looks somewhat like a castle of the middle ages. Three of us share our room: Ted, Walter and I.

5 December

Canadian currency is worth 3.6 times the Chinese money and since the Chinese work for very low labour rates, we can afford our personal butler to look after our room, our clothes and laundry. Strange country China! At least this part of it. It's different than what we learned of it in Canada. The earth is arid with few edible plants. Their ways are so strange. Women at work is a case in point. Everywhere we see them carrying loads of nearly 100 lbs. and they walk miles like this. They are of all ages incredible: the Chinese are frail but not lazy. The majority live on the water in junks. The two cities are like ant colonies. I have never seen so many people at one time and girls by the thousands.

At thirteen, they are sold to a prostitution company and they must earn their living in a manner that our mothers would not approve. In places like taverns, hotels and clubs, you have to fight your way through a horde of females to reach the door. They hook on to your clothes and invite you to their room ($1.00 short time, $5.00 long time) they whisper. Some guys have bought themselves a woman for $60.00 a month. She performs all the duties of a faithful wife (which is more than we can say of Canadian wives). The Hong Kong girl is very delicate and pretty and certainly not bashful in bed. The prostitutes have developed a liking for Canadians and I believe that the blokes are envious.

There have been many fights with other regiments with gory results.

During October and November 1941, as war clouds gathered across Asia, British planners began to send what reinforcements they could to imperial outposts in Asia. One of the most bizarre developments was the decision to reinforce Hong Kong, a location that had long been regarded as almost impossible to defend. Georges Verreault was part of this effort and had arrived at Kowloon near Hong Kong on 19 November 1941 on the Australian ship Awatsea, *together with 2,500 fellow Canadians. Tom Forsyth, whose diary also appears in this anthology, was part of the same contingent. They found the local customs and arrangements in Kowloon and Hong Kong strange and not a little enticing. In China, the Philippines, Malaya and India it was usual for soldiers to retain the local population for washing, cleaning and, as Georges observes, a range of other services. Georges himself, as his diary testifies, was a romantically minded individual and was in search of love rather than mere carnal experience. SEE ALSO PP. 164–7, 593–4.*

Saturday 29 November 1941

Marquis Kido and ten former prime ministers listen while the Japanese Emperor asks about the current situation

At the end of November the Japanese Emperor invited his most senior statesmen to convene at the Imperial Palace. This was not a formal meeting, more of a roving discussion, reflecting the fact that the decision for war had already been taken. Participants included ten former prime ministers as well as Hara, President of the Privy Council.

From 2:00 to 3:00 P.M. the Emperor asked the ex-premiers for their opinions on the current political situation.

Mr. Wakatsuki said that we were equal to a prolonged war with the U.S.A. in spiritual power; but, regarding national power, we must make a careful study. Admiral Okada had grave doubts about our supply capacity for war materials, in spite of the optimistic view of the government. Baron Hiranuma agreed with Mr. Wakatsuki's opinion concerning our spiritual powers, urging further measures for the awakening of patriotic sentiment.

Prince Konoye said that it was quite regrettable that our negotiations were going to be a failure, in spite of our strenuous efforts for four months. But he was of the opinion that there was no need to resort to a hasty war just because of the rupture in the negotiations, since we might be able to reach a solution in some way or other while continuing our struggle toward better things.

Admiral Yonai said that he could not base his opinion on definite data, but that it had been his desire that we should be careful not to become poorer by inches in the struggle against our national poverty, losing the little we had in our hands.

Mr. Hirota said that the diplomatic situation was approaching a serious crisis, but that we should have iron nerves in order to reach a true solution to the problems, nerves which could courageously meet a crisis twice or thrice at least. We should be able to seize an opportunity to solve the problems between the two countries even after a declaration of war, if we are sincere enough in our diplomatic efforts.

General Hayashi said that since he had no data for his opinion, he could do nothing but accept the decisions of the Imperial Headquarters and of the government.

General Abe said that, according to the government's explanation, the negotiations had come to a deadlock in spite of the strenuous efforts on the part of our government. He was sure that the government had studied the world political situation from various angles with laborious minuteness, and we were thankful for it. But it would be quite necessary to pay much more attention to the attitude of the Chinese people toward a war with the U.S.A. Otherwise we would lose the fruits of the China Incident.

Mr. Wakatsuki said that the war with the U.S.A. should be fought to the last, even if there was no chance to win, if it was a defensive war for our national existence and independence. But we should avoid the war if it was to be fought to realize ideals such as 'the Asiatic Co-prosperity Sphere' or 'the stabilizing of power in Asia,' because such a war would be very dangerous.

One of the interesting features of this discussion was Japan's evaluation of its chances of success in war, since the participants assessed their country's power as much in terms of 'spiritual strength' as in terms of industrial capacity. The decision of a small country like Japan to declare war on a country as powerful as the United States now appears very odd; however, Tokyo's thinking had been influenced by the course of the First World War. The Japanese expected to make rapid initial gains, then fight to a stalemate in the mid-Pacific and finally negotiate an armistice from a position of strength. SEE ALSO PP. 75–7, 86–7, 586–7.

DECEMBER 1941

BY 1 DECEMBER 1941 a Japanese fleet consisting of six carriers with 423 aircraft was already taking an elliptical northerly route towards Pearl Harbor, the US naval base on the Hawaiian island of Oahu. Japanese troop transports were heading south around the coast of Indochina and taking on infantry ready for a push towards the invasion beaches of Malaya and southern Thailand. Although the 'noise' of Japanese preparations for an attack had been audible on the ground in south-east Asia for about ten days, the authorities in Malaya did not declare a state of emergency until 1 December, and thereafter moved in a leisurely fashion.

On 2 December the *Prince of Wales* and the *Repulse* arrived at Singapore from Colombo. Japan's decision for war had already been taken, and so any deterrent effect from their presence was already lost. The two capital ships had been sent to Singapore without air cover.

On 4 December Japanese troop transports in the South China Sea appeared to be heading for Thailand, but a day later they changed course to head for the beaches of northern Malaya. The following day a Japanese invasion fleet set out from Palau bound for the Philippines.

On 7 December at 0755 the Japanese attacked Pearl Harbor with the carrier fleet and five midget submarines. Two waves of aircraft were sent in and damaged all eight battleships in port, sinking five of them. Three cruisers and three destroyers were also lost. Airfields were attacked as well: the United States lost 188 aircraft, though all its aircraft carriers based at Pearl Harbor were out at sea at the time of the attack. The Japanese declaration of war was not handed to Hull in Washington until late that afternoon. Local warnings had been received from an American destroyer that had attacked a Japanese midget submarine at 0630, and from radar operators at 0700 who spotted the incoming waves of aircraft, but these warnings were disregarded by junior officers.

Many have speculated that either Churchill or Roosevelt was given some secret forewarning of Pearl Harbor, but found it convenient to do nothing. There is no evidence that this was the case. It is more likely that both London and Washington expected Japan to attack only the soft targets available in southeast Asia. There is some evidence that British intelligence officers speculated about the sudden absence of Japanese carriers from the waters around Japan in early December and even talked of Pearl Harbor as a possible target. However, if they did so, they were playing a hunch and had nothing substantial with which to support their suspicions.

Japan attacked the Philippines on 8 December. Despite the fact that the local US commander, Douglas MacArthur, had by now had ample warning of what was afoot, Japanese aircraft were able to attack almost with impunity at midday. They surprised American forces and destroyed two-thirds of the aircraft on the ground, leaving MacArthur with only about fifty operational aircraft. Although he presided over a notional force of 130,000 troops, most were Philippine army soldiers who were poorly equipped and trained. MacArthur decided to retreat to the Bataan peninsula just north of Manila, hold out and wait until they could be relieved. However, the attacks on Pearl Harbor meant that no relief operation was possible, and a long siege ensued.

On 8 December Hong Kong was attacked by a Japanese division. Despite the recent arrival of reinforcements, the local British commander had only six battalions and thirty artillery

Japan's Attack on East Asia, 7 December 1941

pieces with which to repel this attack. On 18 and 19 December the Japanese made a number of landings on Hong Kong Island, supported by heavy artillery fire. The garrison surrendered on Christmas Day and many of the prisoners were transported to Japan, where they were employed as forced labour in dockyards.

In Malaya, Japanese forces were landing on the north-east coast and also moving south across the border from southern Thailand, where Thai forces initially fought both the Japanese troops and also British troops crossing the border from Malaya to try to seize this vital strategic area. Late on 8 December the government in Bangkok ordered its forces to cease firing and eventually allied itself with Tokyo. On 9 December the *Prince of Wales* and the *Repulse* headed north and approached the Japanese beachheads on the coast of Malaya in the hope of inter-cepting enemy troopships. A Japanese submarine sighted them and on the following morning they were sunk by a force of ninety Japanese aircraft, operating out of southern Indochina. On top of the strike at Pearl Harbor, this left the Allies without a single operational battleship in the Pacific theatre. Japanese forces then made steady progress across Malaya. Although small in numbers, they were hardened troops who enjoyed armoured and excellent air support. Their opponents were more numerous but were mostly fresh recruits who had never seen an enemy shot fired. They were also poorly led. On 27 December the aged and ineffective British commander in the Far East, Air Chief Marshal Brooke-Popham – nicknamed 'Old Pop Off' by the locals – was replaced by the energetic General Henry Pownall, but such measures were already too late.

The diary of the German propaganda minister, Joseph Goebbels, shows that Adolf Hitler was elated by the entry of Japan into the war, declaring: 'We have an ally that has not been defeated in 1500 years!' On 11 December 1941 Hitler gave a speech to the Reichstag in which he declared war on the United States. Italy followed in Germany's footsteps. There was no need for Germany to declare war on the United States at this point and it is hard to fathom why Hitler did so. One can only conclude that perhaps as a general principle he had always found that escalating a conflict had worked to his advantage. Winston Churchill was perhaps more accurate in his estimation of the meaning of Pearl Harbor. Realizing that the United States was now on his side, he remarked: 'So we have won after all!'

Wednesday 3 – Wednesday 10 December 1941

General Kawamura Saburo, commander 9th Infantry Brigade, lands in southern Thailand and advances over the frontier into Malaya

During the 1930s General Kawamura Saburo had been the Japanese military attaché in London. During late 1941 he was one of the senior officers with the Japanese forces moving south through southern Thailand into Malaya. His brief but spirited diary captures his feelings at the outbreak of war and during the initial advance across the border from Singora in neutral Thailand into northern Malaya.

3 December

0800 ending the exercise return to Sana about 1300 and drop anchor.

By news learn that Ambassador Nomura had a tête-a-tête talk with Wells. It seems that the negotiation is now in its final stage. In the P.I. special defence precaution is now taken and America is requesting China to let her have S.W. China defence rights, news says also that at Singapore Adm. Thomas Philips arrives on the battle ship Prince of Wales leading a number of ships and thus Singapore defence is strengthened. The die is now cast, one may aver.

1630 S.O. Tsuji informs that an order has been issued by the Emperor. Tomorrow we will sail. Things have now come to this pass, the only way is to press on and get through. Quickness is vital in war. This very quick decision reveals Toojoo Cabineet's quality and a matter probably for congratulation at this juncture. What I feel keenly is, it is a statesman's burden to make good a victory after the war. (It may be, however, that things will take care of themselves once begun, as the saying is. God's thoughts are always on us; Go resolutely on! Yes, will go on resolutely).

4 December
0700 starts, all keyed up and valiantly are bent to reach the landing point. Temperature rises immensely.

5 December
Parade on the deck and pay homage towards the Imperial Palace.

About noon enemy submarines reported cruising heading north. Sharp lookout kept, but nothing happened.

Evening passed south point of French Indo-China at a point S.E. off it. Recall Camran Bay & of Russo-Japanese War times.

6 December
From today Army planes escort us. English planes reported reconnoitring; redouble our precautions.

Morning, course changed towards Bangkok. (Reported downed one English plane this day).

7 December
From noon change course for S.W. and proceed direct to the point of landing. Uno and Wabiyoshi Detachments also proceed to their respective landing points. Speeds are about 15 knots. It blows and the sea is rough; but the morale of the troops is very high.

8 December
Shingora at last! (zero o'clock[midnight])

At once get on the lighters and land. 4 o'clock landing succeeds, although high waves contributed difficulties. At once act as have been ordered. Some lighters have run aground. At dawn we attempted to disarm the local Thai Army, but it resisted and fighting ensued. 1500 our attack and orders from their highest source made the Siamese to cease fire, and we march on for Pajai. 2000, arrive in Pajai. There, Ichikawa Unit joins Miyamoto Unit (both Hongoo and Imai Units). Receive welcome from Japanese living there.

10 December

0600 start Sadao. 10 to 10 arrive at the frontier roads south of the frontier have undergone complete destruction, but enemy resistance at present is slight. Tomono Unit was ordered to repair it . . . S.O. Tsuji contacts us and tells that road destruction is the means of enemy resistance. But, there is need of swift advance . . .

General Kawamura Saburo's diary captures a number of fascinating aspects of the Japanese invasion of Malaya. Although some Japanese forces arrived by infantry transports on the beaches of north-east Malaya, others landed inside Thailand and made their way south down the Kra Isthmus towards the border with Malaya. Despite the fact that the military leader in Thailand was sympathetic to Japan, the country was neutral and so the Japanese first had to fight local Thai forces on their arrival at Singora. Eventually, after a few hours, the local Thai forces received orders to capitulate. In January 1942 Bangkok would declare war on the Allies.

Kawamura Saburo was made Governor of Singapore upon his arrival and it was during his short tenure, through to mid-March 1942, that the Chinese population would be brutally purged by the Japanese military police, the dreaded Kempetei. This crackdown was organized locally by Colonels Oishi and Tsuji, and perhaps as many as 50,000 Chinese were killed. SEE ALSO PP. 236–8.

Saturday 6 – Wednesday 10 December 1941

Captain Malcolm Kennedy, a codebreaker at Bletchley Park, is surprised by Pearl Harbor

6 December

Owing to the critical situation, was on duty at the office from 9 a.m. yesterday until 9 a.m. to-day. From now on, for time being, we are to take turns about at night in case anything calling for immediate action comes in. Incidentally, the All Highest (Smith's [a colleague's] name for Churchill) is all over himself at the moment for latest information and indications re Japan's intentions and rings up at all hours of the day and night, except for the 4 hours in each 24 (2 to 6 p.m.) when he sleeps. For a man of his age, he has the most amazing vitality. His chief form of recreation, I gather, is to get out onto the Admiralty roof whenever there is a raid on London and shake his fist at the raiders! As there have been no serious raids on London now for 6 or 7 months, he must be missing this recreation!

7 December

A message recd. just before leaving the office this evg. had indicated that the outbreak of war was probably only a matter of hours, but the news on the 9 p.m. wireless, that Japan had opened hostilities with an air raid on Pearl Harbour, more than 3000 miles out in the Pacific, came as a complete surprise.

10 December

Something like a gasp of dismay went round the dining room at B.P. when the 1 p.m. news opened with the an[noun]c[emen]t that the 'Prince of Wales' and 'Repulse' had been sunk off Singapore by J.[apanese] air attack.

Britain and the United States could read high-grade Japanese diplomatic traffic, but only low-grade military traffic with any consistency, and so did not have a complete picture of Tokyo's military preparations for war. Therefore diaries kept by intelligence officers in key locations record surprise at the news of the attack on Pearl Harbor. The same is true of diaries kept by members of the British War Cabinet. The British chiefs of staff had spent the period between 6 and 8 December worrying about the possibility that a limited Japanese attack on areas of south-east Asia might leave the United States without a pretext for war against Tokyo; so they were somewhat relieved to find that Japan had encompassed Pearl Harbor in their plans.

In 1944 Malcolm Kennedy would transfer to the counter-intelligence section of MI6. After the war he was moved to the new anti-Soviet component of MI6, known as Section IX, which was headed by Kim Philby. SEE ALSO PP. 58–60.

Sunday 7 December 1941

Ginger Leonard, aged seventeen, watches the attack on Pearl Harbor

Ginger Leonard was a seventeen-year-old high school senior who was living at Hickam Field, Hawaii, at the time of the Japanese bombing on 7 December 1941. Her father was a medical officer who was serving on the nearby base.

I was awakened at eight o'clock on the morning of December 7th by an explosion from Pearl Harbor. I got up thinking something exciting was probably going on over there. Little did I know! When I reached the kitchen the whole family, excluding Pop, was looking over at the Navy Yard. It was being consumed by black smoke and more terrific explosions. We didn't know what was going on, but I didn't like it because the first explosion looked as if it was right on top of Marie's house. I went and told Pop that (He in the meantime had gotten dressed and was leaving) and he said, 'Who cares about Marie when you and Mom might be killed!'. Then I became extremely worried, as did we all. Mom and I went out on the front porch to get a better look and three planes went zooming over our heads so close we could have touched them. They had red circles on their wings. Then we caught on! About that time bombs started dropping all over Hickam. We stayed at the windows, not knowing what else to do, and watched the fire works. It was just like the news reels of Europe, only worse. We saw a bunch of soldiers come running full tilt towards us from the barracks and just then a whole line of bombs fell behind them knocking them all to the ground. We were deluged in a cloud of dust and had to run around closing all the windows. I got back to the front door just in time to see Pop calmly walking back to the house through it all. He said we could leave if a lull came. Also that a Mrs. B was coming down to our house and to wait for her. Then he left again. In the meantime a bunch of soldiers had come into our garage to hide. They were entirely taken by surprise and most of them didn't even have a gun or anything. One of them asked for a drink of water saying he was sick. He had just been so close to where a bomb fell that he had been showered with debree. He said he was scared, and I was too, so I couldn't say that I blamed him. I saw an officer out in the front yard, so Mom said to ask him if he thought it would be wise for us to try to leave. He said, 'I would hate to say because we don't know whether they are bombing in town or not, and besides this is your home.' I no sooner got back into the house than a terrible barrage came down just over by the Post Exchange. That's just a block kitty corner from [diagonally opposite] us, so the noise and concussion was terrific. Mom and I were still standing in the doorway and we saw the PX get hit. I was getting more worried by the minute about this time as they seemed to be closing in the circle they had been making around us. (The Japs were flying around in a circle bombing us, Pearl Harbor, and machine gunning Fort Kam.) A second terrific bunch of explosions followed the first by a few minutes only. I found out later these had landed in the base-ball diamond just a second after Dad had walked across it. He ran back to see if the men in a radio truck there had been hit. All but one had and they were carted off in an ambulance. I went dashing into my room to look and saw that the barracks was on fire, also the big depot hanger. I hated to go into my room because the planes kept machine-gunning the street just outside my window and I kept expecting to see a string of bullets come through my roof any minute. We had all gotten dressed in the meantime and had packed a suitcase and were ready to leave any time. Finally, after two and a half hours, the planes went away and we left. I gave the soldiers in the garage two and a half packages of my chewing gum before I left and they nearly died of joy at sight of it. Poor guys!!

Ginger Leonard noted that the nearby barracks, depot and camp theatre were all badly damaged or on fire. Within a few minutes the roads were jammed solid with traffic because the radio had appealed for all service personnel to return to their units. The next day school was discontinued and Ginger noted in her diary: 'there goes my graduation'. On 14 December it was announced that all dependants of service personnel would be evacuated, and she was anxious about having to set off with her family for the United States, leaving her father behind. However, a few days later her father was posted to a military hospital in San Francisco, and so towards the end of the month the whole family would set sail for the United States.

Helen Clarke Grimes on Rhode Island listens to the radio on Sunday afternoon

Helen Clarke Grimes was born in 1905 in Mystic, Connecticut. In 1941 she was a mother living at the village of Spragueville on Rhode Island outside New York. She was a remarkable diarist and had kept a careful log of daily events since she was ten years old. On the afternoon of Sunday 7 December she recorded what she heard on the radio as information came in moment by moment.

This is a sleepy Sunday afternoon at home. We are in the little upstairs sitting room – Mother sewing, I writing, and Dorrance listening to the portable radio. I haven't anything to write about, really, and the Philharmonic is fast putting me to sleep although the broadcast is interrupted now and then with news bulletins on the tense 'Far Eastern Situation'. After all we have been more or less tense for months.

Later – I guess this is it! Japanese dive bombers have attacked Honolulu!

4:30 News bulletin. Taken down as given. Parachute troups sighted – Pearl Harbor attacked by dive bombers – Manila bombed – smoke of anti-aircraft guns over Pearl Harbor – from 50 to 100 planes from Japanese aircraft carrier – attachés of Japanese government at Washington burning secret papers.

We are shocked silent. Dorrance who is coming down with a cold is too carried away by the intermittent bulletins to realize how rotten he feels.

The Albert Spalding program, Victor Herbert selections, Carmichael's Stardust Castelanetz [*sic*] orchestra.

5 P.M. At last more news – fragmentary, probably inaccurate.

Washington: President Roosevelt is dictating message to Congress. Probably declaration of war tomorrow. Heavy damage and loss of life in Hawaii. It was a dawn attack, all aerial observation posts in Los Angeles ordered manned. Naval engagement reported. Pearl Harbor under bombardment.

Well, here it is: we're at war.

We hang close to the radio listening to program after program afraid we may miss a news bulletin no matter how vague or unconfirmed the reports may be. The Prudential (Insurance) Hour with Deems Taylor, Gladys Swarthout singing Paradise in Waltz Time from the motion picture Champagne Waltz.

At last, another bulletin. Japan announces she has entered a state of war with Britain and the United States from dawn to-day Dec. 7th, 1941. Government order just issued comes over WPRO: The Secretary of War orders that all plants working on defense orders institute a guard against sabotage.

Jimmie Cat jumps on my lap. The news has come to an end, the program returns to Gladys Swarthout.

5:45 – William L. Shirer, [CBS] news commentator. Speaks of 'flagrant aggression . . . a war after 23 years ~~of~~ and one month of uneasy peace . . . the battleship Oklahoma set on fire by Japanese bombs.

I should be reacting to this in some~~where~~ way, but I remain incredulous and interested, nothing more as yet.

An attempt has been made to contact overseas – no result. Honolulu – CBS calling Honolulu – no answer. Calling Manila – CBS calling Manila, go ahead Manila – no answer.

We take time out for supper, our ears on the radio.

6:30 – All marines notified to return to their stations . . . order from Quonset.

Guam has been attacked by a squadron of planes . . . Elmer Davis, commentator. He must have seen this happening months ago. Senator Wheeler, isolationist says sensibly enough that 'there is nothing to do now but lick the hell out of them.' . . .

We ~~know~~ hear Albert Warner, Washington news commentator – and next, Maj. Elliot who says the Japanese plan plainly underway for two weeks during treacherous negotiations at Washington. I have a conviction we have been sold down the river again. A year ago Oliver said every navy man on Jamestown said we'd be at war with Japan shortly. I suppose <u>Major Elliot</u> didn't know, or our beloved President! Well, this is no time to think of that. We <u>are</u> at war.

Notice: all recruiting offices open to-morrow.

7:00 – censorship on all out going cablegrams and radio messages. The Jack Benny Program . . . Don Wilson, the announcer . . . 'J-E-L-L-O with that locked in flavor.' An interruption; news from the office of the Providence Journal – Providence police are requested to round-up all enlisted men. War Extra editions are on the streets.

I am surprised at Mother. I expected her to be shocked, horrified, but she seems excited, stepped-up, her asthma forgotten.

The programs continue . . . a Dennis Day song. How are the performers reacting? – they must be getting this awful news.

More bulletins; Shanghai: the Japanese have taken over the American Light Company.

7:30 – Providence Cake commercial . . . the Fitch (Shampoo) Band Wagon program with – Oh, another news bulletin, from the Prov. Journal: Gov. McGrath has called a meeting . . . Newport takes immediate precautions . . . six Japanese planes said to have been shot down. Unconfirmed report that Wake Island is occupied by Japanese. A black-out of Panama Canal ordered for to-night.

Back to the scheduled program again: Horace Heit [*sic*] and the 'Spheheard's [*sic*] Serenade,' with Frankie Carl [*sic*] at the piano . . . 'I'll Never Forget,' this weeks [*sic*] Band Wagons [*sic*] top tune.

Just happened to remember that Elizabeth Colby and her husband are stationed at Honolulu.

News bulletin: 104 dead and 300 wounded, not including civilian population as a result of Japanese raid on Hawaii.

Horace Heit again, featuring a new arrangement of Ezekial Saw the Wheel.

8:00 – A Pinkerton Fur commercial . . . the Chase and Sanborn Coffee Hour with Charlie McCarthy and Mortimer Snerd on Edgar Bergen's knee. Just ordinary Sunday night listening mixed in with a world shakeing [*sic*] event.

Ray Noble's Orchestra . . . Abbott and Costello . . . Judy Garland, the guest star.

<u>News</u>: The Governor of the Dutch East Indies has declared war on Japan . . . likewise Costa Rica. Well, that will be a help!

In Shanghai bombs fall on the International Settlement . . . and Judy Garland sings, Zing Went the Strings of My Heart. Commercial: Shop at Newberry's <u>first</u>. News flash: All women and children in Manila ordered evacuated. Mayor La Guardia has issued an order that all Japanese nationals remain in their home until their status is settled.

Back to the regular programs – this one Carter's Little Liver Pills and it is terrible. A long wait this time lasting through an Inner Sanctum mystery story and into the Ford Musical Hour which comes on at 9 o'clock. Jimmie Cat in my lap again, mother is embroidering a bureau scarf for Constance. Somehow small things seem important – things I can understand like the radiator clanking as the steam comes up, or the small spot of nail varnish flaked from my thumb nail.

9:30 – At last more news. Washington officially announces 100 dead and 300 wounded. Wake Island is said to have surrendered to a superior Japanese force. There has been one – perhaps two – ship casualties. Japanese of San Francisco under careful watch . . .

10:00 – Commercial: This Christmas shoppers are using Gerber's lay away plan. News Flash: Canada has declared war upon Japan.

Grand Central Station is jammed with men in uniform

rounded up by Shore Patrol and Military Police from theatres, restaurants and bars. All officers on leave called back to their posts. State of emergency declared in San Francisco. Mother says thank God Constance isn't there . . .

10:30 – Following a Nylon hosiery commercial comes a CBS special broadcast. There is an unconfirmed report of a big naval engagement at sea. Eric Severied reports from Washington: the city is swarming with reporters, the portico is lighted; there are lines of shiny cars and a mass of faces standing in the cold waiting news.

There has been heavy destruction at Hawaii. Unconfirmed reports state that we have lost two capital ships and the airfield has been leveled. President Roosevelt will address joint session of Congress at 12:30 to-morrow.

It is 4:30 in London. Parliament meets today to declare war on Japan directly after America.

A Columbia broadcast: Guam is in trouble . . . Shanghai bombed. I have smoked until my mouth is dry: I am too tired to write more. It is now eleven o'clock, we have been glued to the radio for hours.

In 1941 radio news was still in its infancy and in most countries there were only short hourly news bulletins. In Providence, Rhode Island, there were several local commercial stations, including WPRO, which had been set up in the 1920s by companies selling radios to advertise their products, and which gradually evolved into proper commercial music stations. In-depth current affairs programming in the United States would develop later in the war in response to public demand.

Sunday 7 – Wednesday 10 December 1941

Richard F. Tamabayashi, a boy scout in Honolulu,
experiences the Japanese bombing of Honolulu and
moves house

*Richard F. Tamabayashi was one of the many Japanese Americans living
in Hawaii, a boy scout in the 2nd patrol of Troop 26 at Honolulu. All the
scouts in his troop were encouraged to write diaries of the Japanese
attack on Hawaii and its immediate aftermath.*

7 December
During the morning I helped my mother to clean the house.
About 11.30 a.m. as I went to the store next door to shop, a
Japanese bomb fell and killed my neighbors. Soon after a fire
was raging and I helped move our things as well as the
neighbor's across the street to safety. By this time firemen
came and tried to stop the fire but it was very hard because
the fire had a bit of a start. When they had it under
control, the whole block including my house was burned
down. The rest of the day we moved over to my uncle's
home. I was very much in grieve.

8 December
After settling down on our things, I helped to move school
furniture into Lunalilo School. It was also hit yesterday by
the Japanese.

9–10 December
I stayed and cleaned up Lunalilo School. It was a hard job. In
the afternoon of December 10, I moved to Punahou district
into a new home with my family.

*After the war Richard F. Tamabayashi was employed by the Honolulu
Gas Co. He died on 7 March 1999.*

Reginald Carter watches a sleepy colonial Burma move
from peace to war

*Reginald Carter was born in 1903 and spent the inter-war period work-
ing for the Indian Civil Service in Rangoon, Burma. He lived with his
family in the Prome Road on the northern side of Rangoon, and in early
December 1941 they were looking forward to some well-earned leave.*

7 December

I have had no long leave for five years and the Burma
Government have granted me leave as a special case. We
should have been in Singapore by now on our way to
Australia. But, owing to the uncertainty about Japan's
intentions, it has just been cancelled, though we hope to get
it later. Rangoon and Burma are their usual semi-peace-time
selves.

8 December

Po Chone, our Burmese head servant, brings us our early
morning tea and the Rangoon Gazette, which tells us that the
Japanese have attacked Pearl Harbour and Singapore and
landed on the coasts of Siam and Malaya. So the war has
come to the east at last. A good deal of talking, and not so
much work, is done in the offices. The Army say there is no
likelihood of Burma being invaded by land but there may be
air raids. I collect some coolies to dig air raid trenches
in our garden in Windermere Park, a V for ourselves and
Grace (our child's nurse) and a W for the servants nearer
their quarters. It is one of the first trenches in Rangoon and
an object of interest to our neighbours, who soon follow our
example and profit by our mistakes. We put boxes of sand
upstairs and down, to smother incendiary bombs. A police
Sub-Inspector brings a bucket for each house and hands over
to me a stirrup-pump, to serve for our neighbours too.
I arrange with them how they can get hold of it in an
emergency. We all practice working the pump, including
Vicky (aged five). Dorothy buys a First Aid outfit, to be kept
always in the passage on the ground floor.

9 December

A blackout is ordered and we are busy, fixing sheets of dark paper over our windows and lampshades.

10 December

We hear chilling news that the Japs have sunk 'Prince of Wales' and 'Repulse'. They are evidently stronger and more efficient than we thought. We shall be weak on the Eastern seas now but comfort ourselves by thinking that other ships will soon come and that the Americans will soon be arriving in large numbers.

If anything, the defence of Burma was even less well organized than that of Malaya. Most defence planners had considered a landward advance through Burma to be impossible because of the very dense jungle and had presumed that British sea and air power would prevent an advance up the coast. Japan's invasion was accompanied by widespread bombing, which would reach Rangoon later in December. Quite quickly, British troops in Burma would find themselves fighting not only Japanese troops but also Thai troops, whose government, after much fence-sitting, decided to join Tokyo. SEE ALSO PP. 212–13.

Monday 8 December 1941

Shu Xiangcheng, a civilian in Hong Kong, gradually realizes that the disturbance is more than a practice air raid drill

Shu Xiangcheng was born in 1921 in Guangdong province in China. He was typical of the local writers and historians in Hong Kong, whose books and articles enriched the colony's cultural life. Although he had never received any formal education, he was renowned for his poems in both the traditional and modern styles.

Today was a sunny day. At 0800 in the morning, there had been already many people sitting at the seaside in Saukeiwan [a small town at the eastern end of Hong Kong Island] chatting, fishing and relaxing. Last night I slept very early, so this morning I woke up early and so I was also walking around in there.

When I was looking for the boats between the harbours, there was a man who said loudly: 'Oh! Look! Smoke. That side.'

Then most people looked over to Kai Tak Airport on the opposite side and really did see some white smoke there. That prompted a discussion amongst us.

'Would the Japanese come?'

'Do not make us afraid.'

'Look! The Japanese were bombing the airport.'

'No, I don't think so. It may be an air raid drill only.'

Then, the air raid warning was issued by the broadcast systems in the area where we were living. I could not exactly remember whether the warning or the air raid occurred first. Anyway, everything occurred suddenly without any preparation. Even if there was an air raid warning, no one actually wanted to escape. Quite the opposite, more and more people came to the seafront to look at what was happening. Most people hoped that this was only an air raid drill. But a few minutes later, we saw several planes in the sky and we were not sure if they were Japanese or British.

Then after the warning broadcast ended, everything seemed to become silent and people again suggested this might be a practice drill only.

After two hours, one of our neighbours who came from Kowloon warned us, 'The Japanese are coming.' And this news spread out among the town in the fastest way.

When mother heard that news, she became extremely worried about the food and our future. She discussed it with our neighbour immediately and went to the market to get more rice.

After lunch, I told my mother that there was no need to worry and then I went back to our Store, 'ee-kee' which my daddy left to us. It was located at the opposite side of the Tram terminal in Sau Kei Wan and each month we paid HK $30 for rent. Everyday I went to there from home on foot. It only took 15 minutes.

When I arrived at 'ee-kee', most of the neighbours there were discussing the future of Hong Kong. Someone argued that if the Hong Kong defence force could resist for a short period, other troops from mainland China or the British would come to help us. He believed Hong Kong could hold off the Japanese attacks for three months. Another man replied: 'Two or three months? That's nearly impossible.' He explained that the Hong Kong defence force was made up of the British, the Indians, and the young guys from Canada and also some Chinese. Their numbers were very limited and most importantly, they did not have any experience. He concluded that it was difficult for them to face the highly-experienced, organized and mobilized Japanese troops.

'How about you? What do you think?' the third man asked.

'I do not think the British can win.' the fourth man replied.

The answer from the last man seemed to reflect most peoples thinking, although no one wished to accept the fact that Hong Kong would soon be occupied and under the governance of the Imperial Japanese. It was because in the past several years, we have heard many stories about how cruelly the Japanese have ruled in China.

When we were having the discussion, an elderly man came and bought a pack of cigarettes. Then he sat down and told us that a large group of Japanese troops had already attacked Hong Kong from Shenzhen. Many of the defence forces were killed. The situation was very dangerous.

At the same time, there were 'Special Issue Newspapers' being sold outside and we bought two. The headlines said that the Japanese had raided Pearl Harbor, declared war on the US and the British and so this morning they were bombing the Kai Tak Airport.

At that moment, everyone knew that Hong Kong was entering into 'War Era'. They all went off home and some began to buy food, rice as much as they can.

In the evening, no one was in the street. That was very unusual compared to normal weekdays. The silence in the street made me feel afraid and it was the fear before the war came.

I do not know when the tram was suspended and at night, the air raid warning was broadcast again and there was an official from the Hong Kong government reminding all families that they should black out so as not to guide enemy bombers. Our house was in completely dark. I was waiting with time passing and I could not do anything. I heard the sound of planes and then somewhere was being bombed. My heart 'jumped' very fast and highly excitedly until the all clear was sounded.

I just think, 24 hours ago, I was living in a happy and peaceful world. But now we are already at war. So, how about tomorrow? What will happen to us? In the past, when we talked about the war and Japanese, seemed we were outsiders. But now, we have become the insiders. If, one day, the Imperial Japanese army really occupy Hong Kong, what shall we do? What will be our life?

In the autumn of 1942, in order to escape the Japanese occupation, Shu Xiangcheng left Hong Kong and went to live with friends at Guilin in nationalist Free China. Although life was hard in this poverty-stricken region, he enjoyed freedom there.

Shu Xiangcheng would return to Hong Kong at the end of the war. During the 1960s he was a well-known columnist for several newspapers. He died in 1999.

Monday 8 – Tuesday 16 December 1941

Martin Ogle takes part in the defence of Penang beach in northern Malaya

Martin Ogle was a schoolteacher in Penang and also a volunteer part-time soldier – the colonial equivalent of a 'territorial'. Until November 1941 he had told his pupils that Japan was far too preoccupied in China to have the resources to attack Malaya and believed this firmly himself. He was mobilized on 1 December 1941 and arrived at his unit head-quarters in Peel Avenue, Penang, at seven the same evening. His unit was soon allocated to beach defence duties in pill boxes and bunkers made of the trunks of palm trees. Ogle's pill box was close to the Penang Swimming Club.

8 December

We heard on the radio of the Japanese landing at Kota Bahru. We had hardly had breakfast before there was the distant sound of bombing, and up rose a great pall of smoke. Sungei Patani aerodrome was being 'blitzed'; it is believed that most of the Blenheim aircraft were caught on the ground, some of the pilots being on the Penang side of the water, waiting for the ferry to take them across. Alor Star aerodrome was done for at the same time.

9 December

Butterworth aerodrome, opposite Penang, was attacked, and reconnaissance planes appeared over Penang, without dropping anything. This gave the Asian population the illusion of safety – a fine view of the bombing over Butterworth and no harm to themselves. A.R.P. wardens and police were powerless to disperse the thousands that congregated on the Esplanade, gaping at the excitement. The Safety First propaganda that had been drummed into them for so long was no match for their curiosity . . .

10 December

About 11 a.m. a swarm of bombers appeared, and at first it looked as if they were going to have another go at Butterworth airfield. But they came on and on, in a dead straight line for Beach Street, Penang. We Volunteers were a mile or so to the right of their line of flight, cowering in slit trenches, but when it became evident that they were not coming directly for us we had a ring-side view of what followed. There were twenty-seven Japanese bombers (a favourite number with them), flying at eight to ten thousand feet. There was not a single anti-aircraft gun or fighter to oppose them so they came on in tight formation directly for the town from the north. We felt they meant business, but everyone was shaken by the horror of the reality. One moment there was nothing but the drone of twenty seven engines, next moment the pandemonium of bombs; they all seemed to let go together, yet the explosions kept up a continuous rumbling for several minutes, like an earthquake. The planes went on, out of sight; they may have turned round the island because – twenty minutes later – a 'V' of nine appeared, again from the north. Smoke and flames were already piling up from the town. These nine dropped another load and were hardly out of sight before the second nine appeared and then the third. And finally, after half an hour they all came back again, twenty seven in close form- ation and dropped what they had left. In effect, 81 bombers had passed over in little more than an hour. Whether there were really 81 or whether they were the same 27 making three visitations I could not say; if the latter, they must have made their turns out of sight. It had the appearance each time of a fresh lot appearing from far away to the north and disappearing due south.

We spent the rest of the day hastily pulling down tents that were in an exposed area (the Old Race Course) and putting them up again under the trees in private gardens. Western Road, close by the camp, was soon thick with Asians fleeing to the safety of the Botanical Gardens, Penang Hill etc., and in the afternoon we met civilians who had been caught in the 'blitz'. Those I spoke to had taken shelter in the new shelters built in and around Fort Cornwallis which had not been hit. The bombs were evidently of light calibre as not many substantial buildings were flattened, but older build- ings and the flimsy houses of the Chinese quarter were said to be badly knocked about. Far worse, of course, was the loss of life. It was announced later on the radio that 506 casualties were brought to the General Hospital on this day alone; these were people still alive when found so there must have been many times that number found dead or never found at all. The Fire Station had been hit and most of the appliances put out of action in the first attack. An A.R.P. organisation had been built up but there were not nearly enough Europeans in it, and in any case this first (and almost last) of its air-raid experiences was altogether too much for it. I believe the Chinese wardens did wonders in a hopeless situation, but the panic and destruction were beyond them. The greatest need was for drivers of cars and lorries but the great majority of local drivers had run away.

15 December

. . . The Japanese had achieved their object – the terrorizing of the population and the breakdown of normal life. The town was practically empty of Asians who were camping out on the lower slopes of Penang Hill, and a handful of Europeans were struggling with an impossible task to keep things going. Forty-eight hours after our move out to the coast our quartermaster appeared with some food. He told us that the Singapore Cold Storage plant and bakery had been taken over by the Army, some bakers etc. impressed from somewhere, and that some semblance of order was being restored out of chaos. The few European civilians and fewer European Volunteers on Headquarters staff were working day and night distributing food to Asians who came in on bicycles, in cars, with hand-carts etc. to collect rice and other foodstuffs of which there were plentiful stocks. But those native shops not destroyed were bolted and barred, the owners having run away, and in some cases the Army had to break them open. As for general news about the situation, he knew little more than we did. The incredible news of the sinking of the 'Prince of Wales' and the 'Repulse' shook morale badly, but we kept up a pretence before the Malays that there was nothing to worry about. Meanwhile the days passed idly with less and less to do, while we waited for a possible attempt at a landing.

16 December

. . . About 6.30 p.m. we got moving at last, in lorries and with many stops, down to Swettenham Pier. It was pitch dark before we got there and it had started to rain heavily so I saw nothing at all of the town or of bomb damage. There was no light anywhere – it was rumoured that Butterworth Power Station had been blown up (by us), and in any case no lights were allowed for fear the Japanese might get wind of what was going on and try a night raid. But the bad weather was in our favour, and a night raid was improbable as they had it so much their own way in the day-time. At the Pier we found the Straits Steamship Company's s.s. 'Pangkor', but before we could embark we had to load up piles of equipment, machine guns, ammunition boxes which were lying on the wharf in the rain. Everything and everybody piled in somehow, leaving the sorting out to be done in the morning as the Captain wanted to get as far as possible from Penang before daylight. We cast off about 11 p.m. The ship was totally blacked out and crowds of people were milling about in the dark. Presently all Volunteers were called for, to go to a lighted room and clean machine guns etc. for Ac-Ac mounting in the morning. We had a chance, then, to see who was who, and some appeared to be missing, though whether left behind in the confusion no-one knew.

Had I known that we were bound for Singapore, leaving Penang to its fate (and not, as some said, going to land further down the coast to 'form a line' against the enemy), I should have felt very much inclined to slip away in the darkness before embarking and remain in Penang. The thought of scuttling away in this shameful manner, leaving thousands of people – including all those I had myself been teaching to trust us, was extremely depressing.

On the first day of the invasion, Martin Ogle observed hopelessly outdated RAF Brewster Buffalo fighters performing poorly against their Japanese opponents and saw at least one Buffalo shot down. Stragglers from the Leicester Regiment began to move through their area on 15 and 16 December, bringing news that defences at the front were crumbling. At this point Asian volunteers were given the option of disbanding, throwing away their uniforms and going home to put on native dress. The majority did so.

After an eventful voyage to Singapore, Martin Ogle would evade capture by sailing to Sumatra in a small fishing boat on 15 February 1942. He donated his diary to the Bodleian Library, Oxford in 1966.

Tuesday 9 – Sunday 14 December 1941

Anne Morrow Lindbergh, an American isolationist, discovers that 'we are completely in it'

Anne Morrow Lindbergh was a world-famous writer and aviation pioneer. She was born in New Jersey in 1902; her mother was the women's education advocate Elizabeth Cutter Morrow. Anne had married Charles A. Lindbergh, Jr in 1929. In 1933 she was awarded the Cross of Honor of the US Flag Association for her part in the survey of transatlantic air routes. She was also the first licensed woman glider pilot in the United States.

Anne Lindbergh

9 December

C[harles] and I listen to the President speak at 10. It is a very dramatic speech, well written and given (in spite of some bald contradictions. Why, if that long list of countries had been attacked 'without warning,' were we so appallingly ill-prepared in the East as we seem to have been by the damage done?). Evidently things have gone very badly in the Pacific. 'Up to now *all* the news is bad.' He implied that it would be a long hard war. He did it very well.

'The Star-Spangled Banner' is played after the speech. It is very moving. I feel as if all I believed *was* America, all memories of it, all history, all dreams of the future were marching gaily toward a precipice – and unaware, unaware.

10 December
The British have lost a great battleship and a destroyer, the *Prince of Wales* and the *Repulse*. Our navy badly hit also. Japan still getting the best of it. Talk of investigation of navy. How were we caught so off guard? The interventionists are blaming it all on us. And Fight for Freedom has come out with a gloating exultant full-page ad, starting with a huge headline: 'It's America First now'! This makes me sick.

11–14 December
Friday morning we discover at breakfast from Pat, who heard it on the radio, that yesterday Germany and Italy declared war on us and Congress declared war back – with only one dissenting voice. It is no shock. So now we are completely in it.

Charles and Anne Lindbergh were never entirely comfortable with the fame that their aviation exploits had brought them. In the 1930s they had spent some time in France and Germany, returning to the United States in 1939. Anne Lindbergh's diary records one of the more puzzling developments of mid-December 1941: Germany and Italy declaring war on the United States. They had no particular reason to do so and it was probably not in their strategic interests. However, in making this move they saved Roosevelt from a potentially awkward predicament and allowed him to join the war against all the Axis powers. Anne's diary also captures the suspicions entertained by many 'America First' advocates concerning the lack of warning about the surprise attacks on American forces in the Pacific. These concerns would eventually translate into some of the first conspiratorial interpretations of events at Pearl Harbor. SEE ALSO PP. 336–7, 625–6.

Wednesday 10 December 1941

Journalist Cecil Brown escapes from HMS *Repulse* as she sinks off the coast of Malaya

On the afternoon of 8 December Brown and O'Dowd Gallagher of the London Daily Express *had been the only two correspondents given last-minute invitations to travel on the fateful voyage of the two capital ships. They agonized, knowing that any stories that happened in Singapore would go uncovered in their absence. Neither could resist the opportunity and both had their kit – typewriters, diaries and cameras – aboard the* Repulse *within an hour. They sailed out of the Straits of Jahore at 1820 the same evening. The following morning, over breakfast, they listened to the radio as Roosevelt spoke to Congress, declaring war on Japan. Both ships attempted to intercept Japanese troop transports that were landing invading forces on the coast of Malaya. At 1100 on 10 December they were attacked by Japanese bombers and one bomb penetrated the* Repulse *in the area of her catapult deck, killing fifty crew. The* Prince of Wales *was also hit. Over the next hour the commander of the* Repulse, *Captain Tennant, would zigzag successfully, dodging no fewer than nineteen torpedoes. At 1220 the ship was hit by a further torpedo and began to sink.*

It is streaking for us. There is a deadly fascination in watching it. The watcher shouts, 'Stand by for torpedo.' The torpedo strikes the ship about twenty yards astern of my position. It feels as though the ship has crashed into dock. I am thrown four feet across the deck but I keep my feet. Almost immediately, it seems, the ship lists.

The command roars out of the loudspeaker: 'Blow up your lifebelts!'

I take down mine from the shelf. It is a blue-serge affair with a rubber bladder inside. I tie one of the cords around my waist and start to bring another cord up around the neck. Just as I start to tie it the command comes: 'All possible men to starboard.'

But a Japanese plane invalidates that command. Instantly there's another crash to starboard. Incredibly quickly, the

Repulse is listing to port, and I haven't started to blow up my lifebelt.

I finish tying the cord around my neck. My camera I hang outside the airless lifebelt. Gallagher already has his belt on and is puffing into the rubber tube to inflate it. The effort makes his strong, fair face redder than usual . . .

Captain Tennant's voice is coming over the ship's loudspeaker, a cool voice: 'All hands on deck. Prepare to abandon ship.' There is a pause for just an instant, then: 'God be with you.'

There is no alarm, no confusion, no panic. We on the flag deck move toward a companionway leading to the quarter-deck. Abrahams, the Admiralty photographer, Gallagher and I are together. The coolness of everyone is incredible. There is no pushing, but no pausing either. One youngster seems in a great hurry. He tries to edge his way into the line at the top of the companionway to get down faster to the quarterdeck.

A young sub-lieutenant taps him on the shoulder and says quietly, 'Now, now, we are all going the same way, too.'

The youngster immediately gets hold of himself . . .

The *Repulse* is going down.

The torpedo-smashed *Prince of Wales*, still a half to three-quarters of a mile ahead, is low in the water, half shrouded in smoke, a destroyer by her side.

Japanese bombers are still winging around like vultures, still attacking the *Wales*. A few of those shot down are bright splotches of burning orange on the blue South China Sea.

Men are tossing overboard rafts, lifebelts, benches, pieces of wood, anything that will float. Standing at the edge of the ship, I see one man (Midshipman Peter Gillis, an eighteen-year-old Australian from Sydney) dive from the Air Defence control tower at the top of the main mast. He dives 170 feet and starts to swim away.

Men are jumping into the sea from the four or five defence control towers that segment the main mast like a series of ledges. One man misses his distance, dives, hits the side of the *Repulse*, breaks every bone in his body and crumples into the sea like a sack of wet cement. Another misses his direction and dives from one of the towers straight down the smokestack.

Men are running all along the deck of the ship to get further astern. The ship is lower in the water at the stern and their jump therefore will be shorter. Twelve Royal Marines run back too far, jump into the water and are sucked into the propeller.

The screws of the *Repulse* are still turning. There are five or six hundred heads bobbing in the water. The men are being swept astern because the *Repulse* is still making way and there's a strong tide here, too.

On all sides of me men are flinging themselves over the side. I sit down on the edge of the *Repulse* and take off my shoes. I am very fond of those shoes. A Chinese made them for me just a few days ago in Singapore. They are soft, with a buckle, and they fit well. I carefully place them together and put them down as you do at the foot of your bed before going to sleep.

I have no vision of what is ahead, no concrete thoughts of how to save myself. It is necessarily every man for himself. As I sit there, it suddenly comes to me, the overwhelming, dogmatic conviction. I actually speak the words: 'Cecil, you are never going to get out of this.'

I see one man jump and land directly on another man. I say to myself, 'When I jump I don't want to hurt anyone.'

Down below is a mess of oil and debris, and I don't want to jump into that either. I feel my mind getting numb. I look across to the *Wales*. Its guns are flashing and the flames are belching through the greyish-black smoke.

My mind cannot absorb what my eyes see. It is impossible to believe that these two beautiful, powerful, invulnerable ships are going down. But they are. There's no doubt of that.

Men are sliding down the hull of the *Repulse*. Extending around the edge of the ship is a three-inch bulge of steel. The men hit that bulge, shoot off into space and into the water. I say to myself, 'I don't want to go down that way. That must hurt their backsides something terrible.'

About eight feet to my left there is a gaping hole in the side of the *Repulse*. It is about thirty feet across, with the plates twisted and torn. The hull of the *Repulse* has been ripped open as though a giant had torn apart a tin can. I see an officer dive over the side, dive into the hole underneath the line, dive back inside the ship.

I half turn to look back on the crazy-angled deck of the ship. The padre is beside one of the pom-poms, administering the final rites to a gunner dying beside his gun. The padre seems totally unconcerned by the fact that the *Repulse* is going down at any moment . . .

The jump is about twenty feet. The water is warm; it is not water, but thick oil. My first action is to look at my stopwatch. It is smashed at 12.35, one hour and twenty minutes after the first Japanese bomb came through 12,000 feet to crash into the catapult deck of the *Repulse*.

It doesn't occur to me to swim away from the ship until I see others striking out. Then I realize how difficult it is. The oil soaks into my clothes weighting them and I think underwater demons are tugging at me, trying to drag me down. The airless lifebelt, absorbing oil too, tightens and tautens the preserver cords around my neck. I say to myself, 'I'm going to choke to death, I'm going to choke to death.'

Next to confined places, all my life, I've been afraid of choking to death. This is the first moment of fear.

I have a ring on my left hand which Martha bought for me on the Ponte Vecchio in Florence when we were on our honeymoon. It is rather loose on my finger. With oil on my hands, I'm afraid I will lose it. I clench my fist so that it won't slip off.

I start swimming away with the left hand clenched. With my right hand I make one stroke, tug at the cord around my neck in a futile effort to loosen it, then make another stroke to get away from the ship.

That ring helps save my life. Something like it must have helped save the lives of hundreds of men. Your mind fastens itself on silly, unimportant matters, absorbing your thoughts and stifling the natural instinct of man to panic in the face of death.

I see a life preserver eighteen inches long and four inches thick. It is like a long sausage and I tuck it to me. A small piece of wood appears inviting and I take that too. A barrel comes near, but I reject that because the oil prevents me getting a grip on it. All around me men are swimming, men with blood streaking down their oil-covered faces.

The oil burns in my eyes as though someone is jabbing hot pokers into the eyes. That oil in the eyes is the worst thing. I've swallowed a bit of oil already, and it's beginning to sicken me.

Fifty feet from the ship, hardly swimming at all now, I see the bow of the *Repulse* swing straight into the air like a church steeple. Its red underplates stand out as stark and as gruesome as the blood on the faces of the men around me. Then the tug and draw of the suction of 32,000 tons of steel sliding to the bottom hits me. Something powerful, almost irresistible, snaps at my feet. It feels as though someone were trying to pull my legs out by the hip sockets. But I am more fortunate than some others. They are closer to the ship. They are sucked back. When the *Repulse* goes down it sends over a huge wave, a wave of oil. I happen to have my mouth open and I take aboard considerable oil. That makes me terribly sick at the stomach . . .

As I swim in the water, other men are hanging onto pieces of wood, floating life belts and debris . . . A small table, about three feet square floats by . . . I scramble up on top and lay there for a moment. And then I watch the *Prince of Wales* go down, a big, dark thing sliding into nothingness.

Cecil Brown's account of the sinking of the Repulse *and the* Prince of Wales *must constitute one of the most remarkable diary entries of the Second World War.*

After clinging to his floating wooden table, Brown would eventually be pulled aboard a raft and then rescued by a destroyer. Brown records that, after he was picked up, a friend went through the pockets of his coveralls for him and located 'the precious notebook' in which he had recorded the battle. Brown was worried that it might have been destroyed by seawater; however, he wrote, 'I open the notebook, and see every page is water-and-oil-soaked but still legible.' SEE ALSO PP. 83–6, 94–6, 185–7.

Saturday 13 December 1941

John Kennedy on Winston Churchill and the chiefs of staff after the Japanese attacks in the Far East

John Kennedy was Director of Military Operations at the War Office and was in constant contact with the chiefs of staff and others around Churchill, including 'Pug' Ismay, Secretary to the War Cabinet, and Alan Brooke, the Chief of the Imperial General Staff. He was close enough to witness their constant vexations but thankful to be distant enough not to have to deal with Churchill personally.

The news about the Prince of Wales and Repulse was a great shock. This and the results of the attack on Pearl Harbor seem to spell the doom of the big ship. Aircraft carriers, small and many of them, will be of tremendous value in the future. It was a relief to hear that 2000 men had been saved, but sad that Tom Phillips is missing. The naval people in London seem to think that he would have preferred not to survive because of the fear of feeling he had committed an error in handling the ships as he did. We do not yet know the full story however.

I dined with Ismay one night at the Carlton Grill. He told me Winston had been tired and irritable and difficult and no wonder. Winston seems to suck the vitality out of his entourage like a leech. Ismay looks very tired and unwell. I am thankful to have so little to do with him.

Winston broadcast on Monday and I listened in the club. He was either very tired or not quite sober. He spoke badly. I wish we had someone in sight in case he breaks up. It is frightful to be so dependent upon a man who is so old and of such luxurious habits.

Winston has held several meetings of the COS [chiefs of staff] this week and has been very difficult and dictatorial about strategy and detailed movements of troops. He will not leave the COS to decide or even issue orders. We have directed the 18[th] Div[ision] to India. Brooke had g[rea]t difficulty in stopping him sending it to Burma to carry out a sweep behind Japanese units into Siam – He would not realise that the country in Burma with its mountains and jungles was quite impossible for a British mechanised division and moreover that no administrative facilities have been built up for British troops.

I fear that Hong Kong will not last long – perhaps a month or six weeks. And Singapore is not too secure. For it will be very difficult to send out supplies and reinforcements with the Japanese aircraft dominating the Malacca Straits. However, we must go on doing our best, fighting where we can and as long as we can.

Churchill was especially irritable and unpleasant to work with in December 1941, seeing his much-cherished Middle East offensive delayed and regretting his decisions on the Far East. December 1941 was certainly a terrible month and John Kennedy knew worse was soon to follow. Yet British military planners also knew now that, in the long term, they would win the war, having the United States, with its enormous productive capacity, on their side. In terms of major world powers, only Russia and Japan now remained at peace, standing uneasily by their non-aggression pact concluded in the spring of 1941. Churchill's prestige was at an all-time low in the six months following Japan's attacks in the Far East.

John Kennedy would continue to serve as Director of Military Operations until 1943, when he became Assistant Chief of the Imperial General Staff. After the war he was made Governor of Southern Rhodesia and was knighted in 1952.

Sunday 14 December 1941

Mollie Panter-Downes observes 'mass misery' among the population of London

Mollie Panter-Downes was born in London in 1906 and grew up in Sussex. At twenty-three she had become the London reporter for the New Yorker *magazine. Her writings provided one of the principal windows through which New Yorkers viewed London and the home counties during the Second World War.*

Events of the past week have been so closely packed and the emotional pressure has been so intense that items of news which at most times would have made headlines for days . . . were received with practically no comment. On Monday, December 8th, London felt as it did at the beginning of the war. Newsdealers stood on the corners handing out papers as steadily and automatically as if they were husking corn; people bought copies on the way out to lunch and again on the way back, just in case a late edition might have sneaked up on them with some fresher news. Suddenly and soberly, this little island was remembering its vast and sprawling possessions of Empire. It seemed as though every person one met had a son in Singapore or a daughter in Rangoon; every post office was jammed with anxious crowds finding out about cable rates to Hong Kong, Kuala Lumpur, or Penang.

The initial shock and anger resulting from the Sunday evening radio announcement of the Japanese attack on the United States were terrific, but comfort was taken in the assumption that these early blows would be returned with interest at the earliest opportunity. When nothing happened except new and harder hitting from the Japanese, there was gloom which culminated in the stunned silence that met Wednesday's news of the loss of the *Prince of Wales* and the *Repulse*. For sheer mass misery, this was probably England's blackest day since the collapse of France. The satisfaction over the arrival at Singapore of the *Prince of Wales* with her consorts was still so recent that her loss seemed at first almost incredible. It was as if some enormously powerful and valuable watchdog which had been going to keep burglars away from the house had been shot while exercising in the front yard. The big battleship's disappearance made the landscape look so menacing that British spirits, which always react better to disaster than to triumph, promptly rose to a new high pitch of belligerence. This found immediate outlet in angry questions as to how the *Prince of Wales* disaster had been allowed to happen in the first place. Mr Churchill's preliminary statement to the House of Commons didn't stop people from asking why capital ships had been given inadequate air support . . .

Because most people's store of excitement had been used up on the entrance of Japan into the war and the events surrounding it, the United States' declaration of war on Germany and Italy was received quietly. There was little outward jubilation over an event which every intelligent Briton has been quite frankly praying for ever since it became evident that, for all the fine phrases, something more than the tools was going to be necessary before there could be a possibility of finishing the job.

The level of responsibility born by Churchill for the loss of the Prince of Wales *and the* Repulse *is still debated. In reality the Japanese enjoyed regional air superiority and it is unlikely that support from a single aircraft carrier would have made a difference. All countries were learning expensive lessons about the importance of air power at sea and the growing obsolescence of the battleship. Britain's debacle in the Far East probably had as much to do with poor co-operation among the different armed services and the colonial authorities as with any decisions taken by Churchill. The Japanese also had their strategic blind spots, notably in logistics, and were making progress in Malaya partly because of the vast amounts of supplies and fuel abandoned by the retreating British, which they referred gratefully to as 'Churchill stores'.*

Mollie Panter-Downes would continue to write for the New Yorker *long after the war. She died in 1997 at the age of ninety.*

Mid-December 1941

Charles Ritchie, a Canadian diplomat, takes secret pleasure in a lesson on the 'facts of life' for the Americans

Charles Ritchie was a young Canadian diplomat serving in London. Born in Halifax, Nova Scotia, he studied at Oxford, Harvard and L'École des Sciences Politiques in Paris before joining the small Canadian diplomatic corps in 1934. He had spent most of 1940 and 1941 in London observing the Blitz.

The Japanese have taken the Americans by the scruff of the neck and bounced them into the war. The picture is that of an over-cautious boy balancing on the edge of a diving-board running forward two steps and back three and then a tough bully comes along and gives him a kick in the back-side right into the water! And only yesterday they were still hovering, saying they felt almost sure they might back us up if the Japanese attacked the Kra Peninsula, but they would feel happier if we could give a guarantee of the territorial integrity of Thailand before we invaded its territories. The President had a hot tip that the Japanese objective was Rangoon – but, lo and behold! it was Pearl Harbour. For years I have seen movies of the United States reconnaissance planes ('the eyes and ears of the US Navy', as the announcers portentously described them) circling away from the US base at Pearl Harbour to spy out the Pacific for just such an attempt as this. What were they doing when those five air-craft carriers sneaked up close enough to disgorge those planes? Mr Massey [the Canadian High Commissioner in London] says, 'They have been living in a Hollywood world of unreality.' We listened to Roosevelt's address to Congress on the wireless in Mr Massey's big office at Canada House under the great glass chandelier – the room where he told us of the declaration of war on Germany. Roosevelt was moving and had dropped his mannerisms. He sounded pro-foundly shocked and bitterly angry. His speech was exactly right.

At the Admiralty they suggest, 'Why not a British naval adviser on every American battleship.' At first the news of American unpreparedness and its results was an immense *soulagement* of a long-stored, carefully restrained grudge in this country, but when the number of US battleships sunk began to come in an Admiralty official said, 'This is getting past a joke.' I have not heard one word of sympathy for the United States here. The note of outraged American indig-nation at the treachery of which the USA has been a victim meets with no real echo here. It is like a hardened old tart who hears a girl crying because a man has deceived her for the first time. We have become very much accustomed to treachery – now let the Americans learn the facts of life and see how they like them.

The somewhat bitter reflections of Ritchie, who had watched the bombing of London over a period of two years, were not surprising. He hailed from a North American country that had been at war since 1939 and had already suffered significant losses. His remarks reflected particular irritation at the attitudes of isolationists, who saw war as a 'disease of Old Europe', a symptom of moral decline which should be kept at a distance. However, Ritchie's observations about the tardiness of the United States might equally be applied to other countries that had stood by during the attacks on China in 1937 and Czechoslovakia in 1938. SEE ALSO P. 729–30.

Monday 15 – Wednesday 24 December 1941

Juan Labrador experiences 'fifth column' panic in the Philippines

Friar Juan Labrador OP was a Spanish priest who by 1941 had been working in the Philippines for twenty-three years. He had taught at Santo Tomas University in the early 1930s before becoming Rector of the Lectran College in 1936. As an academic and a trained political scientist, he was unusually prescient on the subject of international affairs and had forecast the Japanese invasion of the Philippines in a published article in 1935.

15 December

Night before last, rumors spread like wildfire that the tap water has been poisoned by the Japanese, or by the Germans, or by fifth columnists ... or by ghosts. The Japanese, the Germans and the fifth columnists have been put away in safety. Only the ghosts can be walking around freely. The police and the members of the CEA (Civilian Emergency Administration) are greatly responsible for spreading the false rumors.

'Do not drink tap water. It is poisoned!' they shouted in the streets. All of a sudden, a number of gullible individuals started feeling stomach pains. Fortunately for us, we got wind of the news quite late, and no one among us suffered the minimum of discomfort either in the stomach or in the imagination. The more enterprising ones set up stalls with their original concoctions of sure antidotes.

Otherwise, the city has returned to normalcy. There are no more explosions at night. All the sympathizers of the Axis were nabbed after the 'heroic' street to street and house to house encounters. I tried to find out where they were confined, to know what has become of my friends and some other people I know. I had to be very discreet, as we were all under suspicion. There is a news black-out about the fate of citizens of the enemy countries. A number of German and Italian priests were arrested on the first day and imprisoned. But they were released after two days. An Italian parish priest, on returning to his parish, found out that his cook had been manhandled and robbed. He complained to the authorities but they said to him: 'You are an Italian and you are complaining?' And they locked him [up] again . . .

17 December

Bamboos are no longer being burned at night. Nobody can explain such fantastic illuminations in different places during the first nightly raids. They tell us they are the Japanese, pro-Japanese spies who burn assortments of multicolored lights which signal to the enemy pilots the different places and the nature of their targets: friends, enemies, military installations, etc., depending on these colored lights' combinations . . .

24 December

A tragi-comic note was added to the situation when someone – musician, poet, or fool – shouted: 'Poison gas! Poison gas!' The panic spread as he ran about wildly, like one possessed, covering his nose with a wet handkerchief, and shouting: 'Poison gas!' Some people scampered up trees, others on top floors, where they thought the poison gas would not ascend, while the Chinese and the street vendors abandoned their wares.

Shortly afterwards, improvised laboratories sprouted with a fantastic quantity of bottles, expensive concoctions which they declared to be sure antidotes against all kinds of poison gases. They were sold at P2 to P5 and they really turned out to be sure antidotes, since no-one was poisoned by those imaginary gases.

The possibility that gas or poisons might be used was an ever-present worry during the Second World War. Although large stocks of gas were maintained by the protagonists in Europe, deterrence prevailed and they were never used. In contrast, in Asia the Japanese conducted substantial operational trials with chemical and biological weapons, using them against its opponents in China – activities that were perpetrated by the now notorious Unit 731. In 1995 Japan agreed to pay large sums to China to cover the cost of cleaning up large stocks of chemical warfare munitions uncovered in Jilin Province. Conversely, some British and American officers would later advocate carpet bombing areas of Japan with mustard gas in the final stages of the Pacific campaign, but the advent of atomic weapons curtailed these discussions. SEE ALSO PP. 229–31, 456–7, 563–4, 689–91.

Friday 19 – Monday 22 December 1941

Canadian soldier Georges 'Blacky' Verreault watches officers and men under fire for the first time during the battle for Hong Kong

Heavy Japanese bombing and shelling formed a prelude for an amphibious attack on the island of Hong Kong, prefiguring the pattern of events at Singapore two months later.

19 December

The situation is getting worse. Last night enemy sharp-shooters landed on our island. They're close. Their machine guns are spitting deadly bullets. Christ what noise. More bombs, more airplanes. We are trapped like rats. We can't escape. We've been told that the Japs do not take prisoners. What a way to die. I feel sad, I will never see good old Montreal again. Still it seems so stupid to die this way. Charlotte! Will I see you again? My queen, I must. Do you think of me?

Someone must be thinking of Georges at times? I'm

depressed for the first time in my life. I don't want to die, I want to see my home again, my old ptit Louis, my brothers, my sister, Mrs. Gaudet, Paul . . .

The atmosphere is getting tense. The enemy is closing in. I think I hit one a minute ago, but I'm not sure. The future looks dark!

My night work will get very dicey with Japs everywhere in the hills.

Charlotte my duchess, it's getting worse. Well that's all we needed, an earthquake.

20 December

The battle is fierce on the far side of the hill. Cannons, machine guns, tommy guns all spitting death. I think that if we win this war (I'm beginning to have my doubts) it won't be due to the brilliance of our brave officers. It's a shame how nervous they are. This morning a few Japs appeared about a mile away. An English lieutenant with us since last night lost his cool. He almost had us fire at them from that distance. It was pathetic to watch him go from one group to the next asking 'are you nervous? Now keep cool boys.' Finally the enemy disappeared.

The stinking rats got two of my buddies. My captain also disappeared.

If I ever come out of this, I don't think I'll ever be able to tolerate a Jap in my presence.

Sharp, Fairly, Orvais died recently. All three recently married. Three more young widows in Canada.

22 December

Denante, Greenburg, Thomas just died, crushed under some fallen rocks on the mountain. Adios comrades. Sooner or later the little stinkers will pay for this.

We are now back in our barracks in the city. Bombs are falling in great numbers.

Last evening, general alarm was sounded. Everybody on guard around the building, the Nippons are all around us they say. Maybe in the building next door we don't know. It's terrible not to know.

Mitchell and I were sprawled on our stomachs behind a

tree. Suddenly I need a leak. I stand up to satisfy nature then ta!ra!ra!ra! tommy gun. Bullets whistle around my head. Zoum! Zoum! Zinc!!! There's a dent on my helmet. I escaped a brutal end by falling on my stomach with you know what hanging out.

I'm totally exhausted. No sleep. It's war but after the war, I'll rest at will but I hope not six feet under.

The Japs are desperately trying to take the island. Many are disguised as Coolies and the first thing you know, you're being shot at by a 'civilian?'

Rumour goes that a Chinese bomber has bombed Kowloon. It seems that the Chinks always try to sneak up behind the enemy. Will they be there in time?

Charlotte, I miss your majesty, your lips, your eyes, you.

Three weeks of war and already it feels like two years. What a different kind of Christmas day. I just saw my captain. He's not dead but shivers continuously, poor sob. So much responsibility for a type like him. What a pity. In dangerous moments, he disappears. He hides. Disgusting! All the guys are disgusted.

It's been quite a while since I enjoyed the luxury of a bath. Water lines are all cut. This a.m., fed-up with my whiskers, I shaved in a glass of beer. I tore half my face off. I didn't have the courage to cut my mustache . . .

My skin is encrusted with dirt and my joints are in dire need of lubrication. Cheer up lads. 'Fuck em all' as the song goes. Presently while the bombs are falling, I'm at the canteen with a few guys while one guy is on the piano playing to his heart's content.

I'm in a joyous and noisy crowd; our good old parties. The piano, the music: melancholy. Something strange stifles me. My throat constricts, my soul drains it seems.

Will I ever see home again?

Georges Verreault's diary gives some of the many reasons for the rapid fall of Hong Kong. Most obviously the Japanese enjoyed larger numbers and massive air superiority, which quickly demoralized the defenders. No less important was the fact that most Allied officers and men had never been under fire, while most of the Japanese troops had enjoyed four years of experience since 1937 campaigning in the war against China.

Georges records the psychological impact of direct fire on unseasoned troops without fear or favour, including 'the shakes' and a need to urinate frequently. To his disgust, Hong Kong would surrender on Christmas Day 1941, and Georges remarked in his diary, 'So many lives for such shameful results . . . We are prisoners of war and the pigs are laughing at us.' SEE ALSO PP. 121–3, 593–4.

Tuesday 23 December 1941

Robert T. Smith, a Flying Tiger, watches the war arrive at Rangoon in Burma

In 1937 Claire L. Chennault, a captain in the US Army Air Corps, accepted an invitation from Madame Chiang Kai-shek to come to China to make a confidential survey of the Chinese air force. This had coincided with the beginning of the Sino-Japanese war. Chennault stayed on and organized the American Volunteer Group, a freelance collection of American pilots committed to the Chinese cause. Robert T. Smith was serving with these 'Flying Tigers' in southern China.

Boy and it all came today! We got a report at 10.00 am that large numbers of bombers were on the way. 14 ships from our Sqdn. and 14 Buffaloes from RAF took off. We intercepted them at 12,000 ft. 15 minutes east of Rangoon. Two waves of bombers, 27 in each wave, and about 40 fighter escorts. We started making runs on them and shooting like hell. After a bit I couldn't see any of the fellows up there. Found a bomber away from the formation, made about three passes, and on the last one went in to about 50 yds., firing all guns and he blew up right in front of me + down in flames. Went after another and McMillan and I together put out his right engine and smoke trailed out. He was losing alt. last time I looked, but about that time I was jumped by three Jap fighters. Shot at one and drove away. Went back up and fired at more bombers till ammo. out. Greene was shot down by fighters, bailed out, + they strafed him going down. Wasn't hit. Landed OK. Martin and Gilbert both shot down and killed. My ship had a few holes in it. Several killed at the field here and about a 1,000 in Rangoon. Fires all over and smoke very thick. After the raid refuelled and went on patrol. A busy day. Let 'em come. We got about 15 ships to their 3.

Robert T. Smith would soon find himself attacking the Japanese as they advanced quickly into Burma. His own unit was equipped with the reasonably effective Curtiss Hawk aircraft, while neighbouring RAF units in Singapore had the outdated Buffalo – dubbed the 'flying coffin' by its crews. Neither was as good as the fabled Japanese 'Zero'. Smith observed that few appreciate just how incredibly busy the pilot is during combat. As well as controlling the throttle, the left hand must be used for making changes in rudder and elevator trim tabs required with changes in speed and power settings. The right hand grasps the pistol grip, a squeeze of which will fire all six machine-guns. All this time, if the pilot is to live, his head is constantly turning in every direction to locate the position of enemy planes, trying to make sure that one or more of them haven't swung in behind him, ready for the kill.

Robert T. Smith would continue to serve with the Flying Tigers, later the 14th Air Force, until the end of the war; he returned to his home in California in 1945.

Christmas Day – Boxing Day, December 1941

Corporal James A. Roxburgh, an Australian at Singapore, watches a new officer arrive at his unit

James A. Roxburgh was serving in the 2/30th Battalion, Australian Imperial Force, at Singapore. His unit had arrived in Singapore in July 1941 and had immediately begun jungle warfare training.

25 December

Still on guard, we have all been issued with Bren equipment. For our Xmas dinner we were given tomato soup, turkey, ham, baked potatoes, plum pudding & sauce, a bottle of Tiger beer & a bottle of orange drink. We were then given 4 pkts of cigarettes, a hank. With a 30th Bn colour patch, & a box of comforts from the Lord Mayors Fund. This contained

1 lb Arnotts Xmas cake, ½ lb Joyce plum pudding, boot polish, Nestles cream, Ipana tooth paste, tooth brush, 2 oz Log Cabin, cig. papers, tin peaches, ½ lb Nestles chocolate ration, small Kraft cheese, razor blades. We had barely finished dinner when we were given a 'red' air raid alarm & had to make for the shelter of the rubber trees. We were so full after our big meal that it was a struggle to get there. During the afternoon a new officer took over the guard & before he had been there an hour he had one of our guard in the clink, & another under open arrest for refusing to take over this man's work. When I called out for the relieving sentries at 6p.m. a lot of them refused to leave their tents. These men were put in clink & we also found that 3 of our guard were A.W.L. The M.P.s brought these 3 men back later on & put them in with the others. Before 'Lights Out' we had a total of 23 men in altogether & they were singing, yelling out & giving abuse till after midnight. As the guard was short handed owing to the trouble, we N.C.O.s of the guard had to do sentry duty during the night. What a perfect Xmas day.

26 December

The men in the clink were quiet this morning & gave no trouble. Our breakfast was late & we had just started to have it at a quarter to ten, when the 'red alarm' sounded & we had to make for the rubber. It is a funny co-incidence that most of these alarms are at meal times. We were relieved at 6p.m. & I was immediately put on as Depot Ord. Cpl. I was on this till 5.30p.m. Saturday night.

In October 1940 Major-General Frederick Gallagher 'Black Jack' Galleghan had taken over command of the 2/30th Battalion. He was a strict disciplinarian and expected his subordinate officers to follow his example. Some of his men said they feared Galleghan more than the Japanese. SEE ALSO PP. 183, 185.

1942

'I MUST BE VERY CAREFUL from now on with this diary. The Japs did a search of our huts today. No bullshit, they turned the place inside out. I have got this diary shoved in a bamboo pole. They gave no warning and I was quite worried about it . . .'

Don McLaren, a POW recently arrived in Changi, diary entry for 26 March 1942

JANUARY 1942

THE EVENTS OF DECEMBER 1941 had delivered a terrible psychological shock to the western powers; but worse was to come.
While western leaders had expected Japan to carry some initial
victories as the result of its surprise attacks, they had not anticipated the staggering strategic reversals that followed during
January and February 1942. Britain and the United States maintained significant military forces in Asia and the Pacific.
Everywhere these forces were defeated by Japanese units that
were often inferior in numbers, but superior in commitment
and battle experience. Japan had always been viewed as a
country that pursued a conservative foreign policy, seeking only
limited gains. Uncharacteristically, Toyko had chosen to take
huge risks – and the gamble was paying off.

This was nowhere better illustrated than in Malaya, where a
force of some 50,000 Japanese troops pushed a demoralized
defending force more than twice its size into a headlong retreat
southwards towards Singapore. Much of the explanation for the
success of this advance lies in Japanese air superiority, along
with the existence of new roads and rail links within Malaya,
developed to support rubber and tin production, which had
removed many of the barriers to invasion previously presented
by impassable jungle. Accordingly, the Japanese could deploy
tanks, and their forces raced past Kuala Lumpur. Indeed, by 18
January British troops had been ordered to move back to the
Jahore Line, no more than 50 miles north of Singapore. Almost
all of Malaya had already been abandoned to the enemy,
together with its Asian populations. The Japanese proceeded to
treat the local Chinese community with particular savagery.

In the Philippines, the Japanese quickly occupied the capital,
Manila, and the major US naval base at Cavite, both located on
the main island of Luzon. The Philippine army successfully
held a defensive line, permitting the organized withdrawal to
the peninsula of Bataan to continue. Some 15,000 US and 65,000
Filipino troops prepared to defend these limited positions,

although they were already short of supplies. US submarines attempted to conduct covert supply runs to beleaguered American garrisons on the nearby island of Corregidor with limited success. During mid-January Allied forces fought off Japanese units attempting to infiltrate Bataan from the rear, but by the end of the month the defenders had been forced back across Bataan to secondary positions. Throughout January, Tokyo was already so confident of its control in the Philippines that it felt able to withdraw an entire division for service elsewhere, leaving the Allied garrisons on Bataan and Corregidor penned in.

While attention was focused upon these dramatic developments in Malaya and the Philippines, Japan was also sweeping into the Netherlands East Indies (now Indonesia) and advancing from Thailand into Burma. Allied forces in the region had already been placed under united command, a testament to secret contingency planning during mid-1941. Archibald Wavell was designated overall commander of a new American–British–Dutch–Australian headquarters called ABDA Command, but unification did not result in invigoration. Indeed, there was no time to adopt common operational doctrines or even arrange proper intercommunication. On 27 January a motley Allied force of ageing cruisers and destroyers attempted to engage the Japanese invasion force heading for the island of Java, but were defeated by a superior Japanese force in what became known as the Battle of Java Sea. ABDA was the shortest-lived of the wartime commands and was soon preparing to liquidate itself and flee. On the last day of January 1942 British forces in Malaya informed Wavell that they had withdrawn to Singapore Island, leaving all other territory in Japanese hands. Defeat was only days away.

The situation in January 1942 also presents a curious unevenness in terms of the duration of the war. For the Chinese, this was merely the expansion of a war that had been under way on the Asian mainland since 1937. Britain, Australia, Canada, India, New Zealand and all other countries of the Empire and Commonwealth had been at war for more than two years. Now the United States was embroiled in what had become, indisputably, a global conflict. However, even at this point Russia remained firmly respectful of its neutrality pact with Japan.

Despite all these very different starting points, in January 1942 a consensus was emerging about what an end point might look like. In Washington delegates from more than twenty countries, calling themselves the United Nations, declared themselves in favour of the abstract freedoms set out in the Atlantic Charter that had been framed by Churchill and Roosevelt in August 1941. These were effectively the war aims of the free world. They also agreed that they would push on together to absolute victory, and that none of them would make a separate peace with the enemy.

Thursday 1 January 1942

Sheila Allan, aged seventeen, heads for the boat from Singapore to Australia

Sheila Allan was born in 1924 in Taiping in Malaya, where her Australian father, Charles Allan, was a mining engineer with Osborne and Chappel Company. Her Malayan mother had died some years before the war and Sheila had been educated in a number of convents, her father often travelling to Thailand on business. At the beginning of 1942, with Japanese forces advancing rapidly on Singapore, the mining company offered to evacuate Sheila and her Thai stepmother to Australia.

New Year's Day! Happy New Year – that's a laugh! Wonder what the year will bring – will we still be here next year?

Just imagine I was nearly bound for Australia today. Dad received a note ordering Mum and me to be ready to leave today.

The Company was evacuating the women and children and paying their passage to Australia. I didn't want to go but Dad insisted. Mum, at the last moment, broke down and refused point-blank to leave him. Without realising it she was the means of making me stay too. When the manager found out that she wasn't leaving, he had to send our ticket away to be altered. Consequently I'm left behind. Somehow, I believe it's Fate. I'm glad I'm staying with Dad.

Well, our things are gone. Dad had permission to look in the yard for the truck. To our horror we found the truck broken into and had been looted by the Malays. In fact, two of them were shot by the MPs [Military Policemen] on duty the night before. All Dad's clothes and his twenty years collections in Malaya had all gone. Mum and I were lucky with regard to clothes. We found them untouched. They must have only wanted men's clothing.

There are some soldiers stationed not far from us. We've made a few friends among them. Dad sometimes invites them to a meal and they talk late into the night about things that I don't understand. But I like listening.

The decision of Charles Allan's family to stay behind underlined the extent to which, even in early January, no-one could believe that Japan would conquer the great imperial city of Singapore. This was self-delusion, partly based on racial ideas of superiority: it was not so much that defeat by Japan was impossible, more that it was unthinkable. Nevertheless, law and order were already beginning to break down. Charles Allan's wife and daughter were fortunate to be offered passage, even though they did not in the end avail themselves of the opportunity, since elsewhere the authorities refused to evacuate anyone who was not white, even if they were family members of Europeans. SEE ALSO PP. *187–9, 209, 459–60, 587–8.*

Friday 2 – Tuesday 13 January 1942

Freddie Mathieson of the Australian army experiences the snow in Damascus before heading east to fight Japan

Freddie Mathieson was born in 1920 in Newcastle, New South Wales and grew up in Sydney. He had served in the militia from the age of sixteen and joined the army full-time at the start of the war in Europe. By 1942 he had already seen plenty of action in the Middle East and was serving as a driver in an ammunition supply unit stationed near Damascus. Their accommodation was a tented encampment poorly equipped against the unseasonable weather.

2 January

Woke up to a strange sight. Everything is white about 6 inches of snow on the ground and still snowing like mad. What a sight. We have seen just about everything as far as weather goes since we have been in the Middle East. This is the first time most of us have seen snow, so snow fights are on. The cabs of our trucks are half full of snow. What a mess. We also find out a number of our trucks are U.S. [unserviceable] with cracked heads or engine blocks, about twenty in all. This puts the company in a very bad position if we have to move quickly . . .

4 January

When we go to the latrine you must take a bayonet with you to scrape the snow and ice off the seat. We just can't get over the thousands of cement slabs and other material for the troops' winter quarters we delivered. The snow is here and what are we in. Nobody is very happy about this, from the O.C. [Office Commanding] down. We believe the boss has sent a few signals to C.H.Q. [Company Headquarters] using some colourful language concerning this state of affairs. We believe this has been the heaviest snow fall here in forty years and it is now −12 degrees.

13 January

At last we are informed we may be going to Palestine and then to Burma, but who knows things change so very quick.

By 7 January the snow was disappearing around Damascus and Freddie Mathieson's supply unit had been able to move its trucks. On 18 January the men were formally told that they were striking camp and heading for the port of Suez. From there they would be sent east to fight Japan and to reinforce an increasingly desperate Allied situation. Movements were always shrouded in secrecy but the locals soon got wind of their general destination. The Egyptian dock workers enjoyed baiting the Australian soldiers with the phrase 'Japan man eat you'. By 5 February, Mathieson would be in a convoy heading east – 'into the Red Sea and who knows what'. SEE ALSO PP. 215–16, 511.

Sunday 4 – Monday 5 January 1942

Richard C. Malonnee, US instructor to 21st Field Artillery
Unit, Philippine army, finds that confusion reigns

Richard C. Malonnee was an adviser to the army of the newly in-
dependent government of the Philippines. Malonnee confronted the
problem familiar to his American successors twenty years later in the
Vietnam War, and indeed in numerous other wars: how to become a
successful and effective adviser without appearing to display a colonial
mentality.

[W]e continued to have CP's [Command Posts] located in
prominent houses which were always an invitation to bombing or shelling. In addition to the CP location other matters
were very much to my dissatisfaction. The actual occupation
was never smooth and orderly. Even though a considerable
interval of time always elapsed between the time the
personnel arrived and I tailed in at the rear of the column,
things were always at sixes and sevens. Confusion reigned.
Trucks stood on the road. Officers evinced no interest in the
establishment of anything except their own comfort. After
commenting about these matters informally many times,
I finally called a staff meeting during a lull at Pabanlag. I
emphasised that the reconnaissance purpose was to allocate
specific locations to the various installations of the CP: that
the officer in charge of that section had to sub-divide his area
to best meet his needs; that the definite and specific place for
each vehicle and installation be designated; and that guides
knowing those locations meet and guide in each vehicle and
get it off the road and into its covered position in an
expeditious manner. The shelling we received at Pabanlag
illustrated the necessity of avoiding prominent locations. We
had enough battle experience to make evident to all the need
of systematic order of occupation. This was evident to all,
and an amiable and lengthy discussion took place as to the
proper technique of occupying the CP location. I
recommended strongly to Colonel Catalan [the commander,

21st Field Artillery] that he sub-divide his CP into a command and an administration echelon. I had been harping on [about] this throughout the campaign but I could not persuade Catalan to divorce himself from his supply officer, mess officer, motor officer, doctor, dentist, chaplain, and several utility officers.

I gave a sigh of relief and thought that the matter was ironed out. When I arrived at the new CP I found things even worse than usual. The CP was in the only bario on the road – the only one for miles around – a perfect invitation to bombing. It was about as far from the battalions as it was possible to get without going to Dinilupithan. Instead of spreading installations out over several hundred yards to minimise potential losses, the entire CP was less than 50 yards from one edge to the other. Trucks were parked along the road in the 'shade' of the buildings.

I regret that I lost my temper. I can only say in my excuse that the entire period of the campaign had seen little, if any, improvement in the standard of performance of the regimental staff. They have been almost valueless to Catalan and have been the only section of the regiment which has not responded to training. Despite constant failures I had kept my temper – at least tried to do so – and pleasantly and with even temper pointed out the defects and indicated the correction. I found opportunity to speak privately to each officer and explain in some detail the relation of a staff officer to the commander – how the latter was dependent upon the assistance of his official family – and how invaluable the assistance of the staff could be. I had outlined in some detail the duties and the many other matters in which they could help Colonel Catalan. All of this father–son attitude had been unavailing and this night's experience was but one more fact to convince me that collectively the staff were – and would always be – nice, pleasing, young men of polite habits, courteous speech and well-timed applauding laughter, – but perfectly valueless in the campaign.

I informed Colonel Catalan publicly and with muleskinner language that the command post was an impossible one which violated every known consideration of command post selection and organisation – that if it was the best his staff, including Villa-Real, could do after so many similar failures had been repeatedly pointed out to them, then I would suggest and strongly recommend that he clean out the stable and start afresh by surrounding himself with a staff which could secure results.

This was inexcusable on my part from the standpoint of tact and diplomacy. But emphatic action was indicated as absolutely imperative from a military standpoint. I find fault with myself only for taking the action while I was out of temper and with unrestrained language. Colonel Catalan obviously sided with and defended Villa-Real and the staff by saying that they, the CP, would move anywhere I desired and they would await my orders. This made me even madder. This was in keeping with the political juggling which has so many times evidenced itself in American–Filipino relations. The attempt to put me in a hole by this tongue-in-cheek lip service to my wishes when it was obvious that I could not give any sound and reasonable command there in the pitch-darkness in territory which I had never seen even in daylight, infuriated me. I told him to leave his rear echelon where it was, to be blown to hell if it was, as it seemed, their desire . . .

Not unlike the British, who had extended a limited independence to Egypt between the wars, the United States had offered the Philippines a qualified independence in 1935. The Philippine army now had American advisers, rather than American officers, much as the Army of the Republic of South Vietnam would have twenty years later and with the same effect. While veteran Japanese forces were making inroads in 1941, the novice Philippine army was retreating to Bataan. Malonnee's problem was how to persuade the headquarters staff to abandon peacetime exercise mode and to take the war more seriously. He knew the situation was becoming dangerous. Some of Malonnee's fellow advisers even took to manhandling their charges in an attempt to obtain results, but this proved counter-productive. Later on 5 January Malonnee's troop would receive news that the 11th Division, which lay between them and the enemy, was crumbling badly and in a state 'which is aptly expressed by the word "fluid"'.

Richard Carvel Malonnee would remain as a regimental adviser to the 21st Artillery Regiment of the Philippines army during the Bataan campaign of early 1942. He took part in the Bataan Death March of 1942 and was held prisoner in the Philippines throughout the war, thereafter returning to the United States.

Tom Forsyth experiences conditions in a POW camp in Hong Kong

Canadian Tom Forsyth had been a farm worker from Pipestone, Manitoba. On 30 September 1939, aged twenty-nine, he had enlisted in the Winnipeg Grenadiers. New recruits had spent a short month training in civilian clothes before being issued with 1916 uniforms and elderly rifles. Initially he had spent a quiet war guarding prisoners of war in Jamaica. However, on 8 November 1941 his unit had been embarked on a ship at Vancouver and sent to reinforce Hong Kong, together with other recently arrived units from Britain and Australia. By the end of December they were prisoners of the Japanese.

4 January
In HONG KONG the day never passed without the camp staff or the guards inflicting sheer wanton cruelty on helpless innocent Chinese civilians. The guards loved to practice Ju-Jitsu on ten year old boys: to make old women kneel for hours in the middle of the road at Shamshuipo, while at North Point camp when ever any Chinese women attempted to gather firewood on the higher hills above the camp the guards used them for target practice, taking turns firing, laughing and joking. The camp was on the very edge of the water, there was always a lot of small craft in the bay. A small rowboat with two women in it came just within rifle range; an officer was making his rounds, he seized a rifle from a guard and fired, one of the women dropped her oar and sank forward in the boat, the other rowed frantically to get out of range. Cold, calculated butchery, that's all it was. A Chinese girl about 18 was tied to a tree for two days for gathering firewood close to the camp.

Close to Bowen Road hospital two Chinese were wired to trees, soaked in waste oil and set on fire. Their screams were terrible to hear.

Now we are Prisoners of War back on the mainland in Shamshuipo barracks.

5 January

I got my diary back from Colonel this morning. Lack of personal kit is proving a great handicap and inconvenience. Few men have any soap or razors. The problem of feeding 5,000 men, Grenadiers, Royal Rifles, Royal Scots, Middlesex, Hong Kong volunteers, Hong Kong Singapore Royal Artillery (the latter were Hindus) all big men with turbans and bushy black beards, was a difficult one. Old gas drums had their heads knocked in (or out) and they were propped up on stones, a fire lit underneath and rice boiled that way, a cupful morning and night, no salt, a most insipid mess. The fortunate who have money can buy over the fence from the Chinese a few things like buns and canned goods that really help. I'll never forgive myself for leaving $25.00 in my kit bag up among the hills on the island. We had a lecture from Baird, he advised us to make wooden clogs or sandals to save our shoes.

The reinforcement of Hong Kong with fresh troops in the autumn of 1941 now appears as one of the most criminally stupid decisions of the war. As early as 1939 British defence planners had been moving key installations from Hong Kong to Singapore precisely because they knew that Hong Kong could last only a matter of weeks if subjected to Japanese pressure. Britain's main signals intelligence listening post was one such facility to be carefully relocated. As predicted, the colony had held out only until the end of December 1941 and Allied troops had quickly become prisoners of the Japanese. By early January 1942 Tom Forsyth was already enduring cold and hunger, but had little idea of how much harder life would become for him. SEE ALSO PP. 433–4, 501–2, 802–3.

Saturday 10 January 1942

Hilda Lacey evacuates from a hospital in Kuala Lumpur as the Japanese advance

Hilda Grace Lacey was born in Devon in 1891. Unmarried, she had worked in the medical field for many years. Having been a nurse during the First World War, by 1941 she was working at a hospital in Kuala Lumpur in Malaya. In January 1942 the Japanese arrived on her doorstep.

I had just arrived on duty when Mr. Wakefield the new CMO [Chief Medical Officer] rang up to say that we were to be ready to evacuate the convoy in 2 hours. I said this was impossible – as we had not begun to pack. I spoke to the sisters and we all decided to remain if possible. In the middle of a hurried breakfast Dr. McGregor sent for me and . . . I said . . . 'What is the position if I refuse to go'? He replied 'you will be forcibly removed'.

There were dreadful scenes, the nurses were crying. The Annah's [a family] and the T.B. children who had been in the hospital for months, and we, were heartbroken. We had arranged the previous evening for the Kuru's to take the children. When they arrived to take them away I completely broke down. There was also a baby of one month old whose mother had died. I gave . . . biscuits and chocolate for them and they left. It was dreadful saying goodbye to . . . the Chief Clerk and Cornwallis the Steward . . . they looked like wounded animals.

With Kuala Lumpur, the main city of Malaya, about to fall, all British staff were evacuated. Hilda Lacey regretted leaving, not only because she was deserting her patients, but also because the Asiatic staff were forced to remain behind and face the Japanese. Dire scenes had occurred at the harbour where British families were evacuated while passage was refused to Malays, Chinese and Allied troops on the run. Other troops were used to keep them back from the quayside. SEE ALSO PP. 193–5, 219–20.

Monday 12 January 1942

Corporal James Roxburgh of the AIF watches the efforts of
two Brewster Buffalos against the Japanese Zeros

Today was a very busy day for us. At 8.30 p.m., 160 enemy
planes came over in batches to attack Singapore. They had
barely passed over us when the A./A. [anti-aircraft] guns
started shelling them & also some of our planes went up to
have a crack at them. Directly above our heads we could see
a dogfight going on, with 10 Jap planes attacking one of
ours. The poor chap had the odds against him with his
Brewster Buffalo & we saw his plane come down in a steady
spin until it landed behind some trees about a mile away
from us. Our officer & sgt. went over to investigate but when
they arrived at the scene, the pilot had been taken from his
plane dead & was covered over with part of the fuselage,
until the ambulance arrived. He was a N.Z. chap & he had
put up a real good scrap before he was brought down. His
plane hit the ground & tipped up, & the body of the plane
snapped off & was some yards away from the engine. There
was a line of bullet holes from the tail of the plane right up
to the cockpit. We believe there was only 18 of our planes
against the 160 Japs. The raid never finished till 11.30 a.m. At
1 p.m. they came over again in bunches, & the A/A. started
again – landing their shells right amongst them. We saw one
of their planes come down. Above our heads another dogfight started, & again it was a number of enemy planes
against one of ours. The chap had no chance either. His plane
nosedived to earth, after he had brought down 2 of the Japs,
& he bailed out in his parachute, landing not too far from our
camp. The plane hit the ground, engine first, about half a
mile from camp & made a hell of an explosion. The officer,
sgt, myself & 2 others made for the plane, but when we
arrived there, there was not too much of it left. There was a
hole where she crashed about 10 feet deep & 20 feet wide, &
buried in the bottom of this was the engine. The rest of the
plane was just a heap of junk about 30 feet away from

The War in Malaya, December 1941 to February 1942

the hole, with small pieces scattered over an area of 100 yds. Although it only took us 5 minutes to reach the smash, it had burnt itself out & was just smouldering here & there. I found out later that the pilot had landed safely & only got a broken leg out of it, caused by a bullet. He was a Dutchman & his plane was a D.I. [Dutch Indies] Buffalo. English airforce chaps have told us they will be glad, in one way, when these Buffalos are finished as they are too slow against the Japs. They will get Spitfires then & as these are faster & are quicker to manoeuvre in the air, the yellow cows will get a very warm reception. This second raid finished about 3.30 p.m.

The Japanese Zero was superior to most types of Allied aircraft operating in 1942. By contrast the Brewster Buffalo was a pathetic aircraft with low power and poor stability that had been sent to the Far East to free up Spitfires and Hurricanes for use in Europe. The Dutch operated a superior variant of the aircraft with a more powerful engine. However, all dubbed this aircraft 'the flying coffin'.

After the fall of Singapore, James Roxburgh became a prisoner of war of the Japanese. While he continued to make regular diary entries, it appears that the problem of keeping the diary concealed necessitated a resort to smaller handwriting, which is in large part almost illegible. He would survive the war and return to Australia. SEE ALSO PP. 168–9.

Sunday 18 January 1942

Cecil Brown, a CBS correspondent covering the fighting in Malaya, asks the troops about the enemy espionage and 'fifth column work'

Cecil Brown, having survived the dramatic sinking of the Repulse, *was now back in Malaya. As he had noticed, the scale of subversion and sabotage – often referred to as 'fifth column activity' – was immense. In the weeks before Pearl Harbor the Japanese secret service had triggered its networks in Malaya and Singapore.*

'What about the Fifth-Column work?' I asked.

'The Malays, Tamils and Indians and even a few of the Chinese have been bought up by the Japanese. Where we would pay $50 or $100 for information they would pay $500. In Seremban there were just the usual Japanese – a photographer, a barber, a masseur, and one or two others. It was a very small colony. When they were interned we made a thorough search of their homes and officers found $350,000 in Straits currency . . .

'It's damned discouraging,' the captain said, 'to take up a position in the morning and find three banana leaves laid out in the ground pointed directly at your position. That's what happens all the time. You move a battery or two during the night and the very next morning the Japanese aircraft is flying and circling around it trying to locate the precise spot in the jungle to drop their bombs.

'In Kelantan there were a dozen Indians on guard duty and they heard a voice cry out in the darkness, "We are wounded; we are Indians." The guards were suspicious and told them to advance a half dozen feet. They did and were again challenged. One of the men called out in the darkness, "I am a Punjabi. Is Sergeant so-and-so there? Is Corporal so-and-so there?" They named a half dozen men in the camp. That convinced the Indian guards. The group advanced out of the darkness. Japs they were. They killed most of the Indian regulars, except six.

'Oh, yes,' the captain said, 'this is an authentic story. You see, the Punjabi was a civilian who had been living in the area and grew friendly with the men stationed there. He was bought up by the Japs and they contacted him when they came through.

'This scheme,' the captain said, 'was followed the other day when six Japs dressed as Indians went running toward the Aussies yelling, "We are Indians, don't shoot!" But,' the English captain chuckled, 'the Aussies wouldn't play. They shot all six.

'Throughout the country lights flash at night for the Jap raiders. That,' he said, 'shows lots of preparation and planning.'

Japanese immigrants, nationalist Malays and paid Chinese agents all moved from passive espionage to active sabotage. The unnamed 'captain' quoted at length in this extract is almost certainly working for the Malayan Security Service, the local branch of MI5.

Perhaps influenced by the huge success of his CBS colleague William Shirer with the publication of Berlin Diary *in 1941, Cecil Brown would publish his own journals in late 1942. He would survive the war and by 1945 be recognized as one of the great reporters of the conflict, having made numerous on-the-spot broadcasts from the notable battlefronts. He was awarded the Overseas Press Club's prize for outstanding radio reporting as well as many other prizes. In the 1950s he would move from broadcasting into the academic study of journalism and become a professor of journalism at Cal Poly Pomona University near Los Angeles in 1970. He was named 'outstanding professor' when he retired in 1980. After he died in 1987 his wife Martha established the Cecil Brown Memorial Endowment. S*EE ALSO PP*. 83–6, 94–6, 152–6.*

Monday 19 January 1942

Sheila Allan and her family endure a Japanese air raid in the Rex Hotel at Singapore

We reached the shelter just in time as the first bomb was dropped. We flung ourselves flat on the floor and whizz-shiss-ss-ss, crr-crr-rump, crash came the bombs one after another. I heard the whistling of each of them as they hurtled down the sky and waiting for the rest – the explosion – to follow. The building rocked beneath us. An orange flame from a bursting bomb flashed in a downward streak as it passed an open window. Screams of human fear and pain penetrated through the sound of the crashing and open windows. There was dust everywhere. Mum had her head buried in her arms, sobbing. Dad had his arms around her. I, for that split second closed my eyes and thought 'this is it!' The danger had passed – no sounds of planes or firing. The 'All Clear' rang through our fuddled minds as we lay on the floor, shaken and white-faced. The raid was over and we are alive!

We got up, rather dizzily, dusting ourselves and feeling ourselves all over to ascertain if any bodily damage had been done. No, we were safe and sound in limb and body. Mentally and emotionally, I'm not sure. I think I grew old, very old and very frightened during that short time when I had my face down on the floor!

We made our way through the debris of plaster, splinters, broken furniture and dead bodies – poor souls, they hadn't reached the shelter in time. Dust, smoke, foul-smelling fumes seemed to fill the atmosphere as we choked and gasped for a breath of fresh air which was non-existent!

It was too much for Mum. She was on the point of collapse as we helped her upstairs.

When we got to our room which was facing the VHQ [Volunteer Headquarters] we stared into a wreck of a room. There was a huge hole in the ceiling. The floor was littered with pieces of armour, broken wooden frames, broken glass and brickwork. Dad picked [up] several pieces of the metal, turning them over in his hands. He reckoned that they must have come from the dump of machinery outside the Headquarters. Our windows and walls were no longer as such and if we had stayed in the room – well, it would have been 'Kingdom come' for us three. Mum became hysterical at the state of the room and refused to stay another day there, so off once again we went seeking somewhere else to stay.

Dad went across to hand over the metal he had picked up. When he came back he announced that we've had a very lucky escape as there were two bombs lying not fifty yards away – unexploded! Duds perhaps! Whew! Certainly we weren't meant to die – not yesterday anyway!

Beach Road was closed to us so we decided to go through North Bridge Road. We came upon the dead and dying. Many were badly injured. Ugh! It was awful seeing them lying around uncovered with blood that was still warm and from some, the blood seemed to flow steadily on, making a pool of red. In fact, crimson seemed to be the dominant colour. No matter where we looked our eyes rested on dead bodies, dying people – men, women and children and so many of them with horrific injuries. How could I describe such a scene?

As Sheila Allan's family discovered, Singapore's civil defence system was hopelessly inadequate to cope with the scale of air attack that Japan inflicted upon it in January 1942. There were few civilian shelters or emergency medical facilities. Inexcusably over-confident civil servants had doubted their necessity and concluded that air raid precautions or expanded emergency services might cause panic. Others had resisted the recruitment of Asiatics into their ranks, doubting their loyalty and capability. Sheila Allan's family were surprised by the rapid collapse of Malaya and now realized that everyone was gradually falling back on Singapore island. SEE ALSO PP. *174–5, 209, 459–60, 587–8.*

Saturday 24 January 1942

Betty Hu and Alice Lan, two evangelical missionaries, take the bus in Japanese-occupied Hong Kong

In 1929 Dr Alice Lan had completed her university studies in the United States and returned to China to lead the Bethel Bible Seminary in Shanghai, a college of divinity. This evangelical organization sent missionary teams all over war-torn China. However, in 1937 the main seminary in Shanghai decided to evacuate to Hong Kong and settled into new premises at Grampian Road in Kowloon. By the end of 1941 war had caught up with them again and Alice Lan struggled to run the seminary under occupation, assisted by her friend, Betty Hu.

This diary is an example of a rare phenomenon, the jointly authored journal. It is hard to distinguish entries made by Alice Lan from entries by her friend and assistant Betty Hu. Another example of this rare phenomenon is the joint diary of the factory workers Kathleen Church-Bliss and Elsie Whiteman, extracted in the first volume of this anthology, Witness to War.

Betty records:

I took my first ride with Alice since the Japanese occupation. There is a new technique in getting on the overcrowded bus. We could wait all day and not get a bus going in the direction we wanted to go. Our plan was to board one going in the opposite direction and ride to the end of the line. That was our only hope of ever getting a ride.

Alice Lan and Betty Hu

Even so, we waited forty minutes before we secured even standing room on the bus. If one is fortunate enough to find a place to hold on, one's arm may ache for days from the jerking of the bus and one's effort to keep that hold. Coming back was worse. We were tired and our arms were loaded with what canned food we could buy from the peddlers on the streets. Japanese could hail the bus anywhere they happened to be. We waited impatiently, sweating outwardly and boiling within with resentment, for it was getting late in the afternoon. This is the fortune of war. We were defeated and we had to take it. Finally, we got into a bus and saw a friend, a Christian business man living on our street, crawling into the bus from the front window. He grinned at us as if he had been doing that all his life – he, formerly, a man with three cars and liveried chaffeurs!

Kowloon is a changed city indeed. The Japanese ordered that all English signs should be abolished. All over the city we saw black marks smeared over the English street names and shop signs, but we could still clearly see the English underneath. Is this symbolic?

After the Japanese occupation, Hong Kong was ruled as a captured territory and was subjected to martial law. Isogai Rensuke was the first Japanese Governor of Hong Kong. All trading activities were strictly controlled, with the majority of factories being taken over by the Japanese. Local dollars were replaced by military yen, whose steady devaluation resulted in chronic inflation. Food was rationed, with rice, sugar, flour and cooking oil particularly restricted, and public transport gradually disappeared. Alice Lan and Betty Hu were already thinking about moving on from Hong Kong to a new location. SEE ALSO PP. 290–1.

FEBRUARY 1942

THE FIRST WEEKS of February offered the Allies some respite. Naval operations allowed the Americans to begin to slow the Japanese advance in the Pacific, with raids by US carriers against Japanese bases in the Gilbert and Marshall Islands. Using aggressive air patrols, the Americans had already begun to find the Japanese Achilles heel: an inability to move sufficient supplies to over-extended forces spread out across innumerable small islands. Elsewhere, some American garrisons were holding out against Japan. On 3 February at Bataan, American and Philippine forces pushed the Japanese back to their preferred line of defence, the Bagac–Orion line.

By contrast, Britain was about to suffer the gravest defeat in its military history. Although the British had anticipated almost every aspect of Japanese strategy and tactics in the Malayan campaign, they were still swept aside by superior fighting. Japanese troops began crossing the Straits of Jahore and landing on Singapore Island on 8 February, and a week later the British army commander in Malaya, General Arthur Percival, surrendered. His inexperienced forces had suffered a collapse of morale largely as a result of the loss of air superiority, but they had also been poorly led. At this time Japanese forces numbered less than half the Allied garrison and, moreover, the Japanese had almost run out of ammunition. The Japanese commander could hardly believe his luck and feared a trick. He repeatedly asked: Do you really mean to surrender? The British replied emphatically: Yes. Over 100,000 British, Australian and British

Indian Army troops fell into Japanese hands. Thereafter, British and Australian troops were used in large numbers for forced labour, while Indian troops were encouraged or coerced to join the pro-Japanese Indian National Army. Across Asia, Japan had begun sponsoring numerous indigenous anti-colonial military formations.

Air superiority is perhaps the key to understanding Japan's dramatic success during early 1942. The ageing Brewster Buffalo fighters that constituted the bulk of Allied aircraft in Malaya were too slow to catch Japanese bombers. Combined American and Australian efforts to send convoys to reinforce bases in the Netherlands East Indies were turned back by heavy Japanese air attacks. On 19 February Japan launched a heavy bombing raid on the Australian port of Darwin. The psychological consequences of this raid for the Australian population and for Allied relations were enormous. Australians now prioritized the defence of their own homeland and demanded that their troops be brought home from the Middle East. A week later the Americans were also under attack at home when a Japanese submarine shelled the town of Ellwood in California.

Although the Japanese advance by sea had slowed, on land it continued. In Burma the American commander, the irascible General 'Vinegar Joe' Stilwell, brought Chinese forces in from the north to try to stem the Japanese tide, with some initial success. However, there was no stopping the Japanese as they advanced along the vast island chain of the Netherlands East Indies – increasingly referred to by the local inhabitants as Indonesia. Here, Wavell's ABDA Command was liquidated on 25 February. Direction of the war in the south-west Pacific would now fall to General Douglas MacArthur.

Monday 2 – Tuesday 10 February 1942

Hilda Lacey, a British nurse in Singapore, makes preparations in case the Japanese take over

Hilda Lacey had been evacuated south to Singapore, where she worked at the Malacca and Jahore General Hospitals.

2 February

One day, on my way to Outram School, I went to the mortuary with Mr. Havidar. It was piled with dead bodies of various nationalities, some visibly mutilated. They were awaiting burial. The municipal coolies refused to work, probably due to fright from the incessant bombing, and MAS [Malay Administrative Service] members and volunteer's were collecting the bodies after the raids – bringing them into hospital in any available conveyance and bagging the dead.

MAS were made up of Indians, Malay, Russians, British and other nationalities. Some Chinese were very good. The dock coolies also refused to work, and unloading of ships, fire fighting parties were mostly Europeans. Miss Tostee, whose husband worked on the docks, said there were only 3 Europeans left at the last, and the looting of Gowdowns (?) by Asiatic's – mostly Chinese – was beyond belief. 24 docks were burning everyday at least . . . it was found that there were only about 3 fire hoses which were in full working order, the others were defective. We heard the European responsible for this was sent home. The thick black columns of smoke when the docks were burning could be seen from the Hospital.

3 February

Women and children are leaving on every ship that arrives. When doing my round in Ward 5 on Sunday evening I had a chat with Miss Turner from Malacca. She had been down to the docks to embark for Australia and after waiting in the darkness for a very long time, the ship sailed leaving at least

100 passengers' behind – some women with their babies in cradles. They were taken alphabetically and the last in the queue were left. There were some disorderly scenes. Australians who were helping with luggage were given big tips . . . later . . . one heard of men scrambling on the ship in front of the women! Not Australians. They were just under the influence of too much beer.

MAS women and nurses are daily resigning, and waiting for passages, and many Sisters are getting married with only a few days notice. Servants are leaving daily and life becomes increasingly difficult, whilst with constant raids the hospital becomes more congested. The Japanese now have our main water supply and I am trying to impress on everyone in my wards the necessity for economy. Before they took over the reservoir 'al-Pontiau Ketchel' the main had received a direct hit.

10 February

The aerodromes had been severely bombed, the Naval base had been evacuated previously which was very depressing news . . . Amidst all this turmoil I went down to get my hair permanently waved. I had made the appointment the week before and thought if the Japs did take us over it would be more convenient.

There were raids all morning and an alert as I was starting out. Miss Steward sent me down in her car – for some time a taxi could not be had for love nor money. I fell into the hairdressers . . . the ladies hairdressing salon was on the top floor of the new building with the sun-roof, and I must admit I felt a little nervous – there were three alerts during the process of perming, and each time we rushed down a back stair case of concrete and sat on the stairs on a lower floor, a mixed assembly of men with soap on their faces in the act of being shaved . . . the managing director of Robinson's herself with hair in curlers (it was a new method) and I was hot strung up to an apparatus. The hairdresser – a Dutch man – was one of the few remaining as they had all been ordered back to Java. He told me the Consul had also gone, so he could not have attained a visa had he wanted to. He did me very quickly and I was ready to leave for the hospital before 5 pm . . .

Singapore seemed so deserted except for a few people, mostly men, in Robinson's. I was really very worried, when Mr. Spence came along and gave me a lift to the hospital. It was good of him because petrol by this time was very limited. He had just returned from leave in Australia. He said the Japanese had broken through our lines . . .

Hilda Lacey was most struck by the ability of the Japanese to bomb Singapore at will, seeing formations of up to thirty enemy planes meeting no Allied opposition. By 13 February the water supply had been cut off and some patients in her hospital were dying as much from thirst as from the results of their wounds. The hospital was also subjected to artillery and machine-gun fire, despite the prominent display of Red Cross insignia. SEE ALSO PP. 182, 219–20.

Saturday 7 – Sunday 8 February 1942

Clyde Berwick, an Australian army engineer, watches the activities of a Japanese 'chaffcutter' above Singapore

Clyde Berwick was born in Launceston in Australia on 15 October 1921 and was one of nine children. After finishing school he began work on the Tasmanian railways. In July 1941 he joined the army at the age of nineteen and was quickly transferred to the Engineers. He was still in Sydney on 10 January 1942, where he joined 3,500 troops on the Aquitania *that arrived in Singapore on 29 January 1942, being among some of the last Allied forces to arrive in the colony before its surrender. He was soon injured by the incessant bombing.*

A small reconnaissance plane, which caused us some considerable trouble whilst moving our wounded by gunning us from the air, and which we named 'the Chaffcutter', owing to the sound of its engines, carried pilot and observer. It generally hovered over us at 100–200ft and it was practically impossible to move without being machine gunned, or if it was a body of men a salvo of shells would soon be heading in our direction, quite often after he had sighted us we would bang away at him with the rifle, but to no avail.

By midday there wasn't a gun pit that didn't have some portion, if not all of it, blown away. His barrage was still as constant as when he'd started in the morning and there was hardly any returning fire from our side . . .

Not long after daybreak our friend 'the Chaffcutter' spotted us. We were in position on the crest of a hill, but did a hasty retreat, after the plane headed off for home, to a higher ridge about 200 yards in the rear. Very shortly a nice little artillery barrage was falling around our last position with an occasional long shot falling amongst us.

We were all ragged out and sleeping on and off when six of us were called out for a patrol, which we did covering about five miles and whilst we were away the bombers paid our position a visit and caused some havoc . . .

Once more, after a few miles, we ran out of our shelter rubber on to the roadway and we moved along in the drain, evidently we were well covered for our good friend 'the Chaffcutter' wasn't far above us and was searching all the while.

Passing around a turn in the road we sighted about 500 troops squatting around the railway eating, and thinking they were Indians, we passed on till our good friend 'the Chaffcutter', (and for once he was a friend as he showed us what breed they were), swooped down over them and we saw the big red circle displayed by these troops. Following the old proverb 'Let Sleeping Dogs Lie', we broke from the roadway and took up the bush, the type of country we came to was thick mangrove swamp and it was none too pleasant squelching to break through the mangrove thickets, but it was a shelter from the air and that was all that mattered.

We succeeded in circumnavigating the Nips quite success-fully and we breathed a sigh of relief when we were a good half hour's march away from them, we were all feeling very weary on it, and I was rather weak from loss of blood, but the urge to push on was there and that was the mainstay.

It was with relief that we once more stepped on to solid ground again although we still had very thick jungle to push through and the country was rather rough with plenty of ups and downs over the slight rises.

Imagine our surprise to walk over the crest of one of those

rises to be met by a Nip officer with a white flag and an Argyll prisoner (Argyll Regiment is a Scottish Regiment) standing on the pipe line which ran through the valley. (The pipe line runs through Singapore Island from Johore Baru on the mainland and is Singapore's only water supply).

As we came over the crest an Argyll was shouting out to us, and then the Nip officer spoke in perfect English. 'You'd better surrender as we have machine guns trained all around you', one of our boys shouted back to him, after we'd got over the surprise, 'Don't worry mate, we have a few ourselves' to which the Nip replied in a very sarcastic voice, 'You Australian fools', and he jumped down one of the pipes and disappeared in the undergrowth.

He certainly never told any lies, for they sure had the machine guns and used them also. We lost three of our boys during the action whom the Nips took prisoners, also several other lads were killed.

Clyde Berwick was stationed on Singapore Island looking out over the Jahore Straits, where his unit watched out for Japanese amphibious attacks with landing barges. Although Allied forces were superior in numbers, Japan's troops were experienced and enjoyed support from tanks and aircraft. This in turn gave them other facilities, including precise aerial spotting for artillery. Constant bombing and accurate shellfire were instrumental in breaking the morale of Allied forces who, unlike the Japanese, had seen little active service and were poorly directed. Most had never been under fire. Japan also deployed 200 tanks during the campaign while the Allies could boast no armour at all. SEE ALSO PP. 488–90.

Thursday 12 February 1942

Thomas Kitching witnesses a historic evening at the Singapore Club

Thomas Kitching was Chief Surveyor of Singapore and had worked in Malaya for thirty years. He was offered the opportunity to leave by ship but, although married, chose to stay at his post. Being a surveyor by training he was fascinated by the way in which the bombing was changing landmarks such as the Golf Club and the Swimming Club.

The 'Singapore Free Press' is reduced to a single sheet 11 x 8 inches. It says 'Enemy held on all fronts', and contains an announcement by the Governor, all spirits in anybody's possession are to be destroyed by noon tomorrow! Six months or 2,000 dollars is the penalty for infringement . . . I shall probably risk it! My office has the most wonderful hiding places. It may be a precaution in case we capitulate, we don't want drink-inflamed Japanese soldiers about the place – but a contributory cause is certainly some heavy drinking by our own men – the Navy rifled the drink stocks when they took over the Royal Singapore Golf Club, and the Aussies put the lid on it yesterday – they have broken and behaved very badly. The town was full of them last night, many were tight and many were demanding to know when they are going to be evacuated! And these are the men, who when we entertained them in our house before the War reached Malaya, used to have one stock remark: 'all we want is a chance to get at them bloody little Jappos before we are sent back to Australia! D'you think I can get 2 on one bayonet?' Yesterday the Japanese invited us by a polite letter to a parley, no use carrying this resistance on any longer, they said. We were to send a car with a special flag along Bukit Timah Rd. We refused . . .

The Aussie troops seem in many cases to be completely out of hand. They have looted Clark-Walker's house, drunk 4 cases of booze and eaten a case of tinned food . . . Nelson went down from the Fullerton Building this evening to look at his car, which is parked just across the river in Empress Place. It was immobilised, and he arrived just in time to see them tear out all the wires and ruin it generally – when they saw him approaching they took pot shots at him as well, so he beat it, very incensed. So I thought I'd go down and have a look at my car, the little Morris 8, but they all said NO! The Aussies are down there in force, full of booze, and they take pot shots at anybody . . .

The Singapore Club has a historic evening, the last stengahs [whisky and sodas] are being quaffed prior to the destruction of stocks, they have over 200 cases of whisky alone, which must be got rid of ere noon tomorrow. Obviously the members can't drink it, but they have a good try. I went down from the 5th Floor to assist in the obsequies. Just imagine a Singapore Club in which you can't have a stengah! All the Fathers of Singapore will turn in their graves, and a new name will have to be found for the time-hallowed 'stengah shifter' . . . It's an astounding scene, wish I had the pen of Frankau to describe it. The Club of course is absolutely filled to capacity with refugee members from up-country and Singapore members washed out of hearth and home by the ever-advancing wave of hordes, of Nippon: all the fossils of Malaya are there, paleozoic (Abang), mesozoic (E.N.T.C.) and cainozoic (me): all the boys have disappeared, except one faithful retainer, duping out stengahs behind the Bar, with Broadbent, the Club Steward, perspiringly assisting. And what stengahs! You still go through the formality of signing for them (though I doubt if anyone now expects to get his bill at the end of this month) but you can have 'em any strength you like, it matters not, one, two, three, four fingers, take what you want, the rest will be down the drains and into the Singapore River before noon tomorrow . . .

Thomas Kitching's diary is one of the most revealing. It is merciless in chronicling the bungling incompetence of the colonial government and the refusal of many of the troops, whether local volunteer units consisting of planters and miners, or recently arrived Australians, to fight the enemy. He insists that when the Perak and Selangor Volunteers were given the option – 'Do you wish to defend your country or not?' – with almost one voice they replied 'Not' and were allowed to disband.

Kitching was interned in Changi in February 1942 and died there in 1944.

13 February 1942 '(and a Friday)'

Lieutenant-General Sir Henry Pownall in Java reports on Singapore's last days

Henry Pownall was born in 1887 and boarded at Rugby School before joining the British army in 1906. An artilleryman, he served repeatedly in India and by 1940 had held key appointments as Director of Military Operations and Intelligence and Chief of General Staff in the British Expeditionary Force. Late 1941 and early 1942 were hectic days for Pownall. In November 1941 he had found himself ordered out to Singapore to try to inject some vigour into efforts to defend the garrison. However, it was far too late for him to implement new measures and he lacked up-to-date aircraft; by the time he arrived on 24 December, war had broken out in the colony and things were already going badly. That month, somewhat belatedly, he was made Commander-in-Chief Far East, replacing the ineffectual Air Chief Marshal Sir Robert Brooke-Popham. By 13 February he had shipped out to Java, where he became Chief of Staff in Wavell's short-lived ABDA command.

Henry Pownall

It has been a bad week and today is the worst day of it. Singapore is on its last legs. Six days ago the Japanese crossed the Jahore strait onto the north-west side of the Island, always the most likely place and we have not been able to hold them. I do not know why for I do not believe they were in greater numbers than ours. I fear that we were frankly out-generalled, outwitted and outfought. It's a great disaster for British arms, one of the worst in history, and a great blow to the honour and prestige of the Army. From the beginning to the end of this campaign we have been out-matched by better soldiers. A very painful admission, but an inescapable fact. Not even the Australians, for all that they started so cock-a-hoop and critical of others, put up a good showing at the end.

Wavell spent a day there at the beginning of this week and no doubt his visit did temporary good, but morale seems to have fallen to a low point and could not recover.

Soon the Jap forces that have attacked Singapore will be freed for other theatres, one obvious one is Burma where, if successful, they would get to Rangoon and stop supplies to China, which would just about finish China's war effort and probably end the China war. But most of the Jap forces are likely to be directed further south ... There's nothing on those islands – one Dutch battalion – to stop them! ...

In his diary Pownall is frank about the chronic under-estimation of the qualities of both Japanese troops and their generals. He is also clear that British intelligence had actually performed fairly well, broadly predicting where and how the Japanese would attack. After the collapse of ABDA, he would become Commander of Ceylon in March 1942.
SEE ALSO P. 518–19.

Friday 13 February – Thursday 5 March 1942

Colin Inglis is selected to attempt an escape from Singapore to Java on a small passenger boat

Colin Inglis was a British engineer employed by the Department of Public Works in Singapore. For the last six months he had been occupied mostly on Fleet Air Arm projects. Selected as 'essential personnel' for evacuation to Java in early February, he was forced to pack his office bags alongside local Asiatic staff who were to remain. He then reported to a heavily bombed quayside at the Telok Ayer basin to board the SS Kuala.

The *Kuala* was built to carry about twenty-five passengers, but about 600 odd people were eventually put aboard – all very matey. We sailed at dusk, leaving Singapore blazing in a hundred different spots, but nevertheless the City proper looked comparatively unharmed! . . .

Returning to the poop deck, I squeezed into my place between Roger Steed and Burke-Gaffney. Supper began. Corned beef, tinned fruit and assorted cream biscuits, washed down with whisky and water. Shortly we settled down for the night, as there was nothing else to do – even smoking being forbidden owing to black-out regulations. Using my tin hat as a pillow, I lay down as far as possible on the hard deck. Being unable to stretch fully outright, it was some time before I managed to get off to sleep, but not for long. The hardness of the deck and the little bumps of oakum which came through the planks, added to a wind which was distinctly cold, woke me shivering . . .

On return to our poop deck, Hutton, always resourceful and thinking of others, went off to see what he could do about a bucket of tea, and shortly returned with it – milkless, sugarless, steaming hot, and very welcome. We were just dipping our cups into it when the cry went up that bombers were approaching. We all trooped down to the main deck, which had the steel promenade deck over it, and hoped that it would be sufficient protection. The planes, however, flew over us, paying no attention and directed their attack on to the abandoned *Kwang Wu* further out. This they sank with one salvo, and went on towards the horizon. A wild relief went through us, that perhaps they hadn't spotted us, and I said as much to Hutton. He looked graver than I've ever seen him look before and shook his head. We watched the other ship sink by the bow, milling about before the small main deck portholes, when somebody yelled from the promenade deck that the planes had turned and were coming back. The whole crowd of us sank to the deck like a *corps de ballet* and waited for what seemed like a year before we heard the planes. Their roaring was soon drowned by the whistle as the bombs began to fall, and we all snuggled closer and lower trying to burrow under the next-door person. With a series of roars the bombs exploded and the ship heaved and shuddered (so did we!). Immediately a loud hissing broke out and clouds of steam came pouring from the engine-room, the first bomb having broken the main steam pipe. All, then remembering the old saying about rats and traps we surged up into the air again to find the bridge and upper deck well ablaze.

A start was made putting women and children into the ship's boat which we had left alongside when we came back from Pompong, while the rest of us dashed about throwing overboard lifebelts, seats, chairs, drawers, anything in fact that would float. I then took my shoes off to be ready in case we had to jump for it, and wandered around looking for a safe place in which to put them, not realizing that it didn't matter where they dropped. Alec Niven and I then saw a Chinese woman with two children hovering on the brink before jumping into the boat; we went to her and took her children and told her to jump and we'd pass the children down. She jumped and missed. So I passed my child to Alec and went after her. When I came up to the surface she was being dragged into the boat, so Alec passed the children to me and came in, too. Between us we got the kids into the boat and looked around to see what we could do next. It was then that I realized the difference between paddling about in a swimming pool in trunks and splashing in the ocean fully dressed, but lighted on a piece of wood about 2 ft. long, 9 in.

wide, and 2 in thick. This I tucked under me and then heard the planes returning. This time they were aiming at the *Tien Kwang*, and I saw one bomb coming down quite close. Most of the missiles exploded in the water, which gave those swimming a feeling as though their tummies were being pummelled by quickly wielded sledge hammers. Several bombs, however, fell on the rocky shore of the island, flinging great boulders and splinters in all directions, and causing a number of casualties amongst those who'd already landed. The explosion of one bomb near me in the water swamped me in its filthy black wash smelling utterly putrid, and I surfaced again alternately praying and cursing with fervour and fury. The two probably cancelled themselves out! Never have I felt so completely helpless as floundering in the water while these bleeding Japs dropped their eggs – helpless and at times petrified.

When things had quietened again I paddled around on my little bit of board collecting odds and ends of boards, sticks, etc., and passed these around to those who looked as though they needed them. Feeling rather like Father Christmas, I found a kapok mattress floating, so grabbed it and towed it off to two women keeping up on an oar.

Then these ruddy Japs paid a third visit, and once more our insides were subject to rough treatment. More bombs dropped on the island again, causing many casualties . . .

I thought I'd make for the island almost due west of Pompong, about two miles away, and started off again. And then it was I suspected that a fairly strong current was running away from Pompong, and this was confirmed soon by coming on a dead woman, who, despite my efforts, would not be shaken off, but kept up with my by now somewhat hysterical swimming with the greatest of ease.

Eventually I outstripped her and, swimming on, discovered that no matter what I wanted to do, I would pass the island I'd chosen well to the south. I then began to look around for somewhere else to land – somewhere to which the current would bring me without much effort on my part. It was now about 1.30 p.m., and I'd already been in the water for two hours and was beginning to feel tired, and, strangely enough, bored. My watch, which had been so cheap, was proving its worth, if never before, by ticking valiantly . . .

Deciding that it was now no time to be finicky, that I must get out of the water before nightfall, I set off in the opposite direction for one of the swampy islands – 4.30, 5.00, 5.30, 6.00. This was awful! If I was getting nearer it was so slow as to be imperceptible to the naked eye. And with the open sea beyond and nothing else in sight, I began to wonder just what life was all about. Had I escaped all injury in Malaya in the two months of raids, escaped hurt when the docks were bombed yesterday evening, the *Kuala* this morning, just to float to an unidentified grave somewhere in the Pacific? It didn't make sense, although it looked as though nonsense was going to win. It was beginning to grow dusk and I was feeling distinctly rattled. I pulled myself up on my board to rest my arms, and, ye gods! there was a fishing boat with two Malays in it about 200 yards away!

That fishing boat picked up no fewer than ten survivors from the Kuala. *Dozens of other survivors were dotted about on neighbouring islands. Colin Inglis eventually continued his journey to Padang in Sumatra and was soon in danger again from the advancing Japanese. On 3 March he would be evacuated to Colombo on Ceylon by the Australian ship HMAS* Hobart; *less than two weeks later, Padang fell.*

Saturday 14 February 1942

Joseph Hodder makes a record of the behaviour of the Japanese in the Princess Alexandria Military Hospital, Singapore

Joseph Hodder was a civilian electrical engineer working on the installation of generating equipment at a maternity hospital in Singapore. On 10 December his superiors told him that it was time for every man to look after himself. The following day he noticed British and Australian soldiers 'wandering aimlessly about', having lost their units and discarded their rifles and equipment, and realized the end was near. By 14 February his family had already been evacuated and he was seeking to get on a boat headed for Java. At this point he copied into his diary the text of a diary entry for 14 February 1942 by a member of the medical staff at the nearby Alexandria Military Hospital, recording the moment the Japanese arrived there. He did this in order to preserve the record, but the name of the medical staff diarist is not known.

Enemy drawing near and approaching the hospital in Ayer Raja Road direction . . . Japanese troops were first seen at 13.40 hours and were attacking towards Sister Quarters. As fighting troops were about to enter from rear entrance of Hospital Lt. Weston R.A.M.C. [Royal Army Medical Corps] went from the Reception Room to this entrance with a white flag to indicate the surrender of the hospital to the Japanese. They ignored the flag and Lt. Weston was bayoneted to death by the first Japanese to enter. They then ran amok on the ground floor, highly excited and neither pointing to the Red Cross brassard nor shouting 'Hospital' had any effect. The following incidents then occurred and only a few are recorded here.

(1) One party of Japs entered [the] operating block (operations were being performed). Japs climbed over walls into the corridors and fired through windows, wounded Pte. Lewis. Approx. 10 Japs came in one corridor and the Medical personnel held up their hands. Capt. Smiley [pointed] to the Red Cross on their arms but the Japs took no notice and set upon this unarmed staff with bayonets. Lt. Rogers was bayoneted receiving two through back of his thorax and died. Capt. Parkinson was bayoneted and killed. Also Cpt. McEwan and Pte Lewis (previously wounded). Capt. Smiley was bayoneted but the blade was struck aside by his cigarette case in his left-hand breast pocket. He was then lunged at again and wounded in the left groin, one previous thrust had cut his thumb and made a wound [in] his left arm. Capt. Smiley pretended he was dead and fell on top of Pte Sutton who was unharmed and remained still . . .

(2) Another party of Japs went into the Medical Ward and ordered all patients who could walk and the orderlies to go outside the Hospital. In another ward two patients were bayoneted. Another two Japs went upstairs to the 1st floor and gave similar intimations. They motioned to patients on

crutches and otherwise helpless to remain behind. About 200 were taken outside the Hospital. Their hands were tied behind their back, with slip-knots, one length of cord used for 4 or 5 men . . . Everybody then marched off in a circuitous route which ended at the hospital water and oil storage tanks. Here they were herded together in the servants rooms, 50 to 60 in a room 9' × 9' or 10' × 10' or 10' × 12', jammed in tightly so that it took about ten minutes manoeuvring to raise ones arm, sitting down was impossible and people urinated on each other. All suffered greatly from thirst and the foul atmosphere.

By afternoon shelling was at a maximum. Shells bursting all round. One struck the roof and blew open the locked doors and windows, injuring some of the hospital staff and patients held as prisoners. When the doors burst open by blast about 8 attempted to escape, some were successful, others were hit by machine gun fire. Prior to this Japs had been leading off parties out of sight, ensuing yells, screams coupled with Japs returning for more prisoners, wiping blood off their bayonets, left little doubt as to fate of those led away. Except for the very few who escaped none of the 200 have been seen again.

On 14 February invading Japanese troops reached the Princess Alexandria Military Hospital in Singapore. The building was guarded by a detachment of Gurkha troops who refused to lay down their arms. Once the Gurkhas had been killed, the troops then entered the hospital. Widespread slaughter followed, some patients even being beheaded by swords. The doctors were killed, the nurses beaten and raped. Although this incident was untypical of Japanese behaviour during the last days of Singapore, a similar event had occurred in Manila at the headquarters of the Philippine Red Cross. The diary of the member of the medical staff who survived has a 'report' quality that suggests from the outset a determination to document the incident in detail in the hope that the perpetrators might be brought to justice. This was precisely what happened. Although Hodder was interned in Changi until 1945 his diary, and the further diary within it, were preserved. This was later employed as evidence during the extensive post-war investigations of war crimes at Singapore. Hodder himself would survive the war and return to Britain.

Sergeant Len Baynes, a British soldier, surrenders at Singapore and meets his Japanese captors

Len Baynes was serving in the 1st Battalion, the Cambridge Regiment in Malaya in 1941 and retreated to Singapore. His unit surrendered the afternoon before the general ceasefire during fighting on Singapore Island.

At 3 o'clock the Japs stepped out from among the trees all around us. One even came sliding down a coconut tree right beside BHQ [Battalion Headquarters] where he must have been since the previous night . . .

The enemy approached with their rifles held at the 'ready'. They were evidently taking no chances. Every man had his finger on the trigger. They halted a few yards away and what we took to be an officer stepped forward. He was wearing one of the traditional two-handed Japanese swords, its scabbard knocked his leg with every step he took and nearly banged on the ground. We later became familiar with the sight of these swords. They told us they were handed down from father to son . . .

The ordinary Jap soldiers were our biggest surprise. They looked like walking bits of jungle, and their camouflage had to be seen to be believed. Their uniforms were so completely hung about with twigs and leaves, that if they stood still their form disappeared into the jungle screen behind them.

Another surprise was the stature of these men. Although I suppose we had all heard that the Japs are small, when we saw these little fellows below our shoulders, and realised that it was to these mites that we were surrendering, our amazement and shame were complete.

Sergeant Len Baynes was moved from Singapore to a work camp on the Thai–Burma border. He was fortunate to survive five years of terrible deprivation. On 22 August 1945, a week after Japan's surrender, he was still in a prison camp in Thailand and had not yet seen any Allied soldiers. He was eventually evacuated to Rangoon on an American aircraft on 1 September 1945.

Sunday 15 February 1942

Sheila Allan, civilian teenager, hears of the surrender of
Singapore

At a quarter to ten we heard an officer commanding his men
to line up. Not long after, one of them came with the
shattering news, 'We've given up!' 'Boss' came in, dazed-
looking. His face working up as if he wanted to cry. He kept
repeating to himself, 'I can't understand it – it's not true. We
were told we were pushing them back. I can't—' tears ran
down his cheeks. He sat down and unashamedly buried his
face in his hands and wept as if his heart would break. We
tried to comfort him but what was the use – what words
could we say. We, too, felt like sobbing our hearts out. There
are no words to describe how I felt; how any of us feel!
Shocked, disbelief, horrified, anger perhaps. Then there's
fear as to what is going to happen. All at once, everybody
started talking – trying to convince ourselves that this nightmare is not true.

The firing has ceased. The night air was no longer
shattered by the bursting bombs and shells. In fact, the silence
is quite frightening. For the first time in weeks, there was no
throbbing droning of the planes; no sirens; no guns. I found
this silence from the artillery fire more threatening and
unnerving to say the least. It gave me the creeps to realise that
this is 'Surrender!' We slowly trekked upstairs to our flat with
some of the boys. 'Boss' came up later with their stores saying,
'You – you better have these instead of those yellow dogs'.

*Sheila Allan soon found herself moved to the internment camp at
Changi gaol, at the eastern end of Singapore Island. This had been a
former naval base and barracks and was now used by the Japanese to
house the vast numbers of Allied prisoners and internees. Her father was
also interned, but in a different part of the gaol where she could not see
him. Throughout her internment, and at considerable risk, she would
maintain her diary in exercise books and on scraps of paper.* SEE ALSO
PP. *174–5, 187–9, 459–60, 587–8.*

Sunday 15 – Monday 16 February 1942

Stan Arneil, an Australian soldier, enjoys wine from the
cellars of the French consulate in Singapore on the eve of
surrender

*Stan Arneil had four brothers and a sister, but his mother had died when
he was young and his father in 1938. He joined the Australian army in
June 1940 as an infantryman. By the time he was despatched to
Singapore a year later he had already reached the rank of sergeant. He
served in the 2/30th Infantry Battalion commanded by the legendary
Black Jack Galleghan.*

15 February

The odd types of food, at least odd from an Army point of
view, came from the buildings within the perimeter we were
holding.

Our particular area included the French Consulate. It was
to our eyes the ultimate in luxury and included an enormous
wine cellar stocked with, we were told by Frank Tuckey, a
wine buff, the choicest of wines.

The rare wines were wasted on us. Most of us were in our
early twenties, some not even that old, and our previous
drinking experience was that of the average Australian male,
beer. Still we drank it by the tin pannikin, and if it were
almost sacrilegious to do so then at least many of those alive
on that day never returned to Australia to enjoy Australian
beer.

During that morning we were talking of another Tobruk. We
were great admirers of the Rats of Tobruk and believed that
here was a chance for us to emulate their example. It was an
exhilarating day and we did not give a thought to the civilians
in Singapore who were under constant bombardment.

About 4 p.m. somebody said something about a
surrender. It was an odd thing to say and did not really
register as something which could happen to us. We did not
know then that General Percival had agreed to an
unconditional surrender to the Japanese. The rumour

persisted and as it did so the bombardment and the shelling in our section of the perimeter increased. A piece of shrapnel glanced off my tin hat and I recall my sudden surprise: it was the first time I had been touched by an enemy missile during the war. I recall thinking how stupid it would be to be killed after the surrender had taken place.

About 5 p.m. all firing had ceased. It was uncanny, one could almost hear the silence.

We saw no Japanese that night and spent hours talking about the prospects for the morning. Some men got drunk on French wine whilst others were so shocked they could hardly speak.

We were told that the reason for the surrender was to prevent wholesale slaughter of the civilian population together with the hopelessness of our own position. We understood the first but could not accept the second: but what amazed us was that not one person in the Unit had even contemplated that the Allied Forces could ever surrender.

16 February

There was almost a blind fear within the Unit on the morning after the capitulation. There was no noise which was strange to us and only occasionally did we see one or two Japanese, through the rubber trees. They looked quite demoniacal with their cloth head coverings fringed at the back with pieces of cloth something like the French Foreign Legion caps.

Our fears were not so much of what would happen to us in a physical sense but the fact that we had not the haziest idea of what to do next; we were like people on a boat without a rudder. Our army training had conditioned us to carrying out orders from superiors.

Stan Arneil's diary confirms the observation made by many civilians that during the closing stages of the Singapore campaign Allied troops were poorly directed and often keener to find untapped stocks of alcohol than enemy forces. Arneil is one of the few soldiers to have kept a diary from the period before his capture through his entire imprisonment, including his time in the infamous Thai–Burma railway camps, his return to Changi and his repatriation to Australia in 1945. He would marry in 1947.

Sunday 22 – Monday 23 February 1942

Reginald Carter, colonial official, gets ready to flee the
chaos of Rangoon as the Japanese come nearer

22 February

One of us from the Food Department is on duty each night
at the Mogul Guard. This is my turn. The lights remain on
and people are coming and going all night. I sleep badly and
dream that I have a weak heart and am sent on sick leave to
India, where I rejoin Dorothy and Vicky. I awake to find no
such luck. The houses in Mogul Street have a bright pink
glow on them from the Suratee Bazaar and other burning
buildings. The Gloucestershire Regiment is doing its best to
keep order in Rangoon and its patrols are out all day and
night in their Jeeps. They shoot or capture looters, return to
Mogul Guard to report, hand over prisoners and loot, drink
a bottle of stout, and are off again.

23 February

If only we found someone to pay our salaries, we would be
very rich. For food and petrol are free, there is no time to
spend on other things and no shops to spend in.

Most of the few remaining police are to leave for
Mandalay by train. They parade outside the Mogul Guard,
see shops near-by being broken into and join the looters.
When they return, they find their own kit has been looted in
the meanwhile.

We are armed. I receive a Greener gun and ammunition. I
keep it in the armoury while at the Mogul Guard and load it
each time I go out. Frank triumphs over me by displaying a
revolver he has wangled. His triumph is short-lived. For (a)
he gets no belt and holster and (b) the ammunition does not
fit. The revolver makes a hole in his pocket and proves a
thorough nuisance. Someone promises to get him a belt
and holster but never does. Someone else tells him that only
Major So-and-So can issue the required ammunition. Frank
seeks him for several days but never finds him. I collect

Galstin and his coolies. The train may take several days to reach Mandalay or may never get there. So I collect much food for them and water in many beer bottles. We go to the station by lorry and contact Major Mayne. There are still large crowds, locked out of the station. The train is very late, as it takes hours to collect a train crew. Mayne has a difficult situation well in hand. We are priority three. He marks each carriage with the name of the body to whom it has been allotted and their priority. He then broadcasts to the batches to enter their carriages when their turn comes. Our coolies travel first class, clutching their beer bottles. They and Galstin are staunch fellows, who deserve well, and I am immensely relieved when the train finally steams out. It is the last passenger train that will use the Mandalay line.

Reginald Carter's diary captures the general collapse that affected Rangoon in early 1942. Efforts at an orderly destruction of stores and equipment that might be of use to the Japanese quickly disintegrated in a whirlwind of looting and civil disorder.

Carter and his family evacuated successfully to India, and he would spend the rest of the war there as a colonial civil servant. SEE ALSO PP. *141.*

MARCH 1942

ON 1 MARCH THE JAPANESE were busy consolidating their hold on the island of Java. They were gratified to discover that they could reinforce this operation by using troops that had been released by the surprisingly early termination of the Malayan campaign. The Allies attempted to intercept Japanese forces moving between Malaya and Java. In a naval battle off the port of Surabaya, the Japanese sank the HMS *Exeter* and two destroyers. HMS *Stronghold* was sunk two days later off the coast of Java, while the Dutch quickly scuttled their remaining naval vessels as they prepared to evacuate. More than 20,000 troops, including some recently arrived reinforcements, failed to escape from Java and surrendered. Meanwhile, Japan continued to demonstrate that it understood the importance of naval air power, bombing the Dutch base at Tjilatjap and sinking several further ships. Remarkably, this was followed by a further Japanese air raid on Pearl Harbor which, while inflicting no serious damage, underlined that the base remained pathetically vulnerable.

Burma was now developing as the site of the major land campaign. General Harold Alexander was appointed as the British commander, but his forces continued their headlong retreat towards India, evacuating Rangoon on 6 March. British troops were mostly engaged in demolitions and destruction in a 'scorched earth' campaign to prevent the Japanese from benefiting from any of the infrastructure of the colony, including Burma's oil. By the end of the month the Japanese had over-run the town of Toungoo, forcing both British and Chinese troops back towards India and breaking the line around which they were trying to focus their defence.

American naval raids around New Guinea, using large carriers such as the *Lexington* and the *Yorktown*, continued to inflict significant losses upon the Japanese navy and, more importantly, sank large numbers of merchant ships carrying supplies. Admiral James Somerville arrived in Ceylon to command the combined Australian, British and Dutch fleet in the Indian Ocean. He found himself preoccupied with the Japanese 1st Air Fleet, which had moved its carriers into the Indian Ocean and seemed to be about to mount an attack on his headquarters in Ceylon in the fashion of that inflicted on Pearl Harbor in December.

In the Philippines, American and Filipino troops fought on in a dogged rearguard action under General Wainwright at Bataan and Corregidor. Meanwhile, General Douglas MacArthur reluctantly departed for Mindanao after being firmly ordered out, against his own expressed wishes, by Roosevelt. On 17 March he was flown to Australia in a US B-17 bomber to begin his new command role in the south-west Pacific.

By the middle of March fresh American troops were beginning to make their way into the mid-Pacific in large numbers. The Americal Division occupied the New Hebrides, while significant formations were en route for Australia. This would become the rear area for MacArthur's operations, which focused on the successful defence of New Guinea and the gradual shift of his headquarters from Melbourne to Port Moresby.

In London and Washington, important strategic questions remained to be resolved. The Pacific was declared an American sphere of responsibility and was divided into two zones or 'areas'. MacArthur was to own the South West Pacific Area, while Admiral Chester Nimitz was to own the Pacific Ocean Area. This was not only a division of territory between two extremely egotistical individuals, it was also a division between the US army and US navy. Somewhat ironically, co-operation between the two services was not much better than that between their Japanese counterparts. In both countries the rival services had to be kept apart. Meanwhile, Roosevelt and Churchill, together with the combined chiefs of staff, agreed on the doctrine of 'Germany First'. The US navy, led by the irascible Admiral King, remained a dissident element, anxious to avenge Pearl Harbor and never in any doubt that Japan was the 'real enemy'.

Sunday 1 – Tuesday 3 March 1942

Freddie Mathieson, an Australian army soldier, sails east from Ceylon on a troopship and just escapes imprisonment in Java

1 March

The early hours of the morning, all hell broke loose. The destroyers were tearing all over the place relaying signals, flashing lights, sirens going. Everyone upon deck to see what was going on. We soon found out as the whole convoy did a complete turn around and headed back to Colombo. At dawn we are in the outer harbour. Our destination 'was Java' but it has fallen, we are very lucky indeed. We hear that some of the ships that sailed from Colombo while we were there got to Java, landed troops without their equipment as it was on other ships. They were just in time to be P.O.W.'s. What a way to go into the bag, if we had sailed a day sooner that would have been our fate. Just after breakfast, we up anchor once more, out to the assembly area. Fourteen ships now, all troopers and freighters, with trucks and equipment, the cruiser H.M.S. Cornwell and two destroyers, looks like Aussie now. Our course is a general S.S.E. The convoy looks a picture, the Cornwell to our stern and the destroyers like sheep dogs, very busy. Also a tanker with us. As we departed Colombo we all noticed something that was not there before, two Australian Soldiers wearing all new gear have 'appeared' one plays guitar, the other clarinet. They just sit around playing great music and it goes down well with all the troops – a real touch of home. No one knows where this pair came from and who cares, their playing in the early evening settles the whole ship down, this could be one of those strokes of genius the Army has at times, to smuggle a couple of good musicians on to all the troop ships, as good music could help soothe the lousy news we have had on this trip . . .

3 March

Rained all night. My hammock as usual is slung under the canvas but that did not stop the rain coming through. My ground sheet is U.S. My blanket is soaked. I had a couple of inches of water in the hammock, but at least it was cool, better than down below. Rumour is we may still go to Java. Don't think so.

Freddie Mathieson was quite unaware how politically contentious his journey east from Suez had become. Once Java had fallen, the British and Australian prime ministers fell to arguing over whether Australian troops that had been diverted from the Middle East should be sent to protect India, or else sent to defend their Australian homeland against a possible Japanese assault launched from Java. Canberra stuck to its guns and, to Churchill's dismay, insisted that substantial numbers of Australian troops were brought home. Psychologically this was an important moment for Canberra, reflecting a realization that Australia would be increasingly responsible for its own security and that the imperial relationship, in which they had placed so much faith, would not protect them. SEE ALSO PP. 175–6, 511.

Friday 6 – Wednesday 11 March 1942

Vera Brittain in London watches the impact of news of defeat in the Far East

In 1942 Vera Brittain was already beginning to sense that her pacifism was being eroded by the sheer scale of atrocities committed first by Nazi Germany and now by Japan.

6 March

Conditions worsening in Java. First civilian casualty lists from Malaya & Hong Kong published in *The Times*. Long list; greatest number are the missing – always the most sinister, as in the Blitz here. I recall the gruesome item of the Bristol taxi-driver after the Blitz there – 'five sackfulls of human remains'.

'Observer's notes' (J.M.M.) [John Middleton Murry, a prominent British pacifist] point out this week the change of atmosphere in the H. of C. due to the sudden collapse of the Churchill legend. Churchill remains P.M. because there is no one else, but the faith in him as an inspired leader has gone . . .

7 March

Losing battle in Java nearing its end. Dutch, British, Americans hopelessly outnumbered. Batavia gone, Surabaya besieged, attack on Bandoeng – where the Government is – shortly expected. Doubtless we shall have similar conditions here before the end. Tragedy moves so swiftly from territory to territory that it is impossible to keep pace with it. The *Evening Standard* leader remarked to-night that in the S. African war it took the British 2½ years to conquer the Boers, but the Japanese have conquered an Empire in 2½ months . . .

8 March

Newspaper filled with accounts of the tragedy of Java. The Juggernaut rush of events is overwhelming. It seemed just incredible that our Eastern Empire built up, however unjustly, over two centuries, should have vanished, with that of the Dutch, in 2½ months. So much for Imperial power – a house built on the sand . . .

11 March

Jap atrocities splashed over all the main pages of the daily papers, coupled with a good deal of hypocritical blah about the Govt. keeping it all back till it was confirmed out of consideration for the relatives of the victims. They could spare the feelings of the relatives still if they wished, by keeping it out of the Press, but it serves their purposes too well. The effect of it on the common people in this country was seen immediately in a poster put up by a news-vendor outside the cinema on Richmond Hill: 'WAKE UP ENGLAND. GIVE THE B JAPS A BLOOD BATH.' It might be more becoming in us to refrain from righteous indignation over the Japanese until we have refrained from starving children on the Continent by our blockade.

Although she would continue to campaign for an early peace, by 1944 Brittain's work in wartime pacifism was all but abandoned. However, she felt vindicated in late 1945 when her name was found on a list of 3,000 people that the Germans wished to imprison or shoot after they had invaded Britain in 1940, offering her much-needed confirmation that her pacifism, however unpopular at home during the war, was fundamentally anti-Nazi. The atomic bombing of Hiroshima and Nagasaki in 1945 lent her campaigning zeal a new lease of life. In 1957 she came together with J. B. Priestley, Bertrand Russell and many others to form the Campaign for Nuclear Disarmament. Vera Brittain died, at the age of seventy-seven, in March 1970. SEE ALSO PP. 71–3.

Sunday 8 March 1942

Hilda Lacey and the rest of the hospital staff walk for 9 miles in the heat to their place of internment in Changi gaol

We were up very early packing the rest of the equipment in the servery – most of which we never see again! The buns arrived very late and several people had their tea without them. Our orders were to line up at the front entrance at 9:30am; lorries on one side and walkers on the other.

It would be difficult to describe all the costumes of the women walking and their contraptions for carrying their kit. Miss Williams ('Betty Bond') had a Japanese lampshade with fringe hanging all round, a bath towel round her shoulders to protect her from the sun, and a small child's Go-Kart for her luggage. This came to grief soon after starting out and upset the whole squad. There were also perambulators, bath chairs and anything they could get that would wheel. Many had bath towels round their heads and shoulders, every kind of haversack and contraption strapped to their backs. I carried a thermos and a bag with my tin of tongue and a bun.

We were lined up in four or fives with a Sentry at intervals and started out at about 10:30am. We walked down the street watched by many sympathetic natives, singing 'There will always be an England'; 'Roll out the Barrel' and so on. We did not sing for very long as it was so hot and when we walked some little distance some older people began to fall out from exhaustion. Lorries came along and picked them up. At one stage of the journey we passed a Japanese staff car with a British Officer in it. He hung his head as if he couldn't bear to look at us as he passed.

Our formation . . . did not last long, the more fit pushing to the front and the weaker ones lagging at the back. The Sentry's [*sic*] allowed us to rest fairly often; they seemed to be feeling the heat and were glad to rest themselves. One pushed roughly with his bayonet when we first started when I did not keep in close formation. We got water occasionally but our own supplies were soon finished. We were given water by one or two natives from ... pumps along the road with the Sentry's permission. Some distance from Changi we met lorries of soldiers going out to fatigues and one lorry with civilian internee's ... going out to cut wood. We cheered wildly, gave the 'V' sign and they cheered on out of sight.

... I was offered a lift a short distance from the Gaol by an ambulance driver, which I refused as I was determined to finish on foot. We arrived into the prison courtyard at about 3:30pm and as we poured into it ... we were photographed by the Japanese on all sides. There were a number of men in the yard who were detailed to see to our luggage.

Hilda Lacey left the hospital in Singapore on 18 February as the staff were moved to several temporary holding locations. Rumours circulated that they would all be shipped to Formosa (Taiwan), but in reality she was to spend the rest of the war in Changi gaol. After the war she settled in Kensington, London and in 1966 presented her diary, which was always kept in a small black pocket notebook, to Rhodes House Library in Oxford. SEE ALSO PP. 182, 193–5.

Sunday 8 – Thursday 12 March 1942

Lord Halifax, British ambassador in Washington, discusses the race riots in Detroit

Lord Halifax was born Edward Wood in 1881. He was the fourth son of the 2nd Viscount Halifax; however, his three elder brothers died in childhood, making him heir to the title. Becoming a member of the Conservative Cabinet after the First World War, he was appointed Viceroy of India in 1925. As Foreign Secretary in the 1930s he supported Chamberlain's policies of appeasement. Halifax remained Foreign Secretary with the advent of Churchill's new government in May 1940, but at the end of the year he was sent to Washington to become British ambassador to the United States.

8 March

After dinner with [Sumner] Welles [Assistant Secretary of State] last night, he and [Francis] Biddle, Attorney General talked a good deal about their negro problem, and are evidently very much concerned with it. They say trouble is being made by German and Japan agents on radio, and evidently thought that the [US] army and navy were a good deal to blame for the reluctance to take negro recruits. The more I hear the more I resent their criticism of us in India. We have been a bit slow politically, but socially and administratively we are miles ahead of them . . .

12 March

I happened to have a talk with Mrs Morgenthau [wife of the US Secretary to the Treasury] last night about the negro business. She is very worried about it, and said that recent rows in Detroit had been quite bad. According to her the whites had got some machine guns and there had been some bloodshed. Negroes kept saying to her, was it not a racial war? I asked her what had done it. Apparently the war has accentuated racial discrimination. Negroes have been refused offering their blood to be made into some serum; they weren't allowed to recruit, and I suppose many other things. As regards votes in many States the negro is not allowed to vote unless he has paid his poll tax, and he is not allowed to pay his poll tax and therefore doesn't vote.

As a former Viceroy, Halifax was sensitive to the frequent American criticism of British rule in India and of colonialism in general. He regarded this as hypocritical because of the widespread American discrimination against African Americans, both in the armed forces and in civilian life, which he regarded as worse. Factories and shipyards involved in war production often had separate black and white shifts. In February 1942 there had been minor race riots in Detroit, but these would be overshadowed the following year by much larger disturbances in the same city in which 34 people were killed and 700 wounded.
SEE ALSO P. 786.

Monday 9 – Thursday 12 March 1942

Corporal Tom Fagan, an Australian soldier at Bandoeng in Java, finds that he has been 'sold out'

Tom Fagan had served in a motor transport unit in Syria during December 1941. After the outbreak of war with Japan his unit had been hastily sent south to the Red Sea, where they boarded the SS Orcades *and were sent eastwards as reinforcements. They had hoped to move to Australia, but were in fact heading for Singapore. En route to Singapore, the news came in that the city had fallen and so they were sent further east, to Java, in an ill-advised effort to reinforce the doomed ABDA Command. While much of Java had fallen to the Japanese by 1 March, in fact the island did not formally surrender until 9 March. Being a few days in advance of Freddie Mathieson and his unit, who were also heading for Java, Fagan's unit made landfall just ahead of capitulation.*

Tom Fagan

9 March

The worst has happened. The Dutch have capitulated and we have been sold out. We made a break from Bandoeng last evening at 5pm and we are now camped at the Grand Hotel, or rather in the grounds of the hotel. I believe the Japs have already marched into Bandoeng, so we are only one jump ahead of them.

It was raining like heck when we arrived here last night. We were making for the beach when we had to stop here, as the road down is impassable, so we are 40 miles from the beach. There are trucks, cars and Bren Gun carriers everywhere. There is quite a lot making a break for the hills and some are trying to make our way down to the beach. Personally I don't like the idea as we would have Japs, natives, malaria and dysentery to contend with. Also we've heard there are no boats here – so what's the use.

Our officer let us down badly and is not worth the ink it takes to write his name. The boys are hitting the whisky and gin and are drowning their sorrows in a big way. This evening we had to destroy and bury all our arms and ammunition as we have been handed over by the Dutch unconditionally. The Dutch, who are the bravest and best fighters in the world! (Oh yeah). I really don't think they fired a shot at the enemy.

There is a large swimming pool here and we have made good use of it. There are quite a few women and children here at the hotel; their husbands are supposed to be prisoners in Sumatra. We are just waiting around there until we are picked up. The boys are throwing their money around – the natives are doing well. All souvenirs have been dumped and we are down to bare necessities. Quite a few Tommies here with us.

10 March

Today we had orders from Togo to go back to Bandoeng and here we are, back in the hospital grounds. We are allowed to carry on our jobs as ambulance drivers until further orders. We are not allowed out of the grounds except by special orders from the Japs. The town is full of them now. The natives have changed their tune and are all waving Jap flags and booing us when we go past.

11 March

We have been visited by the Japs and they made us promise we would stay put and not try to escape. Well, that was easy as we have no earthly chance of getting off this island, even if we did make the beach.

12 March

My birthday today. How different it was 12 months ago. We were then in Tobruk and now we are POWs in Java. As much as I hated the desert, I'd rather be free there than under these conditions.

The Dutch in Java probably offered the Japanese even less determined resistance than the British had done in Malaya, capitulating very quickly. However, the loss of seasoned troops like Tom Fagan and his comrades, some of whom had fought doggedly at Tobruk, was a disaster, and the decision to send Australian troops there, rather than to Australia or India, was foolish in the extreme. For Tom Fagan the cost was high. By April 1942 he was appalled to find that he had become a prisoner before much resistance had been offered. SEE ALSO PP. 442,–4, 474–6, 484–5.

Monday 9 March – Saturday 18 April 1942

Edgar Wilkie, an Australian POW, attempts an escape from Japanese captivity in Singapore

Edgar Wilkie was born in Radcliffe, Australia in 1917. His family endured rural poverty in the inter-war years and in 1939 he joined the Australian infantry at the first opportunity. He was part of a late batch of reinforcements sent to Singapore and arrived there at 1100 hours on 24 January 1942. Within three weeks he was in captivity at Changi gaol and was being used as labour on a gardening scheme which gave him the opportunity to escape.

9 March

Today I was working in garden scheme, and the camp is just driving itself mad with false rumours. Where they come from I don't know.

10 March
We found the camp is being enclosed by barbed wire fences so we decided to put our plans in operation.

11 March
Left Changi about midnight and after some solid work got a boat afloat and paddled over the Strait of Johore with two shovels for paddles. Nearly ran into a Japanese guard. Landed at a jetty and pushed the boat off. Found we were on an island so we camped in weeds all day, found a boat again and set off to go round the island, but again ran into guards. Landed and camped for the night.

12 March
Found a Chinese who although in peril of his life gave us a bit of food and promised to help.

13 March
Moving to Johore. It rained like fun all day. Chinese rowed us from the island to the mainland early last night. We found some pineapples this afternoon that someone had left, and were they good!

14 March
Crossed Kota Tinngi Road this a.m. Got a good handout last night. Brought pancakes and tea at 2030 and we never felt so good . . .

9 April
Camped in a patch of jungle. Worried. We were seen by two Tamils and thought we saw a Jap at a plantation house. First sun for days.

10 April
After a successful night in passing through Segamat. It took a couple of hours. Camped in good rubber with under-growth. Water laid on. Mosquitoes in droves. Sun again today. 14 miles more. No food except rice twice daily now. Tea and coffee without sugar is the rule. Country flogged out for food by Japs. Told of many ** of **** ****. [These words

are deliberately obscured.] Who could help us? Very sore feet. I washed everything and myself. Best camp we have had. Beautiful day.

11 April

We started well last night. Tried for a bit of dry rice and got a feed as well. Caught in the yards at Batu Enam by a train. The place must have been an engineers' stores dump and fuel depot. We struck Gemas about 0100 and cleared it by 0230 and started on a new line. Walking very rough. Sore footed and weary. Covered about 15 miles. Having trouble finding water. Shifted to jungle 0900. Malays about us and didn't like their behaviour. Got some bananas from them. Had good sleep and bananas and rice for tea. Our camp was on the S. Muar River in the jungle.

12 April

We covered about 20 miles last night. Found that the railway on the map had been demolished. Trouble in finding a camping place and water. Rice for breakfast. Thoughts of home. Bahau, our goal on one railway was passed. We start on road travel tonight. 1100hrs we were captured. Taken to Bahau for lunch, rice, tinned sausages, pineapple. Believe we are to be taken back to Singapore. Such is life. Being well treated. Rice, vegetables, stew for tea . . .

17 April

Brought by truck from Seremban to Kuala Lumpur into prison. Believe should we try to escape again we will be shot. Plenty of Australian men here. No breakfast. Lunch of rice and a little stewed pork. Tea was rice and green vegetables. Lit by two electric lights in corridor. Lights out 2030hrs. So ends the first day in Pudu Prison, Kuala Lumpur. In time for an issue of cigarettes and soap.

18 April

Reveille at 0600hrs. Count of troops, washed. Breakfast 0800. Rice and vegetables. Talking to the boys on the various atrocities that have been committed on them and what they have seen. Shooting of prisoners tied together with signal wire, machine gunned and petrol poured over them then fired, many still living; massacre of wounded. Lunch of pork, rice and 'gyppo' (name for a cross between gravy and soup). Very tasty. Stomach trouble seems to be passing. Tea of a little fish and rice. Rumours of Tokyo being bombed. Feeling very weak from the diarrhoea.

Escape was almost impossible for POWs in Asia because of the vast distances to be covered and the likelihood of being turned in by the local population. The exception was Hong Kong, where an effective escape and evasion system was in place.

In 1943 Edgar Wilkie would be transferred to Formosa and then on to Japan. He worked on the wharves at Kobe and was then moved to a coal mine at Fukuoka on Kyushu Island. He would die there in July 1945 at the age of twenty-eight.

Thursday 12 March 1942

Robert Moody Smith meets escapees from Japanese-occupied Hong Kong

Robert Moody Smith kept an excellent diary during his year with the American Volunteer Group (AVG), a unit that eventually became known as the Flying Tigers, made up of pilots who had volunteered to fight for China long before the attack on Pearl Harbor. Smith had attended college before joining up and spent his spare time in China reading literature, being especially partial to Anthony Trollope's Barchester Towers. *Like many members of the Flying Tigers he joined partly for adventure and partly out of a sense of outrage at the violence that Japan had perpetrated upon China. Based at Kunming in southern China, he soon began to encounter refugees from Hong Kong.*

Doreen Lomberg (now Doreen Reynolds) arrived yesterday noon by truck at my station, which is on the main road to Chungking. My sedan parked in front has AVG painted on it in big letters. When she saw it, she had the truck stop and let her off. She is engaged to Davis, who is on our staff in Kunming.

Doreen had escaped from Hong Kong. She had been there during the siege and fall of the colony. Her stories tell of muddling and inefficiency. A friend of hers, Bran Fay, saw the first Japanese troops land on the island. He was one of the volunteers raised to defend the city. He rushed to the telephone and called military headquarters. He told them what he had seen. The officer on duty refused to tell the commanding general 'for he was asleep.' The British announced that all 'British' women and children were removed from the colony. They did not include anyone with any Chinese blood. On the day the women were to register many Eurasians possessing British passports, thinking and looking like Englishmen, came to report. They were refused transportation – yet the husbands of these women were volunteers in the Hong Kong forces. They were the best troops the city had. They spoke English and considered themselves British. One English woman of 'pure' blood was told that she could be evacuated to Australia, but her three small children must remain behind. Her husband was part Chinese.

During the two and one-half week battle with the Japanese, the authorities refused to publish any casualty list since 'it would be bad for morale.' After the surrender, the British postal head asked the Japanese for their help in getting the names of the Hong Kong dead, many of them Eurasians. The Japanese agreed, but the British commanding officer refused to permit it; it still would be 'bad for morale.' Thousands of Hong Kong women did not know whether or not their husbands were dead.

'It wouldn't have been so bad, you see,' Doreen said, 'if they knew. Women can face it. But the uncertainty the not knowing – some of them are mad with worry.'

Hong Kong had 12,000 Canadian soldiers with two months' training. They were all young and inexperienced. Many of the officers of the Royal Scots were killed in a pill-box the first night of the battle. Although mobilized, they had no sentries and were engaged in a poker session. The Japanese threw a hand grenade into the cement building.

Hong Kong had 4000 volunteers, a goodly portion Eurasians. Their casualties were heavy.

If the Allied defence of Singapore was incompetent then the British direction in Hong Kong was worse, although on the ground a number of units, especially locally raised volunteers, fought bravely. When it came to evacuation, racial division was strictly enforced by the colonial government and families of mixed race suffered especially harsh treatment. Curiously, Doreen Reynolds had escaped from Hong Kong with the assistance of a German officer who was on liaison duties with the Japanese. He loathed the Japanese and was happy to assist her. SEE ALSO PP. 268–70.

Juan Labrador, a Spanish academic and priest, watches the Japanese police and local police deal with road traffic offences in occupied Manila

The Filipino traffic policemen have gone back to their posts at the corners of avenues and principal streets. There are also a number of other peace and order agencies whose members carry no weapon other than a wooden stick, which replaces the rattan stick with which the police were armed when the Japanese arrived. The policemen direct the traffic while their Japanese counterparts stay under shade of trees or in alleys adjacent to buildings, giving the orders. It is typical of what is happening in the civilian administration.

In many cases, the Japanese apply rules obtaining in Japan but unknown in the Philippines. Whenever a Japanese traffic officer spots a violation – according to his standards – he would blow his whistle, and the Filipino policeman would run after the infractor and bring him to his master, who would then furiously reprimand the violator. The latter, not understanding the Japanese language, would merely bow continuously to pacify the Japanese. Sometimes the violator is released. At other times he is tied to a tree for a long time in punishment of a violation he never knew he committed. The poor Filipino, who could not understand a word, would end up not complying or doing the opposite infuriating the Japanese who would start dealing blows with his saber.

I never thought the Oriental imagination could be so fertile as to be able to invent such refined and painful torments. There are three classes of offenses which the Japanese punish with unusual rigidity; thievery and looting, traffic violation, and disrespect for agents of the law.

Thieves and looters are kicked or dealt saber blows. Recidivists, or those who rob military installations, are made to walk on their knees and whipped, or their hands tied behind the head which is placed between the legs all tied up, and then hurled rolling against the wall, like a human ball.

Traffic violators are tied to a tree or post and kept there under the sun in public view for two days. In a few cases, when two infractors are caught at the same time, they are made to deal blows on each other until they are both hurt and exhausted.

Sometimes while the hands are tied behind the back the infractor is pushed from the front, tripping him at the same time and sending him rolling on the ground. This is repeated over and over until the poor fellow is bruised and bleeding.

Those who fail to salute the sentries posted in many strategic places are made to bow twenty times or more and if the performance is not satisfactory, the infractor is given saber blows.

These acts do not serve the new masters well in the sight of the public which talks about, compares, criticizes and is horrified by these novel methods. The repertoire of exquisite torments is inexhaustible. Those mentioned are the most common. Each day new forms of cruelty are being invented or imported.

However, it should be noted that the same rigidity and strictness are applied to delinquent Japanese, civilian or military. The same punishments are dealt in the same public manner, although the Japanese either are less sensitive or are simply accustomed to such practices. They accept the blows without wincing, in stoic passiveness, firm as a statue before their henchmen.

Father Juan Labrador's diary was kept as a deliberate attempt at 'scientific record', capturing the small but revealing details of the

Japanese occupation, seeking thus, in his words, to make 'the actuality more acute'. His observations on the enforcement of traffic regulations are a beautiful example of this approach, with an eye for the quirky but illuminating details of everyday life. His diaries also reveal the true nature of the Japanese treatment of the Filipino people, whom Tokyo claimed to have 'liberated' from western dominance. SEE ALSO PP. 162–4, 456–7, 563–4, 689–91.

Monday 16 March 1942

Freddy Bloom arrives at the women's camp at Changi and chooses her accommodation

Freddy was a New York graduate working as a newspaper correspondent in Singapore. Her first husband, a British army officer, and her father had both died of illness in 1940. During 1941 she had met Philip Bloom, a British doctor serving in the Royal Army Medical Corps, and fallen in love. On 8 February 1942, her twenty-eighth birthday, they were married 'in between air-raids'. A week later, after the surrender of Singapore, she was interned in the civilian section of Changi gaol while her husband was detained in a different section of Changi as a POW. Freddy Bloom worked with another internee, Mrs Graham White, to run the NAAFI stores in the General Hospital at Changi. There she was able to obtain an account book, which became her diary.

The prison is not a very happy-looking place. Nothing but grey walls and bars. Not a single tree or shrub. Hardly a blade of grass.

Katherine greeted us with rolls she had picked up on the way and a tin of sardines. I don't remember anything ever tasting so good. While we munched she told us the awful state of affairs.

There had been absolutely no preparation made for our arrival. There was one big room in which fifty people could lie down, if they had no luggage and were willing to lie skin to skin. Otherwise nothing. What luggage of ours had arrived she had dragged into a corner of a corridor and now we would have to wait and see.

I just didn't care. My mattress was there and in no time I was three-quarters asleep. My getting worried and running about looking was not going to help things any.

After perhaps an hour word came round that a new wing had been opened and that we should choose our cells. Up we went – to the Chinese part of the prison – rows and rows of nine-by-twelve-foot cells with great concrete slabs on which to sleep and Chinese lavatories [slits in the floor, known as 'squatters'] (dirty) in the corner. The walls were high, bleak and filthy, and up about ten feet were little windows. We could have a cell each. There was privacy but, my God, it was hell . . .

Some of the women did not seem to mind so much, which was good, for most of them are still living in those holes of concrete. We waited while they moved in and then went off searching. Luckily we found a helpful officer who took us around, and down on the ground level at the end of what had been the recreation room we found a tool-room, fairly large, full of implements, instruments and shelves. He said that if we took care of the stores we might stay in the tool-room. Feeling much better we moved in – Katherine (DeM), Kate, Ethel, Mrs Moir and me. And there at the moment of writing we still are.

Now we love our tool-room with the same passion as we had for Woodchoppers' Cottage. Our five beds are put up about three feet apart. The others all had table-cloths or regular bedspreads with which to cover theirs, and I felt rather left out until I remembered the heavy green canvas that had been our impromptu bed rolls. By splitting one length and sewing the halves on either side of the whole with thick green wool I made a really fine spread. The green cushions that were to be my bed before you copped the mattresses, blend beautifully. Next to my bed are my three shelves. The bottom one holds a few books, sewing materials, soap and toothbrush, etc. The second shelf is the important one, for besides comb, brush, eau de cologne, it holds your picture (and Mother's).

You know, Philip, I never like that photograph at all but now it's become the most understanding thing in my small world. When I'm happy you smile. When I'm worried your picture regrets that it hasn't a shoulder for me to cry on. Sometimes when I stare at it very hard wondering whether you are taking care of yourself (we are told there are one hundred new cases of dysentery at Changi every day), whether circumstances are not too terrible for you, your picture seems to wink.

The women of Changi consisted largely of the wives of those who had worked in industry or the colonial administration, together with some civilian nurses who had volunteered to stay on. The women's prison at Changi was run differently from other areas of the gaol. Although the internees were provided with only the minimum of food and other supplies, the restrictions were very few and the women were left to organize themselves. Many tried to bring their dogs with them, but these were not allowed into Changi. The women were required to dose their own pets with veronal, or else hand them over to a party of male prisoners tasked with shooting them. However, on her arrival Freddy Bloom managed to save a stray fox terrier called 'Judy' who sneaked into Changi and took up residence in the tool-room. SEE ALSO *PP. 352–3, 404.*

APRIL 1942

APRIL MARKED THE LOW point in the war against Japan. By the end of the month, the beleaguered American outpost on the Bataan peninsula in the Philippines had fallen and almost all of Burma was under the control of Tokyo. With a fleet of Japanese aircraft carriers roaming the Indian Ocean at will, there was near-panic in British India, where the invasion of the east coast around Calcutta now appeared a real possibility.

Two separate struggles – Japan's war for imperial conquest and the efforts of Asian nationalists to overthrow colonial rule – now seemed about to join forces. British rule in India was already strongly challenged from within by Gandhi's Quit India movement. Now Japanese forces were approaching the eastern gates of India and a Japanese landing was anticipated, perhaps by carrying forces the short distance from Rangoon across the Bay of Bengal. Few colonial administrators expected the Indian population to offer any resistance. In private, officials in London and Delhi began to think the unthinkable, contemplating the loss of India to Japan. Meanwhile, Germany too was advancing towards the western borders of India, having reached the Caucasus. India, and in particular Indian military manpower, had already made a vast contribution to the Allied war effort and accordingly the situation for Britain could not have been more serious.

During early April the American and Filipino troops holding out on Bataan ran out of supplies, penned in by the effective Japanese naval blockade. Counter-attacks failed to throw back the Japanese advance and by the second week of April the defence of Bataan had crumbled. A general withdrawal was ordered, but only a few escaped to join the guerrillas in the hills. Over 75,000 troops surrendered to the Japanese and were put on long forced marches to prison camps. Many died along the way. American forces continued, however, to hold the island of Corregidor.

In the Indian Ocean, Somerville's Eastern Fleet searched for the Japanese carrier force in the hope of locating it before it could attack the Royal Navy's base on the island of Ceylon. On 4 April Japanese raiders were detected to the south of the island, and the Japanese launched an air strike on Colombo, but the two fleets failed to meet in battle. During the hours of darkness they passed within 180 miles of each other, yet were mutually ignorant of each other's presence. This was fortunate for the Allies, since the Japanese were undoubtedly the superior force in terms of capability, tactics and training. Meanwhile, other elements of the Japanese fleet raided the Bay of Bengal, sinking a dozen merchant ships and increasing fears about a potential Japanese landing. After the Japanese sank the British carrier HMS *Hermes*, the rest of the British Eastern Fleet was withdrawn to Bombay and to Mombasa in East Africa, leaving Ceylon undefended. Vital personnel, including the naval code-breakers, were also evacuated to Kenya and would not return for a year. Japan could have taken Ceylon almost without resistance but did not realize the weakness of its opponent.

The War in the Philippines, December 1941 to May 1942

Although Japan continued to advance in the Pacific, landing at Bougainville in the Solomon Islands, the pace of that advance slowed markedly. By contrast, in Burma, despite the arrival of further Chinese troops, combined Allied efforts failed to hold the Japanese and a general withdrawal began. The Japanese commander was determined to make all possible gains before the onset of the monsoon. By 26 April General Alexander had accepted that Burma was lost and that efforts would have to be concentrated on the defence of India.

Notwithstanding these reverses, the United States was determined to strike back at Tokyo in the most dramatic fashion possible. On 18 April it offered a dramatic demonstration of this resolve. The aircraft carrier USS *Hornet* advanced to within 700 miles of Japan and launched sixteen B-25 bombers on raids against Tokyo, Kobe, Nagoya and Yokohama. Many of the aircraft did not have enough fuel to return and were abandoned over China, their pilots normally recovered by local Chinese troops, nationalist or communist, and assisted in returning to their units. Although the damage inflicted by these light bombers on Tokyo was limited, the symbolism of the 'Doolittle Raid' was important, representing the first attempt at a 'payback' for Pearl Harbor. At a time when the main Japanese carrier fleet was far away in the Indian Ocean, this attack had an important psychological effect. Japanese fighter aircraft were moved from the front line to defend Tokyo and other cities. More importantly, it would help to draw the Japanese into a crucial naval air battle at Midway in June 1942.

Wednesday 1 – Thursday 9 April 1942

General Kawamura Saburo visits senior commanders in Manila, observes the fall of Bataan and feels 'tip top'

General Saburo had completed his tenure as Governor of Singapore on 11 March 1942, handing over to Major-General Suegiura. In late March he set sail for the Philippines, arriving in early April for discussions with local commanders and also witnessing the end of the fighting at Bataan.

1 April

It is April! From midnight the breeze blows and it is pleasing. The sea has ripples . . . It is scarcely half way of first lap of the voyage. Today perhaps Fumiko started her primary school and her brother, Middle School. I call to my minds eye the image of their going to school!

5 April

About 1300 as scheduled, drop anchor in Lingaen Anchorage . . . Hills around are bald, quite different from Malaya, and the scenery austere.

6 April

In order to report to Corps Commander and concert matters, start at 0830. After about four hours journey arrive at Orani. Find Lt. General Homma in very high spirits. Major General Wachi downwards are in very high spirits. Conversed on various topics. Feel tip top. Regarding [operations] against the North, General Homma concurs with my views. Climb a belfry and take observation of Bataan fighting. Just then there was bombing from the air and it presented an impressive and majestic scene. 1600 took leave and came to Manila City and put up at Manila Hotel. A beautiful hotel, and is in control of the Army, I understand.

Evening, Sub-Chief Major General Hayashi Yoshida inviting. Eat with Colonel Sukesagota, Lt Colonel Maki, S.O's Inuzuka, Tomita and others, and those from Centre Unit – Colonel Kaji, Lt Colonel Orita and others. On account of having many old friends, conversation went on lively from the beginning. Besides the dishes were very tasty. Surprised to have caviare! Manila's Pilsen beer is also good. Finding oneself a guest of a fine hotel feel like myself again after long roughing. But I was piqued if this is right, this extravagance and luxury when one thinks of conditions in Japan. It was rather comical that my thoughts run on many things.

Manila has the leisurely aspect of a place not war-scarred and it has quickly recovered its peace and order. Because of this it is a common assertion that it has not been sufficiently impressed by Japanese awe . . .

9 April

From 1700, all drink toast with sake given by the Emperor and call three cheers for him, and thus celebrate our majestic expedition. Morale raise high.

At this juncture there comes report that the enemy at Bataan has sought to surrender . . .

Saburo's diary captures the ecstatic feeling of Japanese commanders in the early summer of 1942 at the apogee of their success. Although Saburo was delighted by his experiences, his thoughts repeatedly strayed homeward to his daughter Fumiko and his son Tsukasa. Later in the year he received a letter from home dated 2 May 1942 and, noting that his son had been made sub-monitor of his class, remarked: 'My son, after all, is not so bad. I feel some respect for his plodding on somehow when I give no hand in his education . . . I think of his mother's efforts and sympathise with her.' In June 1942 Saburo would travel on to the island of Corregidor. At the end of that year he was appointed Chief Staff Officer to the army in Indochina; he remained there until the end of the war. In 1947 he was tried, condemned to death and hanged as a war criminal for his part in the 'cleansing' of Singapore's Chinese population in February and March 1942. SEE ALSO PP. 129–31.

Sunday 5 April 1942

Don McLaren, an Australian prisoner in Changi, attempts to teach a Japanese guard some vernacular English

Donald McLaren was born in Adelaide, Australia, together with his twin sister Betty, on Christmas Day in 1922. His father owned a butcher's shop on Churchill Road in the suburbs of Islington. The family was badly hit by the depression and moved frequently. After he left school, Don became an apprentice with Amber & Sons, an Adelaide company of furniture makers. In 1940, at the age of seventeen, he had volunteered to join the army. On 15 August 1941 his unit had been despatched to Jahore and by October he had been moved to Singapore. After the surrender he found himself in Changi gaol with thousands of fellow Australian soldiers.

Had a very unusual experience today, we were taken out, or indeed marched out, to where we are expected to build some sheds for the Japs. During a break, a Jap captain came up to me and said, 'You're very young to be a soldier.' I replied that I was only 19. His English was excellent, he continued talking to me, he even sang 'God save the King.'

Somewhere close by a few blokes were having a bit of an argument. One of them said, 'Pigs fucking arse.' The Jap captain looked at me with a very puzzled look on his face and said in English, 'What does pigs fucking arse mean?' Bloody hell! Well I said, 'A pig a hog.' He said, 'I know quite well that a pig is a hog, but what does it all mean?' I was flabbergasted trying to explain that it was an expression meaning 'I don't believe you!' I said, 'It actually means exactly the same as "bull shit".' 'And what is bull shit?' he said. I thought, 'here we go again.' I tried as hard as I could to tell him both expressions meant the same thing, that is, 'What you're saying is not true.' He gave me a look of disgust and walked off. I made a point of it from that day, whenever any English speaking Japs were around, I pissed off.

The entries to my diary from now on will be recorded only if it's worth the risk.

Not all contacts between Japanese guards and Allied servicemen were unpleasant. The Japanese armed forces, and especially the Imperial Japanese Navy, had received considerable training and advice from the Royal Navy and British arms companies until the mid-1920s. Many Japanese officers had enjoyed exchange postings to Britain and boasted an excellent command of the English language – although not all its vernacular expressions. SEE ALSO PP. 387–8, 807–9, 821–2.

Saturday 11 April 1942

Renton Hind, an American civilian internee, gets ready for
a move to a new internment camp at Baguio in the
Philippines

*Renton Hind was born in 1885 and had been President of the Philippine
Sugar Association in the 1920s. He maintained a diary describing more
than three years of daily life in a Philippine civilian internment camp
under the Japanese. Here British, Chinese, Dutch and American men,
women and children were in 'protective custody', which was designed in
reality to prevent them from helping to organize the active guerrilla
resistance. Hind had initially been held at Camp John Hay at Baguio,
north of Manila, but in April 1942 he was to be moved to the nearby
Camp Holmes.*

While at four o'clock dinner on the 20th there was great
excitement when it was announced that we were to be
moved to Camp Holmes, Trinidad Valley, on the 23rd.
Trinidad was the vegetable center of Baguio, being farmed
mainly by Japanese. In this valley was located the Trinidad
Farm School where 650 Filipino students were given an
academic and agricultural training under American supervision. Less than a mile away was Camp Holmes,
headquarters of the local detachment of the Philippine
Constabulary or Insular Police and used as a training center
for the Philippine army.

The next morning a crew of fifty of our men, including
fifteen Chinese who were to prepare quarters for their own
nationals, were transported by truck to Holmes armed with
all manner of tools, including the complete equipment
associated with a modern janitor service. Included were
some of the kitchen crew who were to enquire into the needs
of this important department and to lay the groundwork for
our reception and feeding when the general exodus from
Camp John Hay took place.

After a six o'clock breakfast on the morning of the 23rd,
married men were permitted to go to the women's barracks

to assist in the final packing. What a mad-house it was! Hammering of nails, moving baggage out of the building, howling children or children so excited over the prospect of moving that they were entirely unmanagable, and un-attached women yelling for someone to come to their aid in rolling up mattresses and blankets or in closing bags which were packed to the bursting point. Everyone was in a holiday mood and the transfer took place under circum-stances reminding one of an excursion. For better or for worse it was a break in routine and we were off to the other side of the mountain 'to see what we could see.' Some of us, the writer among them, had not been outside the fenced enclosure since coming to Camp Hay. Our movements had been limited to a 250-foot concrete walk in front of the two barracks and the area of one of the two tennis courts.

There were three barracks at Camp Holmes, all facing west. The North building, an old one-story affair built in 1927, was assigned to the men. The center and south build-ings were new, having been erected shortly before the war. These were two-storied buildings, equipped with self-contained kitchens and messhalls ... At the right of the compound the land gave way sharply to a level piece of ground on which were tennis courts and two officers' residences, the larger becoming our hospital and the other a nursery for camp-born children. Round and about stretched attractive roadways with rock gardens and flower beds and vine bedecked trellises ... We were quick to agree that our new location was preferable to the old. We had ten times the area to wander around in, we had a superb view and we had better living accommodations.

After a late supper of stew and boiled rice we were off to bed. The Japs insisted that lights remain switched on all night but this did not affect our ability to drop off to sound sleep at once for our stamina was not what it used to be. After a breakfast at eleven the next morning, the task of getting settled was undertaken. This required a couple of days hard work, saws and hammers being busy with shelv-ing and other conveniences. Everybody wanted his job done first and barracks floors were strewn with everything from handbags to umbrellas and bawling children were under

foot. We had been at Camp John Hay 116 days. How long
would we be at Holmes?

*The Japanese authorities had not made sensible plans for the occupation
of conquered territories and many of the instances of ill-treatment and
poor provision for captives stemmed from this unpreparedness. In
particular, Japan's military culture had not prepared them for the large
number of POWs, since they did not expect many fighting men to
surrender. Nor had they considered the large numbers of civilians from
enemy countries that they would have to intern. In the Philippines the
numbers interned were simply too great to be managed, and during May
1942 they decided that they had no choice but to release all Chinese
because of their large numbers. The remaining detainees of other nationalities quickly took over the additional living space vacated by their
departure. Despite the release of Chinese internees, some 5,000 civilian
American men, women and children on the Philippines would be
confined for the duration of the war. SEE ALSO PP. 348–9.*

Sunday 12 April 1942

Colonel Paul Bunker engages in an artillery duel with the
Japanese as Corregidor Island in the Philippines fights on

*Paul Bunker had graduated from West Point in 1903. He married
Landon Beehler, the daughter of an admiral, and they had three
children. Paul Bunker was very familiar with Corregidor, having served
with the 59th Coastal Artillery there in 1915 and later, after many tours
of duty in the United States and South America, returned to command
the same unit during the mid-1930s. By 1937 he had become a reserve
officer in California, but in 1940, with war looming, he volunteered to
return to his old unit on Corregidor. In mid-1941 all dependants were
ordered off the island and so his wife had returned to the United States.*

A rough day all day. The Japs started at 6:00 A.M., shelling
us from the Bataan side with numerous guns, probably
mostly 105mm but with some 150mm mixed in. Maj. Julian
and Capt. Schenck were right on the job with their flash
ranging and we cut loose with Btry. Geary at a Jap

concentration near Lokanin Pt. After destroying an enemy battery here, we shifted to another battery, got it and its adjacent ammunition dump and then landed a few in a bunch of tanks and set them afire. Observers said the fire was perfect and the Japs were hurriedly leaving the place.

More Japanese guns opened up and we started counterbattery with our 155mm, 6″ disappearing and all other small and medium calibre guns which would bear on the Bataan shore. Because of our inexperienced personnel it took so long to get corrections applied to the guns that the enemy had time to bring lots of fire to bear upon our guns. Our guns and emplacements are very vulnerable. Two men were killed at Btry. Kysor (an officer – Arnold? had to have his leg amputated this afternoon) and at Fort Hughes. Many of our guns suffered direct hits and other damage. The only gun of Btry. Sunset which bears on Bataan will be out of action for days.

This artillery duel kept up all day and we worked furiously to combat the accurate fire of the Japs. In the afternoon, they started shooting at us from Cavite side also, aiming at Ft. Hughes, at Kindley Field, and at our shipping.

In the morning we tried to register Btry. Craighill on the pier and boats at Mariveles, but had to give it up as a bad job, the shooting was so erratic. General Moore was in C1 at the time and was not particularly impressed with the shooting.

There were air raids and bombings throughout the day, and all on Corregidor. I don't know where they all landed but the Japs seemed to try mostly for James Ravine and the post power plant – which has been already hard hit. Some say that the plant has lost all its ammonia. There is no post power now at most of our batteries and we have to run our emergency 25-kw sets – and the staff won't give us enough gas for that! In our C1-G1 set up, we use my little 6-kw Air corps alternator.

Although the Bataan peninsula had fallen by 7 April 1942, bringing resistance on the main island of Luzon to a halt, American forces held out on Corregidor. The series of forts and artillery emplacements on this island represented a veritable Maginot Line of the Pacific, guarding the entrance to the important harbour of Manila Bay. Although the defences had not been upgraded since the 1920s because further work had been forbidden by the Washington Treaty of 1931, they remained formidable. The key to the ability of the garrison to hold out was the safety of its power plant. Fresh water for the island had to be pumped from its twenty-one deep wells. Food could be kept fresh only by power-driven refrigeration plants. The large sea-coast gun batteries, though equipped with emergency power sets, also relied on the power plants, and much of the heavy equipment was moved over an electric railroad with 13½ miles of track. SEE ALSO PP. 270–3, 310–12, 326–7.

Monday 13 – Thursday 30 April 1942

An unknown Japanese soldier finds himself guarding POWs at Bandoeng on Java

This pocket diary was captured on Guadalcanal in early 1943, translated, and circulated for intelligence purposes. Although the soldier's name is not known, he had sailed from Cam Ranh Bay in Indochina on 18 January 1942 on the Heian Maru and arrived in Java on 1 March 1942. Four days later he was placed on POW guard duty at No. 86 temporary stockade at Bandoeng, which by 15 April had become a permanent POW camp.

13 April
The prisoners are very well disciplined. They have a bugle to call them to roll-call, to mess, and to their other activities.

14 April
In the afternoon I commanded a squad and 10 prisoners. We constructed wire entanglements around the stockade. The escape of prisoners is frequent but unavoidable since the surrounding fence is not completed.

15 April
As I had planned to take today off and go out in the afternoon, we worked hard in the morning (putting up wire entanglements.) However, it took us till noon and today, as it

happened, was the day for transferring prisoners; so I found I could not go out this afternoon after all.

The BANDOENG Prisoners Assembly Area was changed to the BANDOENG Prisoners Stockade and the Comdr of our unit was ordered to become the Comdr thereof. Now the Co will do nothing but guard the prisoners and wherever one looks around this place he will see nothing but prisoners. (Today about 2000 prisoners came from the 2d Co and were placed in the stockade behind our Co).

16 April

Today the transfer of prisoners was carried out. It began early in the morning and was finally finished about 1400. This time they were put into stockades according to their respective races. Put up wire entanglements this morning. In this Prisoner Stockade about 3000 prisoners interned. The 4 races of INDONESIA, MENADO, MAMPON (TN.phon) [translation phonetic] and CHINESE are interned. These are watched by the 4th Sqd with myself and 10 men.

17 April

There seemed to be a difference between the number of men in yesterday's and this morning's roll call; therefore at 1300 an unexpected roll call was taken by order of the outpost Comdr. They are in groups of approximately 50 prisoners each according to their race. A sergeant is the leader of 50 prisoners. The total number of men is the same as yesterday. The prisoners are somewhat accustomed to conditions and have become friendly toward us.

20 April

There's a report (radio news) that three places, NAGOYA, WAKAYAMA, etc, were bombed by the US Forces. The people back home have probably become tense.

21 April

In the evening at supper time the road leading to the west side of the 2d outpost was so crowded with visitors that it was hardly passable. Most of them were wives. Some had gained vantage points from where they could see better and were waving their hands, and others even threw goods into [the stockade]. If it were our Army, the wives would feel ashamed; they would look down upon their own husbands and probably could not face anyone. It must be the difference in races. That is the reason they surrender without fighting.

22 April

At 0100 some prisoners escaped and 30 soldiers were sent out to search for them. Three of them were captured and at 0400 they were returned. At about 1230 the 3 escaped prisoners were killed by stabbing as a warning to the others. Everything which might be used as a weapon was confiscated by evening. By an order everyone brought in his weapons and the guardhouse was crowded with people.

23 April

The articles confiscated since yesterday were being brought since early this morning into the guardhouse, and crowded it. Today a prisoner became ill and went to the hospital. 3 new prisoners came in.

In the afternoon Cpl NAGASAWA and 4 men inspected the personal belongings of the prisoners but found nothing of value.

24 April

Nothing unusual happened today, but up until the present 11 prisoners are said to be missing. How they escaped is indeed disturbing. The guard will become from now on even more strict and a night watch has been established to make its rounds among the prisoners.

28 April

In the near future they may release a part of the INDONE-SIANS. Therefore, there were many officers of the BUTAI coming in and out for personal history examinations, etc. The prisoners understand our Army and carry out our orders. Even when we are on guard they approach us in a friendly manner.

29 April

We celebrate the Emperor's Birthday for the first time since the outbreak of the Great East Asia War. At 1015 we performed at the outpost the ceremony of worshipping [the Emperor] from afar. The Co also took part in the ceremony at the Bn Hq. At the same time the prisoners performed it in their respective stockades.

30 April

Today too, was the celebration of the Emperor's birthday and I think the city was more crowded than it has ever been. I spent most of the day guarding the prisoners. Even when their officers are hit over the head by our soldiers they cannot complain for they are prisoners of war. When I think about the prisoners, I keenly feel that we must not lose the war.

It was unusual for Japanese soldiers guarding POWs to keep diaries, not least because Japanese combat units regarded looking after prisoners to be a demeaning duty. This diarist was delighted when his unit was told it was to be relieved. By late May they were busy conducting security searches of villages on the outskirts of Bandoeng. Initially, the POW camp had held some Javanese who had been serving in the Dutch military, but on 2 May they were released. On 10 May more Dutch prisoners arrived and he noted that the 'Indonesians are friendly, but the Dutch seem arrogant and hard to get on with'. By 19 September 1942 he seems to have been on his way to Guadalcanal. His eventual fate is unknown.

Tuesday 14 – Monday 20 April 1942

Colonel Lewis Brereton, US Army Air Force, meets with Wavell and watches the journalist Clare Booth Luce leave India by air

During early 1942 Brereton had been placed under Wavell in command of the Allied air forces in Java, but this headquarters melted away almost as soon as it appeared. By April 1942 he was organizing the newly arrived US 10th Air Force in India. Like most prominent Americans in New Delhi, he felt that the eyes of the Indian Bureau, the local British Indian security service, were always upon him. Clare Booth Luce was an accomplished playwright and journalist. In 1942 she was undertaking an extended tour through India, China and Burma for Life *magazine.*

New Delhi, 14–15 April

Heard some interesting and somewhat disturbing information that most of our business is known to the British, undoubtedly through their Secret Service which does an efficient job on everybody. Had a staff meeting on the subject of security and told them I would not tolerate any more leakages.

New Delhi, 18 April

General Wavell is very gloomy about the Burma situation. Friction continues between the Chinese and the British. General Stilwell also is having difficulties with the Chinese generals. A definite threat is developing against the Chinese east flank and the Chinese are complaining bitterly that the British withdrawal of the past 36 hours left Chinese west flank completely unprotected . . .

Karachi, India, 19 April

Awarded decorations for the Rangoon and Port Blair raids and then inspected the troops. After the review, the messes and kitchen were inspected by a party, including war correspondents. The only wood available for shelter construction was boxes from motor and airplane crates . . . After the inspection went for a swim. Clare Booth Luce, on her way back to the States, fell overboard in her swimming suit and Captain Mahoney, General Brady's aide, and Col. Merian C. Cooper, former movies producer, gallantly went to her rescue, but in the end Mrs. Luce very nearly had to rescue her rescuers.

Karachi, India, 20 April

Mrs. Luce left for the States today. She seemed genuinely sorry to be leaving, as I believe she had formed a liking for the members of the Tenth Air Force. I'll bet her departure was better than anything she wrote in *The Women*. She

arrived at the airport 40 minutes late and threw the British
Overseas A.C. into a complete state of confusion. She staged
one of the best helpless-woman acts I have ever witnessed.
She lost her coat; then she lost her camera; and finally had
everyone in a dither. She walked right by the customs and
immigration people who had their mouths open. As we
walked down the gangway she grinned and whispered she
didn't think she would have any trouble with her papers.
Previously she had been worried for fear of censorship on
the manuscript she was carrying. As she entered the plane
she gave the captain a very calculating glance and melted
him down to her size, too.

*There was much three-way friction between the British, Americans and
Chinese in India. British imperialists feared Chinese designs on Burma
and were even more nervous about Roosevelt's proclaimed sympathies
for Gandhi's Indian independence movement. Americans in India were
conscious of constant surveillance by the British Indian secret service,
ever watchful for some ingenious political outburst in favour of independence. British paranoia also extended to intense censorship of
newspapers and broadcasts. Clare Booth Luce had interviewed
Jawaharlal Nehru, Chiang Kai-shek and General 'Vinegar Joe' Stilwell.
As she well knew, there was tight control on the material that journalists
could take out of India.*

*In October 1943 Brereton would move to become Commanding
General of the 9th Air Force in the European Theater. After the war he
was Chairman of the Military Liaison Committee to the Atomic Energy
Commission in Washington. He retired in 1948. SEE ALSO PP. 117–19.*

Saturday 18 April 1942

Robert J. Casey, a journalist with the Pacific Fleet, hears the impact of the Doolittle Raid on Tokyo

Robert J. Casey lived with the men of the fleet, as he had previously endured the war with forces in France, Luxembourg, Belgium, England, Africa and the Mediterranean. A writer and journalist for the Chicago Daily News, *he was an assigned reporter on the aircraft carrier USS* Hornet. *The Doolittle Raid, launched from the* Hornet *on 18 April 1942, was one of the most innovative operations undertaken by the United States in the war in Asia and the Pacific. Although conceived as an operation to divert Japanese resources from other theatres, and to boost Allied morale, it also had strategic consequences.*

It was a weird experience this, listening to what you might call Japan's Pearl Harbor. That afternoon we weren't given much information about whose they were or what had happened to them. But we were kept in no doubt at all about what they had done. We were close enough to hear the crescendo of Tokio's hysteria, to read in the tone rather than in the substance of the popular outcry the fear that had seized upon the capital. And there at sea, fluttering about on a patrol that seemed too timely for pure coincidence, we got perspectives on the raid that never did come out in the official reports.

Whatever might have been the effect of bombs on factories and railroad centers and the like, the upheaval in the morale of a people whose stoicism had seemed their chief national characteristic was complete. We weren't to know for many a day what material damage had been done on Honshu Island. But had we based our estimates on what we heard that night as relays of hysterical announcers pushed a somewhat un-intelligible commentary in English over the beam to America, we should have thought the whole of Japan in ashes.

On one of the domestic frequencies a shrieking woman broke in repeatedly, hour after hour, to call for donors to a hitherto neglected blood bank. The captain of our ship, who had been listening to the bulletins with close interest, interpreted her plea with some surprise.

'The woman's had a shock,' he said, '*a bad shock.* Japanese women don't get that way over nothing. Maybe this bombing amounts to something after all . . .'

The woman was chattering disjointedly of the horrors of bombing – broken bodies and tenuously held lives. She spoke when she was coherent at all in the language of the hospitals, of first-degree burns and amputations, severed arteries and tourniquets, blood types and blood transfusions – an amazing program for a people supposed to care nothing about human life. But even if she'd been talking about nothing more unusual than new ways to cook rice you'd have known that the terror had arrived in Tokio. It was her voice rather than her subject matter that conveyed her message of panic. Her choking intensity gave you the notion that she was one citizen of Japan who wouldn't give much for her chances of being alive tomorrow.

The captain, long a student of the Japanese language and philosophies, read the principal message of her jeremiad in the things she left unsaid.

'It's fear, of course,' he said. 'She thinks this is going to be something like the 1923 earthquake only worse. But she's bewildered, too. The Japanese high command said that it couldn't happen. And it has happened. However it was done, it was done. And the generals, the protectors of the Emperor, have lost face – and death would be preferable to that. This woman sees catastrophe threatening the country's leadership . . .'

The woman went on with her keening: 'Give your blood as the men at the front are giving theirs. Your lives are in danger. Your country is in danger. Tomorrow – even tonight – your children may be blown to bits. Give your blood. Save them. Save yourselves. Save Japan.' The captain nodded gravely . . .

Noon dispatches mentioned that General Muto, former chief of home defense, had been ordered to a line regiment with a possible stopover at Hara-kiri. Muto was asked how the bombing happened and apparently he didn't know any more of the answers than anybody else.

In early 1942 a chance observation that it was possible to launch army twin-engined bombers from an aircraft carrier accidentally caught the attention of US fleet commander Admiral Ernest J. King. He assigned James Doolittle to organize and lead a suitable air group. Volunteer aircrews embarked on a vigorous programme of special training. The new carrier USS Hornet was sent to the Pacific to undertake the navy's part of the mission, but even her commanding officer had no idea of his ship's secret mission. The Hornet steamed towards a planned launching point some 400 miles from Japan. However, on 18 April enemy picket boats were encountered much further east than expected and so the planes took off while still more than 600 miles from Tokyo. All sixteen B-25s attacked the Tokyo area, with a few hitting Nagoya. Afterwards, none of the planes reached their planned landing grounds at Chinese airfields and most had to bring their aircraft down in the countryside. The Japanese high command was deeply embarrassed and this event would spur an acrimonious debate in Tokyo over strategy, leading to an effort to eliminate the risk of further raids by the early destruction of America's aircraft carriers. This decision pointed the way to the Battle of Midway in late May 1942. SEE ALSO PP. 278–9.

Monday 27 April 1942

Angela Bolton, a British nurse in India, visits the Calcutta bazaar

Angela Bolton was born near Preston in Lancashire in 1918 and had attended Winckley Square Convent School. She had qualified as a State Registered Nurse in 1940 and had joined the Queen Alexandra Imperial Military Nursing Service in 1941 after training in Liverpool and Manchester. By 1942 she had been posted to India, where she served in military hospitals and on the hospital boats that plied Burma's major rivers.

I tried to disentangle the odours that assailed my nostrils as I entered the Aladdin's Cave of curiosities: cow dung from the fires, spices from the stall near the entrance, horse urine from the passing *gharies* and an all-pervading coconut smell from the barber's stall, which took me back to my aunt's shack on Formby shore. The ripe fruit brings its own gallimaufry of scents, attracting flies in their hundreds. The poor babies' eyes are covered in flies too and their pathetic pot-bellied bodies are wasted and shrivelled. By observation we discovered that the brick-red spittle on the pavements was the result of the native habit of chewing *pan*, a mixture of areca nut and betel leaf.

We noticed a terribly disabled man without fingers shuffling around on a little cart, begging for backsheesh. Is he a leper, I wonder? There are so many poor people wandering about who look as if they never have enough to eat. No one takes any notice! Little boys offered to carry our purchases in baskets on their heads, first twisting a grey rag of padding turban-wise to protect themselves. They all swarmed around shouting for attention until a smart, khaki-clad Indian policeman raised his baton to chase them away. It is quite alarming to see the desperate need for a few annas.

The stall-holders in their clean white *dhotis* look fairly prosperous. Many of the young men own a bicycle, which they share with a friend, one of them sitting on the handle-bars. Other young men go about in pairs holding hands, reminding me of the way young English girls walk about arm-in-arm at a certain age to give themselves courage in facing the world – and in particular the young men in it. The bicycle bells ring in the time as their owners try to break through the solid phalanx of overloaded buses and Jehu-driven taxis.

When we went into a bank to change some money there was a white cow lying by the counter chewing his cud. No one attempted to drive it out. It was rather lovely with a hump on its back, the eyes as liquidly dark as a Jersey cow's. What a contrast the great granite buildings make with the dusty excremental street outside, where the heat blasts you with its foetid breath. Beggars accosted us all the way back to the Grand Hotel where we were rescued by the rick-shaw wallahs, who drove us home.

Angela Bolton was serving in a well-appointed hospital ward reserved for officers in Calcutta. There she soon discovered there were many more patients in the hospital through tropical illness, especially malaria, than through battlefield injury. Free time was spent socializing in the various local clubs and cinemas with officers from the Royal Artillery, interspersed with occasional visits to the bazaar. Most people recently arrived from Britain were shocked by social conditions in the major Indian cities. Angela would not be in Calcutta for long, since she was soon posted to a military hospital nearer to the front line in Assam. SEE ALSO PP. 289–90, 467–8.

MAY 1942

IN MAY 1942, only six months after Pearl Harbor, the Japanese 'New Order' in Asia and the Pacific reached its furthest extent. Surprise, audacity and extraordinary effort on the part of ordinary soldiers had permitted Japan to conduct an eastern version of Blitzkrieg warfare not unlike Hitler's in the west, the extreme brevity of some campaigns allowing a great deal to be achieved with relatively small numbers of troops. Tokyo's forces had also moved with astonishing speed across some supposedly 'impassable' terrain and in Burma, which it now controlled almost completely, only 8,000 Japanese casualties had been incurred, while the Allies had suffered five times as heavily.

During May a Japanese seaplane, launched from a submarine, undertook a reconnaissance of southern Africa, including northern Madagascar and the South African port of Durban. Operations were planned against the Aleutian Islands, and Japan seemed poised to achieve its dream of an Asian–Pacific destiny. However, in India and Burma it had failed to recognize the vulnerability of its British opponent, and so hesitated, while in the Pacific it began to run up against the industrial power of the United States. For both these reasons its advance was slowing and would soon stop. This was an outcome that Japan's supreme naval commander, Admiral Yamamoto, had predicted before the war had begun.

On 6 May General Wainwright surrendered all American

and Filipino forces on Corregidor, although some fighting continued on Mindanao. From this point on the Philippine campaign would be increasingly a matter of guerrilla warfare. General Douglas MacArthur began an operation in New Guinea and the Solomons designed to prevent the Japanese from capturing Port Moresby and to bring their southward advance to a halt.

At sea the dominant mode of warfare was the aircraft carrier. During the Battle of the Coral Sea, two carrier task forces searched for each other and then fought the first major naval engagement in history in which the two fleets did not come into contact with one another. The Japanese formation, consisting of the carrier *Shoho* and four cruisers, was heading for Port Moresby in the hope of strengthening Japan's position on Papua New Guinea. However, on 7 May aircraft from the *Yorktown* and the *Lexington* sank the *Shoho*, forcing the Japanese fleet to retire. The following day the two fleets – out of sight, but within aircraft range – continued to engage each other. The US carrier *Lexington* was sunk and the Japanese carrier *Shokaku* badly damaged. The situation on the *Lexington* in particular reflected the problems of damage control, the first serious explosion occurring about an hour after she had been attacked. Over the next seven hours, spreading fires and further explosions culminated in her destruction. After this sea battle Port Moresby would cease to be a serious strategic objective for the Japanese.

The increasing numbers of submarines deployed by the United States began to take their toll. On 11 May the US submarine S-42 sank the Japanese cruiser *Okinoshima* off the coast of New Britain. A week later the submarines *Tautog* and *Triton* sank two Japanese submarines.

In Burma almost all territory was in Japanese hands and commanders such as 'Vinegar Joe' Stilwell were lucky to escape capture. At various points Japanese troops even entered India. Their new forward headquarters was set up in the mountainous area of Imphal on the border. To consolidate their hold on the peninsula from Burma south into Thailand, the Japanese set about constructing the notorious Thai–Burma railway using slave labour drawn from local populations and prisoners of war. The initial group of POWs, often referred to as 'A' Force and numbering more than 3,000 men, were transported from Changi gaol in Singapore in the early summer of 1942, enduring unspeakable conditions on the Japanese ships *Tohohashi Maru* and *Celebes Maru*, packed in the holds with almost no food or water. Many died during the journey north. Those who survived came ashore at Margui and Tavoy in Burma, whence they marched about 20 miles to a base camp at Thanbyuzayat. Gradually they were distributed to work camps throughout Burma and Thailand along the length of the 265-mile railway they were to help construct.

Behind the scenes, intelligence was slowly becoming more important, and throughout 1942 Allied efforts to read Japanese signals traffic improved. Although not all the Japanese codes were broken, more and more trained operators and Japanese-speakers were becoming available. It was through signal intelligence that Admiral Nimitz learned of Japanese efforts to concentrate its naval power for actions against the island of Midway in late May, paving the way for American success in a major battle the following month.

Monday 4 May 1942

Charles R. Bond, an American pilot with the Flying Tigers, is shot down over Kunming in southern China by Japanese Zeros

Charles R. Bond Jr was born in Dallas, Texas on 22 April 1915. He began his military career in July 1932 in the Texas National Guard. He entered the Aviation Cadet Program in March 1938 and was commissioned in February 1939 at Randolph Field. In September 1941, before America had entered the war, Bond joined the 'Flying Tigers' commanded by General Claire Chennault.

What a sight. Before, the city had been spilling over the evacuees, and now they were jammed all over the place. The Japanese bombs had caught them without any warning. Fires engulfed the city. Many buildings and houses were blown to bits.

After one last look I concentrated on my landing

approach. I slowed down and moved the lever for the flaps and landing gear forward. Suddenly I heard several loud explosions. The noise stunned me. I immediately concluded that my landing gear hydraulic system had blown up. I had been having trouble with it operating correctly the last several days but couldn't find anything wrong with it. I decided to try to recycle the gear lever. When I reached down, I cried out in pain. I had stuck my left hand into a raging fire!

I swung my head around and looked to my rear. There they were. Three Jap Zeros right on my tail and firing like mad! The explosions were their rounds of ammunition hitting my armor plate behind my seat. The bullets had gone through my fuselage tanks, which still had a few gallons of fuel in it, before impacting the armor plate. The fuselage tank had exploded, and the fire was shipping into my lower rear cockpit and then up around my legs.

What a stupe I had been, I had become so engrossed with the bombing scene below that I had made the fatal mistake that a fighter pilot should never get·caught doing: I didn't suspect enemy fighters in the area.

The Japs had laid this attack on a little differently. They knew our situation from the two reconnaissance flights that preceded the bombers. They decided to forgo the fighters as bomber escorts and hold them off and away from the field with the hope of catching all of us when we returned – low on ammunition and gas.

For a split second I considered giving up, but something wouldn't let me. I leaned forward as far as my seat belt would permit, closed my eyes because the fire had begun to engulf me, and reached over with my right hand to grasp the canopy crank and rolled it fully back. I unhooked my seat belt with my left hand and put both hands on the stick to make the ship climb abruptly and roll over one-half turn to the right. I took my hands off the control column and reached for the right side of the cockpit to get out of the seat.

The airstream grabbed me as the upper part of my body protruded outside the cockpit. It dragged me out. I had forgotten my earphone connection to the radio plug, but the force of the wind tore it loose. I knew I was out of the airplane and opened my eyes. One second the blue sky and the next the ground. I was tumbling. I looked down to find the metal ring to pull my parachute and jerked it wildly. I felt a tugging and then a violent jerk. I was in the parachute straps, floating.

Suddenly I became terrified. Those dirty bastards will strafe me like they did Henry Gilbert at Rangoon. Automatically I started praying – out loud. I prayed devoutly to God with my eyes closed, and then opened them to look for the Zeros. Fortunately, they had pulled away and were heading south.

Looking down, I saw the ground rushing at me. I would hit backward if I didn't do something, so I tried to kick around in my harness, and I did get about halfway around when I hit. I fell across some large clods of earth in a rice paddy. The parachute gradually floated to the ground beside me. I sat up and realised that I still had the rip cord right tightly grasped in my right hand.

I landed in a Chinese cemetery ... I felt a burning sensation on my neck and shoulder and suddenly realised that my scarf and flying suit were on fire. I hurried to a small stream flowing through the cemetery and laid down on my back and wallowed in the water.

Charles Bond had been saved by the armour plating behind the seat of his fighter aircraft. Although his hands and upper body were badly burned, by June 1942 he would be back on active duty. In October 1942 he rejoined the Army Air Corps. A year later, he became Chief of the Air Division in the United States Military Mission to the USSR in Moscow. Bond was credited with ten victories, was shot down twice and was awarded China's Fifth Order of the Cloud Banner and Seven Star Wing Medal. He survived the war and returned to America.

Lieutenant Miyoshi escapes death for the fourth time on Mindanao in the Philippines

Lieutenant Miyoshi served with the 7th Company of Japan's 124th Infantry Regiment. Little is known about him. He was fighting on the island of Mindanao in the southern Philippines, where some of the last American and Filipino troops had held out against the Japanese invasion. Although Japanese troops had arrived at Davao on 20 December 1941, they were few in number and the Japanese had not sent enough to control the island until April.

This morning we washed our faces and bathed in LANAO Lake, and I felt very refreshed: even the breakfast was more tasty. After a short march, we engaged the enemy, and the rifle fire in front was intense. Wondering what the situation was, I concealed myself on the side of the road, and while I was concealed, an enemy mortar shell burst close to me. Everybody was frightened. Apparently the enemy had guns because I heard their fire continuously. There were loud voices calling for the medical offr and the men to advance forward. There must have been some sacrifices already. My platoon received an order to contact 6 Coy and besiege and attack the enemy. Immediately after coming to the mountain, we discovered enemy movement. We fired the LMG continuously and watched the enemy fall. The enemy did not seem to know our position. We advanced again because of the danger of remaining in one place too long. We tried to cut off the enemy line of retreat but due to the complicated terrain, the severe continuous fire from the enemy, and the shells from our troops which were falling short, we could not advance. We mainly observed the enemy movement. Our position being higher than the enemy's their situation, trenches, MG emplacements, etc were clearly seen. In the area around the foot of the mountain and the road, severe fighting was in progress and the violent sound of the rifles and the guns continued. The enemy attempted to flee in a small boat to the small island in Lake LANAO. Our MG's and A/tk fired violently at the boat, splashing water all around it. Probably the men in the boat were unconscious or they must have been close to death. However the boat was still heading slowly toward the island. Life must have hung in the balance for those in the boat. The remnants who went into the ravine were spotted, and 15–16 of them were shot. 2 Sec rejoiced. At that moment, Sup Pte YOSHIMATSU became a casualty with a bullet through his left knee, and then I turned my head when Sgt YOSHIMURA cried out, and I realized I had been hit by an enemy bullet. Very fortunately, the bullet hit my sword, pierced through my wallet tearing the bills, and stopped. I must have been under the protection of divine grace. If the bullet had been 1/8 of an inch off, I would have been wounded in the thigh. This was the fourth escape from death. During this time, we saw the enemy retreating from the hill in front of us, but we attacked and captured them.

Allied forces made their last formal stand in the Philippines in the area of Mount Dansalan and Lake Lanao. Miyoshi's diary underlines the point that soldiers on all sides were highly superstitious, attributing fortunate events to divine providence or lucky talismans that they carried. It is also interesting for its references to resistance by the indigenous population, to whom he referred as the 'savage Moros'. Miyoshi's diary would eventually be captured on Guadalcanal and translated for intelligence purposes.

Early May 1942

Donald Peacock arrives at a new POW camp in Surabaya in the Netherlands East Indies

Donald Peacock was born at Stapleton in North Yorkshire in 1919 and went to Darlington Grammar School. He was training as a journalist when he was called up in 1939. By early 1942 he was a leading air-craftsman serving at RAF Seletar near Singapore. He had escaped from Singapore in February 1942 on the Empire Star, *only to be taken prisoner during March at Batavia (now Jakarta). He was then held in POW camps further east, at Semarang and Surabaya, with many Dutch and Australian soldiers.*

Late that night, after ten hours on the move, we were turfed off the train at Surabaya, Java's second city, in the east of the island. The place was either blacked-out or the power had failed. We picked up our loads and dragged ourselves blindly through endless pitch-black streets, goaded on by guards anxious to be rid of us.

At long last we turned through a gate in a tall bamboo fence. We stumbled, still in the dark, on to a muddy square. There, weary and drenched in sweat, we were herded about while Nips counted us, recounted us and counted us again. When it was finally decided that no-one had gone off to lead a resistance movement, we were addressed by an interpreter. He impressed upon us that our sole purpose in life so long as we remained in his camp was to salute or bow to all Nip soldiers who came within range. Otherwise we would be pukuled. So we came to learn the Malay word pukul, to clout, perhaps the commonest word in the Malay-speaking Nip's vocabulary. A little more bumbling about in the dark and we were pushed and shoved into what had apparently been a school. Now every classroom, in fact every cupboard it seemed, was bulging with hungry Dutchmen. But somehow or other, after a little juggling of bodies, space was made in the corridors for us to get our heads down.

We understood why the Dutch were so hungry when we queued for breakfast next morning. We got a mess-tin of watery glue garnished with the bloated bodies of a few rice-weevil grubs. This was our introduction to what the Dutch called pap. And it was as well to get used to it, for it was the dish with which we were to start every day, with very few exceptions, until the war ended.

We gathered that the camp consisted of what had been Surabaya's Lyceum School and playground. Our arrival meant that there were now 2000 prisoners milling miserably about inside its 15 ft bamboo fences, under the watchful eyes of armed guards posted in sentry towers. There was little time to glean the full facts of life Lyceum-style before we newcomers were hustled back on to the mud square, together with all our possessions . . .

Next came the kit inspection. We stood in line, each with all his worldly goods piled in front of him, all ready we thought for the Nips to plunder them. But, to our surprise, they didn't take much. The odd super-optimist who had hung on to a camera was quickly relieved of it. They were contraband. So too were tin helmets, which was a minor disaster because, later, helmets which survived in other camps were to prove first-class frying pans. On top of my little heap in a purposely prominent position was my diary. I thought that if I placed it under their noses the Nips would be sure to ignore it. But to my consternation an English-speaking guard picked it up and began thumbing through it. There wasn't really much chance of his reading my short-hand; it often baffles me. But I was very relieved when he gave up and tossed the book back on my heap.

Fortunately neither at this time nor at any time during my captivity did the Nips attempt to steal any money we might have. And some of us had what to the Nips must have been quite considerable sums. We had been getting paid right up to the surrender with little chance to spend it. In my case my parents, showing admirable foresight, had sent me £50 just before I left Singapore. It formed the foundation of a last-ditch emergency fund which I managed to eke out over most of my time as Pow. At last, the indignities of the kit inspection over, we were dismissed. We were now free to get together with the camp's established residents to swap experiences ... and in many cases a few possessions as well ...

The only chance of supplementing what seemed to us at the time a starvation diet was to get on an outside working party where, if you were lucky, it might be possible to do a quick cash deal with a street-trader. There was tremendous competition to join these parties, particularly among the Dutch. Many of them had families living, so near and yet so far, just on the other side of the bamboo fence. Wives and children, who had not yet been interned, kept watch on the working parties from a discreet distance in the hope of exchanging a smile or a wave with the men who had been taken away from them.

The work consisted mainly of filling in air-raid shelters ... We had some thug-like Nip navy types as foremen. With continual shouts of 'Koorah' and 'Lakas' and the occasional clout or kick they made us work non-stop all day and we never got even a glimpse of a street-trader.

There was just one crumb of comfort. Working nearby were some Nip sailors who were being treated as badly, if not worse than we were. And they, we gathered, were men who had helped to rout the Allies in the Battle of the Java Sea. Unfortunately for them, however, their ship had sunk and they had failed dutifully to go down with her. For this gross misconduct, we were told, they were in disgrace and banned forever from returning home.

Don Peacock's observations about the treatment of Japanese sailors are telling. Many have pondered why Japanese treatment of POWs was so bad, but in reality it was in line with Tokyo's general military culture of brutality in which their own servicemen were very badly treated. SEE ALSO PP. 369–71, 557–9.

Tuesday 12 May 1942

Hatsuye Egami, a Japanese American woman, spends a last morning in her home town of Pasadena in California before heading for internment

In May 1942 over 100,000 people of Japanese descent, most of whom were American citizens, were rounded up within the United States and interned as enemy aliens. They were kept in camps for the duration of the war. Hatsuye Egami was a first-generation Japanese woman who, together with her four daughters, joined 5,000 other internees at the Tulare Assembly Center in central California. In the United States, German Americans and Italian Americans were not treated in the same way.

Up at five. We had thrown ourselves on the hardwood floor spread with thin blankets and slept. Very simple. The fire that had burned in the fireplace the whole night through is still burning faintly. The fireplace that the whole family loved. Beside it we had talked and laughed through that last night. And must we really part from this room now?

'It's war! We can't be sentimental, we can't,' I had thought, but the urge to become sentimental which I had suppressed with each event seemed to gush forth as I gazed on the fire that still continued to sparkle a bit. But that was for only a moment; I raised my eyes, gave my head a shake, and stood up, my good spirit restored.

The children woke up, too, and we all began our last preparations with much hullabaloo. Evacuation was to be carried out in three days and we were to go on the first day. Mr. Matsumoto, who lived across the street and who was to leave on the third day, came over to help us.

'Baggage is limited to the amount that can be carried in both hands,' was the Army's orders. From what we had heard from people who had already evacuated, however, it seemed that, in the end, those who took a great deal had the advantage, and we certainly racked our heads about the baggage.

'This won't do. That won't do either!' we said as we packed and repacked our bundles, and now the final results were stacked up in the living room. Just about the time preparations were done and we felt relieved, Mr. Castro, whom we were accustomed to calling in, showed his robust form, wrinkling his dark-red face into a smile. He carried off lightly the bags which my eldest daughter and I had sweated so to jam full of things and had thought so heavy!

Since yesterday, we Pasadena Japanese have ceased to be human beings – we are now simply numbers or things. We are no longer 'Egamis' but the number 23324. A tag with that number is on every suitcase and bag. Even on our breasts are tied large tags with this same number – 23324! Again, a sad and tragic feeling grips my heart!

Our neighbour, Mrs. Rasparry, brings cocoa for the children and coffee for the elders. Feeling a warmth of affection, I drink the coffee. The taxi that we had called yesterday arrived at 7:15 sharp, and now we must start.

Pursuing Mr. Castro's truck, which left a moment before us, the taxi carrying our little family of six, picks up speed – we are going! Mrs. Rasparry waves her hand, as if, I thought, they would tear off, and sees us off. For five years we had lived as neighbours, forgetting racial differences entirely. As if we were relatives, we had associated with her. I don't think that we shall ever forget how much she has done for us since the evacuation problem came upon us. On May 10, Mother's Day, I sent her bright red roses. The fact that she shed tears and showed her appreciation will surely remain with us as warm memories for a long, long time.

At half-past seven the taxi reached California Street, where the train we were to board was lined up – car after car after car. The faces of Caucasians seemed to overflow the place. It was a deluge of sad faces. Beautiful city. Educational city. City of the Rose Parade. City that has been friendly to the Japanese to the last! This is our last morning with Pasadena! Whether we laugh or what we do – it is no use now!

We do not know at all where we are going or what is to become of us even in the next moment, but among the Japanese no one is crying. Those who are crying are rather white Americans and Negroes and 'foreigners' who came to see us off. They are honest and simple. It seems that when they want to cry, they can raise their voices and cry as they wish. It is the Japanese, who are being sent off, who are consoling them! . . .

The train runs on. It continues to advance into the famous and expansive Mohave Desert. Presently, we pass places where water is trickling in the creek. Pretty mountain birds are gathered cheerfully. In the green meadows cows are grazing and, above, white clouds are floating gently. In contrast to the giant cacti that could be mistaken for large trees, that I gazed on with surprise, I find wild flowers whose names I don't know, smiling at me. While nation fights nation, and people kill each other and suffer, how peaceful nature is. Was nature always so peaceful and so immense and so beautiful as this? I gazed as if for the first time.

I hear a burst of joyous laughter, and turn around. Four or five pretty girls are talking with some soldier-boys and they are laughing together wholesomely. These seem to be harmless and cute soldiers. I would not like to see these innocent soldiers sent to war to be killed or maimed.

The train carrying its load of disturbed thoughts finally approaches its destination. The sun of the desert suddenly disappears, and the surroundings are enveloped in a grayish dusk. The journey required eleven hours, and it is about eight PM. Tulare at last. People are looking out of the windows and I do so, too. Beyond the road by the tracks there is a place that looks like a race-track. The grandstand is filled with Japanese, clustered together, silently, like ants. Can it be that those who arrived in the Assembly Center before us are out to welcome us newcomers?

The train comes to a standstill. Those in the front car begin to get off in an orderly way. Our historic entrance into an internment camp has begun. As I am in the last car, I observe the line quietly. Mothers with children in their arms, sturdy youths, tottering old men leaning on sticks, cheerful children, beautiful lasses – I was too far off to see the facial expression of each person, but the flow of the moving human line, how silent and gloomy!

The wave of the line flows gently along. And pretty soon our family, too, becomes one more wave in the silent stream and we find ourselves moving slowly forward. I am carrying two suitcases and a blanket. The camp lies beyond the road, and, as soldiers guard us, we reach the gate.

Tulare Assembly Center!
My eldest daughter says, 'Mama, if we enter this gate we shall never be able to come out again until the end of the war!' It seems so obvious, but no one laughs. Someone answered: 'Really, let's remember this feeling. This is probably an event we shall never experience again during our lifetime.' In the next moment we finally pass the gate and become residents of the Center.

When Hatsuye Egami arrived at the Tulare Assembly Center she discovered that they were located at a camp in the middle of a semi-desert. Family accommodation consisted of the most basic barrack-type huts. Her family's room was located in a cement-floored hut, furnished with cots. The women's toilets and wash facilities offered no privacy. The occupants did their best to make a show of normality, organizing talent shows and a popular Fourth of July parade. Some Japanese Americans had presented themselves for internment wearing their First World War US military service uniforms with medals. Most Japanese Americans

The Japanese Advance into Burma, 1943

living in California ran small family farms or local stores. The Bank of America took over much of their property and sold it to local agricultural businesses which benefited considerably from these cheaply acquired assets.

Nothing is known of the post-war fate of Hatsuye Egami. Her diary was preserved by American Quakers working with the American Friends Service Committee, who assisted many internees during the war.

Sunday 17 – Monday 18 May 1942

Robert Moody Smith, a pilot with the Flying Tigers, observes the English on the run in Burma

Rangoon in Burma had been evacuated at the beginning of March and by the end of that month Robert Moody Smith's colleagues, flying with a unit of the American Volunteer Group in Burma, had also been withdrawn. During April the Japanese had entered Lashio, cutting off China's only land transport route to Burma. As a result all supplies from the Allies had to be moved into China by air. General Alexander, the British commander, decided to withdraw to new positions in the Chindwin and Irrawaddy.

Before the British evacuated Rangoon, they burned the supplies on the docks. Over 400 brand new trucks were burned. They could have been loaded with gasoline and supplies and sent up the road to China, but there was no organization. Every one of our men got a jeep to drive. Before the supplies were destroyed, everyone helped himself to gin, shotgun shells, radios, bolts of cloth, perfume, shoe polish, and anything else of value. The goods would have been worth a fortune in China.

Most of the physical work in Burma was done by imported Indians. When the bombs started to fall, they left. The Chinese owned most of the shops, the British ran the government, and the Burmese became monks and wore yellow robes.

On February 22 the British let the lepers and insane out of

the asylums and prisons. Rangoon was in flames. Shaper and his convoy left the next day, heading for the airfield at Magwe in central Burma. Many of the trucks were driven by RAF enlisted men. Some of the trucks towed jeeps; some jeeps had another jeep dragging from the rear. Shaper had a dismantled airplane in his International truck – a Stinson 105 that had belonged to U Saw, the Burmese leader. The trucks were loaded with spare parts for the P-40s, ammunition, and much loot picked up from the Rangoon docks. They had two Studebaker gas trucks driven by RAF men. Paul Frillman, our chaplain, led another convoy loaded with miscellaneous supplies and many cases of whiskey. He also had about 20 Eurasian girls who had been quite friendly with the members of the AVG.

Many of the shopkeepers gave their keys to the AVG when they left Rangoon. 'Take what you want and then burn it,' they said.

When Bill left Rangoon there were only nine pilots and their P-40s remaining in the city. Bob Neale and Snuffy Smith were the last to fly out on February 28, retreating to the field at Magwe. Rangoon fell to the Japanese ground troops on March 1. All of the loot was carried on one truck. In an accident on the Burma Road the truck and all of its cargo was completely destroyed . . .

British trucks, mostly empty except for gasoline and driven by Englishmen, are passing daily, escaping from Burma; 30 or 40 a day have gone by for the past few weeks. Most of the trucks are American-made.

London radio broadcasts talk of the heroic British soldiers in their withdrawal from Burma. They put their shoulders to the wheel to get the trucks out of mudholes. BBC seems to be proud that the Japanese cannot keep up with them. Yet the Chinese are dying in Burma in a desperate fight against the Japanese. The Chinese live on a handful of rice a day, are shod in straw sandels, have no trucks and little mechanical equipment. Even their supply of guns is limited. I know, for I have seen them pass here on the way to the front. They are ill-clad and poorly paid, have little food, and are walking down to Burma. The British are taking empty trucks the other way.

In early May Mandalay had fallen and Japanese troops had even crossed the Burmese border into southern China. By 15 May retreating British forces were arriving in India. With the monsoon season starting, the Japanese had completely over-run Burma, and had increased pressure on China. In the process they had suffered 2,500 casualties, compared to British and Chinese losses of 8,000.

Robert Moody Smith would continue to serve with Claire Chennault's Flying Tigers. When they became the 14th Air Force in mid-1942 he was made responsible for the development of their communications in China. After the war he was treasurer of the Air Volunteer Group Association. SEE ALSO PP. 227–9.

Sunday 24 May 1942

Colonel Paul Bunker, US artillery commander, arrives in Manila after being captured on Corregidor Island in the Philippines

To Parinaqua, Bilibid and Pasay.

Along toward dawn the ship got under way and headed toward Manila. I gazed on Corregidor with mixed feelings. Most of us said we wanted to never see those desolate ruins again. Our crowded deck crawled with life. There was hot drinking water available and Pvt. Robinson made me some tea and another soldier gave me some Vienna sausages.

The ship was slow. Another freighter, with 2 AA guns forward, passed us and steamed toward Pier 7. We sheered right, toward Parinaqua and anchored. Meanwhile, with all deck space jammed, crazy Pyzick said the Japs wanted us to form in order of Groups and debark in that order! A manifest impossibility. Now they brought 'invasion boat' (landing boats) alongside, and our men tumbled aboard via a gangway and a Jacob's ladder on port side forward and another Jacob's ladder on starboard side aft. These boats ride with bow out of water and are quite fast. The scow bow lets down to form a ramp.

On nearing shore, near the Parinaqua beach, we were all forced overboard into water chest-deep, and waded ashore with our stuff on our backs. We still didn't know our destination. We formed on the beach, but groups were so mixed up that we could only form in a column of fours, regardless of Groups. As we landed, we could see long columns of our predecessors moving south along the beach to the main road. The whole bunch was, unfortunately, guarded by cavalry not infantry.

After a short time, 1000 or so of us were counted off and moved out to the highway, the extension to Dewey Boulevard and sat down there until the gang ahead of us moved out in the broiling heat for it must have been nearly noon by now. I shouldered my clothing roll and started, and my burden did not seem excessive at this time. The tar on the pavement stuck to our shoes which were, of course, wet on our feet, making blisters.

Gen. Moore luckily was landed on dry land with all of his baggage and was transported with said baggage to our destination.

As we marched along we could see Filipino curiosity seekers being kept back by Jap sentries. Many grinned at us, but whether in derision or otherwise we could not tell. Downtown, more people lined the streets, but were very quiet.

My load, water soaked as it was, kept getting heavier and heavier, and then Pvt. della Marva and Julian relieved me of it and carried it for me for some hundreds of yards. Three soldiers also took turns at it – and I offered one of them, a husky-looking man, P20 if he would carry it the rest of the way. He refused the offer but spoke cheerily of getting the bundle to our destination. I shouldered the load again and toted it to our first stop, which was probably near the Admiral Hotel. Here some of us got drinks of water. I interviewed the Jap officer in charge of our bunch, pointing to my white stubble of beard and motioning that I wanted to be picked up in the Red Cross truck that was patrolling the column. He roughly repulsed me, barking 'Sit down.'

Our stop was for only a few minutes and then we started again. I knew now that I could never carry that clothing roll much farther, so I just left it where I'd dropped it and had no time to remove anything from it. So I stepped off, bereft of every single article of worldly goods except what I had on my person!

Even so, lightened, I found the going tougher and tougher. As far as you could see, ahead, the prisoners were plodding along, with no sign of a stop for rest. We marched to the Elks Club, turned right in front of the Bay View, then slanted left past City Hall to Post Office, over the bridge and onto either Rizal or Quezon Blvd. all this without a rest. I was staggering by this time, and soon fell down in a daze. The Jap guards came and prodded me up and on a bit, but I couldn't make it. They gave me a gallon bottle, empty, and a gas mask case and urged me on. After standing their persecution all I could, I turned on them, tore open my shirt and, with a melodramatic gesture, indicted them to go ahead and shoot and be damned to them. Then they put me through some sort of test (I was dazed and forget what it was) to see if I meant what I said, and then they did a queer thing. They made me kneel and raise my hands over my head and lean backward. Then they made me lie down on the strip of ground in the middle of the boulevard and brought *ice* and put it on my head and chest. They hailed one truck which passed us up. At one time I thought the guards were leading me off into a back street to shoot me, as they are said to have done with 3 officers in Bataan on their march to San Fernando – when they fell out. But instead, they were very kind, and kept ice on my head and solar plexus. (How I enjoyed gnawing hunks off the ice and swallowing them!) Later, they led me across to the sidewalk and I lay there for a long time until the sentry stopped a light pick-up truck and loaded me into it. As I lay there, before starting off, a rock rattled into the truck and hit me on the rebound! I wondered if this was a sample of the feeling the Filipinos have for us now.

The Japanese had initiated what became known as the Bataan Death March for POWs from Bataan on 10 April. Soldiers who fell behind were usually killed and the prisoners were beaten at random. They were also forced to sit in the sun without any shade, helmets or water. A similar fate awaited most soldiers captured on Corregidor in May, since they were ferried to the Bataan peninsula and also forced to march to

their POW camp. Bunker seems to have enjoyed slightly better treat-
ment, perhaps because of his officer status, but he was still lucky to make
it to his final destination. He was soon at Pasay hospital, from where he
was transferred to Bilibid prison in Manila. SEE ALSO PP. 242–3, 310–12,
326–7.

Late May 1942

Rena Krasno, a Jewish teenager in Shanghai, begins university classes and acquires a skeleton

Rena Krasno was a Russian Jewish girl whose family was living in exile
in Shanghai and was therefore under Japanese rule. They were long-
standing residents of Shanghai's famous International Settlement,
having moved there shortly after the Russian Revolution of 1917.
Although conditions there were tolerable, Rena found reading, studying
and especially writing in her diary a vital mental escape from the
pressure of war. In late 1941 she had begun to read medicine at the local
Catholic university.

To escape Shanghai's tightening trap – at least mentally – I
plunge into intensive reading. The need to reach levels
above and beyond the one where I exist has become almost
obsessive. In discussion with friends I quote, I fear
pompously, the Chinese saying:
    'To realize that our knowledge is ignorance is a noble
insight.'
    After much brooding I resolved not to return to teaching
this autumn and instead to enroll in the first year of the
Faculty of Medicine at the Jesuit Université de l'Aurore, to
which my baccalaureate diploma entitles me. This decision
is in some measure the result of my friendship with a French
classmate of mine who early in high school decided to
become a Jesuit priest. During our prolonged walks in the
Koukaza (French) Park we discuss our widely differing
philosophy and aims in life. Although we appear to disagree
on almost everything, we both admire moral and intellectual
ideals – a pursuit from which I, alas, occasionally stray

because to tell the truth I love frivolous pastimes such as dancing and flirtation . . .

The Université de l'Aurore was established by the Jesuits in 1876 in the heart of the French Concession near the Cimetière des Soeurs. Today, its spacious grounds extend on both sides of Avenue Dubail, a wide and busy thoroughfare. Intended at first only for male students, its policy was later liberalized to include women. I spoke to the incredibly handsome Jesuit Père de Breuverie regarding my admission, which he welcomed. He suggested that I buy a skeleton now from a former medical student who no longer needs it. Owning a skeleton is a requirement for our osteology class and, later, when the semester starts I would most probably have to pay more. My parents gladly gave me the necessary money and I brought home 'Oscar,' complete with 'coffin,' a rather nice hinged wooden case which rests under my bed – a silent, friendly presence at night!

Due to the increasing number of deaths in the streets of Shanghai, skeletons are readily available. On the university grounds I saw coolies roll wheelbarrows in the direction of the Salle de Dissection with chemically treated corpses piled topsy-turvy. By the way, Oscar's former owner – who had named him after Oscar Wilde! – explained that students were assigned in pairs to each cadaver and he also suggested that I always select a male for dissection. He told me that no matter how emaciated a woman may be there always remains a thin layer of fat that complicates dissecting.

Shanghai had been one of the first cities to fall during the Sino-Japanese war and so its Chinese-controlled areas had been under Japanese rule since 1937. In 1941 the Japanese then took over the remaining quarters of the city, which had been designated the International Settlement. In the intervening period some additional 20,000 refugees had arrived from central Europe, most of them Jews hoping to escape oppression. Japan had little interest in Hitler's anti-semitic programmes and so Shanghai became a curious Axis refuge for many Jewish families.
SEE ALSO PP. 419–20, 493–4, 665–6.

JUNE 1942

O N 1 JUNE the Japanese combined fleet took up station off the Pacific island of Midway, which Tokyo saw as a useful staging post for a subsequent attack on Hawaii. The Japanese were below strength, having lost two important fleet carriers at the Battle of the Coral Sea the previous month, and were also unaware of two American carrier task forces converging to the north off Midway. The Americans also enjoyed the advantage of reading Japanese signals. While Japanese aircraft were launched in an attack against Midway, the Americans attacked the Japanese carriers, sinking four out of Japan's remaining complement of only nine such vessels. The Americans did not escape damage themselves. The carrier *Yorktown* suffered a tremendous assault and had to be towed from the battle area. Yamamoto ordered the Japanese fleet to retire, but before they could escape American aircraft sank one cruiser, the *Mikuma*, and damaged another, the *Mogami*. Shortly after the battle the badly damaged carrier *Yorktown* and its escorting destroyer were sunk by Japanese submarine action. By 9 June the scale of the Japanese defeat was clear to the high command in Tokyo and it was clear to them that their eastern advance across the Pacific was over.

The events of June 1942 struck a blow to Japan's overall war strategy, which had been based on the course of the First World War, in which countries had fought to a standstill and then sought an armistice. Japan had sought to do the same this time around: that is, to establish dominance in the western Pacific and then simply hold on to the perimeters until the end of the war allowed it to cash in its chips at some reprise of Versailles. However, Japan's failed attempt to capture Midway underlined the difficulty of finding defensible positions in the mid-Pacific.

Nevertheless, Japanese submarines continued some remarkable ventures during June 1942. Submarine operations allowed Japan to dominate the area around the Aleutians, and Australians awoke on 1 June 1942 to discover that three

Japanese midget submarines had managed to penetrate Sydney harbour. Individual boats shelled the coast off Vancouver and then Oregon. Submarine warfare by both the Japanese and German navies created tensions in Washington, with simultaneous calls for more naval resources to guard both the Pacific and the Atlantic coasts of the United States. In fact, unlike their German allies, the Japanese never fully recognized the real potential of submarine warfare.

In the south-west Pacific MacArthur continued his preparations for a major offensive throughout New Guinea and the Solomon Islands, and the construction of support airfields at Milne Bay began. Dominance in the air and eradication of Japanese supply vessels through submarine action would play a central part in the Allied strategy to retake the Pacific islands.

Monday 1 June 1942

Australian diver W. Lance Bullard puts his hand on a Japanese midget submarine in Sydney harbour

Petty Officer W. Lance Bullard was a leading seaman diver on a naval diving boat that was working from the depot ship Kuttabul *at Garden Island in Sydney harbour. The* Kuttabul *had previously been a ferry but had been taken over by the Royal Australian Navy at the outbreak of war. To his amazement, this ship was the victim of a raid by Japanese midget submarines.*

I caught the 7.30 a.m. ferry to Garden Island and one of the ferry hands told us that *Kuttabul* had been torpedoed and sunk. One rating wisecracked, 'Did they sink Garden Island as well?' On arriving at *Kuttabul*, we were amazed to find her on the bottom, with only her funnel and wheel-houses out of the water. To make matters worse, the diving boat and all the gear on board had been blown to pieces.

A torpedo had passed under *Kuttabul* and two Dutch submarines tied up on her southern side and then exploded against the stone wall of Garden Island, immediately under the diving boat and *Kuttabul*. One of the submarines was also severely damaged. While the second one escaped and was still seaworthy.

From then on, we had plenty to do. A motor launch was requisitioned with Wally Messenger as driver. Naval stores supplied pumps, air hose, breast ropes, ladder, etc. which we fitted up and tested. We were in business again and under water by about 9.15 a.m. which was fast work.

I will never forget the scene when we arrived on the sleeping deck of the sunken ship. The sun was shining through a gaping hole in the deck head, giving a green glow to the still water. Blankets and clothing were scattered round the deck. Hammocks were still slung with their occupants as if asleep. There were two men sitting on a locker leaning towards each other as if they had been having a yarn before turning in. There was not a mark on them of any kind. The blast from the explosion must have killed them instantly. I think we passed up seventeen bodies before we were called up and ordered down the Harbour at Taylor's Bay to investigate an oil slick and bubbles coming to the surface there. Roy Coote and I remained dressed. Work on the *Kuttabul* was carried on by members of a diving class which was under instruction.

When we arrived at Taylor's Bay, Lt. Whittle dropped anchor about 50 yards upstream from the bubbles as the tide was running out. The depth was about 85 feet. Roy Coote finished dressing and dropped down. He made a complete circular sweep, trailing his lines. He reported nothing and was called up.

Lt. Whittle then moved the boat further upstream and I dropped down. While descending, I heard a continual throbbing noise in my helmet but assumed it was caused by some boat on the surface. On the bottom I walked out to the full extent of my lines and started to sweep. The bottom was about six inches of mud on hard sand. Walking and trailing heavy breast rope and air hose was hard going and the stirring up of the mud made for poor visibility.

After about 10 minutes I stopped to let the water clear and have a breather, and as the water cleared I caught a glimpse of a steel wire stay about 20 yards away.

I walked towards it and saw a submarine lying practically on an even keel and apparently undamaged. I put my hand on the hull, which was quite warm. Suddenly I realised that the sound I had heard from the time I entered the water was coming from the sub and was quite loud.

Lance Bullard approached the midget submarine without knowing if it was still capable of action or if its crew was still alive. He could hear what seemed to be a motor running, although it eventually turned out to be salt water reacting with the submarine's batteries. In fact the submarine had been depth-charged and was now out of action. Eventually three midget submarines were recovered and put on display. For weeks delighted Australian schoolchildren could be seen scrambling over them. Although the Japanese had come close to hitting their target, the American cruiser USS Chicago, *and although twenty-one sailors were killed in the sinking of the* Kuttabul, *the Japanese raid on Sydney harbour could not be called a military success. In psychological terms, however, the impact was enormous, bringing home the fact that Japan could not only attack northern outposts like Darwin but also raid the populous eastern coast. Japan followed up this raid with further operations, but in subsequent attacks the submarines merely shelled the coastline from a distance.*

Thursday 4 June 1942

Robert J. Casey, journalist with the Pacific Fleet, hopes for the turning of the tide at the Battle of Midway

12:00. Mickey Reeves signalled me to come down to the bridge for a sandwich. So I was right at headquarters when first reports began to come in from our planes. The first message was brief. The Jap carriers had been located, a little belatedly, and they were virtually without air cover ... Apparently all their planes had been sent out to make the conquest of Midway quick and easy. However, the squadron commander of the TBD [Douglas Torpedo Bomber] unit reporting, said that his planes were virtually out of fuel.

'Request permission,' he called, 'to withdraw from action and refuel.'

The admiral's answer was terse.

'Attack at once.'

So as I sat down in the chartroom to bite into a ham sandwich, the planes had begun to move in on the carriers. Whatever might be the result, we'd never be able to criticize the quality of our opportunity . . .

I sat there thinking. The Jap air admiral undoubtedly had figured us as permanent fixtures in the southwest Pacific where last he had had word of us. So just about now he'd be looking up at the sky suddenly clouded with SBD's [Douglas Scout Bombers] and asking himself the Japanese equivalent of 'Where the hell did those things come from?' . . .

If these planes have failed in their mission or fought a draw or left the Japanese carriers usable we may expect a quick and vicious attack in return. If by some remote juju we have put all four carriers out of commission we have just about gained mastery of the Pacific . . .

Presently the word filtered back to us that the attack had been a complete success. All the carriers had been hit and severely damaged. At least three of them were burning. One, apparently, had been sunk in the first two or three minutes of the engagement.

One battleship of the north group of the force that we had attacked was afire. A second battleship had been hit. Reports from the Army told of hits on two more battleships and another carrier. Discounting these messages to the fullest extent and recognizing how easy it is for one observer to duplicate the report of another, it was still obvious that we had had something of a field day, still obvious that the bulk of Japan's attacking planes must presently be going into the drink for want of any other place to land.

Casey kept a meticulous journal of Midway, an extraordinary battle in which several groups of American forces, dispersed but with good co-ordination, worked closely together. The Americans also benefited from improved radio intelligence, which was making headway against Japanese naval codes. The result was an American victory in a battle in which no ship fired at another ship, and all combat was by aircraft. The Japanese suffered irrecoverable losses to their carrier fleet.

After his dramatic sojourn on a heavy cruiser, Casey opted for an attachment on a submarine – probably the only wartime journalist to undertake this experience – and, as ever, he kept his journal. However, the resulting book was so revealing about submarine operations that the censors would not allow it to be published in wartime. It appeared in late 1945 as Battle Below.

Casey continued to work for the Chicago Daily News *after the war.*
SEE ALSO PP. 250–1.

Wednesday 17 June 1942

Elizabeth Vaughan, an American civilian, observes separate family life at Bacolod internment camp on Negros in the Philippines

Elizabeth Head was born in 1905 in Athens, Georgia, the fourth child of a wealthy merchant. A successful scholar, athlete and pianist, she moved on from school to a select women's college. A downturn in the family fortunes forced her to leave college, but she entered the local state university in Athens, where she proved to be an outstanding student. Winning a scholarship, she went on to complete a master's degree in sociology at Vanderbilt University in Nashville, Tennessee. In the mid-1930s she had travelled to China and, returning via the Philippines, had met Jim Vaughan, a civil engineer. They married and enjoyed a comfortable life with a company house, servants and a car on the island of Negros. In 1939 their first child Beth was born, followed by their son Clay in 1940. After the invasion she was interned with her children in a camp for civilians.

The hot, humid days are enervating. Flies are thick in the bedrooms, the toilets, and on the food at mealtimes. There seems no way of controlling the flies as Japanese army horses are kept in fields adjoining the concentration camp grounds, and the doctor says flies probably come from there.

The nights are too hot to sleep – mosquitoes terrific – and we are forced to come indoors at dusk. We fight them until bedtime and even then they sometimes come through the nets. We are anxiously awaiting the heavy rains which had already started in the mountains, though do not know yet how we will eat – there is no dining room, the kitchen is out of the doors, there are no covered walks. We eat on small children's desks scattered around the yard.

Toilets are huge concrete affairs on which the students climbed and stood with feet apart after removing inner underwear. The custom here is not to sit on the toilet but climb up on it. More sanitary than our custom but inconvenient for those accustomed to American plumbing fixtures.

'Men must sleep in one room together and women in other rooms,' the Commandant instructed us upon arriving and so instructed seven newcomers today. 'But you may live freely,' he concluded. Husbands are assigned yard duty during the day, women to kitchen and housecleaning tasks, or laundry. Wives and husbands see little of each other except at meals and after 10:00 in the evening. Couples, all married, are seen strolling about the building hand in hand between 6:30 (after roll call) and 8:30 P.M. (Everyone in rooms ready for lights out at 9:00). Husbands and wives kiss each other goodnight on verandah, before eyes of others crowded in this narrow space before bedtime to get what breeze there is. The bedrooms are stuffy hot with many beds, each with its mosquito net hanging from wire near ceiling – cutting the breeze, if any. A strangely isolated family life: seven wives in one room, their seven husbands in the next, and so on down the long corridor: men, women, men, women, in alternate rooms.

Although Elizabeth Vaughan gives us a precise picture of the separate lives of couples under internment, her own husband was not one of the men she describes here. Jim Vaughan had joined the US army after the Japanese invasion in 1941 and ended up on the Bataan Death March. By April 1942 he found himself in Cabanatuan POW camp. Elizabeth Vaughan and other civilians living on the island of Negros had evaded internment for two months before being confined at Bacolod. SEE ALSO PP. 340–1, 371–2, 402, 417–18.

Thursday 18 – Monday 22 June 1942

Captain Hyman Samuelson of the US army watches the locals clear a runway and construct a pier at Milne Bay in New Guinea

This morning, the Empire flying boat left the wharf at Port Moresby. We were headed for Boston Island. But Boston Island was not an island at all; that was only a 'code' name. It is a coconut plantation located at the western end of Milne Bay. Later the name of this particular place was changed to Fall River. Actually there are no large rivers around either, but again that was no particular disadvantage. General Scanlan was the big shot aboard the flying boat. There was a reception committee at the Gili Gili Pier to meet us. This consisted of Captain Rich, the local Native administrator, and a number of missionaries and other personnel from ANGAU [the Australian New Guinea Administration Unit]. I was amazed at the perfect rhythm with which the Natives rowed our boats from the plane to the pier. Never once did they look to see where they were going; yet they made a perfect land fall.

We drove out to the site of the proposed airdrome. The place looked reasonably level, and for nearly a mile along its length it looked well-drained. The eastern extremity seemed to be poorly drained and presented a problem which could be solved only by months of work. However, there was very little clearing and grubbing to be done; perhaps a hundred coconut trees, that was all. And already the Natives were busy cutting the grass along the proposed landing strip. The women worked as hard as the men. They swung their knives wildly, apparently without any regard for the welfare of any of their co-workers. They all seemed to work faster and faster, and their chant grew louder and louder. It had a sort of rhythm which was different from the kind we are used to seeing in the movies. At length they broke into loud shouting, and they swung their knives very vigorously at the grass. Then altogether they stopped work and let go a wail which was a single note and faded into nothing. Then after a few minutes rest, they started the cycle all over again. They produced amazing results. A new pier had to be built. We were told that the first ship would arrive in one week . . .

The morning of the first day we were in Fall River we went out to see about constructing the new pier. 'Yes, I've had some experience in pier construction,' I told them, 'but I don't think you will ever be able to put in a pier within a week. And it will take a devil of a lot of material. Anyway, I don't know what can be done with this Native labor.' While I was thus beating my gums and looking around for material and at an old pile driving rig, the ANGAU got busy with the Natives. They shook piles into place, forming a rectangle 40 feet by 80 feet; this jetted out into about eight feet of water. Then they placed coconut logs on the inside of the piles, forming a wall. Finally the Natives came along with rock and coral, all carried by hand, and filled in the rectangle. They put on a smooth surface of beach sand. In the meantime, another group of Natives under the supervision of Mr. Latterman, the local carpenter, commenced work on an oil-drum pontoon – about 25 feet × 50 feet. This thing when floated into position at the end of the rectangular quay reached out into fifteen or twenty feet of water. Presto! There was adequate unloading facilities!

These Natives gave a good demonstration to a college-graduate civil engineer of how to build a pier – quickly! The whole job was completed in less than four days; but to look at the Natives working at any one particular moment, you would swear that the job would never be done. For instance, you might see fifty or sixty of the strongest men tugging at a palm-tree log, all of them shouting 'oh-oh-Op!' And the log doesn't move. And they just keep tugging, keeping up that 'oh-oh-OP!', each time pulling just a little bit harder than the time before. Finally the log gives 'way. They all look very much surprised. The women are used for carrying lighter stuff, such as basketsful of rock and coral. But if you observe closely, you will see that the women's baskets are always fuller than those of the men.

The peoples of the South Pacific are the invisible characters of the war in Asia and the Pacific. Yet they contributed enormously to the war effort, either through assisting with the remarkably rapid construction of ports and airfields, or through acting as scouts and guerrillas in terrain they knew well. In Papua New Guinea, military operations often took the form of three-way co-operation among local tribesmen who acted as scouts, Fijian soldiers, who were extremely skilled jungle fighters but did not know the local terrain, and Australian officers and NCOs who were there as advisers. SEE ALSO PP. 102–4, 338–9.

JULY 1942

BY JULY 1942 the main flaw in Japan's strategy had been exposed. Japan had chosen the concept of perimeter defence, hoping to hold an outer ring of Pacific bases and islands far from Japan. But it lacked the capacity to build or supply such bases, which were far away from the resources of south-east Asia. Critically short of merchant shipping even at the outset of the war, it was unable to replace the losses inflicted by Allied submarines and aircraft. As American industrial production swung behind the war effort, the eventual outcome became all but inevitable. Matters were made worse by poor Japanese organization, particularly the lack of communication, even active dislike, that existed between their army and navy.

American forces had now begun the long drive back across the Pacific. On Yamamoto's instructions, every island was defended vigorously by the Japanese and it soon became apparent that the task of liberating each one would be slow and costly. Nevertheless, the US navy began to push the Japanese out of the Solomon Islands while MacArthur focused his attention on the northern section of New Guinea and then on the major Japanese base of Rabaul on the neighbouring island of New Britain. Japan committed considerable forces to the struggle in New Guinea, focusing on the islands of Gona and Buna before moving up the Kokoda trail to fight Australian troops near Port Moresby. The Japanese continued to pour reinforcements into this area in the latter part of July and there was bitter fighting around Kokoda. Australian forces held on, despite the weight of attack on their positions south of Kokoda, and then launched a counter-attack, taking Kokoda on 28 July in a fiercely contested assault, only to be forced out again on 29 July.

In the Indian Ocean, Britain's Eastern Fleet cautiously made its way back to the naval base at Ceylon. The British force had retreated after the Japanese 1st Air Fleet had moved into the Indian Ocean in April 1942 and used its superior air capability to attack Allied bases at will. Although this Japanese naval foray into the Indian Ocean had been successful, it was not repeated, for Japan's naval resources were now increasingly focused on the island war in the Pacific. Here, American submarines and aircraft continued to take their toll of Japanese transports and destroyers seeking to resupply their garrisons. As a result the British now enjoyed naval supremacy in the Indian Ocean from mid-1942, largely as a matter of default.

In both Burma and China fighting was at a standstill, although for different reasons. In Burma, very significant fighting had seen the Japanese run into trouble with their over-extended supply lines, allowing the British to hold them on the borders of India; however, the defending forces were weak and vulnerable to pressure should the Japanese manage to resupply their troops. The British were assisted here by significant numbers of Chinese troops under the command of 'Vinegar Joe' Stilwell, and by guerrilla activities by the Burmese hill tribes. By contrast, in China fighting was limited because neither side wished to pursue active campaigning. After five years of war, communists, nationalists and Japanese alike were often content merely to make a show of combat and sometimes engaged in peaceable trade across established borders and positions where there had been no hostilities for some time.

Throughout July, US marines in New Zealand began to prepare for Operation Watchtower, the operation to retake Guadalcanal in the lower Solomon Islands. They unloaded their own stores at the docks because of a local labour dispute. Washington had designated Europe as the first priority and so the resources available for this operation were limited. Only one division could be deployed, and the majority of US naval power in the Pacific, including most of the large aircraft carriers, had to be focused on this objective. The United States was not fully ready to undertake a large operation, but commanders were determined to exploit the momentum developed by the victory at Midway.

Thursday 9 July 1942

Eddie Stanton reflects on native reasoning versus 'civilization' in Papua

Eddie Stanton was born in the Sydney suburb of Waverly on 8 September 1915. His father had been a signwriter and Eddie left school at fifteen to join a shipping firm. He had spent much of the inter-war years at sea as a purser on large freighters. His pastime was amateur magic and just before the outbreak of the war with Japan he had tried his hand as a stage magician, working under the improbable name of 'Edamonde – Last Word in Magic'. In January 1942 he had joined the army as a private and was soon en route to Port Moresby. As operations in that area expanded, he was promoted from private to warrant officer in a matter of weeks. Enjoying somewhat distant relations with his family and receiving few letters, Stanton confided private thoughts and feelings to his diary.

It causes a slight hardening of the arteries to observe Europeans in the Tropics pursuing the same vicious system of life that prevails in 'civilised' communities. Many of these men pride themselves on their ability to think black, to fathom the natives' system of reasoning. Yet, with all their knowledge and understanding, they have been unable to grasp the importance of certain principles of native life, principles so obvious that their adoption would seem only a matter of course.

Most Europeans must be continually doing something, occupying most of the day & night with trivial tasks. They can't take an hour off and sit in a chair, and do nothing. No, that is laziness. Instead, one must type, fiddle around with the anatomy of a wireless, walk around in circles, annoy natives with one's presence, get up at five in the morning, and continually think about what to do next.

Observe such people closely, and one will find them fidgety, irritable, indifferent companions. Unable to relax, the sight of a native or European doing so, vaguely annoys them.

If it has not been ruptured too severely by white intrusion, native life consists of three essentials – food, sleep, women. Food, the native has in abundance. Yams, bananas, coconuts, pineapples, oranges, crabs, oysters, turtles, fish, and pig, constitute his diet. Sleep is obtained in the shelter provided by the native house, a dwelling easily constructed. The elements are kept without, and so long as this condition is preserved, nothing further is required of the house.

Women combine with the men to participate in the joys of living. As soon as rounded breasts and supple body show that a girl has got to the age of interest, and her eyes send out messages to come and get it, most eligible bachelors pursue the quarry to earth. As the girl is looking for just what they're looking for, they are rarely refused.

So, the nights pass away in love, for there isn't anything else to occupy their attention. They have no radios or newspapers to tell them to use body-odour soap, that efficiency is the secret of success, that it's fun to work for someone else, that the war is getting worse, or that one must take out some kind of policy so that one can live comfortably ever after. No their ears are spared such tripe, and they are so much better off. All matters that have no bearing on food, sleep & women, are left to the white man to worry over. Of course the native gets yaws, ulcers, & malaria; but he isn't too old at forty, or gets knocked down by motor-cars, or evaporated every twenty years by a load of bombs from the sky.

Once, however, a native loses his sales resistance and adopts the artificial wants of the European, he begins to lose his independence. He finds that he has to work long hours to procure his acquired necessities, and soon becomes a miserable slave. The majority of natives, however, prefer to live after their own fashion, because they instinctively sense that a swing towards white man's fashion can only lead to destruction of their independence.

The Second World War accelerated a process that has come to be called 'globalization'. Only small numbers of people had travelled extensively before 1939, and even then it was rare for them to penetrate areas inhabited by native peoples unless they were colonial administrators. Worldwide conflict brought a vast range of isolated cultures into contact with each other. Stanton came from a society that still practised a 'White Australia' policy and certainly revealed attitudes in his diary that reflected the prejudices of his generation. However, he was also an intelligent man who could write critically about the impact of the war on the carefree lives of the islanders, manifesting little time for the paternalistic attitudes of the Australian civilian administrators. SEE ALSO PP. 377–9, 533–4, 760–1.

Sunday 12 – Monday 13 July 1942

Private Jim 'Bluey' Armstrong, Australian army, watches the Japanese 'go to town' on the Dutch

James Frederick Armstrong was born on 21 February 1919 and came from Noorinbee North in Victoria. He was part of 2/21st Gull Force AIF. He was kept a prisoner at a POW camp on the island of Ambon for most of 1942 and took on the role of cook in the camp kitchen.

12 July

Another fine day, but one to be remembered by all the men in the camp as BLACK SUNDAY. The Japs had 32 Dutchmen in a hut standing to attention all the morning and in the afternoon a truck load of Japs came out of AMBON. Each one armed himself with whatever piece of wood he could find, then the Dutch were marched up to the Jap headquarters, we could not see them very well. They were made to stand with their hands over their heads then the Japs went to town on them for about ¼ hour. Most of them had to be carried back on stretchers. There were 28 broken arms and legs, one bloke had a go at the Japs and he came back with

ABOVE: General Tojo Hideki (centre) proposes a toast to the Axis with the German and Italian ambassadors to Japan during the ratification of the Tripartite Pact in September 1940. Despite this treaty of alliance between Tokyo, Berlin and Rome, there was little joint Axis planning for war.

BELOW: The Japanese surprise attack on Pearl Harbor (pp. 131–140). Airmen dealing with bomb damage at the Ford Island Naval Air Station watch the battleship the USS *Arizona* explode.

LEFT: Japanese troops fight their way through the streets of Kuala Lumpur in Malaya in January 1942. General Kawamura Saburo's diary records the opening of the Malayan campaign (p. 129).

BELOW: First aid personnel deal with casualties during Japanese air raids on Singapore in January 1942, which Sheila Allan records in her diary (p. 187).

ABOVE: The disorderly British retreat in Burma in March 1942 is described by Reginald Carter and Robert Moody Smith in their diaries (pp. 212, 268). Here an abandoned motor bus is deliberately set on fire to prevent its use by the enemy.

BELOW: The 'Flying Tigers' were American volunteers who took on the Japanese Zero fighters in the skies over China and Burma against enormous odds. The diary of Charles Bond captures their dramatic experiences in aerial combat (p. 256).

LEFT: Children experienced all aspects of the war against Japan. Here a ten-year-old boy soldier serves in the Chinese army that attempted to slow the Japanese advance in northern Burma during 1942.

RIGHT: Japanese American children heading for the internment camps of California in May 1942. Hatsuye Egami's diary records the experiences of American citizens kept behind the wire for the duration of the war (p. 263).

OPPOSITE PAGE: W. Lance Bullard's diary (p. 276) describes his underwater encounter with a Japanese midget submarine that took part in an attack on Sydney harbour in late May 1942. After this submarine was captured it was put on display, to the delight of local schoolchildren.

CONNING TOWER

CONTROL ROOM

ABOVE: Australian troops befriend the locals while on patrol in Papua New Guinea. Bitter fighting near Port Moresby halted the Japanese southward advance here in September 1942.

ABOVE: Happy days in the southern seas. Japanese naval personnel under the command of Vice-Admiral M. Kamada shortly after arriving in Borneo in 1942.

ABOVE: US army troops cautiously probe a Japanese dugout during fierce fighting near Sanananda on Papua New Guinea in 1943.

BELOW: Brigadier Orde Wingate plans an attack in his socks on a vast map of Burma in 1943. Leo Amery's diary (p. 431) records how he lobbied Churchill for the appointment of this unconventional figure, loathed by staff officers.

LEFT: A Japanese transport ship runs aground off Muschu Island, New Guinea, after being hit by bombers of the US 5th Air Force. Losses inflicted on an already inadequate merchant marine crippled the Japanese war effort.

ABOVE: POWs laying railway track on the Thai–Burma railway. Despite the huge cost in human life, the railway barely functioned. Logistics and transport were the Achilles heel of the Japanese war effort.

LEFT: The infamous 'Pack of Cards' bridge on the Thai–Burma railway near Hintok is described by Don McLaren in his diary (p. 387). It collapsed several times during 1943.

his hands bashed to pulp. We are hoping it won't be long before we are relieved, everyone was horrified with their doings.

13 July

A very wet day, and we had fish for dinner. One of the Dutch died after yesterday's doings, and what should the Japs do but make wreaths and go and put them on the coffin. One day they are savages, and the next day they are humans. Everyone is trying to forget the episode. It is just 2 years since I left home to join the A.I.F., never thinking I would be landed in a place like this.

James Armstrong left Ambon Island in October 1942 and was moved to Hainan Island off the coast of China, where he spent most of 1943. He was killed in an ambush at Hoban on 8 April 1944, when Chinese guerrillas attacked a prisoner work detail on the island. His family were only notified of his fate after the end of the war and had received no communication from him since 1941.

Mid-July 1942

Angela Bolton, a British nurse in Assam, feels sorry for the rickshaw-wallahs

What a relief to leave the smells and sights of Calcutta. It was good to talk to Charles again and I was interested in what he had to say about the arch-villain (from the British point of view) Subhas Chandra Bose. He is far more impatient than Gandhi and wants independence straight away even if he has to foment trouble amongst the population and side with the Japanese to put pressure on the British.

The other thing that concerned me in Calcutta was the plight of those rickshaw wallahs. Charles said that they had very short lives because they work on so little food and are riddled with diseases such as hook worm and tuberculosis. I saw both Indians and Europeans kick out at puny little men who pull them along in rickshaws to make them go faster. It would give me great pleasure to put such bullies between the shafts and drive them for miles through the crowded streets so that they would know how it felt to be a rickshaw wallah.

While Gandhi led a Quit India movement that focused on civil disobedience as a means of protest, the nationalist Subhas Chandra Bose advocated support for Japan. He had travelled to both Berlin and Tokyo to gather support for Indian independence and led the Indian National Army (INA), which fought alongside Japan during the war. In practice, few Indians were given front-line roles, and they were more often exploited in ancillary duties such as guarding rear areas. The Japanese-sponsored INA was at its most successful between 1942 and 1943. Thereafter, as the Axis cause waned, enthusiasm for the INA, and other Japanese-sponsored armies such as the Burmese Independence Army, also decreased. These 'independence armies' were never given genuinely equal status by Tokyo, although Bose and the military leader of the INA, Mohan Singh, became important nationalist icons. SEE ALSO PP. 252–4, 467–8.

Thursday 23 July 1942

Missionaries Alice Lan and Betty Hu prepare to flee from Hong Kong and wrestle with occupation currency problems

A letter today helped us to decide that we will leave Hong Kong soon. Mr. Chi, one of our Bible Seminary teachers, has everything ready for us to go inland to open school. The Faith and Love Mission in Kwangsi (eight days' journey from Kowloon) has kindly offered us their school building to be used for Bethel. Mr. Chi is getting everything ready to move. He has also sent out notices asking all old students to come back, and we hope that many will be there when we arrive! Another factor that would force us to leave soon is the money question. Since the Japanese came they lowered the value of our currency by 50 per cent – two dollars for one Yen. Now, unexpectedly, they have made it still lower – four dollars for one Yen. Our money, already inadequate, has been reduced to half its original value overnight. It may again be reduced – then we will not be able to leave. So we had better hurry and get away while we can. This news of currency depreciation is throwing the whole city into panic. It means that the Chinese are all poorer, while the Japanese can buy many more things with their worthless paper, and who dares to raise an objection? All must suffer silently while the Japanese go around buying all they can. If a store refuses to sell to them that is the end of that store. We know a rug store that suffered a great loss one day in this way. A Japanese came in and said that he wanted some rugs. He asked their price and picked out the best ones. He told his coolies to carry them to a truck. After this was done he threw down only one hundred dollars. When they told him it was not enough for even one of the rugs he drove off and was never seen again.

A friend sent me a beautiful powder box last Christmas and I kept it, for it was too pretty to be used. When we were hard up we asked someone to sell it for us so a teacher took it to the street to sell. He is making a living this way. He sells and he takes ten per cent. Well, that day a Japanese picked it up and asked the price. He said 'Four yen', but the Japanese threw down one yen and walked away with the box. He chased after him for more money. The Japanese turned around and slapped his face. We were terribly sorry when we heard this and told him not to chase them any more but let the things go. The box is worth four yen because it is American. The Japanese dislike Americans but they are crazy about American goods.

Alice Lan and Betty Hu eventually decided that conditions in Hong Kong were too oppressive and evacuated their forty-four students to Guangxi on mainland China in batches, escorting the last batch themselves and deploying considerable ingenuity on their troubled journey. Merciless manipulation of the currency by the Japanese made their task infinitely harder.

Both women would survive the war and go on working at the seminary until 1970. The Bethel Bible Seminary in Shanghai became affiliated with Acadia University in Canada, and continues its work today. SEE ALSO PP. 189–91.

Tuesday 28 July 1942

Tadahide Hamada, a Japanese soldier, suffers exhaustion on a route march across China

Tadahide Hamada, a student at the Japanese Institute of Physical Culture, had been called up for military service in December 1941. By July 1942 he was suffering from malaria and beriberi.

When I am too tired, when I am bored or when I have malaria, I tell myself: 'I am fed up with war.' How many miles are there still to be covered, how long must I go on sleeping on the ground?

When I see the bad road stretching out in front of me, I think that I would prefer to lie down and die. That is truly my profound conviction. Besides, I am angry with myself, for I feel that I have forgotten many *characters*.

After having dug a ditch with a shovel, I had to take my rifle and drag myself as far as a pass like that of Karikaza. I was tired to death. As we got further up the mountain, we found ourselves surrounded by bamboos. We discovered a peaceful sunlit spot, the sun was reflected by green leaves and there was a small village. I had the impression that we were coming back to the paradise of Chinese legend. Had there not been the war, life in that village in the heart of the mountains would have been peaceful and pleasant. There was a stream of sparkling clear water.

The soldiers march and march without stopping. Why must these men who lived so peacefully in Japan be made to suffer so much? When I ask myself that question, a voice within me answers that it is not true . . . that I do not really hate the war so much . . . that it is merely the nervous strain that makes me think so much. As I drag myself along the road that has become groundless through the torrential rains, sinking in the mud up to my knees, I repeat to myself: 'March, march on until you fall by the roadside . . .' How many forced marches through the night, without any light at all! I drag my feet, following the shadowy outlines of the men in front of me. Sometimes, I fall asleep without noticing it, and I wake up because I get splashed in walking through a puddle. Then I go on following the column. Once I very nearly fell off a bridge.

Tadahide Hamada was eventually evacuated by air and then sent to a military hospital near Yosu in southern Korea. He would eventually return to his infantry unit in China and was killed fighting at Chang-cha on 3 November 1944.

Friday 31 July 1942

Richard Tregaskis, a reporter, watches US marines prepare to assault the beaches at Guadalcanal

Richard Tregaskis was born on 28 November 1916 at Elizabeth, New Jersey. He had attended Harvard University and then begun a career as a journalist, beginning work for the Boston American Record. *At the outbreak of the war in Asia and the Pacific he covered Pacific Fleet operations for the International News Service.*

In the afternoon, I watched a group of marines cleaning and setting up their mortars and light machine guns on the forward deck. The lads were taking almost motherly care of the weapons. And I could see that the working parts were cleaned and oiled so that they worked like the conjunctive parts of a watch.

Some of the lads were sharpening bayonets, which indeed seemed to be a universal pastime all over the ship. I saw one with a huge bolo knife, which he was carefully preparing. Others worked at cleaning and oiling their rifles and sub-machine guns. Some of the boys had fashioned home-made blackjacks, canvas sacks containing lead balls, for 'infighting.'

While working over their weapons, the marines passed their inevitable chatter, 'shooting the breeze' about the girls they had known here or there, their adventures in this or that port, a good liberty they had made here or there. But now, a large part of the chatter deviated from the usual pattern. A lot of it was about the Japs.

'Is it true that the Japs put a gray paint on their faces, put some red stuff beside their mouths, and lie down and play dead until you pass 'em?' one fellow asked me. I said I didn't know. 'Well, if they do,' he said, 'I'll stick 'em first.'

Another marine offered: 'They say the Japs have a lot of gold teeth. I'm going to make myself a necklace.'

'I'm going to bring back some Jap ears,' said another. 'Pickled.'

Richard Tregaskis was one of only two reporters allowed to accompany the US marines to Guadalcanal, and he noted that even in July 1942 they had a reputation for much greater aggression than other units. SEE ALSO PP. *296–7, 309–10.*

AUGUST 1942

THE INVASION OF Guadalcanal began on 7 August. This was the largest Allied operation in the Pacific during 1942 and continued until Christmas. The US marines were the first ashore and enjoyed a remarkably unopposed landing, advancing westward to over-run a Japanese airstrip. This was quickly named Henderson Field and was pressed into service in the battle for the island. However, at sea the Allies encountered disaster. In an attack at night – Japan's preferred time of attack – Japanese cruisers armed with formidable oxygen-breathing torpedoes surprised an Allied squadron, sinking four cruisers and one destroyer. This engagement, which became known as the Battle of Savo Island, was the worst single Allied naval defeat in the Pacific. The only compensation was the sinking of a Japanese cruiser by an American submarine some time after the battle.

The victorious Japanese naval cruiser squadron subsequently missed a vital opportunity by failing to attack the main force of transports carrying the US marines. Instead they sought to withdraw rather than expose themselves to the possibility of air attack. Even so, the engagement left the Allied supply situation on Guadalcanal in disarray and US marines found themselves short of rations. Once air operations were established at Henderson Field, emergency supplies could be flown in. On 21 August the newly arrived Ichiki detachment, a crack Japanese unit, attempted a surprise dawn offensive against the marine beachhead but was repulsed with heavy losses. It was the first of a number of Japanese attempts to recapture the vital airfield.

On 24 August the US carrier *Saratoga* sank the Japanese carrier *Ryujoin* in an engagement off the eastern Solomons. The US carrier *Enterprise* was damaged in the same engagement and transferred many of her operational aircraft to Henderson Field, which was in an exposed situation and was still being shelled by Japanese ships. A week later, the *Saratoga* was damaged by a Japanese submarine attack and forced to retire. Japan attempted desperate resupply operations, losing a number of destroyers and transports; however, some Japanese reinforcements, including the Kawaguchi detachment, reached Guadalcanal.

Little fighting had occurred in China for some time, but in August 1942 the Japanese army began an offensive in Kiangsi province, which was eventually defeated by the Chinese. In Burma, the dire military situation had forced a significant rethink on the part of the Viceroy of India, under whose control the British colony of Burma lay. Up to now, the Indian government had wanted neither Chinese nor American forces on Indian soil. The British authorities in India feared the arrival of American personnel because Washington had expressed fervent support for Gandhi and the cause of Indian independence. During August the political situation deteriorated badly after the British decided to imprison Gandhi and some of his followers, an action that provoked rioting in many cities. Colonial administrators feared that Roosevelt's frequent proclamations about the need to end European colonial dominance in Asia would reach the ears of an already restless Indian population. The Viceroy also feared Chinese territorial ambitions in northern Burma. But in the face of the military pressure these political considerations were put aside and the Americans were permitted to open a training camp for Chinese soldiers at Ramargh, just inside India close to the Burmese border.

Friday 7 August 1942

Richard Tregaskis arrives on a silent beach with the US marines at Guadalcanal

At 9:05 the intense bombardment on the shore was ending. A haze of dirty black smoke hung over the edge of the land. And we were heading straight for it.

We followed, not too distantly, the first wave of landing boats, which we could see as an irregular line of moving white spots against the blue water, each spot dotted at the centre with black. The white spots, we knew, were foam; the black, the boats themselves, making maximum speed toward shore.

We could not see the boats strike shore; but signals rose ahead of us on the beach. The colonel turned to the rest of us in the boat and smiled. The agreed signal for a successful landing. A signalman stood on our motor hatch and wig-wagged the good news back to our mother ship.

It was quickly acknowledged.

The fact of a successful landing, however, did not mean that our effort to take the beach-head would be unopposed. We ducked well below the level of the gunwales as we reached a fixed line of departure, a certain number of yards from shore, and forged ahead.

At 9:28 we passed the boats of the first wave, coming out from the beach to the ships to get another load of troops. We poked our heads up to see that they showed no signs of having been damaged by enemy fire. We gathered a little more courage now and raised our heads to see what was happening. Lieut. Cory, squatting next to me, shouted to me over the rumble of the motor that perhaps there were no Japs. Still, it seemed that this would be too good to be true. Perhaps the Japs were merely drawing us into a trap.

At 9:40 we were close enough to land to see isolated palm trees projecting above the shore – sign that we were coming close to whatever trap the enemy might have prepared.

In our boat there was no talking, despite the excitement of

the moment. The motor was making too much noise, at any rate. We sat and looked at each other, and occasionally peeped over the side to glimpse other boats plunging shoreward in showers of spray around us, or to cock an eye at the strangely silent beach.

Guadalcanal was the first major Allied offensive of the Pacific war, and many were surprised that the landings went unopposed. However, fighting soon developed further inland. The operation was undertaken with some haste and this led to a number of problems. Some 14,500 marines were tasked with seizing and holding a Japanese airfield, subsequently called Henderson Field. Although it was a new Japanese airfield and was not yet operational, it was within easy striking distance of Japanese bombers and warships based at Rabaul. Australian intelligence operatives were active on the island, but their intelligence was not passed to the marines before the landings. SEE ALSO PP. *293–4, 309–10.*

Sunday 9 – Saturday 15 August 1942

Oliver Harvey, Anthony Eden's private secretary, follows the internment of Gandhi in India and the ensuing riots

9 August

... We are on the verge of removing and interning Gandhi. The old fox has us in a fix, he thinks. But after the Cripps offer, however bad our record up till then may have been, he has no excuse and even the Americans have begun to look on him as a hopeless twister. The real problem for Gandhi is the Moslems, not us.

10 August

I was away from the Office Sat. and Sun. and on returning today learnt the shocking news that Gott had been killed on Friday in an aeroplane crash. But this is something like a national disaster – our only first-class desert general killed like this, on the eve of his recognition and appointment. What frightful luck pursues us! Rapid decisions had to be taken and it is now decided that Montgomery is to be the general to take his place. He has the reputation of being an able and ruthless soldier and an unspeakable cad. However, it is the ability and ruthlessness which count, but he has no desert experience. Otherwise the changes so remain, Alexander as C. in C. Mid East and Auck. C. in C. Iraq and Persia.

P.M. goes on to Moscow via Tehran today plus Wavell. I expect he will get killed in a crash next.

Gandhi and co. locked up yesterday. Some disturbances. He is not being removed from India.

15 August

Both Roosevelt and Chiang-Kai-Shek are showing a tendency to intervene in India. Chiang is anxious for American or 'United Nations' mediation and an under-writing of the Cripps' offer of independence at the end of the war. This is most distasteful to Winston and indeed to all here. We have made our offer and it stands. Gandhi has tried to twist us into immediate independence. Jinnah, the Moslem, says he won't have a Gandhi solution at any price. Rioting is still sporadic and not too serious.

Although India was in a state halfway to civil war over the internment of Gandhi, civil servants felt that London had made an honest effort at a settlement. Sir Stafford Cripps had led a mission to India in June, and the major impediment had proved to be Hindu–Muslim power-sharing rather than British obstinacy. Although the Cripps mission was a failure, it pointed the finger at Gandhi as someone who was reluctant to compromise. It was all the more important that Britain should seem reasonable, given American and Chinese interest in Gandhi and Indian nationalism.

During August, British policy-makers in London were less concerned with problems in India than with those in the Middle East. Here, Churchill had decided to make significant leadership changes, acceler-ated by the unfortunate death of General Gott in an air crash. Oliver Harvey remarked that they had suspected for months that 'Cairo was rotten' but it had taken a lot to break 'the trades union of generals'. The peppery Montgomery, much disliked by his fellow officers, was now in charge.

Oliver Harvey would continue to work in the Foreign Office in London until 1948, when he became ambassador to France. SEE ALSO PP. 107–8.

Wednesday 12 August 1942

Leo Amery, Secretary of State for India and Burma, contemplates widespread riots and the Whipping Act in India

Leo Amery was directly responsible for British policy in India as devised by London. He was continually dogged in his work by interference from Churchill, who was obsessed by India. Britain's tough line on the protests reflected the failure of the Cripps mission earlier in 1942 which had sought a settlement. London now felt justified in postponing political change until the end of the war.

News of rioting etc. in India not too bad in itself but woefully exaggerated by masses of unnecessary detail in the press and bad headlines. Having with some difficulty persuaded Attlee that the Cabinet, even if it could not come to any decision on his broad proposals for Burma, should at any rate hear him. He stated his case very fairly and reason-ably and John Anderson made the helpful suggestion that during the period immediately after reconquest and pend-ing the restoration of self-government Burma should be governed by a commission. Apropos of this Cripps seems to have suggested that the Commission should consist of two British, two American and two Chinese! I didn't hear this or I should have certainly exploded. I did in fact explode prematurely when I heard Anthony [Eden] say something to the effect that he hoped we weren't going back, meaning apparently 'backward' politically, though I took it to mean that he didn't want us to declare our intention of going back into full occupation. My excuse for misunderstanding him was a terribly woolly telegram I had just seen about Hong Kong telling our Ambassador at Chung-King to fence as regards the future of Hong Kong and to listen with interest if the Chinese made suggestions about cooperating in the administration.

This appalling defeatism about our mission in the world horrifies me. The place seems full of people who really think that the solution of everything after the war is to hand it over to the Americans, or the Chinese, or the Russians, or some mixed committee of all of them. I only wish sometimes I were in a free position to say what I think about the Atlantic Charter and all the other tripe which is being talked now, exactly like the tripe talked to please President Wilson . . . Just before the Cabinet I saw a further telegram from Chiang Kai-Shek to Roosevelt urging him to interfere in India; I sped it on its way to Winston with a strong telegram urging Winston to tell Roosevelt to tell the Generalissimo to mind his own business. At the Cabinet they were also rather fussy about the unnecessary flood of news from India while Bevin reported that the Labour people, while otherwise sound, were much agitated over the revival of the Whipping Ordnance which permits of flogging for sabotage and arson. I telegraphed to India to find out more about this.

Amery may have taken a calm view of the riots, but in fact August 1942 saw the height of the Quit India movement's campaign of civil disobedience and a dangerous wave of mass protests in response to the arrest of many of the movement's leaders. In the first week after the arrests, 250 railway stations were damaged or destroyed, and over 500 post offices and 150 police stations were attacked. The cutting of telegraph lines was also common. The police used gunfire against crowds, and rioters were also machine-gunned by low-flying aircraft. The whipping of suspects and burning of villages were especially controversial, and caused argument with the Americans and anger among the Labour members of the coalition in Westminster. By the end of 1942 over 60,000 Indians would have been gaoled. The government's line remained that little could be done about Indian independence until after the war was over. SEE ALSO PP. 87–9, 431–3, 637–8.

Mid-August 1942

Ursula Blomberg, a teenage Jewish girl in Shanghai, works in the General's house and befriends the 'three sisters'

When Ursula Blomberg was eleven years old she had emigrated with her family from Germany to China – one of some 20,000 European Jews who had left for Shanghai in the 1930s. In Germany, Ursula Blomberg's family had been wealthy with a large house and horses. Now in Shanghai they were poor, and she found work teaching languages wherever she could. She had been engaged by a Chinese general to teach English to his three concubines, who were all sisters, but not related to the General.

By late summer General Yi's three sisters – who had long confessed their concubine status to me – had acquired a good smattering of English. I insisted that their sentences be grammatically correct, would not let them pick up Pidgin English, and made it a rule that at each session they learn ten new words. With childlike glee, and after much searching for the right one, the girls each selected an English name for themselves from a long list of suggestions. Sister One called herself Connie, Sister Two became Madeleine, and Sister Three opted for Anna. Through Madeleine, who was the quickest to learn, General Yi conveyed his pleasure at the progress his sisters had made, and predicted that in six more months they would be fluent in English, and French classes could begin.

In between lessons we turned into four giggly girls, playing croquet in the garden and Ping-Pong and gin rummy when the weather kept us indoors. The sisters loved to gamble, show off their jewelry, freely spend the General's money, and satisfy their unbridled passion for American cosmetics and French perfumes. Accompanied by bouts of laughter – their dainty hands coyly cupping their ruby-red mouths – the sisters discussed the most personal and intimate details of their times spent in the General's bedroom – no shame, no show of jealousy, no hands-off-this-is-my-man attitude.

I kept on learning.

One day an older Chinese lady burst unceremoniously into the sisters' pleasant sitting room where we were reading. I had caught a glimpse of her several times on my way to the east wing, but had not bothered to ask who she was. She was dressed in a showy bronze-colored brocade gown, dripped gorgeous gold and jade jewelry, and sported a slick, tall hairdo that towered above a cold and angry face.

No sooner had she entered the room, when she started to yell and scream at the three sisters, who had jumped up from their chairs. With their heads bowed and eyes trained to the floor, they let the barrage of anger pass over them. On and on went the furious lady, yelling and hissing and sputtering all the while spittle trickling down her chin. Suddenly, she stepped towards the girls and, one-two-three, slapped each one a hefty smack on her cheek, let go with one final colorful string of curses, turned on her high-heel leather pumps, and stomped out of the room. I just stood there with my mouth open.

'Hey, girls, what was that all about?' I shrieked.

Before any one of them would answer, they broke out into uncontrolled laughter, holding on to their sides. Tears ran down the faint red bruises the older woman's harsh hand had left on their silken, ivory cheeks. Mascara ran in fine trickles and smudged their glowing skin.

'No matter! No matter!' Connie finally caught up with her breathing. 'That *I-Tai-Tai*, General Yi number-one wife. She has bad temper. She does not like us. We are young and pretty, she old and ugly. But she *I-Tai-Tai*. She has two sons for General Yi, very important. But she gets angry at us; we have a good time. No matter, she old and ugly. All her friends are *I-Tai-Tai*, they also old and ugly.' Anna, the more scholarly one, went to great length to explain the way the Chinese household works – the pecking order of the wives and concubines. It seemed rather complicated.

Totally undisturbed by the incident, and still chuckling to themselves, the sisters returned to reading their lesson for the day from *Little Women* – which we would discuss the following day – just like Fräulein Amanda used to do.

The four girls had the run of the General's luxurious mansion. The General served in the collaborationist regime of Wang Chin-wei, which dominated northern China and ran the area on behalf of Tokyo. Although it was not unusual for a prominent person to have 'minor wives', it was still clearly a cause of tension in this household. SEE ALSO PP. 360–1.

Friday 28 August 1942

Lieutenant Kiyoshi Yamamoto, a medical officer, bids a gloomy farewell to comrades heading for the battlefield at Milne Bay

Kiyoshi Yamamoto was born in 1915. He had trained as a medical officer and had been part of the task force that the Japanese had sent towards Midway in 1942. After the Battle of Midway was lost his own transport ship was sunk, and he had eventually ended up at the major Japanese base of Rabaul on New Britain. This was a staging post en route to his final destination of Milne Bay, the current front line in the fighting for control of New Guinea, where he knew fighting was bitter. On 28 August he watched No. 2 Company of his battalion departing for Milne Bay, knowing he would soon follow them.

On 28 Aug No 2 Coy left for RABI [Milne Bay]. They assembled at noon and received the CO's instructions. OC 2 Coy, usually nonchalant, on this occasion showed an exceptional air of resolution.

The pl[atoon] comds [commanders] and the Senior Nursing orderlie(s) seemed bravely prepared to die although exhausted and with bloodshot eyes. The farewellers and the farewelled doubtless thought this was their final parting.

When No 1 Coy was seen off at GUAM there was still some room for exchanging smiles, but now we were on the verge of tears after the hardships we had gone through and knowing this was no ordinary battle-ground. However we watched them march off in a style befitting the 2 Coy of a splendid force until they were out of sight. I then returned to my tent and smoked.

The CO (Capt YASUDA) then came up quietly, put out his hand, and I gave him a match. We were both silent – nothing to say. Without speaking, we each knew what the other was thinking.

A car came and we went to the jetty to see them off again. The CO shook hands with all WOs [Warrant Officers] and above, encouraging them. In farewelling 3rd (Class) Nursing Orderlies, Nisimura and Sasaki, I patted their shoulders, and also the four dvrs [drivers] who had just been attached to the SB unit. This was also my parting from the chief Nursing Orderly who was looking extremely grave.

Later, when I was on the way to visit the Submarine base unit, someone called to me. It was Ide (one of my contemporaries). He was well and said he would give me anything I needed as I must have lost everything. I asked him for underwear . . .

As it grew quiet, insects could be heard outside the tent. By now those in the expeditionary force would have recovered their spirits and found something to joke about. But while they joked, each would doubtless be thinking secretly either of tomorrow's fate or of their families.

I put out the candle on my left which I had used to write up my diary, but could not get to sleep although utterly weary. Remembering that my wife, on the night we parted, had washed my back, it weighed on my mind that I had not washed hers. The tiniest things strangely remain in one's head and recur at the oddest times.

Kiyoshi Yamamoto joined his comrades and headed for Milne Bay on 1 September, noting in his diary 'no hope of victory, but I must go'. However, on arrival he was soon tasked with caring for wounded who were being brought away from Milne Bay back to Rabaul and so escaped the worst of the fighting. He survived the war and later became professor of endocrinology at Gunma University in Japan. He retired in 1980 and thereafter lived in Nagasaki and Tokyo.

Sunday 30 August 1942

Peter Vladimirov, Comintern agent, spends an evening with Mao Tse-tung and his inner circle at Yenan

Peter Vladimirov was born in 1905 at Voronezh in Russia and in his youth worked as a fitter at a railway repair yard in Tikhoretsk. He joined the Communist Party in 1927 and in the 1930s went to university in Moscow, specializing in Asian Studies. For several periods from May 1938 through to the end of the war he served as a Tass correspondent in China and also as an agent of the Comintern or Communist International, the Russian-controlled international organization that linked communist parties around the world. By August 1942 he was a Comintern liaison officer at the headquarters of Mao's Chinese Communist Party in Yenan.

Mao Tse-tung

In the evening Mao Tse-tung invited Aleyev and myself to call on him. Judging by the flushed faces of the members of the Politburo, I realized that they had just been in conference and that the session had been far from peaceful. The invitation struck me as unusual because it was not accompanied by the usual dry official ceremonies.

Besides the stiff bearing which is meant to inspire awe in the visitors, Mao Tse-tung has another, purely Chinese way about him. This time he asked us solicitously about our health and about our needs, seated me into the leather armchair which is usually reserved for guests of honor, then he himself brought rice, khanja, and tea. Chiang Ching moved up the beach chair and he stretched on it by our side. The guard handed him a cup of khanja, and Chiang Ching dropped a few peanuts into his hand.

We asked him what he thought about a possible Japanese attack on the Soviet Union and about the CCP's attitude to such a war. Mao Tse-tung replied absent-mindedly, 'Of course we shall conduct operations against the Japanese.'

The question obviously rubbed him the wrong way. Mao Tse-tung tried to conceal his irritation with a vagrant smile and proceeded to expound the current tasks of the CCP:

'All that does not contribute to unity must be destroyed. We must banish complaisance and excoriate the unhealthy style.' (He failed to elucidate this point.) 'It is necessary to check on the probity of the personnel and to judge it on the merit of their work,' etc.

Sitting left of me was Kang Sheng. From time to time I looked at this bespectacled man with a receding hairline and thin tightly pressed lips and thought about the tremendous power he had and the authority he exercised over so many human lives . . .

Mao Tse-tung suddenly fell silent and ordered that pimiento pepper be brought in. We took it as a sign that the official part of the meeting was over. Mao Tse-tung pointed at me, and a plate loaded with red pimientos was passed to me first. A similar plate was given to Mao Tse-tung.

Mao Tse-tung bolted the pepper and, stretching in his chair, threw his questions: 'Is Stalin a revolutionary? Does he like red pepper? A genuine revolutionary must eat red pepper . . .' He sipped out of his jug and remarked, 'Alexander the Great adored red pepper for sure. He was a great man and a revolutionary in his own right. As for Stalin, he surely eats pepper, too. You must also eat pepper, Sung Ping. Come on, do, if you are a revolutionary . . .'

Mao Tse-tung put away one pod after another, washing it down with khanja. One must admire his strong head, which can carry so much alcohol.

Kang Sheng was in raptures over Mao Tse-tung. Squirming and smiling from cheek he noisily inhaled the air . . .

After a while Mao Tse-tung's face became as red as the pepper on our plates . . .

Chiang Ching kept putting on Gramophone records . . .

We were joined by Wang Chia-hsiang. The conversation now drifted to the current events.

Wang Chia-hsiang and Kang Sheng took a jibe at our often fruitless efforts to study their information, which by all standards can hardly satisfy anyone: scant and false . . .

About an hour and a half later Mao Tse-tung turned logy. He yawned and stretched in his beach chair. Chiang Ching put on a Gramophone record of an ancient Chinese opera – Mao Tse-tung nodded approval and began clapping his hands by way of accompaniment. His slow and measured clapping gradually put him to sleep.

Mao's headquarters were situated in the caves of Yenan in northern China where they were secure from Japanese air action. Peter Vladimirov and his team were effectively the local Soviet embassy. Although they were fellow communists, there was immense distrust and Kang Sheng, the notorious head of Mao's secret police, did not hesitate to let the Soviet group know that they were under round-the-clock surveillance. Nevertheless, living in such close proximity to Mao they learned a great deal about the Chinese communist leader and his circle. Vladimirov recorded the more sensitive material in his diary, which had to be kept away from locally employed Chinese servants. SEE ALSO PP. 321–3, 451–2, 575–6.

SEPTEMBER 1942

DURING SEPTEMBER, fighting remained focused on the island of Guadalcanal in the Solomons and on New Guinea. Both sides struggled to win the war of resupply and reinforcement at extreme range from their supporting bases. Japan employed destroyers and successfully landed the remaining elements of the Kawaguchi detachment on Guadalcanal, at the same time sinking many US transport ships. Japanese air power was very much in evidence and made US daytime resupply operations extremely hazardous.

On 8 September a battalion of US marine raiders on Guadalcanal effected a dramatic surprise attack on the Japanese rear area and broke up preparations for a major offensive by the recently arrived Kawaguchi detachment. Marine raiders also occupied a number of undefended neighbouring islands. Four days later the Japanese detachment, having regained its poise, attempted yet another offensive against the air base at Henderson Field and, during what became known as the Battle of Bloody Ridge, was thrown back with heavy losses. The US carriers *Hornet* and *Wasp*, together with the battleship *North Carolina*, provided heavy protection to an important convoy carrying the 7th Marine Regiment to reinforce Guadalcanal. The operation was costly, for the latter two vessels were torpedoed and the *Wasp* was sunk. Nevertheless, the 7th Marines landed on 17 September together with a major resupply of ammunition, food and fuel. Allied troops on Guadalcanal began to enjoy full rations for the first time since they had arrived.

In New Guinea, Japanese forces had come within 50 miles of Port Moresby. Five fresh Japanese battalions placed extreme pressure on the defending Australian units, who were in danger of encirclement. On 15 September the first US infantry arrived on New Guinea in an attempt to restore the situation. American survey parties began to locate sites for new airfields on Papua to support their operations.

In the Indian Ocean, the British were still anxious about the scope and scale of Japanese ambitions and the possibility that the Germans and Japanese might somehow link up. The Middle East campaign had been going badly for the British, and some feared that the Germans might push through Cairo and reach the Red Sea, gaining access to the Indian Ocean. The Allies knew that Berlin and Tokyo did not co-operate especially well; nevertheless, their forces in the field seemed to be in danger of joining up. Accordingly, on 10 September British commandos attacked Vichy French-controlled Madagascar, fearing that it might be taken by the Japanese. By 23 September the British had occupied the capital, Tananarive (Antananarivo). At the end of the month South African troops arrived to consolidate the hold on the island.

In Burma, British forces began their first tentative offensive in the Arakan area, using amphibious landings to approach the difficult terrain. At the end of the month an undercover team from Special Operations Australia conducted a raid on Singapore harbour. Deploying only a handful of personnel transported in three canoes, the raiders used limpet mines to destroy more than 40,000 tons of Japanese shipping.

Monday 14 September 1942

Richard Tregaskis, a journalist with Allied troups on Guadalcanal, hears Japanese soldiers shout 'Banzai!'

Beyond that firing line, the ridge curved and dipped. It rose like the back of a hog into a knoll, beyond the dip. It was on this knoll that the Raiders had been doing their fiercest fighting.

I worked my way out along the ridge to the firing line, to get a look at the knoll where the Raiders had been fighting. I lay flat next to a machine gunner while the Japs fired at us with a .25 light gun. A man to our right, farther out on the ridge, was wounded. We saw him crawling back toward us, a pitiful sight, like a dog with only three serviceable legs. He had been shot in the thigh . . .

I worked my way back to the CP and got some coffee. I was cleaning my mess cup when I heard a loud blubbering shout, like a turkey gobbler's cry, followed by a burst of shooting. I hit the deck immediately, for the sound was close by. When the excitement of the moment had stopped, and there was no more shooting, I walked to the spot, at the entrance to the CP on top of the ridge, and found two bodies of Japs there – and one dead marine. Gunner Banta told me that three Japs had made a suicide charge with bayonets. One of them had spitted the marine, and had been shot. A second had been tackled and shot, and the third had run away. These three had been hiding in a bush at the edge of the ridge road, evidently for some time. I had passed within a few feet of that bush on my way out to the firing line and back. The animal-like cry I had heard had been the Jap 'Banzai' shout.

Richard Tregaskis remained with the Allied invasion force on Guadalcanal until mid-September. At the end of the month, he would join a combat aircraft on a perilous reconnaissance of the island of Bougainville, before being transferred to the European theatre of operations.

Tregaskis became one of America's more prominent war reporters, covering the Chinese Civil War in the late 1940s and then the Korean War. He travelled to Vietnam in the early 1960s and worked there for a decade. Tragically, he died on 15 August 1973, at the age of fifty-six, in a boating accident off the coast of Hawaii. SEE ALSO PP. 293–4, 296–7.

Wednesday 16 September 1942

Colonel Paul Bunker, an American POW on Formosa, reflects on the Japanese culture of ferocity

Bawled out a Limey early this morning for making excessive chatter with his clogs. Our rice ration increased slightly today; not temporarily, we hope. Acquired a piece of bamboo near our rear fence and will use it to make a shelf and stops for my dishes. Our urine pit is overflowing but the Jap OD says that is all right! About 30 Japs in ranks at the guard house at 1:00 P.M. Seems they are changing our guard on us.

The governor of Hong Kong arrived last night with one other officer. He wouldn't sign the oath to not try to escape, so they locked him up in the guard house instead of giving him the big separate room upstairs. This morning I saw a big rangy civilian in his shirt sleeves, being escorted from the guard house to our building by the Jap OD ringed about by 6 soldiers with fixed bayonets! A most ludicrous spectacle. He has been in prison for 6 weeks, I hear.

This morning at 9:00 I met with Brigadier Curtis, who commanded all the big guns at Singapore – the job corresponding to mine in many ways. He had five 15" guns (ex-Navy) and the armament, like ours, was emplaced primarily for defense against *naval* action, and not against land attacks. They also had only armor piercing ammunition. Their air force pulled out and left them flat, and with no trace of observation for their guns.

The Japs moved many truckloads of cement into the fenced building that we thought might be the punishment cells. Perhaps they will build a wall between us and the river, also screening us from the school on the far bank. Much singing takes place in that school, also very complicated calisthenics.

The Jap culture is queer in one respect, the stress that is laid upon a Jap's ferocity. Soldiers of all grades utter the simplest commands in blood-curdling yells and howls, as though they were frantic with rage and hate and were suffering extreme torture. And, worse, they are inculcating this technique into the school children of all ages. Over across the river, for example, the children will be singing along calmly when suddenly their music stops and instead, sharp short yawps of hateful noises come in unison from them. Like the snarling yells of 'Ga-a-ah' which the soldiers bark as they bayonet the straw dummies. A nation is being trained to animal ferocity, presumably for war purposes.

Worthington et als gathered and cooked more snails today but, having learned all I had to tell them, omitted me from the party. I whittled on bamboo strips in the shade on the parade ground. Meat? ... Tonight, mirabile dictum, our soup had flecks of meat in it, but *not* a single globule of oil on its surface – so it was mostly fake. But the flavor was good, even though no nourishment existed.

We evidently changed guards today. The new gang is better dressed, more snappy and howls, grunts and yells with much more bestial ferocity than the old gang did. One of their sentries is relieved hourly just outside our window and the barking wakes us all up. They inspected our room at 8:30 while I was still up, reading. Checking for smokers!

Colonel Paul Bunker, veteran of the siege of Corregidor, had arrived at Takau on the west coast of Formosa on 15 August. He enjoyed distinguished company in his new POW camp, which contained many senior officers captured by the Japanese. He rubbed shoulders with the Governor of Hong Kong, together with General Wainwright from Bataan and General Percival from Malaya. Bunker's comments on the attempts to inculcate military ferocity are important and revealing. Japanese treatment of POWs in the First World War had been remarkably gentle, but twenty years later it had changed markedly. Many have attributed this to a general shift in the norms of military behaviour during the 1930s. Training of their own troops was increasingly accompanied by shouting, screaming and petty violence. SEE ALSO PP. 242–3, 270–3, 326–7.

Thursday 17 – Saturday 19 September 1942

Commander Thomas Hayes gets ready for the big inspection by General Shinichi Tanaka at Bilibid prison in the Philippines

Thomas Hirst Hayes was born in Philadelphia on 8 February 1898. He studied at George Washington University Medical School and later joined the US navy as a medical officer. Attached to the 4th Marine Regiment, he had been captured on Corregidor along with his whole medical team on 6 May 1942. As a POW he was initially chief of surgery at Bilibid prison hospital in Manila, later becoming the prison's senior medical officer. He maintained his voluminous diary in a small green notebook, and when this was full continued on whatever scraps of paper he could find.

17 September

One hell of a day! We received word early that there would be an inspection of our compound this afternoon by a senior medical officer of the Japanese Army. Then the following Sunday we would be privileged with an inspection by General Tanaka.

At two o'clock, Sartin, Joses, and I strolled up to the front office to greet the visiting dignitary. However, instead of a medical officer, Major General Miramoto stepped out of the car. There was the usual saluting, etc. We then stood at attention for about an hour while the General made himself comfortable in Nogi's office – drinking tea and ordering the furniture moved about. He rearranged the entire interior of the room, while at the same time making the guards stand at attention and recite their ritual and creed. But that wasn't all. Next there was a drill for us as to the correct manner of saluting and bowing to the Japanese.

About an hour later, Nogi and the missing medical officer finally showed up and the inspection began. During the walk through the wards, everyone was admonished as to the proper manner of greeting a general of the Japanese Army – the call to attention – the salute – the bow. But the one thing that the General objected to most strenuously was the fact that no one faced toward him. That's very important to these boys.

Later in the afternoon we learned that this was only a dummy run for the big inspection on Sunday. My impression of the whole affair is that our Army and Navy aren't the only services which have generals and admirals who find it necessary to find fault at inspections, and manufacture their own importance by overwhelming themselves in piddling unimportant details while exhibiting a total lack of sense of values.

The most amazing thing about the whole episode is that immediately after the inspection a rumor ran rampant through the camp that a German officer had accompanied the inspection party. However, since I had been along the tour, I knew that this just couldn't be. But later I learned the origin of the rumor. The only clean clothes I had to wear were my dyed blue shirt and shorts. All the other officers were dressed in khaki. I guess that with my blue uniform and jodhpurs I did look like a Prussian officer. Anyway, I was the German man in blue . . .

19 September

Soon after I turned in last night there was a lot of commotion outside in the yard. About 400 prisoners from Cabanatuan had just arrived in the camp. The 'Field Marshal' was in charge of getting the men settled down for the night. Gooding was drunk and abusive to everyone.

This group is a mixture of Army, Navy, Marines, and most of the crew from the *Canopus*. The men believe that they are on their way to Japan. These Cabanatuan boys looked in good shape. Their camp conditions have improved, and the death rate has dropped considerably. The men receive a prize of three cigarettes for every can of flies that they kill. They also have a baseball diamond and volleyball court. The tension in that camp has eased quite a bit. However, three prisoners were shot trying to escape. They were taken to a prominent hill where they were executed in full view of the rest of the camp.

General Tanaka arrived at exactly ten o'clock for his inspection. We were lined up to receive him and gave the General his usual honors. Tanaka then proceeded to a desk where he heard Nogi's report on the hospital. Next a whirl-wind tour through three wards then off he went. The General is an elderly man with coal black hair and a handle-bar mustache. He acted very quiet and dignified. Tanaka is reputed to have been a military attaché in Washington at one time, and the Manila newspapers report him as being a 'humanitarian and poet' . . .

General Shinichi Tanaka was part of the Japanese army general staff and one of the key planners behind Tokyo's war strategy. As Thomas Hayes was a senior officer, his diary gives us a larger overview than many, covering issues such as the administration of the prison, relations between the Japanese and American officials, and the medical problems of imprisonment. Before the war the old penitentiary at Bilibid had been declared unfit for further use and was a condemned building. It was reopened by the Japanese in April 1942. Located in Azcarraga Street in downtown Manila, it was a square building about 600 feet across. Prisoners lived in cells, which held about fifteen men each. Some Filipinos seemed to be able to move in and out of the prison fairly freely and so acted as couriers for messages and smuggled goods. Food, tobacco and newspapers were the main items that were sneaked into the prison. SEE ALSO PP. 657–60.

Wednesday 23 – Friday 25 September 1942

Louis Dusting, an RAAF corporal fitter, endures illness and air attack as the Japanese put pressure on Port Moresby in New Guinea

Louis George Dusting was born in Arncliffe, New South Wales on 16 February 1912. He joined the RAAF in Sydney in February 1941 and was initially sent to a large aircraft depot at Richmond. After a course on Beaufighter engines at No. 1 Engineering School he was posted to No. 30 Squadron. His unit had been moved to Townsville in Queensland, then to nearby Bohle river, and finally to Port Moresby in September 1942.

23 September
Back to camp today. Felt very weak and useless but I suppose I'll pick up. All the chaps seemed glad to see me. Later met Jack Crowe who is camped on the other side of the valley. There was much exchanging of news and afterwards I went over to his tent and cracked a couple of bottles of beer with him. We were just enjoying a mug when the ack ack started, then the sirens. We went into the trench and took our beer with us. The Japs came straight over our heads and dropped their loads over at the 7 Mile. The trouble with these night raids is you never know who they are going for. The Japs don't seem to be doing much day raiding lately, probably because of our greater air strength. Lost a machine today, A19-1 with George Sayer. What a bloody shame. He had had his share over the other side.

Mos Morgan stayed behind to see the results of the raid and was set on by Zero fighters. He saw them while he was in a turn so just kept turning until he was headed for home and then opened everything up and just walked away from the Zeros. Sayer was down low strafing when he copped the ack ack. Last seen heading for the jungle. The machine wasn't on fire so there may be a chance.

24 September

Did a bit of washing this morning and discovered that another bloke had been wearing my best shorts. He'll have to wash them. Tried to do a bit of trench digging but got knocked up very quickly. Went over to see Jack tonight.

The Japs came over again and dropped their bombs much closer this time. The ack ack and bombs make an awful bloody noise and at times it's hard to tell one from the other. I thought we would be free of them last night as it was cloudy and windy but the bastards still drop their bombs through the clouds. They always get somewhere near the target too. It's a fair cow when you can hear them but not see them.

25 September

Just got into bed last night and was settling down when terrific explosions started nearby. The bloody Japs had sneaked back and caught the whole place flat-footed ... There was quite a scramble and I seemed to get tangled up in the mossie net and so I rushed out with just my tin hat on and no show. Just finished breakfast this morning when they started again. They seem to be very persistent over something. 'A' Flight is coming back today so will see Ron. There is a standby flight of our kites at Milne Bay.

Louis Dusting had been in hospital with fever up to 23 September, when he returned to his unit. Its main role was to support the heavy fighting on Buna. They were involved in air-to-ground attacks against Japanese pill boxes, barges and airfields in New Guinea. The Japanese were attempting the same, using Zeros to strafe his airfield on a regular basis. Louis Dusting was not only concerned about the bombing, he was also made miserable by the huge numbers of flies and mosquitoes. Local conditions were uncomfortable, with vast numbers of insects, intense heat and a high incidence of illness. The Americans and Australians had learned to move air power as far forward as possible in support of their troops, and this meant continually building new air bases in inhospitable places. SEE ALSO PP. 346–7.

Thursday 24 September 1942

General 'Hap' Arnold attends a stormy command conference at Noumea in New Caledonia

Henry Arnold graduated from West Point in 1907. Although he received a commission in the infantry, he had always wanted to join the cavalry. In the event, four years later he opted for the Aeronautical Division of the Signal Corps. After instruction by aviation pioneer Wilbur Wright, Arnold won his pilot's licence and began a career in what was to become the US Army Air Force. In 1938 Arnold was elevated to Chief of the Army Air Corps and three years later, in 1941, became Commanding General, Army Air. During the war Arnold proved to be an adept politician as well as a strategist, dealing comfortably with his contemporaries, and persuading Congress to move ahead with the new B-29 Superfortress bomber.

First Nimitz, then Ghormley, finally McCain: 'Your bombers are doing no good over in England; your fighters are being wasted in Europe; here is where they can be of use; here is the only place where they can get results; MacArthur may need them but we need them more than he does.' The whole question revolves around: Where is this war to be won? What is our plan for winning the war? Is this not a local affair and should it not be treated as such? In any event, everyone from the Chief of Naval Operations on down should be indoctrinated with one plan for winning the war. So far everything we have seen indicates the necessity of having one theatre extending from Honolulu to Australia; one commander who can dictate an operating policy against one foe; one man who can move his forces to the place where they will be most effective; one plan for using all our forces and rotating them to be used as reinforcements and as replacements . . .

Emmons getting along 100% with Nimitz. Thinks Nimitz about the most brilliant naval officer he has met. Trouble in Pacific is Navy doctrine of having and retaining control; will do everything to retain control. Put Naval officers in command

and give them higher rank so that they will retain command. Under no circumstances must an Army officer command a Navy unit. Navy does not understand ground or air operations. They have no idea as to planning logistics or supplying troops. Their plan for putting air units along islands is lousy. Think that very soon the whole show in Solomons will break down due to lack of supplies . . .

In 1942 'Hap' Arnold was engaged in numerous strategy conferences with America's top commanders. There was little consensus. Admiral Ernest King, the US Chief of Naval Operations in Washington, and his subordinate Chester Nimitz, based in Hawaii, demanded a 'Japan First' strategy. They opposed the deployment of most American heavy bombers to Britain to begin daylight raids on Germany. However, King and Nimitz were fighting a political 'war' on more than one front. They also wished to see the entire Pacific come under navy control, resenting the role of General MacArthur and the predominance of the US army in the running of the South West Pacific Area. SEE ALSO PP. 367–8, 749–50.

Monday 28 September 1942

Corwin Mendenhall joins the bucket brigade on the US submarine *Sculpin*

Born in Beaumont, Texas, Corwin Mendenhall went to South Park High School and entered the US Naval Academy in 1939. Racing into action immediately after Pearl Harbor, in 1942 he was a junior ensign in charge of torpedoes on the US submarine Sculpin. *Although he enjoyed rapid promotion, he always regarded himself as 'an enlisted man's officer'.*

At eight minutes past midnight Cape Lambert, New Britain, was sighted, and before dawn *Sculpin* submerged for the day in the northern approaches to Rabaul. Right at sunrise a seaplane tender of the *Chiyoda* class was sighted, moving north. *Sculpin* tried to close but got no nearer than 20,000 yards.

An hour later masts were sighted to the west, and *Sculpin* commenced closing. The possibility of an attack was evident after twenty minutes of tracking, so we went to battle stations. The target was a large tanker of the *Omurosan* class, with only one small escort visible. They were zigzagging wildly on an easterly base course at a speed of eleven knots. After an hour of maneuvering to gain firing position, we fired a spread of four fish at the tanker from the stern tubes at a range of 1,860 yards.

The captain saw two hits, and three explosions were heard throughout the boat. After watching for only a few seconds longer, the captain took *Sculpin* to deep submergence as the escort headed for us with a bone in his teeth [at speed]. Sonar reported hearing the screws of two escorts.

Long before reaching *Sculpin* he commenced dropping depth charges. We knew that he was way off target. All was quiet for about twenty minutes. The crew was released from battle stations, and I went to my bunk for some rest.

No sooner had I gotten in the bunk than I was almost knocked out of it by a string of four very close depth charges, seemingly right over me. I could hear water spewing into the compartment. I ran to the control room to report that water was coming into officers' country in the vicinity of the head (toilet), and then went back to find the leak.

A gauge line to sea, located in the officers' head, was broken. Water was building up on the splash-tight deck over the forward battery. We dared not let that saltwater get into the battery below, because deadly chlorine gas would be formed when the saltwater reacted with the hydrochloric acid in the battery.

Calling for damage controlmen to come quickly, I went into the head and, by draping myself over the commode with my head back of it, I was able to use my hands to hold the gauge tubing and cut off the flow of water. The position was very awkward, and the pain of holding the water back with my hands was too much for me to stop the flow for more than a few seconds. It was incredible how much water could come in through a quarter-inch tube at a depth of 275 feet.

Baldwin arrived with plugs, turnbuckles, and other equipment to plug the leak. With him and a helper working on that job, I went to the after end of the compartment to help remove the water.

A bucket brigade was hurriedly formed. Jack trimmed the boat with a ten-degree up angle so the water would accumulate at the after end of the deck, in the officers' country. He had to maintain two-thirds speed to keep *Sculpin* from going deeper. *Sculpin* was tons too heavy, having taken on water from a number of leaks throughout the boat.

I took on the job of dipping up buckets of water, handing them through the compartment door for the bucket brigade to pass on aft and dump. The most comfortable position I could find was in the yeoman's chair in the ship's office, facing aft, filling buckets to be passed aft. The brigade was dumping the water into a bilge and into the canned-goods storeroom just aft of the control room.

We were able to keep the water level below twelve inches at our bailing location for the half hour that it took Baldwin to stop the leak. Then we bailed out the residual water and dried the deck. Fortunately, no water got into the battery.

Corwin Mendenhall

During her first eight patrols, mostly around the Solomon Islands, the Sculpin *sank nine ships. The American submarine effort was vital to the turning of the tide against Japan and accounted for over half the*

Japanese shipping sunk in the Pacific. Each attack was fraught with danger, as this diary entry shows. Mendenhall served no fewer than seven tours of duty with the Sculpin. *SEE ALSO PP. 569–71.*

Late September 1942

Peter Vladimirov, Soviet representative, visits Mao's 8th Route Army and finds it peacefully co-existing with the Japanese

On 15 September Peter Vladimirov and his friend Aleyev had left Yenan on a ten-day journey to visit the Chinese communists' 8th Route Army.

The Army doesn't get a cent from Yenan, and it doesn't provide any supplies. Besides the troops and territories they control, Ho Lung, Liu Po-cheng, Nieh Jung-chen, Cheng Kuang, and Hsiao Ko have their own industrial arsenals and issue their own money. Each commander imposes his own tax on the peasants. There is no single system of taxation.

Old arms are repaired here in workshops; several discarded rifles are taken to pieces to assemble one good rifle. Production of grenades and mines is well organized. Metal for their casings is produced in primitive furnaces.

Army leadership is not free from feudal survivals. I got acquainted with a commander who has two very young wives, almost girls. And no one seems to be outraged.

The commanders and their deputies report to Yenan by telegraph to the extent they consider fit. Directives issued by the center are discussed from the viewpoint of their expediency, and not as to whether they should be fulfilled. The commanders disdainfully refer to the leading Yenan comrades as 'scribblers'.

Among the troops there is an atmosphere of indolence, waiting for the events to take their course. No one sincerely helped us get information about the combat actions. We were met affably, but then they immediately sought to get rid of us . . .

The Eighth Route Army peaceably coexists with the

enemy. The Japanese had comfortably settled for the winter in built-up areas (we stayed well out of their reach as we went by). Meanwhile, the Eighth Army's units idled their time away in the vicinity.

In the area of Hsin-hsiang very small Japanese garrisons, of five to forty soldiers, occupy villages which are invested by the numerically superior forces of Ho Lung. I asked why they did not recapture the villages, since it was easy to destroy the punitive forces. The men of the Eighth Route Army watched them have a good time. I was corrected: 'They have four hundred soldiers there, not four!'

We dismounted, had a smoke with the men, and they admitted, 'We are told not to touch them. If we destroy the garrison, they tell us, the Japanese will bring in reinforcements. What's to be done then? So we do not touch them and they don't touch us . . .'

As we could see, the Kuomintang forces are the main concern of the Eighth Route Army. Propaganda in the units is spearheaded against them; combat actions are also expected against them in the future. Consequently, nearly all operations undertaken by the Japanese are successful. Yenan has ordered the preservation of the Eighth Route Army at all costs, so the Army is backing away, although the forces of the advancing enemy are insignificant.

Mao Tse-tung doctrine: The war is waged to preserve his own man power, not to exterminate the enemy. It is achieved by slackening resistance to the enemy and by yielding more territory.

The years of inactivity have had a degrading influence on the armed forces of the CCP. Discipline is slack, and cases of desertion have become more frequent. The men neglect their weapons. Training in the units and in staffs is not organized. Co-operation between the units is not organized. Staff officers play cards and gossip. Operational orders are issued in the presence of peasants.

For many years historians considered that the Chinese communists were much more effective opponents of the Japanese invaders than the nationalists. But more recently it has become clear that both Chinese factions had traded space for time and were avoiding conflict with the

Japanese, expecting either the Americans or the Russians eventually to defeat their external enemy. Meanwhile they stored weapons and supplies for the civil war that all knew was coming. Both the nationalists and the communists ran their armies on a semi-feudal basis, with each general serving as a warlord in his own area and raising his own local taxes. As Vladimirov rightly observed, the communists commanded allegiance over the peasantry the more effectively by the simple expedient of giving them land. SEE ALSO PP. 305–7, 451–2, 575–6.

OCTOBER 1942

O N 5 OCTOBER the Japanese attempted a last, rather half-hearted attack on the air base at Henderson Field on Guadalcanal. Two days later the US marines began a new offensive with the objective of pushing all Japanese forces back out of artillery range of the vital base. The marines advanced on all fronts and were more seriously impeded by torrential rain than enemy action. However, Japan continued to reinforce Guadalcanal successfully, if at considerable cost in lost transports. The Japanese 2nd Division landed from destroyers on 9 October. Thereafter the US navy began to assert its superiority and two days later, at the Battle of Espurance, US cruisers destroyed a major Japanese convoy, sinking a cruiser, a destroyer and a number of transports. US aircraft sank two more destroyers the following day. On 15 October Japanese transports were forced to beach on Guadalcanal under intense American air attack and, although they landed their troops, the ships were destroyed. Nevertheless, Japanese cruisers remained in the area and periodically managed to shell Henderson Field.

On 25 October Japan attempted to move up a task force of carriers to tip the balance at Guadalcanal. At the Battle of Santa Cruz Islands, the US carrier *Hornet* was badly damaged and later sunk, but the Japanese carriers attempting to move towards Guadalcanal all suffered severe damage and were forced to withdraw. By the end of the month the Japanese had voluntarily disengaged from the front line on Guadalcanal and withdrawn towards new defensive positions on Koli point and Kokumbona.

During October, American and Australian forces were preparing a new offensive in an attempt to throw the Japanese out of Papua. Meanwhile in Burma, after a long period of argument, the British and Americans agreed on a strategy for an offensive in the north that would reopen the Burma Road supply route into China. Since the Japanese incursion it had been necessary for all supplies for the Chinese nationalist army to be ferried from India to China over the Himalayas by aircraft, a hazardous mission known to pilots as flying 'over the hump'. The effectiveness of nationalist operations against the Japanese in China remained hard to judge, and some regarded Allied efforts to resupply China as a waste of time. Churchill, in particular, was sceptical about Chinese military potential, and wished to see the Allies press south along the coast of Burma towards the lost imperial possessions of Malaya and Singapore.

In America mobilization for war was still gathering pace, with the creation of large recruit training camps all over the United States and a steadily accelerating programme of ship and aircraft production. Meanwhile, in less than a year Japan had lost more than 10 per cent of its merchant fleet, losses that were hard to replace.

Thursday 8 – Friday 9 October 1942

Lieutenant Tadayoshi Matsumoto encounters US artillery fire near Henderson Field on Guadalcanal

Tadayoshi Matsumoto was a junior officer attached to the headquarters staff of Hyakutak Force, which was assisting with the defence of Guadalcanal. Periodically he had served as acting company commander of the 3rd Company in his infantry unit. He was part of a Japanese force of some 2,500 soldiers and 1,000 marines at Palau that had been ordered to Guadalcanal by Tojo during late August in the hope of removing the toehold established by the US marines. They were joined by other Japanese forces from Guam. On 12 September they had tried, but failed, to push towards the US-held air base at Henderson Field. On the night of 5 October they made a further attempt – but were soon retreating.

We failed in our second attack ... We suffered enormous casualties due to the accurate artillery barrage and strafing of the enemy.

The Bn Comdr [Battalion Commander], 5 other officers, and approx. 180 men were killed. More than 100 men were injured so badly that they had to be carried away on litters. There were countless numbers of men who were hit but still able to walk. The transporting of so many patients by only a small number of men who were physically sound created a very difficult problem. The rations had been completely exhausted by the end of the night attack. Although it was possible to march 2 or 3 days on the difficult road without food, the men were tiring from hunger, day by day. It was a pitiful sight ...

We had never experienced this retreat march in the China Incident and it is a very distressing event. When I read this diary in the future I believe I'll be carried away with some very deep emotions. The faithful heroes in battlefield are not always found in the attack, but also in the distressing aftermath. The sight of those men who are enduring hardships and hunger, the kind affections of transporting the wounded, is even more beautiful than the picture of them in victory. These are the qualities of only the faithful and well-trained armies. I cannot help from crying when I see the sight of these men, marching without food ... and carrying the wounded through the curving and sloping mountain roads. Hiding my tears I encouraged the ones with weak will to march on. Try to imagine the trying heart of the Co Comdr [Company Commander].

The wounded could not be given adequate medical treatment because of lack of medical supplies. There wasn't a one who didn't have maggots in his wounds. I felt sorry and it was trying even to look at them. The swinging motions of the litters during the march, the fatigue, and excess loss of blood were too much for the patients and many died. There were 3 or 4 of the bearers, too, who died of fatigue and hunger. By exalting their spirits the majority of the other sick persons arrived at the Regt. Hq. [Regimental Headquarters]. Next day we received 6 to 7 GO of rice. The men showed some vigor for a change and I can see them cooking their meal.

During early September the 'Tokyo Express', a night transport service for troops provided by fast destroyers, had brought Japanese reinforcements to Guadalcanal from Rabaul and Palau. By 12 September General Kawaguchi Kiyotake, the local commander, felt strong enough to lead his men in a new attack designed to take the vital air base. Fighting focused on a low grassy ridge south of Henderson Field, soon known as 'Bloody Ridge', and his forces came within a mile of the airfield. He tried again in early October, but the weight of firepower from aircraft and in particular from naval bombardment broke up the attack and inflicted heavy casualties.

Later in October Matsumoto was attached to an engineering unit and was kept busy reconnoitring defensive positions around the Lunga river. His diary ends abruptly on 7 November 1942 but his fate is not known.

Friday 9 October 1942

Colonel Paul Bunker and fellow American POWs in Formosa receive the gift of a pig from a visiting Japanese general

Fine day. Our guard changed today and a new bunch takes over. Great bustle everywhere over the inspection: we did last minute sweeping, etc. and then turned out at 8:35. The CO of the Taiwan army arrived on dot of 9:00 A.M. He was a chunky, moon-faced man with wide-spread luxuriant mustache. He received our 'eyes right' and we had to follow him with our eyes as he crossed our front and took post in front of our center. Wainwright and Sir Percival ran out in front of him and Wood read their speech. The CO brought in a small package (cigarettes, etc.) to them, also some small, cheap books for us. Then he went up to HQ for tea and later came back and walked through our barracks, wherein we were lined up.

Pork! For 2 days we've been excited over the Jap promise that we would get a pig to eat today. But it develops that the pig is a present from the Jap general, and when it reached our kitchen, the local Japs cut off both hams, to include the loins! Now, when our enlisted cooks steal what *they* want, if we get more than a *flavor* we'll be lucky.

With Carter's help, I started surveying a new line of markers for our assembly formation. For evening meal we had more rice than usual and real soup with rich pork flavor – and even a crumb or two of the pork in it. Universally hailed as the best meal that we've had here at this camp. Everybody more cheerful, as a result. Gosh, how little it takes to please us now! We repaired our electric lighter this P.M. A couple of Jap newspapers (in English were given to us: 'Japan Times and Advertiser' – Practically nothing but propaganda.)

The new guard is less savage than the old. No racket at benjo tonight or in posting guards.

Colonel Bunker shared his POW camp with Generals Percival and Wainwright, both of whom would survive their imprisonment and attend the Japanese surrender ceremony at the end of the war. Bunker, however, died of malnutrition-related illness in March 1943. He passed his diary to a friend, Colonel Delbert Ausmus, together with a piece of the American flag that he had hauled down on Corregidor in April 1942. SEE ALSO PP. 242–3, 270–3, 310–12.

Tuesday 20 October 1942

John Nevell, an Australian soldier, watches frog racing in Changi gaol at Singapore

John Nevell began work as a bank clerk at the age of fourteen, but during the 1920s depression found himself unemployed. He had spent a period farming before joining the Australian army at the outbreak of war. He was assigned to the 2/10 Field Unit and sailed from Sydney for Singapore on the Queen Mary. *He had arrived in Singapore on 18 February 1941 and almost exactly a year later found himself in an over-spill POW camp near Changi gaol.*

The latest rumour about our Xmas celebrations pleases me. It is that the Japs have stated they will issue each man with two bottles of beer. If the privilege is abused, there will be no issue the following Xmas.

The Thompson Road lads have started frog racing. Each frog has a name and pedigree such as 'Easy Money' by Petrol out of Nippon. The frogs are painted in colours for easy identification. All frogs go under a box in the centre of a marked square, about a foot wider than the box. The odds are laid, the race starts when no one else wants to bet. The box is lifted and first over the outside line wins.

The trainers have found that their steeds jump best on a white ant diet, so much of Nippon's working time is spent bottling white ants.

Rather an unpleasant incident tonight. A few of us with money bought bananas, as we had done before, at work. Most chaps ate them on the spot. As the guards have never worried about them, a couple of us brought them home. We are searched each night before coming into camp. I always carry my mess gear in a respirator bag with a compartment at the back, which the little fellows have never discovered, as the opening flap folds back over it. For no reason, except my natural cunning, I put my spoils, including bananas, in the back compartment, and got them through. The other chap put his bananas in his bag as usual, and the guards pulled him out of the ranks and took him to the guard house. The officer in charge of us explained that they had been bought, not stolen. This was of no avail. They bashed the chap until unconscious, threw water over him until he revived, then bashed him again. He is now in hospital.

Arbitrary violence over small issues such as banana smuggling ensured a high degree of obedience from POWs. In mid-September the big issue in POW camps across Singapore had been the 'no escape clause'. John Nevell and his friends had by now heard about an incident at Selarang barracks at Changi. The POWs had refused to sign an agreement not to escape and so had been kept in the sun in a courtyard for several days. The rest of the POWs in Changi had then agreed to sign the clause, on condition that it was marked as signed 'under duress'. John Nevell's commanding officer said he would not order them to sign the document, but advised them to do so. All agreed that escape was, in any case, virtually impossible. SEE ALSO PP. 353–4, 499–500.

Saturday 24 – Wednesday 28 October 1942

William Leaney travels north from Malaya by train towards Ban Pong work camp in Thailand

William Leaney was a sergeant in the Royal Artillery who had been captured at the fall of Singapore in February 1942. Kept first at Changi, he was now being transported north by train towards the work camps that had been established on the Thai–Burma frontier for the purpose of building what would become known as the 'railway of death'.

The nights were horrible – absolutely. I was unable even to sit with my back against anything and several of the nights I just didn't close my eyes. I felt very sad as we trundled thro' Malaya and unhappily contrasted our stop at Kuala Lumpor with the last occasion I had been there. That time I was leaving after a short stay with the F.M.S. [Free Malay States] Volunteers, a small party of whom had seen me off – hospitality (of course) from the station buffet. I was to spend the night journey in a 1st class sleeping compartment and it was the termination of one of my happiest memories of Malaya. Now we were Nip captives, were given rice and dried fish and actually allowed to go to the rear, this was the only time on the trip that we used the latrine officially and it was the first time I have ever had to squat . . .

Much of the country was under flood it appears. Some of the lads claimed to see wild elephants tho I didn't myself. We seemed to get 3 irregular meals of rice and some other stuff (veg. Stew, or fish) in 24 hours. But thank the Lord we had Red Cross tinned stuff and to a great extent were independent of this hog-wash. By this time we had bought fruit from the natives and many of us were suffering from 'squitters' and, as at no time did they let us know how long we were stopping at any station it became very, very awkward. Some chaps of course dirtied their trousers while others 'crapped' out of the train as it was moving held by another chap. I have never seen anything quite like that before. Eventually we arrived at Ban Pong at 7.15 (in a drizzle of rain) on Wed. morning 28th. From the station we marched to the Camp – still not knowing where we were going. The first glimpse of the camp filled me with horror. It is quite impossible for me to describe. It was almost completely under water – what part wasn't completely under water was a slithery, slippery morass of mud . . .

Here were treated to the picture of the 'amiability' with which the Nips treat the Thais for practically all day long outside the guard room they had Thais bound to posts and indulged themselves in the face-smackings and corporal punishments that they seem to love so much. Here also we were very surprised to meet 'Hub' Garland who had been living in this hell-hole for 4 months and, curiously enough, was as fit as a fiddle. It was a strange feature of this place that, despite appalling sanitary conditions and vile living conditions they had very little disease. Most of us had the 'squitters' by this time and I sampled the open trench latrines many times. Gosh the maggots that were in those trenches!

William Leaney

Ban Pong was the Thai end of the Thai–Burma railway. The task of the first prisoners sent here in June 1942 was to construct the camp for larger groups who would arrive later, but the site selected by the Japanese was low-lying and prone to flooding. Leaney's diary captures the treatment of the Thais at this location. Many more Thais and Burmese than Allied POWs were forced to work on the railway project and suffered terrible treatment. SEE ALSO PP. 344–5.

NOVEMBER 1942

IF THE BATTLE OF Midway in June 1942 marked the turning point of the war against Japan at sea, then on land the critical moment was the struggle for Guadalcanal in November 1942. Elsewhere the tide of war was also turning against the Axis. In the western desert Rommel was retreating after a decisive defeat at El Alamein. On the Eastern Front the Germans were bogged down in the battle for Stalingrad, an epic struggle from which the Wehrmacht would never recover. Japan had hoped that Hitler's preferred strategy of a southward push through the Caucasus and onwards towards Iran and Afghanistan would draw resources away from the British effort in Burma. However, this tantalizing prospect of assistance never materialized. German forces ground to a halt in the Caucasus, and German plans for activities in south Asia never progressed beyond secretive assistance to rebels in Afghanistan.

Heavy support weapons were an additional advantage for the Americans on Guadalcanal. Accompanied by a fierce bombardment, the US marines crossed the Matanikau river on 1 November. Although small numbers of Japanese reinforcements continued to arrive, American operations became more adventurous, with a number of amphibious outflanking operations. American success on Guadalcanal had been likely from the outset because of the sensible decision to begin by capturing and protecting the air base at Henderson Field. With this came air superiority and, thereafter, eventual victory.

Nevertheless, the waters around Guadalcanal continued to be the site of hard-fought naval engagements, following one another in quick succession. On 12 November Japanese cruisers and destroyers employed their favourite tactic of night attack with torpedoes to deliver a crushing blow to the US navy, sinking several cruisers and destroyers. The following day US aircraft managed to sink the Japanese battleship *Hiei*, while a US cruiser sank a destroyer. On 14 November aircraft from the USS *Enterprise* inflicted severe damage on a Japanese convoy, sinking a cruiser and forcing the transports to beach with their reinforcements. The following night the Japanese attempted to bombard Henderson Field with a large force of ships, but the US battleships *Washington* and *South Dakota* were waiting for them: in one of the few battleship-to-battleship engagements of the Second World War, the *South Dakota* was damaged and the *Kirishima* effectively destroyed and later scuttled.

On 20 November the Japanese launched a surprise counter-attack on Guadalcanal to the west of the Matanikau river, but the scale of US air and artillery support brought it to a halt. US marines began to encounter skilfully constructed Japanese defences and deep bunkers designed to withstand heavy air and artillery bombardment. Although the Japanese fought another successful naval engagement by night at Tassafarogna, their troops on Guadalcanal were fast running out of supplies and their defeat was only a matter of time.

In New Guinea, Australian forces captured Kokoda and its airfield. Heavy fighting continued up and down the Kokoda trail and a major battle developed for the town of Oivi. Later in the month, the Australians also took the town of Goravi. MacArthur was now confident enough to move his headquarters from Australia to Port Moresby.

Early November 1942

Henry Traill, a former rubber planter, observes the
domestic economy of POWs and attempts some fishing at
Kinseyo camp in Thailand

*Henry Traill was born in Northern Ireland in 1911 and had come to
Malaysia as a rubber planter in 1935, working in Jahore. He later served
in the Royal Ordnance Corps and had been taken prisoner in February
1942. By November 1942 he had been moved north from Changi to a
camp on the Thai–Burma railway at Kinseyo.*

Every day, one or two little canoes appeared round the bend
of the river and paddled in beneath the tree-hung bank. Each
was propelled by a woman, usually accompanied by a child
or two, and they brought duck-eggs fresh and hard-boiled,
bananas, coconuts, home-made cakes, and peanut toffee, to
sell to us. Their coming was yet another example of how
many more inhabitants there really are in these lonely
stretches of road or river, than one would think.

We generally bought our gula malacca from the Thai huts,
where we also got banana fritters. An old woman used to
make these, squatting on the ground underneath her hut,
which, as is customary, was built up on posts about six feet
high. The fire was a tiny heap of charcoal in a depression in the
ground, over which rested the small cooking-kuali,
a plain round metal utensil shaped like a deep saucer,
measuring a foot across. In this was the boiling pig-fat, and in
a bowl beside her she mixed a batter of tapioca flour. The
bananas were cut in half lengthways, dipped in the batter, and
fried till their covering was brown, and crisp at the edges.

It could not be claimed that throughout the whole process
these fritters were 'untouched by human hand', nor that the
hand that touched them, as well as the clothes, dwelling, and
all the belongings of the old woman were anything but worn
and grimy; but as a sop to our hygiene-educated feelings we
could reflect that the last act in the process was an
undoubted sterilisation in boiling oil.

One of these families of Thais was impressed by the Japs as official slaughterers of our occasional pig. The pigs were kept in a bamboo pen on the river bank, and if one were passing that way when a killing was imminent one would know the fact by the piercing squeals that preceded it. The squealing started when the pig was being manhandled out of the pen and down the path to a spot convenient to the river, but it stopped completely during the few moments when, being held down on its side, it actually awaited the knife. The latter was so sharp that it cut through the pig's gullet with a single dextrous stroke, much more easily and quickly than a butter knife through butter. No squeal, but only a grunt, accompanied the coup de grace.

For this slaughtering service the Thais were given the head, tail, trotters, blood and offal – except that the Japs kept for themselves such delicacies as the liver and kidneys. Most of these by-products of our own precious rations were then sold back to us individually by the Thais; and one occasionally passed a fire outside one of our huts on which some part of a pig simmered delectably in an old kerosene tin.

I remember the first time Bill and Robby and I bought some duck-eggs. We could have boiled them, of course, but decided that to get real satisfaction out of them they must be fried. For by this time we must have had about a hundred consecutive meals consisting of rice and stew, or mushy mixtures of some kind, and a fried egg seemed to us the last word in gastronomic pleasure.

Cooking was my province, and Bill was chief provider, by his fishing . . .

Towards the end of our stay at Kinseyo the Jap commandant proclaimed a whole holiday and a fishing competition. There were to be prizes for the heaviest five fish; one hundred, fifty, forty, thirty and twenty cigarettes respectively.

Bill, Robby and I decided to try our luck. It was a pleasant way of spending the day, anyhow. Hooks and some rough line we had bought from the Thai boatmen. Rods of bamboo were growing in a hundred assorted sizes around us. We all had knives, and very sharp ones too – especially Bill's, as he had a pocket whetstone, and took a great pride in keeping his knives in good order . . .

I must admit that my fishing efforts were rather un-productive. The fish in this river were abundant. Many were caught, of great variety, and ranging up to twenty pounds or so in weight. Below the cookhouse, where the swill and the vegetable peelings were thrown in, one could see scores of fish constantly on the lookout; and when a basket of scraps was thrown onto the water it floated down-stream accom-panied by a catherine-wheel gymkana of carp-like fishes, twirling and cavorting around it.

I tried floating a baited hook on a long line, but not a fish looked at it, though they were gobbling up exactly similar delicacies all round. Then I attached my mosquito net (torn and useless for its proper purpose) to a huge bamboo frame measuring eight feet across, and carried it down to the river bank amid the derisive looks of fellow-prisoners, Thai barge-men, and Japs, alike. Sinking it in three feet of water I chucked vegetable rind into and over it, and waited with growing concern while fish after fish gave me the cold shoulder.

But at last I found my metier. A little way up-stream, the bank was lined with bushes which extended into the water, and past them and round them we frequently saw shoals of little fish about three or four inches long. Remembering childhood's days, when we sat on the harbour rocks and caught 'cudding' with bent pins and walking sticks, I collaborated with Bill, who, from an invaluable little tin work-box, produced both a pin, which he bent and sharpened, and two yards of blue silk sewing-thread.

With these and a bamboo cane and the tips of some small worms I justified myself at last, and spent a happy morning yanking tiddlers out, with the smiling encouragement of a Thai woman on an anchored barge. Of course I missed a lot too, but I came back with half a dozen on a bamboo twig. Bad luck dogged me still, though, for after we had toasted them we left them to keep warm by our fire during evening roll-call, and when we came back they were gone. Thereafter I stuck to cooking.

Henry Traill and his friends were kept at undeveloped POW locations in Thailand and found themselves sometimes quite literally camping. His friends sold most of their valuable possessions, including pens and watches, for local currency – the Thai tical – in order to buy extra supplies of food from the locals. These included salt and a locally produced variant of sugar. They enjoyed some freedom to enhance their diet by picking edible vegetation along the edge of paddy fields and fishing for shrimps in nearby pools and streams. Frequently wandering alone and unguarded with a shrimp net through pools at the edge of the jungle, Henry found this time oddly pleasant and peaceful, reflecting that this was a 'strange and unimaginable situation' for a prisoner of war. SEE ALSO PP. 408–11.

Saturday 14 November 1942

Anne Morrow Lindbergh visits an iron foundry in the Ford motor plant at River Rouge, now turning out B-24 Liberator bombers

After supper C [Charles Lindbergh] takes me to see the big iron foundry at the River Rouge factory. It is like a great city – a factory city with railroad, coal dumps, boats (ore boats come up the Rouge River), cranes, dumps, derricks, cars, and of course blocks and blocks of factory units. We go into the foundry, where they are melting the crude iron ore and pouring it out of the furnace. We climb up grimy stairs. It is black and not much lit and seems empty. We pass by one furnace – a great fortlike stack or tank that goes up into the darkness – and get to another that is pouring. Five or six men are standing about, grimy, tough looking, with smoke glasses on and great forks or iron poles. The heat is terrific, even standing back where we were, and a great roar from the furnace, and the streams so bright you could hardly look at them.

The darkness, lit only with the great mouth spitting out molten metal, gas, and sparks, and those roaring, tumbling, flaming streams of metal, the dark soot-covered figures with their poles glowing red on the end gave an infernal impression. And when you heard the foreman talk of 'we used to do this [lift the gate] by hand but a man got burned so . . .' when you considered what those men were handling – liquid torture, liquid death, liquid fire – one false step would mean instant shriveled death, then you had the impression that it was hell – really hell.

I was afraid – full of fear before that terrible power and nearness of torture and death. And I had the feeling that one could not stay long there and believe in God or trees or sky or children. It was dreadful. A poster on one of the grimy walls showed a soldier flat on the ground with a machine gun asking for more – more production. To work in that furnace is war, too. There were two men who did not seem to belong there. One a dark-eyed, soft-voiced Mexican whose face lit up quickly and sympathetically when you spoke to him. The other a Negro, bent and oldish, who at the orders of the foreman opened the small holes inside the furnace and you could hear a great blast of air from it. When he had done this he made a slight gesture with his hands – a gesture you might make if you had set down a tray of food before someone or some flowers. It was an awkward gesture but a gesture of grace, just the same – an 'I have given you what I could' gesture.

Those two men did not belong there. But then – who did? An inferno – the 'creation of Faustian man,' C[harles] said. And 'Blood out of Rocks.'

Anne Morrow Lindbergh's husband, Charles Lindbergh, spent the war working as an aircraft consultant for the Ford Company and for United American Aircraft. Some of Henry Ford's largest car plants were turned over to wartime aircraft production and in November 1942 the Lindberghs were given the opportunity to tour one such plant. The United States enjoyed fantastic productive capacity and this was one of its main contributions to winning the war. In 1942 Germany was still producing more tanks than Britain (9,300 against 8,600), and the German tanks were of superior design and quality. However, some 23,000 American tanks were produced that year and were certainly of increasing quality, including the reliable Sherman. With such differences of scale in production, Allied victory was only a matter of time. SEE ALSO PP. 150–1, 625–6.

Thursday 19 November 1942

Captain Hyman Samuelson, US Army officer with the
96th Engineers (Colored), goes on a date while on leave in
Sydney

I had a date with Peggy again last night, the date which we
had made last Sunday evening. She looked prettier than she
did Sunday night, and I had put on a fresh uniform, brass all
ashine, clean shaved, wearing a big grin. We looked like a
decent sort of couple. Jimmy was in a bad mood, and he and
Irene didn't click very well. But Peggy and I were right there.
We went to see two British motion pictures, which turned
out to be excellent productions. As we sat in a little tea shop
on Pitt Street after the show was over, I realized that Peggy
was at least twenty. Her lips were very pretty and her small,
shapely body was quite feminine. The way she inhaled a
cigarette proved she wasn't just a kid. While we stood on the
corner waiting for a taxi, I put my arms around her. The
streets are very dark with the 'brown out' and making love
in public is dern common on the streets. She leaned her body
against mine so that I felt goose bumps rise all over. I said to
myself, 'I'll kiss her when we get into the taxi. Say she resists.
You'll feel like a fool. You're married. You can't force yourself on a girl. Sure, I know, it's nearly nine months since you
have kissed a girl. That's longer than you've ever gone in
your whole life without kissing anyone. And sure you'd like
to be kissed. That's what you'd really enjoy. Her mouth is
very pretty. It is – oh, well, go on – I don't blame you. The
drive to her house takes only ten minutes. This might be
your last chance to take a girl in your arms until you get
home – home – Dora! Gee, isn't it worth while waiting for.
Just think of coming home and having her throw her arms
around your neck and really kissing you. No other girl can
kiss like her. This girl will disgust you. You'll be disappointed. And remember – you're married. You're not at
college anymore! You're a man – a married man!
Behave yourself – But no harm will be done by kissing

her. I need it. She is clean and decent – It will do me good –'

'Why so quiet?' Peggy asked 'What are you thinking about?'

'Oh-er-nothing! I'm tired I guess. I'

'I'm tired too.' We got into the cab. I looked at Peggy. She looked into my eyes, and I looked at her lips. I smelled the powder she was wearing. I leaned my face to hers and touched my lips gently to hers. She didn't turn away. We kissed. It was absolutely wonderful. Her lips were full and soft and she knew how to kiss. At her doorstep I took her hand.

'Don't guess I'll see you any more Peggy. It has been good knowing you.'

She put her arms around my neck and gave me a big kiss. Then she started to turn, but I pulled her back to me and kissed her again. Then we looked at each other a minute.

'Have a good trip back. God be with you,' she said half choked for some damn reason. She then gave me a quick kiss and before I could take hold of her, she had turned and run into the house.

'I must be going crazy,' I told Jimmy back in the cab.

'What do you mean?'

'I swear I feel like I have been out with my wife. I'm all muddled. I need some sleep. This is the strangest thing I have ever been through.'

'Aw, snap out of it. Haven't you ever kissed a girl before?'

'Yes, but – aw, give me a cigarette.' We drove a way in silence. 'I don't think I've ever felt so homesick before in my life.' Jimmy laughed.

Hyman Samuelson's diaries are uniquely personal and sensitive to feelings and emotions. His diverse reflections on race, love and death are thoughtful and the diaries are remarkably full, even seeking to capture the texture of his conversations with friends and compatriots. Hyman's story was ultimately a tragic one. He had married Dora in December 1941 and spent the Pacific War longing to be reunited with his wife. Although he would succeed in being posted back to Virginia in late 1944 and was able to see his son for the first time, he also discovered that his wife was terminally ill. She died on 30 December 1944. SEE ALSO PP. 102–4, 282–4.

Friday 20 November 1942

Elizabeth Vaughan, a civilian who has been interned for
five months, visits the toilet in total darkness at Bacolod
Camp in the Philippines

Up in total darkness at 6:00 A.M. (Electricity is off from
6 A.M. to 6 P.M. daily to conserve fuel for running the small
electric plant of Bacolod.) Stumbled around room, as did
other adults in their dressing, trying not to disturb the
children, then down the dark verandah, trying not to collide
with other gliding figures or bump into makeshift seats.
Then down the concrete steps for which the camp's
carpentry committee has this week secured secondhand
lumber and nails (which they pulled from walls here and
there) for badly needed banisters. Steps are dangerous at any
time and treacherously slippery when wet. Then along walkway to toilet, walkway irregularly dotted with large and
small puddles from which frogs hop with a splash as
pedestrians approach, only to splash back in again when
footsteps have passed. On to the wet, foul-smelling toilets,
so continuously wet at this time of year that mushrooms six
inches in height spring out from wooden partitions separating
one narrow stall from another. Then in darkness an eerie
sound from roof of toilets and, as heart stops, one wonders if
it's a python (a few small snakes have been seen around
toilets), a nest of scorpions, large cockroaches scurrying, or the
lizards which abound in the Philippines – and a cock crows on
the roof and you realize with relief that the sound came from
this fowl changing position. A kerosene tin can is filled and
poured in toilet for flushing. In the darkness the toilet seat cannot be seen and it is hardly possible to pour water in with force
necessary for flushing without splashing water over sides of
toilet and on walls and already wet floor.

*One of the puzzling issues concerning the 7,000 American civilian
detainees in the Philippines is why so very many of them chose to stay
on in late 1941, when it was plain to all that the military were busily*

evacuating all their civilian dependants. Part of the answer lies in the secluded life of many Americans in the country. Working for large companies and banks, universities and hospitals, they lived a protected middle-class existence, often in exceptionally comfortable purpose-built American-style townships. Some of the local population had a good idea of what was about to occur, but contact with the locals was minimal. When the Americans were transferred to the camps, it must have been a sharp shock. Bacolod had no medical facilities at all, and the latrine facilities are vividly described by Elizabeth Vaughan. SEE ALSO PP. 280–1, 371–2, 402, 417–18.

Monday 23 November 1942

Mack Morriss, US army, goes on leave with his friend Brodie and discovers the city of Auckland

Mack Morriss, from Elizabethton in Tennessee, was a sergeant in his early twenties and also a newspaper correspondent. He worked on the US army newspaper The Yank. *He was despatched to Bougainville and Guadalcanal to report on the front line of the war, and compiled a superb and often extremely frank diary. Interspersed between his accounts of military life in the South Pacific were narratives of his periods on leave in Auckland with his friend Brodie, an official war artist.*

Brodie and I debarked in the middle of a madhouse . . . Our hut-mates were two regular army crewmen on B-17s, back to this 'Paradise of the Pacific' for a ten day rest after 11 months of combat. They took us to town and bought us drinks at the Royal Hotel bar. There we ran into Frank McCarthy, UP correspondent, and Jack Dowling of the *Chicago Sun*. They are just back from Guadalcanal . . .

Went back to the Royal. Mack and Mac bought us more drinks and we had dinner with them and some dates they procured for us. Brodie went out to a dance hall and I took mine home. I had a terrific headache, and didn't feel like fooling. It was a wild day.

I've been in a daze since we landed. I just can't absorb this all at once. It's fantastic – like something out of a movie or Hemingway.

Everybody here is crazy about Auckland. They refer to it as the last outpost of civilization, and a wonderful town to come back to. The women, they say, are easy and from what I saw in the lounge of the Royal, it is so. Gin is plentiful, some Scotch and wine and beer.

But the people we've seen are the most amazing. In the Royal: A staff sergeant with a wild eye, a punchy expression which couldn't have been natural or intoxicated, ate lunch with us. He had been 'up', he was going back. I'm trying to think of something he said: he didn't say much of anything. Maybe that's why I remember the look in his eyes.

A master sergeant, one of our hut-mates, explaining that the Japs have a neat trick of wiring their gear, so that when the dead are searched a grenade explodes. He advised that Jap prisoners be made to search them – if there are any prisoners.

A staff sergeant of Marines, very drunk, who insisted on joining our party in the lounge. I have never seen a man with that little regard for convention. Nobody would say much to him except Mac, who very bluntly told him to stay out. The Marine did – for a couple of minutes, and then back again. We didn't know what to say: the guy was just back from 'up north.' He had a picture which he handed around, telling us it was his wife whom he hadn't seen in over a year. We looked again. It was a snapshot of Betty Grable.

A drunk New Zealander who wandered over to our table, bellowed something, shook hands all around, and wandered off.

The group of young Air Corps officers and men who moved in on four girls, laughed a little while and then moved out with them. One man had a hand in a cast.

The women in uniform, the little waiter who does 'anything just for you, Mr. McCarthy,' the hodgepodge of uniforms on the street – practically none of them New Zealand. The ads in the *Herald*, on the front page, 'in memoriam, in memory of so-and-so, beloved husband and father, killed in action Nov. 23, 1941, in Libya.'

Auckland is the backlog of the war. The streets are

jammed with men who have seen this war, and now want to see some peace. They live high, wide and handsome while they can.

The New Zealand cities of Auckland and Wellington were transformed by the war. Not only did they become the primary leave destinations for Allied servicemen fighting in the South Pacific, there were also many thousands of troops encamped about them. One of the manifestations of this was a huge rise in the illegal production and selling of liquor. Although there was no prohibition, licensing laws were very strict. Hotels and grocery stores were forbidden to sell liquor for off-site consumption, but in practice a huge network of so-called 'sly-grogging' developed. The business was highly organized, with selling from hotels, stores, milk bars, houses, dance halls and clubs. Distributors used an effective monitoring system to evade the police and delivered direct to military camps. Grog-touts and 'droppers' roamed the streets looking for buyers. Auckland residents complained that many of the temporary visitors were so drunk by six in the evening that if an air raid occurred at that time they would not notice. SEE ALSO PP. 363–4, 372–4, 396.

DECEMBER 1942

DECEMBER 1942 effectively marked the end of the Guadalcanal campaign. Final attempts by the Japanese to land reinforcements were halted by growing American air superiority and the activities of 'PT boats' – fast, lightly armed motor torpedo boats. One of these, PT-109, was skippered by a young John F. Kennedy. By the second week of December the United States could afford to pull away the 5th Marine Regiment for service elsewhere. The US army's Americal Division took the strain and rotated fresh troops into the island for the last phase of the campaign. At the end of the month General Tojo decided that the few remaining Japanese forces on Guadalcanal must be evacuated. Both the American and

Japanese forces on the island had suffered badly from disease, including high rates of malaria.

Elsewhere, the Allies ran into difficulties. In Papua the Japanese managed to reinforce their activities in the areas of Buna and Gona. The overall US commander on Papua New Guinea, General Eichelberger, decided to replace the commander of his lead unit, the 32nd Division, and a number of other subordinates before pressing forward with renewed attacks. Later he took direct command of the division when the replacements were wounded on the battlefield. Here too, American air superiority disrupted Japanese attempts to bring reinforcements to their positions. In Papua the major objective of Gona was secured, although Buna held on for another few weeks. Eventually the Japanese began to fall back to a prepared defensive front at Sananda. Japanese troops had fought doggedly in Papua but had suffered from divided priorities. The Japanese garrison on Guadalcanal had been given much attention but had nevertheless been lost, while Japanese forces in Papua had been starved of resources.

In Burma, the British were advancing slowly in the Arakan region, meeting surprisingly little resistance from weak Japanese forces. Arriving at Muagdaw, they were astonished to find that the Japanese simply turned and fled. Recognizing that they were over-extended with impossible supply lines, the Japanese had decided to fall back to a defensible position at Akyab (Sittwe).

Tuesday 8 – Thursday 10 December 1942

William Leaney, a British sergeant at Ban Pong POW camp in Thailand, sells his gold watch to buy food

I sold my gold watch yesterday afternoon. I think Mum and Dad will understand. I can buy a new watch when I get out of here but I want to *get* out of here that's the important thing and much longer on their food and we definitely won't get out of here. Yesterday was a 'Yasumi' supposedly to celebrate the declaration of war. I had had this tick fever for

2 days and didn't go sick for I was sweating on the holiday allowing me to recover but the Nips held a big check roll-call at 10 a.m. and I am afraid, for the first time in my army career I fainted and had to be carried off. Of course their food for the last few days has been bad even for this place and I suppose that had something to do with it also. Then at dinner time the Thai people who are allowed to come up and sell stuff in the camp brought up fritters and cakes and toffee and we ('Brum' Benjy Wilbur and I) had to sit and watch some of our people eating it then to go down to dinner and get just salt water and rice. It was too much, so after another roll-call at 3 where I once more had to sit in the shade to avoid 'passing out' I took myself down to the river and sold the watch for 35 dollars. I shan't go into the details of how I tried to get 40 (the Thais who bought it even put it in a bowl of water when I said it was waterproof) but the bastards know we're desperate and of course they are cashing in. Today since we've had the money we've been unable to buy damn all except a few cents worth of toffee but please God we'll be able to get some eggs or some sunfish soon. I feel a lot better today and so hungry. I'd like to describe adequately the abject misery I felt at parting with my watch, sat on that river bank haggling with the Thais. I kept thinking of home and I could remember Mum digging it from the sideboard to give me it. Any-way they got a bargain, for it's been a damn good watch.

Another poor chap died last night – a sergeant was found dead in his bed this morning. Only about 28 years of age and he makes the 15th in this camp – it's astounding when one comes to think of it. We managed to buy some food after all yesterday and we had some fritters and some eggs – very good – as Wilbur said quite the best watch he'd tasted . . .

William Leaney's efforts to stay in reasonable health were successful, for he survived the brutal period of the building of the railway, which came to an end in late 1943. He was then taken to Singapore. However, on 6 September 1944 he left Singapore for Japan in a convoy of six trans-ports and five escorts, and on the night of 12 September the convoy was attacked by a pack of American submarines led by Commander T. B. Oakley. A number of ships, including Kachidoki Maru *and* Rakuyo

Maru, *carrying some 2,300 POWs, were sunk, and Leaney is presumed to be one of those who died as a result. By chance, some 159 of the POWs were rescued a few days later by the same submarines when they were patrolling the area, but Leaney was not among them. SEE ALSO PP. 329–31.*

Monday 14 – Wednesday 16 December 1942

Louis Dusting, an RAAF corporal fitter, dodges enemy bombs and Allied ack-ack at Port Moresby in New Guinea

14 December

I was right about last night. The Japs raided 4 times between midnight and 0230. As usual the noise of their motors woke us first and we just had time to get in our trench when the bombs came whistling down. It was then that the dopes here decided to sound the alarm. The bombs landed between our camp and the strip. The concussion made some more bits of our trench fall in so we had to wait about till he made another run. Sure enough, back he came so into the trench again. This time the lights and guns were waiting for him. They've got a lot of new guns installed around here lately and when the Japs came sailing serenely into position the guns hurled everything into the sky. Because of the overcast they put their lights out and relied on their predictors. It was a marvellous sight to see our ack ack [anti-aircraft fire] bursting inside the clouds. There were brilliant white flashes reflected on the clouds as the guns fire and then winking red stars as the shells burst in the clouds. The ack ack claimed one bomber shot down: the others just dumped their loads and fled in a dive. Nothing could live in that sky.

The noise was terrific and there were big pieces and our ack ack shells falling everywhere – makes it dangerous to look up. When the Jap dumped his load there was a terrific scream that made us duck down low in the trench. It was a bomb that landed right very close to us but didn't go off. Another one landed right alongside the duty pilot's tower and it didn't go off either. We found that the only damage was a hole in one of our Beaus from a piece of our ack ack . . .

16 December

They sent 6 bombers over last night in a very determined effort to get our Wards strip. They came in over the overcast and let go some red signal lights to try and fool us, but the ack ack opened up using their predictors. The noise was absolutely hellish and in the middle of it all the little bastards let their loads go. They were big bombs but they landed on the other side of the strip in a Yank camp killing five men. But the guns on Slap Happy Hill got one of the Japs which came down in a dive and exploded in the Harbour.

After the kites had passed an unearthly noise began to come out of the sky just like a million dynamos. We couldn't make it out until one particularly loud buzz landed near our trench. My God, how we took cover! The shrapnel continued to fall for about 20 minutes . . . It was queer to hear it slapping on the Mess roof and on the ground all around us. We picked up a piece this morning about 8 inches by 4 inches. There were plenty of holes in the tents and the Mess. There was another alert about 0200 this morning. After listening for a while I went back to sleep and never heard the all-clear. There are pictures tonight. Hope we can have them in peace to try and finish a letter by moonlight.

Louis Dusting's unit was subjected to heavy air attack throughout December 1942, although the ground crews were in as much danger from pieces of their own anti-aircraft shells as from enemy bombs. Their own targets were transports and convoys of Japanese troops trying to reinforce positions on the island of Buna. In the days before Christmas, Dusting hoped for some leave in Australia, but instead he was posted to a Rescue and Communications flight. He was not happy and wrote in his diary: 'I could tear things to pieces . . . I want to go home.'

Louis Dusting would end his diary when he completed his active service overseas in late 1943 and returned home to his family in Sydney.
SEE ALSO PP. 315–16.

Mid-December 1942

Renton Hind, civilian internee, regrets the uncovering of the bootlegging operation at Camp Holmes in the Philippines

For several months liquor in small quantities had either been brought into camp for sale or had been made on a very limited scale in a home-made still located at the rear of the shops at the west end of the grounds. This was, of course, contrary to regulations but their violation was never on an extended scale. Occasionally a birthday party, where liquor enlivened the affair, would develop into a noisy gathering from which two or three would wander and disport themselves to the amusement or disgust of the rest of us, depending upon one's point of view on the subject of demon rum, and the receipt of good news from the war fronts would sometimes call for a celebration with the aid of John Barleycorn. In truth it must be pointed out that neither barley nor corn ever figured in the manufacture of camp liquor. The lowly sweet potato and pineapple pulp and peelings were the basic ingredients in the local moonshine. Smuggled liquor was almost wholly confined to native gin or 'squareface' dispensed in the familiar square glass bottles, the contents having been distilled from fermented sugar cane molasses. That our standards of taste had sadly deteriorated was plain for so long as a drink had a 'kick' to it it satisfied all requirements. After all, beggars can't be choosers.

The chief 'bootlegger' was Clarence Mount who, with the full knowledge of the committee, smuggled into camp as much of the firewater as demand dictated. His customers were many, not the least of whom were some of the committee men themselves. In doing this, Mount was not censured by any of us, except, of course, those missionaries who are opposed to traffic in liquor under any circumstances but we all felt that sooner or later he would run afoul of Mr. Jap, the consequences of which might be painful to him. Sure enough, on the 4th he was caught by the guard in the act of retrieving four bottles of gin from a point down the hill east of the camp. He was promptly marched off to the guard house. He was grilled by the sergeant and to clear himself of any complicity with a liquor ring, told the story that the discovery of the cache was accidental for he was near the spot only because he was working on a detail of housemoving in the abandoned non-commissioned officers' village which was part of the Camp Holmes reservation. As he had been under suspicion for sometime, his yarn was not taken seriously. Aggravated by his unconvincing attempt to clear himself the guards proceeded to beat him most cruelly with a heavy club to the point of insensibility. His shrieks of pain could be heard in the barracks across the parade ground, a matter of a good two hundred yards. Satisfied that he had suffered sufficient punishment when he collapsed the guards sent for four or five internees to carry him to the hospital where it was ascertained by a camp physician, Dr. Dana Nance, that he was painfully, tho not seriously, hurt. Here he remained for a week. A sidelight on the incident was the visit to Mount on the 10th by one of the guards who participated in his beating to apologize for his part in the affair, stating that he was merely acting under orders. Thus ended the bootlegging chapter at Holmes. Mount had learned his lesson and there was no one else with sufficient hardihood to take over the traffic for the Japs made it clear that the next offender would be carted off to Intelligence where, by reputation at least, we knew that no kid gloves were worn.

Liquor was not the only thing in short supply at Christmas 1942. During December rationing was introduced in the Philippines and essential supplies such as soap, salt and sugar became scarce.

Renton Hind and his wife would both remain interned until the liberation of the Philippines in February 1945. They were offered accelerated passages home to the United States and on their way to the harbour they passed their former guards, now sitting behind the wire. On 2 March 1945 they finally sailed for home. SEE ALSO PP. 240–2.

Monday 21 December 1942

David E. Lilienthal, lawyer, comes across American deserters en route to a court martial on Union Station in Washington DC

Growing up in Morton, Illinois, the son of a struggling Jewish family that kept a grocery store, David Lilienthal hoped to be a writer or a journalist. He attended the local DePaul University, graduated when he was only twenty, and went on to Harvard Law School. As a young lawyer he handled cases for the city of Chicago and, still in his twenties, won important public utility cases. In the 1930s he was chosen to be one of the directors of the large-scale hydro-electric project in the Tennessee Valley that became known as the Tennessee Valley Authority and remained in that role during the war.

I am writing these notes in the waiting room of the Union Station. It is ten minutes after seven, and so far my five o'clock train for home hasn't even been announced. I have been here almost three hours.

I wonder if there is anything like the scenes in this station to be seen anywhere else in the world. To say that the huge station is jammed with a milling crowd of every kind of human being in the world is as near as I can put it. Soldiers, of course, by the hundreds, every kind of uniform. Some rather bedraggled, lugging their shapeless barracks bags. Some very jaunty indeed, and definitely out for a good time, and a low, appreciative whistle when a suitable pair of gams go by. A young fellow in the uniform of Venezuela, a tall, very young-looking fellow; any number of British and Canadian officers; a Free French officer telephoning. A Polish officer painstakingly writing out a telegram. Sailors, very cocky-looking. A group of parachute troops, the angry eagle and the word 'Airborne' on their left shoulders, tall, fine-looking fellows who stand out from the crowd.

The most tragic thing I have seen in a long time: a group of young men in a kind of tan coverall, hatless, and large letters, fore and aft: 'P-W,' and in smaller letters: 'officer.' For a moment I thought: Is this a time for fraternity initiation stunts, for somehow the 'get-up' and the youth of the men made me think of that. Two of them had full beards, the soft brown of young men. I asked a soldier. He said, 'They're deserters, prisoners of war.' Then I noticed the cordon of armed guards in a semicircle, and the whole thing suddenly froze me with the horror of war. Captured, on their way to general court-martial; I could fill in the details. Such young faces, one of them defiant as the crowd in the station stared, one acting as if he were amused or didn't give a damn. What was the history back of their standing there, with those hideous signs on their backs, on their chests, even the letters P and W on their legs?

If railroad transportation doesn't break down completely this week, it will be a marvel. Soldiers are denied furloughs, except for 10 percent; so Mamma, the big woman next to me, explains, is going to South Carolina to see the boy before he goes overseas. And government clerks, here in Washington from Iowa, can't travel home during Xmas, so the relatives come to see their girl in the big city . . .

Well, they have called the train, thank goodness. It is 7:45. Started out three hours late; we shouldn't be more than five or six hours late into Knoxville.

Some 21,000 deserters from the US army were caught and convicted during the Second World War. Technically the punishment for desertion was execution; however, fewer than 200 deserters were hanged between 1941 and 1945, and those usually because their offences included murder or rape.

As an administrator and government official, David Lilienthal had helped to develop some of the infrastructure that contributed to the atomic bomb project during the war. Accordingly, President Truman appointed him the first chairman of the Atomic Energy Commission, which managed the peacetime use of nuclear power. Later he served as a consultant and as chairman of the International Development and Resources Corporation, working on projects in Colombia, Peru, Brazil, Iran and Vietnam. He died in 1981.

Saturday 26 – Wednesday 30 December 1942

Freddy Bloom meets her husband for thirty-seven minutes in Changi gaol

Freddy Bloom had been interned in the women's camp at Changi since March 1942.

26 December
Philip, we were together yesterday. I can't write any more. Oh, Philip – my own.

30 December
Have you managed to get over the thrill of it yet? It was so crazy – thirty-seven minutes in the sun outside my prison walls, and yet it was the first normal, real half-hour in the last ten months. When we're not together things don't count. Of course there were a score of things we did not discuss but when you held me in your arms it seemed as if nothing could separate us again. We were 'at home', You looked very lean and gaunt and I am more worried than ever about your health. What fun it will be to feed you up. You said you were not bored – of course not, you could not be – I worry about your reaction to the damned futility – it's funny to think of you going in for languages in a big way – still wish you'd try carpentering, etc. You say you're good with your hands – I don't believe it – anyway you must develop into 'something useful round the house'. It's grand about your stories – please keep them safe. Loved my presents – am in your pyjamas right now. Perhaps we will meet again soon. Look, darling, a whole page without blubbering! Take care of yourself, I love you so.

Unable to write to her husband in Changi gaol, Freddy Bloom poured out her heart into her diary as if she were addressing him, adopting a letter style. This was very common: other civilian internees, including Natalie Crouter and Elizabeth Vaughan, did this in their own diaries. At Changi on Christmas Day most of the army wives had been allowed to meet their husbands for just half an hour outside the prison. SEE ALSO PP. 231–3, 404.

Tuesday 29 December 1942

John Nevell enjoys the Christmas pantomime in Changi gaol and talks with a 'bad lot' from western Queensland

The concert last night vindicated the need for the competition for tickets.

It was a pantomime Cinderella with local additions. They have a good stage and excellent scenery. The lighting was professional. The costumes are surprising, considering the limited scope. The two bad sisters ran a skit on the prevalent rumours: Have you heard the Yanks are ten miles off the shore? What, off Ireland, Mrs Gallagher? No, America, Mrs Shean!

Had a long talk this morning with a bad lot from Western Queensland. They had spent a fortnight in jail, for selling petrol extracted from the Jap trucks. They had a Jap interpreter with them, who had spent 15 years in America. Two days before they were caught, he addressed the parade as follows: 'You boys are number one gentlemen of the world. Number one gentlemen do not steal petrol. If you steal petrol, you are not number one gentlemen. Mr Mandai (Japanese Camp Commandant) says if you want petrol for cigarette lighters to come and see him. He cannot understand who would want two hundred gallons per day for petrol for lighters.' When the interpreter drove off, after the parade, he only went half a mile, as someone had milked his petrol tank, while he extolled the folly of petrol stealing . . .

Another day a Japanese guard was explaining to the men, that they must not steal, when loading ships. To show them he knew their little tricks, he put a tin of condensed milk at his feet. Then he looked around and dropped his hat over the tin of milk. He then harangued them on what would happen if they continued stealing in this way. He bent down and picked his hat up and the milk was gone. They said the expression on his face was worth recording, but he happened to be an unusual Jap and he eventually laughed, although he didn't see the tin of milk again.

POW and internee camps in both Europe and Asia provided steady employment for racketeers, smugglers and thieves. Perhaps the most lucrative trade was in cigarettes, matches and lighter fuel. Most men and more than a third of women smoked in the late 1930s. Once incarcerated they were literally a captive market and were prepared to pay almost anything for cigarettes. By December 1942 John Nevell finally had his craving under control. He noted that earlier that year he had paid a $1 a packet 'and thought I would die without it'. Now he had managed to reduce his needs to one cigarette a day, just before bed. SEE ALSO PP. 327–9, 499–500.

1943

'THIS MORNING WE WERE issued with kit to make up full battle gear of a hundred rounds per rifleman, eight magazines per Tommy gun, three days' rations, groundsheet and shared blanket and so on. And Simon said:

"We move out tomorrow, Johnno. We walk back across the big mountain . . ."

"I got you a new waterbottle," the big man added. "The old one was no good no more, the moths had been at it."

"Shit! What did you do with it?"

"Oh – I put it in the bush."

And this diary was inside it! But luckily he had not put it very far.'

Peter Pinney in New Guinea, diary entry for Tuesday 23 March 1943

JANUARY 1943

AMERICAN TROOPS had been fighting for the island of Guadalcanal in the Solomons since August 1942. In January 1943 they launched a major attack on the Japanese stronghold of Mount Austen. The Japanese held their ground, but secretly they were withdrawing as many troops as possible from the island. The decision to do so signalled that they had reconciled themselves to losing control of the Solomon Islands – and with them the mastery of the north-eastern approaches to Australia and New Zealand.

Evacuation was conducted on destroyers visiting the island by night. This was the 'Tokyo Express' commanded by the talented Rear-Admiral Tanaka. The Americans had 50,000 men on Guadalcanal by January 1943 and the Japanese a garrison of only 15,000. The US forces advanced slowly with continual heavy fire support but did not manage to disrupt the Japanese timetable for an orderly withdrawal and a tough rearguard action, which inflicted considerable casualties on the Americans.

In New Guinea, on the island of Buna, General Eichelberger's forces finally overcame the enemy, but fighting continued at Sanananda. On 19 January the local Japanese commander, General Yamagata, finally decided to withdraw from Sanananda and left the area himself by sea. By the end of the month the Japanese were completely cleared from Papua, the southern territory of Papua New Guinea.

In Burma, the British attempted an offensive in the area of Donbaik in the Arakan but without success. The offensive had been undertaken as much for political and psychological as for military reasons and had little prospect of success, in part because insufficient resources were devoted to it. This was a mistake on the part of the British, who failed to appreciate how over-stretched the Japanese lines of communication were here and missed a major opportunity in not pressing harder.

In northern Burma and China, General Stilwell continued to

try to persuade the Chinese to launch an offensive in Burma and to supply more troops for that campaign, but without success. On 8 January Chiang Kai-shek, the nationalist leader, sent a formal message to Roosevelt rejecting the suggestion that he should launch a major spring offensive, claiming he was not ready. Personal relations between Stilwell and the Chinese were deteriorating fast. This decline was charted precisely in Stilwell's outspoken diary, in which he referred to Chiang as 'the Peanut'. He was no better disposed towards his British allies, whom he considered to be backsliding and scared of fighting, referring to them in his diary as 'the Pigfuckers'. Some of Stilwell's criticisms of his Allies were well founded, but he scored no points for inter-Allied diplomacy.

During January, Churchill and Roosevelt met at Casablanca to discuss overall Allied strategy. The Americans argued, with some justification, that the British were not doing enough against Japan. The British countered that the US navy in particular had not fully subscribed to the doctrine of 'Germany First'. They agreed on a likely offensive in Sicily in 1943 and on the invasion of France thereafter, probably in 1944. Although the British promised to do more in Burma, one of the problems there – as everywhere else – was a serious shortage of shipping. Most importantly, on 24 January 1943, at a press conference, Roosevelt and Churchill announced the doctrine of unconditional surrender agreed privately a year previously, whereby all the Allies agreed that they would enforce complete defeat and occupation on each Axis nation and only end the state of war together, not separately.

Thursday 7 – Friday 8 January 1943

General Joseph Stilwell has dinner with T. V. Soong, the Chinese foreign minister

'Vinegar Joe' Stilwell was born in Palatka, Florida in 1883 and commissioned into the army in 1904. He had fought in the First World War and then served for thirteen years in China, where he acquired fluent Chinese. He considered himself an experienced 'China hand'. In early 1942

he was sent back to China to fulfil a curious double role as both Chiang Kai-shek's chief of staff and also the commander of US troops in the China–Burma–India area. Stilwell disliked Chiang and his whole entourage and did not restrict his frank remarks to his diary, enjoying confronting his Chinese allies in the most direct way.

7 January

Social note: Last night I had dinner with T. V. Soong. Chinese food and damn good, though he insisted it was just *pien fan* [casual food]. The pièce de résistance was the cook's speciality and he was so proud of it that he peeked in to see how we took it. It was fried, in rings about the size of a thumb ring. Nice brown crackly skin and chewy on the inside. I had swallowed one and was enjoying the second when I asked T.V. what it was. 'That's tripe. You know, the *gut*. The end of the big gut in the pig.' In other words, fried pig bowel. Roast sphincter. Well, now I've bitten a pig's backside. All I've got to do now is take a bite out of a skunk and I'll be fully qualified as a dietary specialist. When our Thanksgiving goose came on the table, his head and neck were sticking out stiff and straight at a rakish angle, his eyes had a surprised look in them and there was an electric light in his mouth. The boys had stuck a flashlight down his throat and produced a most novel and elegant effect. No, he did not have a tail light but I expect to see one on the next big occasion.

You know about Chinese plumbing. Well, my bathroom is right over Powell's bed and the drain pipe is hung on his ceiling. The pipe developed a hole about the size of a dime, so that when the handle was pulled upstairs, Powell [one of Stilwell's staff officers] had to leap for his life. A brand-new brigadier general, too, has his dignity to think about. Luckily, Powell used to be a pole vaulter, but in his palmist days he never made a quicker start.

8 January

Black Friday. T.V. gave [Frank] Dorn the Peanut's answer to F.D.R. (Afraid to see me with it on account of a possible blow up.)

Peanut says he won't fight. 'The Japs will fight

desperately. They have had time to prepare. Our supply lines are not good. The British force is inadequate. We risk defeat . . .'

Joseph Stilwell

Stilwell's troops had been defeated in Burma in May 1942. During 1943 and 1944 he would build up forces for successful counter-attacks in the north of Burma. However, the Chinese nationalist government had not wished to commit resources to this campaign, preferring to hoard weapons for a future fight with the Chinese communists. Relations between the outspoken Stilwell and Chiang Kai-shek were already deteriorating, with many 'blow-ups'. Accordingly, communication between the two was often conducted through subordinates such as the Chinese foreign minister T. V. Soong and Stilwell's Chief of Staff, Frank Dorn. SEE ALSO PP. 421–2, 615–16, 806–7.

Mid-January 1943

Ursula Blomberg, aged fourteen, orders food in Chinese in the Golden Jasmine restaurant in Japanese-occupied Shanghai

Since arriving in Shanghai from Germany, Ursula Blomberg had earned her living by teaching. Her close friends were three indifferently behaved girls to whom she taught English at the house of a Chinese general.

I had always joined the sisters in their merriment when one of the silly pranks (which they loved to play on each other and on the servants with great regularity) was successful. But that was only until the day I turned out to be their victim.

I had told the sisters that Mr. Yung and my father were planning to entertain several important customers at a dinner to be held at Tsu-Chen Li's Golden Jasmine Restaurant. I asked the girls to teach me how to order four of my favorite dishes in Chinese – Peking Duck, Mandarin Fish, Beef and Bamboo Shoots in a ginger sauce, and Sour/Sweet Pork. The girls giggled a bit too much, I thought, as I carefully wrote down the names for the dishes phonetically. The three sisters were having a good time, probably chuckling about my pronunciation of some of the difficult syllables.

The night of our dinner arrived, and as we took our places at the big round table at the Golden Jasmine, I announced proudly to Mr. Yung that I had learned the proper Chinese names for my favorite dishes, and may I please order?

No sooner had I rattled off my order, than the waiters roared with laughter and were joined by our Chinese guests at the table. When everyone kept on laughing, holding their aching sides and wiping fat tears from their cheeks, I wondered just what I had said to result in such hilarity.

Finally, Mrs. Yung took pity on me, pulled me over to her side and behind her cupped hand, put her mouth to my ear and still giggling furiously, whispered the awful truth.

According to her, I had ordered male and female genitalia in a wide range of preparations – from fried, chopped, sauced, diced, pickled, and gingered, to braised, steamed, and God knows what else. My cheeks flamed hot red, I buried my face in my hands, and hoped for a hole in the floor to open and swallow me.

When I told Mrs. Yung that the three sisters had taught me how to order, she laughed out loud, and, still chuckling and speaking in Chinese, explained to our guests and their wives how General Yi's three naughty concubines had played a joke on me. Our guests thought it a remarkably clever prank, cheered for the three sisters, and assured me that I was not to blame. It was quite all right, and not to worry. Not to worry.

Ursula Blomberg's family would spend eight years scratching out a living in a ghetto in Shanghai. Her father did his best to sustain a business until they were able to emigrate to Denver in the USA in 1948. Ursula Bacon (Blomberg) was still writing and lecturing about her wartime experiences in 2004. SEE ALSO PP. 301–3.

Saturday 16 January 1943

Brigadier E. V. Bowra of the British Indian Army receives confidential instructions regarding 'the Americans'

Brigadier Edward Bowra was a regular officer in the Royal Engineers and had fought in the First World War. He had been serving in India with the Military Engineering Services since 1931. He had spent the last three years at Poona, where he was responsible for overseeing contractors building infrastructure for an expanded Indian Army, including barracks and workshops. He was now dealing with similar work near Moradabad on the River Ganges in the Uttar Pradesh district of India. Increasingly, however, British, British Indian and American forces were located on the same bases and training areas.

Army Commander issues a confidential manifesto about our attitude towards the Americans. Apparently the British and

American troops have been having rows. British troops resent the high rates of pay their American equivalent ranks get. A sergeant gets as much or more than a captain with us. The American troops resent the attitude adopted towards them, and a vicious circle ensues. Relations between officers here is very polite, but by no means friendly. Numbers of them living in the hotels with us. They will not move out into the hutted quarters built for them as they get Rs 20/- a day allowance whilst in a hotel, a profitable situation, as the hotel rate is half this, and also the hotel is far more comfortable than huts. They are well behaved on the whole, but a middle class, provincial lot uninteresting to talk to, except the odd one who has previously travelled abroad. The men here are a superior type, being technicians for the Air Corps workshops, but are singularly unmilitary in their turnout and bearing. Their varieties of garments can hardly be termed uniform and saluting appears to be unknown. Their expenditure in the shops has turned the 'bunyas' [traders] heads and prices are now preposterous.

While frictions at a high level between the British and the Americans related to issues such as the future of India within the British Empire, at a lower level they were about more practical matters. Differences in pay caused difficulties in every wartime theatre, notably on the European continent in 1939 and 1940, when the French had considered their British allies to be disgracefully over-paid. In India, there were different rates of pay for American, British, British Indian, British African and Chinese forces, not to mention local levies raised in Burma. All were serving alongside each other and doing much the same job.

Brigadier Bowra would retire from the army in 1950.

Monday 18 January 1943

Mack Morriss, a soldier working on *The Yank* newspaper,
contrasts US army and marine attitudes to taking
prisoners on Guadalcanal

Dowling, Cromie, Jackson were on the Marine front, came
back green at gills from seeing too many dead Japs. They
said it was awful. I fail to see how this can last much longer.
By actual figure there are 51,000 of us here and something
like 8,000 Japs – all of which aren't effectives – and this still
drags on. It must be incredible to people who have never
seen this place. But I wouldn't be surprised if we're not still
rounding up strays a year from now unless they all starve to
death. It isn't the Japs so much as it is this god-awful terrain:
but at the same time the little bastards are as hard to get rid
of as a dose of crabs. They dig in and come hell or high water
they won't come out unless you drag them out. They're
fighting the worst kind of war there is – a sort of fatalistic
desperation. They must know they haven't got a chance, but
apparently they mean to die hard. But they're beginning to
break.

This thing wouldn't have to drag on if some of these men
had any sense. It's disgusting. Higher headquarters is breaking a leg to get all prisoners possible, but look at all these
incidents.

On the Marine front last night a Jap came in with his
hands up, saying 'Me sick, me sick.' The major, knowing
there were other Japs watching, motioned him to come on in
– told his men not to fire. One Marine raised his rifle and the
major knocked it down – but on the other side of him
another dope brought up a shotgun and blew the Jap apart.
The Japs watching melted away – they'll never give up as
prisoners now. Things like that are always happening – guys
get trigger happy or think here's a good chance to kill me
a Jap and let 'em have it. As long as this situation exists, the
Japs will naturally fight to the last man.

On the Army front the men had sense enough to know

that if they shot a man who would surrender they were just making it hard on themselves – and they haven't done it, at least, not the 35th. Those Marines must have been trying to live up to their reputation. It's not a matter of humaneness, but purely a matter of practical military operation.

I've heard some pretty bad stories of savageness on the part of our boys. Dowling said they shot a sniper 100 yds from him and before he could get there they were kicking his teeth out for souvenirs. That was the Marines, a bunch of kids who get ferocious in a fight. The Army is a little different. At the 35th I saw a Jap ear passed around. The men didn't have much stomach for that. But then there's the case of my young 'killer priest' who hacked off heads for the fun of it or something. When the bars of civilization come down, they hit with a bang. I can understand part of that, but there are other things I don't get at all. Perhaps that's because I haven't seen enough.

But in either event, war in my book is a lot of crap. Even up on the 35th, where there weren't but two casualties and we had everything our own way – like in the movies – I still got a bad taste in my mouth. It was the exact opposite of our experiences with the 132nd – infinitely a cleaner, more glamorous type fighting – but I still keep thinking 'What's the use?' I mean the isolated things – taken by themselves – seem not worth the effort.

Despite an open line of retreat from Guadalcanal provided by the 'Tokyo Express', many Japanese chose to stay in place until starved or shot. To encourage surrenders, substantial efforts were made by the American high command, using fluent Japanese-speakers, equipped with megaphones. These were often Japanese Americans, known as Nisei. Exactly how many Japanese attempted to surrender in the field only to be despatched when they reached the Allied lines is uncertain. Clearly it was not an uncommon occurrence. Japanese soldiers had been taught to expect torture and death if they surrendered, and so few attempted to give themselves up. The practice of taking the ears from enemy dead was an indigenous rite in some areas of Burma and the Pacific, and was not widely adopted by Allied troops. SEE ALSO PP. 341–3, 372–4, 396–7.

Dr Charles Huxtable, an Australian POW in Changi gaol, learns of a remarkable act of kindness by the Japanese authorities

Charles Huxtable was born in Sydney on 30 September 1891. After passing his medical exams in 1914 he volunteered for the British army and served as medical officer with the Lancashire Fusiliers for most of the First World War. A surgeon in various Australian hospitals between the wars, he married in 1928 and had four children. In 1941 he rejoined the army at the age of forty-eight and was sent to Singapore with a military hospital unit. He was soon a prisoner of the Japanese.

Captain Laurie West of the Gurkhas came to see Alan Carrick today with interesting news. He has been to the Gaol today under orders to attend the Japanese authorities there and he was handed a wireless message from Delhi, India, from his wife. It was to the effect that, last May, his wife had given birth to twin boys and all were well. He was allowed to send a message in reply. Old Laurie, of course, is filled with delight and pride. We later gave him a special evening up here and, in the presence of a dozen of his friends, drank his health in black coffee and shared a fairly good feed of fried rice cakes and fruit salad made of pineapple and paw paw.

I had about this time a surprise visit from V. T. McGuire of Southport. How strange that we should have met here. His wife used to show me photographs of him on active service in Palestine and Egypt way back in 1940 before I ever had any prospects of serving abroad. He looks well, though thin and weatherbeaten. Whilst in the Middle East, he was taken from his Battalion and attached to Headquarters of the 7th Division. He left Suez early in February for Australia on *Orcades* but, unfortunately, they were sidetracked and landed first at Sumatra and then at Java shortly before the surrender, and that is how he came to be here. He came twice to see me, a longish walk from the 18th Division area, but I was able to help him with some socks, etc., and a little money. He left again with the Java party on 21 January for up-country; we think probably near Bangkok but nobody knows for certain.

This striking incidence of kindness encountered by Charles Huxtable, was a notable exception to the rule. Many prisoners waited for mail that arrived only months, even years late, if at all, and communication with families back home was minimal. Nevertheless, Japanese treatment of POWs varied enormously and cannot be stereotyped. The worst treatment was often meted out by veterans of the China campaign, where there had been numerous massacres. In contrast, officers who had served as attachés in the west were often courteous and considerate. In some cases officers refused to carry out orders that involved ill-treatment. For example, Rear-Admiral Sadamichi saved the lives of 1,600 American prisoners on Wake Island in late 1942 by countermanding orders to execute them.

Charles Huxtable would survive the war and went to work with the Flying Doctor Service in the highlands of New Guinea. He died in 1980 at the age of eighty-eight.

FEBRUARY 1943

ON 8 FEBRUARY 1943 the first Chindit raid was launched in Burma. The Chindits were officially known as the 77th Indian Brigade, and had been trained to operate behind enemy lines. Unlike other special forces, the Chindits operated on a large scale. Their eccentric leader, Brigadier Orde Wingate, had already notched up considerable successes with other irregular forces in Palestine and then in Abyssinia. The British army hoped that his operations would show that the British soldier could fight the Japanese soldier in the jungle on equal terms. However, Wingate also hoped to demonstrate how large-scale units could operate independently, attacking targets of opportunity, without taking orders from a hierarchical command structure. Such novel concepts did not endear him to his military superiors; however, he was protected by lofty patrons, including Winston Churchill. Whatever the value of his operations – and they are still fiercely debated – the Chindits were one of the few British units taking the fight to the enemy in Burma in 1943. In February 1943 their plan was to cross the

Chindwin river and then destroy vital Japanese rail links between Mandalay and Myitkyina.

By 9 February almost all Japanese troops had left the island of Guadalcanal and a week later the fighting was over, allowing the island to become a major stepping stone for future American operations elsewhere in the Solomons. Over the next few days the Americans managed to occupy a number of smaller islands nearby that had been abandoned by the Japanese, and these also became valuable bases.

If the Battle of Midway in 1942 had been a turning point for the Pacific war at sea, then Guadalcanal was a turning point in the conflict on land. Indeed, by the end of February 1943 it was clear that Axis fortunes were in decline everywhere. The Germans had lost in north Africa and had been put on the defensive on the Eastern Front. Events in Russia were of considerable importance in the Far East. Allied commanders had feared that the Germans might continue their southward drive through the Russian Caucasus towards Iran and Afghanistan, ending up at the gates of India. This was certainly the German intention: 3,000 Indian POWs captured during the desert war were being trained up as a special German unit for this eventuality, and Subhas Chandra Bose, the pro-Axis leader associated with the Indian Nationalist Army (INA), had been spirited between Tokyo and Rome by German U-boat for secret talks. However, defeat at Stalingrad in February 1943 halted the German advance through southern Russia and the threat to India's north-west frontier melted away.

Thursday 4 – Friday 5 February 1943

General 'Hap' Arnold flies from India to China and wonders what shoes to wear in the jungle

General 'Hap' Arnold was the commander of the US Army Air Force. While he was visiting various commanders in the field in India and China his aircraft had become lost at night. At this time the Japanese occupied most of Burma and the danger of landing in enemy-occupied territory was very real.

Well, the Japs occupy country extending well into China from the coast. There is always the possibility of Jap planes being abroad. They probably have radar and plot the course of all visiting aircraft such as ours. If we turn back into the wind do we run out of gas in the mountains? Do we jump? If so, when? Will we be captured over by Mandalay? What should we take with us if we have to jump? What will the people back home think if they hear that the Commanding General, US Army Air Force and the Commanding General, 10th Air Force and others with us have been taken prisoners? What are the best shoes to wear in hiking through the jungle? Can we take emergency rations with us if we jump?

Well to make a long story short I told the pilots to cut out the plotting and turn back on the reverse of the course taken going out. Then asked the navigator to get a position at once, the radio operator to start working on any station. He replied that he could get Chinese and Japanese stations but no American stations. Where were we and why?

It was some time before the navigator gave us two fixes about [sic]: the first 300 miles east of Kunming and the second about 50 miles to the west of the first. In the meantime, having been at 19,000 feet for over five hours we were all getting somewhat goofy. Soon our radio operator picked up a station, then another after getting a new frequency, then the navigator got another fix that clinched our position. We landed at 1.45 A.M. at Kunming. Everyone on the station was alarmed and concerned. But not more than we were, for there are a lot of things I would rather do than have coffee with Japs in Hanoi.

The capture of Arnold and his party would have been disastrous, not only because of his knowledge of future Allied plans, but also because of the danger that might result if the Allied reading of Japanese codes were revealed. There were several moments when the capture of Allied officers, or poorly controlled press stories, might have given this priceless information to the Japanese, but did not. As the war progressed, regulations for senior officers with such information visiting front-line areas became progressively tighter, but were not always obeyed. SEE ALSO PP. 317–18, 749–50.

Early February 1943

Donald Peacock, an RAF technician, is transferred to the Jaarmarkt POW camp at Surabaya on Java

It was too dark to see much of the Jaarmarkt camp when we arrived . . .

'Jaarmarkt' means a fairground, and some remnants of the old structures remained. Some of the Dutch prisoners were housed incongruously in what appeared to have been an oriental tunnel of love. The whole area was surrounded by a high bamboo wall broken at intervals by sentry towers manned at all times by armed guards . . . I can't say how many of us were incarcerated there but there were certainly a few thousand. The British were nearly all RAF with a sprinkling of Army and Navy lads.

The sailors were survivors from the destroyer *Jupiter*, one of four British warships lost in the Battle of the Java Sea. The *Jupiter* lads had learned the new rôle in life very quickly. After sinking, they told us, they had struggled to the safety of dry land only to be met by a Nip invasion force. It seemed that at that time nothing could go wrong for the Nips. Just when they needed coolies, a bunch of half-drowned Brits came crawling up the beach.

The majority of the Jaarmarkt inmates were Dutch. Some had been well-heeled Surabaya businessmen until the invasion wrecked their lives. They either had large sums of money with them, or access to it on the outside. They had got themselves, and somewhere along the line some Nips or Koreans too, very well-organised. And they were generous enough to spread the benefits around. As a result Jaarmarkt had by far the best food I came across as Pow. Incredibly there were even occasional handouts of eggs, bananas and sugar, all acquired somehow by the Dutch. We half-naked newcomers were also treated to a handout of badly-needed clothing. I was fortunate enough to acquire an old green Dutch Army tunic and a more or less matching pair of shorts.

But everything in life has to be paid for, particularly in Pow life. And the price of the Jaarmarkt goodies was the Jaarmarkt discipline. It began with the dawn bugle call. We were hounded out of our huts on to the camp square, hounded by a bunch of whooping Koreans competing with each other for the pleasure of beating up any stragglers. On the square, encouraged by more Koreans yelling 'Koorah' at frequent intervals, we formed ourselves into what could loosely be called a parade, facing east. Then, as the light of the bright new day tinged the sentry towers with rose, a falsetto Korean voice shrieked 'Ki-oss-ki', and those on the fringes of the parade brought themselves grudgingly to something like attention. 'Kirri,' screamed the voice, and those under the close scrutiny of the surrounding guards bowed stiffly to the rising sun and its close relative the Emperor Hirohito . . .

We also had to follow a precise routine on feeling the call of nature after curfew. The procedure was to approach the nearest sentry tower, wait until you were sure you had been observed, bow and then bawl out: 'Banjo Mickey Mouse!' This unlikely combination apparently bears some resemblance to 'May I go to the toilet?' in Nipponese.

The 'toilet' turned out to be a super-luxury latrine by Pow standards. No open-trench fly metropolis here. Instead, sunk into the ground, we found a huge metal tank with holes spaced out over the surface at appropriate distances. To watch the once high and mighty Europeans at this mass squat must have given great satisfaction to our guards, but at least it was all very hygienic. It appeared, however, that this bizarre multi-loo could have been installed for economic rather than health reasons, for quite incredibly the Nips made money out of it. A contractor came along from time to time to drain out the tank with a suction pump, and paid quite handsomely for the privilege. For while the Nips may have demoted the white man from demi-god to coolie, the manure he produced was still at a premium to the Asiatic variety.

This entry in Peacock's diary illustrates the value of meeting POWs from other locations: they often brought news of more recent events elsewhere

*in the war. Although Peacock was now a non-combatant, military action
continued to have a direct impact upon him. Guadalcanal had finally
fallen to US forces and this resulted in increasing American air raids
around the Bismarck archipelago during the spring of 1943, hampering
Japanese shipping of reinforcements. The Japanese badly needed air
cover and so began the construction of new airfields and the expansion
of existing ones. Plans were drawn up to use POW labour for this
project. During April 1943 a group of about 2,000 British and Dutch
POWs – including Don Peacock – would be shipped from the relative
comfort of Java to the remote island of Ambon to be used in the
construction and expansion of airfields.* SEE ALSO PP. 260–3, 557–9.

Sunday 14 February 1943

Elizabeth Vaughan and her children, American civilian
internees, celebrate St Valentine's Day at Bacolod camp

St. Valentine's Day. Wonderful alliterative beauty of the
English language – from mendicity to mendacity. While
thoughts were on such a lofty terminological plane, I heard
a strange gulp from Beth's bed where she lay quietly for a
mid-day siesta. Scattered around her in bed were many
paper valentines, an exchange of which had taken place
between children this morning. Beth has a way of keeping
new acquisitions at her side until something still newer
crowds out older playthings for lack of space. She simply
wallowed in volutions made from old Christmas cards and
bits of colored paper and ribbons hoarded squirrel-like by
foresighted parents. Yellow, green, and brown wrapping
paper had also been transformed into heart-like symbols of
the day. Beth's and Clay's more prized 'valentines,' however,
were pasteboard with a shiny old-currency ten-centavo
piece pasted in the center.

I feared, when I heard gurgles and gulps from Beth's bed,
that it might be this coin passing down her throat. It was.
Childlike, she had given the new toy the test of taste of well
as of touch. For an awful moment Beth gasped as the coin
hesitated in its downward course, then a smile broke on her

face as she gave one final swallow and the coin passed safely to depths below. A glass of water, hastily handed her, helped lubricate the pathway of this indigestible item . . .

Beth's silver valentine coin is rare now – Japanese money is of course paper, even one-centavo papers are now in circulation. Needless to say I salvaged Beth's precious coin and put it in safety in her piggy-bank.

As civilians, Vaughan and her fellow internees were treated relatively gently by the Japanese and lived in conditions that were considerably better than those to be found in POW camps. Though food supplies were limited, they were equally poor for those living outside the camps. Until 1944, when the Japanese became paranoid about the impending invasion, internees were also allowed to receive additional food packages from friends and former domestic staff outside the camp. Elizabeth Vaughan's diary captures the anxiety of so many mothers coping alone with young children, with the additional knowledge that their husbands were imprisoned in even worse circumstances. Vaughan's diary, like the diaries of many other internees, was a lettre manqué, *a text that began as a letter to her husband, incarcerated some distance away in the notorious Cabanatuan prison, but which could not be sent. SEE ALSO* PP. *280–1, 340–1, 402, 417–18.*

Friday 19 – Sunday 21 February 1943

Mack Morriss and Brodie satiate themselves in Auckland – the US Army's liberty town

Mack Morriss was a US army journalist, working on the official news-paper The Yank. *Together with his friend Brodie he had already discovered Auckland in 1942, and was now revisiting it.*

19 February
Six and one-half hours from Tontouta to Auckland.

20 February
This is the Army's liberty town and nobody bothers to make anything else out of it. When we came in yesterday we were

given a long official song & dance on what we could & couldn't do, but it didn't mean a thing. We reported in at Victoria Park and were told that we could stay at a hotel if we liked, altho the sheaf of instructions we were handed said such was absolutely prohibited. So is the buying of liquor by officers for enlisted men, but it's done. So we registered at the Royal – all we have to do is report to the top sergeant at Victoria every morning before 11:00. Our first night passed with only a mild drunk – very mild. Ran into Dowling – he gave us gin & scotch. We couldn't seem to really get started, even with gin and beer by the gallon. It was wonderful to sit down to a meal – a real honest meal – with chinaware and silver. Oh boy!

21 February

I am writing on my bed – clean white sheets – at 12:15 a.m. This has been the damnedest day I've spent in months. I'm so full of solid food I'm almost popping – what a place this joint is. Perhaps I should start at yesterday noon.

Brodie & I were in the lounge when we spotted two wenches giving us the eye. We invited them to lunch. After eating they took us to their apartment. We had already drunk until our eye teeth floated, altho we never did get drunk, but we drank more there and pawed around awhile. The babe I had was married and she expected her husband, so Brodie made a date with her friend for 8:00 and I was to come back this morning. So we came back to the hotel, Brodie & I, ate and lay down. Naturally, we slept thru Brodie's date – oh, boy was he burned up. I was supposed to wake him – ha. Anyway, this morning we went around. To make a bad story short, we got it. I have never seen anything like these women – my God, what animals. I'll believe anything. Not to go into the gory details – I probably established a world's record for fast work . . . me and the rabbits. Four months layoff does things. I was not, shall we say, exactly pleased with mine – she was as evil minded a bitch as I ever saw – both of them – they had sex books of the dime variety all over the house. For pure carnal knowledge, which was all we had in mind, they were all right, but I couldn't stand a steady diet of that stuff. Phew!

This day has been one round of meals – we eat like kings. New Zealanders are meat lovers and that's down my alley – steak & eggs, fillet, pork – anything. I'm stuffed – and on top of that there's the beer. After three tremendous meals and a gallon of beer, we went out a few minutes ago & got an order of steak and eggs.

Auckland was one of the most popular destinations for US army soldiers on leave, and had changed to accommodate the requirements of men briefly back from the front. Mack and Brodie enjoyed a period of leave or a 'furlough' every six or nine months and followed the regular pattern of so many soldiers who were allowed brief liberty, indulging to the maximum in all the pleasures that were not available at the front. SEE ALSO PP. 341–3, 363–4, 396–7.

Thursday 25 February 1943

John Gaitha Browning, war artist, crosses the equator and becomes a Shellback

John Gaitha Browning was a thirty-year-old artist when he joined the US army on 7 May 1942. As a Boy Scout he had done a lot of work among Native Americans in the United States and was already an admirer of aboriginal art. He began his diary while training at Fort Ord in California, and it describes his initial journey aboard the transport ship Willard A. Holbrook *to Brisbane in Australia. This foray into the Pacific would allow him a vast opportunity to pursue his interest in indigenous art and culture.*

On the morning of February 25, we crossed the equator, and our officers arranged for the traditional ceremony. Lieutenant Callaway called for me. When I went to the state-room, he wanted me to help with the make-up of the principals in King Neptune's Court. We went down to the carpenter's shop where one of the ship's officers waited with an assortment of ridiculous costumes and a collection of greasepaint.

Lieutenant Callway was the Royal Baby, wearing diapers

made from a sheet, a lace baby cap, and a large green butterfly painted on his ample stomach. Captain Gudgeon made a good subtle Neptune, and Captain Shaul was a ruthless Royal Barber. The cast included a wife, and also a mistress for Neptune, a jester, and others.

Court convened on B deck aft, where a tank had been constructed of framework and heavy canvas. Neptune opened the court with a thump of his tridon and a wave of his long white whiskers. The fun was on, beginning with indignities on the colonel himself, who was led out blindfolded onto the raised square of the hold, clad only in his shorts. He was charged with issuing orders that no WAVE or WAC could come aboard the ship at any time. The barber proceeded to give him a Royal Shampoo by first covering his head with pancake batter, then breaking two eggs into the mess and rubbing it in well. Next he was given the Royal Zoot Suit to wear. This was a larger rubber suit open only at the top and equipped with a drawstring. When the colonel was safely inside the suit, a large hose was suddenly dragged out, and the suit was filled with water until he was a large rubberball with hands and feet. The colonel was ordered to walk around, presenting an awkward and hilarious sight.

Others were brought out and charged with various crimes of a somewhat indecent nature and were given a real clipping with the barber clippers. Some culprits went away with paths cut to the scalp. Neither hair nor dignity was spared. Some men had their hind parts painted in designs with indelible inks. Afterwards, each man on the ship became a Shellback, and all were pronounced members of the Shellbacks forever.

Innumerable US army soldiers enjoyed or endured the ceremonies that accompanied the 'crossing of the line', with their fanciful figures drawn from the myth of King Neptune and his court. Some of these affairs were gentle and good-natured – as here – but others were rather rough and unpleasant, with more than a whiff of bullying. SEE ALSO PP. 506–8, 605–6, 622–3.

MARCH 1943

O N 1 MARCH 1943, a US B-24 Liberator bomber spotted a substantial Japanese convoy off New Guinea. Between 2 and 4 March the United States attacked the Japanese convoy in what would become known as the Battle of the Bismarck Sea. Admiral Masatomi Kimura was in command of eight destroyers that were escorting eight transport ships moving 7,000 Japanese infantrymen from the base at Rabaul on New Britain southwards to Lae and Salamaua in New Guinea. First of all, General Douglas MacArthur ordered raids on neighbouring Japanese airfields to limit any possible air cover. Then the convoy was attacked by American aircraft by day and PT boats (motor-torpedo boats) by night. All the transports were sunk, along with four of the destroyers. More than half of the Japanese infantry who were being transported were also lost. Thereafter, most Japanese supplies in this area would be carried by submarine.

In mid-March, at a major strategy conference in Washington, MacArthur's deputy, General Eichelberger, proposed a plan for the capture of the Japanese base at Rabaul and achieved a measure of control over Admiral Halsey, the naval commander in the same area. US strategy conferences were often accompanied by tussling between the army and the navy.

In China, General Claire Chennault's organization, originally a band of American freebooting volunteers who styled themselves 'The Flying Tigers', was expanded to become the 14th Air Force and he was promoted to brigadier-general. Despite this elevation, he continued to prefer to operate as a virtually independent commander, reflecting his roots in a maverick volunteer service. Although his air operations were highly successful, poor performance by Chinese nationalist ground troops meant that his airfields repeatedly came under threat.

In Burma, Wingate's Chindit force succeeded in its objective of cutting the railway between Mandalay and Myitkyina; destroying it in no fewer than twenty-five different places.

However, the Japanese then attempted to respond, hoping to trap the Chindit columns deep in the jungle. Few were caught, for on 24 March, to Wingate's dismay, he was ordered to return to India and safety. His Chindits would retreat in small groups over a period of weeks. This withdrawal was probably a sensible decision, as one-third of his force had already been lost in the operation up to this point. In the Arakan, the more conventional British offensive was not making any gains and eventually withdrew in the face of Japanese infiltration that threatened their supply lines.

Sunday 21 – Tuesday 23 March 1943

Australian soldier Eddie Stanton watches a Japanese prisoner fail to take the plunge near Goodenough Island

By early 1943 Stanton's unit had been moved from the Trobriand Islands to Goodenough Island, where the construction of an airfield was under way to support the dogged advance of the Australian army through the jungles of Papua New Guinea. He was serving as army liaison with the local Papuan police force. Together they spent much of their time dealing either with a number of Japanese stragglers who were giving themselves up, or else with bodies that were being washed ashore as the result of the nearby Battle of the Bismarck Sea.

21 March

About 1.30 p.m. what appeared to be a small barge was sighted about 15 miles off Goodenough Island. Looking out from Mapamoiwa it appeared to be bobbing all over the place. Perhaps some Japanese might be on board; if so, out boys and get 'em!

At 2.15 p.m. we all, six white, & 3 police, went out to intercept it on 'Kismet', with about 4 sub-machine guns & 3 rifles. As we approached, a figure in the stern was seen. Right up to the barge we went, guns cocked.

One Japanese was in the back. He stood up, resting on his sword. Apparently, he wanted us to shoot him. He should have been.

We were told to hold fire. When he saw he was not going to be shot, he took his sword out of the sheath & went to run it thru his stomach, then his throat. However, he couldn't make the plunge. Who could?

He was taken prisoner & brought back to Mapamoiwa . . .

At this minute he is outside the office, praying, on his knees, and looking skywards . . .

He was suffering from malaria, but otherwise he was in good health.

A clean, starched Australian uniform was given him to wear, whilst a native washed his own clothes. I was appalled to see white men treating the Japanese bastard as if he were a brother. Would we be so attended, were the position reversed? I think not. I still remember the Australians who were burnt alive at Tol last year.

22 March

About 12.30 a.m. team of enemy bombers overhead. Later it was learnt that they had bombed Milne Bay.

At 7.15 a.m. left on 'Kismet' to intercept a barge that we had sighted on the horizon. With Tommy guns, rifles & pistols out we went, Jap hunting. Our quarry, however, proved to be a brand new American barge. We brought it back to Mapamoiwa.

I left on 'Gudara' for Vivigana at 11 a.m. with Japanese prisoner. Turned him over to the Military authorities about 4 p.m. A devil of a job. No-one wanted to take him. Was told NOT to take any more prisoners.

Shortly before 6 p.m., 36 Japanese, who had been captured at the Trobriand Islands (my late stamping ground), were towed in to Vivigana. They did not appear to be very worried. Japanese are still being shot all over the place. The necessity for capturing them has ceased to worry anyone. From now on, Nippo survivors are just so much machine-gun practice. Too many of our soldiers are tied up guarding them.

Arrived back at Mapamoiwa with 3 spotters about 10 p.m.

23 March

. . . The Nippo whom we caught on Sunday probably left Goodenough Island on account of the death of his companions. I learnt, yesterday, that 23 Japanese had been shot dead on Sunday just near the place which he had left. Maybe he thought he stood a better chance in flight. He did.

Stanton's diary captures the ambiguity of Allied treatment of Japanese POWs. On the battlefield, American and Australian practice was often to take no prisoners – an attitude, as Stanton underlines, that was partly a reaction to documented Japanese barbarities, partly a fear that Japanese surrenders might be a trick. However, his diary also mentions another reason for disposing of prisoners summarily: namely, that guarding and caring for prisoners in remote areas was an enormous administrative burden. This aside, if Japanese soldiers managed to surrender to rear area troops they tended to receive much better treatment than that meted out by front-line soldiers. SEE ALSO PP. 286–8, 533–4, 760–1.

Tuesday 23 March 1943

Peter Pinney listens to his friend Whacker offer his views on army officers

Peter Pinney, known to his fellow soldiers as 'Johnno', was already an experienced soldier by 1943. He had joined the Australian army in 1941, serving in the Middle East as a signaller. Now he was at Salamaua in New Guinea with a commando unit – often referred to as an 'independent company'. Independent companies were effectively special forces, given some of the most difficult and demanding tasks posed by fighting in the dense jungle.

Whacker is an uncomplicated man, but pretty old – like Roy and Simon. All three must be getting on towards their thirties. He has travelled the outback shearing, mining unsung hills, droving in the Territory and riding the Marree-Birdsville track. Mildura, Milparinka, Mallapunyah . . . the names of distant places are milestones marking adventurous years of challenges, achievements and disasters . . .

Whacker snorts with disgust. He was with the Sixth Div in the Middle East, and he fears no god or devil or any kind of man. He despises Pommy publicans and Egyptian gulli-gulli men, brummy coppers and Italian barbers and all provosts, poofters, pimps and Japs and poons. When contemplating women, his satanic grin suggests the morals of a well-hung ferret. But, with few exceptions, his keenest derision is reserved for army officers.

'Grow up, Johnno.'

'But I mean, he is an officer, and that.'

He regards me with a sort of patient scorn. He has the ethics of a blinkered wombat, Whacker has. Whenever provoked or under pressure he moves in a dead straight line, regardless of intervening hazards, to his goal. And he talks that way too, whether under pressure or not.

'Johnno, I don't know where you growed up, but it weren't nowhere I been. You don't know your arse from Pancake Day.'

He takes a half-smoked durry from behind his ear and strikes a vesta. As he puffs his smoke alight:

'I been a lot of places, boy. I done a lot of things. I've fought a lot of bastards too; and one or two was better than me, but not many. I've met ponces and drongos and dimwits and villains and pricks and plain damn fools: but the biggest menace in this man's world is some ninety-day-wonder from the ROTC [Reserve Officer Training Corps] what pushes good men into action without knowing what he's about, and gets 'em killed.'

It is almost sedition. If someone overheard, he could be arraigned for 'spreading despondency and alarm'.

'Just you remember this,' he goes on. 'Don't let yourself be conned. Don't believe the lies. You got to look beyond the wrapping and see the man inside. Right?'

'I guess.'

'Wrap a pisspot in silver paper, or in a doublebreasted suit, and all you've got is still a pisspot. Right?'

'Yes, Whacker.'

Who, in his right mind, would disagree?

'Most officers are only peanuts wearing pips. There's only one way they can earn respect: and that's by proving they got at least as much guts as the men they command.'

He squints at me through the smoke.
'You remember that!'

Diaries reveal numerous examples of disrespect towards military officers, usually related to their limited ability. The general subject of military discipline during the Second World War remains somewhat mysterious. Although reliable figures exist for courts martial and desertion, more routine aspects of officer–soldier relations remain hard to gauge. Desertions were high in 1941 and 1942, at about nine men per thousand. Later in the war the figure would halve. During the Vietnam War, officers who were regarded as either dangerously incompetent, or excessively keen to engage the enemy were reportedly 'fragged' by using grenades to injure them on the battlefield. There is little evidence of this practice before Vietnam, although in tough units such as Pinney's commando outfit respect had to be won by officers and was not given by the men freely. SEE ALSO PP. 670–1, 735–7.

Tuesday 23 March – Saturday 17 April 1943

Malcolm Foord observes the battles between two armies on the island of Tonga

Malcolm Foord was born in 1921 and grew up in Dunedin in New Zealand. He had worn a military uniform since the age of twelve, having joined the cadet corps in his secondary school. In 1939 he attended Otago University and continued his part-time soldiering in the Otago Territorial Regiment. In 1942 warfare had become altogether more serious, and Foord was transferred to the 6th Battalion of the Canterbury Regiment and sent to garrison the island of Tonga. There was no active fighting on Tonga, and so he had time here to maintain his schoolboy interest in the local flora and fauna.

23 March
I have been having some fun with the ants. In the ground beside my bed there is a small colony of them, and I watch them hunting for food. I put a tin on a box, and on top put a piece of Army biscuit, about 2' 6" off the ground. One ant foraging about came across it, and reconnoitred it

thoroughly, running over it and around it and touching it everywhere with his antennae. Then he made for home as fast as he could go, a walking distance of five feet in all. On the way he met a few of his cobbers, and it was interesting to watch how he communicated with them. Both would stop and agitate their feelers together, and then the two would set off at high speed, the one on his way home, the second straight for where he had been told there was something good to eat. And when the first one arrived back at the nest a stream of ants would immediately set out for the biscuit, hurrying as fast as they could go. It is certain that they follow the scent, for they go by the route used by the discoverer of the goods, even if it isn't the shortest. In this case they all went in a wide sweep over the top of the box instead of cutting across it. As they arrived on the scene they were immediately tugging at the biscuit, and when enough were there they pulled it home, tumbling over two big drops en route.

In the centre of the tent lives another colony, a very populous one this, and belonging to a different species. They look very like the Small Blacks, but there is just enough difference to distinguish them when all mixed up. They are slightly smaller, and a shade browner. Their soldiers are faster in their movements than the Small Black soldiers, and are quite distinctly smaller than they. The Brown soldiers generally lose their lives to the Blacks in close combat. The Browns specialize in hit and run tactics, a swift approach, a savage nip, and away. The Small Blacks' soldiers are heavy cruisers when the Small Browns' are destroyers.

Emulating Sir Basil Zaharoff and the war-making capitalists of his ilk I have been engineering wars between these two ant colonies. The principle I work on is the innate greed that makes one colony refuse to share its wealth with other colonies. To put it more simply, if I put a piece of biscuit where both colonies will find it at one time, both will soon have scores or hundreds of workers upon the scene; but they will not work peaceably together, and a battle royal will result. The Small Blacks are not nearly so numerous as the Small Browns, so to equalize their positions as much as possible I have to put the biscuit fairly close to the Blacks' nest. On the earth of the tent floor the ants do not attempt to carry a large piece holus-bolus, but break little bits off it, necessitating thousands of individual ant-loads to get it all home. When food-carrying activities of Browns are at their highest, they have a wide two-way stream running continuously from biscuit to nest, and in a five-foot long stream I have counted ants going past a given point in one direction only at the rate of 100 a minute.

When the two sides join in battle the Blacks send their workers home, and the soldiers come out to meet the foe. They are much bigger than the workers, with tremendous heads and big jaws, indeed savage creatures. If one comes upon a Brown worker from behind he will grab him about the middle, reverse hurriedly with him, and cast him to one side, where he will lie writhing on the ground, lying to be gathered in after the fight.

If a Black soldier grips a Brown worker from in front, however, the latter usually succeeds in freeing itself and dashing away in great agitation.

The Small Browns, however, adopt a different method in battle. They have not got such a large percentage of soldiers, and while they are valiant fellows, most of the fighting is done by the *workers*. Against a Black soldier one of these is usually outclassed, but it often happens that while a soldier is dashing a poor Brown worker to his death one of his mates will come to the rescue, perhaps a soldier or two with them, and by sheer weight of numbers overpower the big brute, tear him to bits and carry the pieces home in triumph.

And when two opposing soldiers come face to face they grip each other by the jaws and don't let go, so that the Black by his superior strength usually succeeds in pulling the Brown home for his children to eat. Obviously, since the Blacks cannot put more than a score of fighters on the field at one time, the Browns with their vast manpower resources could pour hundreds of men into the fight and win every time, but this does not happen in practice. If the Browns manage to get a steady stream of ants running before the Blacks get going, the latter will not dispute it, but keep well clear, and vice versa if the Blacks get in first . . .

17 April

I trust you don't mind the number of squashed ants on this page. I am writing in the I-Room, and lots of them are walking around. One common species has a few nests in the folds that the walls make when they are rolled up. The topmost ant on page 2 is a good example of this ant. Not of a large size, but with long, thin legs, which enable it to get along at a terrific speed. I will call them the 'greyhound' ants. Very hard to time them, for they won't keep a steady course, but they can cross this page in less than two seconds, which other ants of larger size take 7 seconds to do.

Malcolm Foord would survive the war and return to Dunedin. He became a wildlife specialist, preparing reports for the New Zealand Forest Service and compiling a descriptive dictionary of New Zealand wildlife. In 1990 he took one of the squashed ants from the page of his wartime diary and sent it to the British Museum for a formal identification which was successfully performed. Six years later he typed out his wartime diary and published it privately.

Friday 26 March – Monday 5 April 1943

Will Wilder, a British POW, works on the Wampo viaduct near the River Kwai on the Thai–Burma railway

Will Wilder was called up in August 1940. After training as a signaller, he was attached to an artillery regiment and his unit was despatched from Britain to reinforce Malaya in late October 1941. Sailing via Cape Town, they paused in Mombasa in Kenya on Christmas Day and finally arrived in Singapore on 13 January 1942. Air-raid sirens sounded continually as they disembarked and the situation was already 'serious'. Following the surrender a month later, Will Wilder spent much of 1942 in Changi gaol, before being sent north to work on the Thai–Burma railway.

26 March
[K]illed a snake that was amongst our kit where I am bivouacked with five other fellows . . .

28 March
[A] scorpion ran out of my boot today . . . It did not sting.

The last 24 hours or more have been, and still are, the most unpleasant I can remember. Sent on a Jap working party unexpectedly to a spot about 6 or 7 miles away in torrential rain wet through. Japs chivvied us and there were incidents of brutality, slapping fellows and then their own men by their superiors. Wretched lot. Did get a ride back on a train. Clothes dried on me. Wretched feeling. Then had to stand to attention for nearly the whole time: we came into camp by the wrong entrance. Favourite Jap punishment this. More rain, then kit wet. Dried what I could by the fire and went to sleep on a damp bed. More rain before daybreak and I found myself in a puddle wet through again, all my bedding soaked and nowhere to keep dry. Why don't they put us under cover? What have we done to deserve this? Raining all morning.

1 April
Camp a quagmire. Nowhere to sleep or rest. Oh for a home and a roof. This book is spoilt in places. I've just discovered my pack wet. It's too bad. More rain to come too.

5 April
This point is as far as the rail track has gone and it will have to run on an embankment by the side of the cliff with a drop of some distance into the river . . . Really having a rough life. Anything in England will seem palatial after this. Hurry up war and end.

By early 1943 the Japanese were applying maximum pressure in the attempt to finish the Thai–Burma railway. For Will Wilder this meant working twelve hours a day on a cliff-edge above the river, carrying heavy wood with the guards continually shouting 'speedo'. Remarkably, despite the impossible conditions, he recorded his experiences in a diary and also by sketching. Both the diary and the drawings have survived and have since been exhibited. SEE ALSO PP. 430–1.

APRIL 1943

FOLLOWING THE JAPANESE defeat at the Battle of the Bismarck Sea, the commander of the Imperial Japanese Navy, Admiral Yamamoto, felt it necessary to respond with an offensive. However, Japan lacked the naval resources or military manpower to retaliate at sea or on land; so instead an air offensive was chosen, and a large force of planes assembled in the Solomon Islands. On 7 April the Japanese began a series of large-scale raids on airfields and harbours in the area of Guadalcanal, sinking the US destroyer *Aaron Ward*. A few days later, two merchant ships were sunk at Oro bay. Although this operation made an impact, in the course of it Yamamoto lost many experienced carrier-based pilots. On 18 April his own aircraft was intercepted by P-38 Lightning fighters and he was killed. This dramatic event was witnessed by his staff officer, Admiral Ugaki, who was following in a second aircraft and who was also shot down, but survived to write up the experience in his remarkable diary. Yamamoto's death was considered a disaster and was not announced in Tokyo until the following month, when there was an impressive state funeral. Admiral Kogo replaced him as commander-in-chief of the Japanese Combined Fleet.

Throughout early 1943, more Allied prisoners were being moved north from Changi gaol to serve as slave labour on the Thai–Burma railway, on which the Japanese were pressing ahead with a view to establishing a logistics network and extending their hold on northern Burma. By the end of the year there were almost 60,000 POWs engaged in this work. Much of the railway would be complete by October 1943. The workforce also included 200,000 Asian labourers, who were treated no better than the prisoners. Estimates place the number of Asian deaths as high as 80,000. The Allied death toll was nearly 13,000. All in all, for every mile of track laid, 393 men died.

Thursday 1 April 1943

Don McLaren, an Australian soldier on the Thai–Burma railway, labours to build the 'Pack of Cards'

On 1 April Don McLaren and many of his fellow prisoners had been moved by truck deep into the Thai jungle near the border with Thailand to help construct a railway bridge over a gulley near Hintok using teak logs.

It was still dark when the guard was yelling. 'All men out, all men out.'

Here we faced an enormous natural gully. A timber framed bridge would eventually span this gully, we called it 'The Pack of Cards.'

We hauled these teak logs in from the jungle. First we had to drive the logs, sharpened at one end, into the ground. Next we shaved off one side with crude axes to make it possible to keep going up and up. The Jap engineers rigged up this pile-driving apparatus. We had long ropes. Hundreds of Australians would walk back until the rope was taut, then we'd sing, 'Ichy, nee. Nisio, nisio, nisio.' (One, two. Pull, pull, pull.) As we sang these numbers, we'd pull on the rope. This huge great lump of steel would rise up. On the last 'nisio' we would all let go. Down would come the pile-driver and the pole would sink another inch. All day, seven days a week, for weeks on end, with not a single day off, we drove these bloody things into the ground.

Quite a few Japs had sore heads. Every time a chance came along, some items would fall from the bridge and hit a Nip on the cranium.

The stupidity of the Jap guards was their continuous screaming of 'More sing, more sing!' We would all be yelling 'Ichy, nee, nisio!', but it took more out of our emasculated bodies to sing and tug at the same time.

The bridge is equal to a four storey building. While we were still hauling timbers up to complete it, every Australian saw this bloody Jap fall off the top. Next thing, an arm comes out and grabs the falling object. So here's this Aussie holding this Jap by the neck of his shirt. We were all yelling, 'Drop the bastard, drop the bastard!' The Aussie yelled back, 'I can't, the bastards are on to me!'

We did an enormous amount of sabotage to this structure. Over half the timbers that were cased out with another piece shaped to fit into the cased area were broken. Often the cased out section would be filled with sand and small stones. It was the crudest bridge one could ever wish to see. I hope I never have to go over it in a train.

The Thai–Burma railway stretched for 265 miles from Bam Pong in Thailand to Thanbyuzayat in Burma. The intended purpose of the railway was to offer an alternative supply route for the Japanese army, instead of the vulnerable Singapore to Rangoon sea route. By mid-1943 Allied aircraft and submarines had driven almost all Japanese transport shipping from the Bay of Bengal. The bridge would collapse three times while it was being built – hence its nickname – and at least thirty-one people died during the various phases of construction. SEE ALSO PP. 238–9, 807–9, 821–2.

Sunday 11 April 1943

Tamura Yoshikazu endures night-time bombing at Wewak airfield in New Guinea

Tamura Yoshikazu was twenty-six years old in 1943. He came from the Tochigi prefecture north of Tokyo. His family there consisted of his father, two sisters and a brother, his mother having died some years before. He had previously fought as a soldier in China and Korea, enjoying some leave at home in 1942. He resumed service in January 1943, joining the 239th Infantry Regiment (Toto 36 Unit) of the 41st Division and travelling to the port of Shimonoseki, where his unit joined a ship bound for Korea. By April 1943 his unit had been sent south to oppose the Australians at Wewak in New Guinea.

Through the quiet of the night, we could hear the sound of a plane engine. I gradually woke up, wondering what time it was. The guard shouted 'Air raid!'

Soon, enemy planes approached above us and search-lights lit up the sky. The anti-aircraft gunners started to open fire. The special music of the night began to play.

Fine continuous rain, characteristic of the tropical rainy season, keeps falling. It seems it is raining hard as we listen to it beating on the jungle leaves. However, the enemy planes dare to fly in this weather to bomb our position.

The sound of the explosions becomes quite numbing and the next one shakes the ground and the sky. Boom! Boom! We can hear the explosions one after another. Here they come!

We have experienced many air raids since our landing. We are no longer surprised by them and think, 'Oh, it's just another air raid'. However, this attack was executed so beautifully that we cannot help admiring the enemy.

When the enemy plane flew over us, we anticipated a direct attack and bombs to fall down. Yet, none of us got out of bed. All the soldiers were very much relaxed and I was impressed with their boldness.

Finally, we felt relieved when the dawn came and the sky began to grow light. We did not know the extent of the damage, but we could hear the morning reveille. We celebrated that we were beginning another day uninjured.

I believe people back at home are really lucky, as they can sleep through the night with their heads on pillows. It clearly reflects the great power of the nation. The soldiers are engaged in protecting the future of the nation.

Tamura Yoshikazu was subjected to continual heavy air bombardment almost from the moment of his arrival at Wewak. During airfield construction the business of breaking off from work to head for the air-raid shelters seems to have been so frequent as to have been regarded as routine. Elsewhere his diary records grabbing reading matter to while away the time there when an alert sounded. His attitude to this night-time raid was no less phlegmatic – although clearly this particular attack found its mark. He noted that the bullets and shells that came from the enemy planes and Japanese artillery 'glowed in the dark beautifully and looked like grand fireworks'. SEE ALSO PP. 399–400.

Thursday 15 April 1943

Augusta Clawson goes under cover as a woman welder in an Oregon shipyard

In early 1943 American shipyards faced a problem. Because few men were left on the home front and ships were desperately needed, more and more women were being trained as shipyard welders. However, few stayed in the job for more than a few weeks. Augusta Clawson, a graduate from Vassar College in her twenties who was working for the US Department of Education, was recruited to go under cover. Her task was to work as a welder for two months in an Oregon shipyard to identify the problems and explain why women were leaving. She had begun training at the welding school on 8 April.

I crowed too soon. Today was horrible. I went in expecting to conquer the world, and was thrown by a vertical weld. I'd get it smooth about eight inches up – and then let a huge bubble roll down and spoil it, I don't understand it. Usually when you learn a thing you retain it. But that isn't so with welding. You think you have the hang of it beautifully, and then you do welds that are inferior to the day-before-yesterday's. And tonight I'm so much more tired than before. In fact I came back from dinner, sat down in my big chair for a few minutes, and fell sound asleep . . .

Just after I reached the school we were all huddled together around the table putting new glass in our helmets when Missouri yelped, 'look at what's all dressed up', and in walked Shorty complete with new leathers in all their yellowish newness. And they are so *very* mustard yellow when they're new. Her overalls were so long she had to walk with a weaving motion to keep them from catching her heels . . .

Missouri was in rare form. She took two years of medical training at St. John's in Springfield, Missouri, and did practical nursing for a long time. Then she did waitress work – 'but I want to tell you, that just about killed me. It's harder by the jugful, and what you have to take from the public!'

Several there who had waitressed agreed with her . . . I was talking with Jeanette Mattox. She has two girls of twelve and fourteen, and also supports her mother. Another daughter, older, is married and has a child. This class seems to be full of young grandmothers. She looks very young and is as pretty as a picture . . .

We were called to another safety lecture – good sound advice on Eye Safety. Pontocaine 1/2 sol. is the best treatment. Potato juice or juice from tea-leaves is good. Report to First Aid immediately in case of arc flash. The safety man urged that we help new workers coming into the Yard, that we clean up our work areas . . . The lecturer brought up the rumor that arc welding causes sterility among women. He said that this was untrue, and quoted an authoritative source to prove its falsity. In the Girl's Room afterwards, this question was the topic of conversation. Two of the women had completely misunderstood him. One said: 'I'm not going to stay in welding if you can't have babies. I don't like the idea.' Another agreed: 'I don't like it, either. I am going to get out too'. I interrupted: 'But you're all wrong. He said there was no truth in the rumor. Welding does not cause sterility . . .'

I am today the proud owner of one check drawn by The Shipyard and payable to one A.H. Clawson, badge 44651 – $20.80 for three days of last week. I'll have to pay it over to Uncle Sam, but it's fun having it even go through my hands. And I shall keep the stub as a record for posterity. I must have a grandchild, even if I have to adopt one, so that I can say, 'Darling, in the last war your grandmother built ships.' (Probably by then my granddaughter will be an Admiral and won't be impressed at all.)

Augusta Clawson recorded her information in a journal on which she based her report. Although the material was never meant for publication, it was eventually decided to turn it into a wartime book to reassure other women about industrial work. SEE ALSO PP. 401–2.

H. L. Mencken worries about the scarcity of silk pajamas in Baltimore

Henry Louis Mencken was born on 12 September 1880 to German American parents. His grandfather had been a cigar-maker in the German section of Baltimore in 1848, and eventually his father had started his own tobacco firm, which ensured a comfortable existence for his family. Although destined for the family business, Henry was more attracted by writing and journalism. He went to the Baltimore Sun *as Sunday editor, became an editorial writer, and in 1911 started his own column, the 'Free Lance', in the evening edition of the paper. A vigorous opponent of prohibition, he was known for his pungent opinions and soon became an institution.*

H. L. Mencken

I had lunch yesterday at the Merchants Club as the guest of Spalding Albert, advertising manager of the *Sun* papers. Don Tobin, the new manager of the O'Neill department store, was also a guest. He is an extremely charming young man, and greatly resembles F. Scott Fitzgerald. He is a Dartmouth college graduate and felt an inclination toward store-keeping even in his college days. He has been extremely successful, and came to Baltimore from Hartford.

He told me that the life of a department store manager is now one grand series of headaches. He said that in the O'Neill store there was little difficulty about counter help, for most of the saleswomen are oldsters who have been on the staff for years, but he said that in the office there was a constant overturn of labor. Girls came in knowing nothing. They were taught laboriously, and after a while reached pay of as much as $40 a week. Thereupon they quit to go to work in a war plant at even more money and the whole grind had to be repeated.

Tobin said that there was absolutely no stock of silk in the Baltimore stores. He said that Bonwit Lennon some time ago advertised ready-made silk dresses at $99 and that all of the other department store people are still wondering where they got them. Tobin said that the new rayons are not only as good as silk but even better. I complained that those I had tried for pajamas washed badly, but he said that in the new ones that difficulty has been overcome. He said that rayon dyes better than silk and is more durable. I'll bear this in mind whenever the time comes to renew my stock of pajamas. I used to buy lengths of silk at Hutzler's annual silk sale and then have pajamas made up by McPherson, but for two years there have been no silk sales.

Even before the war broke out, silk imports from Japan had come to a halt as a result of escalating trade embargoes. Moreover, in August 1941 silk supplies in America were commandeered by the War Production Board for use in parachutes. This set off a run on all silk goods, including women's hosiery, and trade papers carried headlines such as 'Stocking Panic'. Once war began, most nylon production was also absorbed by war manufacturing. Consumers complained that substitutes were inferior and wondered whether the absence of silk and hosiery was a result of the war or of profiteering. Servicemen in the Pacific would buy up any silk goods and stockings they could find, feeding a black market. Official efforts to suppress black markets in the United States were not especially effective. See also p. 796–7.

Sunday 18 April 1943

Admiral Matome Ugaki is shot down with Fleet Admiral Yamamoto in the Pacific

At 0610 Fleet Admiral Yamamoto, who had commanded the attack on Pearl Harbor, left Rabaul on an inspection visit in a medium torpedo bomber with six fighters as escorts. US signals intelligence units based on Hawaii had intercepted signals sent out, unwisely, by the Japanese on Rabaul announcing his flight. Quickly decoded, these had informed the United States of Yamamoto's flight in advance, and sixteen P-38 Lightnings of 339th Fighter Squadron commanded by Captain Thomas Lamphier, Jr were tasked to attack the Japanese aircraft.

After we had evaded about twice, I turned to the right to see how the first plane was evading. What I saw then was astounding. Lo! The first plane was staggering southward, just brushing the jungle top with reduced speed, emitting black smoke and flame. It was about four thousand meters away from us. I just said to myself, 'My God!' I could think of nothing else. I grabbed the shoulder of Air Staff Officer Muroi, pointed to the first aircraft, and said, 'Look at the commander in chief's plane!' This became my parting with him forever. All this happened in only about twenty seconds.

In the meantime, my plane turned sharply to evade another enemy attack, and we lost sight of the commander in chief's aircraft. I waited impatiently for the plane to get back to the level while full of anxiety, though the result seemed apparent. The next glance revealed that the plane was no more to be seen, only a pall of black smoke rising to the sky from the jungle. Oh! Everything was over now! . . .

Making a rising half-turn and then a quick turn, a P-38 came upon us at last. Here he comes! Our machine gun opened fire on him desperately. Though it worked well it didn't seem to hit him. The enemy P-38 rapidly closed in, taking advantage of his superior speed. His gunfire caught us splendidly. And oncoming bullets were seen on both sides of our plane. I felt them hitting our aircraft from time to time.

Now we were hopeless, and I thought my end was very near at hand.

The sound of our machine-gun fire was reduced by this time, and the skipper could not be heard any more. I thought quite a number must have been killed in the plane.

Staff Officer Muroi was leaning on a table with his face down and arms outstretched. He must have already been killed . . .

Everything went black and I felt the sea water rushing all over my body with fair pressure. I could do absolutely nothing. I told myself, 'This is the end of Ugaki.' Since I thought it was all over my mind was a blank. I don't think I struggled or made any impatient effort, but that wasn't clear anyway. (I can't think I became unconscious; I didn't swallow any water. I suppose it must only have been a few seconds until the next moment.)

Right after I gave it all up, all of a sudden it lightened. When I opened my eyes, incredibly I found myself floating on the sea surface. What a miracle! The fuselage had already disappeared and the right wing was already standing upside down in the sea right behind me and was still burning fiercely.

*Yamamoto was killed by machine-gun fire even before his aircraft crashed into the jungle. Admiral Matome Ugaki and other staff officers were accompanying Yamamoto in a second medium torpedo bomber, which was also shot down. However, Ugaki survived and a year later, on the first anniversary of the attack, recorded the events in his diary. Admiral Nimitz, the American naval commander at Hawaii, had initially agonized over this interception operation, fearing the possibility that the removal of Yamamoto might result in his being replaced by someone more capable.**SEE ALSO PP. 105–7, 632–3, 740–1.*

Mack Morriss reads the diary of a Japanese truck driver
who experienced 'Hell's Front Line' on Guadalcanal

*Mack Morriss, with his friend Brodie, was still located on Guadalcanal
in April 1943 and continued to work as a GI war correspondent at corps
headquarters. The fierce fighting on this island, the most southerly of the
Solomon Islands, had ended in January 1943 and it was now a major
base for the US marine regiments assembling for amphibious attacks
against Japanese positions further north and a vast focus of American
air power.*

At Corps today read excerpts of translations from a Jap
diary. The guy landed here around Nov. 14 and was scared
to death from before the time he got off the boat. He repeated
time & again: 'The people at home would never understand.'
He certainly had a hellish time. The best line was his
description of Guadalcanal, 'Hell's Front Line.' . . .
    The translator said he was a truck driver, but there was no
name. The guy came in on that convoy which we pounded
to pieces and he was bombed and strafed dizzy. There was
no rice and after the third day here he & his outfit were
wobbly. We shelled the hell out of them. The Jap kept saying,
'Really, I am miserable.' He had to make trips up to the front
and told of seeing 'defeated remnants:' and in the same
breath he said, 'I pray that the day shall soon come when we
shall conquer.' And then he got malaria. He seemed to think
that inevitable. Two or three times he said, 'I can not describe
it by tongue or brush.' He heard he would be relieved
around the first of the year and he was sweating it out. The
constant pounding had him groggy – even hysterical in his
writing. 'I too am going mad . . . all people are the same.'
From early December until the last of the month he didn't
write because of his illness but when he did resume things
were no better. Then: 'Jan. 1, 1943 – New Year's Day – I can
think of nothing but my homeland . . . I can write no more.'
    And that was all. There was no clue as to how he died.
Guadalcanal for him was 'hell's front line' and he went over
the top. I think this campaign must have had some effect
on the Japanese soldier – at least he must realize that there is

such a thing in war as defeat. The Jap gave a hint as to their psychology once while he was very sick. He said: 'I cannot die here like this.' I think that he didn't so much fear death as he disliked the idea of dying of sickness or starvation rather than in battle. He seemed absolutely dumbfounded that he and his buddies were taking such a licking. 'If the Imperial Army told of this to the people at home they would never understand – no matter how many times they were told.'

Really, that boy didn't like this place or anything about it. I wouldn't have either, in his place.

Morriss and Brodie found that their main opportunities for action were hitching rides with B-24 bombers heading out for targets over the Pacific. It was only now that the scale of the battle for Guadalcanal struck Morriss, and this was underlined by the diary of the Japanese soldier. Just previously, Mack had visited the cemetery on the island, which had recently doubled in size but was already full. He was struck by the personal ephemera that soldiers had left to commemorate their friends – mess tins, aircraft propellers for pilots, sometimes snapshots of the fallen in happier times – 'all just grinning kids with their garrison caps tilted on the back of their heads'.

Mack Morriss would go on to cover the war in Europe and was present during the Ardennes offensive of December 1944. He was demobilized in July 1945 and after a period as a freelance writer and journalist went to work for the WBEJ radio station, ending up as station manager. He died in 1975. SEE ALSO PP. 341–3, 363–4, 372–4.

MAY 1943

IN BURMA, DESPITE being over-stretched in terms of manpower and materials, the Japanese continued to keep the British off balance. During early May they infiltrated in the area of Buthiduang and Muangdaw and disrupted communications. By the second week of May the British were forced to withdraw from these areas; on 11 May the 26th Division pulled back from Muangdaw, which the Japanese soon occupied. In southern Burma, the 1943 Arakan campaign had now come to an end with the onset of the monsoon and was regarded as a colossal failure. In contrast to the Pacific, where the Americans were inflicting far more casualties than they were taking, the British account was unimpressive. In the Arakan campaign the British had suffered 3,000 casualties, about twice the number suffered by opposing Japanese forces. Morale was extremely low. On 15 May the commanding generals in Burma, Irwin and Lloyd, were sacked and replaced by William Slim, who became commander of the 14th Army. Meanwhile, in London, plans were being put into place for a new regional theatre called South East Asia Command in the hope of injecting more vigour into the Burma war.

During late May a particularly vicious struggle was fought for the control of the Aleutian island chain, stretching across the northern Pacific, with US forces attempting to prise the Japanese infantry out of rocky positions on numerous small islands. On 29 May the Japanese mounted a vigorous counter-attack on the island of Attu. By the following day this attack had been repelled and the island had been captured. The cost was high, with the Americans losing 600 men and suffering twice that number of wounded. The Japanese had lost 2,350 men and only 28 were taken prisoner, all of whom were wounded.

In the Solomons, the Americans used the substantial air-fields they had recently constructed on Guadalcanal to begin an aerial mining campaign, dropping sea mines from aircraft with the aim of closing the Japanese harbours around New

Georgia. Three Japanese destroyers were soon sunk by these mines.

In mid-May Roosevelt and Churchill met in Washington for an important strategic planning conference codenamed Trident. Arguments over the war against Germany continued, with the Americans voicing their unhappiness about the idea of invading Italy and the British criticizing the Americans for giving too much priority to the Pacific war. In reality the main problem was the efficacy of the U-boat war in the Atlantic. The U-boat offensive had ensured that the Allies were short of merchant shipping all around the world; moreover, a great deal of time and resources had been devoted to building escort vessels to counter the U-boats, which in turn meant the Allies had fallen behind in constructing assault shipping and landing craft. Admittedly, in May 1943 the Allies were winning the Battle of the Atlantic, with Admiral Dönitz forced to withdraw many of his submarines in the face of growing losses. However, the massive depredations he had inflicted on Allied shipping over the previous two years were now having profound consequences for Allied strategy across the entire conflict. There was nowhere near enough shipping to launch offensives in all theatres. British planners in south-east Asia were lowest on the priority list in their requests for landing craft to launch their amphibious operations down the coast to Burma and towards Malaya.

Tuesday 4 May 1943

Tamura Yoshikazu, a Japanese soldier in New Guinea, encounters the locals for the first time

When I saw real naked natives for the first time, I felt frightened. But they did not do any harm. They were very well hung, and proudly decorated their hair with bird feathers. It was a surprise for me to see the way they showed off their decoration.

When we reached our destination in the late afternoon, we rested by the regimental barracks. Forty to fifty natives came, and they were all naked. Some were carrying thick ropes and bush knives. A few were wearing crosses on their chests. Furthermore, about half of them were completely naked.

The soldiers stared at them strangely. The natives were also staring at the soldiers intently. They went around the building about twice and disappeared. When I asked other soldiers who had been here previously about them, they told us that the natives came to have a look at us. To them, the soldiers looked very weird. Probably, we looked very foreign to them.

I asked for bananas in the mountains. They seemed to be saying that they did not have bananas at the moment. I felt I understood their language a little bit. Compared with Chinese people, the native children did not have any traces of gloominess and looked so innocent, as if they were blessed by God. They seemed to regard the soldiers as a peculiar group. They were not frightened and did not cry although we were still new to them.

Tamura Yoshikazu's main contact with locals was through trade, and relations with them seem to have been good. He noted in his diary: 'I gave twenty sen for two bananas. These are the first bananas I have had in New Guinea. They tasted very, very sweet. The size of the fruit was as big as my arm or even bigger. They were astonishingly large.'

Yoshikazu was killed, probably by shellfire or aerial bombardment, in December 1943. It appears his diary was then captured and found its way into the hands of Allan E. Connell, a soldier from Melbourne. He had joined the 57/60th Australian Infantry Battalion in October 1941 and had moved into military intelligence, where his duties included translating captured material. Connell was clearly fascinated by the diary and kept the original as a souvenir of his wartime service. More recently it was returned to the family of Tamura Yoshikazu in Japan. SEE ALSO PP. 388–9.

Augusta Clawson, a welder, witnesses casualties on the home front in an Oregon shipyard

At breakfast today I saw the headlines. 'Ten Escape Death After Ship Blaze' and read how ten men were trapped in the forward hold of a tanker at The Yard. All ten had been overcome by fumes from a broken welding lead line, and were rescued by fellow workers who cut into the gas-filled chamber from an adjoining tank.

When I reached the Ways, I was assigned to work for Harry in the bilge tank (Frank's crew was sent to another ship.) As I tugged at my lead line to get it into the tank I looked down on the remains of a charred ladder and a pile of lead lines which had melted into a shapeless mass of rubber and copper wire. Then I knew on which ship the accident had occurred. This hull is well numbered – 13. By lunch time rumours began to seep through explaining the accident. One said that a welder's broken lead had struck an arc, starting a fire that ignited the scaffolding, burned through a burners' hose, flamed up into an inferno of flaming gas, and burned one man to death. Nine others had been overcome by the smoke and fumes of melted rubber, and burners had had to cut through from the next tank to get them out. They were all unconscious.

Another version says that a burner left his hose below without turning off the gas. A welder struck an arc and the whole place exploded. Reports say that five were killed and twenty were injured, and that the ambulance had to make four or five trips at midnight last night. No one knows the truth. The paper reports no deaths. Nothing has been said of the welder who was hurt on Sunday.

The worst part is that it was probably all unnecessary. Workers are careless. When we see welders' lead with copper wires showing through, it seems no one's responsibility to repair it. I don't think I've mentioned the one I showed to Bill. All he said was, 'The next shift will fix it' . . . There is too much carelessness. But The Yard is new and the tasks of the Safety Department are endless.

Although Augusta Clawson's diary was published in 1944 as part of a US wartime work education campaign, it does not appear to have been much sanitized and clearly highlights one of the major problems of the rapid expansion of wartime industrial production. With large numbers of new workers being brought into heavy industry, despite the best efforts with training programmes accident rates were bound to increase. In 1988 a welding historian, Margaret Sondey, located Augusta Clawson and put her in touch with the Smithsonian Museum. Her welding mask is now in a permanent collection there. In retirement Augusta H. Clawson lived in Washington DC; she died on 13 May 1997. SEE ALSO PP. 390–1.

Friday 7 May 1943

The efforts of Elizabeth Vaughan, civilian internee, to get a letter to her husband Jim at Cabanatuan POW camp go badly wrong

Turn quickly the spigot of my mind. Cut off this debilitating flow of war fears which leaves my life a dry and devitalized thing!

The agent who promised to deliver a note to my husband in Cabanatuan Military Prison brought harrowing and chilling news today. The 'agent' is an American newspaper correspondent, wife, and their two and one-half-year-old daughter. The baby had infantile paralysis before coming into camp and is permitted to be taken outside once each week for therapeutic massage in a private hospital in Manila. One week the father takes the baby, the next week the mother. On one of these trips to Manila, this father set out with a note I had written to my husband. He in turn gave the note to a Filipino friend of his who was to deliver a consignment of medical supplies to the Cabanatuan Hospital. The letter began 'Dear Jim' and was signed 'Libby.' My husband's full name and army rank were written on a separate piece of paper. There were no names on the communication itself.

Ordinarily medicines are permitted into the prison

hospital after only a cursory examination at the prison gate. But five prisoners had escaped from Cabanatuan the day the medical supplies arrived and cartons of pills were emptied and vials of serum, worth thousands of pesos and badly needed by sick and dying internees, were broken open in the search for messages which might give a clue to the escape. No less than eight or ten notes to prisoners were discovered in the destroyed medicines. The fate of those who could be identified from the messages is not known. It is known, however, that three of the escaped prisoners were recaptured near Cabanatuan, and shot, and that the remaining five prisoners who made up the work-group of ten who were together at the time of the escape were shot also.

In May 1943 Elizabeth Vaughan and her children were moved to Santo Tomas, near Manila. Incarcerated with her children along with some 5,000 others, she knew that her husband Jim was being held as a POW in one of the most notorious Philippine camps, Cabanatuan, a former military training base 6 miles east of Cabanatuan city. By late 1942 it had become the largest single location of American POWs anywhere. Some 9,000 Americans would pass through the camp and nearly 3,000 failed to return to the United States. Cabanatuan eventually became a forced labour camp: those considered fit for work were sent out on details with the Japanese to build bridges and airfields. Conditions had been at their worst during 1942, when the high death rate was caused mainly by neglect. Simple medicine was not made available and as a result over 500 men died in June and nearly 800 in July. By 1943 a system for supplying basic medicines to the camp had been agreed with the authorities. SEE ALSO PP. 280–1, 340–1, 371–2, 417–18.

Sunday 23 May 1943

Freddy Bloom and Cicely consider the idea of an 'open mating season' for internees at Changi gaol

Freddy Bloom, the American wife of a British medical officer, Captain Philip Bloom, continued to write the diary she had kept since her intern-ment in March 1942. It took the form of an extended letter, that could not be sent, to her husband, who was a POW in another part of Changi. Unlike their counterparts in the Philippines, the civilian women interned in Singapore were occasionally allowed to see their husbands from mid-1943 onwards, and indeed on 20 July 1943 put on a show for them. However, no cohabitation was allowed.

The Camp remains incredible – for over a year the main clamour of the women has been to see their husbands – they have just been allowed fortnightly meetings. While our hosts were 'restless' they ordered all the men in from the ex-Sikh quarters, now called Golders Green. Cicely put up a suggestion that the large families be allowed to live in these houses and that the other marrieds take turns, a week at a time, with the odd houses left over. Sounds a pleasant suggestion – no? But did it rouse controversy! The older and fatter the wives, the louder they proclaimed that they weren't going to spend a week with their husbands à la Brighton. What, prosti-tute themselves! Give the black and tans a chance to breed more brats (our children are not universally popular)! Open mating season! Oh, you should have heard them. Many sug-gested kicking Cicely out for the infamous suggestion. Most of us just looked with open mouths, scratched our heads and wondered. Darling, I love the British. Also I am getting a type-writer. Also the food has improved considerably and we have received masses of presents each; four clothes pegs, sandal-wood soap, one towel, four yards of materials, toothpowder. Internment is becoming positively sissy.

Freddy Bloom would survive the war and in September 1945 was reunited with her husband. SEE ALSO PP. 231–3, 352–3.

JUNE 1943

O N THE AMERICAN HOME FRONT the war production effort was dogged by strikes in the summer of 1943. On 1 June some half a million coal-miners went on strike after a long period of difficult wage negotiations. Most went back to work later that month. Production in the United States had also been affected by severe flooding in the midwest.

In the Solomons, mid-June was characterized by a series of significant air battles as the Japanese attempted to break up concentrations of shipping and aircraft that were being brought together for an attack on New Georgia. Japanese air attacks were extremely successful and over 100 Allied aircraft were lost. At the end of the month the Americans began a major offensive in New Georgia with the objective of capturing the airfield at Munda. US marines began to advance across Viru harbour. On most of the islands there was rapid success, and the airfield was taken on 30 June; however, the Japanese offered tough resistance on the island of Vangunu.

In New Guinea, the 3rd Australian Division was gradually making its way towards Salamaua, fighting a number of desperate battles during the summer of 1943. The size of New Guinea meant that all forces were somewhat dispersed. A number of independent companies were used to probe Japanese positions, and where these seemed to be lightly held, attacks were launched. This approach led to the capture of Bobdubi Ridge close to Salamaua. Continual advances allowed General Krueger to move the headquarters of the US 6th Army to Milne Bay. Islands such as Kiriwina and Woodlark at the eastern extremity of the archipelago were occupied without incident and quickly used to construct airfields. However, on 30 June a large combined force of Australians and Americans landed closer to Salamaua at Nassau Bay and met heavy resistance. The ultimate objective of these operations was to clear Papua New Guinea completely and prepare for an assault on the major Japanese base at Rabaul at the northern tip of the nearby island of New Britain.

Following the miserable performance of the British in the Arakan campaign, Churchill 'promoted' two senior British generals to remove them from the direction of the war in Asia. General Wavell ceased to be commander-in-chief of the Indian Army and became Viceroy of India – a move that allowed Wavell, for the first time in his career, to keep an excellent diary. General Auchinleck replaced him as commander-in-chief of the Indian Army; however, this role would soon be rendered supernumerary by the creation of South East Asia Command under Louis Mountbatten. It would be Mountbatten and Slim who would direct the war in Burma during 1943 and 1944.

Tuesday 1 June 1943

The identity of Frank 'Foo' Fujita, an American Japanese POW, is discovered by his guards

Frank 'Foo' Fujita was one of only two Japanese American combat soldiers to be captured during the Pacific campaign of the Second World War. Fujita was a Texan who had joined the Texas National Guard in 1938 and sailed for south-east Asia in 1941. He served with the 'Lost Battalion' of the 36th Infantry Division and was captured during the defence of Java in early 1942. In March 1942 he was briefly in the same POW camp as Don Peacock at Jaarmarkt (see pp. 369–71), before being moved to Singapore and then to Fukuoka camp at Nagasaki, Japan. There he laboured in the shipyards as a stevedore until June 1943. Remarkably, despite his Japanese name, his ethnicity had not previously come to the attention of his Japanese guards.

On June 1, 1943, almost one year and three months after we were captured in Java, a Japanese guard realized that my name was Japanese, here in Nagasaki, Japan. This guard, like so many people in Japan, could read something printed in English, but they could not understand when it was read back to them. On this particular evening he was going from one room to another, showing off how he could read the roster, which was posted at the front of each room just inside the door. I was standing by the front table (tables were placed in a row between the bunks) when he came into the room. He called everyone to come close to him, and he motioned to the roster board indicating that he was going to read it to us. As room chief my name was at the top of the roster and when he saw it, his eyes liked to have popped out and he pointed to my name and said: 'Fujita! Fujita Nippon no namai!' ('Fujita is a Japanese name!') And then he asked me where Fujita was, and I told him that he had gone to the *benjo* [toilet]. He said that he would wait and I moved towards the back of the room with my heart in my mouth and shaking like a leaf. I was as close to being scared to death as I will ever come. The guard remained at the front of the room and asked everyone that came into the room, where Fujita was.

Almost everyone in the room was as keyed up as I was, for they had sweated my being found out, too, and now that the time had come they all stood around with bated breath to see what would happen next. Another man came into the room and the guard asked him where Fujita was and he looked around and saw me, and before anyone could caution him, he pointed to me and said 'There he is!' The guard looked surprised and also a little put out with me for having told him that Fujita had gone to the *benjo*. Any other time I would have been beaten up on the spot, but this time he was much too excited over his discovery to think of bashing me about.

He called me back up to the front of the room and looked me up and down, sucking his teeth and muttering something incredulously about Fujita being a POW. He tried to carry on a conversation with me, about me, and finally decided that I really could not speak the language. He would feel my skin and then put his arm next to mine and compare them, and like the guard at the wash rack, he said '*Somma, Somma.*' He would turn to the other guys in the room and then point to me and then to himself and tell them that we were somma, somma. Finally he could not stand it any longer, that he was the Japanese to know this so he took off for the guard house. I really became frightened then and felt very strongly that my untimely demise could be forthcoming posthaste! Even though I felt like this, I still felt hope way down deep that I would survive the war in one piece.

In a little while he brought another guard with him to look

me over, only to have the lights go out, for it was bedtime and all room lights were turned out at 10:00 PM. Well, there was no sleep for me this night and Sgts. Heleman and Lucas were trying to comfort me and convince me that maybe they would not kill me after all. I was in such mental anguish that even the bedbugs, fleas, and mosquitos were not bothering me. During the night, each time the guard shift changed, the guards would take turns coming to my room and looking at me, even those who normally patrolled the other side of the camp . . .

After subjecting Frank to several interrogation sessions with the camp commander and visiting Japanese officials, the authorities considered that he would be more forthcoming if he could speak Japanese. He was provided with a text entitled Japanese in Thirty Hours, *but decided to 'play stupid'. On 6 June Frank wrote in his diary that the Japanese had tried to persuade him to join the Japanese army. He added: 'They got mad as hell when I laughed at them and told them they were doomed.' He was soon back at work in the dockyards.*

Frank was one of many Japanese Americans or 'Nisei' serving in the US armed forces. Many fought in segregated military units, such as the 442nd Regimental Combat Team, and were among the most highly decorated soldiers of the war. In June 1999 a memorial to the Japanese American war efforts was opened in Los Angeles. The majority of Nisei fought in the war against Germany, but others were used individually as interpreters and translators in the Far Eastern war. SEE ALSO PP. 638–9.

Mid-June 1943

Henry Traill's POW camp at Kanyu confronts the 'icy clutch of death'

Henry Traill's arrival in the work camps of the Thai–Burma railway had not been traumatic. Initially, at Kinseyo, the diet was good and he had even been allowed away from camp on solo fishing expeditions. However, by June 1943, at Kanyu 3 camp, matters were very different. Even before cholera struck it was known to be coming, for it was striking other camps along the railway and therefore threw a long and unavoidable shadow.

In the midst of our stark life of endurance there now came upon us a new and vastly more horrifying threat. All the beatings and insults, the weariness, discomforts and hunger, were insignificant compared with this, which was just coldly terrifying. There was nothing, during all those years, which confronted us so suddenly with the prospect of death as did those first rumours of the outbreak of cholera in the camps.

In our minds we thought of cholera in the same terms as the Plague or the Black Death of medieval times, pestilences which had no cure and which decimated whole populations. These diseases bring with them a feeling of inescapable doom, and now that this epidemic of cholera was coming upon us how could any one of us hope to be singled out among thousands to survive it? I for one, when I heard of the outbreak, felt in my heart, and understood for the first time, 'the icy clutch of death' . . .

Then one day, when we came back from work, we found ourselves confronted with the thing we had known must happen. There was cholera in our camp. Not only was it in our camp, it was amongst the officers. It was in our own tent.

The victim was Madden. He had been back and forwards to the latrines all morning, and by midday the well known and frightening signs were unmistakable. So quickly does cholera act, that in a few hours the flesh seems to turn to water, and the body becomes wasted as though from weeks of starvation.

In the afternoon of that day Madden was carried to Hospital. On the following morning, at Roll call, we were detailed for his funeral. It was to be by cremation, so we spent the morning digging a fire trench and preparing a large pile of bamboo and hard-wood.

At lunch time we found that two others from our tent had got it, Johnson and Tyler. They were moved to the new cholera compound, about eighty yards from the camp. There were also three or four patients from the men's tents.

It was now apparent that somehow the infection had become seated in our tent, and the prospect was, that one after another of us would go down with it. Fortunately, if there was one thing the Japs feared it was infectious disease, and especially cholera, and to prevent it spreading they would do almost anything our Medical Officers suggested. The eleven of us who now remained in the tent were allotted an isolation area some hundred yards from the camp. Each of us was to build his own individual bivouac, and these were to be separated from each other by a ten foot interval.

We cleared out of the tent at once. The canvas was taken down, and it and we were sprayed with disinfectant by a Jap done up in goggles, respirator, gloves and rubber boots. The sleeping platform and all the bits and pieces which we had left behind were soaked in oil and burned on the site.

In the afternoon we completed Madden's cremation.

It was a good thing we had no time to brood. It was now mid-afternoon, and before dark we had to provide ourselves with a bed and shelter. The materials at our disposal were, as usual, what grew around us. To start off with we had to cut down the scrub which covered the ground. While some did this, others cut bamboos for the beds, which we made as simply as possible. Three thick pieces of bamboo about two and a half feet wide were laid on the ground as the head, middle and bottom of the bed frame; and long pieces, flattened out, were laid on top of them. These were the standard pieces which we supplied by joint labour. Over them we each built the best shelter we could devise, most of us using our groundsheets. We had also to dig ourselves a latrine.

Tyler did not survive the night. On the following morning we again had the melancholy job of preparing a funeral pyre. Johnson still held on.

At one's first meeting with him out at work, Johnny had seemed a cantankerous sort of person, always nagging and complaining about something. But as we knew him better we found this was only on the surface. Moreover, it was his protective armour, assumed in order to hide one scarcely knew what, unless it were indifferent health, and a too-much-felt sensitivity to his unpalatable surroundings.

We found that the real Johnny had an unconquerable spirit. However much his body might fail him, his spirit never did. Now, stricken with a deadly sickness, and alone in a small tent in the muddy compound, he remained doggedly cheerful and lightly sarcastic. As one day and then a second passed and Johnny still struggled against the disease, we almost allowed ourselves to hope he might survive . . .

A new party of 1,500 prisoners had just made a camp beside us, their job being to put the final touches to our piece of the railway line. With them they had an M.O. who had already dealt with many cholera cases before coming up here. He helped rig up an apparatus for making distilled water for saline injections, and we had high hopes that Johnny might benefit from it. These injections are one of the few positive aids that can be given to cholera patients, and without them recovery is seldom made.

The saline injections came too late for Johnny; and courage alone was not enough to retain the spark of life. After three and a half days of pitiful brave struggle, his poor body was finished.

Johnny was not cremated, as the Japs now allowed our cholera victims to be buried in deep graves. The sun was shining on the muddy paths and sodden scrub of our clearing when we brought him round the graveside . . .

From under the rice-sack that covered him, a stray lock of Johnny's hair blew gently in the wind. Impassively we saw it. Could we then feel no sorrow? No fear? No deep emotion? We saw only that the sun was shining; felt only that it was warm on our shoulders. We saw the jungle around us; we comprehended the Japs, our being prisoners, the epidemic of cholera. And we saw the frail form, outlined in the sacking, that was Johnny; and a stray lock of his hair which was blowing in the wind.

Medical attention was available, for the Japanese did not wish their labour force to be wiped out and had laid in a large stock of serum for anti-cholera injections. However, to be effective the injections had to be given over several weeks and the programme of inoculation was begun far too late. Cholera was endemic in Thailand in the rainy season, but hit particularly hard among the weak and under-nourished inhabitants of the camps, where cooking and sanitation facilities were poor.

Throughout his three and a half years as a POW Henry Traill kept a diary in indelible pencil on 'whatever scraps of paper I could find'. Despite the atrocious conditions, he would survive the war and in 1947 returned to the Kuala Selangor district of Malaya to resume work as a plantation manager. SEE ALSO PP. 333–6.

Saturday 19 June – Monday 26 July 1943

Genta Kamimura, a Japanese soldier in training, admires America and longs to breathe the air of freedom

Genta Kamimura was born in 1921. A student of Chuo University, he was called up for military service after his graduation in January 1943. Having been granted a few days' leave, he attended a farewell party for friends who belonged to a military unit being sent to fight in the Solomon Islands. It was a dismal affair, for they could all foresee their fate.

19 June

My weight is 10 stone 8 pounds. I have just passed the oral part of my examinations. Never before have I felt such a need to give full expression to my sentiments. When I was asked what I thought of the United States, I revealed my innermost thoughts and replied that I had a great admiration for America's democratic policy. The administrative officer, Tsuchiya, was at pains to conceal his fury. I also affirmed that the Americans were as ardently patriotic as we were, and that there was no sense in hoping for victory in this conflict.

The commander looked at me and said:

'So, according to you, they are perfect?'

'We say they cannot win because they are a people without history. That is not a sound argument. The goal they have set themselves is very human . . . They want to enjoy life.'

At that moment the commander interrupted me and reproached me for using the language of our enemies. I took the opportunity of protesting against the suppression of certain English words which have become current in our language, such as the word *news*, which we are now forced to replace by *hôdô*.

He continued:

'You have said quite enough about your sentiments towards the enemy: you are a materialist.'

We then began to discuss the principle of total mobilization. I experienced a sense of relief. Faced with all these officers, I had dared to express severe criticism of their principles.

21 June
Written examination.

I shall certainly fail. I should hate to be passed.

I dream of being demobbed. What a dilemma! I long to breathe the air of freedom once more . . .

Since I received my calling-up papers, I have been afraid of death and my one desire is to live. It is becoming ridiculous. I am like a man buried in his grave who would like to taste hot rice once more. I must really free my mind from all these thoughts . . .

26 July
I came back yesterday after having spent three days and four nights on leave. My mother is convinced that she has seen me for the last time. I comforted her by telling her that the war would not last more than three years. Actually, it looks more like lasting four to five years, and I believe that I must give up any hope of returning. I know that it does not help to dwell on the past, but why, why did I pass that exam?

Genta Kamimura was anxious to survive the war and to avoid the fate of so many of his friends who had gone before him. He was almost successful and would survive until April 1945, when he was killed fighting on Okinawa.

JULY 1943

IN THE SOLOMON ISLANDS, the American units tasked with seizing the airfield at Munda on New Georgia landed and met no initial resistance at the beachhead: the Japanese had chosen instead to fight in the jungle terrain further inland. On 5 July an American naval flotilla attempted to intercept ten Japanese destroyers trying to bring in reinforcements. The Japanese demonstrated their flair for fighting at night by sinking the American cruiser *Helena* and the destroyer *Strong*, but lost two of their own destroyers. On 12 July there was a similar battle in which the Americans suffered damage to many ships as the result of torpedo strikes, but managed to sink the Japanese cruiser *Jintsu*. Both American and Japanese infantry began to run short of supplies during this campaign. By mid-July the local Japanese air force was too weak to carry out daytime operations and restricted itself to night bombing. Although the main American objective, the airfield at Munda, would not be reached until the first week of August, American aircraft were already mounting heavy air attacks on Bougainville, the next target in the island chain.

Air power was also of increasing importance to the Allies in New Guinea. On 7 July an amphibious force landed at Nassau Bay under the command of General MacKechnie but held back momentarily while a massive air bombardment was launched on the neighbouring town of Mubo. By 10 July Mubo and Salamaua had been isolated by Australian and American forces that had managed to link up. Advances in New Guinea were continually accompanied by the building of new airfields and this month a large air base was completed on the Trobriand Islands.

On 20 July Roosevelt approved an Anglo-American deal for co-operation on the atomic bomb project in which Britain provided some expert theoretical physicists who were soon busy working at Los Alamos. Officials began to draw up a formal treaty in which London and Washington agreed not to share atomic information with third parties, not to use the bomb without each other's consent, and never to use the weapon against each other. This agreement would be finalized during August 1943 and eventually included Canada. One of the signatories' objectives was to try to monopolize world stocks of uranium, and secret missions were despatched to numerous countries to begin this process.

Saturday 10 – Saturday 24 July 1943

Robert T. Boody, a pilot training for the war in Burma, is briefed on his survival kit for life in the jungle

Robert T. Boody was born on Staten Island in New York in 1920 and grew up there. At the age of fifteen he was sent away to boarding school at Phillips Exeter Academy in New Hampshire. Although he had a place at Yale, he was unable to begin his studies because his family had insufficient funds, and so went to work for American Airlines at La Guardia. In December 1941 he was already training to be a reserve pilot in his spare time and by July 1943 was conducting advanced training on the Curtiss P-40 Kittyhawk aircraft at Karachi in eastern India. This included detailed briefing on escape and evasion kits designed for those who had to bail out over the jungles of Burma.

10 July
All pilots of the 80th Fighter Group were treated to a briefing on combat tactics against Japanese 'Zero' fighters and 'Betty' bombers by Lt. Barnes who had flown and fought over there for one and a half years. For many of us, his talk proved to be a life-saver in the months of combat stretching out into the future. Bus rides were made available to all personnel into the town of Karachi whenever we were off-duty and wanted, as individuals, to see and enjoy what the town had to offer.

22 July
Our 90th Fighter Squadron moved this day to Landhi Field at Karachi. This would be our tactical base from which we

would receive all our combat-transition training. Our objective was to increase our effectiveness and teamwork as P-40 Warhawk pilots in combat against the Japanese in the skies over India and northern Burma when we moved east the following month to Assam Province.

23 July
This was our first day of actual P-40 tactical training missions in India.

24 July
We practiced dive-bombing with live bombs; also flew two, four and eight ship formations. Gene Jenkins became a 'poppa' that day. We received an 'intelligence' briefing on Assam and northern Burma from Captain Kehoe. The correct use of all the items in our parachute-pack escape-kits was also carefully explained in detail; fish-hooks and line, pocket-knife with can opener, Hershey bar, vitamin capsules, iodine to purify water from jungle streams to make it drinkable, polished-metal signalling mirror, detailed silk map of the terrain we'll fly over in combat – showing rivers, mountain contours and elevations as well as populated areas, pocket compass, water-proof matches – container made of metal, a container of 'atabrine' tablets to reduce the effects from the ever-present 'anopheles' mosquitoes, a clip of .45 caliber ammunition, and several messages written in Urdu, Hindustani and Burmese asking help from any friendly natives if we were forced down.

On the back of our flight jackets we wore a 'blood-chit', a Nationalist flag of the Republic of China on which was printed, in Mandarin Chinese characters, a request to friendly forces for assistance in case we were forced to 'bail-out' in our parachutes or crash-land.

Before each mission we would check out from our Intelligence Officer the following two items which we were required to return to his custody on coming back from a mission, while we were being 'de-briefed':- a canvas money-belt containing silver 'rupees,' each the size and weight of an American half-dollar; and a plastic belt containing sugar-lump-sized chunks of compressed, sickly-smelling opium for trading, for cooperation, with the head-hunter Naga tribesmen who lived in small villages and were all addicts from poppies they cultivated in the mountains of Assam as well as in the dense jungles of northern Burma.

Robert T. Boody had arrived in Karachi by freighter in late June 1943. A shipment of P-40 Kittyhawks arrived on the next freighter and were assembled from crates in a vacant balloon hangar at Camp Malir. The pilots were soon training over the Sind desert and listening to a series of talks from experienced pilots on everything from air tactics to survival. If they were required to bale out, the financial inducements they all carried could make the difference between receiving local co-operation and being handed over to the enemy.

At the end of August Boody would be sent east to his new base at Jorhat in Assam to begin operations over Burma. SEE ALSO PP. 537–9.

Saturday 10 July 1943

Elizabeth Vaughan, a civilian internee at Santo Tomas in the Philippines, hears definite news about her husband

Was mopping floor of room, my chore this week (each of eight mothers in room is responsible for sweeping and mopping entire floor each day in turn), when Millie Booth called me to door. 'Let me talk to you,' she said. 'Wait until I wash the mop at the faucet and fill the bucket with water and hang it on the fire prevention hook,' I replied, 'then we can talk while I polish Beth's shoes for Janice's birthday party this morning.' The expression on Millie's face caused me to stop my chatter about the morning activities. 'Is it bad news about Jim?' I demanded hastily and frightenedly. 'It is,' she said as she handed me a little square of notebook paper, a full sheet folded and refolded till it was no larger than a two-inch square, sealed together with narrow strips of adhesive tape. My name was written on the outside of this packet. In my haste in ripping off the tape I tore the outer paper. A penciled note from Mr. Booth was still legible. The typed note wrapped tightly, almost wadded, inside. Mr.

Booth's note gave me the definite and heartbreaking news.

'Don't let Beth and Clay know,' I asked Millie, whose own note from her husband, which came via the same underground route as mine, had told her the news. 'They are going to a birthday party this morning and they have been looking forward to eating the ice cream which Janice's mother has prepared.'

In a way the truth is better than the suspense of these past few months since fears that Jim had died first entered my mind. After a squeeze of the hand Millie was gone. A mother bumped into me with a baby tub of warm water as she passed down the corridor, always crowded with children and mothers. Instead of apologizing she swore at me for standing so stupidly in the middle of the corridor.

Beth and Clay appeared from nowhere to tug at my skirt and to ask had I forgotten to dress them for the party. I suddenly remembered that I had an overdue library book which must be returned to the library before it closed, which meant go to the Main Building before taking the children to the shanty where the party was to take place. Also the alum crystals which I asked the personal shopping service of the camp canteen to buy for me (interned women have discovered that alum crystals in water make a very sharp and effective underarm deodorant), and for which I had paid 0.50 in advance, would not be held beyond today. Saturday.

I shook the children loose, told them to stay indoors – a drizzling rain made the bleak day more dreary – and set out, my mind calling 'Oh, Jim, Jim, why did this have to happen? You to die alone and suffering two days before our fourth wedding anniversary. Why couldn't I have come to you, to give you medicine, to answer your feverish calls for water?'

'Please take your place in line to return a library book. You cannot crowd to the desk ahead of others who have been waiting,' I was admonished as I absentmindedly placed my book on the library 'return' counter.

Although Elizabeth Vaughan heard news of her husband only in July 1943, he had in fact died of cholera almost a year before this. Together with her two children, Beth and Clay, Elizabeth would survive her incarceration at Santo Tomas and return to the United States in March

1945, arriving first in California, and then returning to the family home in Athens, Georgia. Vaughan went back to university in North Carolina and was soon writing a sociology thesis on life in Japanese internment camps. She was granted a PhD and her work was published by Princeton University Press in 1949 – one of the first substantive studies of the wartime internment of civilians. She eventually became head of the Department of Sociology at Meredith College. In 1953 she was diagnosed with cancer and was told she had only months to live. Drawing on the remarkable strength of character that had served her so well in Santo Tomas, she fought the disease for several years, living to see her daughter Beth go to college and her son Clay enter his last year of high school. She died in 1958. SEE ALSO PP. 280–1, 340–1, 371–2, 402.

Mid-July 1943

Rena Krasno, a Jewish teenager in Shanghai, contends with 'the Monster'

Vast areas of Shanghai, including dockyards, factories, private businesses and houses, were being requisitioned by the Japanese. These appropriations were now affecting Rena Krasno's family.

However, not only have the Japanese requisitioned real estate of supposed military value, but they are also taking over private residences among which, unfortunately, is our apartment located on the top floor of a modern building called Tower Apartments. A couple of weeks ago, a Japanese couple rang our bell, bowed slightly as I opened the door, entered politely and made us understand they wished to 'inspect' our home. They were young, rather shy, and the pretty woman wore a delicate kimono. In spite of the fact that Mama well knew we would be forced to give up our home without any reimbursement whatsoever, she spoke in a friendly manner to the visitors and showed them around, opening closets, explaining the use of the hot water boiler, and even pointing out the view from our balcony. Her behaviour did not surprise me, because I assumed it was a reflection of the famous 'Siberian hospitality' in which she (and we) were brought up. But my sister thought that perhaps Mama was actually trying to avoid an unpleasant situation that she could not control. Having found our residence to their satisfaction the Japanese couple announced in broken English their intention to move in within a week.

Mama treated them so politely it seemed as if she were doing them a favor. 'I hope you'll enjoy it,' she said. They seemed surprised. They didn't expect hospitality from a person whose home they were taking.

Such a turn of events during a period of catastrophic housing shortage would have shattered anyone but my indomitable little mother who has stood up to the challenge and somehow found three rooms to rent in a large villa in a lovely residential section of the French Concession. Unfortunately, she had not reckoned with the ferocious landlady whom my sister and I quickly dubbed 'The Monster.' A heavy, large, vulgar, foulmouthed woman with a jarring voice, her accent sounds like something from the East End of London. But she is obviously not a British citizen because the Japanese would have interned her, so I have no idea what her nationality might be. She carries a huge bundle of keys at her waist which jangle as she moves, sneaking about the house snooping on her tenants and checking her secret hoards of food. She consumes her cakes with her pallid husband at her side and throws her three Scotch terriers boiled potato peels which keep the miserable dogs on the edge of constant starvation. Whenever the poor animals come within her range she yells and kicks them away sharply while my sister and I – both passionate animal lovers – quiver with fury. My sister's normally sparkling, mischievous hazel eyes fills with tears and I have to control myself from physically attacking The Monster . . .

Despite the war, Shanghai had somehow maintained its international character. There were in fact a remarkable number of people of British descent at liberty in Shanghai, some working for the Japanese. An Enemy Aliens Office issued armbands stamped with different letters for each of the many nationalities. Curiously, in the summer of 1943 the diverse residents of Shanghai were not following news from Tokyo or Washington; instead, they were fascinated by events in Rome, where Mussolini had just resigned. This was because his daughter Edda, together with her husband Count Ciano, had lived in Shanghai for some years when Ciano was Italian consul-general in the city. SEE ALSO PP. *273–4, 493–4, 665–6.*

Monday 12 July 1943

'Vinegar Joe' Stilwell extracts a commitment to fight from the 'Peanut' – Generalissimo Chiang Kai-shek

General Stilwell had been attempting to persuade Chiang Kai-shek to launch an offensive since May 1942. The Chinese nationalist government had tended to procrastinate, claiming it was short of supplies and ammunition. In July 1943 Stilwell momentarily seemed to have wrung concessions from Chungking.

Joseph Stilwell with Chiang and Mme Chiang

Red-Letter Day   The answer came from Peanut to the Combined Chiefs of Staff Saucy proposals. In *writing*. And *signed*. After a year of constant struggle, we have finally nailed him down. He is committed, in writing, to the attack on Burma. What corruption, intrigue, obstruction, delay, double-crossing, hate, jealousy and skullduggery we have had to wade through. What a cesspool . . . What bigotry and ignorance and black ingratitude. Holy Christ, I was just about at the end of my rope . . .

——ON PEANUT 'He wants to be a moral potentate, a religious leader, a philosopher. But he has no education! How ridiculous this is. If he had four years of college education, he might understand conditions in the modern world but the picture we see clearly is dark to him. He simply does not understand. If he did, conditions would be better, because he wants to do right. No one tells him the truth . . . no one. He will not listen to anything unpleasant, so nobody tells him anything but pleasant things. It is impossible to reason with him . . . one could with Sun Yat-sen . . . but this man! He flies into a rage if anyone argues against him. Everyone avoids rocks and gets around knotty problems by devious means. He does not know what is going on. He writes orders by the thousand . . . like snowflakes . . . and everybody says 'yes, yes' and he never knows what has been done. He is afraid of the crowd and what people will say, so he tries to stop them talking. This is very foolish. It is like trying to stop the sound of a rattlesnake's rattle while leaving the poison in his fangs. There is no reason for him to fear anything.

When Stilwell was appointed as Chiang Kai-shek's Chief of Staff it was known that they were well acquainted. What few realized was that they had disliked each other from their very first meeting in 1935. Their strategies and ambitions were very different; moreover, they barely spoke the same language. Stilwell spoke excellent Mandarin, but Chiang was from the Chekiang district and spoke a different dialect. The two variants of the language were markedly different, but Stilwell always refused the aid of an interpreter. Accordingly, he often misunderstood Chiang's true response to what he said. However, it was clear that Chiang did understand that Stilwell wished to see the nationalist and communist Chinese armies brought together to fight Japan, something he was never going to allow. SEE ALSO PP. 357–9, 615–16, 806–7.

Friday 16 July 1943

General William Brougher reflects on rumours and the desire for news in prison life

The American General William Brougher had commanded the 11th Infantry Division of the Philippine Army, the last unit to surrender on Bataan in April 1942. A careful observer of human behaviour in his POW camp on Formosa, Brougher recorded many aspects of prison life in a secret diary which he kept hidden inside bamboo sticks buried beneath the floor of his barracks.

One of the phenomenon [*sic*] characteristic of the prison camp is the *rumor*. It is born of our pathetic need for news and usually coincides with desire. Rumors are spread about all kinds of things, war news, indications of war prisoner exchange, prospective moves, new arrivals, changes in food issue, arrival of mail, etc. As to sources, they originate in (1) the kitchen (2) the benjo [toilet], (3) the bathhouse, (4) hospital. Authorities cited, 'Baggy Pants' (Nipponese Lieut.), a 'member of the guard,' Provoo (American Sergt who speaks Japanese), local newspapers, 'somebody said.'

We have deluges of rumors in advance of every important event, fragments foretelling faithfully what is to happen or giving correctly news that is to come in the papers later.

The credibility of rumors is based mainly on two things: (1) how closely they coincide with wishful thinking; (2) whether or not the rumor can be tied to somebody by name. We are incurably optimistic. No rumor is accepted unless it is 'rosy'.

Examples: 'American troops have taken Sicily.' 'American troops are in Rome.' 'Baggy Pants told the kitchen crew we'll soon get mail.'

Two new lows were registered on rumors today: (1) The final farcical form in expression: 'Bluemel said he heard somebody say something but he's forgot who it was and what he said.' (2) The limit of credibility: '*Baggy Pants told General Weaver* that the Nipponese are sore at the Germans for lying to them and letting them down.' (Baggy Pants doesn't like General Weaver and never speaks to him.) Rumors are an important phase of our life . . .

William Brougher was held in three different camps on Formosa and then two more in Manchuria. Concealed radios were the best antidote to the wild rumours that circulated in POW camps, but not every camp enjoyed this secret facility and the penalties for operating a hidden radio could be very severe. One of the most persistent, inaccurate and disheartening rumours was the idea that some POWs would be exchanged, allowing them to return home before the end of the war. In reality, only a few diplomats were exchanged. SEE ALSO PP. 452–4.

AUGUST 1943

ON 1 AUGUST 1943, Japan set up a puppet government in Burma. In Rangoon, a nationalist administration under U Ba Maw took over the running of what was now declared to be an 'independent country', although in reality Burmese autonomy was little more than symbolic and Ba Maw was required to sign a secret treaty with Tokyo. In the Netherlands East Indies, too, an indigenous government had been set up under Japanese tutelage, and the same formula would be repeated in the Philippines in October 1943. Much noise was made by the Japanese about Asian brotherhood, and they spoke of an Asian Co-prosperity Sphere. However, even in these so-called independent countries ruthless exploitation remained the norm, while in others, such as Malaya and the Netherlands East Indies, the Japanese retained formal control. Remarkably, in Vichy French Indochina the Japanese put aside their pan-Asian rhetoric and chose to work alongside the old white colonial masters, although the relationship was an uneasy one.

In New Georgia, halfway along the Solomon Islands chain, the Americans continued to make painfully slow progress towards the airfield at Munda, which they knew to be the key to strategic control of the area. After two weeks of heavy fighting the base fell to the Americans on 5 August, and a week later was put back in operation. The Japanese began pulling their forces away from New Georgia in order to concentrate on the defence of the northernmost island of Bougainville, and infantry were being evacuated by destroyers under cover of darkness. Off the coast of New Georgia near Kolombanga Island two naval battles took place in which Japan lost troop-carrying destroyers.

In New Guinea, American and Australian troops captured the strategic ridges in front of the town of Salamaua, the last major obstacle to an assault on the town. In the north Pacific, the Japanese were evicted from their last remaining toehold on the Aleutians when the Americans landed on the island of Kiska after days of extremely heavy naval bombardment.

In the third week of August Roosevelt, Churchill and other Allied leaders met at Quebec to discuss Allied strategy. One of the most important issues they addressed was an agreement on the development of the atomic bomb. Once this document was signed, the best British nuclear scientists were transferred to Los Alamos where they joined what was codenamed the Manhattan Project. Eventually, nineteen British scientists would be assigned to Los Alamos and a further thirty-five to another site at Berkeley. In the Pacific the Allies decided to push forward on two axes, one with its focus on capturing the Gilbert and Marshall Islands, the second concentrating on capturing Rabaul and then the Philippines. The selection of Admiral Lord Louis Mountbatten to lead South East Asia Command, with Stilwell as his deputy, was confirmed at this conference. Mountbatten would be required to launch an offensive in Burma in early 1944; meanwhile it was decided that Orde Wingate would lead another large-scale behind-the-lines raid into the hills of northeast Burma. Although there was much talk of the introduction of the B-29 Superfortress heavy bomber which would eventually transform the war against the Japanese homeland, there was as yet no overall plan for how the war might be brought to an end in the Pacific.

Tuesday 3 August 1943

Tadashi Higa, a retreating soldier serving with the Japanese infantry on New Georgia, reflects on recent letters from home

Tadashi Higa was a private serving with the Haratake Unit of the 23rd Infantry Regiment, part of Japan's 6th Infantry Division which was fighting American forces in the Solomon Islands chain. In mid-July he had fought on Santa Isabel, before being withdrawn for five days' rest on Bougainville. On 1 August, to his dismay, his unit was embarked on the destroyer Yugiri *and taken to join the fight for New Georgia. They landed near the island of Kolombanga and discovered that other Japanese units there had already been badly broken by American air power and were in retreat.*

We walked along either starving or chewing hard tack. The men in the forces that were withdrawing had pale faces; and there was one casualty in torn clothing who went along using a sword as a cane.

Being just one battalion, we are helpless. We withdrew further. We must withdraw tonight, for our number will be up when day breaks. To advance would have meant death. The situation is indescribable.

The day broke. Enemy planes came roaring toward us, and if we had been detected, it would have meant our end.

The force has spent three days and four nights hiding in the brush without eating, and soaking wet. We were unable to advance a step. We were awaiting the order for an immediate withdrawal to Kolombanga.

Everybody picked coconuts.

The enemy was hurriedly constructing an airfield on the island opposite us. We could see them so clearly that it seemed we could have touched them. It only meant that more air attacks were in store for us. Our lives were worthless, for there was no order for withdrawal after all. I have come to hate the men who cause wars. The withdrawal order didn't come thru tonight either. Our rations have run out. I

New Guinea and the Solomon Islands, 1943

felt as though I had Malaria, and I took quinine tablets and Hinomarin to keep alive. I was merely awaiting my fate and yet I wanted to die fighting . . .

It isn't merely that Japan is being defeated. I felt like crying. Being wet, and in a jungle full of mosquitoes, I thought of home. Ah! The letters from home last month. Ten letters and fourteen or fifteen postcards after a year without any word. There were also letters from my parents. News from HARUKO, I cherish deeply. But the news was that my beloved younger sister has died, has become a cold, black corpse. Oh! When I thought of her fate, the tears came. I really cried. I felt bitter toward Providence. When I realized that fate determines our lives, my mind became calm. Although death comes sooner or later, I felt sorry for my sister who had to die so young. I prayed for the repose of her soul.

Our parents must be bereaved. Furthermore my mother, who is always thinking about me, must be going through an ordeal worse than death. War is sad.

Nature remains unaffected by such things, though. The morning sun shone, the wind blew softly, yet rain fell plentifully. The hard tack was wet and gave out a foul odor; nobody ate it. We did nothing except gnaw on coconuts. Two large landing barges were attacked by torpedo boats while they were transporting material to this island. One squad of our Co was on them. I wonder what happened to them!

We could hear the reports of the enemy guns. The enemy had made landings on the island across from us, and were constructing an airfield. Enemy large landing barges were moving in streams.

Today, I took out the letters from HARUKO and from the school which I had brought from BOUGAINVILLE. They were wet and were barely legible. I have become soft-hearted. Oh! How I long to be home! Some soldiers were saying, 'Although I have not completed my service, I am already disgusted.'

When I thought how my parents must be concerned about my younger sister's death and my younger brother's departure for the front, my heart aches. I have been yearning for the long-cherished homeland so much that I am about to burst.

I thought about my dear HARUKO. She was already twenty-two, and I believe she was a well-qualified and educated woman.

The letter dated November of last year, finally reached me this August. When I looked at the handwriting of dear HARUKO, from whom I shall never receive any more letters, I have an inconsolable longing for her. I looked at the letters which I had brought here, and when I thought that she had written and sealed them, I was overcome with the desire to kiss them. My comrades pondered their lot, each in his own way; they spent every day doing this, and thinking of home.

We talked about home, and we criticized war conditions. We ate no food; our life was just this and nothing else. There was talk that, even today, dead bodies floated up on the north shore. When we thought of their deaths, we were overcome with sorrow.

There was talk that the men of the Southeast Div have not yet arrived. We could not expect them, because our forces, driven hither and thither, must have been roaming about these lonely islands. I wondered what would become of them! I wondered, too, what fate had in store for us!

We often think of sad news as something only those at home received during wartime, but one of the agonies of serving in the war in Asia and the Pacific was a great sense of separation from home, where there could also be tragedies. It is unlikely that Tadashi's sister, Haruko, died as the result of enemy action since there was no Allied bombing of Japan in 1943.

On 13 August he would note that enemy landing barges were approaching their island, and then write the final line of his diary: 'We are determined to resist to the last soldier, and with that intention I lay down my pen.' His diary was found on 20 August, but his fate is unknown.

Friday 6 – Thursday 26 August 1943

Will Wilder, a British POW, endures flooding and disease
on the Thai–Burma railway

6 August
Things are in chaos and upsetting. Most trying, but I'm so
used to such things that I don't worry a great deal. First last
night while I was on the latrine a side collapsed and I got wet
with filthy water. Now floods have come up into the ward I
went into yesterday. Flooded out and having to hang around
all day outside. I am now in a tent on higher ground at the
opposite end of the camp. Just typical of the Japanese. It is
known that the camp gets flooded at this time of the year yet
they are still building huts in the flooded area. It hasn't been
too hot today. Such is life in a PoW camp.

8 August
3 years today since I was called up and sent to Dover. Surely
I shall not complete four years in the wretched army? Am
longing for home so much. Floods still rising and things are
in a poor state. Yet they still bring in fellows from up-
country. Some more came in last night. 2 were dead. The
camp cannot hold them. It is criminal of the Japanese. A
heavy storm in the afternoon. It seems the monsoon has
reached here then. We are in for a rough two months I
believe, but afterwards things will move I think.

12 August
Another fellow died in this tent last night. He looked a
ghastly sight . . .

20 August
Scabies are bad again – itching terribly, feet, thighs, hands . . .
Feeling impatient to get away from this wretched existence
. . . Flies are an infernal pest here. Cannot keep them off one
or the food. Are as irritating as the scabies.

24 August

Had scabies treatment. Was painted with sulphur and did it sting! But should be better for it. 7,400 in this camp to date. 10,000 expected. Nearly all sick men. Many have died. It is wicked.

26 August

6 or 7 more deaths. Tom Evans has been very kind to me. Brought me a lovely omelette made by his friend Lincoln Page whom he brought to see me last night. Tom brings washing water for me ... he is so good-natured. I dearly hope I can repay him some day.

By August 1943 the desperate work on the 'railway of death' had taken its toll of Will Wilder and he was in the camp hospital with many jungle maladies, including periodic dysentery and scabies. He was saved by his friend from the Malay Volunteers, Tom Evans, who realized his plight and gave him ten dollars – a small fortune – which allowed him to buy additional food from the locals. It was probably this act of kindness that enabled him to recover. Will survived the war and returned to home to his wife Joan in Wallingford, Oxfordshire, where he resumed his post as a lecturer in art at Culham College. SEE ALSO PP. 384–5.

Wednesday 11 – Tuesday 24 August 1943

Leo Amery, Secretary of State for India in London, helps to select Mountbatten for South East Asia Command and chats to Orde Wingate, the untidy brigadier

11 August

[Later] a conference with Attlee and Anthony [Eden] on two telegrams from Winston. One was to ask our opinion on my original suggestion, which he had first dismissed, of Mountbatten for SE Asia Command. His previous idea had been Admiral Cunningham, whom the Americans love. Attlee and Anthony still favoured him and as I don't know him I couldn't argue personalities but only that SE Asia was essentially combined operations on a larger scale ...

24 August

Back for tea and a pouch with the interesting news that
Winston with Roosevelt's and Chief of Staff's approval has
plumped for Mountbatten. I had sent him a wire, after seeing
Attlee's somewhat misleading telegram of our meeting on this
point, to say that, admitting I did not know Cunningham, I
thought Mountbatten's experience the right one, especially for
co-operating with Wingate. From Winston's telegram it would
appear that Wingate is also in Quebec and that he and
Mountbatten have clicked. As I rescued Wingate from oblivion
twice, once to get him sent to Abyssinia and once, after his
semi-suicide, and after revising his Abyssinian report, to
Burma, I think I can flatter myself with my contribution to the
new combination. That, with my insistence from the beginning
on the North Africa–Sicily strategy have, perhaps, been my
most useful contributions, outside my Indian work, to the
general conduct of the war ... Even my efforts to press for
more airborne troops seem to be bearing a little fruit, for a new
airborne division is now being formed ...

Then a short talk with Wingate, who looks more untidy
and shapeless as a Brigadier than ever, but looking forward
greatly to working under Mountbatten. He is to command a
whole group of 'Chindit' Brigades, not merely a couple,
which was all that had been envisaged hitherto and is
apparently to have lots of air transport. Then nearly two
hours with Mountbatten, the latter part of it together with
Wavell and also with Jerram, Mountbatten's secretary,
formerly secretary to Chatfield. Mountbatten told me at the
outset that Winston had said to him that this was my idea
and that he had not liked it at first, but had gradually come
round to it. Mountbatten's reply was that he was very glad
to know that he was not only Winston's fancy but was also
thought well of by others and then stipulated that he should
be allowed to talk to the Chiefs of Staff and make sure that
they themselves were not merely giving way to Winston, but
personally favoured his appointment. Apparently Portal
said that after Tedder, whom he could not have spared, and
Douglas, whom the Americans did not want, Mountbatten
had been his first choice, while Pound said the same in
relation to Cunningham who could not be spared from the

Mediterranean and was not anxious to go. I reassured him as to Brooke, who had thought well of the appointment when I first suggested it. We discussed operations to some extent and I found that my Kra Isthmus scheme appealed to him a great deal . . . Altogether we got on famously.

Leo Amery congratulated himself on promoting the fortunes of Admiral Lord Louis Mountbatten as Supreme Commander South East Asia, and Orde Wingate as a local commander in Burma. Both were talented eccentrics with great strengths but also prone to erratic behaviour. Mountbatten was not an improbable choice for the new command, which was intended to preside over massive amphibious landings along the coast of Malaya during 1945. He had previously been in charge of Combined Operations and knew a lot about amphibious warfare. He was also a superb diplomat and would succeed in charming the American components of his command, who were initially highly sceptical about a military organization which they saw as designed primarily to recover colonial possessions and prestige, with little interest in victory over Japan. Wingate was a gifted strategist; however, his eccentricities and excessive demands tried the patience of staff officers in Burma to breaking point. Leo Amery's 'Kra Isthmus scheme' was a secret plan to seize part of southern Thailand after the war in order to enhance the British Empire. SEE ALSO PP. 87–9, 299–300, 637.

Saturday 14 – Sunday 15 August 1943

Tom Forsyth, a Canadian POW, is sent from Hong Kong to Japan for forced labour

I am one of 480 men warned of draft for Japan. 380 Canadians, 25 Dutch Navy, remainder are Imperials. We have two pays one of 24 Yen and a second of 30 Yen. Can buy very little as prices are exhorbit[ant] and supplies very limited. I bought a pound of salty and a pint of Soy sauce. We have been vaccinated and had three inoculations and two stool tests. We have been penned off from the rest of the camp with barbed wire for the past week. The bakery has baked a batch of buns to feed us on the voyage . . .

We embarked on draft for Japan on Sunday Morning Aug 15ᵗʰ, 1943. We were crammed into the hold on top of coal, so closely packed together that there was never room for everyone to lie down at the same time. There were three hundred men in our hold and some days only 10 men were allowed on deck to use the latrines at one time. As many had chronic diarrhea this was a deplorable state of affairs. Red Cross supplies were put on board for us but the Japanese used them theirselves and what they couldn't use they threw overboard. Our buns we took on board were soon covered in a thick greyish hairy mold, we cut the outside off and ate the rest until the mold progressed thru the buns and made us sick. We ate rice and were served a fish stew so rank many of us could not eat it and those who did were sick. But the worst of all was when heavy planks were put over the hatchways and canvas over that and we sweltered in the terrible heat down below. We took off every article of clothing we had and fanned ourselves until we were utterly exhausted. I have a good idea now what it must have been like in the Black Hole of Calcutta or in the dark holds of African slave ships . . .

The mystery man on board was Sub. Lieut. Bush of the British navy. He was said to have married a Japanese girl before the war, spoke the language like a native, still wore his naval uniform and cap and was allowed extraordinary privileges, on deck all the time. He wasn't allowed to do much for us but he did what he could. When we stopped at the southern tip of Formosa he managed to get one pommel for each of us; we were allowed to buy it. They are a poor intimation of a grapefruit mostly peel and pith, but tasted wonderful at the time. He was a tall handsome fellow, looked every inch a naval officer, we often wondered if he would be allowed to join his wife or if it would turn out to be a mixed marriage tragically marred by war.

We lay at anchor for two days at the northern point of Formosa while we had another stool test. Very hot and hard to breathe where we were penned down below. Our drinking water is rationed.

Large numbers of prisoners were sent to Japan as forced labour, working as stevedores on the docks or in industry. Many died in transit, in part because of the bad conditions and in part because they were so weak before their departure. A further hazard was the possibility of being torpedoed by Allied submarines. Concern that POWs might carry infectious disease to Japan caused their captors to quarantine them for a while and carry out inoculations and tests. But the irony of doing this while keeping their captives in terrible physical conditions which bred infection was lost on the Japanese. SEE ALSO PP. 180–1, 501–2, 802–3.

Monday 16 August 1943

2nd Lieutenant Fred C. Robbins of the US army sails across the Pacific on a troopship bound for service in India

Fred C. Robbins was born in 1908. At the age of twenty-two he had graduated from the University of Missouri School of Journalism and in the period before the war he was the editor of the Lexington Advertiser-News *in Missouri, a local daily newspaper. In 1941 he was called up and his skills were put to use in the 18th Special Service Unit, which ran army newspapers and radio broadcasting to the troops. On 3 August 1943 his unit had set sail from California for India via Australia.*

We will cross the International Date Line tomorrow and a large sign in the purser's office reminds us to set our watches ahead twenty-four hours.

I know what first-class passage on a troop ship means, but I am not sure about a difference between second-class and troop-class. Second-class and troop-class all sleep in the same area. Our first sergeant has the only explanation I have heard. He says second-class passengers get their choice of the bunks.

The PX here started out with $100,000 in merchandise. The cigarette supply at least should be ample as there were 47,000 cartons loaded on board, about 1,800 fags per person.

In spite of the restrictions against dogs, the men managed

to smuggle five on board. They probably came up the gang-plank in A bags.

One officer succeeded in getting an extra supply of fresh water from the steward. The officer had to wash a gooey mass of salt water and soap from his hair. He had not been warned.

A rumor in the troop area has it that this is a pleasure trip in lieu of a furlough. The 'small' arms and hunting knives are for sporting purposes. Uncle Sam will pay all expenses. At the end of the road there will be some new scenery, slightly battle-scarred. Oh, everybody is happy, except the poker losers.

We are on the U.S. Army Transport *Uruguay*. A former luxury liner, it was launched in 1928 at Newport, Virginia, as the California and was placed in coastal service. In 1938 the ship became the property of Moore-McCormack Lines and was renamed and made a part of their Good Neighbor fleet (including the Argentina and the Brazil) sailing between New York and South American ports.

Until mustered into troop transport service, the Uruguay was equipped with two swimming pools, elegant lounge rooms, dining halls and spacious staterooms.

Now the swimming pools are filled with barracks bags and the lounges and decks with bunks.

The ship was converted in February, 1942, in four hectic days climaxed with troops pouring up the gangplanks before the workmen could get off. It is 600 feet long and has a gross tonnage of 20,138.

The ship formerly accommodated about 400 passengers with a crew of about the same size. Now she is carrying about 5,000 men with a crew about two-thirds the peacetime size. Soldier details make up for the cut in the crew.

Thirty, and sometimes more, occupy staterooms that in peacetime accommodated not more than two. The fare was from $425 to $2,250 for a thirty-eight day cruise from New York to Buenos Aires and return.

In happier days passengers had seven meals a day includ-ing light refreshments in the morning and afternoon and late night. Now we have to get along with two meals a day and no in-between treats except for candy bars and cookies purchased at the commissary when it can be found open.

The top day's winnings reported so far among the enlisted men is $854 won in the constant crap games in progress over the decks, in the halls, and in the aisles. One of our men was well over $600 ahead in one game, but he did not stop at that point, and so finally left the game with $34.

The payroll has been signed and turned in but the men will draw only five dollars. This is ample for all the spending they can do on board, and will lend new impetus to crap games.

Fred Robbins travelled in luxury compared to those on some troopships, and in relative safety. Troopships sailing to Australia from the United States usually travelled far to the south across the Pacific in order to stay out of range of enemy aircraft and submarines, for the most part successfully. Once in Australia, the men were either transferred to the Pacific islands campaign or across the Indian Ocean to support the war in Burma. It was in 1943 that American troop mobilization really moved ahead. In 1941 the USA had had 1.5 million men under arms; in 1942 this had risen to 3 million, and by 1943 the figure was closer to 7 million. SEE ALSO PP. 465–6, 602–3.

Brian Gomme, an Australian gunner with 2/6th Artillery at Buna in New Guinea, records a Japanese night attack

Brian Gomme joined A Troop of 11th Battery, 2/6th Field Regiment at Ingleburn, Australia, in June 1940. After further training at Bathurst he was sent to the Middle East, where he joined the defence of Alexandria. In 1941 he was involved in action against the Vichy French regime in Syria, before being sent back to Australia. In early 1943 he had been involved in the defence of Port Moresby on the south coast of Papua New Guinea; by August he was involved in attacks against Buna, a Japanese stronghold off the north coast.

Owing to the report of the Jap patrol being in the area, grenades were issued and everyone was on the alert. Around midnight one of the picquets thought he saw someone just out in front of him, he could see what he thought could be a face beneath a tin hat but, after watching for some time and noticing no movement, thought he was letting his imagination run riot. However, when he handed over to his relief he told him what he saw. The relief watched the object for some time and decided it was a stump and did not mention it when he handed over to the next man.

In the meantime, on another post another picquet thought he saw a face but once again thought it to be imagination and that he was seeing things. To convince himself that nothing was there he looked away for a moment. When he looked back the 'apparition' was gone, so he forgot about it.

Just before the moon went down Lt. Gamble woke up and noticed how still the night was. The usual noise of the jungle insects had ceased and all he could hear was the occasional crack of a twig. It was on that evidence and his own misgivings that he went round quietly to each man and woke him. But for this act it is hard to say what would have happened for, before he had woken the last man, the Japs attacked.

The order 'Hoi toi' was heard – apparently being the order to attack, and immediately pandemonium broke out. The Japs opened up with machine guns and at the same time conducted a five pronged attack on the position. The whole time the attack was in progress the Japs were screaming and yelling either as a means of keeping contact or for the purpose of creating panic amongst the attacked. They succeeded in driving a wedge between the command post personnel and the gunners, cutting the defenders into two parties. Incidentally, the main attack came from the swamp which was supposed to be impenetrable. I have few details of the actual fighting.

Dick Payten had just got out of bed and was standing at the end of the tent with his Owen gun ready but not cocked. He heard a voice say: 'Come on out, Aussie'. The darkness was so intense that it was impossible to see but he cocked his gun and fired a burst at the voice. His kill was a Jap Lieutenant and apparently his first. He was wearing a sword which will be a fine souvenir. During the skirmish some of the command post personnel led by the officer in charge of the infantry platoon decided to endeavour to rejoin the gun

:personnel. However, the Japs had a machine gun trained between the two parties and managed to kill Lt. Grove and Gnrs Johnson and George, also wounding one or two others.

At the same time Jack Parker, who was wounded in the leg early in the piece by a bullet before he had time to get out of bed, and Lt. Bryant, were in the command post unarmed when three or four Japs came in. Jack was still in bed and Bryant hid in a corner while the Japs rummaged around looking for documents. They knocked all the command post equipment about, knocking the wireless set to the ground but not damaging it. The two in the command post have only the darkness to thank for their escape. There were, no doubt, many other incidents of which I have heard nothing but I haven't asked questions of those present.

Brian Gomme's diary records a Japanese speciality, the night attack. In this case the fighting lasted approximately an hour and left his unit with three dead and seven wounded. The Japanese patrol had brought demolition charges to try to destroy the gun batteries, but had not found a chance to plant them. Gomme was already aware that the Japanese were short of food and weapons, underlined by the fact that some of their attackers had been carrying captured American M-1 carbines. Although the Japanese were being forced back, nevertheless the following night the Allied unit doubled the guard on their positions and issued extra grenades. SEE ALSO PP. 441–2, 490–1.

SEPTEMBER 1943

IN NEW GUINEA the anticipated Allied attack on Salamaua turned out to be a feint: instead, MacArthur attacked the neighbouring town of Lae on 1 September, with support from a parachute drop by American and Australian airborne units. Once the paratroops had arrived, an airfield was prepared and a whole division was flown in. By 11 September the Japanese had decided to abandon Salamaua and concentrate on the defence of Lae; however, by 16 September the pounding from American aircraft and Australian artillery was too much for them. Lae was abandoned and the Japanese troops streamed away on foot to the north-west. This allowed Australian infantry to press on towards the key port of Finschhafen.

The next targets in the Pacific 'island-hopping campaign' were already being identified and softened up. The first bombing raids were made on the island of Tarawa in the Gilbert Islands, more than 1,500 miles west of Hawaii, using American B-24 Liberators. Later they were joined by aircraft from a new US fast carrier task force, the first fruits of an expanded naval building programme begun by the Americans two years earlier.

Mountbatten arrived at his newly established South East Asia Command. The headquarters were temporarily located in India, close to the old military bodies in Delhi that his new organization was supposed to replace. General Auchinleck, the commander-in-chief in India, and his headquarters were not abolished, they were simply sidelined. Mountbatten was already anxious to move to his new accommodation which was being constructed in Ceylon. On assuming his new command he began a diary, partly for himself, but also to send to the King as a regular bulletin of his activities in a region that was so central to the British Empire. The war in Burma, and also in neighbouring China, was stagnating, and his task was to reinvigorate the Allied effort.

News of developments in Europe had an important impact on morale in Asia. In September 1943 Italy was knocked out of the war, and although it was not the principal adversary in Europe, this confirmed the feeling that the war was moving in the Allies' direction. Having formed a new government, Italy pledged its allegiance to the Allies and declared war on Germany. Dramatic events attended the Italians' switching sides, for there were Italian naval vessels present in the Far East. The frigate *Eritrea* slipped out of the Japanese-controlled harbour of Sabang and made a bid for freedom; although the Japanese pursued her, she finally made it to Ceylon, where she joined the Allies. However, four Italian submarines failed to escape and were turned over by the Japanese to the Germans, who then commissioned them as U-boats.

Friday 3 September 1943

Brian Gomme, an Australian gunner in New Guinea,
wonders about the cause of the accident on No. 1 gun

By September 1943 Brian Gomme's unit had reached ridges overlooking
Salamaua in New Guinea.

This afternoon we've been firing consistently. At about four
o'clock five rounds of gunfire were ordered. I was manning
the phone on No. 3 gun, Lyn Marlin was on No. 2 and Laurie
Hughes was on No. 1. Our gun had just fired the first two
rounds when Laurie spoke into the phone and said,
    'There's been an accident on No. 1, send for a doctor'. He
said something about a 'terrible mess' but other than that we
were in the dark for a few minutes as we could not leave our
posts to investigate. It appears that No. 1 had fired the first
two rounds and then an explosion occurred at the breach.
Lee Stenhouse was ramming, Stormy Evans laying,
Les Mathews loading and 'Stuka' Schulter preparing
ammunition. It is now assumed that the fuse on the shell
being loaded was faulty and must have been knocked on the
breach block before entering the bore. It is enough to say that
the shell exploded, killing Stenhouse, Evans and Mathews
and wounding Schulter severely in the legs. The three killed
were unrecognisable, being terribly mutilated.
    It was a frightful shock to us all. Men were wandering
round with white faces and hardly speaking a word. Laurie
Hughes was badly shaken as it was only by sheer luck that
he escaped injury. He was covered in blood. Charlie Robson
was also lucky as he had just turned his back and was walking away from the gun when the explosion occurred. He
received a slight skin wound in the neck. We buried all three
of them at dusk tonight in the cemetery on the beach. As I
stood there I could see Max's grave behind and a feeling of
great sorrow overcame me.
    Padre Bill Knudsen officiated in a simple ceremony. He
read the burial service and we sang 'Abide with Me'. I could

not help but notice the great variety of sorrowful faces around me. Men were dressed in shorts without shirts, some had hats and others didn't. It was a most impressive ceremony, although so simple, the sincerity was immense. I really cannot express my feelings on paper.

This diary entry captures the morale-breaking effect of casualties result-ing from accidents and friendly fire rather than enemy activity. Indeed, Gomme wondered about enemy sabotage, a natural psychological reaction, although in practice the chances of this sort of sophisticated sabotage occurring were very small. In reality, the likelihood was that some malfunctioning of ammunition had been caused either by damage in transit or by the very high temperatures in which it was being stored. After the war, ammunition was increasingly kept in refrigerated trailers to help prevent such accidents occurring in training or on the battlefield. SEE ALSO PP. 437–9, 490–1.

Monday 20 September 1943

Australian Corporal Tom Fagan on the Thai–Burma railway reconciles himself to medical treatment

During early 1942 Tom Fagan had been transported from Java, where he had been taken prisoner, to Moulmein in Burma as part of 'A' Force, a large group of Allied prisoners sent north to work on the Thai–Burma railway. By July 1943 problems with a heavily ulcerated shin, which prevented him even putting his leg on the ground, had required him to be hospitalized. Despite daily entreaties made to the Japanese camp commander, not a single item of medical supplies had been forthcoming: the prisoners' hospital was such in name only. A large area of Fagan's leg was now green and rotting.

Must be two months since I have been able to put pencil to paper. It has been a terrible time for me – pain, pain, delirium, fantasies whilst hovering on the very brink of the end of my life. Today I have managed to sit up and am deter-mined to record as much as I can of the happenings and the unbelievable horrors I have suffered. Others, too, have had the same experience. As I write of myself so, in a way, I do for others.

There is not a man in this hut who isn't just skin and bone. Features of my mates have become distorted due to the agonies they had had to endure. We are a mob of skeletons who have, miraculously, defied death. How? I just don't know.

The medical officers can only gouge out ulcers in a despairing effort to rid the affected limb of the encroaching gangrenous, killing disease. The gouging is so cruel men scream in expectation of what is to come, even before the doctor gets near them. My innards turn turtle the moment the instrument sets fire to my ulcer.

If only this war would end; all this would then be but a horrible memory, one I'd rather forget. But for now, I'm part of it and it is, I am sure, far from over yet. Despite the morale builders, the jokes, the tender care mates give one to the other, we have much to go through as weeks, possibly months, pass by.

I feel very low down at the moment; the poison, the medicos tell me, has got into my system and is the cause of my inability to get my issue of rice down. Once there, it isn't long before it is on its return journey. At the most, it is only minutes before I lose the food I need so badly.

Worse still, my leg has contracted under me. No matter how hard I try despite the pain due to the effort, I cannot straighten it. I have just been told there is only one possible treatment. Must have it.

I swallowed more than twice when I was told, but come what may I'm all for it. I have been through so much it will be impossible any treatment can hurt me more. Here they come! If I come through it, my diary will know.

Thank God it's over!

Three men held me down as the medical officer went to town with a pair of scissors. He cut through what little flesh I had at the ulcer centre site beneath my shin bone. It is now exposed from knee to instep. My leg looks like a tin one, green and nasty.

When the scissors bit into the flesh all the fury of hell hit me and I was afire. Although the operation took but a few minutes, it was a lifetime for me – of indescribable agony. But it may have saved my life and I am grateful for that. My body revolted at the measures and every inch of me throbbed and trembled. I hope I didn't yell. If I did, no-one said a word about it.

At last, a cessation of pain and I can hold my food down. Best of all, I have had a sleep. So sound I heard nothing for many, many hours. What a blessed relief!

To the MO [Medical Officer] and his helpers, my gratitude knows no bounds.

Almost daily now we hear the plaintive notes of the sounding of the Last Post. It means one or possibly more have gone to rest. Some envy them; others, like me, grind their teeth in anger at those perpetrators of death, the hated Japanese.

In a way I suppose I am a bit lucky. I am bedded down and cannot move but I can see many of my mates hobbling around, forced to work even though they can just put one leg before the other. They are just like ghosts.

The decision to 'gouge' Fagan's leg with scissors would save his life. Many other prisoners had already had legs amputated without anaesthetic. SEE ALSO PP. 222–4, 474–6, 484–5.

Monday 20 – Thursday 23 September 1943

Marcial Lichauco watches the war of spies and informers in the Philippines

In his youth, Marcial Lichauco had travelled to the United States to study at university. By the 1930s he was a prominent lawyer, writer and nationalist. He kept a diary as an act of resistance against the occupation of his country.

20 September
Although the date of the granting of our so-called independence is not far off, the Japanese have by no means ceased their efforts to ferret out the guerrilla elements from

among the civilian population. The latest method employed by them for that purpose is called 'zonification.' When least expected, Japanese troops enter a town and round up all male residents over fifteen years of age. These unfortunates are then confined in the town church, there being at least one in every municipality in the Philippines, and for the next few days they are held there for investigation. First of all they are made to pass single file before a Filipino who sits behind a desk, carefully masked to conceal his identity. If the informer nods his head, the person thus approved by him is led to one side. If the Filipino shakes his head indicating thereby that the person standing before him is in some way or another connected with the guerrillas, the victim is placed in another group.

Following this preliminary test, those who have been identified by the informer as being in connivance with the guerrilla elements are led away and, through beatings, water cures and other forms of torture forced to confess their past activities. The remaining civilians are given lectures and taught to respect the power and prestige of the Japanese Empire. Once a day they are led to the church courtyard for setting up exercises. They get very little food during their confinement and they are, of course, unable to take a bath or change their clothes. After the ordeal is over each citizen is given a small tag which he must carry on his person wherever he goes to prove that he has been duly investigated and found guiltless of hindering Japanese activities in the Islands.

Speaking of Filipino spies and informers in the service of the Japanese, the number of men and women engaged in that dishonorable occupation seems to be on the increase. They are everywhere vieing with each other in the number of arrests or seizures they can bring about. Two friends of mine were recently chatting in a street car. A convoy of trucks heavily loaded with Japanese soldiers drove by. 'I wonder where they are going,' – remarked one of my friends to his companion. Instantly another Filipino who was about three feet away rose from his seat and approached the two men. 'You will follow me,' he said curtly showing his Japanese badge. At Fort Santiago the unhappy victim whose innocent remark had brought about their arrest explained that he had made the statement motivated by the sight of so many soldiers riding on trucks. The investigating officer slapped him severely on the face – 'Next time you be not so curious – understand?' Then the two men were released . . .

23 September

One of the best known and popular characters here in Manila, is Dr. Sixto Carlos, a U.S. trained veterinarian who was in government service for many years and who, before the war, continued to be much sought after by government agencies because of his skill and irreproachable character. To the American-European residents of Manila he was better known for the modern and up to date cat and dog hospital which he maintained in the grounds of his own residence thus assuring his charges constant care and attention twenty-four hours of the day.

Three days ago a truckload of Japanese soldiers drove up to the Doctor's premises. They marched into his tiled floor clinic and, with picks and shovels, proceeded to dig up the flooring. They knew exactly where to dig because within a few minutes, they had unearthed a cache which, when opened, was found to contain two .45 Cal. automatic pistols, one rifle and two shotguns. While some of the soldiers were still busy digging, others went to the Doctor's bedroom and opened his dressing cabinet. There they found a shortwave radio. They turned on the switch and waited a few moments. As the tubes warmed up they heard, clear as a bell, the latest BBC broadcast.

They did not even wait until their return to Fort Santiago to administer the beating which awaited the Doctor there. In his own house the soldiers proceeded to give poor Dr. Carlos a terrific lashing. His wife who had been ordered out of the room during the search could hear her husband groaning with pain until the men had satiated themselves with the orgy. Trussed up securely and with blood flowing freely from his wounds the Doctor was finally carried out and tossed into the truck which drove off to Fort Santiago.

On Luzon, guerrilla operations against the Japanese had begun at the moment of the surrender of American and Philippine forces in April 1942. 'Stay-behind' groups from the armed forces had headed off into the jungle to conduct a campaign of harassment against the occupying forces. Guerrillas were always in real danger from spies and collaborators who could claim enormous bounties for turning them in. One of the main guerrilla forces had initially been under the command of Captain Ralph McGuire, an explosives expert of the US 26th Cavalry, whose principal area of operation was Zambales. In October 1942 McGuire was captured and decapitated, and his head delivered to the Japanese by local spies in return for a bounty. General Douglas MacArthur was anxious that the lives of guerrillas would be lost needlessly if action were taken prematurely and so in 1943 he ordered the guerrillas to carry out only defensive actions until mid-1944, when preparatory activities for the Allied invasion began. In practice, however, many Filipinos continued to operate independently, killing Japanese whenever the opportunity arose. SEE ALSO PP. 616–17, 630–1.

Tuesday 21 – Wednesday 22 September 1943

Andy Fletcher of the Australian army experiences the chaos of a beach landing from wooden barges at Finschhafen

Andy Fletcher was born in 1917 and was one of six children. He attended Walcha Central High School until he was thirteen, when his father died and Andy left school to work on the land. He joined a militia unit in 1935 at the age of eighteen and attended summer camps until called up to join the AIF in June 1940. He was soon on his way to the Middle East with the 9th Anti-tank Company of the 2/13th Infantry and was wounded at El Alamein in 1942. After a period of leave and retraining in Australia, he joined the assault on the port of Finschhafen, to the south of Lae in New Guinea, in September 1943.

Rendezvue was on the beach at 19 hundred hours, we were not to go down until late in case the japs sent a plane over and saw us all lined up, they would know what was on.

Went down to the ships, just coming in to load, nine jap

bombers and a lot of fighters were coming over so we knew that our show had been given away and were likely to strike trouble. The ack ack was pretty solid, the japs were too high, their bombs fell nowhere near any ship. The barges came in, we chugged out and climbed aboard. There was a meal waiting, so everything was teed up pretty well. We yarned and smoked and told just how things had gone. Meals and coffee were fine. Hot shower, a fellow was clean again. The Yanks treated us pretty well, gave us couple of hundred cigarettes, also chocolate and had some souvenirs to sell too. £12 for a small flag etc. Slept in a big armchair – not much. Revelle was at 3.30am. Breakfast, check gear. Zero was 4.45 22.9.43. Was pitch black. The navy wanted to be out of the area by daylight. We were on deck at 4.15 ready to go. Everyone was as quiet as a church mouse.

Pulling up in the barges, 6 destroyers, the barges were lowered and we climbed over into them, a few cheerios and they were off to pick up the other 12 barges. Go in line. Everything seemed pretty well. The destroyers opened up and put on more speed. The shells were well to the left of us.

Our barges were cut out of our position. The barge in front of us veered across us, we went bang into him. We were only made of wood and thought we may have been holed, but things were ok. At the time we could just pick out the dark line of the shore, so things were ok no fire or any sign. The beach small, two headlands at each end so the japs would have enfilade fire to bear on us as we came in. About 300 yards out, the two brownings on the front of each barge opened up the red tracers flying over everywhere.

Things did not go too well, there were barges all firing, some going to different spots on the coast. We could see the beach on our right but were being shouldered away to the left. As yet no fire had come from the shore and none came until the fellows landed – we were on the beach – and luckily no guns were enfiladed or our casualties would have been heavy.

Every gun pointed out to sea. He [the Japanese] could not depress some to water level so a lot went overhead. We did not land on the beach at all but about 300 yards left on a coral

Andy Fletcher (seated on chair, far right)

cliff, lucky there was a flat portion just about enough room to stand on, but water still waist deep. The barge backed away and we were just standing in the water. The fellows in front were trying to find a way up this 15′ cliff of coral. Eventually climbed around and scrambled up. Must have been there about ¼ hour.

All bunched up a couple of grenades would have finished the lot of us. No fire from the front of us, but plenty on our right and some on our left. When the LCI's [Landing Craft Infantry] were coming in, the jap raked them pretty well with fire so they turn all their 20mm guns and blast the trees and the shore generally. That pretty well turned the tide and the japs could not stand up to it and were withdrawing. They left a lot of dead. I wonder – a lot of our fellows on the beach were not hit but they were lying pretty low at that stage. Some of the captains on the LCI's did not like things too well and did not want to take the boats in. A couple went in at the point of a gun. One fellow dropped his ramps too early and they struck bottom and buckled up and the fellows had a job to get off. One LCI pulled up in deep water and Lance Corporal Miller was drowned. He was carrying the base plate of a 3 inch mortar on his back – 37 pounds, went straight down. A lot of mg's were lost and had to be dived for later . . .

The most remarkable thing about the whole show was the way in which things got sorted out quickly just after landing. The mess was terrific – troops who should have landed on the right were landed on the left etc. and vice versa. Battalions and companies were mixed up and everywhere. But each company in the show knew just where to go and went there. Each battalion know each other so well – helped a lot . . .

My gear was wet with sweat, damn tired . . . so slept pretty well except for a two hour shift on the picket. So ended the first eventful day.

By 19 September Andy Fletcher had heard that his comrades from neighbouring Australian units had managed to capture the town of Lae on the north coast of New Guinea. This paved the way for an amphibious operation further along the coast against the port of Finschhafen, in which he participated. Fletcher's diary captures the chaos of landing a whole brigade along several beaches on a jungle shore. The operation was made easier by the fact that many of the units had fought together in the desert in 1941 and 1943 and knew each other intimately. Sadly, in the landing at Finschhafen Fletcher lost several comrades who had fought valiantly at Tobruk and El Alamein.

The consolidation of this northern shore of New Guinea paved the way for a subsequent operation against New Britain to the north. On 25 December 1943 Andy Fletcher would see an American armada setting out to invade Cape Gloucester, the first Allied foothold on New Britain. He would survive the war and return to Australia to marry Phyll on 29 June 1946. Farming sheep on some 3,300 acres near Walcha, the couple had five children and eleven grandchildren.

Wednesday 22 September 1943

Peter Vladimirov, the Soviet representative at Mao's
headquarters in Yenan, meets Jen Pi-shih, 'Commissioner
for the Opium Problem'

The Politburo has made Jen Pi-shih a 'commissioner for the
opium problem.' Besides, Mao Tse-tung often instructs him
to make various communications for us.

It is impossible to conceal the true scale of opium production in the Special Area [parts of China where normal
rules did not apply]. Opium is one of the most important
items of local trade. Jen Pi-shih tried to build an ideological
basis under this 'business.' From a long and tedious talk it
became clear that, contrary to the statements of the CCP
leadership, the Special Area's economic and financial situation was critical. Inflation ravages. Fiscal operations become
increasingly difficult with every day. Six million dollars have
been issued! However, this has failed to improve the
economic situation.

Jen Pi-shih spoke in detail about the economic difficulties.
In the Special Area all people, ourselves included, feel these
difficulties.

Economic difficulties were discussed by the Politburo. A
rather original way out was found. The Politburo sanctioned
an intensified development of the 'state sector of opium production and trade.' In the meantime as an immediate
measure, it was decided to supply at least 1.2 million liangs
of opium to the market (called the external market) of the
provinces controlled by the Central Government within one
year.

Opium – that is, poppy growing and processing – will be
handled mostly by army units. The main suppliers are the
areas of Ho Lung's 120th Infantry Division (which has long
been engaged in this business).

An order has been given concerning the mass purchases of
opium. Opium is not bulky. It is not difficult to bring it to
Yenan or other designated points in the Special Area from

where it will be sent to the provinces controlled by the Central Government and sold at exorbitant prices.

At this time Moscow was anxious for news of the progress of the war in Asia and the Pacific. Although the Soviet Union and Japan continued to abide by their neutrality pact, signed in 1941, this was a precarious arrangement. While the Chinese Communist Party machine was anxious to eradicate Soviet influence, Mao himself was friendly and hospitable towards his Russian guests, making regular overtures to them through emissaries such as Jen Pi-shih or through his wife, Chiang Ching, and frequently joining them for meals. As a result, Vladimirov and his group saw the reality of how the war effort was run, including the expedient of exporting opium to the nationalist areas of China. Opium was then, as it remains now, an essential military currency in Asia. In northern Burma, British officials had raised levies from the local Burma hill tribes who were extremely effective in fighting the Japanese. Here they were paid in 'liangs of opium' recorded by the British in detailed account books. SEE ALSO PP. 305–7, 321–3, 575–6.

Wednesday 22 – Saturday 25 September 1943

William Brougher and ten other generals join prison work details at Shirakawa

By September, William Brougher had been moved to another camp on Formosa at Shirakawa. Here he rubbed shoulders with General Maltby, the commander of Hong Kong in 1941, and countless other British and American 'top brass', although the Japanese appear to have been no great respecters of rank.

22 September
Detail of 10 American Generals turned out with others to carry water from a well outside the camp for the kitchen, Nipponese bathroom and our own use. All were struck over the head with bamboo stick by Nipponese soldier because we misunderstood an order given in Nipponese – tho' the misunderstanding was explained to the soldier by Col. Stuart Wood, our interpreter. In the afternoon 1st Squad

worked (coolie labor) on the farm, grubbing out grass and preparing ground for planting sweet potatoes – soil infected with human feces. When we came in, after handling the soil all afternoon, we had to start serving food immediately – no water to wash in – no time to wash. We will be lucky if we don't all have cholera or something worse. I am more tired tonight than any time since I've been a prisoner.

As a result of General Maltby's talk with Nip. General yesterday, we are supposed to be worked less. Instead, the work is increased by 500% and the work has been made harder – punishment for Gen. Maltby's complaints? . . .

23 September

. . . Officer squads No. 1–5 and all enlisted squads worked until 6:30 PM – got in one hour and ½ after supper is usually served – very tired and dirty – no water to bathe in – after handling soil infected with human feces all afternoon . . .

24 September

. . . Inspection by Swiss Consul and Swedish Consul Kobe (Swiss Consul Maurice C. Champonde, representing U.S. and Great Britain, Swedish Consul representing Holland). Conference held with representative prisoners – Beebe, Seight, Light, Air Marshal Maltby (spokesman for US and GB prisoners) – Gen de Fremery, spokesman for Dutch – many pointed questions asked about food, work, medical, dental treatment, mail, baths, etc. and straight answers given. Inspection of barracks and prisoners in PM. News photographers took many pictures.

Several prisoners got mail – some who had previously rec'd letters getting more – many others getting none. We hear there are many other letters in camp and that others may get letters soon. I got word indirectly from a letter from Mr Rushing, Atlanta, to his son, Sergt. Rushing, that my wife got my radio broadcast message (written Nov. 9, 1942) and stating that she is in good health (March 1943). Hope I get a letter soon – My! My! How hard it is to see others getting letters and still to get none after almost two years without a word from my loved ones! . . .

25 September
... My roommate, Brig. General J.R.N. Weaver was delivered 28 letters today from his family – the third delivery total more than 20. The vast bulk have rec'd none at all! An excellent example of inefficiency or indifference or malicious intent to be cruelly unfair to prisoners ...

One of the interesting aspects of Brougher's diary is a rare glimpse of Swiss and Swedish diplomats serving as 'protecting powers', or neutral intermediaries looking after the interests of countries at war. Tokyo did its best to limit their visits and staged photographs to give the impression that all was well in the camps. The Red Cross was also active in examining POW issues, but its inspection of Japanese POW camps was not effective and it failed to spot the appalling treatment meted out to prisoners until quite late on in the war.

William Brougher would remain a POW until September 1945. At the end of the war he was located in a prisoner of war camp at Mudken in Manchuria, from where he was liberated by Soviet soldiers who had recently entered the war in Asia and the Pacific. He returned to the United States and managed to take with him seven out of the eight volumes of diaries he had written during his captivity. The first volume was lost during the war years. SEE ALSO PP. 423–4.

OCTOBER 1943

DURING OCTOBER, the forces leading two Allied campaigns in the Pacific, one in Papua New Guinea and one in the Solomon Islands, finally moved close enough to begin to provide each other with air support. In the Solomon Islands, naval forces were preparing to attack Empress Augusta Bay on the heavily defended island of Bougainville, and MacArthur's aircraft in neighbouring New Guinea were now close enough to promise significant protection. Although American submarines and aircraft continued to sink large numbers of Japanese ships, Tokyo was still highly successful in using destroyers to evacuate soldiers by night from beleaguered positions. On 6 October nine Japanese destroyers on such a mission encountered American destroyers and beat them in an engagement off Vella Lavella. Ship for ship, and especially at night, the Japanese were still the equal of their opponents.

In New Guinea, Australian forces continued their advance towards Finschhafen. Meanwhile, American clandestine units moved across the straits from New Guinea to Cape Gloucester on New Britain to begin scouting out landing places for a new campaign that would take the Allies north through the island in preparation for an eventual leap north-westwards to the Philippines in a year's time. The expansion of air bases in both the Solomons and New Guinea enabled the Allies to subject all Japanese forces on New Britain to a ferocious pounding. On 12 October 1943 some 350 aircraft raided the island, homing in with particular force on the town of Rabaul, taking the Japanese headquarters there completely by surprise. However, the future intentions of the Allies were given away by this aerial onslaught and so on 21 October Admiral Koga, Yamamoto's successor, decided to send major reinforcements both to New Britain and to Bougainville in the Solomons. On the last day of October, a task force of US marines and soldiers under the command of Admiral Spruance also sailed for Bougainville.

In mid-October Admiral Lord Louis Mountbatten travelled to China, taking the perilous air route 'over the hump' of the Himalayas, to visit Chiang Kai-shek and American commanders in China at Chungking. One of the matters they wished to discuss was who would control territories in mainland south-east Asia such as Thailand and Indochina, which as yet had not been allocated to particular commands. This remained impossible to resolve, for Britain, America and China all wished to extend their influence in this region. Although there was no fighting in these countries, clandestine operations were already being conducted in them by the various Allied secret services. Because of the failure to reach agreement, the various covert operations continued in these Japanese-occupied areas without proper co-ordination. The result was a degree of confusion and mutual suspicion.

Friday 1 October 1943

Juan Labrador, academic and priest, watches the
formation of 'bamboo brigades' in the towns near Manila
in the occupied Philippines

The military police is engrossed in preparing the way for the
advent of the Republic. There is continuous zoning in towns
where they suspect guerrillas to be hiding and arms being
kept. A warning was issued that if the guerrillas in Manila
would not surrender, the capital would also be subjected to
zoning. The people turned chicken at the thought of the
horrors of imprisonment and the search in houses. An order
was also issued to cut the points off kitchen knives, razors
and bolos, and even the toy guns of children are to be
surrendered. Great amounts of these deadly arms were
collected. Many souvenirs such as sabers and pistols
were destroyed, buried and surrendered. The newspaper
reported that more than five thousand guerrillas in Manila
surrendered, and that they made their pledge of allegiance
before the mayor and the chief of the military police, who
delivered lengthy speeches before them.

In provinces near Manila, the army has adopted a measure
which is both meaningless and ridiculous and therefore
humiliating and odious. It consists of requiring all males –
and, in some towns, also females – to carry a piece of
bamboo pointed like a spear which they were to take with
them everytime they went out of their houses. These armed
squadrons are sometimes mobilized and made to march in
parade in plazas to be reviewed by the Mayor or a Japanese
officer. What could be the reason behind these bamboo
brigades? Conjectures vary; nevertheless, no one likes it at
all.

With the increasing terrorism and the state of insecurity
reigning in provinces, the influx of refugees into Manila is
alarmingly on the rise. Shortage of food and of housing runs
side by side and the problem of transportation has gone
beyond solution. It is no rare thing to have to wait for one

hour to take a streetcar ride, just to end up on the running board or finally to walk all the way. Calesas and the carretelas [horse-drawn vehicles] are conspicuously absent. The seats in streetcars have been removed and passengers were packed inside them like sardines.

The formation of local defence forces armed with bamboo spears was especially puzzling to Labrador. Right across south-east Asia, similar local militias were being formed; however, the Japanese did not trust their local recruits and so did not wish them to be armed with anything more substantial than 'suga' or bamboo poles. As the war progressed, weapons were in short supply even for Japanese soldiers, and so when home guard units were formed in Japan they too were armed with sharpened sticks. SEE ALSO PP. 162–4, 229–31, 563–4, 689–91.

Friday 8 October 1943

Marquis Kido and Prince Mikasa discuss three heads and one body in China

Marquis Kido was a senior adviser to Emperor Hirohito; Prince Mikasa was the Emperor's youngest brother, the fourth son of the previous ruler, Emperor Taisho.

At 10:00 A.M. I visited the residence of Prince Mikasa and reported on various matters concerning the domestic and foreign situations, as well as the prospects for the war. The prince told me the following concerning the current situation in China:

At present, there are three regimes in China, viz: Chungking, Nanking, and Yenan. Consequently, whichever direction the world situation may take, China will not be placed in a predicament. If Japan wins the war, the Nanking government will prevail; and if the Soviets win the war, the Yenan government will come to power. Therefore, they are boasting that victory is certain and defeat is not for them. Also, since restrictions on speech are not as strict as heretofore, the effects can be seen in various manifestations in the peace negotiation operation. In Japan, everyone knows of the two regimes, viz: Nanking and Chungking. However, it happens that she is unaware of the Yenan regime. To regard these three regimes as having three heads as well as three bodies is not correct. Of course, they have three heads, but nonetheless, it is one China.

The anti-Comintern feeling is very strong in the Chungking government. We must keep this point in mind with respect to future policy. Wang was not willing to act against Chungking, but since his visit to Japan he has become so earnest that he would do it even by sacrificing himself. The peace negotiations with Chungking chiefly depend upon the result of the Burma operation. Wang has no comrades with whom to consult frankly; therefore, even if he decides on something, he can't put it into practice freely. We have some obligation to aid him on this point. I consider it an urgent duty to send someone like Lieutenant General Kagesa as his adviser. Chiang reportedly said, 'I dislike most Chin Peke-kun; next Wang Ching-wei; and third, the Japanese troops.' The collaboration of Chiang and Wang will be very difficult.

Kido and Mikasa's depiction of China as a country with one body but three heads captures the complex political situation perfectly. The nationalists in Chungking, the communists in Yenan and a Vichy-style collaborationist regime in Nanking each controlled large sections of the country. Kido was exploring the possibility of co-operation between the nationalists and the Japanese-sponsored regime of Wang Ching-wei in Nanking against Mao in Yenan on the basis of their shared anti-communism. At the same time the Americans were hoping to facilitate co-operation between the nationalists and the communists on the basis of anti-Japanese sentiment. All these hopes proved misplaced, and each regime proved resistant to external deal-makers and exhortations for action. SEE ALSO PP. 75–7, 86–7, 123–5, 586–7.

Sunday 10 – Monday 11 October 1943

Sheila Allan, an Australian internee in Changi, feels
uneasy about her diaries

10 October

Last night we were told that there is going to be a Roll Call
in the Rose Garden at 9 a.m. today. Early this morning we
got ready to go to the Rose Garden. Felt very uneasy about
my diaries – what to do with them – stacked them between
the school books and prayed that they'd be safe as before
when the Japs came around the last couple of times.

An hour went by before a troop of about 30 men arrived
and started searching each cell. I felt quite sick. Another hour
went by and we were ordered to go to A garden and E block.
It was really hot today – we had rugs across lines for some
shade. It wasn't until late in the afternoon we were allowed
to go to the Carpenter's Shop. Many fainted and some were
sick with the heat – thirsty and hungry – especially the
children. Later we were given coffee and tea. Coconuts were
opened and eaten and the children had milk brought to
them. I felt rotten – still suffering from the effects of malaria
and wondering if the Japs found my books. Permission
given to cook something. About half-past seven 'All Clear'.
Could go back to our cells. Tried to get to my cell as fast as
my shaky legs would go but nothing was disturbed in ours
– it was just as we had left it this morning. Food arrived –
rice and soup – new batch of men – no guards with them this
time. Felt too ill to eat and had a fit of the shivers again. How
long can I keep up with my diaries I wonder before my luck
runs out should I stop now but I can't – I must go on writing
or I'll go mad not being able to write down my thoughts . . .

11 October

Yesterday's episode is now being referred to as the 'Double
Tenth' – the day the Japanese Kemp-Tai (Secret Military
Police) descended on Civilian Internment Camp. They were
sure they would find a spy ring, transmitters etc. with the

idea that we were going to sabotage the Island of Singapore. The result – 28 men were taken away and a couple of women. Even the Bishop of Singapore was included. They were taken away to be questioned and tortured I guess. We don't know exactly what is to become of them.

Everything appeared quiet. I started to write on a piece of paper about yesterday and what I thought when suddenly there were sounds of heavy boots and voices. Hastily I got rid of the piece of paper and quickly ran outside and lay down pretending to be asleep. Up they went, their boots 'clanging' on the iron stairs, flashing their torches, then down they went. Later I heard them again going into the Carpenter's Shop and I nearly passed out in fear as I remembered that's where I was writing and what have I done with the paper – I can't remember – my mind is a blank. Oh, God! Did I drop it somewhere in my hurry to get over here? What if the Japs found it – Think, think! But I can't – I know I haven't got it with me and I can't leave here to look for it. All quiet at last – dare I go back to the Carpenter's Shop to look for it? Better not and see what happens.

Despite such scares as this, Sheila went on keeping her perilous diary, often writing it using codes and abbreviations for fear that it might be discovered by the camp authorities. While the Japanese provided writing materials, they forbade the keeping of diaries. She also joined a circle of women who sewed quilts. Like her diary, these quilts have also survived. SEE ALSO PP. 174–5, 187–9, 209, 587–8.

Thursday 14 October 1943

Leocadio de Asis prepares to celebrate Philippine Independence Day in Tokyo

Leocadio de Asis was born in 1919 and did well at school, eventually graduating with an honours degree from the University of Santo Tomas College of Law. He joined the Philippine army in 1941 and was captured by the Japanese after the fall of Bataan. After being held in several POW camps, he was selected on the basis of his good record to enter training for a new Japanese-sponsored Philippine Constabulary Academy. Excelling academically, he was soon teaching criminal law on the staff at this establishment. In May 1943 he had been one of ten unmarried college graduates from the Academy, all in their twenties, who were selected to travel to Tokyo for further training.

Philippine Independence Day!

Today we woke up in highest spirits. We marched to school bearing 'home-made' Filipino flags prepared last night by the group at Hongōryō. The Filipino 'propaganda corps,' too, posted attractive placards on the school's bulletin board announcing in bold characters the Philippines' Declaration of Independence.

We were all so excitedly happy that everyone at school, teachers and students, could not help but take notice of us. We were accosted with congratulations and received bouquets of flowers from different groups of pensionados.

At 8:30 a.m. we were in front of the Imperial Palace and shouted '*Mabuhay*' '*Banzai,*' as newspapermen and photographers got busy. We had the rest of the morning to ourselves, and we spent the time roaming about Tokyo's busiest street, waving our home-made Filipino flags, proudly proclaiming to all and sundry the independence of our country.

We imagined ourselves at the Luneta Park in the midst of the thousands upon thousands of our countrymen, rejoicing in the glorious event, waving no longer the Japanese flag, but this time the Filipino flag for which our forefathers fought and died.

At 5:30 p.m. we were all assembled at our dormitory for the 'raising of the flag.' It was a simple but very touching ceremony held with all the solemnity that befitted the occasion. Dusk had crept in, but to us that moment spelled the dawn of a new day for our country; and as the flag was being slowly raised in the gathering dusk of an autumn afternoon, we saw our flag in the full radiance of its glory. (Can this be real?)

After the Flag Ceremony, a sumptuous dinner in our honor was given by the Philippine Society of Japan. Present during the dinner were Mr Okamoto, secretary of the

Philippine Society, and representatives of the Daitōa Ministry and the International Friends' Society. Pepito A Santos and Amado Cayabyab were also present. We had a lot of fun during the banquet, especially when beer had its effect. All sorts of songs, dances, speeches, etc. were featured during the celebrations.

At a point when the highest peak of merriment had been reached, I thought it wise to stand and speak a few words to inject a little seriousness into the affair, lest our Japanese hosts would misinterpret our merriment as mere frivolity. I asked our hosts to please look behind the joy and laughter of the night's merriment, there to find how seriously we are taking the question of Philippine Independence. Although our hosts see us laughing and dancing and singing, I said, deep in our hearts we feel and we know what the day of independence means in terms of liberty and freedom for which our heroes and martyrs shed the last drop of their blood. I was rather inspired, and I think I was able to drive home the point I wanted to bring out.

De Asis and his colleagues were in effect the vanguard for a new Japanese-directed national police force in the Philippines. They were part of Japan's medium-term plans for normalization of the Philippines, which involved granting a form of managed independence and also eradicating 'anarchic' American influences. De Asis did not wish to travel to Japan, and was always conscious of being used for propaganda purposes, but feared the consequences for his family if he resisted. SEE ALSO PP. 481–3.

Friday 15 October 1943

Admiral Lord Louis Mountbatten has a close shave while flying 'over the hump' to China to visit Chiang Kai-shek

Admiral Lord Louis Mountbatten was born Louis of Battenberg on 25 June 1900, a great-grandson of Queen Victoria and a second cousin of King George V. Like the rest of the royal family he had changed his name during the First World War to assuage anti-German sentiment.

Mountbatten attended Dartmouth Royal Naval College and served in the navy during the First World War. He remained in the navy in the inter-war years and in 1941 saw action off Crete before becoming Head of Combined Operations Command in October 1941. He oversaw a number of commando operations, including the disastrous Dieppe raid of August 1942. Many claimed that he had received accelerated promotion due to his royal connections. When he arrived as Supreme Commander in south-east Asia in October 1943 most of his subordinate commanders were older and more experienced than him. One of his first tasks on arrival was to set off to visit Chinese and American commanders at the front line in Assam and then in neighbouring China.

Admiral Lord Louis Mountbatten

Left Palam airfield [in Delhi] 1100. We went in our Liberator, the Marco Polo, whose name had meanwhile been written up in Chinese characters.

I took two sailors, two soldiers, one airman and one political officer with me. The party included Micky Hodges,

Flags, Lieutenant Colonel Dobson (the great Chinese scholar), and last, but on a trip like this, by no means least, John Keswick. We landed at Chabua airfield in Upper Assam at 1700. Here I was met by various American Generals, headed by Stratemeyer, and many other senior officers. We dined in the mess on the old polo ground and later visited a remarkable collection of snakes which a US Medical Orderly at the hospital has collected. In peacetime he is the curator of the Reptile House at Long Beach California. In the same cage as a rock python was a pathetic looking duck which had been sitting there for two days waiting to be eaten. When we arrived they were just feeding a white rat to half a dozen cobras. The cobras kept missing the rat, while our 'curator' kept saying in a pansy voice, 'My, my, their aim is very bad tonight!' I asked him to release the rat, but no sooner had I made a request than one of the cobras got it and proceeded to swallow it.

The Americans are taking the most abnormal precautions for my safety. Armoured cars, and men with tommy guns in jeeps drove with us everywhere and outside my room four men stood with tommy guns loaded and at the ready. I hinted that it was unnecessary to take such precautions, but they absolutely insisted.

When I finally turned in it was extremely awkward. My room was brightly lit, the windows were only covered with wire screens and had no curtains or blinds. The four tommy gunners were thus able to follow my every movement whilst undressing.

I should perhaps explain at this point that Dr T. V. Soong had told me that the news of my impending visit had leaked through to the Japanese and it was probably known that I would be flying through on the day of the 14th. He begged me to change my itinerary and take a fighter escort. I had just changed the day of my departure, as it happened, to fit in with General Somervell's movements, but I did not want to take a fighter escort as it means that extra petrol has to be flown over the 'Hump' to get the fighters back and, in any case, I am no great believer in fighter escorts. We therefore changed our time so as to cross the 'Hump' by night.

Dr Soong was only too tragically correct. The Japanese put

out a terrific fighter sweep on the day of the 14th for the first time for many months and shot down three wretched transport aircraft, as well as damaging others.

T. V. Soong, the Chinese foreign minister, was entirely right about the danger of a Japanese attempt to shoot down the newly arrived Mountbatten. Chungking was a notoriously insecure location and the chances of information leaking about Mountbatten's impending visit had been high. In the event Mountbatten left Chabua in Assam a day late, departing by moonlight at three in the morning on Saturday 16 October and heading for Chungking. This meant putting on oxygen masks and crossing the Himalayas at 18,000 feet. The Japanese effort to intercept Mountbatten was reminiscent of the successful efforts of the Americans to shoot down Yamamoto in April 1943. SEE ALSO PP. 671–2, 770–1.

Wednesday 20 – Thursday 28 October 1943

Fred C. Robbins of the US army takes cover among the tea bushes during an enemy air raid in Assam

20 October
This afternoon we had our first air raid alarm. (The Japanese are only about thirty minutes away.) There is no siren. We just run for cover when our fighter planes take off from the field. We had been assigned no area to go to, and as we have no slit trenches of our own, we hit the tea bushes.

No Japanese planes were in sight but the report is that we knocked down two out of five that pulled the attack.

21–24 October
Another air raid alarm. Again the tea bushes, but this one lasted only about thirty minutes.

Last night we had an earthquake at Jorhat. It happened at midnight and was very violent. Many of the men thought this was a real bombing and streaked for the trenches in their shorts. They had to shower the mud off before they could go back to bed.

There was little damage done in camp, but Jorhat was hit hard. A number of buildings were damaged, some totally wrecked. The jail was split open in several places and the Army hospital was demolished. But the patients were moved outside safely . . .

25–28 October

The men here were telling about their first air raid. The colonel had forbidden the digging of slit trenches. The tea bushes would have to be 'junked' and they are valuable. But after the raid he said, '—the tea bushes.' The digging started. Tea grown in Assam is popular in England, I am told. There are a number of tea plantations around here and some have been turned over to the American Transport Command for airfield installations.

You can't beat a bunch of American soldiers. That first raid came when the women were out picking tea. After the raid seventeen men reported at the VD pro-station.

And the men will drink. Liquor is both scarce and expensive, so they buy this native stuff. It is labeled 'Assam Distillery' so they call it 'After Death.'

When the US army conducted an anonymous survey of its enlisted men in the China–Burma–India theatre in July 1944 it found that more than half of them had engaged in sex since arriving and the majority had paid for it. Although most enlisted men used both condoms and prophylactic treatments, the incidence of sexually transmitted disease was still high. This in turn had the effect of depleting the numbers of men available for active duty at any one time. The earthquake noticed by Fred Robbins was experienced more forcefully by Angela Bolton, also in Assam, who describes it in the next diary entry. SEE ALSO PP. 435–7, 602–3.

Saturday 23 October 1943

Angela Bolton, a British nurse at Assam in India, dashes
out of the mess and into the night

On Saturday 23 October 1943 a terrible thing happened. The
RAMC dance had started and the revelry was at its height
with everyone dancing when I noticed that one of the
pictures on the wall was swinging from side to side. I drew
my partner's attention to it but he merely laughed and said
that someone must have put too much pineapple juice in the
punch. Suddenly a voice shouted – I think it was Colonel
Cawthorn's – 'Everybody outside quickly. Hurry! Hurry!'
and we all dashed out into the pitch-black night leaving the
gramophone playing away eerily in the deserted room. As
we stumbled over tree roots the ground beneath our feet
oscillated backwards and forwards and then up and down.
We all subsided on to the ground willy-nilly listening to the
low grumbling of the disturbed earth. After about three
minutes from the start of it (which seemed like a lifetime) the
tremor ceased.

I am writing this in the early hours as I can't sleep thinking about the earthquake and hoping there won't be any
more tremors. Whatever else moves, you expect the ground
under your feet to be solid, reliable, the one certainty you
can depend on. The horror of that moment when there seems
to be no safety anywhere shakes you to the core. No one
panicked but perhaps the drinks they had had at the party
gave them Dutch courage.

*At 11 p.m. on 23 October an earthquake occurred near Hojai in Assam.
Eastern India was prone to earthquakes and this was one of the largest
of recent times. A fault line opened up and in one village to the north
villagers and cattle were simply swallowed up.*

*Angela Bolton served mostly on the Red Cross river steamers that
moved up and down the river valleys, providing a mobile hospital
service for the army. They were painted with very large Red Cross signs
to discourage air attack. During the war she met her future husband, a*

captain in the Royal Artillery. After the war they lived in Oxford and had four children. SEE ALSO PP. 252–4, 289–90.

Monday 25 – Friday 29 October 1943

Lieutenant-Colonel Arthur Milner, a POW on the Thai–Burma railway, records some problems with abbreviations

Arthur Milner had been a battalion commander in a signals regiment at Singapore. His unit had been captured in February 1942 while evacuating by sea to Sumatra. After an initial period in Sumatra, he and most of his men were sent north to work on the Thai–Burma railway. They were present when the two halves of the line were joined and the railway was declared finished in October 1943.

All inoculated against T.A.B. [Cholera] on 25th. The official opening of the railway was on 25th. The junction [of the two sections of railway] had been affected a few days before that and on 24th two locomotives came through very slowly to test the embankments, bridges etc. with their weight. On the same day all sorts of Japanese officials came through going Northwards for the ceremony.

They found a soldier in my Bn. [Battalion], one Cpl. [Corporal] Moloney, writing up his diary during the lunchtime interval on the line. He had some rather unwise criticism of our captors in it, and referred to them by the usual three-letter abbreviation [Jap]. He was very badly beaten up, with fist, hand and bamboo and an order was issued that anyone using the abbreviation would be severely punished – we must call them 'Japanese' or 'Nipponese'. Hence all the amendments to this manuscript diary. In the last war, we had to issue an order that the Portuguese should be called such and not the 'Pork and Beans' – how naughty our men are!

In November 1943 Arthur Milner would note that since the railway had been completed work on the line had eased considerably. Although work parties were still turned out, in practice 'men stand in groups talking to each other most of the time'. Allied officers were rewarded for the completion of the line with small presents of tins of fish, bully beef and butter.

Milner survived the war, returned to Britain in 1945 and was awarded an OBE for his efforts to intercede with the Japanese on behalf of the POWs under his command working on the railway.

NOVEMBER 1943

ON 1 NOVEMBER Task Force 31, commanded by Admiral Spruance, landed at Empress Augusta Bay on the southern coast of Bougainville in the Solomon Islands. To the north of the island, American carriers tried to diminish Japan's air power by attacking its bases, but the defenders still managed to field a significant number of aircraft against the landing. Nevertheless, a beachhead was established without too much difficulty at the southern end of the island because the chosen landing zone was far away from any main concentration of Japanese troops.

On 4 November a large squadron of Japanese ships, including seven cruisers and a substantial new force of aircraft, arrived at Rabaul harbour in New Britain, with the purpose of attacking the American beachhead on the neighbouring island of Bougainville. In order to prevent this, Admiral Halsey sent two carriers, the *Saratoga* and the *Princeton*, dangerously close to Rabaul to deal with the newly arrived Japanese ships. Attacking with over 100 aircraft, they succeeded in damaging almost all the squadron, effectively neutralizing it before it had a chance to go into action. On 7 November a large force of Japanese aircraft from Rabaul finally located the two American carriers some 200 miles off Rabaul and attacked them, but inflicted little damage. This Japanese failure reflected the use of radar by the American fleet to warn them of approaching attacks and also the superiority of new American aircraft, such as the Grumman Wildcat, which were proving better than the Japanese Zero fighters. Japanese aircraft, which were considered excellent at the outbreak of war, were now being outclassed by new Allied types. On Bougainville, American forces gradually made headway but with very fierce fighting and serious losses on both sides.

On 11 November the arrival of further American carriers under Rear-Admiral Sherman enabled larger raids to be mounted on the base at Rabaul, in the course of which a number of Japanese cruisers and already damaged destroyers were sunk or burned. Although the Japanese were still able to launch air attacks, their losses in the air during this episode were four times those of their American opponents. By mid-November the use of armour by the landing force at Bougainville had allowed the Americans to push the Japanese far enough back to begin the construction of an airfield.

Much further north, Admiral Nimitz's forces had been using carriers to conduct regular bombing raids against the Marshall and Gilbert Islands in the central Pacific to the west of Hawaii. This paved the way for a forthcoming invasion of a number of small atolls and islets to be used as stepping stones on the way to Japan. On 20 November an American invasion fleet of some 100 ships launched an attack on the heavily defended Tarawa Atoll. The first wave of US marines foundered on coral reefs and were thrown back by intense Japanese artillery fire. A second wave had better success using tracked amphibian vehicles, but only a small proportion of marines eventually reached the beach and established a precarious foothold. Had the Japanese launched a night counter-attack – as was their usual practice – the foothold would have been eradicated. However, no Japanese attack occurred and the beachhead was widened. Gradually the superiority of American air support and naval gunfire took its toll on the opposition, whose bunkers had to be reduced one by one. The Japanese commander, Admiral Shibasaki, was cut off in a concrete emplacement and unable to exercise control over his forces. On 23 November the defenders' ammunition was exhausted and the atolls of Tarawa and Makir finally fell to the United States. However, the following day a Japanese submarine torpedoed one of the supporting American carriers, *Liscome Bay*, sinking her with the loss of 700 lives. Nimitz was alarmed by the high cost of capturing two small atolls that were still a long way from Japan.

The picture in Burma during November 1943 was very different. In the north, the Japanese had succeeded in making gains against local Chinese forces and drove the British garrison out of Fort White before occupying the position themselves. In late November the Japanese completely overran the Chinese 112th Regiment, capturing its headquarters and officers. Japan also made a number of successful local 'rice offensives' to capture supplies in China during November and December. However, Japanese activities in Burma were coming under growing pressure from newly arrived American air power based in India. Japan could no longer use merchant vessels off the coast of Burma; meanwhile, road and railway bridges were being systematically eliminated.

The end of November saw the first two stages of a major three-part conference attended by Allied leaders. First Churchill and Roosevelt met with Chiang Kai-shek at Cairo and agreed on a major offensive to reopen a supply route from Burma into China in the early part of 1944. However, despite the attendance of military commanders such as Mountbatten, many issues remained unresolved or unaddressed, including the awkward question of who would control much of south-east Asia at the end of the war. Churchill and Roosevelt then travelled on to Tehran to meet with Stalin on 28 November. Stalin insisted on the extreme importance of opening a second front against Germany in western Europe and promised to enter the war against Japan as soon as Germany was defeated.

Monday 1 – Monday 8 November 1943

Joseph McNamara describes his experience on board a destroyer offering fire support during the invasion of Bougainville Island

Joseph McNamara came from New York and volunteered to join the US navy on 12 August 1942. The following day he was sent for one month of training at Newport, Rhode Island. After some leave in late 1942 he was assigned to the destroyer Anthony, *a fire support and radar picket vessel. In March 1943 they left Portland, Maine, and sailed for the*

*Pacific via Guantanamo Bay, Puerto Rico and the Panama Canal, sink-
ing a German submarine en route. They had arrived at Pearl Harbor at
the end of May 1943 and were then assigned to support the landings
at Empress Augusta Bay on Bougainville in the Solomon Islands.*

1 November

General quarters sounded at 0518, while I was on the throttle
watch. Firing commenced at 055[0]. Target No. 1 Puriata
Island. Target No. 2 Bougainville Island. Fired 457 shells.
Firing stopped at 0735. Secure from general quarters at 1930.
Went at one-third ahead at 42 turns. First Jap plane shot
down at 805. Third Jap plane shot down at 850. Two men
killed and four wounded and a near miss of Dive Bomber on
the Wadsworth, which was just alongside of us. At 1315
stand by for air attack! Driven off by our fighters, our P38s
did a great job. General quarters lasted 14 hours and 15 mins.
Had K rations for dinner and supper. Pretty darn good. Also
cans of fruit and vegetable juices. Marines had little
opposition upon landing. The tactic then we found out later
was to let them land and get them started inland and then to
hit them. 'Wadsworth' opened fire at 540.

Left Bougainville at 730 with 8 other destroyers and
8 troop ships empty for a safe port. We had landed all our
troops.

Task Force #39 met the Japs the same night and 'Foote'
was torpedoed, one of our sister destroyers. She did not sink.
The Jap forces still on the loose, composed of cruisers and
destroyers. Spent Saturday evening patrolling off
Guadalcanal, a typical army post – steamed around Salvo
Island and Florida Island. We had a good plane cover at all
times. Our greatest asset.

Some 17- to 20,000 marines landed – opposed they say by
40,000 Japs. Task Force #39 encountered Jap task force and
sank a cruiser, one can and left two burning. The pursuit was
taken over by bombers. We had a cruiser hit, a hole through
the bow. Not serious – it was the 'Denver.' Also the 'Foote'
was torpedoed in the fantail and killed 19 men. Ship almost
a total wreck. Good only for salvage. The 'Spencer' and the
'Thatcher' rammed each other while making a torpedo
run. In this action was the 'Denver,' the 'Columbia,' the

'Montpelier,' and 'Cleveland' and 8 other destroyers.

The Anthony Task Force #34, destroyer. Squadron #45 that's their designation.

. . . anchored in Purvis Bay, Talagi Island just around the corner from Taluga Harbor. All the damaged ships came in here. This completes our part of the Bougainville marine landing.

8 November

Had 8 to 12 throttle watch. Urgent call for destroyers immediately in Empress Augusta Bay, Bougainville to break up a Jap landing of troops behind our marines. Full flank speed called for not only for as fast as the ship will run but it also calls for super-heated steam at 850 degrees. That temperature makes the steam pipes turn red. You would think they were going to melt. They glow. Of course, the tremendous heat of 850 degrees and 346 RPMs is almost the extreme limit of our engines and that's around 42 knots which is so far as the ship is concerned almost flying.

Arrived with the 'Hudson' Destroyer at Bougainville 2400. At 0030 first fired salvo at a PT boat behind us trying to make a run on us. Just a moment before we fired we got word that they were our friends. They were Americans and they were making a run on us and of course we had them lined up, and if they'd waited another minute we'd have blown them up and killed them off. They were U.S. boats and did not know of our being in the vicinity. Of course we'd come up so fast from the south that they probably hadn't got word that we had actually arrived.

At 0100 fired on Jap barges making a hit. At 0200 Jap dive bombers missed us by 150 feet. Yet his bombs blew out plugs in our ejector lines which causes no end of embarrassment. We had about a foot of water in the forward engine room. Plugs which are used as safety measures in the line were simply blown out, threads and all, so we had to go to work and repair them. This bomb fell just opposite of the forward engine room which is the reason for the plugs being blown out. Fired at intervals all night on Japs on the beach. Now waiting for our convoy to catch up with us.

Joseph McNamara's diary captures the extraordinary peril in which naval vessels operated in the Pacific, even when they enjoyed good air cover. It also illuminates the difficulty of telling friend from foe and the high probability of accidents with friendly fire. At the end of October the Anthony *had been escorting reinforcements towards Bougainville. Before it reached its destination it was diverted to deal with a reported counter-attack by Japanese destroyers trying to land troops near Empress Augusta Bay. The* Anthony *and its sister ship, the* Hudson, *were raced for the area of reported Japanese activity. However, the enemy destroyers had disappeared and instead they had a dangerous encounter with a friendly motor torpedo boat and then endured friendly fire from Allied aircraft. A B-24 Liberator dropped a stick of bombs about 150 feet off the port quarterdeck. The crew of the* Anthony *made efforts to identify themselves to the aircraft when it came around a second time but were strafed from the stern to the bridge by 50 calibre bullets. At this point the* Anthony *returned fire and the Liberator disappeared. At the time of the attack, Joseph McNamara was unaware of the identity of the aircraft and so recorded it in his diary as Japanese. All parties escaped injury during this friendly fire incident, but such situations could be disastrous. A few months earlier, during the invasion of Sicily, US navy ships had opened fire on twenty-three American transport aircraft, killing some one hundred paratroopers. SEE ALSO PP. 741–4.*

Friday 5 November 1943

Tom Fagan, Australian POW, watches a Japanese search party miss four diaries in his camp on the Thai–Burma railway

If it wasn't for the few books being handed around I'm afraid we would all go mad. Some are too far gone, of course, to read. But those who can, read and re-read the volumes available. They won't last too long if someone is able to get tobacco. Even a lot of Bibles have gone up in smoke.

So many sick boys are crammed into this hut it is almost impossible to avoid shoulder to shoulder bed-spacing. The only time we get a bit more room is when deaths occur. Some days a few go almost at the same time, but it isn't long before more are brought in. We are all getting a bit blasé about the death rate. Oft times I feel it will soon be my turn, then an overpowering desire to get home pulls me back into reality and I am glad I had the willpower to overcome the temptation to give in.

The infestation of vermin is now at its height and there is little anyone can do to eradicate the plague. Rats, fleas – millions of them bugs and chats swarm everywhere. There is but one cure, burn the lot to the ground. The boys would, too, if there was a chance the Nips would supply bamboo and atap to rebuild. They won't; said so, and that is that.

A big search was bunged on yesterday and many treasures the lads had hidden were found and confiscated. I was lucky. Well, in a way. Immediately below my bedspace some orderlies had buried two pistols, some maps, a compass and four diaries. Had they been found I would have been tied to a post and now be a statistic.

Luckily, one of the orderlies indicated to the Jap that I was tuxan-bioki (very sick) with cholera. I've never seen a Nip move as fast as that bloke the moment the name of the dreaded disease was mentioned. I breathed a great sigh of relief; so did many others.

If they were after the wireless set they missed out. I don't know where it was secreted, only the operator was aware of that, and he, wisely, kept his own counsel. Last night we heard that Italy had tossed it in. Germany and Japan are still battling it out. But for how long is just a guess. We all hoped it would not be too long before the Axis Powers were a spent force. Had the 'nightingale' been found we would have been unaware of that very important happening.

Apparently the senior Nips had not passed the inform-ation on to their subordinates otherwise another rash of bashings would have broken out. To our surprise, nothing out the ordinary happened. In my opinion, they kept it quiet so that the lying propaganda newspaper would not be doubted by their lower ranks.

Although Tom Fagan did not have cholera, he continued to endure a long spell in hospital as a result of the serious ulceration of his leg. His diary records the remarkable ability of prisoners to hide a range of forbidden items within their camp, including a radio. This would have brought the news that Italy had surrendered in September 1943 and that on 13 October the Italian king, Victor Emmanuel, had declared war on Germany. The news that Italy had not only capitulated but had changed sides was extremely important for morale, and especially to Australian soldiers like Tom Fagan, many of whom had fought against the forces of Rome in the Middle East during 1941. Reverses of fortune in war often resulted in arbitrary beatings administered to the prisoners by the guards. However, as this diary demonstrates, the Japanese guards were sometimes less well informed about the progress of the war than their prisoners. SEE ALSO PP. 222–4, 442–4, 484–5.

Wednesday 10 November 1943

Seaman 1st Class James J. Fahey, on the cruiser USS *Montpelier*, comes across a raft near Treasury Island

James J. Fahey was an ordinary seaman from Florida who defied regulations by surreptitiously compiling a diary on scraps of paper and in secret when no-one was looking. This was not an easy task in the crowded confines of the mess decks of an American cruiser. During October and November his ship was providing fire support for marine operations on Bougainville. Meanwhile neighbouring aircraft carriers were attacking Rabaul.

All hands arose at 5 A.M. It's another very hot day. We had our first good meal in quite some time, the apple pie really hits the spot. This afternoon, while we were south of Bougainville and just off Treasury island, we came across a raft with four live Japs in it. Admiral Merrill sent word to one of our destroyers to pick them up. As the destroyer *Spence* came close to the raft, the Japs opened up with a machine gun at the destroyer. The Jap officer then put a gun to each man's mouth and fired, blowing the back out of each man's skull. One of the Japs did not want to die for the Emperor and put up a struggle. The others held him down. The officer was the last to die. He also blew his brains out.

The *Spence* went to investigate. All the bodies had disappeared into the water. There was nothing left but blood and an empty raft. Swarms of sharks were everywhere. The sharks ate well today.

Fighting for the Pacific islands was particularly savage, with high casualties on both sides. By 1943 the Japanese treatment of prisoners, and their own reluctance to be taken prisoner, were becoming well known. This rendered American servicemen wary of approaching even those Japanese who appeared to be defeated and unarmed. Fahey's diary underlines the importance of officers in enforcing the Bushido code, a set of unwritten samurai conventions developed in the seventeenth century that required soldiers to fight to the last. Japanese were more likely to surrender if they were isolated and not in the presence of officers or NCOs. In this case the Japanese encountered by the destroyer Spence *were troops who were attempting to escape advancing American forces on Bougainville, perhaps by trying to sail to nearby Treasury Island. Their raft had been equipped with a 7.7 machine-gun salvaged from an aircraft. SEE ALSO PP. 702–3.*

Saturday 27 November 1943

David Zellmer, dancer and US army pilot, joins in two bomber raids on Bougainville

As a young man in his twenties, David Zellmer had performed in Martha Graham's famous dance company in New York. From 1943 he served as a bomber pilot, mostly flying B-24 Liberator bombers from his base at Guadalcanal against targets in the South Pacific. During November 1943 his unit was flying missions against Japanese positions on Bougainville.

Koli, Guadalcanal, November 27 – I'm to fly on Ott's plane. Never met him, nor any member of his crew. I caress the little jade goddess Martha gave me to pin on my flying suit. Once I'm aboard, Ott tells me to stay on the flight deck for the take-off. I'm to ride down below with Hill, the bombardier, the rest of the trip. The only extra oxygen hookup is in the bombardier's compartment.

I kneel behind the co-pilot's seat when we start down the runway. I see splashes of first light creep along the bottom of the eastern sky as Ott climbs the plane slowly out over the bay. He then turns us a degree or two to the left, to put us on a course over the Slot that will take us to Bougainville, three hours northwest of here.

The bombardier's compartment is a cramped, noisy, windowless space below the flight deck and directly beneath the nose gun turret. Its ceiling is too low for standing. Switches and indicator lights and instruments cover the bulkhead on the left. The bombsight fits into a floor opening at the forward end of the compartment. Hill must lie flat on his stomach to use it.

I can look down on the sea through the clear Plexiglas floor directly in front of the sight. Hill identifies the islands as they come into view through the rising mists: Santa Isabel . . . New Georgia . . . Choiseul . . .

We're less than half an hour out from the target. Hill reminds me it's time to put on oxygen masks. We begin circling to find our place in the formation. My feet are freezing. Now we're flying due east, towards Bougainville. I see smoke slowly rising from a mountain peak far to the south. A volcano?

The formation slowly turns as one giant plane to begin the bomb run. From the catbird seat, I look down on Buka Passage, the narrow, glistening strait of rushing water separating Bougainville from Buka island on the north. Hill tugs at my arm and points to a tiny white slash in the mottled green-black landscape: Bonis Airfield, our target.

Hill is now lying full-length, peering into the bombsight. The plane shudders as the bomb bay doors slide open. Hill turns knobs and flicks switches. I see lights flashing on a panel to his left. Then I hear him on the Intercom: 'Bombs away!' I cannot see them fall. I look straight down at the Bonis runway and see a scattering of explosions. Several planes are on the tarmac, but none appear to be moving or attempting to take off. Puffs of black smoke brush the Plexiglas windscreen. I feel the plane jolt. Anti-aircraft shells are exploding all around us! Ott does not take evasive action.

I hold my breath. The propellers scream as they claw at the thin air.

Then, abruptly, the formation begins to break up. Each plane is on its own, all descending swiftly towards the other side of Bougainville and down over the waters of the Pacific. Ott aims us directly at the white-hot mirror of the rising sun. When we are only a few hundred feet from the ocean, he levels us off, then reverses direction in a great sweeping turn, holding the left wing nearly vertical. We head back towards Bougainville only slightly above the cresting waves.

The instructions given at last night's briefing called for us to return from Bonis along Bougainville's eastern coast, to fly single file at treetop height, and to shoot up all native structures we see; but no natives, no animals. We are meant to show the natives that allied forces, not Japanese, are still the boss on Bougainville.

We head south, following the palm-shaded strip of white sand, flying so low I can easily see the gunners' 50mm tracer shells streaming into the little leaf huts, setting fire to the thatched roofs, kicking dust after fleeing pigs.

I stare straight down through the Plexiglas floor and watch small naked black men stiffly standing, legs apart, shaking their fists up at us. One of the warriors lofts his spear. Another throws a stone.

David Zellmer's superb diary, which he describes as the journal of an 'artist as warrior', captures the incongruity of modern weapons of war deployed against a Pacific island paradise. What could one usefully bomb when confronted with a landscape that consisted of jungles, mountains and trees? Disturbingly, Zellmer and his colleagues were instructed to bomb native structures. Many pilots recorded their anxiety in undertaking this sort of action, since they had no way of knowing what, or who, might be inside them.

David Zellmer would return to the United States on October 1944, having completed a tour of forty-six missions as a pilot on the B-25 light bomber with the 13th Air Force. After the war he became a writer and broadcaster for CBS. Later in retirement he lived in Warwick, Massachusetts.

DECEMBER 1943

EARLY IN DECEMBER Churchill and Roosevelt returned to Cairo from their meeting with Stalin at Tehran for the third and final stage of this Allied conference. Here they continued their discussions on the war in Asia and the Pacific, but without the participation of Chiang Kai-shek. They agreed that Mountbatten's proposed amphibious operations across the Bay of Bengal against the coast of Burma should be cancelled to keep enough landing craft available for operations in the Mediterranean. China would later use this as an excuse to stall on launching new offensives. Decisions on northern Burma were also postponed, for while Chiang Kai-shek insisted he needed more supplies to fight the Japanese, few believed that he would actually launch any major offensive, whatever his supply situation. With regard to the Pacific, the Allies agreed that they would try to complete the capture of the Marshall Islands and New Britain by the end of January 1944. They expected to capture Hollandia, the last major island in New Guinea, in June 1944 and to be moving against the Philippines in late 1944. The Allies still remained uncertain as to when they should attack Japan's central Pacific base on the small island of Truk, Tokyo's equivalent of Pearl Harbor. On 29 December the US submarine *Sculpin*, on which Corbin Mendenhall had served, was sunk while reconnoitring the area around the vast base at Truk.

The Allied meetings in the Middle East during November and December had been paralleled by pan-Asian leaders' meetings chaired by Tojo at the Imperial Diet building in Tokyo. In attendance were Wang Ching-wei from China, Wan Waithayon from Thailand, Chang Chin-hui from Manchuria, Dr Jose P. Laurel from the Philippines, U Ba Maw from Burma and Subhas Chandra Bose representing 'Free India'. Interestingly, the keynote speaker was Heinrich Stahmer, a former German ambassador to China. Although they pledged themselves to ultimate victory, the direction of the war could not be disguised and the atmosphere was unavoidably gloomy.

On Bougainville a newly constructed American airfield came into operation, allowing a number of attacks to be made against hills that overlooked the beachhead. Highly effective Fijian troops took the lead in conducting reconnaissance well behind Japanese lines.

The major operation launched during December was MacArthur's drive from New Guinea northward on to the island of New Britain. On 26 December American, Australian and New Zealand forces landed at Cape Gloucester in New Britain, at the opposite end of the island from the Japanese base of Rabaul. For weeks B-24 Liberator bombers had pounded the landing area and now the invasion was accompanied by fire support from cruisers and destroyers. The invaders met almost no Japanese opposition and the main obstacle to establishing themselves was the extremely swampy nature of the terrain. Three days later they seized the Japanese airfield at Cape Gloucester with remarkably little trouble.

Sunday 5 December 1943

Leocadio de Asis, a Filipino police officer training in Tokyo, watches an operatic celebration of pan-Asian love

This morning I saw the first winter ice taken from the bathroom. Water easily freezes these cold winter mornings.

Tōhō Moving Picture Studio (Tōhō Eiga Satsueijo). At Setagaya, in the suburbs of Tokyo, at the invitation of Mr Hideo Oguni, author of 'Tear Down That Flag' and 'Bukang Liwayway,' we visited the Tōhō Moving Picture Studio, one of the biggest in Japan. Here we saw displayed many pictures of scenes from the latest picture about Bataan, 'Tear Down That Flag,' which will be shown shortly. We saw the different studios, including one where some scenes of this Bataan picture were shot. It was very interesting to see the different settings used for taking pictures. Artificial villages, trees, farms, etc. have been built within the big studio premises for 'shooting' purposes.

Before leaving the studio, we had picture-taking with

some local stars. Mr Oguni gave each of us a big photo of Norma Blancaflor, star of 'Tear Down That Flag.'

At the Opera 'Madame Rosaria.' We saw the much publicized opera 'Madame Rosaria' at the Kanda Auditorium (Kanda Kyōritsu Kōdō) at 6:00 tonight. This opera, which was highly advertised as a musical masterpiece which is another contribution to Filipino–Japanese cultural relations, was to us a flop. The title alone, spelled 'Madame Rosaria,' [originally Rosalia] shows a lack of research which would have avoided such a big blunder as misspelling the very title of the opera.

We were utterly disgusted when the character, Joaquin Navarro, supposed to be a typical Filipino *padre de familia* appeared dressed in *sarong* (*tapi*) looking more like a Burmese or Indonesian or anything else but a Filipino. The music, though, was rather nice and also the dance scenes performed by ballet dancers from a local dance school.

The story is about a Japanese naval correspondent engaged to an American lady, Mary, resident of Hong Kong. War between their countries forbids their love relation, and Tarō-san, the hero, refuses the love of Mary who in despair takes poison. Tarō-san goes to the P.I., meets 'Rosaria' who at once falls for the Japanese hero (which is not typical psychology of our Filipino women). In the various love scenes, 'Rosaria' may be seen really madly in love with the Japanese Romeo who in the latter part of the opera is seriously ill in bed. Unfortunately (or fortunately), Tarō-san dies, leaving the broken-hearted 'Rosaria' with a perpetual wound in her loving heart. She then dedicates her life as a nurse caring for the war sick, and later she, too, dies with Tarō-san's name on her lips.

The story purports to show the friendship between Japan and the Filipinos personified by Tarō-san and 'Rosaria'. It may be interesting to know that the original story by Mr Taijirō Gō contemplated a 'happy ending' with Tarō-san and 'Rosaria' getting married, but this did not pass the Board of Censors which preferred to see them both die.

We were utterly disappointed on seeing this opera which in our opinion does not represent true Filipino womanhood. Besides, we believe there was not much preparation and research put into this opera.

Leocadio de Asis's diary shows the cultural minefield that awaited the Japanese practitioners of pan-Asian propaganda. Most Japanese had little understanding of the south-east Asian territories into which their armies had moved, and in the Japanese domestic media their peoples were often represented as stereotyped 'natives' in a way that was notably similar to that found in the west. This diary entry also refers to a contemporaneous Japanese film called Tear Down that Flag, *starring the Filipino movie star Fernando Poe. Ironically, in more recent times Poe's son has starred in a film as a guerrilla leader working with the Americans against the Japanese.*

After the war, Leocadio de Asis would enter a private law practice and also taught in universities. Despite the infelicities of wartime propaganda, his mentors in Tokyo did everything they could to ensure that his experience was positive and it left a lasting impression. After a successful business career he became prominent in the Philippines–Japan Society. SEE ALSO PP. 460–2.

Thursday 9 December 1943

Admiral Sir James Somerville watches the dummy parachutists of 'Deception Division' with Peter Fleming

James Somerville was born in 1882 at Weybridge in Surrey. He joined the Royal Navy at the age of fourteen and by the First World War had become the leading naval specialist in radio. He became a rear-admiral in 1933 but retired through ill-health in 1938. At the outbreak of war he returned to the navy, serving at Dunkirk in 1940 and participating in the sinking of the Bismarck *in 1941. In 1942 he was given command of the Eastern Fleet, based at Ceylon.*

Proceeded out to the Bombing Range to witness a demonstration of dummy parachutists being dropped. This was most effective and the parachutists, although dropped quite close appeared to be life size, but on close inspection they were just wooden dummies, not more than 2' 6" with parachutes to scale. Dummy ammo canisters were also dropped, these being provided with time delay actions fireworks to represent rifle fire. Mortars etc. Colonel Fleming stated that at present 150 of these dummy parachutists could be released from one Hudson [medium bomber], and that it was hoped to raise this number eventually to about 350. The smoke bombs, delayed action very lights and other innovations were also demonstrated.

James Somerville was being treated to a demonstration of Britain's increasingly elaborate range of secret weapons, which included elaborate systems for decoy and deception. His guide was Peter Fleming, head of the secretive Deception Division within South East Asia Command. Peter Fleming was brother to Ian Fleming, who worked in naval intelligence and would later write the James Bond novels. The dummy parachutists described here would be employed successfully in 1944 during D-Day to divert German reinforcements away from the invasion beachheads. However, in Asia Japanese commanders rarely responded to warnings about newly arrived enemy formations. For this reason deception worked less well in Asia than in Europe. SEE ALSO PP. 696–7.

Friday 10 December 1943

Australian Corporal Tom Fagan admires the courage of nonchalant traders in his POW camp on the Thai–Burma railway

Tom Fagan had been moved to the 55 Kilo camp in November 1943 and on the last day of the month had eventually suffered the long-dreaded amputation of his badly ulcerated leg. At this point he weighed a little over 6 stone.

Some of my close mates I find hard to recognise, so changed are their features; sunken eyes, gaunt and fearful, they represent the last hold that separates living and dying.

Got to hand it to many of the boys here who are prepared to take their lives in their hands to go out on parties, meet up with the Burmese traders and barter for meat and fruit. They dare to do it in broad daylight. They do it, not for themselves, but their mates who are just hanging on to life by a thread.

They run two risks. If the Nips whack on a sudden body count and they are found to be missing, death, should they return, is what they will have to face.

On the other hand, the known treachery of those they chance to meet, most of them bounty-hunters, could have exactly the same result. Death by bullet or bayonet; they would be deemed to have been attempting to escape.

I have nothing but admiration for these game chaps. One Dutchman I was talking to said neither he or any of his countrymen would even dream of placing their heads on a block, even though such sorties might result in the obtaining of much needed food for the very ill. 'You Australians beat me', he said. 'Only wants one of the guards to change his pattern of patrol, and your friends will die'.

So far no-one has been caught, but the chances are they may go out just once too often. Those who do it are supposed to be the camp maintenance group and are known to the Nips. Some of them are so brazen they come out of the jungle almost on the heels of the patrolling guards. Only wants a Nip to turn around, catch one, and shoot on sight.

We who benefit from the activities of those courageous traders give only a mumbled 'thank you', when a piece of meat or a banana or two is given us. With all our possessions gone, what can we offer but gratitude? When I hear them say, 'she's apples, cobber; eat and enjoy it', I feel so very, very humble. A life risked for me and my mates.

Tom Fagan's diary captures the remarkable selflessness of most prisoners in the indescribable camps of the Thai–Burma railway. Many of those working in the hospital where he was long incarcerated were almost as helpless as himself, but continued to serve their fellow prisoners. The pressure had been reduced for the labourers on the 'railway of death' in September 1943 when the line was completed, allowing some prisoners time to sneak out.

The ingenious efforts of the camp doctors saved Fagan's life and he would survive to enjoy repatriation; he returned to Sydney aboard the Highland Chief *on 11 October 1945. SEE ALSO PP. 222–4, 442–4, 474–6.*

Tuesday 14 – Wednesday 15 December 1943

Sy Kahn encounters poetry and frozen strawberries in New Guinea

In 1942 Sy Kahn had been a studious and quiet eighteen-year-old American high-school student. By 1943 he was serving in New Guinea, the youngest soldier in his unit. Anxious that he might not live to see the end of the war, Kahn kept a detailed diary of his experiences. This journal was a place of personal retreat and reflection which he dubbed his 'foxhole of the mind'. He was acutely conscious that he was not allowed to keep a journal and could be disciplined for it under military regulations. His diary was often written in dark corners, late at night, in tents or on board the ships that he was required to unload. Although immensely thoughtful and a talented writer, Kahn was designated a labourer. He belonged to the 244th Port Company and documents the fatiguing work that he and his fellows undertook.

We were assigned to work in the coolers, and how nice it was to be cold again. It was probably the same temperature in there as it is at home now. We all remembered those starvation days, and we got even with the old ship. We were to unload foodstuffs!! Need I mention the consequences of this bit of luck. The first thing we took out were apples, and we each polished off three or four of those pretty quick. Most of us had not had breakfast, so there was plenty of room for what was to follow. In that same cooler were lemons and grapefruit, but they were not so popular. What a treat it was to have our fill of fruit – and ice cold. In our rummaging, between passing out 60 tons of apples, we found a 28-pound box of grapes, and that was devoured in no time flat. Being a grape addict, I took some! There, of all things, was a whole box of small candies. We all dipped big fists into that and stuffed pockets. We learned that it was candy for the crew for Christmas. Yes, we felt so sorry for the crew – who get back to the U.S. every couple of months. Then Rouse found a cold gallon of pineapple juice, and we made short work of that. I remember bursting out laughing and thinking that we were a flock of locusts descending upon the ripe fields. We moved out boxed chicken, a large liverwurst, salami, and a couple of large pieces of meat which we sent back because they were useless. We took what we could eat, and that's all.

It was funny, really funny, to stand in line and wait to see what would come out next. Then, all of a sudden out came a box of frozen strawberries! Can you imagine having frozen strawberries in New Guinea? They were delicious, and our stomachs had a treat that had been foreign to them for a long time. Never did anything taste so good as those strawberries. To add to all that we got during the day, there was a box of cheese, the one thing I did not get my share of. Also, somebody had a case of K-ration chocolate, so we polished that off. Later came ice-cold oranges. The sailors were moving them on their shoulders, a crate each. One of us suggested that one of the sailors could accidentally trip. One obliged heaving the crate to the floor, smashing it and spilling those beautiful oranges out. We all had from two to six apiece. Well, that took care of what we consumed, which was plenty of poundage . . .

I went to the library and got a book of poetry that I've had my eye on. I stole it, but I have no qualms about it because it was hardly read. This excellent collection contains not only comments on the poems, but information about poetry, metre and copies of original manuscripts! I could not leave it to the dusty shelves. So I managed to get it into my bag, which happily I had not left, along with my other books. It is exactly what I've been looking for. Also have in my possession *Berlin Diary*. Will somehow take it along in my pack if I cannot finish it. Denison stole a calculus book via the 'under-the-shirt' method.

Berlin Diary is fascinating and enlightening on Germany and pre-war intrigue. I am learning a lot about the politics, the game played by the democracies and their stupidity before the war. There were innumerable possibilities for nipping the war in the bud. At times I become exasperated at what I read. If all is true, it is difficult not to become cynical about this war.

Sy Kahn was busily employed unloading supplies in New Guinea. Living in a tented encampment, he moved with the forward supply base and so shifted location on average every three weeks. Although employed on rear area duties, his life was not without hazard, being continually subjected to air raids. His next destination was New Britain.

Kahn, like so many wartime diarists, avidly read other people's diaries, and in particular William Shirer's. Berlin Diary had reached no. 1 in the New York bestseller list during 1941 and was probably the average American's primary source of information about the pre-war Nazi regime. SEE ALSO PP. 508–10, 692–4.

Thursday 16 – Friday 24 December 1943

Clyde Berwick, an Australian army engineer, returns to Changi gaol for Christmas after a year working on the Thai–Burma railway

We disembarked about 12 noon and were all delighted to hear Changi was our destination. We boarded the trucks and moved through Singapore, along the East Coast Road, to paradise, or so it seemed.

A difference about Singapore was noticed by all of us with an air of prosperity seeming to be on the place with the improvements which had taken place since we'd left.

We arrived at Changi about 1:30pm and were billeted in huts on the opposite side of the road to Selerang, the old 11th Div area.

We were all running around like kids who'd just arrived home after a spell away. Any rate, about 3:00pm they called out the hospital patients and loaded us on trailers and we rode in style over to Selerang, which is now the hospital. All the men we struck in Selerang couldn't do enough for us and the orderlies were the same. We were given tobacco and cigars, coconuts and hot tea. After we had our particulars taken I finished up in the building that I was in when I was first in Selerang. I was on the top floor with beds and mattresses and it was lovely. We had our ulcers dressed and then received a very nice tea of rice, towgay, soya bean stew, a fish doover or veg pasties, it was No. 1.

The soft bed was such a change I was unable to sleep last night. Received more tobacco today, Friday 17th, the meals are good and medical treatment extra.

'H' Force, or 1000 of them, are in Singapore, they arrived just in front of us. 93% of 'F' Force have been through hospital. We are in quarantine here for a few days and will be pleased when it is lifted so I can see some of the boys.

Had a great meal last night of greens and stew, 2 pieces of fish, 2 fish doovers, 2 veg pies or 1 veg pastie. I finished up with a lovely hot bath and expect another one on Saturday 18th, today.

Things are going along very well and have seen Maurie and the other boys, they all look well and are looking after us.

More of 'F' Force have arrived down here.

No-one can realise what it is like being back here once more. All the lads are looking better, even in the short period that we've been in quarantine. Received news that the boys up at Kanburri are dying of malnutrition. We were amongst the first to go back to Changi, we had to volunteer, so we are pleased we got in first.

The ulcer is doing well today, Monday 20th, and looks very healthy. If it heals within 7 days I can save my foot.

Food is still very good and we hope we can get a good Christmas ration. On the 18th December I sent a letter card home, so hope it is received by the end of January, would be hopeless to say by Christmas.

My lucky day, the ulcer has recovered 100% . . .

Was discharged back to the unit on Thursday 23rd and had a nice tea back with the lads, though my discharge was due to a shortage of beds, they've had 533 admittances from 'F' Forces so far.

It's Christmas Eve and we are looking forward to a good Christmas. I received a lovely Christmas day present this morning, a letter from Mum, dated August 1st, 1942. I'm glad Mum, Dad and the family are all well.

Our Christmas cake was a bit of a failure, so they fried it and we had it for supper on Christmas eve. They say 'Christmas only once a year, be of happiness and good

cheer.' And we are certainly doing our best. Never thought
we'd have the Christmas we're having.

*Clyde Berwick had been taken prisoner early in 1942 and put to work
on the Thai–Burma railway. Once the railway had been completed in the
autumn of 1943, many of the POWs labouring on the line were returned
to Changi gaol in Singapore. This was a welcome change, for although
circumstances at Singapore were not luxurious, many of the dangers of
the jungle camps, including diseases like cholera, were less prevalent,
while food and medical attention were better. Berwick's weight began to
increase immediately; however, he would be kept in quarantine along
with the other returnees until mid-January. He would survive the war
and return to his family in Fingal near Melbourne on 11 October 1945.
SEE ALSO PP. 195–7.*

Friday 17 December 1943

Brian Gomme, Australian gunner, is awakened by a night intruder near No. 4 gun

Last night at about eleven o'clock when I was just dropping
off into the gentle land of slumber, I was startled rudely from
my midnight meditations by the ominous chatter of an owen
gun fired close at hand. I lay tense and alert for a moment
and started as another burst and then two more following
rapidly broke the stillness of the tropical night. All was quiet
for about five minutes but then a rifle shot rang out and then
three or four more at intervals. By this time I had taken stock
of the situation as best I could in the complete darkness and
had adopted an aggressive attitude outside my tent with my
rifle at the ready, awaiting any impending danger which
may be lurking stealthily through the kunai grass to my
front.

However, after waiting thus for some ten minutes or so,
the silence and tension were broken simultaneously by a
peal of uncontrolled laughter coming from the direction of
the disturbance. I learned later that a pig had ventured

within about four feet of the sentry on No. 4 gun and had met a sudden death at the hands of one gunner McCullough, who apparently collected him with the first burst. He had fired at the noise but had scored about half a dozen hits straight through the pig's forehead. The other shots came from various places as a result of the owen gun bursts. So you see what a pig can do. He was responsible for ourselves, 'B' troop and AA personnel close by losing about half an hour of well-earned rest. The dirty pig! Unfortunately for us, but perhaps fortunately for the pig, the gunners did not treat him then and there so that he won't be fit for consumption. A bit of fresh pork would not have been hard to take. He may have been tough, for he weighed about one hundred pounds and was no youngster, but I'm sure Lew could have made something of him.

In December Brian Gomme's unit was involved in a fierce battle at Fortification Point near Finschhafen as Australian and American forces consolidated their hold on New Guinea. Once the war had ended, Brian Gomme would continue his Pacific experiences by spending some time working for Lever Brothers in the Solomon Islands. He then returned to Sydney and ran two real estate offices before turning to cattle grazing in New South Wales. He is now retired and lives in Nambucca Heads. SEE ALSO PP. 437–9, 441–2.

Christmas Day 1943

Ernest Hodgkin, a former British civil servant and medical scientist, enjoys mail and a full meal in Changi gaol

When the Japanese attacked Malaya in 1941, Ernest Hodgkin was a British colonial civil servant, living with his wife Mary and their four children in Kuala Lumpur. As the Japanese had advanced rapidly through northern Malaya during January, Mary and the children were evacuated on a ship that made its way to safety in Perth, Western Australia. Ernest Hodgkin fled south towards Singapore and had eventually been interned.

Our second Christmas in prison! This time a year ago few of us thought we would have to spend another Christmas here, and now few feel confident that we will not be here for the next – though of course we all hope to be away soon. There is little to indicate that this is Christmas, one day is much like the next, and we have not been allowed the frivolities that last year marked it as a day apart; perhaps it is as well, anything that marks the passage of time only rubs in the futility of existence, the separation from you and all whom one loves. It is difficult to conceive how you and the babes are spending the holiday, perhaps at the seaside, I hope you are enjoying yourselves wherever you are, I can't imagine the babes doing anything else, bless them. It is two years now, I am afraid they will almost have forgotten me, at least Jonathan and Mickey will have, it is a rotten Daddy that does not give them Christmas presents and does not even write to them. How much longer will this stupid war last and keep us apart . . .

We have sent to and received from our lady friends [women internees] what little presents we could muster. I sent some needles and a tablet of Lux soap (beyond price these days) and received some Indian soap of a very powerful odour and some Brylcreem! There is no means of conveying one's thanks, they must be assumed. But the best Christmas present that any of us has had has been our letters, they arrived in the camp three months ago but were only delivered two days past, nevertheless we are very glad of them though they are so old. Only one from you, dated Aug 29th, 1942, no news -- but what is there to tell except that you and the babes are well and of that you leave no doubt. I could wish that you told me of yourself, but it wouldn't be you if you did, and I suppose you would say if there were anything wrong . . .

I am sorry to have to admit it, but the highlight of the day is that we are full, our bellies are distended, we have had as much as we can eat, not with the gentle fare that one is used to eat on Christmas Day, but much better than we have seen for a long time, and enough! Breakfast was the usual watery mixture of rice and crushed soya bean; for lunch mountains of dry rice, chicken curry (2 men to a tin instead

of the usual 10) and a good thick vegetable broth, after which
our kongsi [group] produced Christmas pudding and custard
– food fit for a king! For supper sweetened rice pudding (with
prunes for the kongsi), buns, honey and ersatz butter; and
there is still rice left over for tonight if anyone has room for it.

*Ernest Hodgkin maintained a diary for his wife and young family, with
whom he could not communicate; meanwhile he contented himself
with the knowledge that they had escaped and not joined the many
women and children also detained in Changi. Conditions were bearable
in Changi but not luxurious, with increasing pressure on space as new
internees and prisoners continued to arrive. Food was reasonable,
especially over Christmas, because of the distribution of some Red Cross
parcels, but the cost of black-market goods was rising, with tobacco at
one point reaching an incredible price of one dollar per cigarette. In late
1943 there were instances of the opportunistic local vendors being held
up and relieved of both their cash and their stocks of cigars.* SEE ALSO
PP. 536–7.

Late December 1943

Rena Krasno, a Jewish teenager in Shanghai, enjoys spontaneous friendship in the garden

*Following their eviction in July 1943 Rena Krasno's family had moved
to a boarding house with a tyrannous landlady whom Rena dubbed 'The
Monster'.*

Our landlady The Monster was gone for the day and my sister and I took advantage of her absence to play on the lawn
with her much abused Scotch terriers. In our neighbors' yard
(the villa has been taken over by the Japanese Navy), two
officers who looked like teenagers were reclining on canvas
chairs, their shirt collars open to the unexpectedly warm
winter sun. As we romped with the dogs, they approached
the bamboo fence separating our properties and peered at us
between the sticks, smiling broadly. After some discussion

between themselves in Japanese, they started picking faggots off a pile of firewood and flinging them over to our side, in a generous effort to help us overcome the general fuel shortage. My sister and I quickly gathered the wood, waved at our benefactors shouting the words we remembered from our vacations in Japan: *'Domo arigato!'* ('Thank you very much!') A happy moment of spontaneous friendship between young people. I HATE HATE HATE this War!

Although Krasno's family, which was of Russian extraction, loathed the occupation they did not hate Japan, where they had spent some time living happily before the war. By contrast, they feared Germany and were always anxious to read in the newspapers of any extension of contact or influence by visiting German dignitaries in Tokyo. Rena's own attitudes were increasingly those of an internationalist pacifist and prefigured the anti-war youth solidarity that would emerge more widely in the 1950s and 1960s. SEE ALSO PP. 273–4, 419–20, 665–6.

1944

'THE JAPS MADE AN intensive search yesterday, turning us out of our barracks at 9 a.m., without any warning. All the doors were guarded, goodness knows why, for we have few possessions to hide! Fortunately, I was able to grab my chair which held this diary concealed in the seat, – and was permitted to sit on it, – being an invalid.'

Nurse Hilda Bates in Kuching internment camp in Serawak, north-west Borneo, diary entry for 17 December 1944

JANUARY 1944

IN NEW BRITAIN THE recently arrived US 7th Marine Regiment continued to fight to expand its beachhead at Cape Gloucester. As with most amphibious attacks, the predominantly American invading force found that their landing had been unopposed, but beyond the beachhead the terrain proved immensely difficult and Japanese resistance around the airfield at Cape Gloucester was strong. Nevertheless, by the end of January the Americans controlled all of western New Britain and had mounted an especially heavy attack on the Japanese base on the north-eastern end of the island at Rabaul, destroying eighty-three aircraft.

In New Guinea, Admiral Barbey's Task Force 38 landed troops at Saidor and quickly captured the airfield and the harbour, working in co-operation with Australian forces some 60 miles to the east. Australian and American forces worked particularly well together during this campaign. By 11 January the captured airfield had been put back into service as an Allied air base, enabling more intense air support to be provided for ground operations. This support proved vital as Australian forces made their way towards the town of Maukiryo during late January. Japanese forces were by now desperately short of supplies and this diminished their ability to fight major engagements.

In China, the nationalist government of Chiang Kai-shek was put under increasing pressure by the Allies to launch new offensives against the Japanese. Despite having been supplied with vast amounts of war material the Chinese forces had done little, conserving their strength for what they knew would be a long post-war struggle against Mao's communist forces, now located in Yenan. After vacillating for some time, Roosevelt finally backed General Stilwell in delivering an ultimatum to the government in Chungking, which effectively stated that unless there was fighting, American supplies would be discontinued. Chinese forces were vigorously engaging the

Japanese in Burma, but in China itself the fronts were remarkably quiet, a situation that suited all the local parties. Roosevelt also demanded that the Chinese put more troops into Burma. In southern Burma the British offensive continued to roll forward slowly in the Arakan area, where the town of Muangdaw was captured.

During January 1944 the Japanese mistreatment of POWs became a more public issue. Hitherto this had not been given much attention. This was in part because the Japanese had conspired to hide some of their worst offences from the inspection teams of the International Red Cross, and in part because the British government feared that reports of ill-treatment would be bad for morale. However, by early 1944 the reports of atrocities were too widespread to be ignored. The United States chose this month to publish a report on the 'Bataan Death March' of 1942 in the Philippines. Britain, the United States and Australia now reaffirmed their determination to hold war crimes trials to punish those responsible for such offences when the war was over.

During late January 1944 a number of new elements of the Royal Navy began to arrive in the Indian Ocean. This reflected the drawing down of the war in the Mediterranean and the improving situation in the Atlantic. The battleships *Queen Elizabeth* and *Valiant*, together with the carriers *Illustrious* and *Unicorn*, arrived at Colombo. These would be active in operations off the coast of Burma and the Malayan peninsula.

On the last day of January Admiral Spruance commanded a major offensive in the Marshall Islands, pursuing a classic island-hopping campaign through a series of small atolls and reefs. Majuro Atoll was taken and transformed into an important American base in preparation for further attacks against neighbouring Eniwetok. These islands were among a range of territories in the Pacific that Japan had owned before 1941, some of which it had been given at Versailles for fighting on the Allied side in the First World War. The rapid progress of this campaign alarmed Tokyo and led to growing instability in Tojo's government.

Saturday 1 – Monday 17 January 1944

Freddie Mathieson, transport driver with the Australian army, encounters a pimply-faced sentry at Manbulloo airfield near Darwin

A new day, a new year and still raining. Routine is on again, out to Manballoo [*sic*]. This time a little different. I am lead truck of six. The thing we have done countless times. As I get to near the entrance, I am surprised to see a pimply-faced youth in an American uniform jump out from bushes with a carbine and yell out in a squeaky voice: 'Halt!' Which I did. He came over and put the carbine in my face and said: 'What is the password?' After I told him where to stick the carbine, which he seemed to resent, I said 'What password?' He kept repeating 'What's the password?' A couple of the other drivers came up to see what was going on. He kept us all covered as I tried to explain that we have been delivering bombs etc. for over twelve months to the strip. Reply in his squeaky voice: 'What's the password?' So once more I told him where to stick his bloody carbine and suggested to the other drivers to return to camp as this clown may shoot someone. As a departing remark, I said: 'Tell your boss if he wants his "f—" bombs, he can come and get them.' Trucks we met going out turned them around too. Back at camp, I report to the boss and tell him what has happened. There are twelve trucks in camp now loaded with bombs and ammunition. I was in the orderly room when the boss made a phone call to the adjutant at Manballoo. I have never heard him go off like this. 'What the hell are you bastards doing out there. I will not have any drivers threatened by an idiot with a carbine and what is this crap about a password?' Delay, Commander on phone a misunderstanding, sincere apologies for what happened, will not happen again. Appears this pimply faced guard reported what had happened and what I had said about getting their own bombs. All sweet again. Delivered the loads to Manballoo, no guards. Saw a couple of the senior N.C.O.'s they could not believe what had happened and were all apologies. It seems a brand new Lt. 'ground staff' was posted out there two days ago and decided to make the place safe and without authority, set the guards at the entrance and the only people who knew a password were this Lt and the guard. I heard the Lt has been given a job where he can't do any harm, and the pimply face one back in the cookhouse. Some good rumours about at present. We are all keeping our fingers crossed.

Manbulloo airfield near Darwin hosted a large number of RAAF and USAAF squadrons. Its existence owed something to the reinforcement of the area following the bombing of Darwin in 1942. Relations between Australian and American forces serving together under General Douglas MacArthur in the South West Pacific Area were remarkably good. Indeed, many would assert that they were better than relations between MacArthur and his US navy counterpart, Admiral Chester Nimitz. Accordingly, the sort of incident described by Mathieson was regarded as a source of amusement. However, in Australia itself matters were more sensitive. Enemy propaganda played endlessly on the idea of well-paid Americans enjoying access to eager Australian women. Some of the diaries in this anthology suggest this was not always an inaccurate picture. More broadly, the Australian government was sensitive about American behaviour on its territory. United States officials had to tread warily for fear of charges of American imperialism.

Freddie Mathieson would survive the war and return to Sydney, where he married, worked in the motor trade and indulged his passion for motorcycles. SEE ALSO PP. 175–6, 215–16.

Wednesday 12 January 1944

John Nevell, an Australian gunner, is awakened in the night by shouting at a POW work camp near Kinsyoke on the Thai–Burma railway

You may note we have been off the air for a period. We have had changes, and now settled in a new camp. We are once more on the river, in the locality we were in when we first came up the railway line. We are about a hundred yards downstream from our original camp site. We had to porter our stores, tents, goods and chattels over the mountain, up the ladder and across the railway line, for about 4 miles. We had fairly light loads and for a few days, did two trips per day. We still send a party up each day to collect attap [coastal palms] to make shelters for a kitchen and sleeping huts . . .

Our officer groups are in temporary quarters just across from us, and at about 2:00 a.m. we were awakened by shouting. A Major was the instigator of the disturbance. He yelled 'There look! Grab him! There he is! Somebody get him!' By that time, the whole camp was awake. Another Officer touched his neighbour on the leg to waken him up, and he in turn threw his blanket over the other one's arm, grabbed it, and yelled 'Snake, snake! Quick, I've got him in the blanket.' They each hysterically grabbed each other's wrists through the blankets, yelling 'Snake, I've got him'. The original Major was still giving tongue in even louder, wilder yells. 'A man, you fools, a man! Grab him, don't let him go, there in the shadows', all the time pulling his own blanket tighter about him. At last, in desperation, he yelled 'Bugger you, I'll do it'. He scrambled out of bed, threw himself at a black stump on which another officer had hung his shirt and hat before going to bed. The camp finished up in an absolute uproar.

Every time an officer is sighted today, you will hear someone say, 'There he goes! Grab him.'

John Nevell would be moved from Kinsyoke to Japan in July 1944 and would remain there until he was rescued in late September 1945. His rescue was delayed by six weeks because the route to his camp on Kyushu Island had been devastated by the atomic bombing of Nagasaki.

After the war John Nevell returned to Australia, married and was given a 30,000-acre sheep and cattle ranch through the Soldiers' Settlement Scheme. SEE ALSO PP. 327–9, 353–4.

Thursday 20 January 1944

Tom Forsyth, a Canadian POW, on discipline at Camp
Niigata 5B in Japan

Atrocities in 5B, Niigata, which I personally witnessed. I saw
two men, Tetman, an American and Mortimer of the Royal
Rifles tied to stakes one evening in midwinter, snow on the
ground, clad only in shirt and trousers, barefooted, bare-
headed, hands behind their backs, about 6 feet of slack rope
to let them run around the pole which they did all night to
keep from freezing . . .

Military discipline amongst the Japanese armed forces is
invariably some form of corporal punishment administered
on the spot. While in Hong Kong, in North Point Camp, I
remember an officer making the rounds and the guard being
lax on duty. The officer called him stiffly to attention shouting 'Kiotski' then using the flat of each hand alternatively on
the sides of the man's face, [slapped him] in the regular side-
ways round house delivery till he was panting with the
exertion, and the private's face was red and swollen.

In our camp at Niigata when the camp commandant
became enraged, just for instance if his bath was cold, he
called the orderly Sgt and administered a thorough
drubbing, he in turn beat up the corporal, who retaliated on
the private, and the private had no-one to vent his spleen on
but the prisoners. So he hastened to the huts and if he
couldn't find an excuse easily, why he didn't bother looking
for one. We had no chairs but were expected to sit upright in
a stiff unnatural manner on our sleeping platforms while
eating . . . The guards (privates) used their rifle butts if they
saw us reclining at mealtimes. They delighted in calling us to
salute them many times. 'Kiotski' 'Kerai'.

*Forsyth and his friends endured a terrible winter in Niigata in early
1944. At this camp POWs were used to unload coal coming in by boat
from Manchuria. Some POWs who worked in the coal yard would try to
smuggle away individual lumps of coal for cooking purposes. Rice was*

rarely available and they were mostly fed a kind of millet seed that was hard to digest. This was supplemented by grasshopper – 'I always ate my hoppers head first and gave the head a good crunch' – and snails, boiled and extracted from the shell using a short piece of wire. Out of the 300 Canadians who arrived there, seventy-five died in just four months from overwork, exposure, brutality or disease. When the camp doctor remonstrated with the commandant about the conditions, he laughed scornfully and said there were 'toxon cheesi hookoo' (plenty of little wooden boxes) to hold the cremated ashes of those who died. Forsyth's telling observation here is the manner in which Japanese military brutality affected the Japanese soldiers as well as the Allied POWs. SEE ALSO PP. 180–1, 433–4, 802–3.

Friday 21 – Monday 24 January 1944

Navy surgeon Tetsuo Watanabe retreats with his starving men along the coast of New Guinea

Tetsuo Watanabe began his naval career as a newly commissioned naval surgeon in Hong Kong. He later transferred to the torpedo ship Hiyodori, *operating in the Solomons, and finally to a naval unit in New Guinea. While serving on the* Hiyodori *his ship was bombed and he suffered a wounded jaw from a piece of shrapnel. Later, in Rabaul, Tetsuo's jaw was operated on in hospital and here he met soldiers and marines who had escaped from Guadalcanal and were suffering from malnutrition. In late 1943 he arrived at Sio, New Guinea via submarine I-181, probably one of the last naval vessels to reach the stranded garrison there. Watanabe joined the 82nd Naval Garrison, where his first task was to decide which of the groups of sick and wounded could begin the retreat along the north coast of New Guinea.*

21 January
Preparation for retreat. Surgeon Ikeda came to consult me about wounded soldiers who would not be able to march. I told him that a submarine pick-up was scheduled for the following day, but the allocation for navy personnel was only three to four men. Although the patients were given first priority for the ride, it was rumoured that some healthy

army soldiers always cut in. So, we decided that we would carry all wounded navy men to the beach and negotiate with the submarine commander face to face.

I copied the map, which illustrated the retreat route, in headquarters. I was told it would take around one and a half months to reach Madang. The 51st Division and the naval units planned to cross Finisterre Range, followed by the rear-guard of the 20th Division.

22 January

The commander said that headquarters received a telegram from the commander of the Type-I-171 submarine saying that the submarine had arrived in the waters near Gali and tonight he would make every effort to surface in order to deliver provisions for the retreating troops.

I told twenty patients, who were able to walk, to start marching early in the morning so that they would not be left behind during the retreat which was to start tomorrow. They were so skinny and weak that they could hardly stand straight. I doubted they could endure the one and a half month march to Madang. Those who were seeing them off could not utter a word, knowing the walking patients' very slim chance of survival. How could a doctor send off his patients like this? I handed several malaria tablets to each patient. Every patient made a last salute to the commander and started toddling in one line and disappeared into the deep jungle. At 20:00, the submarine surfaced. The supplies of provisions finally arrived. Seventy five tons of rice were unloaded. And thanks to Surgeon Ikeda's tactful negotiation, all wounded navy patients were able to get a ride. At mid-night one *sho* of rice was rationed.

23 January

The patients who could walk somehow left yesterday, but patients who could not walk had to be left behind. Early in the morning I went to the field hospital with an adjutant. The patients saw us vacantly but never spoke. Some seemed to have realised what was going to happen to them. The adjutant covered each patient with a new blanket. I left a grenade by the pillow of each patient as I was ordered to. I could not stop tears coming out of my eyes; I lamented such a duty for a doctor.

We started retreating today. The retreating troops were formed into:

The 1st Echelon: the 51st Division about five thousand soldiers.
The 2nd Echelon: the naval units about four hundred soldiers.
The 3rd Echelon: the 51st Division about one thousand five hundred soldiers.

The 1st Echelon had left yesterday without waiting for the arrival of the submarine last night. The 2nd Echelon was going to leave today. And the 3rd Echelon would leave tomorrow. The naval units consisted of the 82nd Garrison (Captain Ukai), the N.85 Garrison (Captain Tsuzuki), the 7th Base Unit Headquarters (Surgeon-Sub-Lieutenant Ikeda), the 85th Signal Corps (Lieutenant Tajima) and a part of the Sasebo 5th Special Land-Battle Unit. The 82nd Garrison had about one hundred and fifty soldiers, out of whom twenty four were from an auxiliary platoon. The Garrison's officers consisted of four superior officers: Surgeon-Lieutenant Watanabe (myself), Paymaster-Sub-Lieutenant Ando, Surgeon-Midshipman Mochimatsu and Paymaster-Midshipman Furuie. There were three petty officers in the medical section, fourteen in the paymaster section and three in the signal section.

I packed in my rucksack two *shos* of rice, rations for two meals, two packets of biscuits, taro for one day, salt, powdered soya sauce, medical instruments, medicines, bandages, rubber-soled socks, straw sandals, rubber sheets, two summer shirts, a book (*Naika-shinryo no jissai* [The practice of internal treatment] by Nishikawa), a stethoscope, a torch, matches, candles and a rain coat. On top of them I put in two grenades, a pistol and a sword. They too did not seem to be sufficient for a one-month march which would include crossing the range, but I could not carry more with my present physical strength. The march plan depended on collecting food from natives' gardens en route.

At 11:00, we left Gali, Good-bye, Gali camp! The enemy

might have noticed our retreat. The sound of shelling was closing in. We started the walk on a terribly muddy track. Soon Paymaster-Seaman Okada collapsed suffering lack of blood caused by malaria. His face turned pale and bloodless. He tried to say something while in the arms of his comrade. Soon red liquid began to flow from his mouth. He bit off his tongue to kill himself. He used to tell me, 'Surgeon, please come to my *sushi* bar in Shinjuku when we return to Japan'. He knew his destiny and did not want to be a burden to his comrades. He was only nineteen years old.

Although we struggled on the horrible track, we managed to find a camp site about two kilometres inland. Upon arrival at camp all superior officers were summoned, and the supreme commander, Captain Ukai, repeated instructions about the march. The site was fouled by excrement left by the 1st Echelon that had camped here yesterday. Indeed, it was very difficult to find a clean place to put up a tent. However, when I observed the excrement, which consisted of green fibres and yellow viscid liquid, the soldiers appeared to be eating only grass or roots of trees of low food value. I made a bed of grass and used a stone as a pillow. I was exhausted and had a good sleep.

24 January

We departed early in the morning. I felt refreshed because I slept well. It did not rain last night, and so did not disturb my sleep. We came to the beginning of the mountain trail at last. The jungle was so dense and it was dark inside. I started walking without thinking anything, just looking at the backside of the soldier in front. It was a terribly sheer slope which reminded me of the climb from Nakabusa Onsen to Mt Tsubame in the North Alps. By the track dead bodies were scattered, reeking a horrible putrid smell. Maggots were wriggling in their eyes, ears and mouths although some soldiers were still breathing. This area literally looked like hell. Those who had perished on this climb must have exhausted their last strength in their already skinny and bony bodies.

Tetsuo Watanabe's desperate retreat from Sio up to Madang and then to Wewak took almost six months and involved crossing some of the most inhospitable and difficult terrain in the world. The party encountered mountains, ravines, rain forest and swamp. There were no supplies, and the paths were littered with the corpses of Japanese soldiers. Many died miserable deaths from starvation, disease and insanity, killing themselves or asking to be killed. In addition, the columns of troops were bombed and strafed wherever they were visible from the air. SEE ALSO PP. 551–4.

Wednesday 26 January 1944

John Gaitha Browning, US soldier and an artist, explores Tami Island off the New Guinea coast

The population of the island consisted of six pigs, a hen, and a rooster. All of the natives had gone either to the mainland or to the larger of the three islands. The old sow we called 'Jeraldine', her four shoats were 'the children,' the small pig was 'the baby.' The latter was about the cutest thing in pig form I ever saw, while the shoats and Jeraldine were the same sort of razorbacks that roam Arkansas by the hundreds. The little fellow wasn't more than ten inches long and as striped as a chipmunk. The alternating, dark brown and rust-colored stripe started at his tiny head and continued the length of his body to his curly tail, interrupted only by a white band around his middle.

Jeraldine begged for food and seemed to have been a pet. We gave her various things, all of which she ate noisily, except for our hardtack crackers, at which she turned up her piggish nose and slowly walked away.

The hen and rooster scratched around all day. He was a cheerful fellow, red with white neck and bronze tail; she, a quiet brown lady. The peculiar thing about them was their family relationship. One would suppose that one hen and one rooster on a deserted island would be an ideal couple, but apparently not here. Each evening he escorted her up the island and soon came back alone to the kitchen shack, where he roosted on a high pole. At dawn he crowed lustily, got down, and went off up the island, soon returning followed

by the hen. This happened each day, and we soon concluded
that all was not as well as appearances indicated.

The second day I took a flashlight and decided to look into
the coral rocks where there were bound to be caves – an old
habit I formed with Cliff Pouncey long ago on Gibbons
Ranch, where we poked into every crack of rock and often
found interesting things to repay us for our efforts. Toward
the east end of Tami the rocks rose steep and rugged, and
soon I found large crevices and small caves formed by
'blubbers' in the coral formation. One of these ran into a
room of considerable size – completely bare and apparently
never disturbed by human feet.

At the rear of it I noticed a hole not more than thirty inches
in diameter, and it had a challenging look which I couldn't
turn down. I took the flashlight, squeezed through and came
upon what may be the most interesting find of my life.

Here was a room about ten feet across, at the back of
which was a long shelf supported by poles. On this shelf
rested a variety of native equipment. Several large and
beautifully carved wooden ceremonial bowls with weird,
half-human figures and queer animals in fine carving. A
huge shell horn with a lining of the brightest coral red. (Had
it been used to call the tribe to ceremonials?) A string of
ninety fishnet floats of wood, many of them carved on both
sides. (Perhaps the symbols were to lure the fish into the
net.) Straw baskets and such work were falling apart, for
even though the cave was dry, the low island air is very wet
and penetrates everything. Clay cooking pots were in good
shape, but something I could never hope to get the far
distance from Tami to Texas.

Here was a movie plot come to life, with the things
collectors and students of native lore dream of, but so
seldom see. It was a once-in-a-lifetime experience! Almost
reverently I took up the shell. It had a round hole about the
size of a quarter in the side up towards the end of the spiral.
Most of them I have seen have the end cut off instead. Never
in my life had I been able to blow a conch shell, but I put this
one to my lips and blew. A deep, clear sound came out – to
my surprise – and I had blown a conch for the first time!
Maybe this one was easier, or maybe the gods of Tami had

seen my bare feet, my brief khaki shorts, and the flaming hibiscus in my cap and accepted me as a lover of the tradition of the islands and their magic beauty. At any rate I blew . . .

These things of Tami were made when men had time to be happy. Time – that most precious possession! Tami's people were free to create beauty from a block of wood, a chunk of clay, a bundle of grass fiber. Behind them were generations of free and happy islanders who each gave to successive generations some of their love of Tami and its surroundings.

Now the lagoon was brilliant green with purple patches and streaks of golden sunlight, bounded by the curve of white surf at the reef. Beyond the reef the sea was blue all the way to the hazy mountains of New Guinea. A white puff of cloud was poised above. These are the things of Tami I will remember when I look at the handicraft in years to come.

John Gaitha Browning was an accomplished artist and prided himself on his interest in the peoples and cultures of the Pacific. He decided to take two of the bowls 'together with a number of other things'. Back at camp his fellow soldiers thought the things odd and expressed little interest. They suggested that he was collecting because he could sell the material when he returned to the United States. This made Browning furious, not only with his comrades, but with 'the whole of our money-minded civilization which moulded [them]'. Today, however, we might more readily recognize the acquisitive western spirit in Browning's raid on the secret native sanctuary. SEE ALSO PP. 374–5, 605–6, 622–3.

Saturday 29 January 1944

Sy Kahn, a US soldier in a logistics unit, is troubled by the smell of burning clothes in New Guinea

In the past few days I've seen terrible things. I've seen the wounded and shellshocked come back from New Britain, and if this sight could be seen by the people at home, it would shorten the war by many months. It's not very pretty to see what war does to men. The most horrible event I have ever witnessed was when I recently saw a soldier burn to death at my feet. I was in charge of a detail when an explosion occurred about 60 yards in front of me. A huge sheet of flame burst forth, and for a moment I thought a barrel of gas exploded. Then suddenly out of the flame came a man, a human torch. He ran about 20 yards and disappeared behind some boxes. For a moment I was stunned, then I remembered saying, 'My God, the man's burning alive.' I ran toward the man. When I got there he was lying face down in the sand. As I knelt down I could just hear his voice in an agonizing whisper saying, 'Help, help.' He was a MP. Another man was there before Morales and I. It was horrible. His whole body was smoking, smoke coming even from his eyes. All his hair burned off. His face had screwed into a supreme agony and burned livid white and red. I began to cover him with sand to shut off the oxygen, but the smoking could not be stopped. The pain and his still-burning body were cracking his mind. He made little sound.

Soon there was a crowd and in a few moments a doctor and ambulance. When the doctor got there I stepped back. They rolled him over, and as soon as the air hit the front of his body, he burst into flames again. Because an incendiary grenade, that he had been fooling with, exploded in his hands, the chemical splattered his entire body and made of it a human torch. This chemical was nearly impossible to extinguish. When they rolled him over to get him on the stretcher, his stomach, testicles and penis were afire. Flames were licking around his body, and his boots began to burn. God, it was horrible, the smell of burning flesh and seeing it burn. Luckily I had stepped back when they rolled him over, or I would have been burned as were several of the men helping. The doctor's arms were burned also, but he stayed right in there, yelling for blankets and more blankets to wrap the burning man. The blankets began to burn. Finally the flames were smothered, but the blob of a near-corpse continued to smoke. The burning mass was lost in a confusion of thick smoke, flames and scampering men. The doctor stayed right in there. They finally got the flames out and cut off his clothes.

I knew he was dying. They got him in the ambulance and

took him away. The stench and, on the ground, his still-burning clothes and blankets remained. I turned away much unnerved by seeing a man burn to death within arms' reach and able to do so little in this hopeless situation. His pain must have been indescribable, though probably he was now unconscious. He died that night.

And men use these grenades against one another in wartime – and flame throwers. Civilized world! For the rest of the afternoon I was physically ill and shaken. This man had come to New Guinea to meet a horrible death. I never want to see such a sight or such a face. They haunt me. Now, whenever I smell burning clothes or rags, it makes me ill. However, in the past few days I have been able to harden myself to the memory. It is the first time I have seen a man meet death violently and terribly in front of my eyes. The clothes on the ground had burnt skin stuck to them. I'm afraid that sight and the smell of burning clothes will continue to haunt me. (Good, it is raining). Perhaps this is only the beginning of what I shall soon see.

*In January 1944 Sy Kahn had been moved forward to support oper-
ations in New Britain and was filled with apprehension about being
closer to the front. Nevertheless, he did not expect to see an incendiary
grenade casualty among the military police and stores sections in his
location. The grenade that killed his compatriot was probably filled with
a phosphorous slurry and so reignited even after the fire had been
extinguished. Incendiary weapons were extensively used in the Pacific
campaign for the clearing of caves and bunkers. The first use of napalm
would occur on 23 July 1944, during pre-invasion air strikes by the
Allies on the island of Tinian, part of the Mariana Islands chain in the
Pacific. Napalm was also used against Japanese cities. Kahn spent most
of January unloading transport ships that were ferrying supplies for the
5th Marines. SEE ALSO PP. 486–8, 692–4.*

FEBRUARY 1944

T HE MARSHALL ISLANDS were conquered by American forces during February 1944. On Kwajalein Atoll the Japanese lost over 8,000 troops who fought to the death, while only 265 surrendered. In contrast, American losses were very low – only 370 killed during this battle – owing to the use of heavy support weapons. Later in February, when Eniwetok Atoll was captured, only 66 prisoners were taken out of an original defending force of over 3,000. American forces became increasingly skilled in the patient use of bombing, artillery and incendiary weapons to reduce Japanese defences before advancing. Elsewhere garrisons were cut off and literally starved into submission. The remaining Japanese bases in New Britain were surrounded and then, in some cases, simply bypassed. In New Guinea, American and Australian forces finally linked up near Saidor.

In Burma, the British had their first significant victory in battle against the Japanese. On 4 February the Japanese launched a large-scale counter-offensive in the Arakan region. Some British forces were isolated and had to be supplied by air. The 7th Indian Division eventually repelled the attack. In London and Washington, arguments continued over the strategy to be pursued in Burma. American commanders tended to favour action in the north to free up further supply lines into China. In contrast, British commanders, and Churchill in particular, tended to favour a southward strategy, liberating key imperial cities such as Rangoon by means of amphibious operations along the coast. This would point the way towards the recovery of Malaya, a sentimental imperial objective for London planners. Within the British army a number of 'renegade' middle-ranking officers championed the idea of more behind-the-lines raiding, in the style of Orde Wingate's Chindit operations. Although Wingate was supported by Churchill and Mountbatten, he was detested by most regular army generals for his self-important attitude.

In China, American officials attempted to apply additional pressure on Chiang Kai-shek's government to act against the Japanese by asking its permission to send a mission to visit the Chinese communists in Yenan. Some American officials believed that the communists would provide a more effective anti-Japanese force. In reality, neither Chinese faction was much interested in fighting the Japanese and both were content to await Japan's defeat by the Americans now pressing across the Pacific.

American warships had begun to move around the Pacific with much greater freedom. Carrier forces raided at will, attacking Japanese bases on Truk and other outposts in the Mariana Islands. On 16 and 17 February a massive attack was launched on Truk using six battleships and nine carriers. Remarkably, US warships now sailed with impunity to northern Japan and bombarded the island of Paramushiro, underlining Tokyo's inability to protect the home islands. The extent to which the government in Tokyo now felt itself to be under pressure was signalled by Tojo's decision to take over the position of Army Chief of Staff, effectively sacking Field Marshal Sugiyama.

Sunday 6 February 1944

Kiyoshi Takeda joins the Imperial Japanese Navy and feels himself enter a spiritual void

Kiyoshi Takeda had been a student of literature at Tokyo University. In December 1943, at the age of twenty-one, he was called up to join the navy and the following month was assigned to the anti-submarine defence school near Kurihama. When he joined up he approached the barracks wearing the Japanese flag across his shoulders, which was a traditional display of patriotism on entering the military.

I entered the barracks on the 9th December wearing the flag round my shoulders. That is not two months ago: two months of hectic agitation, during which I have had no time to think. I gave myself up to a number of physical activities which had been completely unknown to me until then. My mind became a blank. During my military career my chief experiences were the physical and moral sufferings which I had to undergo: cold and fatigue, boredom and the longing to read, hunger and its attendant obsessions occupied me all day long. It is a humiliating avowal, but I believe that I must make it in order to be frank.

Now, when I read the papers in barracks, the brutal war news does not affect me in the same way as it used to do before I was called up. While I was a civilian I attempted to ponder and to adopt a personal point of view towards war and its atrocities. But I have not even had time to think since I joined the navy. It is no longer a question of reasoning or adopting a position. From morning to night I am oppressed, exhausted by physical exercises. My life has become empty and passive. I imagined that this would pass in time. After two months, the physical suffering abated a little and I felt myself relieved.

Nevertheless, I was far from having found a meaning in this kind of life, and then I had the impression that my mental faculties were paralysed. I never ceased repeating to myself that my body was weak and my spirit fragile. When I entered the navy I had decided beforehand to become a *spiritual void*. I wanted to do away with all my conceptions of life. It would have been impossible to adapt them to the rules of military discipline. I wanted to begin my new life in the navy by concentrating on the physical problems with which I would be faced.

Kiyoshi Takeda's diary records his feeling of being dehumanized by military training and he responded to this with 'a terrible need to read'. He focused on the writings of Buddhist thinkers who condemned war. He was nostalgic for his leisurely days as a student and frightened at the thought that the enemy had begun to attack Saipan. It was already clear to him that Japan was losing the war and that many of his friends already sent into action had 'vanished like the clouds'. He would not survive the war and died fighting off the island of Saichu near Korea in April 1945.

Monday 14 February 1944

'Dusty' Rhoades, General MacArthur's personal pilot,
visits the battlefield at Soputa Track near Sanananda in
New Guinea

*In 1942 Weldon E. Rhoades – known to his friends as 'Dusty' Rhoades
– had been a civilian airline pilot. By October 1943 he had become
the personal pilot to both General Douglas MacArthur and his Chief
of Staff, General Richard K. Sutherland. Piloting MacArthur's personal
aircraft, a B-17 bomber named* Bataan, *he enjoyed a ringside seat
during some of the most important developments in the war in the
south-west Pacific. Well before this interesting assignment he had
begun to keep a full diary. By February 1944 he was located at Oro Bay,
New Guinea, close to the scene of recent fierce fighting at Sanananda
Point.*

Dusty Rhoades

Today was one of the most instructive days I have ever spent. Early in the day Colonel Baedcke asked me if I would like to accompany him on a trip to the battlefield of the old Soputa Track near Sanananda Point. It was here that he engaged the Japs after his historic march over the Owen Stanley Range.

We drove about thirty miles in a jeep after I had outfitted myself with proper clothing and a gun. (Two Jap stragglers gave themselves up only last week, although this battle was fought fifteen months ago.) On our way we visited the American cemetery, which is located in a beautiful valley and is well kept, but which has all too many graves marked unknown. And in it lie only about 60 percent of our dead because the others could never be found in the dense jungle. We also visited the nearby Jap cemetery, which represents only a token effort on the part of the Australians to abide by international covenants. All of its dead are marked unknown, and what few grave markers have not been stolen by souvenir hunters have been drilled with many bullet holes by our own troops.

We came, finally, to the battlefield, and we set out through the dense jungle on foot. All of my ideas of warfare were upset immediately. This battlefield has never been cleaned up and still remains much as it did when the battle ended. The opposing front lines averaged only about fifty to one hundred feet apart, and the jungle growth was so thick that rifles were almost useless. All of the fighting, except for sniping from the trees, was done by mortar fire and hand grenades. The Jap pillboxes and our own foxholes are still there, although the jungle is rapidly obliterating the scars. The bones and skulls and equipment of the Jap dead lie about in great quantities, and even these last traces will not survive much longer. It gave me a strange feeling to probe among and walk over these bones of what had once been fanatical Jap soldiers, bent on the destruction of our boys for some strange reason which they probably never understood. Before the battle, if they had suspected that they would come to such a ignominious and unknown end here in this lonesome, stinking jungle, I wonder if they would have been quite so eager to die. I'll have to admit that I had no great compunction in walking over skulls. They seemed little different from animal remains. Our boys were in this battle-field for twenty-eight days, and the superior number of Japs was finally defeated, more by the will of our men to win than by any other factor.

During 1943 American and Australian forces had fought their way through thick jungle and over mountain ridges along a track that stretched from Sanananda. The terrain was some of the most difficult encountered by any fighting unit during the Second World War. As Rhoades recorded, a month later the jungle was already reclaiming the few open spaces, and signs that this had been a battlefield were disappearing. SEE ALSO PP. 628–9, 784–5.

Field Marshal Sir Alan Brooke struggles with various commanders and with Churchill to fashion a strategy against Japan

General Alan Brooke had been Commander in Chief Home Forces and in December 1941 was appointed Chief of the Imperial General Staff. His primary role thereafter was standing up to Churchill in arguments over strategy and guiding Allied strategic planning discussions relating to the war against Germany, Italy and Japan. His meetings with Churchill became more difficult as the war went on, since the Prime Minister was increasingly tired and reluctant to read his briefs or follow arguments in any detail.

In the afternoon Lumsden [British Liaison Officer with MacArthur] came to see me and was most interesting concerning conditions in the Pacific. Apparently Nimitz and MacArthur have never yet even met although working side by side! King and MacArthur are totally opposed in their plans. Marshall and King are frightened of MacArthur standing for presidency, Marshall hopes for vice-presidency and consequently won't fall foul of King. General opinion is that King has finished serving his useful period [as Chief of US Naval Staff], etc etc. All military plans shadowed by political backgrounds. God knows how this will straighten itself out!

At 5.45 usual Cabinet meeting which lasted till 7.50. Then 10 pm meeting with PM to listen to Wedemeyer's plan which he had brought back from Dickie Mountbatten [in South East Asia Command]. I had long and difficult arguments with the PM. He was again set on carrying out an attack on north tip of Sumatra and refusing to look at any long term projects or concrete plans for the defeat of Japan. Again showing his terrible failing of lack of width or depth in his strategic vision. He lives for the impulse and for the present, and refuses to look at lateral implications or future commitments. Now that I know him well episodes such as Antwerp and the Dardanelles no longer puzzle me! But meanwhile I often doubt whether I am going mad or whether he is really sane. The arguments were difficult as Wedemeyer and his party were of course trying to sell their goods, namely operations through the Malacca Straits and these operations entailed the capture of Sumatra which the PM wanted. But he refused to argue the relative merits of opening the Malacca Straits as opposed to working via Australia. After much hard work I began to make him see that we must have an overall plan for the defeat of Japan and then fit in the details.

The war against Japan was being directed in the field by four different theatre commanders: Mountbatten commanded south-east Asia; Stilwell commanded American troops in China; MacArthur ran the south-west Pacific; and Nimitz commanded the Pacific Ocean. These commanders, and various individuals in London and Washington, had very different ideas about how the war might be brought to a conclusion. Churchill in particular was more interested in the recovery of imperial possessions than a victory parade through Tokyo. SEE ALSO PP. 832–4.

Saturday 19 February 1944

Lieutenant-General Sir Henry Pownall, Chief of Staff at South East Asia Command, watches Mountbatten meet with Wingate in Burma

Like all of Mountbatten's subordinates, Pownall enjoyed vastly more experience than his commander. Pownall had been Vice Chief of the Imperial General Staff during 1941, and had then been appointed Commander-in-Chief in the Far East at Singapore in December 1941. After a spell with the ill-fated ABDA command in Java during early 1942, he was now at SEAC HQ in Ceylon.

Mountbatten . . . met Wingate at Imphal and as usual a crisis occurred. There was a very big flap . . . It arose from Mountbatten telling Wingate what our proposed strategy is, as carried to London by our party under Wedemeyer. This sent Wingate straight up in the air – he has been ruminating over continental operations right through to Bangkok – Saigon – along the south coast of China and so on. When he found out we proposed no such thing but rather give Burma a miss (as far as possible) and go southabout by sea he went through the roof . . . he wants the best of everything. If his operations are a success he wants all the réclame and most of the Army in India to be turned over to him to convert to L.R.P. [Long Range Penetration]. If he fails he wants to be able to lay the blame on someone else, saying 'I told you I wasn't being properly supported' . . .

I think that at last Mountbatten is beginning to see through him. I shouldn't be at all surprised if within the next three months it is proved that Wingate is bogus; at any rate he is a thoroughly nasty piece of work.

An eccentric and prickly character, Wingate was hated by army commanders and tolerated in Burma only at Churchill's express insistence. His operations were effective but costly to supply, being maintained entirely by air. Pownall was typical in his detestation of the man, but during March 1944 he would be forced to concede that a new phase of Chindit operations had done a lot of damage to the Japanese.

Wingate would die on 14 March 1944 when his aircraft crashed. However, his reputation lived on and had a profound effect on British thinking about irregular warfare, having shown what ambitious special force operations could achieve. Pownall would retire from the army in 1945 and died in 1961. SEE ALSO PP. 200–1.

Wednesday 23 – Thursday 24 February 1944

Jettie Bürger-Duyfjes, a Dutch civilian internee at Ambarawa camp on Java, observes a sinister interview process

Jettie Bürger-Duyfjes was born in 1913 in Limburg, the Netherlands. She married a doctor and moved with him to Poerwodadi in the Netherlands East Indies. Her husband, Wim, was called up as a medical officer at the outbreak of war, and in December 1942 Jettie was sent to Ambarawa women's camp as a civilian internee, along with her two small children.

23 February

Just now all women between the ages of 18 and 28 were called to the guard. Had to notify whether they were married and how many children they had. What is that supposed to mean? I hope they will not make the childless and unmarried plant paddy rice. Dreadful, every day there is something. Of course there are some strange rumours going around, about punish transfers etc.

24 February

Today some of the girls of yesterday have to appear again in front of the 'gentlemen'. The ones who look the best, that is to say, strong, plump and attractive, and who don't have children. Married doesn't matter, one who has two children was called again. Wisely, she took her children with her, and then after she was being asked if these truly were her children, was sent back! The rest had to go into the office, one by one, and tell them whether they were married or not, and again they were extremely rudely looked at and laughed at. Nobody knows what it means. When Mrs Jilderda asked about it, the Nip said, 'Tida apa; maoe tanja sadja!' (It's nothing; we just wanted to ask a few questions!) My neighbour is packing, she was there again as well. She is very nervous. F. wasn't called back, too ugly I presume. The latest news is that it is for a dinner on 8 March.

Every 8 March the Japanese celebrated the anniversary of the Dutch surrender. However, these sinister events had little to do with a forthcoming dinner. Ten girls were eventually taken from the camp by truck to a large house in the suburbs of Semarang. Here they were forced into prostitution. Many of them were very young and were raped with the utmost brutality, inevitably perhaps by the Japanese soldiers visiting the brothel, but also by the Japanese doctors who periodically inspected them for venereal disease. Jettie Bürger-Duyffes was unaware of their fate since they did not return to the camp. She herself would survive the war, as would her children. They were reunited with Wim in December 1945.

Late February 1944

Cecil Beaton, official war photographer, visits the Arakan front in Burma

Cecil Beaton was one of the most celebrated British portrait photographers of the twentieth century and became known in the inter-war period for his images of society elegance, glamour and style. His sensitive work exerted a lasting influence on photography. In 1939 he became an official war photographer, working initially on the home front and then visiting the desert in 1942. During 1943 and 1944 he worked in India, Burma and China. His war work is distinguished by an interest in and a humanitarian concern for the impact of war upon the indigenous populations of these countries that were ahead of their time.

Cecil Beaton

We came unexpectedly upon a battle. A picnic lunch in a ruined temple was interrupted by gunfire. While we climbed a flight of stone steps to discover what was happening, two over-life-sized black satin crows swooped down from the magnolia-trees and carried off the remainder of our meal. So we moved on, down a disused road, through an overgrown village, once bombed, now abandoned and looking like the precincts of the Sleeping Beauty: exotic creeping plants sprawled over the half-destroyed *bashas* and summer pavilions and over the gutted motor car still parked in its neat, cement garage. At the deserted farm, provisions were dumped in the courtyard – tins of bully beef and packages of biscuits lay among hundreds of small eggs, gourds and the exotic vegetation of the tropics.

A group of young officers, with serious expressions on their sunburnt faces, were discussing the situation. During the night some Japs had come down through a nearby jungle range and had taken up their former positions which, inadvertently, we had not filled before advancing any farther. Now this enemy group was dug into the earth snug as moles, and with a two-pounder gun previously captured from us was doing considerable damage to our rearguard. Several men had been killed, and the wounded at this moment were being brought back under fire. The stretchers were placed in the Red Cross ambulances, which the drivers manipulated on the rough roads with dexterity and compassion.

A young major appeared, his khaki battledress stained with dark, dry splashes of blood. 'We thought you'd been killed,' the other greeted him. 'Better have your arm seen to, and if you can cross that ridge, do so quickly and on all fours.'

Meanwhile, in the fields of paddy, Indian men accompanied by their naked children were still working, unmindful of the bursts of shrapnel. Bombing by air alone will send them seeking shelter.

Some of the major confrontations in south-east Asia occurred during early 1944, and it was during this period that the Japanese army in Burma was broken. As elsewhere, supply problems now dogged the Japanese. Their construction of the Thai–Burma railway using slave labour bore witness to the recognition that supplies would be the main problem in undertaking operations; this was also appreciated by their opponents, who used superior air power to destroy railway bridges and shipping. The manner in which Beaton recounts Japanese soldiers conspiring to recover a lost artillery piece emphasizes this point, since such weapons were unlikely to be replaced at this stage of the war. SEE ALSO PP. 540–1, 561–3.

Sunday 27 – Monday 28 February 1944

Lieutenant Hubert Hooper, working at the codebreaking centre at HMS *Anderson* on Ceylon, meets up with an old pal and catches a film

Hubert Hooper came from Gateshead in County Durham and had joined the Royal Navy in 1942. With an aptitude for languages, he had been sent for training at Duchess House, west London, before being sent to the highly secret army codebreaking facility in Delhi, called the Wireless Experimental Centre. On 8 January 1944 he had been moved to the main naval codebreaking centre at HMS Anderson in Ceylon. These two locations provided Mountbatten with a kind of Far Eastern equivalent of Bletchley Park, listening in to enemy signals for intelligence purposes.

What amazes me is the number of Old Pals who are engaged in the Intelligence racket and the ramification of their acquaintance. 'Did old so and so get away from Singapore? Do you remember what's his name at Melbourne? I hear old what-not is running such and such a Department in Hawaii.' It seems that Bris is being sent to Chittagong for the RT [radio telegraphy] course, along with Silkin and Co. I think it is a mistake. Teddy [Poulden] sent various instructions at various times about these people, but they appear to have been either ignored or misinterpreted.

Indulged in the luxury of an idle and leisurely Sunday morning. Wrote to Bris at Chittagong. At lunchtime Worman informed me that Donald had arrived, which was true, for in the afternoon I heard an account of his adventures. He spoke with the air of one who is very intimate with his job. He held us, including Mervy and the Wren, enthralled with tales of captured documents which he had translated, dead bodies which he had searched, natives who had received bribes from Jap parachutists and who were dealt with, Gestapo fashion, by the Indian Police, and the thrills of up-to-date operational intelligence. He brought a flavour of real war in our studious apartment. Nevertheless, even allowing for Donald's sensationalist approach, it would appear that life on the Burma front is not without its excitement. The RT business is not, he says, as difficult as one would have expected. The Japs speak slowly, with ample repetition, and confine their remarks to the matter in hand. Swam with him this evening in the bit of sea adjoining St Thos. He came round to supper, where Mervy was entertaining Teddy and WU [Wireless Unit] C.O. Donald chatted away very easily with them about the organisation at Chittagong, prominent personalities etc. Afterwards we went to see a film – Berlin Correspondent, a poor piece which I have seen in different guises many times before: a Secret Service Agent, a ravishing damsel, a chase by the Gestapo, triumph at the eleventh hour, a heroic death, and a posthumous VC. Rickshaws brought us back by a hidden way and I was half afraid it was a plot to assassinate us.

Hubert Hooper's friend Donald had been on an 'RT course'. This was special training in the local interception of Japanese tactical and operational radio traffic near the front line for battlefield purposes and carried with it the 'whiff of action'. By contrast, Hubert Hooper and his colleagues were working on 'strategic' intercept material in the rather more refined and academic atmosphere of the naval signals intelligence centre at Anderson. This was still the world of intelligence, but one quite different from that reported by his friend, or indeed that portrayed in the 1942 film Berlin Correspondent, *inspired by and loosely based on William Shirer's successful book* Berlin Diary, *published the previous year. Anderson was run by Commander Bruce Keith at this time and its major task was providing intelligence for the commander of the Eastern Fleet, Admiral Somerville. Teddy Poulden, one of Hubert's friends mentioned here, ran Australian signals intelligence after the war and would later become an influential figure in GCHQ.* SEE ALSO *PP. 539–40.*

MARCH 1944

DESPITE SERIOUS SUPPLY problems, the Japanese were still determined to launch offensives where they could, and this month saw their last significant initiatives of the war. On 8 March they began serious attacks on American forces on Bougainville in the Solomon Islands. Their attention focused on the airfields at Piva, and the scale of the artillery fire that poured in forced the Americans to transfer some of their aircraft to other locations. Japanese infantry also infiltrated far behind Allied positions. However, these attacks were very costly for the Japanese and by the end of the month the Japanese position on Bougainville was weak.

Japan also launched a major offensive in Burma close to the

border with India, seeking to destroy British forces in the area around Imphal and Kohima. They hoped to push on into Assam and also cut off American and Chinese forces in the north of Burma from their sources of supply. Through intelligence, British commanders were aware of Japanese intentions well in advance and so planned for their forces to fall back and defend the large and well-stocked base camp at Imphal. On both sides the issue of supply was crucial; the Japanese in particular were short of food, and their campaign depended for its success in part on capturing food from the enemy. Although forewarned, the British under-estimated the scale of the attack, and while the elite 20th Indian Division under Gracey moved speedily to Imphal, the 17th Indian Division had to fight its way through road blocks and ambushes. The defence of Imphal and Kohima was saved by airlifting in additional troops from the 5th Division and resupplying the defenders with food and ammunition by air. However, on 29 March the Japanese cut road communications to Imphal and the garrison's position looked precarious.

Meanwhile, Wingate launched a second wave of Chindit operations, codenamed Operation Thursday. The 77th Long Range Patrol Brigade flew into a pre-prepared landing zone called 'Broadway', well behind Japanese lines at a secret location in the jungle some 60 miles south of Myitkyina. Once the Japanese located this facility they subjected it to heavy air attack. The 16th Brigade was already operating in the jungle south of Ledo, while the 23rd Brigade pushed through the Naga Hills. Later in the month General Wingate was killed in an air crash and was replaced by his most senior subordinate, Brigadier Lentaigne.

In Japan, the cost of war was becoming more and more starkly apparent. The scale of casualties could no longer be hidden from the domestic population, and food supplies were increasingly scarce as the Japanese merchant fleet disappeared from the oceans. On 19 March 1944 General Tojo debated with his fellow commanders whether he should announce to the people that the war was not going well. After several days of consideration they agreed and the announcement was made. However, most of the population still expected that there would be an armistice and did not prepare themselves psychologically for total defeat.

Friday 3 March – Monday 13 March 1944

Eric Murrell, a British cipher sergeant, moves through Burma's 'Death Valley' with the Devonshires and the Gurkhas

Eric Murrell had been a prize-winning scholar at Lincoln College, Oxford, where he had studied medieval French legends. In the late 1930s he became an assistant librarian at the University Library in Cambridge. His academic aptitude ensured that he was chosen for training as a cipher sergeant and earned him the nickname 'Old Prof'. He joined the Royal Engineers at the start of the war, aged thirty-nine, and saw action on the Norway campaign in 1940. During 1944 he was sent forward from India and across the border into Burma's Kabaw Valley, known to the troops who served there as 'Death Valley' because of the very high incidence of disease.

3 March

The British troops here are Devons; the cook I mentioned shows true Devon liberality – won't take much of our rations; tells us to save them for when we go forward (!). He feeds us all right. He comes from Plymouth, where his family have been bombed out four times; and he has been cooking for a hundred or more men in this 'Death Valley' for six months. It is a death valley all right – even empty of inhabitants; and it's odd to see no natives about anywhere, no signs of civilization. Hesin, a few miles back, is now a few burnt skeletons of huts, probably burnt when the Japs came past, and this side of Tamu we have not seen a soul.

We have to take two mepacrin tablets per day to combat malaria – of course I can't swallow them, have to chew them up, and the evil taste lingers for about 24 hours, so is there for ever; and they make my tongue a lurid yellow. We hear the guns now by day and by night.

How patient are the troops here in this heat, doing as we've all been doing more or less since we came up in May '42, playing a waiting game until the European war is over.

4 March

'Death Valley' in another sense. Last night about midnight we woke to very close rifle shots from the river direction of our camp – result, one of our Sikhs killed, three wounded. It is almost impossible to make anyone who has not seen this jungle valley realise how there is no fixed front, and that we or the enemy can penetrate miles behind each other's territory undiscovered. There is no 'line' held by battalions, with Brigade HQ in the rear, and Div. HQ still further back, as in the last war. Here, if a body of troops keeps off the very few 'roads' or tracks, and avoids the usual river crossings, it can go for miles or weeks inside enemy regions and never be spotted, particularly at night. There is no clear land where one can see for more than a few yards or so, save on the hills; even there trees and jungle hide a good deal. We have a brigade HQ and battalions ahead of us; nevertheless this was probably a Jap or Jif patrol which came through the jungle right up to our doorstep. (This Army abbreviation is for Japanese Indian Fifth-columnist, similarly BTA is Burmese Traitor Army, ITA Indian Traitor Army.)

No mail for me yet – it takes a good deal longer to reach us out here.

5 March

Had a delightful swim in the Yu yesterday. We went further down where it was deeper; also there was a tree trunk sloping up out of the water and I managed to clamber on and dive in off it. The water is refreshing, as the weather is as hot or hotter than ever. Sunday afternoon I sit writing this, clad in a pair of slacks and a topee. Bren gun carriers with caterpillar tracks roar up and down the road beside us – especially at dawn, so it isn't exactly peaceful here, altho' so far from civilisation.

6 March

The river is good fun – the 'coloured' troops bathe in quantities. Several here are 'Johnnie Gurkhas' as we call them. (War and roughing it seem just great fun for these grand little fellows.) And many here are Sikhs, who wear their hair long; and when we see a group shrieking and laughing while bathing in their bright-coloured shorts, we usually call out 'Hello, girls'. Teams of horses and mules are ridden down by Indians in khaki turbans to join the humans in a bathe, while the big guns boom and whistle overhead, sending their salvos over the hill ridge opposite to the Japs on the Chindwin. The Devonshire troops here have no entertainment at all – we've lent them a spare wireless set: how they love it in the moonlit evenings! . . .

12 March

It is terribly hot and the flies are a great plague on these wooded steep slopes. Tea-making is my part of the cooking – it's all I've time for – and while the others cook on a fire outside I visit the Gurkhas' cookhouse with the tea dixie. Some heat, pottering around a wood fire in a hut, while the cheery 'Johnnies' do their native cooking. They are most helpful. With their Tibetan looks and close-cut hair, with a few strands left hanging long down the back, they would probably be taken for Chinese by anyone who didn't know them. It all seems like one grand adventure to these 'cheery schoolboys'; to see the cook yesterday, jokingly waving his *kukri* [knife] and rushing at his helpers, because they'd used the *kukri* to carve out some *ghee* (their equivalent of butter and fat) – this was like using mother's best embroidery scissors to cut cardboard – was great fun; one could guess it all without understanding one word of their Nepali tongue. We do indeed owe a debt to Nepal; now there will not be a young man left in the State, and all the beautiful pink and yellow-cheeked Nepali girls with their laughing eyes have their sweethearts or husbands not only serving but in the forefront of the battle, for these Gurkhas just excel in the difficult jungle warfare.

The Japs are just across the Chindwin – we are always gazing at the big river through the glasses. It has been a household word to us for so long, the great Burmese river, across which we finally hope to get ourselves established.

Being Sunday, one of us who hails from Barnsley, is determined to try and make a Yorkshire pudding to go with the eternal 'bully'. A funny idea, making Yorkshire pudding on a wood fire on these steep wood-slopes; at present he is

whisking away with flour and tinned milk in a tea-mug. All
honour to his enterprise!

13 March

The three thin round flat cakes of 'Yorkshire pudding' went
down well; we are thinking of making the same today,
putting jam in, and calling them pancakes.

*Kabaw Valley lay just to the west of Imphal and was dominated by the
River Yu. Eric Murrell was located close to 3/1 Gurkhas and was a great
admirer of both the Sikh and Gurkha troops, who excelled at fieldcraft.
Two days later, on 15 March, he would be ordered to retreat rapidly back
towards India and his base at Langthobal. The Japanese push for Imphal
had moved past them and behind them and they were in danger of being
cut off.*

*After the war Eric Murrell would return to work in the University
Library in Cambridge. He died in 1982.*

Wednesday 8 March 1944

Jesse Gardner, an American pilot flying B-25 bombers, has
a 'close one' at Piva airfield on Bougainville

*Jesse Gardner was born in Pittsburgh and had graduated from Allegheny
College in 1943. He entered the US Army Air Force and after training at
Kissimmee was sent to join the air operations staff of the 419th Night
Fighter Squadron in the Solomon Islands.*

I really had a close one today. When we got up there was a
lot of shelling going on, which we thought was ours, but we
soon found out differently when some boys came back from
the mess hall saying they weren't feeding, because the Japs
are shelling our Piva U strip.

Helmet, gas mask and carbine being required, we all
carried them when we went down to the line shortly after.

We had just gone into Operations when shells began
exploding just across the road from us. I fell flat on the
ground, grabbed my helmet, and jumped into the ditch in

front of the tent. It had been dug just a couple days ago. Several more burst nearby and then Carl Reuben and I straightened up to see what was going on. Marshall Peoples (one of our two or three American Indians) yelled 'duck' and we did. He said a piece of shrapnel passed between Reuben's head and mine and buried itself into the bank behind us. Sure enough, after the shelling died down, I dug in after it and found it; it was so sharp, I cut my finger when I touched it in the dirt. It's a long thin and very jagged piece of steel and looks awfully wicked.

No one in our outfit was hurt, but I've heard that any-where from two to thirty-seven were killed in that shelling. I still have trouble in telling whether the explosion is our guns going off or Jap shells falling unless they're close enough to hear them whistle...

It's funny the things that went through my mind while I was sitting in my hole, waiting for whatever was to come. I regretted not having this diary with me, and thought of the Japs reading it and my letters. But I didn't think once of praying – I don't know why.

Piva airfield in Bougainville was a large base used by American, Australian and New Zealand aircraft. It was a forward airfield used to support operations against the Japanese stronghold of Rabaul. This

Jesse Gardner

Japanese artillery bombardment was part of a softening-up process prior to a major ground attack launched at the airfield on 11 March, triggering partial evacuation. Further attacks would be launched on 23 and 29 March. The attacks were held off by the US 129th Infantry and neither was successful in over-running the airfield.

Jesse Gardner would survive the war and be discharged on 21 December 1945, allowing him to return home to Pittsburgh. In 1946 he began the MBA program at Harvard University.

Tuesday 14 – Thursday 16 March 1944

Kiyosawa Kiyoshi, a Japanese journalist, reflects on the unofficial price of food in Toyko

The diary of liberal journalist Kiyosawa Kiyoshi is one of the most fascinating records of wartime Japan, maintained at great personal risk and used as a repository for subversive social and political observations. As an American-educated commentator on politics and foreign affairs who had worked on the west coast of the United States in the inter-war years, Kiyoshi had become increasingly isolated in Japan as militant nationalists rose to power in the 1930s. During the war many of his friends and associates were arrested.

Everywhere one goes, the core of discussion is the inadequacy of food supplies. Shimura Tamaharu (chief field investigator of the Communications Ministry), who guided me around Hokkaidō, says he has seven children; but families like his eat nothing but gruel. Because of this he says they have lost two or three kamme in weight. I hear that Rōyama gives most of his food to his children, who are still growing, and he and his wife eat what remains. Everywhere there is only rice for two meals, and a third meal is unthinkable. Even in our house Akira says he wants more rice, but of late it is rationed. Ōkuma Makoto says that in his family, 'The children are hungry, but they are already accustomed to it . . . and we have only gruel.' During my twenty-day absence, my family ate well. In the end, no one can survive on these rations. In the magazine *Kōjin konjin* (Ancient people and contemporaries), Ubukata Toshirō writes about this with relative courage.

According to Rōyama, the rice requisition quotas in Yamaguchi Prefecture are becoming more stringent, and there are people who say, 'If it comes to this, please stop the war!' . . .

A certain person came to our house and asked if I wouldn't buy a kamme of sugar for 100 yen. When I inquired into it, I heard that it was selling for 120 yen per kamme. Of course I refused, but this is everywhere the market price. The official fixed price is about 3 yen. It is forty times this price.

The price of one straw bagful of rice is roughly 200 yen, and now it is not uncommon for three bags to be 1,000 yen . . .

Yesterday Eiko and the maid went to the center of the city. They went to Fuji Ice to have lunch and stood in line, but while waiting they were cut off. When they went to the Matsuya Department Store the lunch line filled up three or four floors completely and they were unable to eat. Thereupon they went to Fujiya and at last had lunch. Even there the line was cut off while they waited. When they had lunch there was no rice, and they were served a few ersatz noodles covered with suspicious-looking seaweed, and this cost eighty sen. A man who was sitting in front of them placed the main portion of his lunch in a box that he had brought along and meticulously ate the remaining portion. My wife said, 'It's good to know what is going on outside. Eiko said she will never be finicky in what she eats.' The maid also said she truly understands how thankful we should be.

Of late, cabinet meetings are taking place in the palace. From the beginning, Tōjō has hidden behind his majesty the emperor. Whenever he says anything he claims it is the benevolence of the emperor or an imperial order. This is based on his ignorance that he is unconsciously trying to hide behind the august name of the emperor. Conducting cabinet meetings at the palace is a step in this direction.

Kiyosawa Kiyoshi's diary began as a record of the war, but quickly became a mental refuge and a place in which he could pour out his feelings about Japanese authoritarianism. The country having been at war since 1937, strict government control was exercised over every aspect of Japanese life, from clothing to food. Here Kiyosawa mentions the failing fortunes of General Tojo, soon to be replaced by Koiso. However, he could only write about this in his diary and feared discussing such matters even in small groups for, as he noted, 'there are always spies'. SEE ALSO PP. 589–91.

Thursday 23 – Saturday 25 March 1944

Eddie Stanton, an Australian soldier on police liaison duties in New Guinea, reflects on 'the primitive urge' of the American soldier

23 March
Showery

It is surprising the number of American soldiers who possess filthy postcards, Officers & men. Men & women, in the nude, are photographed in all kinds of intimate positions. Lustful eyes regularly gloat over them.

Soldiers were taking natives in nude poses here by offering copious bribes. The U.S. command tried to put a stop to such depravity but with little success. Sex, to most Americans, seems the only thing to live for. A point of view that is fast leading them into moral decay. They have so much colored blood in them that they lack the power to restrain their primitive urge.

25 March
Showers

Fighters & transports whizz overhead during the morning.

Attending to complaints by Australian & American troops regarding thefts of belongings by natives. Soldiers have repeatedly invited the Fuzzy-wuzzy angels into their tents, given them fists full of cigarettes, tins of meat, & packages of chocolate. Since the angels receive all of these things for nothing, they regard the donors as fools. Fair game for theft. Our advice has never been listened to by the Forces. They knew all, we – nothing. Now, they cry on our shoulders when the angels do a spot of purloining. But the tears just roll off our backs.

Working as a liaison officer with local police forces attached to joint Australian–American units, Stanton regularly reflected on the cultural attributes of his allies. Stanton believed that the Americans were racially 'weakened' as a result of mixing their blood with that of immigrants from Mexico and eastern Europe. Exactly what he considered 'pure' American blood is not made clear at any point in his diary. Stanton's American colleagues also freely offered their views on race, often giving voice to their dismay that Australian women were willing to consort with African American soldiers. SEE ALSO PP. 286–8, 377–9, 760–1.

APRIL 1944

BY 4 APRIL a life-or-death struggle had developed in Burma around the town of Kohima. Road links to the British garrison had been cut off and it was being resupplied by air. However, the besieging Japanese forces had run perilously low on supplies and were dependent on over-running the town in order to sustain their own operations. By 18 April the 5th Indian Division had broken through Japanese positions and restored communications with Kohima. Fighting was still in progress on 30 April, but a lack of food and ammunition was diminishing the Japanese attacks. The position of Japanese forces had been further weakened by accurate American bombing of strategic rail bridges over the Sittang river. In the north of Burma, American and Chinese forces launched a renewed drive for the strategic town of Myitkyina.

In the Indian Ocean, Admiral Somerville's Eastern Fleet began to raid the Indonesian archipelago, attacking the Japanese airbase at Sabang. However, the most significant maritime event of April was an accident at Bombay docks. On 14 April the SS *Fort Stikene*, an ammunition ship carrying some

1,300 tons of TNT, exploded and set off a sympathetic detonation in a neighbouring ammunition ship. The resulting blast destroyed twenty-one ships in total and levelled an area of Bombay, killing over 1,000 people. Similar large accidental explosions at ammunition depots would occur at Hollandia on 19 April and at Pearl Harbor on 21 May.

In New Guinea, Australian and American forces launched an attack on the island of Hollandia. On 3 April the US 5th Air Force caught most of their Japanese opposite numbers on the ground here and over 300 Japanese aircraft were destroyed. By 6 April there were only twenty-five serviceable Japanese aircraft in Hollandia. This remarkable action set the future direction of the campaign. General Eichelberger commanded a force of 84,000 men whose task was to remove a Japanese garrison of 11,000. Their landing was uncontested and the Japanese forces retreated into the hinterland. By the end of April much of Hollandia had been taken with little resistance, and the Japanese airfields here and at Aitape had been pressed into service as US bases. The Allied operations in New Guinea were a multinational operation in which Australian and American troops were joined by considerable numbers of New Zealanders and Fijians – the Fijian soldiers being particularly admired for their excellent fieldcraft – and all units frequently being supported by local militias and retainers. Many diaries record that patrols could not have operated in the dense jungle and intense heat without the assistance of local helpers carrying additional supplies. Even without packs and carrying only personal weapons, the patrols often found it very hard going.

During April, American planners began to tackle the issue of how to bring about the final defeat of Japan. By the end of the month they had concluded that only an invasion of the home islands would suffice, and codenamed this future campaign Operation Olympic.

Monday 3 April 1944

Ernest Hodgkin, a British medical scientist from Kuala Lumpur, on how his fellow civilian internees are drawn to attention in Changi gaol

The Gestapo have pounced again. This time they have taken six people, including Mrs Nixon, poor woman. Three I am told were responsible for the distribution of news. And today others have been questioned (but not taken away) and made to sign declarations that they wouldn't do it again – made to 'write lines'!

A good story, though I am afraid it may be spoilt by necessary explanations. Recently, an order was made that all commands made in the presence of Nip officers ('attention', 'bow', 'carry on', etc) must be given in Nipponese; naturally few except camp officials are familiar with them. One evening a Nip officer was prowling round the camp and entered one part unnoticed; suddenly a P.B.I. [Poor Bloody Internee] noticed him and stood up. In a valiant effort to call his fellows to attention he shouted SUKIMONO (prawn paste), the only Nipponese word he could think of. Luckily the Nip had a sense of humour: he laughed uproariously . . .

The Nips asked a number of camp officials to write letters saying what they think of the management of the camp and of our treatment by the military. They were told that they were to write as though they were writing to their fathers, they were to be honest in the views they expressed, they would not be punished for what they wrote! Mr Tominaga is reputed to have finished his instructions by saying, 'I suppose I shall be the first to have my throat cut.' The letters all said in polite but unequivocal language just exactly how we have been treated.

Ernest Hodgkin's diary illustrates the Japanese obsession with protocol – saluting, bowing and calling to attention – in Changi gaol. He also captures a creeping realization on the part of the Japanese guards that they were under scrutiny by inmates and that their crimes might eventually catch up with them. Later, at the war crimes trials held in Singapore and Tokyo, diaries of the internees featured as evidence. Tominaga Jikko would be sentenced to death by the Singapore tribunal for maltreatment of internees, although his sentence was later commuted to ten years' imprisonment.

In 1945 Ernest would return safely to his wife Mary and his four young children at Cottersloe in Australia and eventually became a lecturer in zoology at the University of Western Australia. SEE ALSO PP. *491–3.*

Wednesday 5 April 1944

Robert T. Boody, a US pilot flying supplies to Merrill's Marauders in upper Burma, loses his propellers on take-off

In early 1944 Robert Boody had been moved from P-40 Kittyhawk fighters to C-47 Dakota supply aircraft. He was kept busy during early 1944 supplying special units such as Merrill's Marauders and the Chindits, which operated independently and required regular air drops.

Our first mission of that day, my 115th completed combat mission while serving with 2nd Troop Carrier Squadron in the CBI Theater, was uneventful into the Hukawng Valley of north Burma. In spite of low-hanging cumulo-nimbus storm clouds over the Naga Hills separating India from Burma, I felt confident that at least one more flight could safely be completed that day before the ceiling closed in.

On arriving back at Dinjan, I found, upon checking our operations office, that a ship containing a much-needed priority cargo for Merrill's Marauders (Galahad target) was being cancelled for that day due to weather – its crew having already returned to their basha-huts. I knew that I could get through to target, run it, and get safely back before the clouds closed in, if we took off right away. I told the operations officer as much, he authorized me, and I assembled my crew to do so.

On our second mission of the day, after one false start

down the runway on our borrowed aircraft #41-38706, we discovered that the elevator and rudder chocks were still in place locking the controls. We had to brake to a quick stop half-way down the runway because the controls wouldn't operate. Then, our crew rectified the problem and we got a green light okay from the control tower to proceed on our mission.

On starting down the runway this time, I pushed the two throttle levers full-forward with my right hand while holding the control column wheel with my left hand. My co-pilot, Evans' right hand was supposed to follow up behind the throttles while with his left hand he should have tightened the knob beneath the throttle quadrant to keep the throttles from vibrating backward.

Because the engine noise was deafening and my vocal command was ineffective, when Evans didn't immediately tighten up the throttle quadrant, I promptly made a circling motion with my right index finger to remind him to do so. He mistook my circling hand for a 'gear-up' signal (right thumb up with fist clenched) and immediately pulled up the landing-gear lever, too soon, before we were airborne.

On hitting the runway, both propellers broke off and spun to the right; the left prop blade cut through the cockpit and got my leg. I yelled 'It's gone; I know it's gone!' – before I passed out. (None of the other seven crew-men were injured.) In my opinion, Fred Evans, a former fighter pilot as I had been, was completely without blame for misunderstanding my hand signal. I had not used that hand signal, before, with him. Again, C'est la guerre!

The medics dragged me through the large cockpit hole made by the prop blade – then injected me with morphine to ease the pain. They put my damaged foot in a cast, after using 'maggots,' an ancient remedy to aid the healing. This took place at the Dinjan infirmary with Doc Carey Legett – our Flight Surgeon – in charge. I was then rushed by ambulance, driven by medic Harrison Vickers III ten miles over bumpy dirt road, to 111th Station Hospital at Chabua. Enroute to the hospital, 'Doc' Vickers and I wryly joked about the depth of the pot-holes until I lapsed again into unconsciousness.

After this accident Boody spent seven days in a coma. Doctors were forced to amputate his damaged foot to check the spread of gangrene. A month later he was invalided home to New York. After further rehabilitation at the Walter Reed hospital he bought a used 1937 Dodge sedan and drove himself home at the end of July, using his good foot for the brake and accelerator while operating the clutch with one of his crutches. SEE ALSO PP. *415–17.*

Wednesday 5 – Thursday 6 April 1944

Lieutenant Hubert Hooper, at the codebreaking centre on Ceylon, has a day off, goes to the beach and catches a film called *Casablanca*

Slept till a later hour this morning. It is exasperating to be constantly missing one's breakfast. Lunch is no substitute. The palate demands something more stimulating after a long sleep . . . Visited Cave's, bought Linklater's Great Ship, a little work on the British Empire by Sir Ed. Grigg and some little verse anthologies. Also consummated the purchase of my mess jacket, begun many weeks ago. John arrived from Delhi a day or two ago looking and behaving like a man newly rescued from a concentration camp and hardly able to believe it. Bris, he tells me, did not go to Chittagong, but is still with Major Thunder, translating documents (lucky devil). I learnt today that I have become Colegrave's 'deputy' and am to be retained at Anderson. This does not please me at all, having hoped for a more active career, but I have not the slightest doubt that the arrangement will be superseded in due time.

Went with Bob to [Mount] Lavinia latish in the afternoon and went through the usual motions. Had the remarkable experience of wading waist deep through an enormous shoal of small fish, which rattled against my legs like raindrops. I cannot bring myself to trust the sea in these latitudes. The legend of the shark is created for us at an impressionable age and it is not easy to shake off the fear of meeting some ill-disposed denizen of the deep. Yet I have never even seen a jelly-fish here. As always at this palm-studded paradise, there were one or two girls very pleasant to behold but as always, adequately attended . . . Afterwards to the cinema to see 'Casablanca', a powerful drama of intrigue, with Bogart, his gangster exterior concealing a heart of gold, and the ravishing Ingrid Bergman. Produced with excellent restraint. Probably the first time in his career that Bogart has traversed the whole length of a film without socking anyone on the jaw.

Hubert Hooper's diary reflects the misery of intelligence officers with valuable languages, such as Japanese, who were kept in boring translation work throughout the war and were not allowed to develop their careers through more exciting roles. His friend 'Bris' appears to have suffered a similar fate. Mount Lavinia was one of the more popular beach resorts near Colombo on Ceylon. Although Bogart does not sock anyone in the jaw during the film Casablanca, *he does despatch the Gestapo officer with a pistol at the end of the film. Hooper remained at Anderson during 1944 and was eventually sent to do more translation work with an interrogation unit that formed part of the British occupation forces in Japan in 1946. A GCHQ listening station was retained on Ceylon until 1963. SEE ALSO PP. 522–4.*

Sunday 9 April 1944

Cecil Beaton, war photographer, chats with the British ambassador to China, Sir Horace Seymour, about the cost of living in Chungking

A small Chinese soldier with a rifle saluted. He was the sentry guarding a dwarf villa. We had arrived, by car, at the top of a mountain. This was the British Embassy.

A minute hall gave on to a tall, octagonal sitting room. The Ambassador, a lanky, overgrown schoolboy with witty eyes and a tired, but benevolent, smile on his long, donkey face, wore grey flannels. He presented his wife. She had humorous eyes, dog-biscuit complexion, and a deep, dry voice. Surprisingly, she introduced me to an owl-like Brooks

Atkinson, the *New York Times* drama critic. We sat talking, maybe for an hour, in a casual atmosphere, about inflation, the Generalissimo and Madame Chiang. 'We're just picnicking here: we get, through the king's messenger, per month one bottle of whisky, a pound of butter, a pot of marmalade, but everything is prohibitive here – especially as the black market is in a panic that it may be officially closed down.'

In this stronghold against the Japs, Chungking, the makeshift capital of China, is thriving as never before. Even the coolies are rich, earning 3,000 dollars a month: to ferry a grand piano across the river would cost 40,000 dollars. Chungking, with its rich, red earth, yields two crops a year and is self-supporting, but aid is being flown over the 'Hump' to China at the rate of one plane every two and a half minutes.

Baffling were the prices they quoted: the official rate is eighty dollars to the pound, but on the black market the pound is worth 1,200 dollars. A candle costs twenty shillings, a pound of boiled sweets thirty shillings; or, in dollars, pork costs seventy dollars a pound, a bottle of ink 200 and a gallon of petrol 900 dollars.

Cecil Beaton visited China in early 1944 and experienced at first hand the reality of a regime cut off from all sources of supply other than by air from India. Later in 1944 a land route from Burma would be reopened. The British ambassador, Sir Horace Seymour, presided over a byzantine network of British agencies in China, many of which were engaged in intelligence and special operations. London was anxious to know more about the precarious government of the Generalissimo and Madame Chiang, which was in essence an uneasy coalition of warlords and regional landowners. Seymour was also required to look after future British interests in areas such as Hong Kong, an imperial possession which neither the Chinese nor the Americans wished to see return to British rule after the war. SEE ALSO PP. 520–2, 561–3.

Monday 10 – Friday 14 April 1944

Natalie Crouter, a civilian internee, witnesses the punishments for circulating news in a Philippine camp

Natalie Stark was born into a wealthy Boston family in 1898. Educated at Dorchester School, she was interested in the political life of Boston and radical causes. She had met her husband, Jerry Crouter, while accompanying her father on a business trip that took them to Manila in 1925. Thereafter, he was employed by a large sugar-producing company and they lived a genteel life at Vigan in the Philippines until the Japanese invasion. In 1942 they were interned together with their two children, June and Bedie.

10 April

At supper time Jim Halsema was given fifteen minutes to prepare his blanket roll for a trip to jail.

Three men out now and the atmosphere is charged. The strain is almost unbearable. Everyone is upset, thoughts scattered and all coming back to one point – the jail. It is surmised that Gene's diary was found, a possible mention of listening to Jim's *News* which may have brought about his being called. Jim will have to explain how he adds two and two from the *Tribune* and the *Nippon Times*. Probably they won't believe it. I am now going to 'bury' these notes and start a new series . . .

14 April

Special Section on Bill, Gene and Jim in jail.

Bill was strung up by his thumbs 4 times in 4 hours. They tied his hands behind him, then tied the thumbs and pulled him up with arms behind him. He could touch the ground with his toes which helped a little, but the back was bent over and the head down, lasting for about 20 minutes each time. They hit him from underneath, in the face, they beat him with sticks, kicked him in the ribs. Once he told them that Americans wouldn't treat a dog like that they beat him unmercifully. The 4th time they strung him up they ordered him to get up on a chair and he wouldn't. Five of them jumped him at once, and he ended standing on the chair where they handcuffed his hands behind him and strung him by the thumbs again. He said he kept hoping he would faint but he is too powerful and could not, so he kept striking his head against the door, trying to knock himself out. They beat him for this too. He said he was not conscious of making a sound until he saw a Filipino crowd gathering outside to find out what was going on, then the Japanese put a gag in his mouth and he dimly realized he must have been yelling. Twice his shoulder was pulled out of the socket and they took him down to put it back in. He had a huge black spot on one leg, another on one arm. He says the Filipinos fed him afterward and he ate like a horse for four days yet he is 12 pounds less than when he left here even after all the food. He sweated so that he stood in a pool of water. What they wanted to know was *where* the men went, who took them and what way they went, how we got the news [bulletins] and who got it. Much of this he could not answer – which made it only worse. At last he lost track and doesn't remember much. He could only give them a vague idea of the destination anyway. After it was all over they told him they had all the information they wanted anyway after torturing Chicay, the meat seller, and two others, one of whom they caught with a script of news from KP, a guerrilla.

Natalie Crouter's diary captures the obsession with news in both POW and civilian internee camps. The Japanese authorities were extremely anxious to control the flow of information and permitted access only to Japanese sources. Meanwhile, the captives, ever anxious for release, were prepared to take almost any risk to obtain 'genuine' information about the progress of the war effort. The desperate hope for relief often led to absurd rumours which made 'real news' all the more valuable. Internees in some camps found ingenious ways of concealing radio receivers. One radio was hidden in the head of a broom; another was carefully concealed inside somebody's sandals. However, Natalie Crouter's companions were often dependent for news on handwritten sheets brought in from outside the camp by those in contact with local guerrillas. SEE ALSO PP. 711–12, 727–8.

Saturday 15 April 1944

Edward Stettinius, US Under-Secretary of State, talks to Churchill about China after a lunch at Chequers

Edward Stettinius was largely responsible for implementing Roosevelt's ideas for a United Nations Organization. In April he had come to Europe to meet with both the British and various governments-in-exile based in London, many of which were already anxious about Soviet ambitions.

Edward Stettinius (left) with Alexander Cadogan (centre) and Averell Harriman (right)

In describing the world organisation that he had in view, the prime minister referred to 'the tripod upon which peace depends.' Taking a sheet of paper on which the seating list had been prepared by Mrs Churchill, he drew a tripod with a head on which stood the three powers and China. He said he did not refer to China and the three great powers as 'The

Four Great Powers.' He could not bring himself to do that. What China is now and what she may become are two different things. She is not a great power now. He thinks the generalissimo is a strong man and 'the generalissima,' as he called Madame Chiang Kai-shek, is a charming woman. But China is not a great power. There is no unity, and there is much communism. For thirty-five years we have had in China unstable government and division. It is nonsense, he said, to talk about China as a great power . . .

He referred to the Chinese as 'the pigtails.' This accords with the President's statement and his warning to Anthony Eden that he must get his skipper to change his thoughts about the Chinese. It led me to remind him that the president was anxious that China fifty years from now should be a world power and have a friendly attitude toward other powers. 'But,' he replied, 'I have little confidence in the pigtails . . . Likewise, France is needed for a peaceful and happy Europe, but France must be reconstituted and what will she be? Eventually she will be very critical of all English speaking peoples, sensitive and very difficult to deal with. In fact, she has already given us no end of trouble.'

Churchill, Eden and Stettinius were spending the weekend at Chequers. After a heavy lunch with roast beef, port and brandy, they had retired to discuss the future world organization – soon to be called the United Nations. Churchill's ideas about the UN Security Council differed from those of the Americans and indeed from those of Anthony Eden, the Foreign Secretary. The idea of the 'Big Three' being expanded to become the 'Big Five', with the inclusion of China and France, was not to his liking. However, although Churchill hated de Gaulle, France was an essential ally in Asia, where both European leaders wished to see their colonies restored to them. SEE ALSO PP. 591–2.

Tuesday 18 – Wednesday 19 April 1944

New Zealander T. E. Dorman fights alongside Fijian troops on Bougainville

Some New Zealand soldiers had been seconded to Fiji during 1942 and 1943, where they helped to train the Fiji Regiment. T. E. Dorman was originally rejected from the New Zealand army on the basis of poor eyesight but by 1942, after repeated efforts, he had been accepted and was seconded to the Fiji Regiment. In 1944 he was deployed to Bougainville in the Solomon Islands.

18 April

We were all glad to see the dawn after a long and rather nerve-racking night. Just before daylight the Japs made a short and vigorous attack but we spotted them before they had even begun to move and gave them a very bad time. After yet another night without sleep most of us now look a bit haggard. Since there is no shaving on these operations, we Europeans look rather more messy than the rest. It is obvious to us that the enemy usually pick out the Europeans easily and concentrate on them. In future we shall have to blacken faces or be allowed to grow beards; the CO favours the latter, I believe.

After the morning attack we were left in peace for a while and we pushed patrols out in all directions and up and down the trail. My platoon has developed into a very good team now and I have a very good man in Sergeant Jo. I spent some of the little spare time we had today talking to him about a variety of things. I still keep finding out new things about my men and how both alike and unalike we are, the Europeans and the Fijians. Amongst other things Jo told me: 'We see a spirit watching beside you, turaga. You will not die.' Thinking over some of the things that have happened to me since we got into all this, maybe there is something in what he says! Like us, most of the Fijians are superstitious, but most of us would deny it. The Fijians are quite open about it and take it very seriously. My 'charm' is a whistle I never leave behind; it always goes into my pocket, though it is never blown out here. My father used it in the last war and it was still in his pocket when they picked him up out of the mud at Ypres. It got him through and I feel it will do the same for me.

The Americans are now in full possession of Hills 500 and 501 and have reached the Saua River beyond them, so the Japs in this area will have to get out before long or be cut off. This afternoon we heard that the First is coming out to relieve us. We also heard from the Americans that the Japs did not like the 'fierce Red Indians' they were using in the area, us!

19 April

The day commenced with a furious attack on our company, but the Japs seemed to be a bit disorganised. The assault was made after dawn and the enemy groups seemed to be un-coordinated. In quite good daylight my Bren gunners used their weapons with deadly effect. The rush by the Japs petered out before it reached our forward foxholes. Once repulsed they began to make off and we went out after them to clear the area and pick up the 'dead meat' from last night. As usual there was a fair amount of it; our score has been pretty good on this operation.

Bougainville had been the scene of fierce fighting in March 1944. The Japanese still held most of this most northerly of the Solomon Islands, although increasingly insecurely, and had attempted to throw the Allies from their small toehold at the island's most southerly edge. Several bloody battles had taken place for mountains and ridges overlooking the airfield and harbour. Japanese frontal attacks had been extremely costly and by April they were petering out. SEE ALSO PP. 571–3.

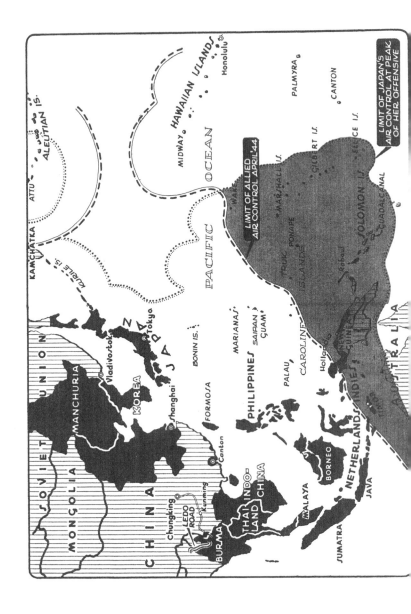

The Pacific, Spring 1944

Thursday 20 April 1944

Arthur Gately, RAAF, has a narrow escape at the air base at Momote in the Admiralty Islands

Arthur Gately had been employed by an engineering company in Rockdale, Australia, and so was in a reserved occupation. It was only with some ingenuity and persistence that he had secured a release to join the RAAF at eighteen years of age. After training as an armourer, in May 1943 he joined 79 Squadron, a Spitfire unit, which was assigned to ground attack, bomber escort and naval liaison duties. Arthur Gately's squadron continually followed the front-line units as they moved forward. He had been posted initially to Milne Bay in eastern New Guinea. From there he followed his squadron forward to Goodenough Bay and then to Kiriwina Island in the Trobriand Islands. In March 1944 they had moved on to Momote, an island recently captured from the Japanese.

The day began like so many others. Our flight was on early standby at the airstrip. This meant an early rise in the dark, a quick cup of coffee (ugh), something hot out of a tin in the Mess, then a scramble onto the back of a truck and a fast run down to our aircraft parked near our workshop area, not far from the airstrip . . .

On this particular morning, with our aircraft in position, we were involved with the routine practice of 'running up' the motors to make sure they reached the required number of revs. While this pre-flight check was taking place, the early morning departure of Liberator bombers was going on – already four or five had thundered past and were gaining altitude to assemble overhead. Our aircraft UP/A was standing at the end of the line, our mechanic Blue Findlay was sitting in the cockpit ready to start the motor. Another Liberator came thundering along the airstrip – using hand signals, Bluey indicated to Tom and me that he would wait until the bomber had passed before starting to run the motor. Tom and I were watching the Liberator closely, it became airborne, its motors were roaring – this is the most critical stage of flight – everything is stretched and straining, particularly the motors, to break the bonds of gravity holding the aircraft back. It had climbed to about 200 feet above the ground, was fast approaching to be above and abreast of us, when, to our horror and shock, we noticed that the port outer motor had stopped. The propeller was feather turning very slowly – the port wing began to drop rapidly until the plane got out of control and nose dived right into the 'Sea Bees' camp, the camp that was originally ours.

This terrible accident took only seconds to happen, and it happened right before our eyes. The explosion, air wave and bang, felt as if our ear drums would burst. Three thousand gallons of high octane aviation fuel, a load of bombs and ammunition, and most tragic of all, nine American aircrew (one airgunner was thrown clear) all disappeared in one unholy, blasting flash. In the camp itself, 40 hard working 'Sea Bee' sailors were killed and many others injured. The blast blew all of us ground crew to the ground. One of our colleagues, Bruce Popel from Western Australia was hit by a piece of metal, which punctured his lung and he was raced to hospital as soon as an ambulance became available. All of our aircraft were showered with pieces of hot metal. Fires had broken out in the camp, ammunition was popping off and the airstrip near us was covered with pieces of red hot metal and smouldering cloth covering parts of bodies. It was the most heartrending, gruesome sight I had seen. All of us were in a state of shock. The fact that we had escaped this holocaust, hadn't properly dawned on us. In no time ambulances were on the scene at the camp, removing the dead and dying and attending to the wounded, while fire trucks started to put out the fires. Bulldozers suddenly appeared and began quickly clearing the airstrip. Steps were taken to replace our aircraft. Before we actually completed our withdrawal, the airstrip was sufficiently clear and another Liberator bomber lumbered and thundered past us to join his waiting colleagues circling high overhead. And so the war went on.

Such terrible accidents as described here were not uncommon on rough airfields where aircraft, fuel, ammunition and tented accommodation

jostled for space alongside the runway. Only two days later a further Liberator, returning from a night bombing mission, would miscalculate its approach and also crash in the SeaBees' (CBs: the Naval Construction Battalion) camp. The next day Gately wrote up no notes in his diary, only recording that he was 'still in a state of shock'. SEE ALSO
PP. 606–8.

Sunday 23 – Friday 28 April 1944

Naval surgeon Tetsuo Watanabe and his men sing songs from their childhood and long for home as they retreat through the swamps of New Guinea

23 April

At 04:30, we started marching. Luckily my stomach was in good condition and I began to have normal excreta. I felt my strength coming back. We walked about two kilometres from the junction and took shelter. We were now in a well-known swamp area in New Guinea where walking was almost impossible for normal humans. I thanked the army's construction unit for their hard work – constructing a trail in a swamp. In this respect the navy on the land was so useless. My troop, consisting of many reservists, had no means or energy to perform such a laborious task. We were too tired physically and mentally and too spiritless to do anything. There was water in the swamp but it was not drinkable. It had a bad smell and seemed to contain much organic matter. The naval unit, unlike the army units, did not have portable filters. We cut down vines and drank clear liquid coming from the cut ends.

There were dead bodies everywhere. Most had no clothes on. We planned to cross the Sepik River at night, and until then we had to wait. While waiting, I sent some petty-officers to look for the soldiers left behind on the march. There were about ten soldiers who could not keep up with the march. But the officers could not find them. We waited for boats until they finally appeared at 20:30. The army man of the marine transport engineer corps began to instruct us to get on the boats. But when I was about to get aboard, a sergeant, who was looking at my collar badge, said, 'That's all for tonight.' He explained the boat had engine trouble. Lieutenant Kakiuchi, already on the boat, shouted from the moving boat, 'Chief-Surgeon, I'll leave the rest of men to you!' The men behind me included medics, paymaster staff and an auxiliary unit consisted of forty eight soldiers. I took them back to the camp. It was so dark that we could not see the trail well. And all we could rely on was the light of fire-flies. At the camp I pitched a mosquito net. There were so many mosquitoes that some penetrated the net. I told the soldiers not to forget to take their malaria tablets. I could not go to sleep for a while, worrying about being separated from my troop. Then when I was about to go to sleep, a telegraphist dashed to me, saying 'Chief-Surgeon, we have got a telegram!' I asked why he was so excited. He reported that the Allies had landed at Aitape and Hollandia. I knew the enemy would land somewhere near us, but did not expect the enemy to land at two spots in the west far away from us. However, in a second I realised that our retreat route was cut off.

24 April

Early in the morning we went into the jungle to escape the enemy's bombardment. In a mosquito net, I tried to make up for the lack of sleep last night. Waking up in the afternoon, I felt my strength coming back. Medic Okudera said to me, 'The soldiers are in low spirits, disappointed at the news of the enemy's landing'. I decided to cheer up the soldiers by making them sing songs. After dusk, while we were waiting for the boat to cross the Sepik River, I told Takasago volunteer Miyagawa and Medic-Ordinary-Seaman Okudera to sing pop songs. I told the two to pick songs which had a plaintive melody or songs we sang in our childhood or songs that were popular when we were drafted. I requested 'Yoimachi-gusa [Evening Primrose]', 'Hanayome Ningyo [Bride Doll]' and 'Byakuren no Uta [Song of White lotus]' from Miyagawa, because they were his favourite songs, and 'Kantaro tsuki-yo uta [Kantaro's song for the night with moon]', 'Kudan no Haha [Mother of Kudan]' and 'Rabauru

Kouta [Rabaul Ditty]' from Okudera. The singing of Miyagawa and Okudera melted into the pitch dark jungle. Many army soldiers stopped talking, suddenly Japanese songs so dear to their hearts.

'Although waiting and waiting, my boy never came.
I was waiting hopelessly like an evening rimrose.
Somebody said there would be no on tonight.'

When the singing finished, a storm of applause rose. Somebody shouted from the darkness, 'Good singer! Who was it?', and somebody replied here, 'It's the navy! Sing, army men!' An army unit began to sing, *'Dare ka kokyo o omowazaru* [Is there anybody who never thinks about home?]'.

'The sun set in the grassland where we picked the flowers.
We went home walking shoulder to shoulder, singing songs
    on the way.
Oh, friends of my childhood!
Is there anybody who never thinks about home?'

Every word from those songs stuck in our hearts. At this moment, in this New Guinea in the southern hemisphere, everybody's mind was just preoccupied with the memory of his home, escaping from a harsh reality where we were hopelessly stuck between enemies. As a last song, I told all naval soldiers to sing *'Taiheiyo Koshin-kyoku* [The Pacific March]'. We sang it sobbingly . . .

26 April
. . . So far we had managed to cross the two big rivers – the Sepik and Ramu – but another tribulation was waiting for us. In the coming week beginning from tomorrow we had to cross a huge swamp where no man had ever set foot.

27 April
After the enemy's routine scouting flight early in the morning, we quickly departed. All day we walked in a knee-deep swamp. Muddy water totally soaked our boots and trousers.

For the first couple of hours we tried to find shallow places to walk, but soon we got tired of searching and walked wherever possible. The life-cycle of this great natural site often left huge fallen logs in our way to impede our march. The constant sound of the enemy's air raids reminded us of their superior performance for they were able to fly even to such a distant interior. We stayed at Gavien that night. The Takasago volunteers cut down trees and made our beds. Without their wholehearted dedication this march could never have succeeded. I was feeling well. The recovery from the diarrhoea gave me the confidence to think I could keep up with the march.

28 April

Departure at 05:30. Today's swamp was more formidable than yesterday's. It was up to our thighs, making our march extremely difficult. Soon we were lost in a sago forest and wandered aimlessly for about one hour. As we walked on, the head of our troop caught up with the end of the same troop to find we had come full circle. During the march I saw a mosquito net in which somebody was sleeping. When I peeped into the net, wondering why he was sleeping in such a swamp, I found two skeletons lying inside. The two had been sick, unable to walk, and quietly passed away. We took almost a day to march a distance of twelve kilometres.

One of the common misunderstandings on the part of Allied soldiers was the idea that the Japanese were somehow 'at home' in the jungles of the Asia–Pacific region. Although they were undoubtedly skilful jungle fighters, there were no jungles in Japan. Nor indeed were there any jungles in China, where the older soldiers had gained their experience in 1937. Scared and increasingly aware that they had been abandoned by their commanders in Tokyo, Watanabe's soldiers and marines, many of them little more than children, longed for a homeland that was far away. Of some 200 Japanese who set out on their long journey to Wewak, only three from this group would reach their destination in early May; the rest had 'vanished in the jungle'. Watanabe held out on Kairiru Island near Wewak until the surrender on 15 August 1945. In January 1946 he began the sea voyage home to Japan. SEE ALSO PP. 502–6.

Sunday 23 – Saturday 29 April 1944

Alf Simpson, a Chindit, pays natives for airfield construction work at Mokokchung in the Naga hills of north-west Burma

Alf Simpson came from London and was a soldier in the Essex Regiment. He had married in January 1941 and two months later was on a troopship heading towards India. By 1944 he was serving in the Chindits, the special force founded by Orde Wingate which specialized in operating behind enemy lines. Simpson's task was to supervise the local tribes in north-west Burma in creating runways for light aircraft, to permit the delivery of supplies to the Chindit columns.

23 April

We were preparing to move forward into the Naga Hills to Mokokchung, there we had some Nagas doing some hill clearing for us and they needed paying. Armed with two heavy bags of silver Rupee coins, I got my first ever air trip. Co-operating with us we had some American light planes, they were like toys with just one seat behind the pilot. The pilot was Mendoza from New York, and he was to fly me over Mokokchung to drop the coins for them, a second plane accompanied us. When we arrived, I could see the clearing where they were waiting for us to drop the bags. We came down low and I dropped the first one after a signal from the pilot, we circled down again and I let the second go. It must have bust on contact with the ground, as we turned back I looked down to see what looked like a swarm of ants as the Naga scuttled around to pick up the coins.

29 April

I thought I was in luck, instead of having to march from Jorhat to Mokokchung, I got a lift in a jeep. The road, or should I say track, was a narrow ledge winding round the mountain with a terrific drop on one side, the wheels of the jeep often coming within about four inches of the edge, I had felt much safer in the toy plane. We heaved a sigh of relief when we eventually reached a plateau surrounded by hills. We had arrived at the Naga village of Mokokchung.

The Naga hills are occupied by many tribes with different characteristics, often hostile to each other. For security, the villages are perched right on top of the hills with just one winding track leading up to them. At Mokokchung, the Nagas were the Ao tribe, easily recognised by the loin cloth they wore showing three red horizontal stripes, each tribe had their own mode of dress. Most areas were governed by the British who gave the elders a red cloak as a mark of authority, but other areas were 'unadministrated' and shown on our maps as just a white space, in the middle, one word 'unsurveyed'. It was a change to meet natives who were not asking for 'Buckshees'. They seemed a proud and cheerful folk who, when given anything, accepted it as a gift and brought something back in return. The Intelligence Office soon had quite an assortment of Naga paraphernalia.

The work that the Nagas were doing when I flew over to drop the money to pay them, was the removal of the side of a hill to make an air strip for our light planes. As they worked, they kept up a pleasant musical chant the whole time. It was completed and the entire population turned out when our first plane, an American Sentinel, came in to land. At one end of the air strip was a sheer drop of about two thousand feet, a plane taking off would shoot over the edge and disappear from sight. We all held our breath until it reappeared again safely airborne. We also stood there and watched a parachute, which had missed the dropping zone float down into the valley. It had thousands of Rupees on it, somewhere down there were some Nagas feeling like the winners of the football pools.

Alf Simpson's first contact with the Nagas had been indirect, dropping money by air; after this he travelled by road from Jorhat to supervise the work more closely. This was part of Operation Thursday, the second major Chindit campaign, which had been launched on 5 March 1944. Alf Simpson was in 23rd Brigade, commanded by Brigadier Bernard Fergusson, a fierce adherent of the Wingate philosophy of independent action and deep penetration raids.

Alf Simpson survived the war but his fate thereafter is obsure.

Saturday 29 April – Thursday 4 May 1944

Don Peacock, a British POW labouring on airfield
construction on the island of Haruku, becomes a leader of
fashion

*In spring 1943 Don Peacock had been moved from Java to the tiny
island of Haruku in the Central Moluccas, just east of Ambon and south
of Ceram.*

April 29, and a gift from the Emperor himself on the occasion
of the royal birthday. To our astonishment each of us was
presented with a 2ft. 6in. square of flower-patterned blue
cloth. How a thousand-odd cotton squares came to arrive in
God-forsaken, starving Haruku must rank as one of the
great mysteries of WWII. What they were supposed to be
used for we never discovered. Presumably the Nips had
asked themselves the same question, and then some genius
had suggested giving them to us.

However, this was the first sign of such generosity since
the Jaarmarkt boots, so some sort of action was called for. I
desperately needed some shorts. Perhaps this scarf, or handkerchief, or whatever it was, could be converted into a pair.

There were difficulties. So far as I knew only one needle
existed in the hut, and it was suddenly in great demand: I
put myself down on the waiting list. There was no cotton at
all, but I kept my diary in a rough canvas holder, and I found
that, with a little patience, I could tease out strands of cotton
from the canvas. Elastic to hold the things up? I managed to
scrounge an old pair of bootlaces to use instead. The biggest
problem of all was how to go about actually making the
wretched thing. To start with, I hadn't the slightest idea, but
during my long wait for the needle it eventually dawned on
me that all I had to do was use an existing pair of shorts as a
template; lay them on the floor and cut around them twice.
And in due course I succeeded in converting a useless piece
of cloth into what I considered an elegant item of menswear.

I was not the only one to show quite unexpected talent

with the needle, and not the only one to appear on working parade with a large flower covering my backside. It did arouse a certain amount of comment, but leaders of fashion can always expect a certain amountof ignorant abuse . . .

3–4 May

On our jobs away from the airstrip we saw more of the islanders. Some, we gathered, were Christians sympathetic towards the Allies. Others were Muslims, co-operating enthusiastically with the Nips. The camp shop was a sort of United Nations operation, supplies for the British and Dutch prisoners being obtained by the Nips from Christian traders through a Muslim intermediary.

After one delivery the go-between apparently thought he could exploit the complexities of the situation. Confident that the traders would be too frightened to protest, he pocketed their money and told them the Nips had refused to pay. Sure enough the traders decided they would be on a beating to nothing if they dared to accuse the Nips of cheating them. They said nothing but, anxious not to be robbed a second time, they stopped coming. The Nips regarded this as an insult, and began making inquiries. The truth came out, and the pro-Nip Muslim found that the Nips were quite impartial when it came to handing out their particular brand of justice. For some reason, perhaps to intimidate us, they chose one of our huts as the torture-chamber.

After savage beatings, the go-between was suspended upside down while boiling water was poured over him. Next he was made to kneel by a cooking fire while Nips burned him about the body with glowing coconut husks. The Gunzo rounded off the session by urinating over him. He was then taken away, presumably to be executed. Another native, who had been selling us tobacco in quiet corners out on working parties, was brought into camp accused of having stolen the tobacco. He, too, tasted Nip justice.

These punishments, with the victims' cries echoing round our huts, resulted in a tense atmosphere, reminding us of the sort of people our captors could be. We pitied the tortured, no matter what they had done, and dreaded that next time it could be one of us.

The territory of Ceram lay well to the east of Bali and offered an ideal location for a new airfield that would allow Japanese attacks on American shipping around New Guinea, and perhaps even on Australia. The POWs were employed to create a level area for airfield construction which involved removing two rocky hills on the island and using the rubble to fill in the small valley between them. Conditions on Haruku were terrible: of the 2,000 prisoners employed on this task, only a third would survive. Donald Peacock was among them; he would return to Britain and resume his work as a journalist, and during the 1970s become a production executive on the Daily Mirror *in Manchester. SEE ALSO PP. 260–3, 369–71.*

MAY 1944

ALLIED AIR POWER was now inflicting severe punishment on Japanese headquarters, supply depots and bases, even those that were far behind the front line. Aerial mining of waterways had rendered the ports of Rangoon and Bangkok inoperative, while most Japanese shipping had been driven from the Bay of Bengal. Admiral Somerville's expanded Eastern Fleet, operating from its base in Ceylon, began more daring operations, including a raid on oil installations and the Japanese airfields at Surabaya in eastern Java.

In the north of Burma, Chinese units, bolstered by new trainees from Ramargh, launched a major offensive. On 10 May three Chinese divisions crossed the Salween river on a 100-mile front and moved forward rapidly, encountering little opposition. Four days later a commando unit called Merrill's Marauders conducted a surprise attack on the Japanese airfield outside Myitkyina. By 19 May American and Chinese troops were fighting in the streets of the town. In the south, the siege of Kohima was finally ended and British units began to advance eastward.

In India, the political situation appeared to have stabilized and, with the threat of a Japanese invasion of the country evaporating, Mahatma Gandhi was released from imprisonment on 5 May. He had been in gaol since the summer of 1942.

In China, a significant Japanese advance, known as the Lushan offensive, had begun in the triangle of territory bounded by Hankow, Ichang and Yochow. Japan had launched minor offensives each year in the late spring to capture rice stocks to maintain its troops, but this was something bigger. Employing tanks, which they had brought up under cover of night, they made surprising headway and on 9 May the town of Lushan fell, giving the Japanese control of the highway and the important railway from Beijing to Hankow. Within China, resistance organizations developed by the British and the Americans were beginning to have real success. The British had been running a large training operation for Chinese guerrillas at Pibu through 204 Military Mission. They had also established an organization called British Army Aid Group which was ostensibly designed to help POWs escaping from Hong Kong but in reality also provided a front for a large operation run by the Special Operations Executive (SOE). One of SOE's most successful operations was the black-market trading of currency, diamonds and rubber through various Chinese ports, turning a huge profit for the British Treasury. Private individuals suffered in China as the result of astronomically high prices, but the British government was determined not to be taken for a ride and acquired all of its local currency through clandestine channels rather than at the extortionate official exchange rate. SOE would be the only wartime organization to turn in a profit at the end of the war.

In New Guinea, US forces used their new base on Hollandia to over-run the neighbouring Japanese base on Wadke Island on 21 May. The Japanese lost 740 men with only four prisoners taken. The island was quickly converted into an air base for a forthcoming operation against the island of Mindanao in the Philippines. On 29 May the Americans attacked the island of Biak and the first armoured battle in the Pacific occurred, with considerable numbers of armoured vehicles deployed. Although the Japanese resistance on Biak was fierce, MacArthur announced that the fight for New Guinea was now effectively over. At Pearl Harbor a transport ship laden with ammunition exploded inexplicably near an ammunition depot. The resulting detonations caused 600 casualties.

On the American home front, the population enjoyed both guns and butter. American wartime rationing was never severe, and on 4 May all types of meat other than steak ceased to be rationed. Certain consumer goods, notably silk and rayon, were hard to come by, as were new cars, but these were minor deprivations compared even to the restrictions and shortages in other Allied countries. By contrast, in Japan the production of consumer goods had all but ceased, and during 1944 and 1945 the civilian population endured a near-starvation diet. Japan was increasingly scoured for every able-bodied man to serve in the military, while schoolchildren of thirteen and fourteen were drafted into the factories to help maintain production.

Early May 1944

Cecil Beaton and Gordon Grimsdale meet with an accident on the mountain road to a special forces training centre in China

Cecil Beaton and Major-General Gordon Grimsdale were making their way by truck through the mountains to visit the British special forces centre at Pibu, where Chinese commandos were under training. Beaton would also visit the British Army Aid Group, which was running clandestine operations into Japanese-occupied Hong Kong.

The first truck went ahead; we followed.

About half an hour later we were halted by an anxious-looking Colonel Larcom, from the first truck, standing alone in the mountain highway with an arm raised. At one side of him, a high wall of rock; on the other, a fifty-foot drop to the river.

'We've had a serious accident,' he told us. 'The truck's gone over there. The General's broken his leg.'

Scattered about on the boulders shelving down to the river lay various members of our vanguard. Bits of luggage, suitcases, umbrellas and pieces of clothing were hanging on the branches of bamboos. Some Chinese boys walked about, their faces marbled with dark dried blood; one of them looked like a prune. A Chinese soldier and Leo, quite undamaged, propped up Gordon, whose leg was giving him much pain. A few paces below him at the water's brink, on its side, lay the dead and battered truck. We were told that the truck had hit a large stone, had jerked over the precipice, before the driver was able to right the steering-wheel, and had somersaulted several times as it crashed down the rocks below. With each somersault people and luggage were thrown clear. But for a very short snapshot exposure I would have been sitting next to the driver, inside the truck, in the place occupied by Dr Young, who now lay unconscious on a crag, his suit and hat gore-blotched, his huge boots looking as if they did not belong to his body.

Bleeding Chinese were sprawled on the roadside, being sick beneath parasols. It was fortunate that a Viennese doctor, who had a huge trunk of medical equipment, was travelling with us. Bandages were applied; a stretcher made for Gordon, who was brave and smiling. How could he be dragged up the rocky slope? How to place him in a truck? How could he endure the three hours' journey back, bumping over the broken road? No, he must go by river. Someone walked miles to the nearest village to try to telephone for a boat, but returned, having found no telephone. Then someone discovered a boat to go back as far as the ferry. The wounded were piled in.

Gordon Grimsdale (left) with Claire Chennault

Accidents like the one described here were common on the dangerous roads that wound through the mountains of Burma and China. Gordon Grimsdale would recover and went on to become the British military attaché in Chungking. After the war, Cecil Beaton returned to a career of portrait photography and by the 1950s had begun work on costume design for Hollywood films. He died in 1980. SEE ALSO PP. 520–2, 540–1.

Saturday 6 May 1944

Juan Labrador, priest and academic, worries about the 'hold-up' merchants in Manila

For the last fifteen days, our streets and parks have been unlighted. We believe that these blackouts are precautions against air raids. I was informed today by a Tepco (formerly Meralco) technician that the blackouts are due to the loss of electric wires and lamps. The Army and the Navy have been paying exorbitant prices for these materials without investigating where they are coming from. Consequently, looters would steal rolls of wire from military warehouses and sell them to these same warehouses. They also stole a one-ton transformer in Caloocan.

Neither private persons are spared from the plague of looting which has become a big problem. They are a prey to all kinds of crimes.

One of the most common these days is the 'hold-up.' Under cover of darkness, a hold-up man would suddenly poke a gun at a victim's back, ordering him to remove his clothes and shoes and leaving him only with his trousers. An easy way of making [an] instant fortune now that a suit of sharkskin costs P400; a pair of shoes, P250; silk socks, P50; shirt and tie, P100; a wristwatch, P400 – in short, a total of P1000 which could be converted into spot cash at any buy and sell store at any time.

Juan Labrador continued to observe the Japanese occupation. His primary duties as a university tutor at Santo Tomas were in suspension, for the university campus had been taken over and turned into an internment camp. Meanwhile he noticed that the Japanese had begun to prepare for an American invasion of the Philippines, which most agreed could be no more than a few months away. SEE ALSO PP. 162–4, 229–31, 456–7, 689–91.

Saturday 13 – Wednesday 31 May 1944

Thomas Price Lewis, civilian internee, poses for photographs as the Japanese record life in Changi gaol

Thomas Price Lewis was born in Scotland and had been a student at Jesus College, Oxford in the 1920s, when he also played international rugby for England. In 1926 he moved to Malaya to embark on a teaching career and also played a part in developing the game of rugby there. In the 1930s he transferred to King Edward VII School at Taiping, where many of Malaya's aristocratic families sent their sons. On the eve of war he had just become headmaster of Clifford School in Kuala Kangsar. He was soon interned in Changi gaol.

13 May
I was able to exchange my tobacco 'issue' for 2 issues of sugar. The boils are getting better.

14 May
A Jap General is reported to have promised a hospital patient repatriation within 2 months. Numerous other rumours are – The Russians have taken Warsaw, we have taken, or landed in Tavoy and Borneo, the Japs have evacuated Flores, Timor and the Celebes.

15 May
A Jap General has given us 5 chests of tea and promised us 5 cows! The women again say they are to be repatriated shortly.

16 May
Doctors Winchester, Diamond and Lowther have been

interrogated by the Kempitai. My eighth boil has appeared on my bottom!

17 May

A roll call was held on the Golf Course outside the camp today. We have had a bread roll for the first time in this camp.

18 May

Emerson, a Sumatran rubber planter, died of dysentery today. The Jews have cornered the Tobacco Market by acting as brokers for the Japs. One cheroot now costs $1.50 each; a packet of cigarettes $15, a tin of sardines $40. Today a Sikh sentry chased away an internee from 'C' Block named Bowen when he went too near the wire fence. Our hut, which is near the fence, has been accused of making insulting gestures, shouting 'Black Bastard' at the Sikh during the chase and even displaying our penises! (We all have to assemble before the Japs tomorrow though most of us never saw the incident at all). Two internees have died, Beddington (P.W.D. Penang) of tuberculosis, and Manasseh, reputed to be a millionaire, who weighed only 46 lbs at death. Both had been ill for a long time.

19 May

We paraded at 10 am outside the Japs' office, where we stood to attention for 1¾ hours in the rain as nobody would own up to something they had not done. Eventually after threatening to beat us all up and keeping us all there all day, they let us all go. Before doing so, they beat up Bowen (Singapore Cold Storage) with bamboo poles, though it was noticed that the Sikh sentry hit Bowen much harder than the Jap did. Some Dutch Railway engineers returned to our camp today. All this time they had been in Pudu Jail, Kuala Lumpur where 2 died of beri-beri. One, in fact, had died on Kuala Lumpur Railway Station last night. The Dutchmen say that there are about 900 Communists and Indian Non-Cooperation in Pudu Jail and that daily hangings take place.

20 May

There are already 40 cases of malaria in the camp and I am lucky that Graham (P & T), my next door neighbour has kindly let me sleep inside his mosquito net, and half underneath his camp bed. John has received two letters from his wife Gwyneldd. 1,400 letters in all have been received in the camp from Singapore, where they are now censored. Reading *Malaysia Mosaic*.

21 May

Our hopes are raised by further unconfirmed rumours of action in Tavoy in Siam. 6 have been taken to the Guard Room for waving to the women over the fence.

22 May

The Jap General has been informed that, in the Committee's opinion, there are 600 potential cases of beri-beri in the camp unless the diet is improved and soya beans provided. There are rumours of an Allied landing in Europe and the rumours about Tavoy and Burma appear to be true. Reading Victor Hugo's 93 [*Quatre-Vingt-Treize*].

23 May

3,800 more letters were given out today – none for me. Three more internees have died: Davies, a Taiping Warder (from anaemia and dysentery), Kerr (who has been insane since 1938) and Southern (tuberculosis). The number of Malaria cases is now 80 . . .

25 May

We have received the great news that 1,000,000 men have landed in the Bordeaux area of France, and also near Cherbourg and that our paratroops have appeared over the Warsaw sector and the Brenner Pass. The Japs are said to expect 1,000 internees to wish to move out of our camp. Today, we again had soya bean flour in our morning meal, presumably because of our protests about our diet. Reading Winston Churchill's *The World Crisis*, Vol. I.

26 May

Bishop Wilson and Yoxall have been returned to our camp by the Kempitai and so has Mrs Nixon to the Women's Block. The two men appear to be in reasonable shape but not Mrs Nixon. We are troubled a bit by rats who will eat anything which is not securely covered up . . .

30 May

The Kempitai have just taken away Hockenhull (Police) and are now looking for missing telephone receivers.

31 May

A mythical Jap doctor now states that we are leaving for home on June 16. We hear that the Japs are planning a great Photographic Propaganda project which will feature the following scenes – 5 clergy conducting a service with a congregation of 50; the Men's Representative accepting mail from Tominara; married men consorting with their wives and children; internees eating double rations of rice; 3 doctors with Hospital patients; 12 musicians playing their instruments, and 50 gardeners wearing shirts and wielding changkols! Reading Drinkwater's *Abraham Lincoln*.

Thomas Lewis's brief but poignant entries give an immediate sensation of life in Changi gaol for the thousands of civilian internees. English society in Malaya, once very hierarchical, was now levelled, and all endured the stark routines of rationing, parades, punishment and rumour that gave shape to each day. The missing telephone receivers had been stolen by internees to make into headphones for illicit radio receivers. Despite the presence of several secret radios in Changi, reliable facts mingled inextricably with fiction. Bizarrely, Lewis heard rumours of the invasion of France almost two weeks before it actually occurred on 6 June 1944! The invasion of France had long been looked forward to, and the rumours that Lewis had heard were almost certainly the product of wishful thinking by inmates rather than genuine information. SEE ALSO PP. 609–11.

JUNE 1944

IN THE PACIFIC, the Americans made strategic advances by attacking the island of Saipan in the Marianas. Operations began on 11 June with heavy air bombardment designed to neutralize Japanese air power. By the end of the month more than half the island had been taken. Saipan had been administered by the Japanese before the war and was home to a substantial Japanese civilian population of some 22,000. Many of them committed mass suicide, by leaping from the high cliffs into the sea, rather than submit to what they believed would be American enslavement. The places where this occurred were called 'Suicide Cliff' and 'Banzai Cliff' by the local population. Thereafter, the Americans began to develop Saipan as a base from which American B-29 Superfortress bombers could attack Japan. On 16 June air raids against Japan were launched from China. These air raids were the first attempts to bomb Japan since the Doolittle raid of 1942 and signalled a change in strategy with drastic effects for the inhabitants of Japan's cities.

The Mariana Islands were also the location of a major naval engagement. On 18 June 1944 Japanese scout planes from a fleet equipped with two aircraft carriers located the American fleet. The Japanese plan was to launch a very long-range strike, using an air base on Guam to refuel before attacking the Americans again on the return journey. The following morning the Japanese launched four waves of aircraft. However, these were detected by radar and were intercepted by US fighters. The Japanese bombers that reached the ships were mostly destroyed by anti-aircraft fire with very few actually able to drive home their attacks on the ships. The only damage suffered was a single bomb hit on the battleship *South Dakota*. The Japanese lost 240 aircraft, the Americans just 29. American sailors were astonished at this easy victory and dubbed it the 'Great Marianas Turkey Shoot'. The two Japanese carriers were quickly sunk by American submarines. The following day, the Americans sank the carrier *Hiyop* and damaged two others, but many American aircraft crashed on returning to their carriers after dark. This series of engagements became known as the Battle of the Philippines Sea.

In China the Japanese offensive continued, and some forward American air bases that had been used for attacking Japanese coastal activities were hurriedly withdrawn. Japanese advances were indeed so spectacular that the Chinese nationalists and communists were briefly forced to co-operate. In Burma, Chinese forces in the north reached the important town of Lung-ling before the onset of the monsoon brought active campaigning to a halt. In the south, the Japanese attempt to mount an offensive at Imphal and Kohima had failed and had now turned into a rout.

American submarines continued to make a major contribution to the weakening of the Japanese war effort, sinking 260,000 tons of merchant shipping in this month alone. These rates of loss made it almost impossible for Japan to reinforce its garrisons effectively. They also made it increasingly hard for the Japanese to import fuel and oil, despite having captured some very large oil-producing areas in the Netherlands East Indies. American submarines also sank two aircraft carriers and six destroyers. No area of the sea around Japan was safe from such attacks.

At the end of June, Emperor Hirohito called a conference of his generals to review the progress of the war. The commanders admitted that outlying bases such as Saipan could not be held and that the focus would now have to be upon defending outposts closer to Japan, such as the island of Iwo Jima, a volcanic island some hundreds of miles east of the Japanese shore.

Thursday 1 June 1944

Corwin Mendenhall, on the US submarine *Pintado*, joins in the destruction of a Japanese convoy

Mendenhall had been posted on board the Pintado *in November 1943 after the sinking of his previous submarine,* Sculpin.

At 0342 . . . [the] convoy made another course change, which placed *Pintado* in a favorable position on the port side of the formation.

We promptly went to battle stations, commenced our approach, and prepared for a surface torpedo attack. There were then two 5,000–6,000-ton freighters in column on the starboard side of the convoy, and one identified as a big *Tarayasu*-type freighter (10,254 tons), alone and heavily loaded, in the port column, with the columns about 800 yards apart. Escorts were on the bow and quarter of the *Tarayasu*.

At 0415 the range to the *Tarayasu* was 4,700 yards, torpedo run about 3,900 yards. Then a lookout reported gunfire from the convoy, so the skipper rashly turned *Pintado*, at flank speed, to open the range, thinking we had been detected. That was a mistake; no one else saw any gunfire. I told him that I thought we should have more evidence than what the lookout 'thought' was gunfire. The movements of the convoy and the escorts gave no evidence that they had sniffed us out, but by turning away and going to flank speed we lost our attack position.

Again *Pintado* maneuvered at full speed to regain position for attack. At 0430 we made our second move in, on the port side of target *Tarayasu*. Ships in the starboard column were in the line of fire beyond our target. Slipping undetected between the two escorts just before daybreak, the skipper fired a spread of six fish from the bow tubes, set to run at six-foot depth and explode on impact. The setup was near perfect: a 1,200-yard torpedo run, near zero gyro angle, ninety-five-degree port track.

Five torpedoes hit the *Tarayasu*. He disintegrated and sank. Other explosions were heard as *Pintado* turned to bring the stern tubes to bear on the remaining freighters, passing only 700 yards from one of the escorts. Both escorts turned towards us, so we went to emergency flank speed, running directly away from them, reaching a speed of twenty-one knots. (The order of speeds, from low to high, was: one-third, two-thirds, standard, full, and flank. 'Emergency' flank meant for the engineers to 'pour on everything including the galley range,' but that speed could not be maintained for very long and could damage the engineering plant.) Surprisingly the escorts didn't press a counterattack, and we pulled clear to regroup and attack the remaining ships . . .

With daylight near, *Pintado* pulled clear on the surface, reloaded torpedo tubes, and prepared to attack the remainder of the convoy. At 0500, in daylight, there were several more explosions, and we saw a second ship in trouble. From our bridge the flashes of the blasts were vivid. The ship broke in two, and the bow and stern sank separately. The tops of one remaining ship were visible at the scene, with escorts milling around, apparently picking up survivors.

From 1943 American submarines increasingly performed duties which might be described as 'sea denial', closing down Japanese supply routes. During the morning of 1 June 1944, Corwin Mendenhall and his fellow submariners on the submarine Pintado *attacked a large Japanese convoy heading towards Saipan. Working with another submarine,* Shark, *they sank four troop and cargo ships. Losses on this scale were catastrophic for the increasingly isolated Japanese garrison. Two weeks later US marines attacked Saipan and the Japanese garrison there found itself perilously short of supplies and ammunition.*

Corwin Mendenhall continued to serve in the US navy after the war and would retire in 1959 with the rank of admiral. Subsequently he worked in Texas as an industrial manager and business consultant. SEE ALSO PP. *318–21.*

Monday 5 June 1944

T. E. Dorman, a New Zealander serving with the Fiji Regiment, comes across the remains of a native village and agrees 'no more prisoners'

The day opened with shelling from the hills behind us, our position now being known to the Japanese, but American dive-bombers swept over and quietened the guns down considerably. We moved off early and speedily, as soon as it was light enough to see, heading for Mawaraka Point which was now quite silent. After crossing a blind river mouth, that is, one that is flowing only at times, we reached the spot appointed for our company's share in the advance to the end of the road to Kahilhi. Our task was now to cut into the jungle on a bearing and strike the road more than half a mile up from the beach, while the rest of the Battalion moved on along the line of the beach itself. We had a laborious task, especially as we struck swamp right across the line of our march and had no alternative but to go right through it. You were in it up to your knees all the time and every few moments you found yourself in a patch that took you into the mud and slime up to your armpits. We managed to get across alright and a little further on came across the remains of a native village, which looked as if it could have been deserted for some time. A very muddy creek ran through the middle of it and there were skeletons in and around that. Much more unpleasant, however, was what we found on a mound of earth behind one of the larger huts. Pegged out on the ground were the naked bodies of two quite young native girls; they had obviously been raped to death. It all reminded us of the kind of enemy we were up against. We paused long enough to bury the girls and skeletons in one deep grave . . .

When C Company arrived and took over the area, we marched back to the beach along the road in about ten minutes and dug in just off the beach. Later in the afternoon the artillery arrived on L.C.T.'s [Landing Craft – Tank] and established themselves about a hundred yards behind us, opening fire as soon as they were ready. It was comforting to have them there, but not the best for our ears. About 1730 there was a burst of heavy fire from one of our pickets, so I was sent out with a two section patrol. It was already starting to get dark, but I stayed out for an hour probing about the area and finishing up with another nasty discovery. We found several patches of blood and evidence that Japanese dead or wounded had been dragged away. Then just as we were turning back we found a body, a man who had been dead by the look of things for a day or two. He was an American, dressed in the remains of a uniform, but with no boots or socks, no equipment, no headgear. His feet were badly cut about. But worst of all was the fact that he was pinned to the ground with a sharp wooden stake driven through each shoulder and both his hands had been cut off. We took the tags that were still around his neck and quickly buried him in a shallow grave at the foot of a tree. The Fijians worked in grim silence, but as we moved away again one of my corporals said to me: 'No more prisoners, turaga.' I agreed with him.

T. E. Dorman's diary is a classic record of the barbarization of warfare and the manner in which atrocity bred further atrocity. His unit was working along the coast near Gazelle Harbour, with excellent supplies, communications and fire support from naval craft. Removing prisoners from this location would have presented few practical difficulties, but after the discoveries of 5 June 1944 his unit resolved that no more would be taken. SEE ALSO PP. 546–7.

Monday 26 June 1944

Charles Lindbergh discusses the practice of war with the 475th Fighter Group on the New Guinea coast

Following the events at Pearl Harbor in December 1941, Charles Lindbergh had abandoned his efforts to champion isolationism. A leading aeronautical engineer, his services were soon in demand with the expanding American aviation industry and he was quickly involved with both Ford and United Aviation. In 1944 it was suggested that he might visit the Pacific as a civilian 'observer', partly to advise local units on techniques to extend their range and partly to explore the possibilities for a new fighter aircraft. After purchasing a uniform from Brooks Brothers, he headed west across the Pacific. On 15 June he landed at Finschhafen, bound for the 475th Fighter Group, a unit that flew under the nickname of 'Satan's Angels'. On 26 June he joined their commander, Colonel Charles H. MacDonald, and some of his officers for the evening.

I accepted the colonel's invitation to spend the night at his quarters. A group of officers were there when we arrived, and we spent the evening until after midnight discussing fighter characteristics and the war in this area.

There were three silk Japanese flags hanging on one wall of the hut we were in, taken from the bodies of Japanese soldiers. The souvenir value of one of these flags was about £10, one of the officers told me ($33.00 American). Someone who has a Japanese officer's sword is asking £250 for it. The talk drifted to prisoners of war and the small percentage of Japanese soldiers taken prisoner. 'Oh, we could take more if we wanted to,' one of the officers replied. 'But our boys don't like to take prisoners.'

'We had a couple of thousand down at ——, but only a hundred or two were turned in. They had an accident with the rest. It doesn't encourage the rest to surrender when they hear of their buddies being marched out on the flying field and machine guns turned loose on them.'

'Or after a couple of them get shot with their hands up in the air,' another officer chimed in.

'Well, take the ——th. They found one of their men pretty badly mutilated. After that, you can bet they didn't capture very many Japs.'

The talk drifted to air combats and parachute jumps. All of the pilots insisted it was proper to shoot enemy airmen coming down in their parachutes. However, several said that they themselves would not do it. 'The Japs started it. If they want to play that way, we can, too.' Accounts were given of American airmen shot down hanging from their parachutes by the Japanese.

The 475th Fighter Group were equipped with P-38 Lightnings and Lindbergh joined them on a combat mission over New Guinea the following day, strafing Japanese barges along the coast. This was the first of some fifty combat missions he would fly in the Pacific as a 'civilian observer'. Already he was somewhat disturbed by certain of the opinions voiced by officers he had met and was busy recording his misgivings in his diary. However, he extended some anonymity to the units that he referred to by blanking out the numerical identifiers and locations in the published version of his diary. SEE ALSO PP. 99–101, 598–9, 611–12.

Tuesday 27 June 1944

Soviet emissary Peter Vladimirov discusses Japanese
atrocities with a 'turned' Japanese POW working for the
Chinese communists in Yenan

*In June 1944 Peter Vladimirov had an opportunity to discuss Japanese
barbarities with a rare category of prisoner. He spoke with a captured
Japanese soldier who was assisting Japanese Communist Party chief
Sanzo Nozaka or, as others called him, Okano Susumu.*

A former Japanese POW, and now one of the most active
Okano assistants, showed me some captured photographs.
These are the blood-chilling pictures of the Japanese
atrocities. I asked him to give me some of the photographs.

It is hard even to imagine that such things were possible!

The photographs show peasants' bodies stripped naked
and crucified on the walls of their houses.

Here is a disembowelled corpse, and then more and more
such corpses.

The Okano worker explained to me that it was the
Japanese soldiers' custom to disembowel their victims. They
do it to most of the Chinese war prisoners and to almost
every male. But they don't stop at it. According to the
medieval belief, liver is the symbol of courage and valor;
that's why in many cases the Japanese soldiers not only disembowel their victims but also cut out their liver and eat it.
I would take it for madman's ravings unless I had such a
photograph right before my eyes.

Here are the photographs of massacres. They show the
victims in the most terrifying poses. The Japanese do not
shoot their victims, and not at all because they save their
bullets. They herd together children, women, and old people
and then stab them with bayonets like dummies for exercise.
Here is one such photograph. It shows the shortish soldiers
in kepi working hard with their bayonets and sabers amid
the frantic crowd . . .

Photograph after photo show heaps of flesh that once

were human beings. And in each photo officers and soldiers pose.

Here is a photograph showing several dozen women with their skirts up and their pants pulled down to their knees, and the Japanese soldiers squatting in front of them. I wish it were the only photo of this kind!

Most of the photos depict scenes of rape and humiliation. Here and there tortured women and the soldiery.

Another typical photograph. It shows the traditional decapitation of the victims. It can be seen even in the photographs that the Japanese regard it as a sport, a competition in skill.

The soldiers' faces are shockingly calm, indifferent, and even sleepy.

Okano Susumu stayed with the Chinese Communist Party leadership in Yenan throughout most of the war and conducted propaganda operations and surrender drives against the Japanese forces for them. Having spent some time in America, Okano also advised a visiting American mission which arrived in 1944. Because Okano's assistant was now a communist working for the Chinese, Vladimirov hoped to obtain frank answers to his questions about atrocities, but while he received full descriptions these did not really help him to understand why they occurred. While all sides committed atrocities during the Asia–Pacific war, Japan was unique in perpetrating crimes against civilians on an almost unbelievable scale. Although this behaviour is documented extremely thoroughly, partly because of the Japanese penchant for capturing it on camera, it remains difficult to explain.

At the end of the war Vladimirov returned to Moscow to join his wife and family, who had left China the year before. He became the Soviet consul-general in Shanghai in 1948 and the Soviet ambassador to Burma in 1952. He died the following year after a short illness. SEE ALSO PP. 305–7, 451–2, 575–6.

Wednesday 28 June 1944

2nd Lieutenant Taiso Nishikawa, commander of No. 5 Company, watches the Japanese offensive at Imphal and Kohima melt away

Taiso Nishikawa's notebook containing his diary was captured at Imphal after Japanese forces were routed and fled during late June and early July 1944, but little is known about him.

The operations conducted by the Supreme Commander, Burma area Army, against IMPHAL which is being described as a second Guadalcanal, have been, on the whole, a lamentable failure. With three divisions, and with the same tactics with which we took Burma, we began attacking before air support had arrived. What with the bad weather, the barrier of the ARAKAN Range, men going down with malaria all the time, and more laid out with diarrhoea, together with the merciless bombing, the three divisions have been practically annihilated. For example, in 33 Division one company finished up with its commander and two men as its total strength.

Although we had occupied hills in the ARAKAN Range, by March of this year, there was not much hope of our taking IMPHAL. At this stage the Army had been asking for re-inforcements. It was planned to send four new divisions, the seven divisions were then to attack IMPHAL. But as a result of transport difficulties and insufficiency of air units we could not win mastery of the air, and completely lost the transport battle.

Again, enemy air-raids were becoming more violent and the result was that our reinforcements were in a bad way; they suffered also from airborne troops landing by gliders to their rear, and other thorns in the flesh; moreover accidents with trucks on the ARAKAN hillsides were surprisingly numerous. It was not merely that the transport of troops – and of course, food and ammunition – was delayed – the thing was practically impossible.

So the troops just had to march through the ARAKAN

Range, carrying a month's rations. More than fifty per-cent fell out and took twice as many days to get there. Although, as a result of fatigue and bad weather, the number of malaria cases and other casualties kept increasing, they managed in some way to transport the troops, but not the ammunition or supplies.

The whole Division, including the Divisional Commander, fought ten days without rice, and, because of things like this, the date of the general offensive, originally 10 June, was postponed ten or twenty days, and left indefinite.

We felt it bitterly, this need for aircraft and motor transport. We wanted to shout to the people at home, 'Send more aircraft to the battle fronts'. The enemy stands firm, having plenty of weapons, ammunition and food. His attacks with tanks and mortars are something terrific – so are his air raids, and we can do nothing.

Today is the 28th of June. Gradually the general offensive is getting under way. My unit is in the front line of all and has begun the final attack, but this is the toughest going, and if we do manage to take a position, the enemy bombards it with mortars, and bombs it from the air to a heart-shaking degree; so that those who have dug deep trenches are buried in them, and those who have dug shallow, have hands and feet blown away.

The Battalion commander and adjutant have been killed. The Company has been virtually destroyed. This is the kind of hell war can be.

The wounded men were sent back but the sick were not. Kept in the front line, they have to pound the unhulled rice. Up to the time of their death they have to pound the unhulled rice, and when they die, they die from sheer exhaustion. It is rumoured that the Regt Comdr too, has been killed. For us it is a matter of days.

The Japanese offensive against Imphal and Kohima was not a surprise for the Allies, yet its sheer speed and ferocity still caught local British army units off balance. The British defenders only clung on by a thread and had to be resupplied with arms and ammunition by air. The defenders would have been surprised to learn that this was a last desperate fling for the Japanese forces in Burma, themselves chronically short of supplies. Already over-extended, the Japanese had staked everything on victory. Once the offensive was halted, Japanese forces found themselves without supplies or medical support and retreated in disarray.

JULY 1944

FIGHTING ON SAIPAN continued until 9 July, with resistance focused on the north end of the island. On the day Saipan fell, the local commanders, Lieutenant-General Saito and Admiral Nagumo, committed hara-kiri – ritual suicide by disembowelment. On the nearby island of Biak, fighting went on. Already American carrier forces were beginning to raid Japanese bases on Iwo Jima, a Japanese island only 600 miles from the home islands.

On 21 July 1944 General Geiger's II Amphibious Force attacked Guam with 54,000 men. Three days later a similar force attacked another Japanese stronghold, the island of Tinian in the Marianas. Japanese counter-attacks proved very costly, not least because American forces now made the first use in combat of napalm, an inflammable liquid mixture of gasoline, oil and gelatine that ran into the bottom of trenches and pillboxes. By the end of July the Americans had taken the southern half of Guam and organized resistance on Tinian had ceased.

In Burma, the poor supply situation, combined with the mounting problems of disease, contributed to the collapse of Japanese operations on the Imphal front. In contrast, the Japanese continued to make gains in China. Henry Wallace, the American Vice-President, had been sent to investigate the situation in China and reported that the government was in disarray. He advocated mediation between the nationalists and the communists in the hope of encouraging a united front to slow the Japanese offensive.

The loss of Saipan, the attacks on Iwo Jima and the bombing

of the Japanese homeland triggered a seismic shift in Japanese politics. Initially, the elderly navy minister, Shimada, was replaced by Admiral Nomura. Then, on 18 July, General Tojo resigned as Prime Minister, followed by all of his Cabinet. Tojo had also held the offices of Chief of Staff, Minister of the Army, Minister of the Interior and Minister of Munitions. General Kuniaki Koiso was chosen as Prime Minister to form a new government and appointed General Umezu as the new Chief of Staff. Many Japanese diplomats were now anxious to seek a negotiated settlement to end the war, fearing the imposition of a harsh peace if they failed to do so.

The American domestic political scene was also active during July 1944. Roosevelt had announced that he was willing to run for a historic fourth term 'if asked by the people', given the unusual wartime circumstances. However, he was anxious to drop his left-wing Vice-President Wallace and so made it clear that he would allow the Democratic Convention to choose his running mate. This person proved to be Congressman Harry S. Truman.

Through most of July the United States hosted an international monetary conference at Bretton Woods. Although a low-profile event this meeting was of enormous importance, representing the beginning of the liberal economic order that would be established by the United States after 1945. More than forty countries attended, and they agreed to set up an International Monetary Fund and an International Bank for Reconstruction and Development, later called the World Bank. Britain took the opportunity to ask for post-war aid, emphasizing to the United States that fighting the Second World War since 1939 had taken it to the very edge of financial ruin, something not yet realized in Washington.

Sunday 2 July 1944

Henry Kasper, a sailor with the American merchant
marine, visits the front line at Garapan on the island of
Saipan

*Henry Kasper records in his diary that he did not want to go to war, he
wished 'to go to sea'. He had joined the merchant marine in early 1941,
but quickly found himself involved in military preparations. By 1944 he
was the Second Assistant Engineer on the SS* Morcacport, *a cargo ship
converted to carry 1,200 combat troops which, although a merchant
marine vessel, participated in the invasion of Saipan and Peleliu in order
to supply the invading marines.*

The town was a mess! Possibly one or two small buildings
were still standing up, but these had shell holes and other
damage. Most of the former edifices and houses were broken
crumbles of rock and sheet metal and brick and wood.

Canned goods and burned commodities made black
heaps here and there. We followed the railroad tracks for a
while until we saw a group of battle-weary marines about a
block away from us to the right. These were actually the first
group of fellows we had seen this far in town.

So we climbed over more debris and ruins and began talking to two of them sitting in the shade of a broken wall. To
our surprise, we learned that the front line was only about
two blocks ahead of us in the direction we had been walking.
These fellows were marines from the front-line group!

Well, here we were! The Japs still had part of the town, and
the line itself was always fluctuating. Sometimes patrols
would penetrate far into the Jap side without making
contact, and other times the Japs would be right on top of
them with machine-gun fire.

These two young fellows – one had just turned twenty –
talked to us for some time and pointed out to us just where
the Japanese were still fighting and what was actually
happening, insofar as they knew.

This group had been waiting in that sector for about five

days without moving ahead. The hills in back of town were full of Japs, and they were to wait until another marine division and the army division came in from behind and established positions. Then they were to move up.

A couple of the marines in this group had been in Guadalcanal, Tarawa, the Marshalls, and now here, without even going back to the States. If they are not wounded, they are still good for fighting.

We were sitting a few yards from a red-painted barn-like structure, and the fellows informed us that the place was a geisha house and they had found materials indicating the same. Also they found cases of Jap beer, sake, cans of pine-apple from Formosa, and even canned tangerines. The one young fellow praised the Japanese canned salmon and canned tangerines.

We could hear the rat-a-tat-tat of machine-gun fire, an occasional Jap .25 rifle shot, and mortar fire also. The hills above us were dotted with puffs of smoke.

The fellows have named the streets here, and we were sitting between Main and Broadway. Main is one block up and parallel to the beach, then comes Broadway, and then Spring.

A fellow was looking through a pair of binoculars on a tripod down Broadway. We inquired why he was sitting in the middle of the street like that. The answer was that this person was observing the road to see if any Japs were sneak-ing across from above town to down toward the beach. They do it every now and then.

The town appears to me like the pictures I've seen of Cassino and other shell-bombed cities.

We were sitting among the remains of a garage, and I picked up a few tools that appeared usable. I also picked up a helmet and a Japanese brass tripod.

As we were talking, the marines were informed to move on and then the word came through to move up. We waved good-bye and wished them luck . . .

We finally made it to the Jap dock and we were walking along when a navy officer asked us who we were. He then informed us that the MP's have orders to pick up any person 'souvenir-hunting' and to put him to work for twenty-four hours at grave-digging! It was high time that we really did leave the island.

Eventually we hitched a ride on a 'duck,' and the fellows took us out to our own vessel, which we boarded shortly before noon.

The marines seemed to treat us all right while we were ashore. It was good to be back. I was dirty and muddy and sweaty, and the cold water of the ship really tasted good. The war was gone from us in the way of thirst, but our minds still retain the sight we saw.

The fighting on Saipan was particularly fierce and, despite their massive superiority in firepower provided by naval vessels firing onto shore, the Americans had been surprised by the tenacity of the resistance. They had not expected the island to be so heavily garrisoned, finding twice the numbers of troops forecast. At one point at an early stage in the invasion the Japanese moved behind the 4th Marines Division and inflicted serious casualties. Interestingly, the MPs met by Kasper were not just looking for illegal souvenir-hunters but also for marines who might have 'wandered' away from the front line, hoping to rejoin their units after the serious fighting had finished. Garapan, the main town on Saipan, finally fell on 4 July 1944. SEE ALSO PP. 623–5.

Thursday 6 – Friday 7 July 1944

Taro Kawaguchi and his comrades prepare to face the end on the island of Saipan

Taro Kawaguchi belonged to the Nakahara Unit, which was part of the Japanese 43rd Division. They had been fighting near the village of Donnay and were now taking part in the last stand on Saipan at the north-eastern end of the island. Here Japanese forces were gradually compressed into a small pocket, subjected to the most formidable American naval bombardment. This made any military action, indeed any movement at all above ground, almost suicidal. Kawaguchi and his colleagues could emerge from their trenches only when heavy rain obscured their activities from American artillery spotters. On 4 July his battalion commander explained that they were not going to move from

their current position and gave out orders to fight to the last, adding:
'My foxhole is my grave.'

6 July

Received artillery barrage during the morning and took cover among the rocks. As each round approached nearer and nearer, I closed my eyes and awaited it. Rifle reports and tanks seemed nearer and everyone took cover within the forest and waited for the enemy to approach. Soon the voice of the enemy could be heard and machine gun fire could be heard over our heads. I thought this was the end and was ready to charge out with a hand grenade when ordered to take cover by the Capt. When I looked from the side of the rock I could see the hateful bearded face of the enemy shining in the sunlight. With a terrific report the rock in front of my eyes exploded, and the Sgt. that joined us last night was killed. Also the Cpl [Corporal] received severe wounds in his left thigh. However, I could not treat the wounds even if I wanted to. Everyone hugged the ground and kept quiet, waiting for an opening in the enemy. As I stood up to get the rifle from one of the dead, a bullet hit between my legs and I thought sure I was hit, but after glancing down, to my happiness, nothing was wrong. A report was heard and as I looked back I saw my friend Cpl Ito lying on his back with a rifle in his hand. Oh! Cpl Ito who has been in my section ever since Nagoya had died. After fierce counterfire, the enemy was repulsed so I approached the body of Ito who had a bullet hole through his left temple, with his eyes half open and lips tightly clenched. 'I'll take Ito's revenge.' Taking Ito's rifle which was clenched in his hands even after death, I waited for the enemy to attack. Cpl Yasukiro also had wounds in both legs. Pathetically he was saying, 'Please kill me,' so 1st Lt. Matsumai beautifully cut his head off. The Cpl pleaded before being cut to the Lt. 'Please cut skilfully.' The Lt. with sweat pouring down his hand, took one stroke, two strokes, and on the third stroke he cut his head off. The rifle reports subsided. Soon however, reports commenced roaring in the frontal area. I pocketed the scroll written by Cpl. Ito as a farewell gift and bid farewell to his spirit. I grabbed Cpl Ono's hand and he stated pathetically that he will commit suicide tomorrow morning . . . Soon a terrific squall started and everyone got drenched.

7 July

While shivering from wetness, orders to move were issued. Facing the dawn, the north, bowing reverently to the Imperial Palace and bidding farewell to the parents, aunt and wife I solemnly pledged to do my utmost. With Sgt. Hasegawa and Capt. Watanabe departed from the rocks and came out of the forest. It is regretful that we depart from Lt. Yamaguchi because we promised that the place of death would be the same. Between the enemy artillery bombardment, approached the cliffs of day before yesterday where we received the artillery bombardment. We tried to reach the shore but could not because of the cliffs. The enemy is surrounding us in all directions. Helplessly we took cover in the jungle. At the crack of dawn, enemy activity commenced below on the road with vehicles, tanks and walking soldiers. At last the end has come. We have separated from the Unit Staff and the members of the second company consisted of Lt. Hasegawa, transport unit. Our group consisted of less than ten men. Even though we wanted to attack we have no weapons, so with the determination of dying for the Emperor we spent our time by preparing for our remembrance. Looking back through the years. I am only 26 years old. Thanks to the Emperor, both my parents, and my aunt I have lived to this day and am deeply gratified. At the same time it is deeply regrettable that I have nothing to report at this time when my life is fluttering away like a flower petal to become a part of the soil. Since the enemy landing, to have fought against the enemy endeavoring my utmost power in carrying out my duty and thus becoming a war lord, I am very happy. It is only regrettable that we have not fought enough and that the American devil is stomping on the Imperial soil. I, with my sacrificed body will become the white caps of the Pacific and will stay on this island until the friendly forces come to reclaim the soil of the Emperor.

Kawaguchi's diary refers to the notorious cliffs at the northern end of the island of Saipan. During the first week of July thousands of Japanese men, women and children jumped from this location, rather than surrender to the Americans. Of the 22,000 civilians on Saipan, perhaps half had leaped to their deaths by the time Saipan fell on 9 July. Kawaguchi's last words, written in his diary, bade farewell to members of his family, especially his aunt. He closed by expressing satisfaction that 'I can die on the anniversary of the Sino-Jap Incident', that is, the beginning of the war against China on 7 July 1937. His diary was found by Master Sergeant J. William Winter on the battlefield on 19 July 1944.

Thursday 13 July 1944

Marquis Kido and Premier Tojo discuss the state of the war after the fall of Saipan

Marquis Kido was Lord Keeper of the Privy Seal and therefore Emperor Hirohito's closest civilian adviser. His task was often to convey the opinions of senior politicians and military chiefs to the Emperor.

Premier Tojo visited me at my office and gave his opinion on the state of the war following the fall of Saipan. This is a summary of his statement:

For a week I deliberated on how to cope with the present situation. At one time I thought it best to resign, but considering closely the domestic situation, the antiwar or pessimistic atmosphere, the criticism of the supreme command, and so forth, I am afraid of ushering in defeat by taking the wrong course through a change in the Cabinet. That is, of course, not the right way to fulfill one's duty as the Emperor's servant. Under the circumstances, I have made up my mind to go ahead to the end, asking leniency regarding my responsibility for Saipan's fall for the time being. I discussed my decision with Shimada yesterday, including also both first vice chiefs. He had the same opinion and said that he also often considered resignation, but when he learned of my resolution, he said that he would make a new determination to go ahead and continue to fight.

As things now stand, it will be difficult for the Cabinet, as it presently exists, to continue, so I want to reform or reinforce it . . .

My opinions should not interfere with the policies of the government, I said, much less those of the supreme command. The present situation not only concerns the Cabinet, but threatens to aggravate the tendency to criticize His Majesty's august virtues. What does the Emperor think will be the future of the war if military operations are left to the part-time strategists? Is it right to entrust Tojo alone with the fate of the nation? Such voices are so often heard that I dared to express my opinions . . .

Met His Majesty in the library at 2:05 P.M. and submitted a general report of my talk with Tojo.

The fall of Saipan had triggered a convulsion in Tokyo. Although Tojo wished to continue as premier, general opinion in government circles had been turning against him for some time. His opponents now expressed their lack of confidence and Tojo would resign a few days after this meeting. Kido continued to serve the Emperor until August 1945 and the surrender of Japan. His diary was then seized by the International Military Tribunal for the Far East – the Tokyo war crimes trials – and used extensively by both the prosecution and the defence. Using his diary, the tribunal found Kido guilty of war crimes and sentenced him to life imprisonment in 1948. He was paroled in 1955 by the new Japanese government and lived quietly in retirement until his death in 1977. SEE ALSO PP. 75–7, 86–7, 123–5, 457–8.

Saturday 15 – Thursday 20 July 1944

Sheila Allan, an Australian internee, varies her diet in the civilian camp at Changi

15 July
Started working in the garden today – while digging to plant sweet potatoes found a worm – fat worm – picked up the wriggling thing and a thought came into my mind – wonder what it would taste like? Didn't fancy swallowing the

squirming creature – threw it away – then found a clod of earth with more of the pink worms – had an idea – collected a tinful and later took it to the hut – decided to cook the worms and see what happens – well! All that was left after the cooking were thin strips of dried-up skins – not appetising – but hunger took over – took a bit of a piece – not that bad – a sprinkle of salt and it tasted like bacon rind – well, I imagine that's how bacon rind would taste – crackly and salty! Did I tell anyone? – No way! They might think I've gone 'cuckoo' – eating worms indeed – what next?

20 July

Did a dreadful thing today – thoroughly disgusted with myself – I swallowed a baby mouse! Found a nest of baby mice in the lalang – so tiny and pink and helpless – I was so very hungry after working in the garden and food was getting scarce. Without thinking I scooped up one and popped it in my mouth and before I realised what I had done, I swallowed it. Immediately I stuck my finger in my throat to make me sick but it was gone and I did feel a bit green after that. Afraid I was very subdued little person and felt really awful about the incident – how could I have done such a thing and I couldn't even tell anyone about it. I don't even want to think about it and even the worms have lost their attraction – I feel sick!!!

Sheila Allan survived her ordeal in Changi, but was never united with her father: Charles Allan, who had been incarcerated in a separate section of the prison, lived only until June 1945.

After the war, Sheila travelled to Australia to live with an aunt in Melbourne, where she trained as a nurse at Queen Victoria Memorial Hospital and married Frank Bruhn. Her diary was eventually transcribed and was published in 1994. SEE ALSO PP. 174–5, 187–9, 209, 459–60.

Sunday 16 – Thursday 20 July 1944

Journalist Kiyosawa Kiyoshi watches the collapse of the
Tojo Cabinet in Tokyo

If one relies upon the announcements of the enemy regarding the Saipan war situation, they state that some ten thousand corpses were discovered, and nine thousand prisoners were interned. These nine thousand were probably women and children.

In the critique of the newspaper of a certain third country (Switzerland?), it said that the war shows that Japan still has reserve strength, but at the same time it is costing extraordinary expenditures. What Japan must avoid is a bankrupting war. The current operations have turned out just as the enemy wanted.

A story of Obama is that it is said that one kamme of sugar is two hundred yen, and one egg is one yen. Even with these prices, many people are buying them greedily.

There is rumor that Tōjō's villa on the embankment of the Tama River was broken into and robbery left it in disorder. Is this really true or not? Rumors are flying around in all directions . . .

Kitada Masanori, who lives next door, was drafted. Of late one has to say that all young persons are being drafted.

I understand that recently the Kempeitai [secret police] rented the house in front of Konoe's home, and a telephone line of the Konoe house was wire-tapped. This exposes the surveillance and burial of a possible Konoe opposition . . .

According to what my wife was previously told by the wife of Ambassador Morishima, the naval marines in the Kamakura area entice the local maids . . . [one] evening about midnight a policeman accompanied by their maid told her that he had discovered that the maid was having secret meetings on the beach and hoped they would pay more attention to this kind of thing. The deterioration of public morals has reached this point.

At the Imperial Headquarters there are conferences for the

exchange of opinions, but a decision-making organ does not exist. There being no opportunity for intelligence to enter into political strategy and military operations, these are decided by the intuition of such people as young advisers and Tōjō. In the Sino-Japanese War, with the Meiji Emperor at the core, senior statesmen such as Itō and Yamagata carefully deliberated. This is what differs in the current situation.

Finally, Navy Minister Shimada has resigned and Admiral Nomura has taken his office. The hostile feelings between the army and navy are profound to a degree unknown before in history. Even in the munitions factories there is a struggle for materials, and the clerks in charge are having a bad time. It is true that the navy's style is in general sophisticated, but even with that, for example, when they invaded an island it was not extraordinary for them to occupy the best part. Because the army has the Kempeitai system, the pressure on those who sympathize with the navy is increased, and it is common for the Kempeitai to behave disagreeably. It is said that it is not rare for navy sympathizers to be arrested. Despite the fact that the bad feeling between army and navy is public knowledge, there is not a single word touching upon this in either the newspapers or magazines. And if it were touched upon it would be disastrous . . .

20 July

The Tojo cabinet has completely resigned. The cabinet that had the responsibility for plunging Japan into misery collapsed as a result of a family quarrel. According to a story of Kasahara, there were a great many anonymous complaints, and even a secret policeman said that if Tōjō had committed suicide it would probably have been alright, but if he lives on in shame it may be that he will have to be killed.

Kiyosawa Kiyoshi's diary records the political situation in Tokyo at the moment that Tojo resigned as premier. It emphasizes the remarkable dysfunction of the Japanese government, unable to take decisive action or receive and process information about the development of the war. In part this reflected the extraordinary ongoing feud between the army and the navy that is still difficult to understand. Hearing of the sacrificial death of all the Japanese on Saipan, Kiyoshi was appalled and wrote at the time, 'Is not this style of death a dog's useless death? Is it in the interest of Japan?'

Kiyoshi died on 5 May 1945 of pneumonia brought on by malnutrition; his diary was published in Japanese in 1948 and, in the more open post-war climate, met with great acclaim. SEE ALSO PP. 531–3.

Tuesday 18 July 1944

Edward Stettinius, US Under-Secretary of State, talks postwar loans with the British in Washington

In July 1944, Richard Law, British minister of state at the Foreign Office, was visiting Washington and held a private conversation with Edward Stettinius, the US Under-Secretary of State. They discussed the dire state of British government finance.

Mr. Law [from the Foreign Office in London] again referred to the serious financial condition of the Empire and referred also to the difficulty that the British would have in accepting interest-bearing obligations. I frankly told Mr. Law that this view was making a very unfavourable impression in Washington – that after America had spent 12 billion dollars seeing them through, to think now that we would have to treat the British as pensioners for an indefinite period, extending them aid perhaps from two to three billion dollars a year without repayment, would react unfavourably with the American public.

While I considered this matter in detail, I could not accept this statement that with the vast resources of the Empire they could not find some way to service a debt of somewhat in the neighbourhood of five to ten billion dollars over a thirty year period at 2 per cent, say.

Mr. Law saw the point and sympathised with my point of view. He continued, however, by saying that we must realise that the British people have gone through five years of, as he put it, 'hell;' that they felt they were in the home stretch; that the flying bombs had been terribly difficult for them to take when they thought they were now safe from anything like that; that if the British population of four or five million people [*sic*] were told, at the end of this long period of suffering and sacrifice, that they could not have some of the niceties of life such as adequate food, new clothes, radios, gasoline, tires, etc. They were apprehensive as to the social reaction, feeling there would be a distinct possibility of an extreme left swing that might take the form of some totalitarian system and might be led by a man such as [Emmanuel] Shinwell, the left wing socialist, who has been raising so much trouble in parliament in recent months. Mr. Law said it was just as important to us as to them to see England through in the middle-of-the-road course, and eventually to bring her into a state of solvency. I assured Mr. Law that I was tremendously interested in hearing his story . . .

London had already forced large British companies to liquidate most of their foreign assets in order to qualify for the 'Lend–Lease' plan and was badly hit by the wartime loss of its export trade. Washington knew that the American public would be unsympathetic to the idea of grants rather than loans for the British, who still seemed to own much of the world through their empire. Like other countries in Europe, Britain was not above taking the 'sore thumb' approach by threatening the possibility that they might 'turn towards communism' if domestic conditions deteriorated too far. In this way they hoped to frighten the United States into giving them aid or grants rather than a loan. Even in 1944, the need for something like the post-war programme of Marshall Plan aid was already being recognized by some. However, many in both London and Washington had no idea how serious the financial problems created by the war would be. Stettinius would replace Cordell Hull as US Secretary of State in November 1944. SEE ALSO PP. 544–5.

Friday 21 July 1944

Georges 'Blacky' Verreault, a Canadian POW in Japan,
gets into trouble and admires his Japanese commandant

I had not gone to work that day as the Japanese doctor,
having seen the infection in one of my fingers, gave me a few
days off. I was enjoying my rice meal in our luxurious abode.
The guys were almost all at work. I had stretched my legs
out with my feet resting on my bunk and was handling my
chopsticks with the dexterity of an old pro.

The Japanese guard came by the hut and noticed my too
comfortable position for a prisoner. This guard's name was
Amoza, also named Snake Eyes, the same man that had
thought of the shovel full of hot coals under my belly some
time back.

He reprimanded me in his frogish tongue, likely telling
me not to sit like that. I pretended not to understand and
remained so seated when a rifle butt on my thigh kind of
awakened my old temperament. Blind with fury, I picked
him up by the scruff of the neck and the seat of his pants,
threw him over the table which landed on top of our hero.
He got up, straightened up the table, picked up his helmet,
his rifle and quietly left. My rage dissipated, I realised that I
had committed a stupidity that Snake Eyes would not let go
unpunished. Shortly after, he returned with two more
guards with their bayonettes threateningly pointed at me.
They took me to the office of the commandant and since he
was not there, they decided to be my temporary judges. A
few shrieks to warm up and they started hitting me for the
next ten minutes. I did not move although my skin was turning blue from the blows.

It was cold and dark outdoors. The solitary box where
West had been kept stood there in the snow. They took me to
it, beating me on the way, then had me stand in it, at
attention until 6 am the next morning when the
commandant was due back. Every fifteen minutes, they
came to beat me up.

When I was taken to the commandant's office, my feet, hands and one side of my face were frozen white, the commandant listened to my story but just by looking at me, he knew what I'd been put through. When I finished, he called in Amoza from the window. Amoza rushed in bent in half. The commandant slapped him, kicked him then punched him out then moving towards me said in fairly good English 'the next time, do not hit a Japanese guard but rather come and tell me'.

Unfortunately, this commandant did not stay with us long. He was the enemy, true but a fair and loyal one. His type is a rare breed among the sons of the rising sun.

Georges Verreault's diary is interesting on many levels. Originally written in French, it offers a uniquely French Canadian perspective on the war. His views on race are also interesting, for while disliking Japanese generally – referring to them as 'yellow pigs' – he appreciated men as individuals and had a strong liking for individual captors who displayed human values. Moreover, personal nicknames that we might now consider to be derogatory were often used as terms of endearment: for example, he called his diminutive friend William Allister 'my little Jew', while William repaid the compliment by referring affectionately to the amply sized Georges as 'my black gorilla'.

Georges returned to his home town of Ville-Emard, Montreal in 1945. He took back his job at Bell Canada and died in 1966 at the age of forty-six, his health ruined by his wartime experience. SEE ALSO PP. 121–3, 164–7.

Major Oscar Conner views the impact of concentrated air power and artillery at Wadke Island near Aitape in New Guinea

During the 1930s Dr Oscar Conner was a practising dentist in Jackson, Mississippi and also a member of the local National Guard. In November 1940 he was called up when his National Guard unit was integrated into the 31st Infantry Division. In 1941 his unit was moved to Camp Blanding in Florida, where he was promoted to major and became the divisional dental surgeon. By July 1944 he was serving in New Guinea and now arrived on the recently captured Wadke Island.

The last thirty-six hours have been the most weird and even fantastic of my life. I doubt seriously that at present I am able to write coherently and I fear that whatever I attempt to place on paper will be nothing more than a jumbled succession of words. But, for my own satisfaction in the years to come, if I survive whatever lies ahead I want to have something concrete to go along with whatever I may be able to remember of the details of these hours.

At dawn on yesterday, an hour which, either by design or accident, seems to be the one time at which we can reach our destination, we sighted land, the low-lying Dutch New Guinea coast, covered with dense jungle and with a chain of mountains rising behind, their summits shrouded in clouds and mist. We moved very slowly inward, engine barely turning, to find that in reality we were approaching an island which lay several miles off the actual coast. The island, the water beyond, the green jungle of the mainland and the clouds and fog around the mountains all combined to provide an unusual sensation of mystery to everything. As we drew nearer we discovered that the island was one gigantic nest of airplanes. We watched with great interest the swarms of large Liberator bombers which rose one by one into the air, each plane apparently following the preceding plane just as soon as there was sufficient room to get off the ground and heading northward without seeming to get into formation. Then came fighter planes, thick-bellied 'Thunderbolts' which followed the Liberators, all hurrying to pay their respects to Tojo, the man who, to the American soldier, is becoming more and more the symbol of Japan. Shortly afterward we heard the drone of other planes high overhead, heading in the same direction, and we decided that these were coming from strips below us to the south. Apparently, the enemy is taking a real pounding somewhere farther up.

As we drew nearer we observed again, as we had done at Buna, something of what concentrated bombing from the air and shelling from the sea can do to an area. This island, which undoubtedly had been covered with trees at one time, was hardly more than a barren, burned-out shell of its former self, with but a few blackened and twisted stumps remaining, interspersed with craters. The word was passed around that this was Wadke Island, wrested from the Japs only a short while ago, and that our landing point was to be Maffin Bay, eight miles or so up the coast and near the native town of Sarmi. We hove to near one end of the island for thirty minutes or so and were surprised that large numbers of planes remained there still, a fact which gave us a real kick as we began to realise something of the strength we must have out here. Also, it was surprising to see at first hand something of what our engineers and the Seabees can do when we take over an area, for in spite of the destruction evident on all sides these miracle-workers had produced in short order a large airstrip and the facilities necessary for a large operation, along with an area containing row on row of tents for living and probably hospital quarters, all in the tidy formation which is the mark of the Army establishment. But I think the one thing which stood out most clearly to my eyes was the all but complete absence of trees or growth of any kind, here in a region which is practically covered with jungle – it was almost weird.

As we pulled out for the final few miles of our journey we were given our breakfast, at seven-thirty – chili, the inevitable dehydrated potatoes, string beans, jelly cake and a pint of coffee. A few more days of string beans or spinach for breakfast and we'll forget that there can be any variation between the day's meals. We viewed various installations and a great many trucks, tractors, jeeps and ducks swarming over the beach as we passed on toward our landing point, finally reaching a small and somewhat murky bay into which a river emptied its sediment and whose water was being churned by large numbers of craft moving between the half dozen ships anchored therein and the beach. There was no pier, and all cargo had to be loaded into smaller land-ing craft to be transported to the shore. Our engineers are busily constructing a landing pier but this early in the game everything has to be done the hard way. Here we sat for at least an hour, awaiting orders to debark, before we realized something was taking place right under our noses. First we saw planes diving low over the jungle four miles or so up the beach, evidently disclosing some kind of target, and then came an unmistakable artillery barrage. Smoke rose from the shells bursting in the jungle and geysers of water spurted into the air as shells landed along the edge of the water. Shortly, an amphibious truck drew up beside us and we began to ply its driver with questions as to what was taking place up the beach. His answers gave us the first example of the apparent nonchalance of almost everybody who is engaged in this operation and we began to wonder if this is actual warfare out here. 'Oh, that', he replied with a careless wave of his hand and as if such activity was an everyday fact of life, 'I think that's a Jap airstrip up there. They take it every night and we retake it the next morning,' his words denoting something akin to boredom with it all. 'How long before we have it?' shouted a voice from the deck. 'Three or four days, maybe,' came the reply as he moved away. As we watched the fireworks up ahead, the bevy of craft of all kinds moved in and out between the ships and the beach, no one paying any attention whatever to the show.

American and Australian forces had begun their attack on Wadke Island in May 1944 and by late July the fighting was drawing to a close. Oscar Conner's diary gives an excellent impression of how the United States had applied its industrial power to the winning of the war against Japan. At Wadke Island the impact of extraordinary air power was visible for miles around. In every aspect of military–industrial production Tokyo's position was now hopeless. During 1944 Japan produced an average of 2,000 aircraft per month. By contrast, in March 1944 American production had peaked at 9,000 aircraft per month, more than had been produced in the United States in all of 1940. By the end of the war the United States had produced a third of a million military aircraft. The spare capacity had been found by ceasing automobile production entirely and diverting factory space and skilled labour. This was done so effectively that the United States was now producing too many aircraft and production had to be slowed down.
SEE ALSO PP. 642–4.

598 THE FARAWAY WAR

Friday 28 July 1944

Charles Lindbergh has a close encounter over Elpaputih
Bay on the north New Guinea coast

Charles MacDonald (left) and Charles Lindbergh (right)

We jettison our drop tanks, switch on our guns, and nose
down to the attack. One Jap plane banks sharply toward the
airstrip and the protection of the antiaircraft guns. The
second heads off into the haze and clouds. Colonel
MacDonald gets a full deflection shot on the first, starts him
smoking, and forces him to reverse his bank.

We are spaced 1,000 feet apart. Captain [Danforth] Miller
gets in a short deflection burst with no noticeable effect. I
start firing as the plane is completing its turn in my
direction. I see the tracers and the 20's [20mm cannon] find
their mark, a hail of shells directly on the target. But he
straightens out and flies directly toward me.

I hold the trigger down and my sight on his engine as we
approach head on. My tracers and my 20's spatter on his
plane. We are close – too close – hurtling at each other at
more than 500 miles an hour. I pull back on the controls. His

plane zooms suddenly upward with extraordinary sharpness.

I pull back with all the strength I have. Will we hit? His plane, before a slender toy in my sight, looms huge in size. A second passes – two – three – I can see the finning on his engine cylinders. There is a rough jolt of air as he shoots past behind me.

By how much did we miss? Ten feet? Probably less than that. There is no time to consider or feel afraid. I am climbing steeply. I bank to the left. No, that will take me into the ack-ack fire above Amahai strip. I reverse to the right. It all has taken seconds.

My eyes sweep the sky for aircraft. Those are only P-38's and the plane I have just shot down. His is starting down in a wing over – out of control. The nose goes down. The plane turns slightly as it picks up speed – down – down – down toward the sea. A fountain of spray – white foam on the water – waves circling outward as from a stone tossed in a pool – the waves merge into those of the sea – the foam disappears – the surface is as it was before.

Charles Lindbergh was flying with Colonel Charles MacDonald, one of the three top fighter aces of the 5th Air Force, who would complete a tally of twenty-seven kills by the end of the war. But for the eagle-eyed protection of MacDonald, Lindbergh might well have been shot down on more than one occasion. SEE ALSO PP. 99–101, 574, 612.

AUGUST 1944

DURING AUGUST THE Japanese garrisons in New Guinea, the Solomon Islands and the Mariana Islands were eliminated. This paved the way for the invasion of the Philippines, where air operations against Japanese bases now began a long 'softening-up' process. Large-scale guerrilla units were becoming more active and received direct instructions from General MacArthur.

Fighting continued on Guam until 10 August. Here the difficult jungle terrain favoured the defenders and hindered American use of support weapons. Small pockets of Japanese soldiers continued to hide out rather than face the indignity of surrender: one defender, Sergeant Shoichi Yokoi, would famously hold out on Guam until 1972, living off berries and snails. When his clothes wore out, he wove himself a complete new uniform from the bark of trees. When he was discovered, Shoichi Yokoi was hailed as 'the last honourable soldier' – but in fact he was outlasted by Lieutenant Hiroo Onada, who fought on in the Philippines until 1974 and who was still shooting local villagers with a working firearm.

Once Guam had fallen, the island was pressed into service as a base for the strategic bombing of Japan. Bombing missions against Japan would soon be launched from here, from Saipan and also from areas of mainland China. As yet the United States did not enjoy bases close enough to Japan to provide its bombers with fighter support. The distances to be covered were still immense and this meant that damaged aircraft, even aircraft with minor problems such as loss of a single engine or fuel leaks, struggled to return to their bases.

On 3 August, the town of Myitkyina in northern Burma fell to Chinese and American forces. For the first time in over a year a land route into China could be opened, sparing the Allies the costly business of flying all supplies 'over the hump'. As a result, the black-market cost of everyday goods in China now began to fall from the dizzy heights they had reached in early

1944, widely thought to have been the highest anywhere during the Second World War. Japan continued to make advances in China, and the fall of the city of Hengyang on 9 August prompted senior nationalist generals and politicians to consider replacing Chiang Kai-shek with a more effective figure.

The early days of the month saw a mass break-out from the POW camp at Cowra in New South Wales, Australia. On the night of 4–5 August, 1,104 Japanese prisoners broke out, believing that dying in the effort to escape would wipe out the shame of capture. In the fighting that followed, 231 Japanese prisoners were killed. Over 300 escaped from the camp and in the hunt that followed, 25 died by shooting. Fearing reprisals against Australian POWs in Japanese prison camps, the authorities kept the whole incident top secret for over six years.

With the virtual elimination of the German and Italian fleets, more and more Allied submarines were transferred to the Indian Ocean and the Pacific. During August, American submarines sank a Japanese cruiser and a carrier. Tokyo could now field only half the number of carriers that it had deployed at the beginning of the war.

At the end of August Allied representatives gathered at Dumbarton Oaks in the United States to consider the creation of some sort of international organization for the preservation of post-war security. They were all conscious of the unhappy precedent of the League of Nations, with its obvious failings. They designed a new body that was not unlike its predecessor, but had greater powers, including an International Court of Justice. This organization would eventually be called the United Nations, and bringing it to life was perhaps Roosevelt's primary wartime ambition. The key figure at this conference was Roosevelt's Under-Secretary of State, Edward Stettinius, himself deeply committed to a future world organization.

Thursday 3 August 1944

Fred C. Robbins, a US army officer, meets an Italian
American and a Japanese American during the capture of
Myitkyina in Burma

Today . . . Myitkyina is completely in Allied hands . . . After
many weeks of hard fighting, Stilwell's Chinese troops and
Merrill's Marauders finally took the town . . .

Among General Frank Merrill's Marauders is an Italian
who has a reputation for never losing his temper.

One incident in the Myitkyina fight was too much for him
though. The men laying assault to the town had dug in as
close as possible to the Japanese positions. The Italian had
dug a fine foxhole and was safely entrenched for the night
feeling not too unhappy with his lot for the night. But he
carelessly left his pack outside and a Japanese sniper sight-
ing it blasted away. That was what finally made the Italian
so mad. The Japanese had ruined his mess kit, and eating
was his chief pleasure. He had to fall back into his mother
tongue to fully express his feelings.

A Nishai [Nisei – a Japanese American] used as an interpreter proved his value over here. He was broadcasting
appeals to the entrenched enemy at Myitkytina to come out
and surrender. But he was beginning to doubt the effects of
his pleas, so being a man of action, he did something about
it. Slipping across into the Japanese lines he went to work.
Walking boldly up to various soldiers he would inform them
that he was general so and so and order them to accompany
him. His ruse was successful enough for him to bring back
twenty-three prisoners safely to the American lines.

*The treatment of first-generation Italians inside the United States
differed markedly from that of first-generation Japanese. While 120,000
Japanese were interned, only 11,000 Germans and 1,600 Italians shared
the same fate. Nevertheless, large numbers of Japanese Americans served
in the American military and many of them undertook either translation
or broadcast propaganda work.*

Fred Robbins continued to serve in India and Burma during 1945 and spent some time with the Naga hill tribes in north-west Burma. He would survive the war and return to the United States. He died in 1967.
SEE ALSO PP. *435–7, 465–6.*

Thursday 3 – Friday 4 August 1944

Hugh Dalton endures a long Cabinet meeting as Churchill gives a long-winded speech about India and Gandhi

Hugh Dalton had been Minister for Economic Warfare during 1941 and 1942, overseeing organizations such as the Special Operations Executive and also much of Britain's propaganda effort. By 1944 he was President of the Board of Trade.

3 August

Then an infinitely rambling discussion on what the Viceroy should write to Gandhi, to whom he owes a letter. The P.M. pours forth at great length about the Indians and speaks ill of Wavell. 'He was a bad General. He let us down atrociously at Crete. I have been too kind to him.' Wavell had, in fact, never been authorised to 'open negotiations' with Gandhi. Amery – as many outside would be surprised to find – is always in Cabinet the warmest advocate of a 'sympathetic' and 'constructive' policy in India, but is over-borne by the P.M. and others. He says that it has long been a habit for successive Viceroys to have a correspondence with Gandhi. The P.M. said that any honourable man would voluntarily return to jail, from which Gandhi had only been released while the P.M. was away in Cairo, because Wavell assured us that, if not released, he would die, that, even if released, he would almost certainly die and that, quite certainly, he would never be able to take any further part in politics. All this had turned out to be false. He is still sticking to his 'Quit India' policy, and there was no doubt that he had been quite prepared to make an arrangement with the Japs whereby the Japanese claw of the pincers could have stretched unopposed across India to join up with the

German claw coming down across the Caucasus. Someone asked Herbert Morrison, 'What would you do, if Mosley, whom *you* let out of jail on much the same grounds as Wavell let out Gandhi, were to start a campaign for 'Make Peace with Hitler now'! Morrison said, 'I should put him inside again at once.' And so they rambled on, for most of the three hours. A dozen of them in turn proposing minor changes in the draft of the telegram. Long debate as to whether one should say 'it is a mistake to say that minority problems are due to the British' or 'it is not true to say that . . .', or . . .

4 August

War Cabinet at 12.30 with further endless talk about India. 'The rottenest show I've ever seen,' says the P.M. to Amery. 'This huge Indian army you talk about is just a gigantic scheme of outdoor relief, as Wingate said to me.' In the Cabinet Amery always stands up for India and the Indians and, as the P.M. said this afternoon, 'You who have become, like Wavell and Linlithgow and all the rest of you, more Indian than the Indians, are attacked in the House of Commons as being a narrow-minded old-fashioned re-actionary! It serves you right.' Amery and the P.M. shouted at one another quite a lot. Amery said, 'India has saved the Middle East.' 'Rubbish,' replied the P.M. . . .

I go off tonight to West Leaze for six days.

In May 1944, with the military threat to India at last declining, the British government had decided to release Gandhi from prison. However, the issue of Indian politics was still a sore point for Churchill, who was obsessed with delaying any moves towards independence and who had single-handedly blocked numerous progressive measures advocated by Leo Amery, Archibald Wavell and others. Churchill's attitude to Burma was much the same. In 1944 Reginald Dorman-Smith, the Governor of Burma, had reportedly told Churchill that what the Burmese needed was the promise of democracy; the Prime Minister had replied that what the Burmese needed was 'not democracy but the lash'.

Hugh Dalton would become Chancellor of the Exchequer in Attlee's post-war Labour government. SEE ALSO PP. 54–5, 93–4.

Monday 21 August 1944

John Gaitha Browning, with the US army at Hollandia
harbour in New Guinea, reflects on prisoners and the
Geneva Convention

Another Sunday has come and gone – another week marked
off. Aside from five letters from Marie and Mae and some from
home, there has been little on the bright side. Still the dullness
of an army camp in a mudhole, of which there is none worse.

For six weeks now the Japanese who are cut off at the
point across the harbor, have been bombed, shelled, and
strafed without mercy. Every day we can see the planes diving on them and hear the thud of bombs and the rattle of
machine guns and cannons. Every night the 155s behind our
tent area shell them from here. They must live in a literal
hell, but they still live – at least enough of them to be
dangerous. Sooner or later, they will be forced to die or come
out. And die they will, rather than surrender, if they are at all
like those before them.

A lieutenant of the infantry that is holding the front there
came by one afternoon and ˙gave us the best firsthand
account of the fighting we have had. He was not a person-
ality to spin yarns, and I believed his accounts of the fighting
there. We lose men every day. The Japanese are still cunning.
Those captured show little signs of needing food and are
tricky and stubborn. Evidently they are better supplied than
the enemy forces to our east.

The best catch of this whole campaign was a group of three
prisoners taken lately who gave more information than anyone had been able to get before. A lieutenant, a warrant officer,
and a sergeant were surrounded and captured alive and uninjured. The two officers offered to talk, but the sergeant, who
evidently spoke English, was stubborn and smart. One of the
[US] infantrymen simply took his sharp machete and severed
his head with one blow. Surprising? Not at all. It is done often,
as I saw with my own eyes, so I have no reason to doubt a
word of the story.

The irony of the whole thing was that just the same day I had read a memorandum on our bulletin board that gave a hair-raising account of an American soldier having his head cut off with a samurai sword. It had been taken from the diary of a Japanese sergeant killed near Hollandia and said in part: 'Today was the greatest day of my life. I was allowed to sever the head of a captured enemy with a samurai sword. My only humiliation was that I had to take two strokes.'

My, my! You should have practiced with a machete, Mr. Moto, for you see, our men need to take only one stroke with that! War is war, and the Geneva Red Cross Convention (quoted often in articles about 'humane treatment of enemy prisoners') is a long, long way from the front line. There is but one law here, KILL, KILL, KILL!

John Gaitha Browning's is typical of the personal 'journals of record' generated during this campaign, which document the real practice of war, rather than the official line. Events of the kind described by Browning were rarely reported in the press. Browning's diary is notably reflective and captures the sense that the American and Australian tendency to execute prisoners was, at least on the surface, driven by a desire for vengeance. This was often encouraged by senior officers who took pains to publicize Japanese atrocities. These practices also reflected a general barbarization of warfare in the Pacific, as well as the sheer inconvenience of feeding and maintaining prisoners while they were transported over large distances. SEE ALSO PP. 374–5, 506–8, 622–3.

Monday 28 August 1944

Arthur Gately, RAAF, is entertained by Bob Hope and friends at an air base in the Admiralty Islands

A special event took place this afternoon. The island was paid a visit by an American entertainment team, headed by the film star Bob Hope and supported by the singer Frances Langford, the comedian Jerry Collona [*sic*] and others. The possibility of such a visit had been made known to us two or three days before over our PA system. Arrangements were made to leave a skeleton crew with the aircraft, so that the majority of the afternoon shift could see the show. A large wooden stage had been erected at the northern end of Momote airstrip near the 7 TMO building. Along with a very large number of USN sailors, airmen and ground crew, our small Squadron group, including Jack, Tom, Bluey and me, took up a position within this crowd about 1.30pm. I understand it was a band from the 13th USAAF Group which kept the crowd in a happy frame of mind – they certainly played some terrific music. A small number, in a group, of American nurses (heavily escorted by officers), joined the group. They were given a rousing reception, and, if they got up to move about, a great roar went up – the men were starved of the sight and presence of women. We stood about in the boiling sun till about 3.30pm. A Dakota DC3 made a low pass over the airstrip, landed, then taxied as close as possible to the stage. The door of the Dakota (named the *Golden Arrow*) opened and out stepped Bob Hope. I have never seen such a mass demonstration of acceptance. The crowd went mad. You couldn't hear yourself. Under close personal guard, he and his troupe made their way on stage. The show started immediately, and over the next hour and half, we were treated to an explosion of laughter, song and music, fun and banter. Bob Hope played the crowd like the maestro of mirth that he is. Golden thrush, Frances Langford sang all the right tunes, and Jerry Colonna was at his craziest best. For a short time, the horrors of war were the last thing on anyone's mind.

Bob Hope devoted much of his wartime career to entertaining the troops through the American USO organization. With his radio troupe he travelled almost every week to perform The Pepsodent Show *at a military training site somewhere in the United States. Of the 144 episodes of the radio programme that would be aired during the war, only nine originated from NBC's studios.*

In the summer and autumn of 1944 Bob Hope was moving from island to island across the South Pacific to entertain the troops. It was a demanding as well as dangerous journey for Hope and his team. He flew some 30,000 miles and gave more than 150 performances. Joining Hope on the trip were guitarist Tony Romano, comedian Jerry Colonna, singer

Frances Langford, dancer Patty Thomas and scriptwriter Barney Dean. Arthur Gately would be transferred back to Australia during 1945, serving at Tocumwal and Brisbane before being demobilized in 1946. SEE ALSO PP. 549–51.

SEPTEMBER 1944

ON 15 SEPTEMBER American forces in the south-west Pacific invaded the Palau Islands group, including the Japanese-held island of Pelelieu (Palau). There followed one of the bitterest battles of the Pacific campaign, which lasted without interruption for ten weeks. The lead element was the 1st Marine Division, together with US army troops, and their operations were preceded by three days of heavy bombardment by navy gunships. Peleliu hosted a large Japanese airfield that was deemed a serious threat to any US advance towards the Philippines, and it was considered essential to reduce this Japanese outpost. The island was heavily defended by Japanese troops dug into a network of pill boxes and coral caverns. Japanese troops would remain hidden and, when over-run, pop up and shoot at the Americans from the rear. The conquest of Peleliu cost 1,529 American lives; the Japanese dead numbered over 10,000. On 14 September, in New Guinea, US forces invaded Morotai in the Molucca Islands, isolating Japanese forces in the western section of New Guinea.

In Burma, the Burma Road was fully reopened, allowing a flow of supplies into China. However, in China the Japanese had begun to stage attacks on a divisional scale against American airfields in the south of the country in response to American air attacks on Japan and on Japanese-held ports on the Chinese coast, such as Shanghai and Hong Kong. On 17 September the major air base at Kweilin was abandoned as a result of Japanese advances.

In mid-September Franklin D. Roosevelt and Winston Churchill arrived in Quebec City to review the strategic plans for the final victories over Germany and Japan. The main issues addressed during their talks were the demarcation of the occupation zones after the conquest of Germany and the policy of post-war administration. The US Secretary of the Treasury, Henry Morgenthau, Jr introduced the Morgenthau Plan, a draconian policy which would have reduced Germany to an agrarian economy. The plan was tentatively approved at Quebec, but political criticism led President Roosevelt to disavow the policy by the end of the year. The parties eventually agreed on a strategy for the final advance on Japan which involved the invasion of the islands of Iwo Jima and then Okinawa. A target date of October 1945 was set for the invasion of the Japanese home islands.

At Los Alamos in New Mexico, work on the atomic bomb had proceeded to the point where a special bomb unit was formed to begin training pilots to drop this special device. Some scientists began to have doubts about the morality of their work and were anxious to share their information with other major powers to encourage international control of atomic energy. The senior American scientists Vannevar Bush and James B. Connant sent a report to Henry L. Stimson, the Secretary for War, emphasizing the need to establish international control of atomic power and to share information with the Soviet Union. In fact two key individuals, Klaus Fuchs and Ted Hall, were already secretly passing information to Soviet intelligence.

Friday 1 – Thursday 7 September 1944

Thomas Price Lewis, a civilian internee in Changi gaol, is issued with honey and marmalade

1 September
The Fall of Paris to the Allies is reported. Two postcards received from England prophesy that the over 40s will be repatriated this month! We received 2 fritters each today.

2 September
An old lady, Mrs Baker, aged 67, has died in the Women's

Camp. A.R. Sirens are being heard again. We have had an issue of 1 oz of honey each. Two of our hut inmates named Paley (an 'Asia' Boy) and Crook are organising some tea racket out on the Dunearn Fatigue. Rumania and Bulgaria are said to be in revolt against their Axis partners. Reading Saki's *Selected Stories*. Two shots have been fired at General De Gaulle, the Free French leader, by unnamed people.

3 September

This is the fifth anniversary of the outbreak of War. We have had an issue of Marmalade (1 lb 8 oz) between 12! We had the first part of a typhoid inoculation, so I am taking the day off from fatigues tomorrow. I have boil No 19 on my bottom.

4 September

One of our Rice Fatigues met 1,500 P.O.W.s at the Docks. They are survivors of those who have been working on the Siamese border and are suffering from dysentery. They and a further 500 Jap wounded are said to be leaving for Japan in 2 ships. The P.O.W.s are from the Argylls and Gordons. Four of our internees have been caught stealing *gula melaka* [a sweetener] from a poor squatter.

5 September

Fatigue parties to Dunearn Road are to be limited to 100 in the morning and 100 in the afternoon and Paley and Crook are to be banned from either party. Gow, one of the 6 drivers of Corpse collecting lorries, and originally sentenced to 2 years' confinement, has come into our camp. Of the other 5 drivers, 3 have died and one is missing. Reading Walpole's *The Bright Pavilions*.

6 September

An ex-Warder named Harris was beaten up by 'Puss in Boots' today for interfering with him when he was 'punishing' some Eurasian girls (including Mrs Begg), 'Puss in Boots' was making them remain in a kneeling position and one of the girls was Harris's daughter.

7 September

We have had a lot of rain today and this has made everything very damp. A British officer contacted in town by a
fatigue says that there is very little happening in either
Burma or Siam (in spite of all the rumours we have been
hearing), but Mountbatten is keeping the Burma Road open.
A few Red Cross cables, dated August 1944, have been
received and some of these indicate we may still be home for
Christmas. We are now being given 'cargo rice', whatever
that may be. One rumour is that General Percival has been
brought back to Singapore from Formosa.

*Thomas Lewis passed much of his time reading, since civilian intern-
ment camps enjoyed a reasonable library of books. Nevertheless, by late
1944 a great weariness is detectable in the diaries of the civilian
internees in Changi gaol. Britain had already been at war for five long
years and there seemed as yet no ending in sight. Moreover, while the
European war appeared to be seeing decisive movement, as in the
liberation of Paris, little seemed to have happened in Burma or Thailand
for two years. Food rations were declining visibly, and everyone was
asking: 'How much longer?'*

*Thomas Lewis would survive the war and become an administrator
in the Malayan Education Service, retiring as Chief Inspector of Schools
in 1955. SEE ALSO PP. 564–7.*

Saturday 9 September 1944

Charles Lindbergh discusses the war with officers on the recently captured island of Roi in New Guinea

Up shortly after sunrise. Natives very friendly. Each one says
'good morning' as he passes the screen sides of our hut and
expects a 'good morning' in reply. Since there are dozens of
them passing, we take turns at the game – one of us nodding
and saying 'good morning' while the other two dress.

Breakfast with Lieutenant [Kenneth] Collyer, Captain
McCall, and other officers. The talk drifts to the original
attack and occupation of Roi Island. Most of our American

losses were caused by an ammunition dump exploding, one of the officers told me. He had landed on D plus 3. The American casualties were buried in individual graves, he said, but the Japanese bodies were loaded in trucks and dumped into a big hollow scooped in the ground by a bulldozer. The natives did much of the handling of the Jap bodies and located many of them by 'smelling for them.'

Before the bodies in the hollow were 'bulldozed over,' the officer said, a number of our Marines went in among them, searching through their pockets and prodding around in their mouths for gold-filled teeth. Some of the Marines, he said, had a little sack in which they collected teeth with gold fillings. The officer said he had seen a number of Japanese bodies from which an ear or a nose had been cut off. 'Our boys cut them off to show their friends in fun, or to dry and take back to the States when they go. We found one Marine with a Japanese head. He was trying to get the ants to clean the flesh off the skull, but the odor got so bad we had to take it away from him.' It is the same story everywhere I go.

Although a civilian, Lindbergh flew some fifty combat missions during the war and contributed considerably to the development of military aviation. After the war he worked as a consultant to the Chief of Staff of the US air force. President Eisenhower restored his commission and appointed him a brigadier-general in the air force. Lindbergh advised on the design of the Boeing 747 airliner and in 1953 published The Spirit of St Louis, *a detailed account of his 1927 transatlantic flight, which won a Pulitzer Prize the following year. In the 1960s his interest in issue campaigning and humanitarianism resurfaced and he worked in support of the conservation movement. He campaigned for the protection of humpback and blue whales. He died of cancer on 26 August 1974 at his home on the Hawaiian island of Maui.* SEE ALSO PP. 99–101, 574, 598–9.

Monday 11 – Wednesday 20 September 1944

Lieutenant Okuma and his men live 'like cats' at Siomapara on Bougainville

Lieutenant Okuma had been fighting at Tiaraka on Bougainville. He was assigned as mortar platoon leader with the 81st Infantry Regiment and travelled to Tiokona to collect men from a mortar unit. They then moved on together to assist in the defence of Siomapara.

11 September

At SIOMAPARA I was put in command of 14 subordinates. Six men including myself, the junior officer, are still alive. Forty days ago there were 14 men in all. How keenly I realise the tricks of fate. Oh, the uncertainty of the future!

The Australian soldiers are having a good time on the NIP HILL. It makes me mad to think that one does not realise that eating can be a war in itself unless he is on BOUGAINVILLE. For, if one doesn't eat anything, he will starve to death. There is no rice or potatoes. What can I eat? Just the roots of papaya, banana and hemp. When one finds a tree shoot he rejoices like a child. The roots of papaya have already disappeared in SIOMAPARA. I had a terrible craving for the stem of a taro plant. When coconuts are issued there is no dignity or decent behaviour. One is driven to greed, and wants to eat it all by himself. I would like to move to a place where I can eat plenty of coconuts and papayas. But one should be ashamed to even think such thoughts here in SIOMAPARA. We must die like men for our country. Defend SIOMAPARA with your very life!

12 September

At the beginning of this great war we had innumerable planes, ships and guns, but now SAIPAN and GUAM are in the hands of the enemy and the BONIN ISLANDS are within enemy bombing range. The Cabinet has been changed to KOISO's. The changes brought about in the present grave situation within the last two months frighten me. And all while our barefooted soldiers on BOUGAINVILLE, wearing just a loin cloth and with a towel around their heads, are busily collecting garden products! Any place where potatoes are the principal food is really a heaven. Next comes a place where the coconut is the principal food. Places where roots of banana plants are eaten such as here, are the worst. Nevertheless, we are in dead earnest because the enemy is in front of us.

13 September

It has been only 1½ months since I arrived here at SIOMA-PARA, but I already noticed how emaciated I am. It starts with the hips and thighs, then in the following order of legs, abdomen, chest, arms and face. Consequently, if one's face grows thin, his whole body is undoubtedly weakened. Furthermore, lack of nutritious food has caused skin diseases all over the body. Day and night it itches. I can't stand it! It itches the most during the first half of the evening. I scratch and scratch until it starts to bleed, but still I am unable to stop. This is all right for us. Our only worry is that the Japanese Empire, whose history has not been marred by a single blotch, is now pressed by its enemies, UNITED STATES and ENGLAND. Something's got to be done! TOKYO is in danger! Even if we starve we shall defend this BOUGAINVILLE ISLAND which is the foremost battle-front and the focal point in the next offensive. I must live until the day when our offensive shifts and until the Rising Sun can be seen flying over these SOUTH SEAS. The fluttering of the Rising Sun will turn this bitterness into happiness. I do wish I could see our planes as soon as possible!

20 September

It is strenuous work for me to go even to the Company Headquarters which is only 2–300 metres walk over level ground. I wonder how it will be to go up and down hills. If I suddenly stand up I feel dizzy. I have hit the bottom. With the food situation as it is, our quarters and clothing are also a sight to behold. Men are wearing filthy clothing which hasn't been washed for two or three months. If clothes are torn, there is not sewing kit nor time to mend them.

Disrespectful as it was to our deceased comrades, we were issued their clothing. We are like cats. We walk into our tents barefooted and we don't wash our hands after going to the latrine. We even prepare food with those hands. We just don't care about the filthiness. There are fleas all over our bodies. However, with but a desire in our hearts to brighten this dark life, we recall how we ate, drank and enjoyed life in CHINA, participated in punitive operations, thought about home and hummed songs. We were so carefree in those days.

At the end of September further Japanese forces arrived at Okuma's location with a view to preparing for an assault on the nearby Allied airfield at Torokina. However, this made him anxious for he considered that either the larger numbers of troops would attract Allied air strikes or they would simply run out of food. Okuma's diary was captured in the Upper Laruma Valley on Bougainville; his fate is unknown.

Tuesday 19 September 1944

General 'Vinegar Joe' Stilwell harpoons the 'Peanut' with a telegram from President Franklin D. Roosevelt

By September 1944 Stilwell was enmeshed in a vast struggle over American policy towards China which was highly factionalized.

Mark this day in red on the calendar of life. At long, at very long last, F.D.R. has finally spoken plain words, and plenty of them, with a firecracker in every sentence. 'Get busy or else.' A hot firecracker. I handed this bundle of paprika to the Peanut and then sank back with a sigh. The harpoon hit the little bugger right in the solar plexus, and went right through him. It was a clean hit, but beyond turning green and losing the power of speech, he did not bat an eye. He just said to me, 'I understand.' And sat in silence, jiggling one foot. We are now a long way from the 'tribal chieftain' bawling out. *Two long years lost*, but at least F.D.R.'s eyes have been opened and he has thrown a good hefty punch.

Although Stilwell believed that he had won Roosevelt's support in press-ing Chiang to assist with further offensives, this was in fact a false dawn and Washington was gradually turning against him. Elements sympathetic to Chiang, especially the American ambassador in Chungking, were already arranging for the removal of 'Vinegar Joe'. SEE ALSO PP. 357–9, 421–2, 806–7.

Thursday 21 September 1944

Marcial Lichauco, journalist and lawyer, shelters in City Hall in Manila during a US bombing raid prior to the invasion of the Philippines

This has been so far the most thrilling day of the war.

I was on my way to town with several friends when the sharp reports of cannon fire suddenly wrent the air around us. We thought at first it was only target practice because yesterday's 'Tribune' had contained a notice to the effect that anti-aircraft practice would be held today and advising the city's population not to be unduly alarmed by the noise. But one of my friends looked up and saw puffs of black smoke just behind several planes that were heading for the port area. 'That's no practice,' he cried as he broke into a run, 'it's the real thing, let's go.'

I heard the roar of many motors above and behind me. I turned and saw eighteen more planes flying in perfect for-mation. From the east an even larger group made its appearance. The sky was overcast thus effectively conceal-ing the attacking aircraft until they were directly over the city when they emerged from the clouds and dove toward their objectives. The raid had certainly caught the Japs napping. There wasn't even time to sound the air-raid sirens. Pedestrians were now running towards the nearest shelters warned only of the impending danger by the popping of anti-aircraft guns which seemed to be coming from all directions.

We reached the City Hall building just in time to avoid being hit by bits of shrapnel which were falling to the ground. But others were not so fortunate. A young boy was brought in with a gaping hole in his stomach. He must have been hit by a stray 50 calibre machine gun bullet. He died a few minutes later. Another arrived with a piece of shrapnel in his forehead, – still another with a terrible wound on the thigh. And yet as the explosions increased in number and intensity, it was impossible to resist the temptation to look out of the windows. We soon recognized the planes as American dive bombers which must have come from aircraft carriers cruising in Philippine waters. There were at least 200 and it was thrilling to watch them dive recklessly towards their objective apparently oblivious of the shells bursting around them. They seemed to be concentrating their attacks on the bay where a large number of Japanese vessels were lying at anchor. Clouds of smoke rising from the south and the east however, told us that the Nichols and Nielson airfields were also being adequately taken care of.

The hallways in the City Hall building were soon filled with thousands of people. But there was neither fear nor confusion in their faces. On the contrary, jokes and wisecracks were heard everywhere and the crowds quieted down only when Japanese officials appeared and made their rounds. A few women were crying but they were laughed at by their companions.

By around 11:30 the raid seemed to be over and so, although the all clear signal was never sounded, the crowds began to disperse. I managed to make my way home where I found Jessie and the babies under the stairway surrounded on three sides by our bedroom mattresses. Baby Cornelia wanted to know why there had been so much 'boom! boom!' going on.

The bombing of Manila paved the way for the return of Allied forces to the Philippines the following month, beginning with the island of Leyte on 20 October. Landings would soon follow on the island of Mindoro and around the Lingayen Gulf on the west side of Luzon. Although liberation was welcome, the Philippines would suffer great loss of life and tremendous physical destruction before the war was over. An estimated 1 million Filipinos died in the war, and Manila was extensively damaged by bombing and then by house-to-house fighting. SEE ALSO PP. 444–6, 630–1.

Wednesday 27 – Thursday
28 September 1944

Captain Elmer E. Haynes, an American pilot with the 14th
Air Force in China, lies in wait with loaded .45s at
Chengkung airfield

27 September

After spending most of the morning trying to straighten up
our quarters, I borrowed a jeep and drove across the field to
check on the mail situation. Imagine my surprise – after two
weeks without any word from the outside world, we had
finally been remembered by the Army Postal Service. My
share was 16 letters. I certainly hope that mail delivery will
be better after this war is over. The rest of the day was
spent in reading letters and exchanging news from
home. After chow, we relaxed with a poker game. I lost – as
usual.

We hit the sack about eight o'clock. However, I had no
sooner turned out the light, when I discovered we had a
problem. Rats! Dozens of rats! They were holding a convention in our room – galloping across the floor and
squeaking and carrying on like they were having an election.

Under these conditions, sleep was impossible. The only
remedy was an all-out assault against our unwelcome
guests. Because of 'lights out' we were forced to rely upon
flashlights and candles for illumination. Wind, Miracle,
McClure, and I entered the combat zone armed with shoes,
machetes from our survival kits, and an old saber that one of
the guys had picked up somewhere.

After several minutes of shouting, cursing, and knife-
swinging warfare, we managed to kill a couple of rodents,
but almost did ourselves in as well. Somebody stomped on
a rat – spreading its slippery innards all over the floor.

Our sudden attack scared away the intruders, and we
finally managed to get back to our bunks after wading
through the debris. The following morning was spent in
cleaning up the mess, and thanking our lucky stars that one

of us had not grabbed his .45 during the riot. But the idea did cross my mind.

It was apparent that we had to devise a better method of exterminating the beasts. Shoes, boots, and knives were definitely not going to do the trick. At the rate these critters were multiplying, we would soon be up to our asses in rats. There were too many of them and too few of us. And they were rapidly eating us out of house and home – literally and figuratively. The damn rats devoured anything that stood still long enough for them to gnaw on – especially if it had the scent of meat. Even wood floors were not safe if food was spilled on them. Candles, and anything made of leather, were delicacies.

At this rate – with Japanese air attacks on moonlit nights, and 'Genghis Khan and his Rat Raiders' holding track meets in our room – we never would get any sleep. Something had to be done. Severe measures were called for.

28 September

Lousy weather this morning and no missions scheduled. However, the day off gave us an opportunity to discuss the problem of rodents using our room for a recreation hall. At breakfast, we formulated a plan of action. I sneaked a few pieces of bread back to the barracks with me, and scattered the crumbs in front of a large rat hole at a rear corner of our quarters. We then loaded .45s with bird shot and set up a watch. Mac and I took the first shift.

Sure enough, within a short time, two large rats – probably scouts for the rest of the pack – poked their heads through the opening and grabbed for the bread. McClure and I opened fire at the same time – three shots apiece for a distance of 12 feet. The rodents were blasted to rat heaven, but we nearly ripped out the wall. Blood, guts, and slivers of wood whizzed everywhere. At this point-blank range, the steel pellets did not have a chance to spread. They smashed into the side of the building like solid shot – blowing the wooden boards to pieces.

The sudden noise and commotion brought the boys of the 3rd Mapping Squadron charging into our room. They figured that it was too early for a 'Jing Bow Juice' party, and demanded to know what the devil was going on.

Mac and I explained the trouble we had the night before, and that we were only trying to run off the rats. The guys next door were not very sympathetic. They chewed us out and said that the rodent problem was comparatively simple to solve. But our raising hell practically all last night, and then again this morning, was disturbing the entire barracks area. There was even a rumor that the Japs had parachuted into camp.

The mapping squadron boys had been at Chengkung longer than us. They knew all the angles and supplied a solution to our difficulty. By chipping in a few bucks apiece, we could hire the building's 'Number One Boy' to patch the rat holes with tin can sheeting from the mess hall.

We followed their professional advice and located the fellow. After a long, frustrating session of sign language – compounded with our pathetic conversational Chinese – we managed to explain the rat dilemma, and the holes Mac and I had blasted in the wall.

The 'Number One Boy' assured us that he would take care of our problem for only ten bucks – American money. I thought the price was a little steep, but this guy was a real businessman. We coughed up the dough and the lad took off like a shot. Minutes later, we heard the sounds and chatter of a repair crew hard at work on our quarters – despite pouring rain.

This had been a long, busy day and I was bushed. I told my gunslinging pals that after our unsuccessful war against the animal kingdom, I could not help wondering if we had enough sense to be let loose by ourselves . . .

By the end of September extensive repairs had been carried out on Haynes's accommodation – which his friends now dubbed 'Rat Hotel'. Two days later he received orders to move to new quarters on the other side of the airfield. He was lucky, finding himself assigned to 'first class' accommodation with no rodents. For many the war was an exercise in constant movement and time spent improving sanitation, drainage or accommodation seemed wasted – for, as soon as the location was made habitable, orders to move were certain to arrive.

OCTOBER 1944

ON 19 OCTOBER US FORCES conducted an amphibious assault on the Philippine island of Leyte. General Douglas MacArthur commanded the invasion force, which would eventually reconquer all of the Philippines. Admiral Thomas Kincaid's US 7th Fleet escorted the first landing parties from General Krueger's 6th Army to Leyte. There was little resistance from the Japanese 16th Division and on the first day about 130,000 US troops came ashore. Simultaneously, Filipino guerrilla forces rose up across the island.

Within a week of the landings the Japanese navy attempted to destroy the US invasion force in a naval engagement between 23 and 26 October that became known as the Battle of Leyte Gulf. This was the largest naval battle of the Second World War and resulted in heavy Japanese naval losses and the sinking of the US aircraft carrier USS *Princeton*. American forces destroyed 40 Japanese ships and 405 aircraft, and damaged 46 more ships, effectively eliminating the Imperial Navy as an offensive threat in the Pacific, as well as ensuring that American forces would overwhelm the Japanese army on Leyte. However, during this battle the Japanese employed kamikaze attacks for the first time, a harbinger of future trouble.

Allied submarines enjoyed their best month of the war, sinking a third of a million tons of Japanese shipping. Surface ships and aircraft sank half as much again. Thereafter their tally would decline, simply because there were fewer targets left for them as the Japanese merchant fleet shrank rapidly. However, one of the disturbing features of this campaign was that some of the ships sunk were carrying Allied POWs to Japan to be used as slave labour.

The war in Asia and the Pacific increasingly benefited from successes in the struggle against Germany. The naval campaign against the Axis powers in the Atlantic and the Mediterranean was drawing to a close, freeing up large numbers of naval vessels and, more importantly, landing craft. For the first time there were sufficient bomber aircraft to meet the demands of both European and Pacific commanders. Moreover, morale in the Pacific was lifted by news of successes against Germany. Some countries in eastern Europe, such as Hungary, were attempting to leave the Axis alliance. The Allies were pushing into southern Germany and in the north-west the town of Aachen fell to American forces on 21 October. Berlin was forced to issue a call for the mobilization of the Volkssturm or Home Guard, which consisted of boys aged sixteen and seventeen, together with men between the ages of forty-five and sixty. Hitler's personal confidence had been shaken by an assassination attempt in July 1944, and since then his public appearances had been few.

Tuesday 3 October 1944

John Gaitha Browning, a US soldier, picks up a
problematic souvenir at his unit's new campsite at
Borgen Bay near Hollandia

This campsite proves to be no exception to our long line of very unhappy places, or maybe we just hit it at a bad time. Here we have sticky, black mud-gumbo ankle deep, and it clings to shoes like glue – slippery as grease when wet. The 532nd Engineers group has been here since April and claims to have packed the ground down for us. What was it when they came?

The place has been defended by a number of machine gun posts until a couple of days ago. Now they are no longer deemed necessary, as it has been weeks since any Japanese have been killed, and even then, only a couple of starved, half-crazy ones. The thick jungle behind camp is full of evidence – their camps and scattered equipment, odd foods in jars and bottles, wooden kegs of pickled fish heads and soybean sauce (still good, or as good as it ever was), two-toed shoes, their little wooden 'pillows,' their blasted foxholes, and their skulls.

I picked up one skull and brought it back to camp and left it on Ed's cot. Later the fellows took pictures of it and will, most likely, never get the photos back either. The army has gotten the holy jitters about the skull question, and we receive repeated warnings of court martial, death, and any number of absurd threats for possession of Japanese bones, teeth, etc. *Life* published a full page photo of a girl with the skull her friend had sent her from Guinea, and such publicity didn't help any. Even Tokyo Rose used the photo as an example of the 'barbarous' Americans' attitude toward a 'superior race.'

John Gaitha Browning's diary mentions the reverberations of the infamous 'skull issue'. Hitherto, American and Australian forces had treated Japanese personal remains in a rather cavalier fashion, taking little trouble to bury or record enemy dead, other than to the extent dictated by issues of hygiene near their own camps. Japanese skulls and other body parts were regularly taken as souvenirs and frequently mounted on boats or trucks as an exercise in grim humour. In retrospect it is clear that these attitudes in part reflected an undertone of racism and a conviction that the Japanese were somehow a lesser form of human being. In 1944 Japanese propaganda had a field day with the controversial Life *magazine cover, and the authorities decided it was time to tighten up on this type of 'souvenir'.*

Browning would survive the war and become a successful artist, working in Texas and New Mexico. He died in 1992. SEE ALSO PP. 374–5, 506–8, 605–6.

Friday 6 – Saturday 7 October 1944

Henry Kasper, with the US merchant marine, watches the fighting at Pelelieu

After participating in the invasion of Saipan in July 1944, Henry Kasper's ship had ferried wounded back to Pearl Harbor. It had then sailed to Guadalcanal to take on troops ready for the invasion of Pelelieu and Angaur, two islands close to Saipan.

6 October
At Pelelieu

A hot day the sun came out and calm seas returned again. Cargo was discharged today from the afterholds, and much progress was made as we cruised back and forth off the island. More shelling visible again today.

7 October
At Angaur

This morning we dashed in toward Angaur from the open sea so as to be off the island for immediate disembarkation of troops and discharge of cargo. So what happens? So we hang around off the northern end of Angaur all day and finally leave at sundown to join the convoy without accomplishing anything. No boats were available . . .

We could see continued shelling of Pelelieu against a Jap resistance pocket.

This weather is hot once more, and most of us feel the increased heat with no slight uncomfortableness. My heat rash is spreading again, and that awful prickly heat sensation is coming back in its irritating style once again. Salt, fruit juice, and lotion and powder are all used to combat the discomfort and cause, but as long as one must work in heat and sweat, the unwanted irritations will remain.

This heat and tropical atmosphere also breeds fungus growth on the men and cultivates mold growth on books and clothing. To combat the mold growth on my clothing, I have installed a 200-watt bulb in the closet, and the dry heat will eventually destroy the bacteria, or at least retard the process, I hope . . .

Well, hurray, the last of the cargo has been discharged! But we don't go back yet, for we have cargo to take on now and that probably will take days yet. We did receive four amphibious tractors, otherwise known as 'alligators,' and a few more are expected tomorrow.

We lay quite close to the shore this afternoon and with the help of a pair of field glasses and clear visibility, I was able to distinguish many features about the island of Pelelieu.

I saw the burned-out hangers, of which only the skeleton frameworks remain. I saw a couple of those thick-walled

LEFT: Chinese stall-holders in a Chungking market. Cecil Beaton (p. 540) visited China in 1944 and was astounded by the extortionate prices.

BELOW: A US navy lieutenant with a Japanese skull, which served as a mascot aboard PT boat 341. As Rena Krasno and John Gaitha Browning (p. 622) note in their diaries, the American authorities would become highly sensitive to 'the skull question' during 1944.

OPPOSITE PAGE: More than 3 million Allied soldiers fighting in the Middle East and Burma came from India. Here an Indian Army tank travels down the long road towards Rangoon.

ABOVE: Burmese hill tribes entertain visiting special forces personnel in their village. Alf Simpson's diary (p. 555) records co-operating against Japan with indigenous peoples who were paid in silver rupees. Some hill tribes were paid in opium.

BELOW: Men read and relax aboard Joe Bryan's ship, the aircraft carrier USS *Yorktown*.

ABOVE: Supplies are unloaded on the beach at Iwo Jima during early March 1945.

LEFT: Unlike formal histories, diaries record the omnipresent dead. Here, a burial at sea follows a Japanese kamikaze attack.

LEFT: Japanese suicide planes inflicted heavy damage on ships during the American amphibious landings on Iwo Jima and Okinawa during early 1945. This jet-powered example was captured by the Allies. Yasuo Ichijima's diary (p. 725) reveals the thoughts of a kamikaze pilot days before his mission.

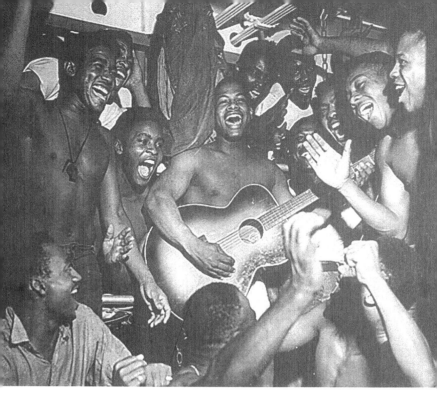

ABOVE: American sailors aboard the aircraft carrier USS *Ticonderoga* celebrate the news of Japan's surrender on 15 August 1945.

BELOW: A street scene shortly after the dropping of the first atomic bomb. Fumiko Amano's diary (p. 774) records the atomic destruction of Hiroshima through the eyes of a fourteen-year-old girl.

OPPOSITE PAGE: Japanese prisoners listen to the Emperor's broadcast on 15 August 1945. Ichiro Hatano, a teenage boy living at Okatani, used his diary to record his mixed feelings of happiness and anger at the ending of the war (p. 794).

RIGHT: Japanese officers surrender their swords in Singapore.

LEFT: A young Japanese prisoner in Burma turns to look at the camera. Most Japanese soldiers believed that capture would mean torture or execution.

BELOW: Rangoon gaol in May 1945 where Lionel Hudson and his fellow POWs had written messages on the roof to the RAF – 'Japs Gone' and 'Extract Digit' (p. 730).

LEFT: Prisoners at Aomori POW camp in Japan greet their liberators in September 1945. Many POWs, including the diarists Don McLaren (p. 807) and Tom Forsyth (p. 501), had been moved to Japan to be used as forced labour.

BELOW: A Japanese war criminal is despatched at Changi gaol in 1946. Numerous diaries, including those of Japanese statesmen like Baron Koichi Kido, together with those of POWs like Joseph Hodder (p. 205), were used in evidence at war crimes trials in Singapore and Tokyo.

concrete houses of which we've heard so much about in the way of near impenetrability. Also I was able to see the landing strip and battle-wrecked buildings adjacent to it. I also noticed tents, water towers, the airfield control tower, 155 millimeter guns, etc.

I also watched fighting continue in the hills above the airfield as the remaining Jap pockets are being slowly wiped out.

A sort of incendiary shell or chemical shell was being used against the Japs. The shell would land and explode against the phosphate hills with a sharp retort and burst into a brilliant flame. Then huge clouds of white chemical smoke would issue forth and spread over the hills.

Flame-throwers were in much use, too, and these were quite apparent as evening drew on. Star shells continued over the hills intermittently throughout the night.

Henry Kasper returned to San Francisco in late 1944 before participating in the landings at Okinawa in May 1945. After a prolonged shore leave in 1946 he returned to the US merchant marine and finally retired in 1970. SEE ALSO PP. *623–5.*

Sunday 8 October 1944

Anne Morrow Lindbergh on inter-racialism in Monterey

Anne Lindbergh's work promoting isolationism had ceased in December 1941. During 1943 and 1944 she took an increasing interest in civil rights. The war had raised these issues partly because Roosevelt's strong stance on freedom for colonies had placed the spotlight on issues of colour inside the United States, and in particular the colour bar in hotels and restaurants.

I went to Margot's Inter-Racial Committee. It was very moving. The little crowd of men and women of good will seated in pews of the small white meeting room of the Monterey Town Hall. Like a New England church meeting it was – everyone rather shy, decent, glowing with good will.

Negroes and whites sat, on the whole, in groups in their own race but smiled and made room for each other cordially. White, Negro, Filipino, and Chinese spoke. It was quite moving, especially the Negro. I was impressed again as always by the eloquence of the Negro, by his deeply moving qualities, his humility, his warmth, his generosity. So ahead of us in all these qualities of heart and spirit.

And how we have pretended to give them freedom, equality, the vote, and in reality have given them no equality, no decent education, no decent living quarters – no chance to earn a decent living.

What is the solution? Complete equality, complete inter-mixture? Certainly the Negro has things we would be better off with. He is superior to us, I feel, in many ways – artisti-cally and spiritually. And yet the principle of complete intermingling looks forward, it seems to me, to a state of sameness all over the world, as though one grafted peach and pear and apple and plum together and came out with just one fruit in the universe. Would the universe be better off with just one fruit? Must differences always make for conflict? I suppose all *separateness* makes for conflict, as Krishnamurti says. But is there no middle ground between a world with no differences and a world of conflicts? I do not know.

Many blacks believed that their wartime service had entitled them to better treatment and increasingly employed the slogan 'those who fought together should eat together'. However, attempts at wartime de-segregation caused difficulties, and where this had been attempted in shipyards and factories there had sometimes been riots. In the American armed services, black troops were primarily used in support capacities such as logistics, and there were few black officers. The military was not fully desegregated until 1948.

The Lindberghs were kept under surveillance by the FBI both before and during the war, not because of their integrationist views but because of their isolationist activities. After the war Anne Lindbergh devoted herself to writing. She died in Vermont in February 2001 at the age of ninety-four. SEE ALSO PP. 150–1, 336–7.

Saturday 14 October – Saturday 21 October

Yashio Shioya lives the life of a fugitive on Lolodai in New Guinea

Yashio Shioya was a private serving with the Takeuchi Force in north-western New Guinea. Cut off from his unit, he kept a diary recording his efforts to hide out with his injured friend Kanetaka.

14 October

LOCKHEEDS flew over constantly again. At 1230 hrs, enemy ships were seen heading north. In the evening the boats appeared again although I didn't know where they had been. The awaited prau has not shown up. Around midnight we received fire from an enemy ship. Tracer bullets, flames, searchlights and explosive cannon shells caused large trees to fall in splinters. The shelling ceased after 20 minutes. The enemy ship was firing again in the distance toward KAILOEPA or POTJAO on HALMAHERA.

15 October

Enemy boats have been around since morning making me nervous. Large trees, coconut trees and native huts are all pockmarked by bullets and look miserable. There were also shell fragments stuck in my bed. I asked the sub-chief of the village to let me hire a native coolie so that I could move into the mountains tomorrow. I stayed in a hollow, full of sago palms, for tonight.

16 October

There is only enough white rice left for one meal . . .

20 October

All I worry about nowadays is concealment. I can't even hang my washing out to dry. Nevertheless, my present location is fairly safe, so I guess I'll stay here a couple of days. There was a set of dishes and bowls, pots and pans, under the floor so I'm using them. The hut belongs to the DOROEME Village chief.

21 October

Enemy airplanes were strafing this area even before sunrise. Four LOCKHEEDS strafed for about 10 min before leaving. After breakfast decided to move farther back into the mountains. Will stop overnight in an abandoned hut. I went down to reconnoiter the village and found it in miserable shape. Houses were down and some burned. I was surprised at the size of the bomb craters. The beautiful church was also demolished. I wonder why the enemy bombs villages in which there are no JAP TROOPS? 10 bombs were dropped and there are two bomb craters of about the size of 50 kilogram bombs.

The islands of Lolodia and Moratai saw the final invasions at the north-western end of Dutch New Guinea before the liberation of the Philippines on 20 October. The islands were recaptured by the 31st Infantry Division during September 1944, meeting only light opposition. At the time, the islands had less than a thousand Japanese defenders. Nearby Halmahera, which was heavily fortified, was bypassed. Many defenders, like Yashio Shioya, fled into the jungles rather than surrender, and some died of starvation. At this stage of the war, the Allies had vast numbers of planes, as this diary testifies, and were content to command the skies, strafing anything that they could see on the ground, even a washing line, that might suggest a hut that harboured a Japanese soldier.

Yashio Shioya and his friend survived for quite a while with the help of friendly local people, but their ultimate fate is unknown.

Friday 20 – Saturday 21 October 1944

'Dusty' Rhoades, a US army pilot, watches Douglas MacArthur return to the Philippines

Aboard U.S.S. *Nashville*, Oct. 20, 1944   2115
What a wonderful day this turned out to be! I was up very early expecting things to start happening, but they were

slow in getting under way. Just before 1000 hours the shelling of the beaches started, but we were too far away to see much of it. The rocket ships poured their short-range rockets into the beaches and then withdrew. This ship did not take part in the shelling. Finally about 1200 hours we started in to the beach in an LCM [Landing Craft Mechanized]. There were ten officers in our party including Generals MacArthur, Sutherland, and Kenney, President Osmeña, Colonels Egeberg, Lehrbas, Whitney, and Wheeler, and myself. We could not get the LCM all the way on the beach, but had to wade ashore in water about knee deep. Dive bombers were making a beautiful show of taking out some gun emplacements on the hills back of the beach, and there was much firing from our guns on the beach. Everything from rifles to 155-mm was being used. There was, of course, much picture taking, and General MacArthur and President Osmeña made radio broadcasts to their respective peoples. Then we plunged into the jungle and were hard pressed to keep up with the general as he visited several command posts in the front lines. Our losses so far have been relatively small. I saw quite a number of dead Japs, but only one wounded American . . .

I forgot to mention that a destroyer off our port side ran into two mines this morning just before daylight. She was badly hurt but managed to beach herself.

Aboard U.S.S. *Nashville*, Oct. 21, 1944   2000
There was an air alert at 0430 hours this morning, which aroused me from a fitful, hot sleep. We all hit the deck, but no enemy planes came within reach of us. They did some bombing on shore.

We had news this morning that the cruiser *Australia* took a hit on her bridge when a Jap suicide pilot flew his airplane directly into her. All ranking officers aboard were killed. Both the *Australia* and the *Honolulu*, now crippled, are on the way back for repairs.

Douglas MacArthur's long-promised return to the Philippines was a major publicity event and was carefully stage-managed. Joined by Generals Kenney and Sutherland and President Osmeña, the exiled

Philippine leader, he strode purposefully through the surf and onto the beach. However, some officers failed to make the picture and so the landing was rerun three months later so that more photographs could be taken with additional officers alongside MacArthur, joining him in the famous landing. The latter photographs are often represented as the real event.

Guerrillas had already moved much of the civilian population away from the coast in preparation for the heavy shelling and bombing that preceded the landing. MacArthur had insisted on landing on the first day of the invasion, at some danger from Japanese air attack. SEE ALSO PP. 514–16, 784–5.

Friday 20 October – Monday 6 November 1944

Marcial Lichauco, a Filipino lawyer and journalist, watches the young men head for the hills as General Douglas MacArthur returns to the Philippines

20 October

Americans have finally landed on Philippine soil. A large convoy escorted by a strong task force has succeeded in disembarking at Tacloban, capital of Leyte province, one of the principal islands of the Visayan group. It was a complete surprise to everyone, Japanese and Filipinos alike, and evidently the invaders met little opposition. Four hours after landing operations began, President Osmeña and his staff stepped ashore. General MacArthur accompanied his forces and his first words on reaching Philippine soil were, of course, – 'I have returned.'

Tonight we heard a stirring address from President Roosevelt. 'America promised that she will redeem the Philippines, and America is fulfilling her pledge,' said the American President . . .

6 November

As was to be expected, there has been a steady exodus of

young men from the city bound for the hills to join the guerrilla units assembling there. Among those leaving town are many constabulary men as well as members of the municipal police force who manage to take along their firearms and as much ammunition as they can safely carry with them. Since the neighborhood association systems collapsed a long time ago when food rations ceased, it is well nigh impossible for the Japanese to find out who is really evacuating to safer localities and who is leaving the city to join the guerrillas. They are doing their best by posting sentries day and night on all thoroughfares leading out of town, and everyone passing through is carefully searched for firearms or other kinds of prohibited traffic. Since it is relatively easy to slip out of the city through any number of paths or by simply crossing the Pasig River in a banca, the only result of these searches is to subject innocent civilians to a lot of fuss and bother. Yesterday I called on a friend living in an adjoining suburb on the other side of the Pasig but, on crossing the bridge, I ran smack into three well armed sentries who proceeded to give me the once over. They found nothing incriminating and so motioned me to proceed but I had just taken a few steps when one of them sidled upto me.

'You got cigarettes?' he asked, flashing a broad grin, 'you give me cigarettes, yes?'

'Sorry,' I replied truthfully enough, 'but I no smoke.'

'O.K., O.K., – maybe next time you bring cigarettes for me – yes?'

And this little incident just about describes the condition in which the mighty Nippon warrior finds himself today.

The Philippines was one of the countries of south-east Asia that the Japanese had found hardest to control. Throughout the war there had been active resistance, and with the return of MacArthur even militia groups and policemen defected, taking their weapons into the hills. Many Filipinos had scores to settle and eagerly joined American forces in hunting down isolated groups of Japanese soldiers as the reconquest of the Philippines progressed.

After the war Marcial Lichauco would continue to practise law and wrote about the history of the Philippines, especially Philippines nationalism. SEE ALSO PP. 336–8, 470–1.

Monday 23 October 1944

Admiral Matome Ugaki watches a near-miss during a
torpedo attack on the Japanese super-battleship *Yamato*
near Palawan

*In the early hours of 23 October 1944 Admiral Matome Ugaki was sailing
with a large Japanese naval force commanded by Admiral Kurita, consisting of several cruisers and the battleship* Yamato, *north through the
Palawan Passage in the Philippines.*

Fair. Although I had expected it, could there be any worse
day than today? I went up on the bridge as usual with the
order 'all hands to quarters' one hour before sunrise. We
were sailing in an alert formation against submarines, with
column abreast with 18 knots on course of 35°. While we
were simultaneously turning to port in a zigzag movement,
at 0625 all of a sudden I saw port ahead the flame of an
explosion and what seemed like a spread water column on
the dawn sea. I shouted involuntarily, 'Done it!' which
proved to be the earliest discovery of it.

Immediately we made a simultaneous 45° turn to starboard with the signal 'green green.' Soon a second explosion
took place in the same direction. The same ship seemed to
have induced another explosion. Asked about the situation
of the Fourth Heavy Cruiser Division, the lookout replied
there were three of them. Then, thinking it might have been
a destroyer, I came to the port side where I saw a ship lying
dead, emitting white smoke, and another one, damaged and
heavily listing, which was approaching us. The former was
Takao, second ship of the line, and the latter *Atago*, first ship.
One destroyer each from the left wing was standing by the
damaged ships, while another was sent to the rescue.
The visibility gradually widened.

Since there were many friendly ships in addition to enemy
submarines, not only did excessive evasion pose a danger,
but as a senior commander I couldn't go too far away
because of the prevailing visibility. Therefore, following the

turning of the Fifth Heavy Cruiser Division, we turned to port and formed a column. At this moment *Maya*, fourth ship of the Fourth Heavy Cruiser Division, sailing starboard ahead, exploded. Nothing was left after the smoke and spray subsided. The firing position of the torpedo could be seen at about 1500 meters port ahead of her.

How dangerous it was! Had *Yamato* been situated a little bit either way, she would have taken three to four torpedoes. Evading to starboard and still advancing, we found another periscope to the port ahead, so we went over to the starboard. By this time the First Force was put into great confusion; some advanced while others turned back. It was certain that there were four submarines.

Ugaki and his comrades were en route to Leyte Gulf, where they intended to attack the American forces landing in the Philippines. Kurita's force was detected by two American submarines, the Darter *and the* Dace, *which attacked in the dark while remaining submerged. They sank the heavy cruisers* Atago *and* Maya *and severely damaged the heavy cruiser* Takao. *Once daylight came they were driven off by screening destroyers. They were unaware that they had narrowly missed one of Japan's two heaviest battleships, the* Yamato. *Shortly after the attack* Darter *ran aground and her crew had to be rescued by the* Dace. SEE ALSO PP. *105–7, 394–5, 740–1.*

NOVEMBER 1944

ON 6 NOVEMBER Joseph Stalin renounced the neutrality pact between the Soviet Union and Japan in order to reassure his allies that he would soon join the war in Asia and the Pacific. Moscow was not yet ready to declare war on Tokyo, but this signalled a clear intention to do so as soon as Germany was taken care of. Roosevelt had been anxious to secure Russian participation in the war against Japan because he did not yet know if the research programme at Los Alamos would deliver a viable atomic weapon. If it did not, then he hoped that Russia would join in the final push against Japan, a campaign in which casualties were likely to be high. The following day, Roosevelt was elected to an unprecedented fourth term as President of the United States; however, his state of health was declining fast as a result of cardiovascular disease. White House aides were doing their best to disguise the fact that even with an increasing number of breaks and rests, the President found it difficult to work even a four-hour day.

China was now the only area where the Japanese armed forces were making territorial gains. On 13 November 1944 the US 14th Air Force was compelled to abandon its air base at Liuchow, and two weeks later was driven out of a further base in Kwangsi Province. The Japanese were desperately trying to limit the ability of the Americans to bomb their homeland. Since June 1944 the Americans had been using bases in China to bomb Japan using the new B-29 Superfortress bomber, with an operational range of 1,500 miles. Nearly 90 per cent of the bombs dropped on the home islands of Japan during the war were delivered by this new aircraft. However, Japanese successes in China were to no avail, for by November 1944 US bombing raids could also be launched from the Pacific: since capturing the island of Saipan, the Americans had restored the Japanese air bases there, and now pressed them into service. On 24 November 1944 Colonel Bob Morgan led the first raid on Tokyo from Saipan in his B-29 Superfortress bomber 'Dauntless Dotty'. Some eighty-eight aircraft bombed Tokyo, but from their operating height of 30,000 feet they were not very accurate. Nevertheless, the expansion of the air bases on Saipan, together with the availability of growing numbers of the new B-29 bomber, paved the way for the massive bombing of Japanese cities.

In late November 1944 the United States also began the aerial bombardment of Iwo Jima, a Japanese volcanic island some 600 miles to the south-east of the mainland, which was the next target for invasion. Concerted bombing continued for more than two months. The Japanese garrison of 21,000 defenders survived this onslaught by hiding in scores of underground fortresses connected by 16 miles of tunnels stocked with food, water and ammunition. The surface was covered with concrete pill boxes and blockhouses housing some 800 guns and mortars.

As American forces closed in on Japan, Tokyo deployed increasing numbers of kamikaze – suicide – aircraft. Japanese scientists were also busy working on high-speed suicide boats and even a manned torpedo called the Kaiten that was launched from submarines. Thousands of young Japanese servicemen volunteered for these 'special services'. Kamikaze attacks were effective, and on 25 November 1944 four American carriers were badly damaged at Leyte Gulf where they were supporting landing operations in the Philippines.

Early November 1944

Joseph P. Kennedy, former American ambassador in London, on Roosevelt's fourth election campaign

Joseph P. Kennedy was born on 6 September 1888, in Boston, Massachusetts, the son of a saloon-keeper. Intelligent and ambitious, he gained entry to Harvard University and then built a fortune in banking, shipbuilding and motion-picture distribution. In 1940 and 1941 he had been the American ambassador in London, and enjoyed excellent political connections.

In discussing Roosevelt's health, which was very bad, Byrnes said that on the day the Supreme Court came to visit Roosevelt – it is the custom for each Justice to talk to Roosevelt personally – that he was in such bad shape that Justice Roberts said to Byrnes, 'I think this is cruel. This man is in no shape to talk, and we should get him out.'

He and Byrnes bundled him out, and when Byrnes told that to McIntyre, he said that Roosevelt was perfectly all right and that he had a Navy dietitian who had just made him thin. When Byrnes met Harry Hopkins and spoke about Roosevelt's difficulty in talking, Hopkins said it was new dental work that he had done, but Byrnes didn't take any stock in that.

Byrnes also said he didn't know what he was thinking of because he had promised Churchill six billion six hundred million dollars on Lend Lease after the war, and this was confirmed when I talked to Admiral Wilson in New York, who told me that at Quebec Churchill had asked for one billion six hundred million, and that he heard that Roosevelt had given him six billion. Byrnes also said that Roosevelt's condition at Quebec was very bad, and at the Press Conference, Churchill had to take it over . . .

On Sunday afternoon at Hannegan's request, I went to Boston to meet Harry Truman. Truman came to see me in my room and begged me to make a speech. They both believe Roosevelt won't live long, particularly Hannegan. He has made this statement to me a number of times before, and they felt that Truman will be President and will kick out all these incompetents and Jews out of Washington and ask fellows like myself and others to come back and run the government. Truman assured me that that is what he would do. He said that he disliked Mrs. Roosevelt very much and that she had snubbed him when she was out west.

I couldn't help but think if the world knew that the candidate for Vice President and the Chairman of the Democratic National Committee were sitting in my room telling me that they hated the crowd that ran things in Washington and wouldn't keep them there five minutes, and that Roosevelt wouldn't live long and they would run things right – no wonder I am not going to do anything. Every time I would make the point – and I did to Truman – that I couldn't in conscience come out for Roosevelt when I have so little confidence in what they do, they both finished up by saying that knowing my experience, they didn't blame me a bit, but they still hoped I would come out for him.

And I haven't made it strong enough before, I state again – both Truman and Hannegan discussed what they would do when the President died.

Kennedy's diary entry offers a fascinating insight into the declining state of Franklin D. Roosevelt's health even as he entered the presidential race for the fourth time. White House aides had long been used to disguising the extent of Roosevelt's illness, but Kennedy's diary entries underline how hard Roosevelt was finding it to be effective by late 1944. Capable and energetic in the morning, he was tired and unable to concentrate by the afternoon. Large-scale events such as Allied planning conferences tired him quickly. His fading powers were visible also in matters of policy. Throughout the war he had stridently maintained that French Indochina should not be returned to the French after the war, but in late 1944 and early 1945 he began to waver on this and other key issues under bureaucratic pressure. Kennedy himself, while retaining an active interest in the political scene, now devoted his time to promoting the political careers of his sons, Jack and Robert.

Monday 6 November 1944

Leo Amery, Secretary of State for India and Burma, has an open row with Churchill in Cabinet over India

Meanwhile in the Cabinet I had the worst open row with Winston that I have yet had. Apropos of the fact that India means to spend some 775 millions on reconstruction over the next five years he had got it into his head that this was to come out of the sterling balances, denounced Wavell for betraying this country's interests in order to curry favour with the Indians, and went on at large about the scandal and disgrace of all that everybody had apparently complacently acquiesced in. I held on to myself for sometime but could not help in the end exploding violently and telling him to stop talking damned nonsense. So the sparks flew for some minutes before he subsided and business continued. At the end of the meeting I told Winston that I was sorry if I had used strong language but wished that he would ever find time to talk to me about these matters and find out how they really stood. It is terrible to think that in nearly five years, apart from incidental talks about appointments etc he has never once discussed either the Indian situation generally or this sterling balance question with me, but has only indulged in wild and indeed hardly sane tirades in Cabinet.

Leo Amery, Wavell and the Governor of Burma, Reginald Dorman-Smith, were forced to endure Churchill's truculent and peevish attitude on India throughout the war. Churchill was obsessed with defending the Empire, but loathed the Indians, to whom he often referred in deeply racist terms, calling them 'filthy baboos'. Leo Amery struggled to fashion an India policy during 1944 and 1945 in spite of Churchill, and then endured a sad end to the war. His son John Amery had been a committed fascist and had made speeches on behalf of Hitler during the war. Captured in Italy in 1945, he was charged with eight counts of treason. Having pleaded guilty, he was hanged in 1946. Leo Amery died on 16 November 1955. SEE ALSO PP. 87–9, 299–300, 431–3.

Tuesday 7 November 1944

Frank 'Foo' Fujita, a Japanese American POW in Formosa, steps forward and volunteers to skin the cat

The food continued to be a soup, made of whatever vegetables were in season and the ever-present maize. The chickens, guinea pigs 'Ole Buck' and even the dogs seemed to subsist on it much better than we did. One day we were surprised to have fresh shark meat brought into camp. That night we had shark steak, and was it ever good. What was not so good is that there was enough meat for one week, and the galley crew was only allowed to cook the daily allotted portion. We had no icebox and the weather was not cold enough yet for the meat to keep sitting out on the table.

That first day the meat was delicious; the second day it was slightly tainted. The third day it was spoiled and the fourth day it was beginning to rot and to smell to high heaven. We would not eat it and the Japanese would not let us throw it out until the time it was supposed to last us ran out. On the fifth day the meat began to resemble jelly and glowed at night like a watch dial.

On the fifth night Nick went to the gallery and immediately began yelling for some of us to come help him catch a cat that had been lured into the gallery by the rotting shark meat. Several of us ran down to help and after almost demolishing the galley we finally captured the cat. I told them that we were not about to let that fresh meat get away. Someone asked if we would really eat the cat and Mickey Parkyns and I said, 'You bet!'

Since I had had a lot of experience in skinning rabbits as a boy back in Oklahoma, I volunteered to skin and butcher the cat if someone else would kill it. That cat was a big old tom and from the size of his accoutrements I figured that he would be awfully tough and strong tasting. He had originally been white but in prowling the alleys he had been turned almost black. I took him out to the bathhouse and dressed and washed him down. The meat was pretty and white and looked like skinned rabbit.

Nick had the galley fire banked and it did not take much to get a fire going. We had no salt or seasoning of any kind except the crushed red pepper, and so this is what we put in the pot. We had gotten in some very large leeks, looking like overgrown green onions, for our next day's soup. We took a poll and all agreed that we could sacrifice one blade from the green top to cook in with the cat. By the time we got the cat boiled to perfection the whole camp was on hand – some to claim a portion and most to see if we would actually eat the cat. The meat looked like boiled chicken and compared to the dog in Singapore it looked like a meal fit for a king. I did not hesitate in eating it and slowly most of the others began to try it. Most of the officers abstained.

The cat tasted so good that we built a wooden box trap and the neighborhood cats began to disappear. Once I was skinning a cat in the bathhouse when one of the Japanese from the front office walked in. He was startled, to say the least, and turned and made a hasty retreat. This was at night and most of the staff had gone home. However, the word was put out the next morning at *tenko* we were told to cease and desist with the cats, for if the neighbors found out about it they would think that we were not fed meat.

By November 1944 it was clear to Frank Fujita that the war was draw-ing to a close. The air raids which had begun in the summer of 1944 had become more frequent. B-29 bombers hit Tokyo hard in November and December 1944.

Frank survived the war and returned to the United States where he was still lecturing about his experiences in the 1990s. SEE ALSO PP. 406–8.

Wednesday 15 November 1944

Tatsu Utagawa, a naval trainee, finds his ship torpedoed near the island of Leyte

Tatsu Utagawa was called up in September 1942 after he had taken a degree in law at Waseda University. After over two years of training he went into active service as a naval cadet in October 1944. He initially served on ships moving between Shanghai, Formosa and Japan, before being sent to the Philippines.

We knew that we would be attacked at dawn and we found ourselves in an unpleasant situation. At last, towards three in the morning, we put the men ashore in the coastguard vessels. This operation was completed at 7 a.m. All that was left to be done was to land the ammunition, but for that purpose we would have to use the launches. This was impossible, and we decided, therefore, to return to Manila. The ship sailed about 10.40 a.m. When we arrived at the spot where the enemy had attacked us the day before, our planes and the Lockheeds started a dog-fight in the clouds just above us. We realized the danger and steamed off as rapidly as possible. In vain – through my field-glasses I could clearly pick out thirty B.25s on their way back from a raid on Tokio; they were flying towards us.

They advanced rapidly parallel to our convoy, flew over our bows and attacked us from starboard in pairs. The first couple were shot down, and crashed in flames into the sea. But the ship was shaken by the bombs which were falling all round us. The second time, two B.25s attacked the bridge with 13-mm. machine-guns. Bullets whistled round our ears. With the third wave two machines almost grazed our funnel as they dropped their bombs. Then there was a fourth attack: four bombers, splitting up into two groups, made for our bows and our stern. The first bomb fell on the first section, the second on the first hatchway; the fourteen men under the command of Kishimoto were reduced to pulp. The bomb which fell into the hatchway set fire to one hundred and eighty cans of petrol. In the stern of the boat, near the sixth hatchway, there was a hole big enough to have let a horse pass through. Another bomb shook up the cases of mortar ammunition, which exploded. Sergeant Fujimoto and Corporal Minato were killed on the spot, and the fire spread to other cases of ammunition on the bridge. The vessel was beginning to break in two, and the captain gave the order to abandon ship.

As I could not swim, I gave up the idea of saving my life. Nevertheless, so as to obey orders, I went to the bridge, wearing my life-saving jacket and carrying my flask, the bag containing my toilet things, with my sword at my side. The ship was now a mass of flame and the enemy planes continued to pepper this furnace with their machine-guns. There was nothing left now to protect me from the bullets. I lit a cigarette . . .

The captain came and asked me to abandon ship. I went back to the bows, where I saw the dead bodies of Fujimoto and Minato, and I watched the soldiers jumping into the sea. It was to that part of the bridge I used to come and dream of my native village while I watched the stars. Finally, remembering the captain's orders, I jumped overboard last of all, for I did not want to make myself ridiculous, even though my rank was not very high. When a ship goes down, it is the rule that the men who cannot swim jump in first, so as to get as far away as possible from the whirlpool which sucks down everything. But I had men under my command, so I did not want to be the first to jump. I knew that Kumiko would be proud to know that I had died nobly. The soldiers had all left the bridge and the ship was keeling over. I slid down, holding on to a rope, having covered my hands with the cotton gloves I had prepared. I had quite forgotten that I could not swim. I had done my duty. From the water I looked at the ship and I saw, just above my head, her name: *Kashi Maru*. As I tried to paddle, I heard a voice calling to me: 'Hi, sir. Hi, sir!' I called back, 'Yes', and started to move my arms and legs again, but I made no headway. I thought this was very peculiar and turned round. Then I saw Sasugawa, who was holding on to my sword with both hands. I called to him: 'I can't swim!' 'It doesn't matter,' he replied. Floating on my back, I attempted to get away from the ship, so as not to be sucked down by the whirlpool. A little further on, I came upon Lieutenant Shimokura, who was holding on to a big board. He called to us, telling us to join him. He could not swim either. All three of us held on to the board and began to paddle. But the petrol flowing from the ship encircled us. We had been floating for less than ten minutes when I had the impression that the surface of the water was lit up and slowly the oil began to burn. The sea was transformed into a sheet of flame. So as not to be burnt alive we tried to go forward against the wind, but the fire spread so quickly that it singed our faces. I thought: 'This is the end . . . I don't mind dying here.' I had all the photographs of my loved ones on me; I did not care.

By October 1944 Tatsu Utagawa knew the desperate odds that confronted him. Following the slowing of the naval war in the Mediterranean and the Atlantic, Allied submarines had focused their attentions on the Pacific, working together with carrier-based aircraft. Numerous Japanese transport ships, each carrying perhaps four or five thousand Japanese soldiers, disappeared without trace, and this was the fate of several convoys despatched to reinforce the Philippines. Utagawa had sailed for Manila on 8 November knowing that the last convoy had lost five out of seven ships. Amazingly, Tatsu survived the loss of his ship this time, but perished when his next ship was sunk on the China Sea in January 1945.

Sunday 26 November 1944

Oscar Conner, a US army dentist, watches Gary Cooper films near Aitape in New Guinea

Last night, Saturday, we spent a perfectly hilarious three hours at the show. Saw Gary Cooper in 'Cassanova Brown' and we all began laughing even before the movie started when Sgt La Costa of the Special Service Section (he of the famous GI woolen drawers episode on the ship coming across last March) and who seems to have the movies in charge, announced the movie's title and told us Gary Cooper was playing. Apparently as an afterthought he remarked, 'Don't ask me the name of the "BROAD".' Just to look at that fellow is to laugh for some reason and he possesses the ability to make even the most commonplace words seem funny. We began laughing, the entire audience, and we laughed the remainder of the three hours. To add to the entertainment, we had an alarm in the middle of the picture and a plane which we thought belonged to the Japs was caught in our searchlights and fled madly with our ack-ack bursting all around him. Again we rooted for a kill and were disappointed when he managed to escape. This morning we learned it was not a Jap plane but one of our very own. I can imagine the consternation felt by that fellow American up there with his own comrades shooting at him, and I can also well imagine the genuine American cuss words which flew thick and fast when he finally managed to return to the ground. Two more alarms came before the night was over, during one of which they really put on a show. For some reason they seemed to fly round and round directly over our heads and I was in and out of my hole so many times I should have grown dizzy. Once while in the depths I heard the boys outside shout that we had a fighter on one of the Jap's tail and I came scrambling out quickly since I have been itching to see a dogfight, more especially a successful dogfight. They were too high for us to see the planes but the tracers were flying thick and fast high over our heads, a rather eerie sight. I am certain that I saw the Jap plane disappear in a blinding flash far above the water toward Halmahera. We do know that our planes got several and I am sure this was one. We were even more glad to learn this morning that we got some of them when we learned that they wounded several of our men with one bomb which landed squarely on top of a tent down in one of the infantry outfits. Fortunately, the occupants of that tent happened to be in their holes, but several nearby were injured. We get even more mad each passing night. It is not hard to understand why men develop real hatred for the enemy.

Servicemen in the front line were occasionally entertained by live shows, but for the most part entertainment was offered in the form of movies. Those were laid on by the army's own cinema organization, the US Army Pictorial Service, which maintained a network of field projectionists and equipment, often showing films in improbable places. They also made movies, retaining a large movie studio in New York for the shooting of training and propaganda films. Casanova Brown, *however, was on general release. Considered risqué at the time, it starred Gary Cooper as a mild-mannered English teacher about to wed his sweetheart when he discovers that his ex-wife has had a child – and that he is the father. When his ex decides to put the girl up for adoption, Casanova can't cope and decides to raise the girl himself.*

Oscar Conner would serve on the island of Morotai off the coast of the Netherlands East Indies until April 1945. The following month he returned to the United States via the Philippines and was discharged in August 1945. SEE ALSO PP. 594–7.

Monday 27 November 1944

Chester W. Marshall, a B-29 bomber pilot based at Saipan, is bombed twice in twenty-four hours

Lieutenant Chester W. Marshall flew thirty bomber missions against Japan, including the first B-29 raid on Tokyo in November 1944. He was based on the recently conquered island of Saipan, which provided a vital platform for strikes against the cities of Japan. These inflicted enormous damage and accordingly the Japanese did everything in their power to degrade the American air bases with counter-strikes, as Marshall discovered on 27 November 1944.

I had my first experience last night of a sound coming from the PA system up at squadron headquarters: 'This is an air raid! I repeat. This is an air raid! Wake up your buddy. Clear your sleeping quarters at once. This is an air raid! Don't forget your gas mask!' Up at the line this AM at 0600 we had found that the Japs had almost wiped our squadron out. There was a complete mess in our 878th Squadron area. A huge hole in the ground was all that was left where

Lieutenant Scarborough's *Hell's Bells* had been parked and we counted more than 300 holes in our ship. We would not be going on today's mission for sure.

Eighty-one B-29s, which had not been damaged in the raid, took off for a second mission against Tokyo. Only two planes from our squadron were airworthy after the raid last night. In the 878th Squadron of the 499th BG alone, one B-29 was totally destroyed and five others were heavily damaged.

The Engineering department had not made an assessment on our plane whether or not they planned to patch it up or scrap it, so we returned to our Quonset huts, with the idea of returning to the line later.

It was almost noon and hot as hell. In addition to battling the hot weather, I couldn't find the combination to beat Navigator O'Donnel in gin rummy. There was no breeze this morning and in order to find a little comfort, the clothing I had on consisted of white G.I. undershorts only.

Cox kept coaxing us: 'Hurry up, you guys, let's get up to the line.' It was high noon and . . . bam! The bastards hit us again – in broad daylight – and again, there was no warning!

I quickly put on my shoes, forgot my pants, and hit the door. In seconds we were all down the embankment among the boulders near the water seeking a safe place to dodge the bullets. Torres and I were both trying to burrow our heads under a small piece of coral rock. My butt was exposed to the elements, and to Jap strafers, it must have looked like a white flag. The noise was terrific. It sounded as if every gun on the island was going full blast, firing at something. I stole a glance up toward the line where all the B-29s not on today's mission were parked. What I saw made me burrow deeper, like a prairie dog. A Japanese Zero fighter plane with the big round red emblem on its wings started a dive across our living area, just a few feet above the ground, with guns blazing. It was kind of a duplication of last night's experience, except this time our machine gun batteries up near the B-29s found their mark. I saw a black puff of smoke come from his engine, and as he zoomed over the top of the Quonset hut, flames broke out and engulfed his plane. As he passed over us, I could plainly see the pilot. I couldn't help wondering what he was thinking at that moment. One thing for sure, he was only seconds away from 'lights out.' He was losing altitude. At first I thought he would hit the water just off-shore from where we were hiding. 'He's going to hit in the 500th Bomb Group area,' somebody shouted. And he did. There was a big fire ball explosion and everybody jumped up yelling and shouting: 'That's the way to get that son-of-a-bitch!'

On 27 November approximately a dozen Japanese aircraft based at Rota flew under the radar screen, taking the newly established American air bases at Saipan by surprise for the second time in twenty-four hours. They inflicted enormous damage. These raids were also costly for the Japanese: half the attacking squadron was lost, mostly to action by fighters launched after the attack had begun. Attacks on air bases at Saipan were also being mounted from the southerly Japanese island of Iwo Jima, a location which the American commanders had already identified as their next objective. SEE ALSO PP. 691–2.

DECEMBER 1944

SOME OF THE FIERCEST fighting during this month occurred in the Philippines. On 7 December, the anniversary of Pearl Harbor, Japanese suicide squads were deployed on the island of Leyte in an unsuccessful attempt to drive off the invaders. On 13 December the American flagship of the group of vessels attempting to invade the island of Mindanao, the cruiser *Nashville*, was seriously damaged by a kamikaze attack. However, two days later a US task force escorted by some thirteen aircraft carriers landed on Mindoro Island in the western Philippines without loss. Several unexpected reverses afflicted an otherwise successful campaign. On 15 December, during the fierce fighting on the islands of Luzon and Leyte, a Japanese prison ship was mistakenly sunk by American aircraft: less than half of the POWs on board survived, and those who did were quickly recaptured. Then, on 17–18 December, Task

Force 38 was struck by a particularly ferocious typhoon: three destroyers were sunk by the storm and twenty-one ships damaged. Bloody fighting continued on Leyte throughout December in a campaign that eventually cost the Japanese 60,000 dead and the Americans 15,000 dead or wounded.

In northern Burma, the Chinese finally took the town of Bhamo after the Japanese suddenly evacuated at night. At Indaw the 19th Indian Division met the British 36th Infantry Division, making the first connected front in Burma. In mid-December the British 15th Corps began an offensive in the south towards Akyab. The Eastern Fleet, operating from Ceylon, began to venture closer to Singapore, attacking oil installations in Sumatra, although these attacks were of questionable value, given that Japan's severely reduced merchant fleet could send little by way of oil supplies to Japan.

In Europe, the German army in the west began Operation Wacht am Rhein, a surprise offensive in the Ardennes which sought to split the Allied forces and capture the strategic port of Antwerp. Attacking forces poured forward from the Ardennes forest, aided by fog and low cloud cover, and achieved a break-through on a 70-mile front. However, by 25 December the Allies had recovered their balance and begun to push the Germans back, assisted by improved weather which allowed them to make use of plentiful air support. By the end of December the Russians had entered Budapest, and Hungary had declared war on Germany.

On 30 December General Leslie Groves, head of the Manhattan Project, reported that he expected to have two operational atom bombs ready for deployment on 1 August 1945.

Friday 1 – Saturday 2 December 1944

Alan J. Brundrett, a British officer, on letters, envelopes and secrecy at the naval headquarters in Colombo on Ceylon

Alan J. Brundrett worked in the naval secretariat of the East Indies Fleet Headquarters at Colombo on the island of Ceylon between 1944 and 1946.

1 December

Among the ships docked there was the cruiser HMS *Cumberland*, which we heard was due in today. The sailors on the quayside were busy manhandling some of her cargo, which was being lowered down to them. No doubt there will be mailbags amongst them, containing letters from home. An event eagerly looked forward to: our lifeblood. There is always the same thrill and expectation when our postman comes round in the office with any letters for us . . .

2 December

George's relief has now arrived so he may be on his way home shortly. He tells me he is just about broke as he has been busy buying stones: rubies, sapphires and water sapphires. The settings are not very good out here so he has this done at home. He has even been including wireless valves and curtain material in his parcels. I haven't caught him crating his portable radiogramme as yet . . . a little too risky! A letter from my father quotes an RAF fellow's remark. 'Tell Alan to lay off the gems, you can easily get stung.' *Caveat emptor.*

Ratnapura, the 'City of Gems', lying about fifty miles south-east of Colombo, is so called because of the precious stones mined in the hills around the district. It is possible to watch miners at work in the gem mine and visit the gem museum, though we ourselves have not been. The famous Star of India sapphire, weighing 536 carats, was found here. The colours of some of the blue sapphires are especially fine . . .

Sydney is hoping to see his friend shortly when HMS *London* calls in here a week on Tuesday, on her way home to UK.

On Friday whilst he was working on Incoming Section, a messenger from C.-in-C.'s office brought some envelopes for him to sign for; one was missing so he signed for the others and against this entry he wrote, 'not received in Registry'. About a quarter of an hour later there was a bit of a flap when an officer hurried in enquiring of Kingswell who had written this. Stand up, Sydney Ingram. He was quietly reminded of the correct procedure by the CWO, who never shouts or raises his voice at any time; always very circumspect, sits there peering over his moon-shaped gold-rimmed spectacles: message received.

Sydney had another incident a few days before. Whilst he was opening the mail, he came across an envelope marked 'GUARD' (envelopes bearing this or 'TOP SECRET' are *never* opened under any circumstances but are passed direct to the Top Secret Registry). Well, Sydney had never come across one of these before, so he opened it! He said later that he got the shock of his life for the moment – rather like opening Pandora's box – as the papers inside were stamped 'HUSH TOP SECRET' in bold red lettering. He hurriedly bundled them all back into the envelope and quickly handed it over to Kingswell: trial pending! He's heard no more about the matter since. As with his swimming, he's willing to have a go.

'Funny what a panic a piece of paper can cause, isn't it?' he remarked. Well, er . . . yes.

There was one amusing incident some time ago. When buying peanuts from a vendor down below someone found the nuts wrapped in a Top Secret signal. There was panic stations! With the large windows open and the fans going it is sometimes difficult to keep control of all the papers.

Occasionally, in the Registry Office, among the dockets which the orderlies deliver, might be a bulky, taped one, marked 'BY MALE HAND ONLY'; these relate to a trial of an officer or rating, and are speedily dispatched through the system. Wrens, of course, are not allowed to deal with them. Nevertheless, peeping goes on!

The island of Ceylon hosted Admiral Lord Louis Mountbatten's vast headquarters, from which he ran South East Asia Command. Some 5,000 staff were arranged in neat huts constructed in what had been a botanical garden at Peredenia near Kandy. Not far away was a major naval headquarters in the town of Colombo. These locations, like other theatre headquarters, were inter-Allied affairs, staffed by British, American, French and Dutch officers. The great game was to keep secrets not only from the enemy but also from allies. British material that was supposed to be kept from the eyes of the Americans was stamped 'Guard', but the existence of the term 'Guard' was itself a secret. Accordingly, any envelope stamped with the word 'Guard' had to be hidden inside another envelope. This surreal system employed by British officials in the hope of deceiving their allies was mirrored by an identical American system, which used the designation 'Control'.

Tuesday 5 December 1944

Joyce Grenfell, an ENSA performer, encounters insect life and takes in a show in Bombay

Joyce Grenfell spent much of the war performing with her close friend Viola Tunnard, entertaining the troops for ENSA – the Entertainments National Service Association. She worked in Britain during the first few years of the war, then embarked on two extensive and gruelling tours for ENSA, performing in the Middle East in the first five months of 1944 and returning for a six-month tour of the Middle East and India in late 1944 and early 1945. She spent most of the last two years of the war on the road.

Insect life has entered into our Room 203. Going into the bathroom late last night – no, early this morning, 2.30 a.m., I was faced by a very horrid and enormous sort of cockroach with a body nearly two inches long (bright brown) and antennae two and a half inches above its beastly head, waving wildly in search of something all over the bath taps. I gave as controlled a cry as I could and Viola nobly took over. That beetle took a great deal of killing. Drowning was the first idea but it could swim and did so vigorously. Finally

Viola held it under the water with a toothbrush handle and it succumbed. The idea was then to pop it in the lav and pull. We did this but it had become as light as a cork and sank not. However a sharp surprise pull this morning has vanished it. *But* – its mate, or its ghost, was in there this morning. With accuracy and courage I have trapped it under a glass vase and it is now staring out from its confined space in a pretty angry way. The bearer says he will fix it later. Meanwhile two separate ant swarms have appeared. We rang for help and a Flit gun has put down the trouble for the moment but I've a shrewd idea those ants will have the upper hand in no time. I do *not* like insect life . . .

We went to the Excelsior to witness the first night of the Navy's amateur show *Men Only* . . . It was full of good intentions, entirely without originality and far, far, far too long . . . There was a chorus of girls – male ratings with nobbly knees . . . There was a top hat and tails number of embarrassing dullness and lack of talent . . . There was a fakir who threw himself about on broken glass and ate a razor blade and an electric light bulb and *fire*. That was impressive but revolting and gave me hiccups.

Joyce Grenfell and Viola Tunnard had arrived in India in late November 1944. ENSA operations in India were organized by the film actor Jack Hawkins. He complained in his memoirs that India was the lowest priority for ENSA headquarters in London, adding that few people 'ever had to handle as many dead-beat acts as were sent to me'. They included actors who were deaf and a stage manager with a wooden leg. However, by the end of the war he had begun to turn things around and had persuaded John Gielgud to join a production of Hamlet *in Calcutta.* SEE ALSO P. 677–8.

Saturday 16 December 1944

John Ciardi's B-29 runs into trouble on a bombing raid over Nagoya in Japan

John Ciardi was born in Boston on 24 June 1916. In 1938 he completed a BA at Tufts University and in 1939 took an MA at Michigan. In 1940 he published his first volume of poetry, Homeward to America. *In 1942, anxious to avoid being drafted into the infantry, Ciardi joined the aviation cadets. After training to be a navigator and an officer he was removed from the programme when the House Un-American Activities Committee turned up evidence of leftist views. Remarkably, in May 1944 Ciardi was still training, this time to be a gunner on B-29 bombers. Only in October 1944 was he assigned to a unit operating from the island of Saipan against targets in Japan.*

Nagoya is the third largest city of Japan with a population about that of San Francisco. Unlike Tokio, it is comparatively unmodernized and consequently highly inflammable. Also it has a Mitsubishi engine plant. The engine plant was our target . . .

We had had lead-navigator trouble all the way and finally hit the coast about 80 miles off course. In the imperative name of SNAFU the formation went cruising about Japan for better than an hour looking for the target finally heading into Nagoya straight across the middle of a major air field we were carefully briefed to avoid . . .

No 4 Engine picked just that moment to swallow a valve and break a rocker arm. The formation was still scouting around for Nagoya like clay pigeons in the teeth of a 100 knot headwind, and with No 4 giving practically no power we couldn't keep up. By the time the Frances's had gotten between us and the formation it was time to clear out. We let our bombs go at a target of last resort left the No 4 prop windmilling to keep from advertising our trouble, and headed out for sea. A few miles out we were clear and had the prop feathered, but still had about ⅓ of the Pacific to limp across. Skipper called O'Hara for an ETA and was told 6 hrs.

Then he called Campbell to find out how much gas we had and was told 4 hrs and a half.

There wasn't much to do but sweat it out. As a last resort we could ditch but even if we landed on the water without cracking up, the Pacific is still no place to be in a rubber life raft. We began to lighten the ship. We depressurized and went on oxygen while we broke open the turrets and hauled out the ammunition to toss into the bomb bays. I was laboring at the belts like a stoker and changing walk-around bottles every 3 minutes. When I wasn't changing a bottle it hung from my shirt like an anchor getting in the way of every move. I finally tore it off and risked 20,000 feet without oxygen, but immediately went faint. The wind was whistling cold through the open turret but I sweated like a pig while the ammunition belts fell in coils around my feet until I was almost caught in my own trap. O'Hara, Franklin, and the radio and navigation equipment have to share one small compartment with the turret and the turret fills most of the space to start with. We had a fine half hour of getting in each other's way and I was limp with exhaustion when I finished and called TJ to help me haul the belts through the turret.

We finally had the ammunition from the upper turret in the bomb bays. The belts in the lower turrets could be fired out and the links and cases would drop out. Doc salvoed the ammunition and our flak suits went with it for good measure. A while later Bob Campbell had the last gas out of the bomb bay tanks and we dropped those. They fell away trailing gasoline vapor and crashing into the radar dome on the way out, putting the radar spinner out of action.

There was nothing left to do but wait and sweat it out. O'Hara plotted a series of shrewd courses that would pick up favorable tail winds, and Skipper fondled the throttle settings to get the last bit of good out of the gas. And the Pacific stayed endlessly below.

Meanwhile the strike report came over. Good hits and large fires. No ships lost to enemy action. But the VHF was full of ship-to-ship distress. One of our crews – Grice's – had picked up some bad flak hits. It hit the water at 1700 and was lost. Some good boys went down in that one. Barry

Campbell was a good red-head, and Kaufman had won a lot of my money by being a good gambler. That's a hell of an epitaph, but what good is an epitaph.

We kept getting VHF distress calls from other ships and sending out a few of our own. A second ship ditched at 1910. Later reports (next day) had them accounted for – picked up by a destroyer. Orenstein kept a log of his calls and position reports and probably was largely responsible for the rescue.

Meanwhile the Pacific stayed where it was and we stayed where we were – not in it. And eventually – Saipan. We called the tower for a straight in approach and they called back for us to land at Gardenia – the B-24 strip.

Ciardi's diary captures the immense distances of the Pacific. Islands such as Saipan and Guam provided bases for the heavy bombing of Japan, but any damage to the aircraft or loss of fuel could mean a disastrous descent into the ocean. The attack on Iwo Jima in early 1945 would be partly intended to provide a base closer to Japan that could accommodate aircraft in trouble and also offer them fighter support. SEE ALSO PP. 686–7.

Tuesday 19 December 1944

Wing Commander Lionel Hudson, RAAF Mosquito pilot, heads off on a low-level 'rhubarb' over Burma

Wing Commander Lionel 'Bill' Hudson came from Kingsford in New South Wales. One of over 1,000 RAAF personnel serving in the air war against the Japanese in Burma from 1944 on, he was commander of No. 82 squadron equipped with Mosquito aircraft and based in Assam during the Burma campaign.

The irony of it all is that sheer pilot error landed me and my navigator in Rangoon Gaol as prisoners of the Japanese. My flight into Burma from Assam that day was my own bright idea. It was a journey that was not really necessary. Group operations had no specific target to offer, but I was keen and wanted to test-fire my cannon. I should have stayed put and played poker.

The morning cloud over the southern spurs of the Himalayas was breaking up as our two jungle-green Mosquito V1 fighter bombers dropped quickly and flattened out just above the tree tops on what we called a low-level 'rhubarb' – seeking targets of opportunity.

My wingman was another Australian, Scotty McKenzie, from the goldfields town of Kalgoorlie. He kept his distance in loose formation.

We used to say no woman could be as sensitive as a Mosquito. You flew it with the tips of your fingers on the control column, delighting in the response. We were flirting with the earth a whisper above coconut-tree height, now lifting the wing to check a jungle village, now zooming down over glistening paddy fields, now swerving to miss a gleaming white Buddhist temple. I recall feeling inside me the reckless rhythm of a Viennese waltz. Perhaps I was fanning the palm tops too closely but that was the spirit of the dance. My partner and navigator, Jack Shortis, a Londoner, who had to share my moods, gave me a furtive, quizzical look or two but said nothing. Trusting birds, these navigators.

The air speed needle was steady at 250 knots. Nothing moved below. Nothing to shoot at. Anyway, it was a beautiful morning . . .

Jack gave me a new course – north to Mandalay. Before us was the Irrawaddy River, broad and smooth and lightly veiled in morning mist. It beckoned. I swished down and skimmed it. Then there was a jolting crash, a jarring note, and a freezing of the music inside my stomach.

Incredibly, we were still airborne and climbing, but my serene and purring Mosquito of a moment before was now vibrating madly. The tips of the port airscrew were curled back and the Merlin motor looked as though it would shake itself out of its bed. White coolant was streaming from it like smoke. I switched that motor off and it seemed to sigh in relief. The starboard motor was still running but it was a struggle to keep straight and level. Anger was my only emotion.

'You stupid bastard, Hudson,' I yelled.

Poor Jack had nothing to do but sit there.

'The port engine's on fire,' he shouted.

I knew it was the coolant but I could not tell him because my microphone was dangling. He swivelled around and pressed a fire-extinguisher button. I suppose it was the right one. Anyway, we were now dropping out of the sky like a falling leaf . . . stick forward or you'll stall . . . straight ahead . . . land it here . . . look for a tree in a wooden aircraft that instructor in Rhodesia had told me three years before . . . put a wing into it . . . put the brake on . . . and I'd laughed. A tree came up on cue, dead ahead, and I put the port wing into it.

When I came to I was standing there on drying mud in a tangle of control wires, with Jack, slumped a little, alongside me. He was still attached to the armour plating by his Sutton harness. I punched the release and we climbed out of the mess of wires. There was a smell of burning, but I have no idea what happened to the rest of the Mosquito. It seemed to have vanished.

Lionel Hudson

Lionel Hudson and his navigator were taken prisoner almost immediately. Their captor was a Sikh belonging to the pro-Japanese Indian National Army, armed with a British .303 rifle. They were quickly passed to a Japanese NCO who made them crawl towards him on the ground. When they were allowed to stand up Hudson discovered that he had failed to remove his wing commander's stripes from his epaulettes and so was immediately identified as a senior officer. Removing such exotic badges of rank was supposed to be standard procedure when flying over enemy territory. Hudson was soon on his way to Rangoon gaol.
SEE ALSO PP. 707–9, 730–2.

Commander Thomas Hayes and his fellow POWs endure a passage by sea to Japan to conduct forced labour

In December 1944, after two and a half years in Bilibid prison, Tom Hayes joined more than 1,600 prisoners who were sent abroad on a Japanese transport ship, the Oryoku Maru. *They were being moved to Japan as forced labour.*

Early that afternoon, the prisoners were divided into three groups and marched aboard the *Oryoku Maru*. Commander Warner Portz was placed in charge of the first group of 850 men. The prisoners were pushed, shoved, and jammed into the aft cargo space (hold #5). The guards met the men with bamboo sticks and brooms as they descended the ladder and forced the first few hundred back against the ship's bulkhead. By the time Commander Portz's men had been packed into the hold, there was neither room to stand nor sit comfortably. The opening for light and air was the eight-by-ten hatch.

The second group of over 500 men was under the command of Lieutenant Colonel Curtis Beecher of the Fourth Marine Regiment. His men were forcibly pushed down into the forward cargo compartment (hold #1). This space was only 60 by 100 feet and the Japanese had installed a horizontal platform about four feet from the floor in order to double the space in the hold. The platform was nine feet deep and the prisoners were forced to sit four men to a row, each man's back against his neighbor's knees. The men in the center had no choice but to stand, packed like sardines against each other. They were then ordered to 'sit down.' . . .

The heat in the holds below deck was overpowering and bulkheads on all sides cut off any air circulation. Wooden platforms had been built over the hatch openings, allowing very little light or air to enter the cargo spaces. Japanese guards, peering down into the dark pits, were able to see the masses of human bodies staring upwards with bulging eyes, their shallow chests heaving for air. Commander Frank Bridget tried to convince the half-crazed men to take off their shirts and fan the stale atmosphere.

About five o'clock in the afternoon, the *Oryoku Maru* hoisted anchor and joined a convoy of four other Japanese merchant ships. All were unmarked and of the same type and tonnage as the prison vessel. They were escorted by a cruiser and several destroyers. The convoy was blacked out as it slipped out of Manila Bay and hugged the coast of Luzon.

The suffocating prisoners shouted for more air and water but the ruckus only angered Wada [Japanese commander]. He threatened to close the hatches completely. However, the clamor of the men only became louder and more insistent. Wada finally slammed the hatch cover shut over hold #5.

Shortly before dark, the guards lowered a few wooden buckets of rice and seaweed into the dark holds. The men who had mess kits scooped up the food while others grabbed blindly with their hands, taking whatever they were able to carry. One canteen of water for about every forty-five men was distributed. Each man received three teaspoonsful.

Along with the food containers, the Japs sent slop buckets (*benjos*) down at the same time and both pails circulated together in the darkness. The men were unable to tell which bucket was being passed to them – food or excrement. Certain prisoners would whisper to a neighbor that one bucket was another, and considered the joke hilarious if a hand was dipped into the toilet bucket, or the food bucket was used as a toilet.

Within the dark spaces, the prisoners soon lost all sense of time and direction. Insane screams, from men already cracking under the strain, terrorized the ones who had any sanity left.

Wada was continually upset by the disturbance and advised the prisoners that he would batten down all the hatches if the racket persisted. Wada complained that the uproar was disturbing the women and children above decks, and if the commotion did not stop, he would instruct the guards to fire into the holds.

An unearthly quiet, born of exhaustion and death, settled over the cargo spaces. The floors were covered with excrement and urine. The prisoners stripped their bodies of clothing so that their pores would be able to breathe.

In hold #5, the scramble for food and air created numerous personal feuds and hatreds. Occasionally a man would awake out of his mind and begin yelling at his tormentors. A prisoner later said: 'The others, afraid the hatch would be closed, shouted, "Knife him! Knife the son of a bitch!" Someone screamed, "Denny, you get him!" There was a scuffle, and then a sharp cry in the dark. Somebody else yelled, "Get Denny! He did it!" There was another struggle, and then a tension-filled silence. Men who owned jackknives unclasped the large blade and prepared to defend themselves if attacked.'

All through the terrible night the men in hold #5 fought, clawed, and tore at each other for a breath of air. Madness, induced by the lack of oxygen, caused many men to pair off and attack their comrades in the dark. They slashed the wrists of the weak and drank the blood. Others urinated into their own canteens and drank the fluid . . .

The first light of day revealed the horror of the night. Fifty men had died, and their bodies had been stacked like wood against the bulkheads. Most of the victims were those who were farthest from the source of air.

Many men died in the first stages of this journey as a result of the appalling conditions; others would die when the Allies attacked the vessel and it sank at Subic Bay off the Philippines. Tom Hayes, who initially survived, was killed a few weeks later after he had transferred to a second ship, the Enoura Maru, *at Takao in Formosa. His diary survived because, before leaving Bilibid, he had handed all his materials over to Lieutenant J. V. Crews, who packed everything carefully in sealed containers and buried it beneath the prison commissary area. Not all the diary was recovered after the war, and the section dealing with January–October 1943 is still missing – presumed to be still buried under Bilibid. The original manuscript of the remaining diary is now in the US Navy Bureau of Medicine Archives in Washington DC. SEE ALSO PP. 312–14.*

Friday 22 – Tuesday 26 December 1944

Harry Hurst, an RAAF engineer in New Guinea, enjoys the surrender of a 'democratic' Japanese lieutenant

Harry Hurst was an RAAF engineer who in January 1944 had arrived in New Guinea, where he was largely engaged on testing repaired aircraft. Weather conditions were extreme that December, with 31 inches of rain during three days.

Harry Hurst (centre)

22 December
W/C Kessey informed me that F/L Cools to replace me as Eng. O. Harry Death's RAAF No1 Concert Party here tonight. Splendid show full of life and movement. Non stop Bass Baritone, Pianist accordian, Violinist all exceptional.

Humerist–Female impersonist, H.D. and his stooge outstanding.

Had a talk with Lt. Jack Carr in mess at night. He told me of capture of Nip 2nd Lt from 41st Div. H.Q.. Small spectacles gave flash salute and bowed from *the* waist. Produced paper inscribed, 'I am Japanese Officer. I wish to surrender and join the American Army.' A bit set back when he found he was in hands of Ausies. Had Chinese coolie carrying immense pack containing changes of everything and supplies of food. He was well fed. Asked if he lacked food & said, 'I am strong. He (the coolie) is weak.' Told by Jack, 'I will give you a receipt for your personal belongings', looked up meaning of receipt in little book, bowed politely from the waist and asked 'you can write?' Boys nearly died laughing & dearly wanted to bump him off and poked fun at Jack about being able to write.

It appears that where there are concentrations the Officers at least are well fed. Patrols and isolated units are very badly off. This Nip had plenty of gen to give. HQ had given orders that Drinamoore was to be taken by Jan 15th. What a hope.

He was a Tokyo university student and claimed to be 'Democratic'. His treatment of the coolie proved it . . .

24 December
First year ends to-day. Harry Death's party again at 8 Sqdn. Flying all night after subs and barges.

25 December
Alex Muirhead invited to *do*.

More than twenty natives hung to day for leading a patrol into ambush and raping Chinese Women held by the Japs. What a Christmas festival. All natives including Marys [*a Mary was the name for a female native*] present at Angan for the execution . . .

26 December
With F/s Watson and McLelland, Sqds P/officer and Thomas to Suwack. Lunch with A.I.F.!! Bat. 6 Div. Out with Patrol to advance post. Saw our bombing among Nip huts and dumps. Good results. Very dead Japs in one hut. At

forward patrol they had killed one Nip and wounded another previous night. Same area as ambush few days ago. Brought back rifle and bayonet of Jap killed by our bombing. Enemy living under filthy conditions and returning at night to sleep. Our lads in Foxholes, but very clean. Position in from rocky point and 2 miles past Danmap.

Had some trouble crossing Drinamuir. Towed jeep going & two jeeps returning.

Had to wade Danmap up above waist.

Will smell dead Nips for the rest of my life.

By December 1944 the remaining Japanese in New Guinea were stragglers and were in a desperate way. Rather than surrender, many had headed into the jungle and were simply surviving rather than fighting. Starving and cut off from their units, after they were captured, some of them confessed to instances of cannibalism. Harry Hurst finished his tour of duty in New Guinea in January 1945 and then returned to Australia.

Wednesday 27 December 1944

Robert Payne listens to a Chinese boy student describe the work of the anti-Japanese underground against Chinese collaborators

Robert Payne was born in Cornwall in England in 1911 and was one of the most prolific writers of the twentieth century, authoring over 100 books and translating many others. Beginning as a shipwright, he found work in China and eventually became a professor of English and naval history at various Chinese universities. He knew China well, partly through the keen eyes and ears of his Chinese students. His diaries reflect a deep love of China and dismay at the horrors the country had suffered at the hands of the Japanese.

'What you must understand is that in the early days of the war, terrorism against the traitors was unorganized, and the bravest of the terrorists were the young students from middle-schools. Perhaps they were brave because it never occurred to them that they might be arrested, or perhaps they were more cunning – knowing they were young and the police were sympathetic sometimes, they preferred to do the killing rather than allow others, who would be tortured. At that time Chen Ti-kung was the Salt Collector in Tientsin. We knew he was working with the Japanese, and this in itself was not perhaps sufficient, for thousands of people were working with the Japanese. What made him dangerous was that he was in a position of great responsibility, very close to the Japanese general staff, and he had given orders for the arrests of some Chinese.

'It was decided to murder him. This happened one day when the students were eating ice-creams. We were eating, and then someone said, "Oh, we must kill him – it is intolerable that we should breathe the same air with him." So it was decided. We followed his movements, and we bought guns and ammunition through our house-servants. You ask them to buy something, and without batting an eyelid they will always obey if you have the money. They said we could buy three revolvers for thirty-five dollars. We gave them thirty-five dollars, and they bought us six revolvers. We were ready then. We would send guards to wait outside his official mansion, and we would spend hours in the ice-cream shop mapping out his movements exactly where he was.

'Then one of the students saw his car outside a cinema. The cinema was showing *Gunga Din*. We had seen the film, and we remembered that towards the end there is a prolonged burst of gunfire between the English soldiers and the tribesmen. This gave us time. We telephoned to all the other students to come, and mapped out a plan of campaign. The campaign was very simple. All of us were to enter the cinema armed, and all of us were to try to shoot Cheng Ti-kung during the time when there was fighting on the screen. It was as simple as that.

'But it was very dark inside the cinema and we couldn't find him. Then K. decided there was only one thing to do. You know that on the side of the screen in China there is another oblong screen where the speech appears in Chinese words. One of the students went to the cinema telephone and called up the manager. Would he please insert into the slide the announcement that Mr. Cheng Ti-kung was urgently wanted in the manager's office. The student spoke as though he was speaking from the Salt Commissioner's own office. The manager complied. The slide was put on. Still no one came to the manager's office, but it was noticed that a man in the third row had half reached out of his seat. His wife had pulled him back. We couldn't be quite sure whether this was our man. We telephoned the manager's office again, asking that a more urgent notice should be thrown on the screen. We were lucky, because at the moment when he rose from his seat there was fusilade of machine-gunning on the screen. Three of us shot at him. The back of his head was blown off. His guards began firing. The whole place was in confusion. One of the girl students found herself trapped into a corner by a foreigner – a Swede. She brought the butt-end of her revolver down on his head, and they say he was killed – he had a very thin skull. Half the audience was struggling to get away, and this helped us, because all the students managed to escape; and we were not so stupid as to throw our revolvers away – they would come in useful afterwards. I remember the smoke and the fumes and the film still going on, and then two minutes later we were out in the sunshine. The Japanese never found us. They arrested hundreds of people. If they had looked in the ice-cream shop, they would have found us eating ice-creams.'

Robert Payne was best known as a biographer of political leaders and film stars, producing accounts of Fyodor Dostoevsky, William Shakespeare, Mahatma Gandhi, Winston Churchill, Chiang Kai-shek, Mao Tse-tung, Adolf Hitler, Karl Marx, Greta Garbo and Charlie Chaplin. He was also a dogged journalist who loved trouble spots. He visited India and Bangladesh in March and April 1972 and wrote an account of the violent birth of Bangladesh.

Late December 1944

Rena Krasno, a Jewish medical student, is caught in an American air raid on Shanghai

In Japanese-occupied Shanghai Rena Krasno could observe the activities both of the Japanese and also of their puppet Chinese government run by Wang Ching-wei. As a Russian Jew finding sanctuary within territory controlled by an Axis power she was already conscious of the ironic and perverse nature of war. This sense was sharpened when she found Jewish friends were being killed by heavy American bombing raids. Nevertheless, all the inhabitants of Shanghai longed for the defeat of Japan.

This morning, just as I was about to leave for the university, the siren screamed: 1 long blast followed by 9 short ones (2 more than the prescribed 7!). A heavy raid. The entire house shook as bombs whined, catapulting downwards and exploding with fearsome bangs when they hit their targets. Nobody was at home, so – before Mama could call and stop me from leaving the house – I grabbed my bike after the all-clear and raced to Aurora University. Some 10 minutes into the lecture when Père Hernault was leisurely checking his 'bone box' in search of a clavicle, the sirens went off again, and again, and again! Pandemonium broke out. Students rushed to the windows staring at the sky and cheering each loud boom, while Père Hernault gazed around with benign bewilderment. He really is a kindly old man. Loud applause clearly indicated the students' hatred for the Japanese Occupation and hope for Allied victory. For the moment, the excesses of white colonialism were forgotten, overshadowed by the horrors of the New Order.

The B-29s pierced the sky like silver darts way out of reach of Japanese anti-aircraft fire and fighter planes. Japanese shells exploded in the air metamorphosing into umbrella-like shapes which we – in our hopeful eagerness – mistook for a U.S. parachute invasion. Previous air-raids had been depressing but this time, since rumors of Allied victories circulate ceaselessly, we are all optimistic and elated by the presence of U.S. boys somewhere miles above us!

As the raid continued, all classes were dismissed. During a lull I decided to walk home with Lee, a Chinese student, crossing the French Park. Both our bicycles – as alas so often happens – were at the repair shop. We strode quickly past Japanese soldiers who merely glanced at our student identifications while they were busy carrying and piling up heavy sand bags. Midway through the park the alarms shrieked again and we froze in our tracks. All around us metal shrapnel from bursting anti-aircraft shells pocked the grass and clumps of earth spurted up in the air.

A young Japanese soldier – he looked like a teenager – started waving and yelling incomprehensible commands at us. As we stood uncertain, not knowing how to respond, he crawled on his stomach very rapidly in our direction, pushed me to the ground indicating to Lee to follow, then half dragged me towards the thick bushes. The three of us lay panting, flat on the ground: a Jewish girl, a Chinese boy, and a Japanese soldier of approximately the same age united in a moment of danger in a youthful spirit of spontaneous friendship. When I finally reached home, I flung myself on my bed and – to my own surprise – burst into tears! The radio was denouncing the 'outrage of Americans bombing residential districts in Shanghai,' which they attributed to the Allies' despair at 'constant losses and defeats.' Papa brought the news that on this same day the Americans bombed the Nanking–Shanghai Railway. A number of passengers were killed, among them three Jews, one of whom was a young man due to be married the following week.

Tension is mounting here. Tales of frantic Kamikaze attacks on U.S. warships persist in spite of Japanese threats again 'rumor-mongers.' According to Papa, nothing can now halt the power amassed by the Americans.

Rena survived the war and eventually moved to the United States. There she served as a simultaneous interpreter for several international organizations and later became a celebrated author. In 2001 she was awarded the Benjamin Franklin prize for multicultural books. SEE ALSO PP. 273–4, 419–20, 493–4.

1945

'SUNDAY. FLASH! 'War can only last three or four days more', followed last night by Flash! – Jimmy Larkin told by two different people outside that the war is over in Japan. Anyway last night, as a result, was a helter-skelter of dreams for me . . . the war may be over – think, my immortal soul – or maybe I have succumbed, having been so long in hospital to its prevailing rumouritis . . . 2.30pm . . . the war is over. Jack's just told me, the four senior Allied officers in the camp have been informed by the Japs. Finish. I can just write now – had to walk twice round the camp to steady my hand . . .'

David Piper, in a prison camp at Shirakawa in Formosa, diary entry for 19 August 1945

JANUARY 1945

THE LAST YEAR OF the war opened with a heavy assault by American and Australian forces on the island of Luzon in the Philippines. On 3 January an armada was launched from US bases on the nearby island of Leyte: 6 battleships, 16 escort carriers, 10 cruisers and many destroyers. The Japanese responded with attacks by midget submarines and kamikaze aircraft. Several ships were damaged and General Douglas MacArthur's flagship cruiser narrowly escaped a torpedo attack. Many of the assault ships were damaged and the US carrier *Ommaney Bay* was so badly affected that she eventually had to be scuttled. This extended naval battle also saw the last surface-to-surface ship engagement in the Pacific, when four American ships sank a Japanese destroyer on the night of 7 January.

On 9 January US marines began landing on Luzon at Lingayen Gulf. General Yamashita, the commander of the Japanese garrison, decided not to fight the Americans on the beaches but instead attempted to draw them into battle further inland. Although kamikaze attacks continued against smaller ships and landing craft, the marines established a significant beachhead and began to land armoured units. On 13 January the escort carrier *Salamuau* was seriously damaged by a further kamikaze attack.

American carrier groups were now sufficiently dominant to challenge Japanese strongholds such as Formosa. Here, despite bad weather, much of the Japanese air force of 100 aircraft was gradually destroyed. These attacks continued into the second week in January with the aim of distracting Tokyo's attention from the major offensive on Luzon. Air attacks on Japanese-occupied ports on the coast of China also intensified.

British commandos and an Indian brigade continued their amphibious campaign down the coast of Burma, landing on the island of Akyab. Further inland, troops of General Bill Slim's 14th Army reached the River Irrawaddy. Japanese units offered little resistance and began to flee south along the river valleys towards the coast in the hope of escaping into Thailand. Arriving at numerous points on the Irrawaddy, the British were able to cross in areas north of Mandalay where there was little resistance, although fierce fighting soon developed in the surrounding areas on the eastern banks. Chinese forces cleared the Ledo Road by the end of the month, facilitating a greater flow of supplies into China, and British forces captured Ramree Island.

During January American carriers began to attack the major Japanese naval base of Cam Ranh Bay on the east coast of Indochina. This Vichy French colony hosted many Japanese bases and formed the rear area headquarters for all Japanese operations in south-east Asia. The relationship between the Vichy French and their Japanese guests had always been uneasy and became more precarious with each passing week. Further south, what was soon to become the British Pacific Fleet was making its way from the Indian Ocean to join forces with US carrier groups. En route it attacked oil refineries in the Netherlands East Indies and in the last week of the month a major air battle developed at Plodjoe. Over 130 Japanese aircraft were shot down; the British carriers lost 48.

Across Asia, Allied prisoners of war were increasingly buoyed up by news of Russian victories on the Eastern Front. This information was often picked up from hidden radios and then circulated secretly. Although it was inevitably subject to exaggeration and rumour, by 16 January 1945 many POWs knew that General Zhukov's Russian forces had taken Warsaw and this, combined with news of advances into Germany from the west, lifted spirits everywhere. It was clear that all Allied forces would soon turn their attention to the defeat of Japan.

At the end of January Franklin D. Roosevelt was inaugurated for a historic fourth term of office as President of the United States, accompanied by a new Vice-President, Harry S. Truman, in place of the previous incumbent, Henry Wallace. Unlike Roosevelt, Truman and Wallace were both active diarists. Roosevelt's health was now declining steeply; those who saw him only infrequently were struck by his physical deterioration and wondered if he would live to see the end of the war.

Saturday 6 January 1945

Peter Pinney, an Australian commando, admires the
Japanese night-time infiltrators on Bougainville

There are a few mavericks who creep around at night; and
you have to admit it, they have talent. And patience. Soon
after the sun goes down they crawl up to the wire, and wait.
As soon as there's a downpour, or an artillery barrage a
couple of miles away, they snip away at the barbed wire and
locate the tin rattles with their fingertips. Sometimes they
start chopping down a tree out there, or using a long vine to
shake our wire; but the odd rifle grenade sorts them out.
They obviously have no mortars, or we'd be copping hell. A
couple have come to grief with booby traps, but occasionally
a Shinto gets inside.

If you shoot at a moving shadow and you miss, likely
you'll cop something in return. Woywoy fired at something
and had a grenade hurled at him for his trouble. Ron's cheek
was grazed by a .256. They killed Captain King, one of our
better officers. They've been sending a few shells over
during the night, too: following a nearby blast something
heavy slammed inside Harry's and my shelter.

'Out!' yells Harry; and we scramble out each end like
goosed goannas. It could have been a Mills bomb, but it was
only a lump of wood . . .

Some enterprising Nip has been stealing our booby-trap
grenades, but we put a stop to that. If you remove the pin
and stick the bomb in an empty bully-beef tin, the lever is
held in place until the grenade is pulled or tipped free of the
tin; but the pop of the detonator still allows the Jap four
seconds to locate and throw the bomb. So now some of us
split the fuse to make it instantaneous, put a loop of string
around the bomb and brace a match against that to hold the
unpinned lever in place . . . and that is a very, very touchy
trap. Even if they retrieve the grenade intact, it kills the man
who throws it. It explodes almost before it leaves his hand.

The high point of the week came this morning.

Checking around out near the wire, Russell suddenly gave a whoop of laughter. One of his booby traps had been stolen in the night. Left behind in the tin was a Japanese ten-yen note. Puzzle: where's that instantaneous grenade? Who is the Jap out there with a sense of humour?

And if we catch him doing it . . . how do you kill a bloke who makes you laugh? How do you warn him against tossing that suicidal bomb?

Peter Pinney preferred fighting in the relatively flat terrain of south Bougainville where the jungle seemed less dense than the vegetation he had encountered in New Guinea. Here, in slightly more open country, Allied troops were able to enjoy support from tanks when advancing. Meanwhile the Japanese were unable to move in supplies either by air or by sea. All sides were short of ammunition and extra supplies were welcomed. In early January Pinney's commandos had taken over from an infantry unit which had left them a supply of 300 mortar rounds. Without mortars to fire the bombs, Pinney's unit employed them as massive booby traps, but well away from their own lines. The Japanese supply lines had now been all but destroyed. Some Japanese units were perilously short of ammunition and, as this extract makes clear, could fight only by stealing weapons and grenades from their enemy. SEE ALSO PP. 379–81, 735–7.

Saturday 13 January 1945

Admiral Lord Louis Mountbatten watches enthusiastic Japanese prisoners under interrogation at the Red Fort in Delhi

I went to the Old Fort, Delhi, to see CSDIC (Combined Services Detention Interrogation Centre). I must say it was most interesting to see how we handle the various Japanese prisoners of war that are being detained for interrogation.

To begin with, it is astounding the way in which they readily, and indeed willingly, and almost enthusiastically, give away information on any point about which they are asked. Only the naval prisoners show any sign of reticence.

It appears that they can in no circumstances bear solitary confinement. 24 hours is enough to reduce the strongest Japanese to tears. Indeed, when a Jap has given some particularly important information and it is desired to protect him from possible retribution at the hands of his fellow prisoners (to whom he is almost certain to confess), it is the custom to separate him from the remaining prisoners, in his own interests. There is no known case for their being able to stand more than a fortnight of this without going almost off their heads, so this presents quite a problem.

I came into one interrogation cell to find the interrogator, a very worthy Oxford don disguised as an Army Captain, red with excitement and emotion. He could hardly wait to say to me: 'Sir, this man has just voluntarily confessed that his platoon was in charge of some 300 British prisoners of war engaged on the building of the railway line from Bangkok to Thanbyuzayat. He states that on an average 120 prisoners of war were flogged a day, many of them so badly that they had to be taken away on stretchers and were useless for further work. He gleefully admits that they were even beaten for no reason at all, other than that their guards did not like their faces!'

When I went into this case further, I found that a Japanese officer had gone so far as to make a gramophone record of a confession, in the first person singular, of inflicting brutalities on British prisoners of war. What their object can be in making these voluntary confessions which, had the cases been reversed, would have involved their probably being flogged to death, I cannot imagine.

I came across one class of Japanese learning basic English with great enthusiasm. It is interesting to note that most of the prisoners assume that they could never go back to Japan and in many cases their ambition is to become Honourable Members of Honourable British Empire.

Many of the more senior officers try to pretend that they are private soldiers. They are dealt with in a very simple way, by being made the batmen of the junior Japanese officers. Altogether, a most interesting morning.

The Old Fort or Red Fort in Delhi was home to a number of remarkable secret organizations, including the secret services of the government of India. It was also the location where the CSDIC attempted to persuade Japanese officers to talk and give up their secrets, which they did with great success. No less amazing is the clear evidence that some Japanese were pressed into service broadcasting propaganda to their own compatriots in the field. Recently declassified documents reveal that the Special Operations Executive had several Japanese agents under training during 1945, although what they did with them remains a mystery. At the end of the war the Allied secret services sent several Japanese soldiers back into Burma to make contact with the Japanese commandants of POW camps to inform them that the war was over and to try to ensure good treatment of Allied POWs. SEE ALSO PP. 462–5, 770–1.

Monday 15 – Tuesday 16 January 1945

George Wright-Nooth, a British prisoner near Hong Kong, watches an American bombing raid on the harbour

George Wright-Nooth had been a police officer in pre-war colonial Hong Kong. He was studying for his Chinese language exams when the Japanese took the British surrender there on Christmas Day 1941. He had now spent three years incarcerated in the Japanese military internment camp at Fort Stanley.

15 January

This morning we had the largest raid since being here. It started at 9.15 am and ended at 11.00 am. Any number between 50–100 planes must have taken part. The noise was terrific with the bombs bursting, the planes diving, and every available gun in the Colony from revolvers to big guns firing. We were waiting for the guards to escort us out to work when we heard the roar of planes and saw fifteen flying in from seawards . . . heading for the harbour . . . We did not wait but made for No. 10 Block where we knew we would have a good view.

One's eyes could not be everywhere at once and our view, though a good one, was restricted, but I saw on one occasion six planes falling out of the clouds like stones on their way down to bomb ... Smoke rose over the hill that blocks Aberdeen from our view. Out at sea near Waglan Island over Lamma Island there was also bombing ... In the camp the guards, having fixed bayonets, were running around like madmen ... Up on 'the hill' the guards had lined the wall. They were highly excited. Every now and then a shot would ring out. They were firing at planes a good 4–5 miles away.

The 'Schoolmaster' was a guard in the garden. He thought it all a great joke. He fixed his bayonet and loaded a clip of ten rounds. 'I have to fire, and when I get back report how many I have fired,' he explained. He took up a kneeling position and said to the gardeners nearby 'You tell me when you see a plane and I will fire at it.'

Just then about 30 more were coming in over Lamma Island and these were pointed out to him. He fired ten shots at these planes which must have been five miles away. The gardeners nearly burst with laughter.

16 January

Hong Kong has had a hell of a hammering this morning. The air raid far surpassed the ferocity of yesterday and lasted for three hours. Our greatest thrill was the attack on the Fort. We have always longed to see this happen. Four planes dived on it firing with their cannons. They did not bother to drop their bombs. When they do bomb the Fort we shall have to keep well under cover. As usual the guards started firing, and so did a machine gun in the village. To our surprise an AA gun hidden among the trees in Stanley village also opened up ...

The planes, 4 or 5 at a time, are diving over the camp and coming straight over our quarters with machine guns blazing. Lying on the verandah we can see them turn and dive with the fire belching from their guns. It is an amazing sight. We are in the front line. The planes appear to be either after our HQ or the guards barracks. I saw one bomb dropping and smoke coming up from near the bungalow. I hope no one was hurt. Another bomb appears to have been dropped near the hospital. A small crater suddenly appeared outside, not fifteen feet away – that was near ...

One of the planes crashed on the hillside to the right of

Stanley Mound. The pilot came down by parachute. I just missed the actual crash, others saw it. We hope the parachutist was the only one in it.

The attacks on Hong Kong were largely undertaken by the American V-20 squadron – known as 'the Jokers' – who were based on the carrier USS Enterprise. *On 15 and 16 January their fighters took part in a series of sweeps and strikes on airfields, shipping and harbour installations at Hong Kong and neighbouring Kowloon. The anti-aircraft fire thrown up by Japanese ships in the harbour and shore batteries was as fierce and accurate as any that the pilots had ever encountered. These carrier-based attacks were followed up by bomber raids launched from bases in China two days later.*

George Wright-Nooth survived the war and returned to his pre-war occupation. By 1969 he was Deputy Commissioner of the Royal Hong Kong Police.

Thursday 25 January 1945

Peggy Wightman, a Wren signals officer, enjoys life at the naval headquarters at Colombo on Ceylon

Peggy Wightman came from west Hartlepool and joined the WRNS – the Wrens – in 1939. Her brother Charles was already serving in the RAF. She was posted to HMS Paragon, *a local naval station. In December 1940 she was selected for officer training, spending a year at Greenock in Scotland and then a further period at the naval signal school, HMS* Mercury, *at Petersfield. She arrived at Ceylon in August 1944 and worked on communications at the naval headquarters in Colombo.*

Great excitement, we have just had parcels from Elizabeth Arden, Sue's mother had written to them and asked to have them sent out to us – they do special packs for the troops – box of powder, lipstick and creams for all occasions, all beautifully packed in a satin lined box.

Someone has given us a wireless set for our cabin, unfortunately we can only get native music on it – very embarrassing as we are all signal officers and should be able to get the thing to work properly. I put an aerial up but Sue says I have put it in the wrong place – a little man is coming to sort us out!!! . . .

Tonight we are having a dance in the Mess; great goings on, an army of sailors on the front lawn stringing up lights in the trees and laying a wooden floor for dancing. It will be very effective and rather like a film set.

Gloom has descended because the Superintendent WRNS has just informed us we have to wear uniform as it is in the Mess. Instead of long colourful dresses against the men's whites, we will be gallumping around in our sailcloth dresses with large white flat feet. Some of our more glamorous members are furious as they always entertain their boy friends in backless dinner gowns. Sue and I don't think we have the sort of escorts who would notice and at least our feet will be comfortable and will take any amount of trampling on . . .

Some of the Wrens are getting very spoilt by the officers, they haven't been used to it and it is going to their heads. A lot of the worthier types don't get a look in, they couldn't possibly live up to what the girls are beginning to expect. It was exactly the same on the way out, the Wrens were treated like first class passengers, for example they were allowed on decks banned to the troops. Consequently many had romances on board with the officers, while the troops were just herded together and never saw a female; what a stupid life it is and what a dissatisfied one after the war is over . . .

Now Angela is back and Shelagh is letting everyone know that lots of things we are doing are not the job of a qualified signal officer! I sometimes wonder myself, especially when as today one of the yeomen came into my office and said 'You are looking very lovely today D.S.O [Duty Signals Officer] if I might say so, I could fall for you', this from a petty officer mark you. I said 'Well thank you very much, but hardly the thing to say to your signal officer'. The answer to that was 'Oh, come off it. I can't be bothered with all this red tape, do you know I have been doing this job for 13 years'. Which job he was referring to I didn't try to find out. I must say he is jolly good at his job and will do anything for me.

The whole set up is priceless out here when your loggist turns up on watch in a sari speaking very little English and a 19 year old sailor says he has never taken orders from a woman in his life!

Peggy Wightman enjoyed her time as a signals officer on Ceylon enormously. Despite the intense heat, mosquitoes and bugs, she quickly developed a full social life and there was time to visit the excellent beach at Mount Lavinia (also frequented by Hubert Hooper, whose diary appears in this collection). Exercising authority over the more experienced petty officers while on duty in the signals centre initially offered a challenge, but it was one that she quickly overcame. SEE ALSO PP. 815–16.

Joyce Grenfell, ENSA performer, struggles on at Barrackpore near Calcutta

The noise was considerable for our outdoor show at Barrackpore on Tuesday. It was like singing from a dock to a liner rising clifflike over one; for the patients were ranged on two balconies, one about twenty foot up and the second ten foot higher. Matron had laid on some ward screens of official green rep set up on the asphalt sweep, in front of a flight of about thirty steps, to form a little background for us. The piano and a small table with my glass of water on it were awaiting us as we stepped out of the CMP's station wagon – mysteriously provided as transport and very comfortably driven by a taciturn Yorkshireman who had the traditional heart of gold under a gloomy exterior. We started off at once. My voice seemed to get to the top tier boys more easily than the lower range; I don't think it made easy hearing for any of them, even though I did my darnedest and got a crick in my neck from looking up. And just to make it harder every crow in the area decided to gather round and join in. So did green parrots. Low-flying aircraft came roaring in just over the treetops; oxcarts rumbled by nice and slowly; motor bikes spurted by nice and quickly; an Indian in immense black boots scrabbled along the asphalt and another, out of sight behind our screens, watered some flowers from a trickling hose that made very suggestive sounds and scared Viola to bits.

In spite of all these little troubles the show went a treat and they were leaning over the balcony rail clapping and calling for more, so we kept on for an hour and fifteen minutes. Can't say I like singing at that angle; kept losing my balance.

Having performed under trying conditions in Barrackpore, Joyce Grenfell and her friend Viola Tunnard set off at 4.00 a.m. the next day and by 6.45 they were airborne in a Dakota sitting among sacked freight on their way to a new performance at Comilla. There they performed in several mobile hospitals, travelling along roads 'which defy description'. By early February they were on the move again, this time to Dacca. Joyce Grenfell returned to Britain in April 1945. She continued performing until 1973. SEE ALSO PP. 650–1.

Sunday 28 January 1945

Atie te Velde, a Dutch girl in an internment camp at Ambawara, watches the impact of leaflet-dropping by the Allies

Atie te Velde was born in 1928 in the Netherlands. She was one of nine children of a Dutch administrator and moved with him to live in Ternate in the Netherlands East Indies. In June 1943, aged fifteen, she was separated from her family and sent to the Ambawara women's camp in Java. There she first worked in the children's kitchen, preparing baby food, before working in the camp hospital.

Oh, a day I will never forget! I had just gone about my work as usual this morning and I was going in and out with the wash basins when I heard a plane. That itself is nothing special, but the sound kept on. It was just as if the plane was circling the spot. I thought, I'll go and have a look. I had just come out when the plane made a big loop and came towards us. And there it came through the bright air and we saw it: Red, White and Blue!

Everyone yelled and waved and cried tears of happiness. The machine came so low that we could see the pilot and when it looped up again, it dropped pamphlets which landed on the kitchen. Everybody ran towards them. It was an overview of the situation on January 22, 1945, that we know for certain, although it was a bit disappointing. Holland is not completely free and here in the Pacific they are not that far either. But it is happening. Who knows how much further they will have advanced in the meantime? Who knows! You tend to believe these good messages now because how can an airplane fly so quietly here without being chased.

The Japanese were dead nervous and the girl who was supposed to be fetching wood for the guards was sent away so that she could not contact the coolies. The camp immediately made it into a story that soon we wouldn't have to work anymore and coolies would come for the heavy work. It's not true but for a short period we can carry on. A while later, a few 'hobbyhorses' [derogatory term for Japanese] came running into the camp and started searching for the pamphlets. They climbed the roof of the kitchen and were looking in the barracks and those who did not want to give the papers were threatened with the death penalty. But we are not mad yet!!!

At around 11 o'clock, they summoned us with the horn and all the women and the older children had to go to the rice kitchen. There, an important man shouted a lecture which basically was this: if an airplane comes again you all have to go into barracks and don't look up. Furthermore, we had to hand in the pamphlets and we were not allowed to copy the contents and we should 'forget' it. (!?!) If they are thrown out again we are not allowed to touch them. Then he gave us the opportunity to hand in the pamphlets. He promised that those who did it immediately would not be punished. 30 people did it. They are still in the *goedang* [storehouse] with the guards. After that we were searched by the ladies, Jilderda, Wielenga and the fire guards. Nothing found of course. Anyone who is found with pamphlets now will be heavily punished. We only came back at around 12.30. Never mind! Be brave! Chin up. The end of the enemy is coming soon!

By January 1945 Allied domination of the skies over much of south-east Asia was almost complete and a great deal of leaflet-dropping occurred as a consequence. The effects could be mixed, boosting the morale of prisoners and internees but also stirring up the sentiments of the Japanese guards in unpredictable ways.

Atie te Velde and her brothers and sisters would all survive the war and were reunited in February 1946 before returning to the Netherlands. She died in 1975.

Wednesday 31 January – Thursday 1 February 1945

First Lieutenant Sugihara Kinryu takes cover and prepares for the worst during an American air raid on Iwo Jima

Sugihara Kinryu was a young officer serving with an infantry company near Osakayama on the north-eastern side of the island of Iwo Jima. He was assigned to the 11th Anti-tank Battalion, commanded by Major Node Tamoji. This was a unit that consisted mostly of reservists from Hiroshima and Shimane and its strength was low, only 262 men.

31 January

Wednesday. Clear. Southerly winds.

It is so warm today that even with a thin shirt I perspire. Submitted a periodic report on the progress of the cave-type road construction. Farewell services held for Sup. Pvt. FUTAOKA (3d company) who had died of malnutrition. He died soon after being hospitalized. How unstable life is!

Received a January 16th letter from my daughter, CHIYIKO. The letter stated as follows:

'Dear father, I am obeying mother and am studying hard to become a great lady. So please hurry and do away with Americans and return home to us.'

Also included in the letter was the fact that they had received the October and December allotments, along with three months pay (279.66 yen).

1130 – Air raid alarm sounded. Looking up I saw a B-29

winging its way majestically Southward. Later, another one came over. Neither plane dropped bombs. I am sure they are returning from a raid on JAPAN. It is indeed annoying.

I met Sgt. HIROZAWA in the vicinity of OSAKAYAMA. He stated that he was discharged from the hospital ten days ago. Sergeant NAKASHIMA of NIJO was also discharged. Night raids, as usual.

1 February

Thursday. Early morn, rainy. Later cleared up.

Reveille at 0300. Attended officers' maneuvers as assistant instructor. It started at 0400 and ended at 0930. 1400 – Accompanied the remains of my fellow soldiers, which were to be sent to JAPAN, to the pier.

It is so warm that one is able to go around nude without feeling cold. Went to take a bath, since it was warm. It was very good.

While taking a bath the fellows were kidding about a raid. Sure enough at 1500, the sound of motors could be heard. Looking up, I saw 11 trim-looking B-29s in formation overhead. I resigned myself to fate and took things easy.

Bombs were dropping all around me. Upon hearing the sound of the bombs as they came whistling down at a terrific pace, I looked up and saw bombs so large they looked like the B-29s of the first formation which had gone by. I thought of escaping but it was too late.

So I slipped in, deeper into the bathtub, and prepared for the worst to come. Then bombs dropped about 10 meters away. However, surprisingly enough, I did not suffer any effects from the concussion.

Peering over the tub, I was amazed. It was a sea of flames in an area 100 meters around. It looks as though the enemy has changed its methods of attack and is now, for the first time, using heavy oil incendiaries. Threw water from the tub on my clothes, which were lying nearby to prevent them from being burned.

Our CO was scorched in a few places, in the arm and back, from the spray of the bomb as he sought refuge. Things cooled down a bit. I took the bath over again and washed off the oil smears.

In a little while there was a second raid. In the nude, and carrying my clothes, I ran for a nearly natural hole, along the sea shore. I perceived that their bombs fell in the vicinity of the bathing place.

Upon hearing 'all clear' I rushed back to my quarters. There I saw the smoldering remains of the 1ˢᵗ Company CP and the lemon grass in front of the barracks. The pigs and chickens of the OTSUKA Unit were all killed.

The island of Iwo Jima, some 660 miles to the south-east of mainland Japan, was being softened up ready for an invasion that would begin on 19 February and would be completed by 26 March. SEE ALSO PP. 687–9.

FEBRUARY 1945

DURING FEBRUARY, American forces met fierce resistance right across the Philippines as they advanced on various key objectives, including Manila and the Bataan peninsula. General Yamashita had not given orders for Manila to be defended, but local Japanese forces put up a tough fight for the city; nevertheless, the second week of the month saw American armour pushing through the eastern suburbs. By 13 February the naval base of Cavite had also been recaptured. Three days later Corregidor Island in Manila Bay was subjected to airborne and seaborne assault. The fighting was difficult as Japanese defenders had to be cleared almost one by one from caves and tunnels.

American planners were already preparing for an assault on the Japanese island of Iwo Jima, and accordingly bombardment by B-29s and other aircraft intensified sharply: some 7,000 tons of bombs were dropped during the first two weeks of February alone. On 19 February two divisions of US marines, amounting to some 30,000 men, began the invasion of Iwo Jima. Despite the massive aerial bombardment, little damage had been inflicted on the extraordinary complex of interlocking defences that had been tunnelled into the island by the Japanese. Their commander, General Kuribayashi, exhorted his garrison to offer dogged resistance. American attackers persevered, knowing that Iwo Jima would be extremely valuable to the Allies. Its proximity to Japan would eventually allow US fighter escorts to accompany bombing raids over Japan and would also provide a vital emergency airfield for damaged bombers returning from the fray. Japanese resistance on the island centred on Mount Suribachi, and every inch of ground was contested. At sea, the supporting fleet of American carriers was subjected to waves of kamikaze attacks and the carriers *Bismarck Sea* and *Saratoga* were sunk. Although Mount Suribachi was taken on 23 February and a US flag was famously hoisted on the summit, Japanese resistance would continue for almost a month longer, focused on the northern end of the island and characterized by more suicide attacks.

In Burma, a second bridgehead was established over the Irrawaddy by the 20th Indian Division, against fierce opposition. But by the time the 7th Indian Division attempted to establish a third bridgehead they found the going much easier, for by then most Japanese forces had been withdrawn to defend Mandalay. By the end of February British forces were advancing on Mandalay against carefully organized resistance.

During early February Churchill, Roosevelt and Stalin met at Yalta in the Russian Crimea to discuss the future course of the war. Although Germany was the main focus of this conference, with plans being made to divide the country into four zones for the purpose of Allied occupation, the war against Japan was now an increasingly prominent subject. Roosevelt was anxious to secure Russian participation in what many believed would be a bloody and costly final assault on the Japanese islands. Stalin gave a firm promise that as soon as the war with Germany was over, Moscow would declare war on Japan. The price would be accepting Russian requests for the rights to the Manchurian ports of Dairen (Dalian) and Port Arthur (Lüshun) and owner-ship of the Sakhalin and Kurile Islands running to the north of Japan – and this was quickly agreed by Roosevelt.

Wednesday 14 February 1945

Hilda Bates, a civilian nurse interned on Borneo, recounts her birthday at Kuching camp

Nurse Bates had a long career with the British Red Cross and had been a health visitor in the British territory of Borneo between 1937 and 1942. She was interned in Kuching camp with the arrival of the Japanese in early 1942.

Hilda Bates

I am back in barracks once again feeling reasonably fit, though a whole stone lighter, which I can ill afford to be.

We are existing under a cloud of depression, due to absence of news, apart from grim rumours, and our hearts sank still further when we learned that one of the male internees has committed suicide following intensive interrogation of the Japanese. Although young, this man already had a brilliant record of service in the Government of Sarawak. Another worrying piece of news is that the Nips have decided that we women are not working sufficiently hard, so fifty are detailed each day to weed tapioca fields for six hours at a time. The ground is swampy, and under the glaring sun such work can prove very burdensome, especially for those who are unfit. There are only about fifty all told – who are in reasonable health, and active enough to do anything except camp duties.

My companions did their best to make my birthday a happy one, and I was the happy recipient of five eggs, one cup of *real* coffee, one tomato, and a sweet potato. These were the most welcome presents I have ever received in my life! Sometimes such little luxuries could be obtained by bargaining with the Jap soldiers, who were greedy for any little valuable or Borneo currency we might happen to possess . . .

The value of everything has risen sky-high. Salt is now £2.10 a pound, and sugar £5. Eggs are 4/6 each, and meat almost unobtainable.

One woman managed to bring in a quantity of soap with her baggage, and this she sells at £1 for a piece of about six inches long. My last towel has now disintegrated, so after washing I am obliged to shake myself like a dog until dry!

Another thing one longs for is real tooth-paste: Soot is not at all a pleasant substitute, though all we have for teeth-cleaning.

By February 1945, internees were aware that the war was drawing to a close. However, the growing pressures on the Japanese, including the disruption of their supply lines, also had an impact on the conditions under which internees lived. Although there were notable exceptions, many civilians had enjoyed reasonable treatment until this point, but conditions now began to deteriorate markedly. SEE ALSO PP. 746–8, 800–1, 812–13, 834.

Friday 16 February 1945

John Ciardi, part of a US B-29 bomber crew based on
Saipan, weighs up payments made in the 'universal
currency'

30,000 or 25,000 [feet]. What loomed so dark in the issue of
5,000 feet? The general was one school of thought. The men
who had the mission to fly made another.

Remember that our missions were flown against two
enemies. The Japanese AA batteries and fighters made one
enemy. The other was 3,000 round trip miles of Pacific
Ocean. There was the third enemy too – metal was our
enemy. Its tiniest flaw, its first imperfection waited to drop
us from air. A loose bolt or a split rivet might spring the
sequence that would end in our symmetry's ruin. In every
engine there is fire and death in more places than any eye
can find, and it waits forever.

The issue made in favor of lowering our altitude was that
too many planes had been forced to ditch due to mechanical
failure. The statisticians pointed out that the added 5000 feet
strained the already strained engines to the point of no
margin of safety. The verdict was that we would lose more
planes over the target, but fewer to the Pacific Ocean. The
ground and staff officers were unanimously agreed.

The flying teams saw it differently. Our bombers were
built for altitude. At 36,000 feet attacking fighters were
reduced in efficiency to the point where we could laugh them
off, and the flak was that much less accurate. Even if the added
strain brought on mechanical failure, the crew still had a
chance to make a ditching and be rescued by the life guard
subs and destroyers. And time and again we cited fighters that
had risen to meet us and couldn't quite make the last few
thousand feet. The extra 5000 feet was our margin for life. In it
we saw home again, and warmth, and wife-flesh, and neon,
and country furrows, and the lost language.

Actually neither argument mattered. We were on the
Island to destroy Japanese factories and Japanese factories

had a price tag attached. We were the price and neither long-ing nor the will to live mattered in the final balance. The General was our bargainer; he bid for those factories at the asking price, and he signed to pay for them in the universal currency that buys all of the world – human life. However we revere the idea of it in the Western World, nothing in practice is cheaper. With it we buy tunnels under the Hudson, steel rails across the Mississippi, skyscrapers in New York, bridge heads in France, factories in Japan. I am reminded of Melville's observation in *Moby Dick*, that not a gallon of sperm oil came ashore to light the lamps of America but a drop of human blood went with it. War only emphasizes it by numbers. To buy one coral rock suitable for air-strips and strategically located: 3,972 lives, 5,764 wounds. To destroy one Japanese oil refinery, damage one toolshed, kill an incidental number of civilians, drop three bombs on an assembly plant, crater so many nearby fields – price blank bombers, blank times eleven men.

John Ciardi, already an accomplished poet in 1940, survived the war to become a cultural phenomenon. In 1954 he completed the best trans-lation of Dante into the English language; he also published more than twenty volumes of poetry in his lifetime. He died unexpectedly of a heart attack on Easter Sunday 1986 at his home in Metuchen, New Jersey. SEE ALSO PP. *652–4.*

Saturday 17 February 1945

First Lieutenant Sugihara Kinryu emerges from the air-raid shelter for a breath of fresh air on Iwo Jima

1830 – Went outside to get a breath of fresh air. In the air raid shelter, it is just like staying in the hold of a ship. It is so stuffy from cooking, etc., and the temperature rises so, one cannot remain inside for a long period of time without getting a headache.

One must live in the nude while listening to the bombard-ment. When I went out to feel the cool evening air, I felt as though I had been reborn. Had some exercise, including deep-breathing. It really is so refreshing.

I climbed to higher ground. Suddenly, as I looked in the direction of South IWO JIMA, I saw a flame shoot far into the sky. The silhouette of a ship that looked like a cruiser appeared on the ocean. Presently it looked as though the cruiser sank. It is possible that it was sunk by our Special Attack forces.

The sound of clapping came from the direction of some soldiers who had come out of their caves and had witnessed the scene. Our morale is rising higher yet.

1900 – Went back to quarters and washed up. With the coming of night, we started to haul food supplies, replenish ammunition, and repair positions, as usual. Repair work was also done at the entrance of the Hq. cave. Message from Capt. HAYAUCHI as follows:

'My thanks to you, for your efforts as acting Bn. Commander. We, of this unit, are at the present time putting up a good fight. In the event of an enemy landing, we hope to have the closest cooperation from your unit. We pray for your success in battle.'

The phrase of 'See what happened, see what happened!' eventually changed to 'BANZAI.'

There is practically no night bombardment. It can be assumed that the enemy is getting reorganized and is preparing in the vicinity of south IWO.

2200 – Received orders from our unit CO to move BN Hq. to the Brigade Hq. cave. We were ordered to start immediately. The sky is cloudy. It is so dark that one cannot see ahead of oneself. Fortunately, we moved taking advantage of the let-up in the shelling. 0130 – The moving to Brigade Hq. is nearly completed. Reported to the Brigade Commander.

Some men went back to get their weapons, food, etc., that had been left behind. About that time, the men who had gone to haul supplies returned. Just as they stepped into the Hq. cave, a shell penetrated through the walls and exploded, resulting in the serious wounding of Lance Cpl. KODAMA and five others of the Hq., as well as three orderlies on duty at Hq. who were from other companies. There were also casualties among the patients in the nearby Field Hospital.

How ironical, that we should have lost as many men from our unit as a result of a single shell as we have lost to date in combat!

In the evening we received 'Imperial Gifts' which consisted of cigarettes and candy. Infinite is the graciousness of our Emperor. We have but one life to sacrifice in repayment for his graciousness.

Although there is no record of an American ship being sunk by kamikaze attack on the evening of 17 February, many ships were sunk or damaged by suicide missions during this campaign. The escort carrier Bismarck Sea *was lost, and the carrier* Saratoga *was so badly damaged that she did not return to service in wartime.*

Fewer than 300 prisoners were taken on Iwo Jima, and First Lieutenant Sugihara Kinryu was not among them. It is presumed that he died during the fighting. The diary was captured and translated by US army intelligence, but probably for historical purposes only, given that the translation was not completed until July 1946. SEE ALSO PP. 680–2.

Sunday 18 February 1945

Juan Labrador, priest and academic, watches the Japanese prepare to abandon the city of Manila

The evenings are a nightmare. They bring a rosary of shocks produced by powerful guns which, from New Manila and Grace Park, strike at Ermita and Intramuros, shaking the air, the earth, the doors and the nerves. Projectiles fly over our heads, whistling their funereal song of destruction. We cannot look at them; we can only follow their trajectory with our ears . . .

But more shattering than the dissonant harmony of war engines is the news about the tragedies suffered by survivors who escaped from the southern part of the city. The accounts are so terrifying and so macabre that my spirit was filled with infinite bitterness, and I wept with tears of pain and indignation. From this sadness and sympathy arose an impotent anger against the infernal forces which vented its desperation and hate among the civilian populace. So many families of acquaintances and friends exterminated. So many mutilated . . .

In the shelter at the German Club, some four hundred persons of different nationalities were attacked and massacred by drunken soldiers. Only about half a dozen escaped. The young Enrique Miranda, son of Telesforo Miranda Sampedro, told me that his mother and five brothers were taken by the Japanese. He did not know what happened to them. We learned later that their bodies were found mangled – those of his two brothers, in the street. Enrique said that he was made to kneel down and they hit him on his neck. He lost consciousness. He came to his senses when a soldier was prickling him with the point of his bayonet to find out if he was already dead. He tried to bear the pain and feigned death. The soldier covered him with earth. He was able to bore a hole through which he breathed. Later, he squeezed himself out and, bleeding all over, he hid among the stones until he was found by the Americans.

In Singalong, the Japanese marines gathered the men to send them on forced labor. The men were made to line up and were herded in groups of ten into houses where their heads were cut off. As those in the streets could not hear anything, they entered the houses confidently, believing that they were only to register their names. A son of Mr. Inchausti, among others, escaped, but was badly wounded.

President Jose P. Laurel, the puppet ruler of the Philippines, had declared war on the United States of America on 23 September 1944. There was little point to this, since the population overwhelmingly favoured the Allies and were jubilant at the return of MacArthur. However, the Japanese defended Manila fiercely, forcing the use of artillery and tanks in a populated urban area, which resulted in many civilian casualties. Far worse were the widespread massacres of civilians. Several thousand died in a range of attacks against schools, colleges and churches, which even extended to the killing of fifty people in the Spanish consulate, including diplomats from this neutral country.

Juan Labrador survived the war and would soon return to his

*teaching work at Santo Tomas University, which reverted from a civilian
internee camp to a university campus in 1946. SEE ALSO PP. 162–4,
229–31, 456–7, 563–4.*

Monday 19 February 1945

Chester W. Marshall, a B-29 bomber pilot, watches a
suicide attack by a Japanese fighter aircraft over Tokyo

We took off on schedule at 7:04 this morning for another raid
on Target 357, known as the most elusive target in Japan.
This time we were briefed to be careful as we passed near
Iwo Jima because the big battleships would be 'softening up'
the island prior to the invasion. We passed within sight of
Iwo and could see the flashes from the big guns from
battleships offshore. It was a sight to behold, and it made
us feel a bit safer just seeing what was taking place. We
figured there would be no way for anybody to live through
such a bombardment, and of course, we knew the B-24s,
along with a few B-29 attacks, had been saturating the island
for at least two months.

As we neared the now familiar airspace above Tokyo we
could see that the 877th Squadron directly ahead of us was
catching hell.

Suddenly, as the flak let up, we saw our first kamikaze
attack on a B-29. We were amazed as the suicide-bound
Japanese pilot made his dive toward one of the B-29s ahead
of us. All the planes in the 877th brought their guns to bear on
him and filled the sky around him with tracers, but he kept
bearing in. As he struck the B-29, on which one of my flight
school classmates, Lieutenant R. L. Nelson, was pilot, the
wings of both the B-29 and the Jap fighter plane crumpled
and flew off. Both planes started spiralling, breaking up and
exploding as they plummeted toward the ground 25,000 feet
below. We watched closely for parachutes opening, but there
were none.

On our way back to base, we got a message that the
Marines had landed at Iwo.

Chester Marshall's B-29 bombers flew at between 25,000 and 30,000 feet. At this great altitude they were safer from anti-aircraft fire and immune from most Japanese interceptors. A few Japanese aircraft, such as the Kawasaki Ki-45 Toryu, could match their altitude and, disconcertingly, they were increasingly used in suicide attacks, simply colliding with their adversaries. This tactic was adopted by the Japanese because many aircraft were too poorly armed to shoot down a B-29. A shift to more night bombing over the next few months would seek to avoid such encounters with 'ramming fighters'. American crews who managed to bail out were often executed and only half of the prisoners taken from B-29s survived to the end of the war.

Chester Marshall would go on to complete thirty missions over Japan. He would survive the war and return to his home state of Mississippi at the end of 1945. There he spent over thirty years in the newspaper and publishing businesses, and also served for ten years as a company commander in the Air Force Reserves. SEE ALSO PP. 644–7.

Tuesday 20 February 1945

Sy Kahn, an American soldier with a logistics unit, goes to the town of Dagupan on Luzon in the Philippines on a 24-hour leave pass

By February 1945 Kahn was working on the ship Blackburn, *supporting the American advance through the Philippines. He was about 200 miles north of Manila at the town of Dagupan.*

Went to Dagupan day before yesterday with Sig and Frank. While there I met nearly everyone in the company. Now having passes we weren't, of course, stopped by MPs. It was a nice day, and I felt especially good going to town for a much-needed change. While there we ate in several one-arm joints that served meagre meals of fish, chicken or eggs, with eggplant or tomatoes as a constant side-dish. No coffee available. It was fun eating in the dirty, shabby little shops with flies using the food as landing strips . . .

At midnight as we came in from work and lined up for the midnight meal, we learned the astonishing news that Cory was dead. Eriksen had been picked up by the MPs and when they noted his outfit, they informed him of Cory's death. A Filipino who was at the scene reported it as follows. There was a gunfight between Cory and a colored soldier. The latter was reported limping away down a road, probably hit in the leg or foot. Cory had twelve bullets in his body, eight in the chest, four in the abdomen. Demers, who saw Cory's body only a half-hour after it all happened, didn't know it was Cory until the next morning. He said Cory was sprawled up when he was hit in the chest. He was found near a house of prostitution situated out in the swamps near Dagupan. Several of the fellows saw him drunk earlier in the afternoon. The last time I saw him was that morning when he signed out on pass right in front of me. I remember, as my name went down, reading Pvt. William A. Cory – and, then, that night dead.

We were all grieved to hear of Cory's death. Because I know his pugnacious attitude, especially when drunk, and his deep-seated hatred of Negroes, it is not difficult for me to construct what probably happened. Most likely he resented the Negro having intercourse with the same girl he had, or perhaps his even being there. One word led to another and blam – blam – blam! Cory's rifle was found with an empty clip that holds 15 shells. We have no further word as to the capture of the killer. It is probable that Cory was shot in self-defense. In any case, he is now buried. A notice on the bulletin board advises that no one will mention anything in reference to this incident in letters. Most likely his mother will get a 'Killed in the line of duty' notice. As Jack Harris said, 'Some men who walk around with a chip on their shoulders are destined to die young.' Cory was 21.

It seems a shame that a man has to go through all the hell of the army and campaigns only to be killed over some slut and because of a bottle of nipa. The occurrence is not unique; it happens frequently. It seems unreasonable that the army should require that troops in this area, which is now secure, carry their rifles and permit them to go to towns where there are liquor and available women. That combination of gun, liquor and women has already made for several deaths. Here frontier conditions exist; it is a place for a man to stay sober. This nipa, or tuber, is powerful stuff. A quarter bottle was enough to make me feel light-headed for several hours. Some merchant marines have been killed; Filipinos and MPs have killed men for rape or attempted rape. Carbines are fired all the time.

Kahn's spirits had been lifted by the knowledge that Russian troops were only 100 miles from Berlin and American troops were on the outskirts of Manila. He now expected the war to go on until the spring of 1946. Kahn himself was subject only to occasional night air raids by single aircraft and very occasional spasmodic shellfire. Enemy action, however, was not the only danger. During the same week Kahn and his friend Norm narrowly escaped being reduced to the ranks for having made one visit to town without a pass. Another friend, 'Pap', had fired off his weapon while drunk and had been court martialled. They regarded these events with fatalism and as part of the normal business of soldierly life.

After the war Sy Kahn returned to the United States and became Professor of English and Drama at the University of the Pacific, California. He is the author of two plays and six volumes of poetry. He has also directed more than 350 plays and musicals. SEE ALSO PP. 486–8, 508–10.

Friday 23 February 1945

G. J. Green, warrant officer in the US marines, deals with a spider trap on Iwo Jima

G. J. Green had served with the US marines since July 1942 and was an artillery specialist often working with observer groups, spotting for targets. He had previously fought on Bougainville and Guam and was now acting as a forward observer with K Company, 3rd Battalion, 21st Marines Regiment.

We moved up to the runway and I kept the team spread out and in the fox holes. We were doing pretty well on communications, as we were in touch with Lt. Pottinger at battalion. He wanted to know why we were not doing any firing – told him I couldn't see anything to shoot at, and the

[American] troops were moving up fast. He said pick some prominent landmark and fire anyway . . . Capt. Heinze, sitting on the edge of the runway about ten feet up from where I am, asked for my compass, as he lost his. As I got ready to toss it to him, he yelled for me to look out. And as I turned around, there was a Nip grenade spluttering about three feet from me. I sat in a small shell hole about two feet deep, looking at the grenade until it exploded. Instinctively I ducked my head then looked back up and started to aim my carbine in the direction the grenade came from. As I aimed, I saw another one come flying toward me from some bushes. It landed just about the same place as the other one did. This time I got to duck my head before it went off. I felt my face expecting a handful of blood, I got only a bit. I have some fine particles of grenade in my face, but fortunately none hit my eyes. Capt. Heinze came sliding down the slope of the runway with his pistol out, holding his right leg – he got a good size piece of one of those grenades in his right leg on the inside, we helped him back to a deep shell hole. I tried to get a BAR [Browning Automatic Rifle] man to spray the bushes, but he walked up to them and toppled over – the Nip shot him in the stomach. Now I could see the Nip in a fox hole with a top that he moved up and down like a spider trap. We got a fire team directed at him, and they dropped a few grenades into his hole. The next time I looked at him we were moving again, and he was plastered to one side of the hole – quite a mess.

Japanese defences were often ingeniously constructed, sometimes offering not only protection but also near-invisibility for the soldiers inside them. In some locations, hidden foxholes were constructed with the only opening facing backwards, so that they could be used after neighbouring positions had been overrun. American marines would not notice them, run past them and then be shot from behind. Green was wounded on Iwo Jima during March 1945 and was invalided back to the United States.

Wednesday 28 February 1945

Admiral Sir James Somerville visits 'the Communications Annex' in Washington DC

Admiral Sir James Somerville had been the British naval commander at Ceylon from 1942 to 1944. By early 1945 he had moved to Washington DC, where he was part of the British Joint Staff Mission, liaising with the Americans on matters of strategy and intelligence.

Admiral Sir James Somerville

In the afternoon I paid a visit to the Communications Annex where I was received by Admiral Redman and Russel Wilson and taken round by Admiral Wenger who was in charge of the establishment. This is the opposite number to B.P. [Bletchley Park] but has been built up apparently regardless of cost and is extremely well equipped and organised. I was shown some interesting diagrams concerning the effect on Japanese cyphers of a release by a US war correspondent after [the Battle of] Midway concerning the ability of the Americans to read Japanese messages. This produced immediate reaction in the shape of cypher changes which had been a continual headache to the establishment ever since. I was also informed that a US cypher machine had been loaded onto a lorry in France for transfer to a divisional HQ and that while the driver was either having a meal or was asleep the lorry had been stolen and there was no trace of the Machine. As a result of this appalling negligence since 60,000 wheels used in the machine will have to be re-wired and the [Allied] cypher is technically compromised until this is done.

James Somerville had trained as a naval signals officer and had made extensive use of signals intelligence in operations against the Japanese during his time as commander of the Eastern Fleet in 1944. He therefore had a clear understanding of the importance of Bletchley Park and its American naval equivalent at the Communications Annex, where Japanese naval messages were decrypted and read. Together with the atomic laboratories at Los Alamos, this was probably one of the two most sensitive and secretive sites in the United States. Anxiety about the security of signals intelligence continually dogged Allied organizations, since a single slip that allowed the enemy to know that their communications were being read might cost months of work and possibly thousands of lives.

Somerville would return to London to become Admiral of the Fleet in late 1945. SEE ALSO P. *483–4.*

MARCH 1945

BY 3 MARCH THE desperate and bloody fighting in the streets of Manila was coming to an end. Over 20,000 Japanese troops had died defending this now devastated urban area and large numbers of civilians and internees had perished during the fighting. Extensive combat continued in the hills and along the ridge lines to the north and south of Manila.

Some 14,000 American troops were landed on the nearby island of Panay on 18 March. Typically, there was no resistance to the initial landing; the Japanese preferred to bide their time and defend prepared positions further inland. In some of the more remote areas of the Philippines, Japanese troops were beginning to withdraw of their own volition, worn down by supply shortages and the vengeful activity of local Filipino guerrillas.

In Burma, British units entered the town of Meiktila and dug in. This small but vital town in the centre of the country sat squarely across the supply lines for most of the Japanese army further north, who now had to face their enemy with dwindling ammunition stocks while trying to clear a supply route to the south. Japanese troops had to be diverted from the defence of Mandalay to try to recapture Meiktila from the British – who only just held on. Once supplies to Mandalay had been cut by deploying units into the countryside around the city, the 19th Division began to advance into the suburbs, and most of Mandalay was recaptured by the third week of March. Large numbers of Japanese forces were drawn into the battles for these two cities, just as General Bill Slim, the British commander of the 14th Army, had hoped. Their defeated remnants were ambushed by guerrillas from the Burmese hill tribes as they tried to flee southwards through the river valleys.

March also saw a historic change in the tactics employed in the American bombing of Japan. Hitherto, attacks had employed high explosive bombs dropped from high altitude, but winds had resulted in poor accuracy. General Curtis LeMay, commanding these operations from the Marianas, wished to retain high altitude to protect his pilots and so redeployed his aircraft in night attacks on cities using incendiary weapons. This new phase in the aerial war began in the second week of March with a powerful attack on Tokyo. This had devastating consequences for civilians: more people were killed in the fire-bombing of Tokyo than in either of the subsequent atomic attacks. Other targets marked out for fire-bombing included the cities of Kobe, Nagoya and Osaka.

Large numbers of US carriers were also operating off the coast of Japan and attacking airfields on Kyushu. As these carriers moved into the Inland Sea to the north-east of the island for an attack on the naval base of Kure, kamikaze attacks in-tensified. Piloted kamikaze rocket bombs, a manned Japanese equivalent of the V-1 flying bomb, made their first appearance.

The US carriers *Enterprise* and *Essex* were damaged, while the carriers *Franklin* and *Wasp* were put out of action. Over 800 men were killed in the attacks on the *Franklin*. Wooden decks on American carriers made them more vulnerable than their British counterparts, which enjoyed armoured decks and often were back in action 30 minutes after incurring a kamikaze attack.

Across Asia and the Pacific, Allied troops were heartened by news of impending victory in Europe. Major cities such as Danzig, Marburg and Frankfurt seemed to be falling day by day. Hitler had dismissed the last of his talented commanders, General Guderian, after a heated argument over strategy, and in Germany the end was in sight.

Saturday 3 – Monday 5 March 1945

Fumiko Amano, a teenage schoolgirl, reports for work at a factory in Hiroshima

Fumiko Amano was a fourteen-year-old 'Patriotic Girl' in the ninth grade who thought that the most beautiful thing in the world was to die for her country. She had stopped going to school to join her classmates working in the Toyo munitions factory. Over the past two years she had worked in the fields, bringing in harvests, and in schoolrooms converted into workshops.

3 March
Clear.

I was tired this morning and slept so well that I overslept. I left the house at seven.

I went to worship at the Hijiyama Shrine and then headed for Mukainada Station. I got to the station at 7:18. A boy accidentally kicked my right leg with his big wooden clog and it hurt so bad I could hardly breathe. How pitiful I was. I finally got to the station but not everyone was there and I had to stand around and wait. In the meantime, all of the students from Jogakuin and Aosaki National People's Elementary School got together and in one line they all did the 'face left!' and went into the factory together. I was so jealous.

Everyone in our group finally got together and we went through the gate but the people at the back of the line were straggling. It made me sad to think that the unified Yamato Spirit had already gone away by the second day.

I put an elastic band in the waistline of my work clothes so they would fit well but Yamaguchi-san tried to fix hers with a string and couldn't cinch hers up. Since I was vice-group leader, I had to warn her that it wouldn't do. 'If the teacher gets angry, cinch it up,' I told her, but I couldn't keep from laughing.

We listened to two people speak this morning. The first was like the colonel yesterday. He said,

1) *Whatever the work is, if you're told to do it, do it with all your ability.*
2) *Be accurate in all your measurements. It is the way of the student-worker to produce hundreds and thousands of units.*
3) *To be a worker is to progress and always to look up.*

The next talk was by the technical manager. He brought up the example of Ninomiya Kinjiro. We need soap to wash our hearts. We need to cast away ourselves and obey.

Before going to bed tonight, I reread *The Mothers of the Nine Soldier-Gods.*

4 March

A beautiful clear Japanese day.

Got up at 6:00. We work on Sundays, too. I left my morning dreams behind and jumped out of bed burning with hope. By train to Mukainada Station.

Our teacher didn't show up for a long while. Finally, just when I had decided to go check on him at his house, he showed up.

In the morning, we heard talks by the managing director of the Toyo Factory and the head of the Machinery Section. In the afternoon, talks by the head of the Weapons Section. It looks like we're going to be working in the Machinery Section.

My hair is growing so long it bothers me but I don't have time to cut it. Kuromoto-san and her friends are always looking at me and whispering. It makes me feel sick. I had a splitting headache today.

I ate supper at 5:10 and went to Ohata-san's house. Ohata-san is one of my best friends. We had a mountain of things to talk about. We just couldn't stop talking. Her little sister, Fujie-chan said, 'I'm going to make an offering to the Buddha,' and made an offering of some flowers and a mud cake. Ohata-san's father was killed in the war.

My eyes and head are so tired. Oh, when can I make friends with the machines? Waiting . . .

5 March
Cloudy then clear.

Got up at 6:30. I felt good and sang all the way to the trolley stop.

We listened to a talk this morning by the Education Section. The manager, Takahashi-san, talked about 'spy prevention.' I wanted to write down the important points but my pen was broken and wouldn't write. Basically, people like me who talk a lot must be extremely careful and keep their mouths shut to avoid leaks.

Fumiko Amano's diary is an exquisite piece of writing that captures the concerns of a schoolgirl in the dark world that was Japan in early 1945. Desperately short of food and faced with the total mobilization of the population, nevertheless she remained in part preoccupied with the childish issues of gossip and friendship. Continual 'education' kept the population docile and accordingly Fumiko knew so little about the progress of the war that she still hoped for victory. The lecture on 'spy prevention' was typically hysterical, since the idea that there were many 'spies' in Japan in March 1945 was plainly silly. SEE ALSO PP. 737–40, 774–6.

Wednesday 7 March 1945

James J. Fahey, serving on the US cruiser *Montpelier*, talks to local Filipinos about the Japanese occupation

While we were loading the LCI [Landing Craft – Infantry], I talked to a Filipino who appeared to be around 35 years old. He was married and spoke good English as most of the Filipinos do. He said that he spent three years with the guerrillas up in the hills . . . If a Jap soldier wanted anything, he just took it. One day the Japs approached him and seized all the clothing he was wearing except his sox. He figured the sox were the wrong size or they would have taken them. After this episode he took for the hills with only a pair of sox to his name. He made a pair of shorts from the sox. He also told how he killed many Japs who held his wife prisoner. He freed his wife and both escaped to the hills. The Japs attacked girls from 10 years old and upwards. After finishing with some of the girls, the Japs would then cut off their heads. A rope would then be tied around their feet and they would be left hanging from a tree. A favourite sport of the Japs would be to take little children and toss them up into the air, then catch them with their bayonets. The only food the Filipinos received was a handful of rice daily. The Filipino then told me how he and his friends would come down from the hills after midnight and kill many Japs in the town. At first guns were scarce, but they got more little by little by killing Japs and taking their guns and food and clothing. When they were through with the Japs, they would bury them. Bows and arrows were used as a silent means of extermination. The Japs were never aware of the noiseless death that awaited them . . . I talked to others there, and similar stories were related to me. These Filipinos still go into the hills at night but this time it's to kill Japs hiding there. I had to laugh when he told me that he worked two shifts. In the daytime he worked at his regular job on the pier. At night he would go into the hills with the rest of the guerrillas and kill Japs.

Guerrilla movements gave the Japanese forces a lot of trouble in both south-east Asia and the Pacific during 1945. In some cases, as in Burma, the guerrillas were extensively organized and supplied by the Allies, but elsewhere the population did not wait for external support and rose up spontaneously to resist as best they could. Guerrillas were particularly active against the Japanese in the Philippines. James Fahey's acquaintances were not exaggerating the brutality of Japanese treatment of the local populations or the vigour with which the guerrillas exacted vengeance upon their former occupiers during the closing stages of the Philippines campaign. American ranger forces and guerrilla groups would still be tracking isolated Japanese units in August 1945.

James Fahey survived the war and returned to his native Florida, where he worked in rubbish collection. In 1964 he was given the 'Garbage Man of the Year' award by Refuse Removal Journal, *the US national magazine for the sanitation industry.* SEE ALSO PP. 476–7.

Monday 12 – Tuesday 20 March 1945

Lieutenant-Colonel R. A. G. Nicholson of the British 115th Field Artillery Regiment directs artillery onto Fort Dufferin at Mandalay

By March 1945 the Japanese were in trouble in central Burma. They were under pressure around Mandalay, their supplies and lines of communications were being interrupted, and they were under constant air attack. Nevertheless, they offered a dogged defence of Fort Dufferin, their main stronghold in Mandalay, and launched a counter-attack against Meiktila in an attempt to open up their lines of communication to the south.

On the 12 Mar, 62 Bde [Brigade] captured MAYMYO the old summer hill station for MANDALAY. They had surprised the HQ of the Jap [Japanese] 15 Army, or rather the rear elements of it, who escaped leaving most of their M.T. [motor transport].

The situation in MANDALAY was as follows. The big feature of MANDALAY HILL (Ht 776) some 500ft above the surrounding country, dominated the entire city and FORT

DUFFERIN. O.Ps [observation posts] on this hill could see directly into the Fort. The latter had sides each a mile in length with a 70 yard moat surrounding the entire Fort. The walls were many feet thick, and to this was added the earth taken from excavating the moat, and piled on the inside of the walls. This made the ramparts, which were 25ft high, some 15 yards thick . . .

From the 12 Mar onwards, fighting took place in the city area lying WEST of the FORT. It was house to house style and arty [artillery] fire was mainly conducted by F.O.Os [Forward Observation Officers] on close targets.

I visited this area daily, and also the O.Ps on the HILL. The F.O.Os [Forward Observation Officers] of 480 Bty had capture a Jap arty director, a good instrument, which they presented to me. I sent this on to Mandalay Hill as its magnification was of value in studying the interior of the FORT. The Japs however, in their usual sensible manner never moved by day and the whole area of the FORT appeared dead. The stairs leading up the HILL to the big pagoda on the summit were littered with Jap dead and the smell of these was pretty grim before they were finally disposed of. On the summit, in a pagoda was an immense Buddha some 20 feet high. Our F.O.O [Forward Observation Officer] parties lived in this pagoda . . .

After the TAIKTAW battle, it was decided to launch a night attack against the Northern wall by 64 Bde [Brigade]. Before this took place, it was planned to attempt to create proper breaches in the Northern WALL of the FORT using air attack and direct fire guns. Medium Guns (5.5) and 25 pdrs accordingly carried out shelling from positions 500 yards or so from the wall. The effect was to gradually break up the brick work, but as this was backed by the earthern ramparts it merely remained as a pile of rubble. As such it would however provide better foothold for an Infantry assault over the wall. Breaches of this type were made at each end of the North Wall. To further demolish this obstacle aircraft attacks with rockets and bombs were attempted. The aircraft tried the method of hitting the moat with their bombs and so 'skidding' them into the wall. It was most impressive to watch, and standing on the HILL just underneath the aircraft as they loosed the rockets was an awe inspiring experience . . .

This form of attack had much the same result as arty fire and no definite breaches were created. The obstacle still remained more or less of the same height. It was then decided to carry out a large scale heavy bombing attack from about 5,000ft with the big American bombers (Flying Fortresses). Three squadrons took part and approached from the WEST, flying directly on the line of the wall. Most of the salvos of bombs fell more or less in the vicinity of the wall, but to our horror one salvo fell right on the Worcesters who were on the EAST side of the FORT, but had been withdrawn 1000yds from it.

This error was criminal, since no clearer target could have been given, with the moat defining its limits with the utmost clarity.

On seeing this occur I left the HILL and rushed off in my jeep to the Worcesters to see if help was required. I passed an overturned jeep and dead driver but found the Worcesters not so badly hit as would have seemed to be the case when the explosions were seen all over the area. They had some casualties but in the circumstances escaped lightly in the ordeal. The bombing had made little difference to the wall, since it was a difficult target to hit. It was however decided to carry on and launch the attack, using such breaches as were available.

Fort Dufferin was captured on 20 March after a daring night attack, and the rest of Mandalay followed swiftly. Meiktila also fell into British hands. Defending Mandalay and Meiktila had cost the Japanese much of their effective strength, and so the Japanese 15th Army had little option but to flee southward, leaving central Burma in Allied control. The Japanese were ambushed all the way by hill tribes operating under the direction of British special forces.

Tuesday 13 – Friday 16 March 1945

Captain Koyanango of the Japanese 3rd Air Fleet HQ
struggles on in the hills of the Philippines

13 March

Got up early to pass rice fields. Collected 5 Kan. In this area
the Negritos [indigenous tribal people] live and when they
see us they try to kill us with spears. They are about 5 feet
tall and wear only loin cloth.

14 March

Koshida was left behind because of illness. Left his baggage
but no hope that he would catch up. No rice after yesterday
morning. Most of those who had fallen were either sick or had
no food. Climbing the hills had sapped their strength. Platoon
leader had fever and Hanana and Torii had slight malaria. If I
laid down now I would die, so I advanced up the gulch. Met
Capt. [Captain] Sato who was slightly injured and was helping
the wounded. He had first class Japanese spirit.

15 March

Met Capt. Munets of Komei Unit No. 1. He was sick most of
his men were sick also and too weak to go on. Our unit
advanced, keeping up our morale to attack the enemy. Takaki
could not go further because of illness. Rice almost gone. Will
have to look for a rice field. Remnants of Tachymoto unit and
other units were retreating. Enemy observation planes
dropped hand grenades on us. If we had planes I would take
revenge. Hoped our planes were repaired and flying so I
looked into the sky, but there were none.

16 March

Staying in the mountains without food would get us
nowhere so I decided to go west to the sea and started to
climb the mountains. I am the only one left of Akinaga Hqs
[Headquarters]. But there is nothing else for me to do but go
west. Platoon leader was sick but I helped him along. On the

way passed through friendly or enemy area. Saw 10 dead friendly troops and about 20 days old. Seeing this moved me, vowed to get revenge. Went forward with ammo, rifle and sword and a box of rations to meet the enemy and kill them. Enemy aircraft was again overhead and hampered my journey. How far will I go with this weight on my back I wondered? I will go until I can kill an enemy no matter how hard it is. I gritted my teeth and advanced to carry on in the Japanese spirit until the last.

Captain Koyanango's diary captures the almost superhuman resolve of Japanese forces in the last months of the war, many of them fighting on in a situation of near-starvation. Koyanango was one of many stragglers who had retreated into the hills of the Philippines, probably on eastern Luzon, after the arrival of the Americans in October 1944. No longer an effective fighting force, they were hunted down by American units, Philippine guerrillas and even tribal people. Koyanango's final diary entry was made on 18 March 1945 and read 'Rice is going fast . . . must find rice field'. The fate of him and his unit remains unknown. By 21 March the diary had been captured and translated for use in assessing Japanese morale by Major Noble F. Sclatter, an intelligence officer working for a forward headquarters element of the US 152nd Infantry. The diary reveals the impact of American air superiority together with the Japanese lack of shipping and supplies. Japanese surrenders increased markedly after March 1945.

Captain Koyanango's diary is now held in manuscript collections at the US Army Military Institute at Carlisle Barracks, Pennsylvania.

Sunday 18 March 1945

Wing Commander 'Bill' Hudson, pilot and POW, discovers a love of spinach in Rangoon gaol

By March 1945, Wing Commander Lionel 'Bill' Hudson of the RAAF was helping to superintend a large unit of Allied POWs in Rangoon gaol. He was gravely concerned when 'Pinkie', one of their most trusted smugglers – an intermediary with the outside traders – was caught conducting his business.

Just watched unpleasant interlude from balcony: Two coolies wheeled in big barrow. Pinkie walked over nonchalantly from his seat in the sun. He lifted the bamboo strip lid and fish leaped out. The action that followed was over in few seconds. Pinkie whipped up 4 live fish and flashed around the corner to hide them. At that moment a Jap sgt – 'Banjo Eyes' – turned corner from main gate. He saw Pinkie, looked at barrel of fish and then called 3-star Q.M.'s stooge who had appeared on the scene. Pinkie was told to return the fish he had taken. He brought back two. Hot words, face slapping, but Pinkie just stood there perhaps a shade pinker. We stood there on the balcony praying. We recoiled at every slap. Then the Jap turned to normal behaviour and, apparently, the incident was finished. I had idea that Pinkie intended to give fish to us for our sick boys. I signalled him if he got away with it O.K. and he gave us thumbs up. He is lucky he did not get solitary cells. Perhaps he is too valuable to Japs. We are now sweating on fresh fish ration.

It won't be our fault if even our real sick boys don't hold out. The two most desperate cases in our hospital are fed 50% of our egg, onion and sugar (jagari) supplies. The other 50% is shared ... eaten by 100 men. In addition, the sick get their share of all compounds' bones which all go to sick bay and the bottom of the soup pot, thick with vegetables, which goes to the sick bay. The fit and near-fit men sacrifice all this without much apparent effect except that most people are breaking out in running sores because of bad blood. Diet is only way to remedy that ...

All is lost! My palate has gone haywire now. All my life I have been a confirmed spinach hater. I cannot remember eating it once outside this gaol. But here I eat spinach because it is important to keep alive. I eat it but I shudder at every mouthful. I still hated it until today when an amazing thing happened. For lunch everybody was served with sufficient spinach for a family of eight. One mess tin overflowing with dark green abomination.

'Toxon,' cried Gus joyfully. He loves spinach. The man alongside him tipped half his helping into Gus's pan. It was heaped high. Gus looked at it with dubious face. Then he was promptly sick – physically. He, a spinach lover, could not face this mountain of weed. What chance had I?

I started eating with temerity but I soon found out that I was enjoying it. My palate had changed face. This was delicious food. I loved that meal . . . and then I came to the stalks of the spinach . . . light green, generally wooden. But I did not push them aside. I ate them. They were tender and succulent and, God help me, they had a distinctive flavour of asparagus. This is the end, I'll be liking red-headed women next.

Smuggling and other 'secret aid' from outside was a vital part of the POWs' existence and allowed the prisoners in Rangoon gaol to maintain a reasonable diet. Hudson recognized that these supplements made all the difference and noted in his diary that without it 'we would be cutting each other's throats'. Nevertheless their diet, although improved by these covert methods, was monotonous and involved a great deal of home-grown vegetables, including spinach. Adequate food gave the men in his gaol the energy to enjoy daytime activities including chess, bridge, deck tennis and even weight lifting. SEE ALSO PP. 654–7, 730–2.

Tuesday 20 March – Thursday 10 May 1945

Les Vancura, aboard the British aircraft carrier HMS *Victorious*, encounters attacks by kamikazes off the Japanese coast near Okinawa

Les Vancura was a petty officer in the Fleet Air Arm who had served on the carrier HMS Victorious *in the Atlantic, in the Mediterranean and now with the British Pacific Fleet. By late March his ship had joined the vast invasion fleet preparing to attack the island of Okinawa, just south of the Japanese mainland.*

20 March

We got into Ulithi Island this morning. There is a full invasion fleet here, the anchorage is a 4 mile by 16 mile reef island and it was in Jap hands 8 months ago, and the battle-ships and cruisers were here before us, we are only allowed to say we are with the US fleet.

1 April

[Pacific, between Okinawa and Formosa] Action stations at 0600. Were attacked by suicide bombers at 0800. One hit the Indomitable and another a destroyer, both still operational. At 1800 one tried to crash on our deck, he was shot to pieces and we skewed to starboard. He skimmed the deck and fell over the side, leaving half his Main plane on deck. We lost one fighter and one bomber.

9 May

Action stations at 0600, the usual strikes went off. During a raid at 1800 THE VICTORIOUS WAS HIT by a kamikaze bomber. We were hit between the gun turret and the forward lift, 3 killed and 18 injured, another plane on fire smashed into two other planes, before going over the side. We lost one plane and shot down 7.

10 May

The hit yesterday made a hole two feet across, as it was forward of the armoured deck, and the bulge is 10 feet across. It was repaired with timber, armour plate and quick drying cement. We oiled [took on new supplies of fuel oil] and passed the injured, then an auxiliary carrier, thence to a hospital ship.

Les Vancura's brief but focused diary reveals the extreme resilience of British carriers, with their armoured decks, in the face of kamikaze attacks, many of which they simply brushed off. Although casualties were incurred, the structural damage to the carriers was slight and often repaired within hours. By contrast, American carriers with wooden decks often suffered more serious problems and burned quickly.

By early September 1945, Les Vancura would be in Sydney enjoying some leave. At 10.30 on 25 September he began the long voyage home to Britain.

Friday 23 March 1945

Natalie Crouter, an American civilian internee, begins her journey back from the Philippines to the United States and suffers a terrible loss

We were up at 6.45 and had breakfast at 7:30 – fruit, and two fried eggs with bacon. We were told there would be two meals a day, but at noon we would fix sandwiches from delicious slices of round sausage, slices of cheese. Hot coffee would be served also. It came to pass at noon and was very good. Everything is being done for us. Their concern seems lavish after the last three years. The ship shines in glass, brass and wood as only Dutch service (or the Army) could make it shine. It is paradise, fairyland, heaven, after what we have come from. But on the other hand it seems to pamper us, and we feel conventions closing in, formality stifling us. How much more will we feel it in cities and in homes, far from insecurity, privation and want. We are as unreasonable as the poor. We are storm-tossed still, between two worlds. I felt horribly depressed all morning, on the verge of flying to pieces, weeping inside.

Then, after lunch, the blow fell. The Intelligence or Counterintelligence came on board and took all my notes. I turned them in, hating it. It was the final squeeze, the last straw. 'It is only paper,' said the young officer, and I answered, 'Yes, it is only paper to you and this is why I hate to turn it over. It means nothing to you, everything to me, for it is all I've saved. It is three years of suffering and experience, and I want to keep it for my children's children.' I begged him to let me take it to San Francisco and turn it over there, to get it that far at least, but he was adamant – said they needed it out there. He said it would be returned to me – 'Don't you trust the Army, the Government?' Passionately I retorted, 'No! I don't trust anybody! I've had things stolen from me, been looted and squeezed even by our own people and this is the last shakedown of all I have left!' I spilled one of the envelopes on the floor, getting the numbered sheets all mixed up, but that is up to them to straighten out now. He asked why I didn't save silver or valuables instead of these paper notes. I said I could not carry it and it was scattered all through our bags when we were given only half an hour to get ready; that my husband was on crutches, and we were not allowed to take more anyway – big bags were ruled out. Besides I can buy silver and I can never buy this record of three years' experience. The young Filipino Intelligence boy with the officer nodded his head. He understood. We talked the same language. People at home just cannot grasp what we feel or try to express. They are too secure and have lost nothing. Poor young man, I gave him a bad twenty minutes. And my old blue bag with large tin box full of three years' notes went off down the stairs in cold blood!

Natalie Crouter, her husband Jerry, and her two children, June and Bedie, had been civilian internees in the Philippines since 1942. They were liberated in February 1945 and it was claimed that orders for all the internees to be shot were found on the desk of the Japanese commandant. Certainly, elsewhere in the Philippines terrible massacres occurred during the Japanese retreat. However, in most camps the commandants failed to implement such orders. There were a variety of reasons for this: in some cases the rapid end of the war and the arrival of the Allied troops simply overtook events; some commandants feared retribution; others took the personal decision to disregard the instruction.

Having left the camp, the Crouters boarded a ship to take them home to the United States. At this point, Natalie Crouter encountered a new enemy much feared by all diarists – the ubiquitous checkers and confiscators of papers. These came in many forms, from customs and excise men to policemen, security guards, counter-intelligence specialists and censors. All were the bane of diarists and journal-keepers. Having been kept from the Japanese guards for three years, her diary was taken by the US army and impounded on security grounds. SEE ALSO PP. 542–3, 727–8.

Monday 26 March 1945

Joe Bryan visits the bakery while at sea on board the
carrier USS *Yorktown* off the island of Okinawa

Throughout the last week of March the Yorktown *was sailing off the
island of Okinawa, conducting softening-up attacks in preparation for
the coming invasion.*

I had to go to sick bay again this morning to get my dress-
ings changed. On the way back, coming along the third deck,
I smelled fresh bread and followed my nose into the baker-
shop, remembering that I had overslept breakfast. The
bakers seemed to welcome drop-in trade, because I had
hardly taken a hungry, beseeching sniff before they produced two thick slices, buttered, a cup of smoking coffee,
and a wedge of cake. It wasn't angel food cake, but an angel
would have blasphemed to get the recipe, I told them so.

One of them said, 'You just hit us on a good day.' His name
was Drum, a skinny youngster with flamboyant tattoos.
'Most days, all we need to start the guns firing is to put a
cake in the oven. The dough's made right, the cake begins to
puff up pretty, and wham!, the 5-inchers begin walking the
dog, and the cake falls flat on its face. It goes in sponge cake
and it comes out pancake.'

Another baker, Volk, said, 'It's either the guns or a sea.
Honest to God, I'm beginning to think we must of done
something wrong somewheres, something we don't know
nothing about, because we sure got somebody mad at us!
You know how your batter is soft and runny one minute,
and a minute later it's set firm? Well, say it's a dead calm
when we put it in the oven. Before it can set, up comes a
wind out of nowheres – *nowheres* – and what happens? The
shop rolls, the batter runs to one end of the pans, and there
it sets. The kind of cake you get, I wouldn't feed to a dogface
– all soggy on the thick end and burnt black on the thin end.
Whoever called this ocean 'Pacific'? It's about as pacific as a
goddam roller coaster!'

One of the things that Joe Bryan appreciated about the USS Yorktown *was her food, which he classed as the second best in the fleet, bettered only by the carrier* Lexington. *In part this reflected the age of the carrier. First launched in May 1943, she had originally been called* Bon Homme Richard, *being renamed the* Yorktown *after the loss of the previous* Yorktown *in 1942. She was in fact the fourth US navy ship to carry the name. Many carriers operated by the major powers during the Second World War were vintage ships that had begun life as cruisers during the First World War and had been hastily modified by adding a flight deck. This resulted in poor damage control if attacked and offered dire living conditions for the crew.*

Tuesday 27 March 1945

Second Lieutenant Fukuzo Obara resists the American return to Luzon in the Philippines

Fukuzo Obara came from Yuzawa City in northern Honshu and was thirty-two years old. He was both a calligrapher and a poet. He had fought mostly in Manchuria and had gradually risen through the ranks, being promoted to warrant officer and then second lieutenant. His unit was dug in on a ridge north-west of Mount Baytangan on Luzon. Obara was enduring the bombardments remarkably well, but attempts to patrol incurred high casualties and he had lost four men killed and injured a few days previously.

It is reported that the enemy has made an audacious penetration of approximately two or three hundred meters into our positions to the west, as far as Futaba Hill.

All along our bunker and foxhole line we receive a simultaneous artillery attack, the intensity of which defies description. Shells from heavy guns, medium guns and light assault weapons, mingled with white phosphorous incendiaries, are falling incessantly. In a period of thirty minutes, the area of the mortar squad and my command bunker is hit by approximately 750 to 800 bursts, of these about 80 or 90 close to my command bunker. How many have fallen in the neighbouring areas I have no idea.

Shell splinters rain down all about us. Bang, bang, boom, boom ... the explosions follow one another without interruption.

I tried counting them. After five or six minutes I had reached 170, but then had to give up because shells seemed to be exploding three, four, five at a time. We are hit, not by one shell per square meter, but by three or four. Even in the side hole of my dugout, I am stunned by the excessive ferocity of this shelling.

All around us, the air is filled with shell fragments, bursts of dirt, the flaring of phosphorous incendiaries and smoke. Inside, there is darkness and the choking stench of phosphorous. I think, this is the end, and I put on my gas mask.

The concussion that follows the explosions shakes my anti-blast curtain and makes it flap. And then the pressure seems to stop my breathing.

I keep wondering, 'is this the end? Now? Now?' I have lost all feeling of being alive.

This intense barrage continues for about an hour and then seems to taper off, but then the shells continue to come in at a rate of two or three hundred an hour.

After about two hours, the rate of shelling has diminished. I creep out of my side-hole, through the crumbling foxhole, and stick my head out to survey the situation. The hillside into which we have dug our position now appears plowed and harrowed beyond description. Directly before me are trees torn out with their roots. Even our reserve foxholes are mostly crumbled or buried.

However, a miracle has come to pass – no, not a miracle, it is divine aid. Not one of my men has even a scratch. Wonderful! Wonderful! The men, all plastered with dirt, cannot help laughing as now here, now there, another blackened face pops out of the ground.

'That was amazing, eh?'

'Pretty awful, wasn't it?'

'That was a brutal pounding.'

'When those big blasts came, my heart seemed to stop beating. Ah, ha, ha, ha!'

And so on, laughing, but with sober faces.

The crumbling foxholes are quickly restored. We are glad now for all the trouble put into digging these positions.

This afternoon an attack using flame-throwers is mounted from the southern slopes of Futaba Hill against our Futaba Hill positions, but is repelled by the spirited fighting of our Futaba Hill reserves supported by fire from our main force, and the enemy retreats in confusion.

We prepare to repel attack but have nothing to do but observe as the enemy retreats with loud howls of pain!

No matter how they were hurt, what a disgrace to bawl like that. Several of their voices sounded incredibly like babies who have burned themselves. Grown men crying as they run away! It is a farce, ridiculous in the extreme, for the enemy to bawl in view of the Japanese Army! It is too much even to speak of it. After watching and waiting for a worthy opponent, it makes one feel as if a treat has been snatched away. We feel puzzled and let down.

We have inflicted about twenty casualties on the enemy. The enemy retreats, and just as I am thinking we are probably now in for the usual artillery attack, sure enough we are promptly enveloped in smoke and flame. It is an insane, blind, vengeful attack.

Fukuzo Obara's beautiful diary captures the intensity of the artillery bombardment being brought to bear on the Japanese forces in the latter stages of the Pacific campaign and also the persistence of the idea of honour. Here we see a tendency common in all armies to call major physical features by familiar names rather than their real names. He refers to a feature called 'Futaba Hill', but the real Futaba Hill was alongside the Kanda river near Hiroshima in Japan. His wish to meet 'a worthy opponent' is especially striking. Even at this stage of the war, the numbers of Japanese surrendering, although growing, were not large. In part this was a matter of honour, but it also reflected a belief that they might be executed.

Fukuzo Obara was reportedly killed in fighting in jungle to the north-east of Manila on 17 July 1945.

APRIL 1945

O N 12 APRIL 1945 the world was shaken by news of the sudden death of President Roosevelt at Warm Springs in Georgia. Those in his immediate entourage had noticed his deteriorating health during the early months of 1945 and by March most strategic decisions were being left to General George Marshall and the American joint chiefs of staff. However, not even his doctor had anticipated his sudden demise in mid-April. Roosevelt's idealistic vision, combined with skilful pragmatic politics, had earned him the admiration of all who worked with him. Partly because of his ability to connect with the hopes of the ordinary person – most notably in his idea of the 'Four Freedoms' – he had enjoyed unique status as a revered world figure, a status that was not shared by Churchill, Stalin or Chiang Kai-shek.

During April America continued to tighten its grip on the Japanese islands through the use of strategic air power. Tokyo, Kawasaki and Nagoya were among the main objectives, and large areas of these wooden cities were burned by the intense fire-bombing. Carrier-based fighter-bombers concentrated their efforts on destroying airfields used to launch kamikaze attacks against American ships, and accordingly the scale of these attacks began to reduce. No less effective was a campaign of using aircraft to mine the ports and harbours, bringing Japan's already devastated shipping to an effective standstill. Food shortages within Japan were becoming extreme and this, perhaps even more than the bombing, had a significant impact on civilian morale and the will to resist.

In the first days of April the invasion of the southerly Japanese island of Okinawa was launched. Defended by over 100,000 men under General Ushijama, the island also contained a Japanese civilian population of almost half a million. In the largest operation of the Pacific war, 1,200 transport ships disgorged 450,000 American soldiers and marines onto the beaches. Once again, they met with almost no resistance during the landing, and a robust beachhead more than 3 miles deep was established on the first day. Ushijama had decided to focus his resistance on caves and prepared positions in the hinterland. More immediate resistance appeared in the air: the Allied fleet provided the kamikazes with plentiful targets and ten ships were hit on the first day, including the American battleship *West Virginia* and the British carrier *Indomitable*. Over the next few days many transports were hit, with serious casualties among the troops on board.

On 6 April the pride of the Japanese fleet, the super-battle-ship *Yamato*, accompanied by a cruiser and numerous destroyers, sailed from the Inland Sea on a one-way mission to fight at Okinawa. The *Yamato* did not carry enough fuel to return and the crew had no illusion about the nature of their task. On the following day she was located and attacked by two waves of aircraft, involving almost 400 planes. After suffering hits by ten torpedoes she was sunk. Far more effective were the continuing Japanese kamikaze attacks, which damaged the carriers *Maryland*, *Jacinto* and *Illustrious* as well as putting more than a dozen other ships out of action by 9 April.

In south-east Asia, the Burma campaign was moving into its final stages. The 5th Indian Division managed spectacular progress along the Sittang valley and at the end of the month Japanese forces began to withdraw from Rangoon back into Thailand. British naval task forces began shelling Japanese installations in the Netherlands East Indies. Sizeable operations also continued in the more remote areas of the Philippines. On 13 April the heavily protected Japanese emplacements and bunkers at Fort Drum on El Fraile Island in Manila Bay were eliminated by pouring in 5,000 gallons of oil fuel and igniting it, resulting in a fire which lasted for a week. On Okinawa, once Japanese defensive lines were encountered, progress was extremely slow. A third wave of kamikaze attacks damaged the carrier *Intrepid* and the battleship *Missouri*; a fourth wave, launched on 25 April, damaged nine destroyers. At the end of the month the units fighting in the front line on Okinawa were rotated to bring fresh troops to bear on what had become a gruelling conflict.

In Europe strategic bombing continued throughout April, but increasingly bomber aircraft were also being used to drop food relief parcels to a starving civilian population in the Netherlands and also to recover prisoners of war and bring them home. Some units hoped that they would be allowed to demobilize at the end of the European war rather than being sent on to fight in Asia. Others, such as the Special Air Service, disliked the idea of disbandment and eagerly offered their services to Mountbatten in south-east Asia in the hope of seeing further action. The SAS units were unsuccessful in their bids to join the war against Japan, but SOE had already begun to transfer some of its more distinguished operators to new missions in Asia. The imminent end of the war in Europe seemed to be underlined by news of Hitler's and Eva Braun's suicide on 30 April.

The end of April was also marked by the opening of the San Francisco Conference, designed to draw up the constitution of the United Nations.

Easter Sunday 1 – Tuesday 3 April 1945

Walter L. Rhinehart, US navy, watches the assault on the western coast of the island of Okinawa

Walter Rhinehart was born in 1909 and was an officer serving on an American destroyer, one of an armada of over 600 ships preparing to take part in the assault on Okinawa.

1 April

In a misty cool morning the mightiest invasion armada in history hit the western coast of Okinawa Jima. Entered transport area at 430 after 2 GQs, two Jap snoopers shot down in flames. After the most intense sea and air bombardment I have ever seen Marines and Army swarmed ashore over the tomb-spotted landscape practically unopposed. At the end of the first day the Marines had gained almost what they expected to gain in three days. We remained in for the night for small boat repairs. 'Sewing Machine Charlie' made his regular visit at 1530 in the form of a suicide bomber which hit the bridge of the West Virginia, casualties unknown.

Heavy calibre shell fire straddled the transports during unloading but it was quickly silenced by our big boys. This is #8 for me and it still gives me the jitters. What a way to spend Easter Sunday.

3 April

Moved to Berth 87 after a snooper missed our mast by inches. Reinforcement group arrived. The Solace Relief stood in today. Japs tried a Banzai charge on the airfield last night. Today a lot of Samurai swords are hanging on leatherneck belts. Japs are trying to land paratroopers tonight. The night is aglow with star shells and heavy shell fire. We leave for Keramo Retta tomorrow.

On Easter Sunday, 1 April 1945, the United States launched one of the most costly campaigns of the Second World War. Over the next few weeks the United States navy would see 36 vessels lost and 368 damaged at Okinawa. More than 5,000 naval personnel would be killed and about the same number wounded. Okinawa would also be the most costly campaign for the US army. The severe losses suffered during the operation reinforced doubts in Washington about the wisdom of any attempt to capture the rest of the Japanese home islands by conventional means.

Saturday 7 April 1945

Yoshida Mitsuru escapes from the bridge of the Japanese super-battleship *Yamato* after it is sunk on its way to attack the invasion fleet at Okinawa

Ensign Yoshida Mitsuru was an assistant radar officer in his early twenties who participated in the last voyage of the battleship Yamato. *On 6 April 1945 the* Yamato, *accompanied by the light cruiser* Yahagi, *and escorted by eight escort destroyers, sailed on a fateful suicide mission towards Okinawa to assist in defence of the island.*

Wriggling through the port, I look back almost longingly, our bridge on its side and completely dark. Surprisingly narrow, burrowlike.

Their bodies lashed together, the navigation officer and the assistant navigation officer reject a second and third time our exhortations to escape; they shrug off their shoulders the hands of their fellow officers.

I watch until the end: both have their eyes wide open and stare fixedly at the water rising toward them.

Thus the end of Commander Mogi and Lieutenant (jg.) Hanada.

Is the responsibility of running the ship so great? . . .

It seems foolish to think such thoughts now, but when I drop my glance to the hull of the ship towering above the water and to its exposed undersides, it looks like a great whale.

That this vast piece of metal, 270 meters along and 40 meters wide, is about to plunge beneath the waves!

I recognize near me many shipmates. That fellow, and that one.

This one's eyebrows are very dark, that one's ears very pale. All of them have childlike expressions on their faces; better, they are all completely without expression.

For each of them, it must be a moment of absolute innocence, an instant of complete obliviousness.

For all I know, I too am in the same condition.

At what do they gaze with ecstatic eyes?

The eddies, extending as far as they can see. The boiling waves, interlocking in a vast pattern.

Pure white and transparent, like ice congealing around this giant ship and propping her up.

And the sound of the waves, deafening our ears, induces still deeper rapture.

We see a sheet of white; we hear only the thundering of the turbulent waters.

'Are we sinking?' For the first time, as if on fire, I ask myself that question. The spectacle is so mysterious, so resplendent, that I am overcome with the premonition that something extraordinary is about to happen . . .

At the instant *Yamato*, rolling over, turns belly up and

plunges beneath the waves, she emits one great flash of light and sends a gigantic pillar of flame high into the dark sky. Armor plate, equipment, turrets, guns – all the pieces of the ship go flying off.

Moreover, thick smoke, dark brown and bubbling up from the ocean depths, soon engulfs everything, covers everything . . .

Perhaps ten seconds after the shock from the second explosion, the agonizing pressure on my chest rises sharply; at last my throat seizes, and suddenly I start to swallow sea water.

Through my nose, through my mouth, I breathe in sea water as if poured in by a pump – unconsciously my body registers the movements of my jaw . . . seven . . . ten . . . fifteen . . . seventeen.

Still, I have no sense of suffocating. Am I unable to die until water fills all the nooks and crannies of my body and spills out my mouth?

Is the peace of death still far off?

Kill me . . . Death, take me.

On 7 April swarms of American aircraft dropped bombs and launched torpedoes that destroyed the Yamato *before she had covered half the distance from the Inland Sea to Okinawa. Some 4,000 Japanese sailors perished in the attacks on the convoy; four mangled destroyers limped back to Japan with survivors, carrying fewer than 300 of the crew of the* Yamato *out of a total of over 2,000. The crews of these ships had expected to die as part of a successful attack. When the survivors returned to Japan they asked to be transferred to 'special attack units' to address the pangs of conscience for having survived, when their ship-mates had perished.*

Yoshida Mitsuru was one of the few to survive the engagement and wrote up his diary shortly afterwards. The editors of the diary succeeded in providing an excellent translation of a very difficult Japanese text written in abrupt bungotai, *a literary form used for military documents and certain types of poetry.*

Friday 13 – Saturday 14 April 1945

Laura Crabill Evans pays her last respects to Roosevelt's funeral train at Greenville

Laura Crabill Evans lived to the north-east of the Valley Pike at Edinburg in Shenandoah County, Virginia. During 1942 and 1943 she had moved around the country with her daughter and son-in-law, Bill Marks, who was serving in the army. She filled her diary with frank observations on many aspects of her daily life and on the world at war as revealed to her through news from her radio.

13 April

Yesterday evening when the word came that FDR had passed away the fireman at the station tolled the firebell every few seconds for 20 minutes. I could not sleep last night with such a heavy sorrow weighing down the country. The funeral train stopped here in Greenville for services enroute to Washington. It was thought 15,000 people were at the station and tomorrow will be a day of mourning. Fala [Roosevelt's dog] was taken off the train here and allowed to relieve himself and limber up his cramped limbs. President Truman said that the weight of the sun and stars had fallen on him and he asked that the people pray for him as he dedicated his heart and soul to carrying out the wishes of FDR. I saw the announcement of Allie Evans' daughter, Lelia Ann, to Earl Miley Jr. The wedding will be May 6 at St Andrew's Church in Mt Jackson.

14 April

I turned on my radio and heard the news from Union Station. Pres Truman, James Burner, Henry Wallace, Chief Justice Stone and Roberts were there as were 8 bearers and the Marine Band. The president's body was to be put on a caisson, drawn by 6 fine white horses and a lead horse. W A V E S, Blue Jackets, Marines and a police guard to follow. The empty caisson got to the Union Station and the body put on and thousands of people lined the streets. All the way from Warm Springs an airplane circled over the train all night. In cars directly behind the caisson were Mrs Roosevelt, Anna and other members of the family. In the procession the cadets from Annapolis were the smartest looking. Everyone in the cars wore black and had sad faces. Liberator planes circled around [and] the largest plane in the world flew over. The band struck up the dead march. There was no other sound. This is the first time FDR was passed along this line of march without booming cheers. The Navy band played a funeral march. A troop of colored engineers marched behind the Navy Band. I could hear the hoof beats of the horses and would hear the wheels of the caisson. From every window people leaned out looking pensively at the procession creeping along towards the White House as gov. workers were permitted to leave their offices on that day. People had tears in their eyes. The people took the president's death hard. As the caisson came into the White House grounds soldiers stood at attention and the gates closed. The band played the 'Star Spangled Banner'.

President Roosevelt's body travelled from Warm Springs to Washington, and then on to his home at Hyde Park, north of New York City, by special train. Tens of thousands of ordinary Americans mourned the death of Franklin D. Roosevelt and waited for hours to watch the funeral train on its way to the presidential burial site in Hyde Park. Roosevelt had served a historic four terms in office, and most young Americans serving in the armed forces could remember no other president. Public attachment to Roosevelt was particularly intense, a popular connection having been established largely through his skilled use of the radio. Moreover, most people believed he was responsible for bringing them within sight of the end of the war.

Friday 20 – Tuesday 24 April 1945

Yasuo Ichijima, a 23-year-old kamikaze pilot, waits for
death quietly, in the days before his mission

*Yasuo Ichijima was a student at the University of Waseda in Tokyo. He
was called up to join the navy in December 1943 and underwent training as a pilot.*

20 April

I have spent a very quiet day. I did not see my family but I
met some former comrades and I was able to chat with them
at my leisure. It was really very pleasant.

We will never see each other again; it was wonderful to be
able to bid each other farewell like this, without sorrow or
regrets disturbing our conversation.

I cannot believe that I shall die within a week. I feel neither
depressed nor nervous.

When I try to imagine what my last moments will be like,
everything seems like a dream. I am not sure whether I will
remain as calm as I am now when the time comes, but it
seems to me that it ought to be easy . . .

23 April

On my way for a swim I wandered slowly through the countryside. It may be that I will receive orders to take off for the
attack tomorrow.

Twenty-three years of life are approaching their end. I do
not feel as though I am about to die tomorrow. Here I am, in
this far-off country, but I cannot bring myself to believe that
the sole reason for this is that I must attack the enemy fleet
by hurling myself against their guns and their aircraft.

Loitering on the edge of the fields with my towel under
my arm, I listen to the chirping of the crickets and the croak-
ing of the frogs. I am reminded of my childhood. How lovely
the lotus blossoms look, bathed in the moonlight . . . The
landscape reminds me of Kawazaki in summer. I recall the
memory of my native country and of our family outings.

I went back to my room, but the electric light had failed. Oil burns in a tin and the flame throws the wavering shadows that we cast against the wall. It is a calm evening. I go to sleep looking at a little doll . . .

24 April

In a nearby room they are being rather rowdy and drinking spirits. They probably have the right idea. Personally, I prefer to wait for death quietly. I am anxious to behave well up to the last moment, all the more because I belong to the 'specialized attack' group, the incarnation of the chivalrous spirit of Japan. I must remain worthy of it. It is by the grace of God and thanks to the affection of those who surrounded me that I have been able to spend my life in an honourable way. Up to now the road I have trodden has been far finer than was to be expected. I am very honoured and proud to have the opportunity of offering to my country, which I love more than I can say, a pure life.

Yasuo Ichijima died at sea on a kamikaze mission against the invasion fleet off Okinawa shortly after writing these entries in his diary. Admiral Takijiro Onishi had founded the first kamikaze units in July 1944 after the fall of Saipan. Saipan was Japanese territory, and some argued that special measures were now called for to defend the homeland. A call went out for young men to volunteer to die for their country and thousands came forward. Training was often rudimentary. However, because the aircraft had to approach ships at low altitudes they were likely to be shot down by anti-aircraft guns and only a small proportion reached their target. During the Okinawa campaign of April 1945 some 1,400 suicide missions were launched, perhaps accounting for some twenty-five American ships that were sunk. The Japanese navy also developed suicide attack boats and manned torpedoes, but these were less successful.

Saturday 21 April 1945

Natalie Crouter, an American civilian who has spent the
war interned in the Philippines, arrives in San Francisco
with her family

The officers ate at 7 and we women at 8. Almost at once they
began taking the Army off. At about 7 we left the cold green
choppy sea and entered smooth waters with soft rolling
green hills on either side. Ahead of us was the Golden Gate
Bridge. We stood up on the forward deck in the icy wind
with officers and G.I.s, watching our ship approach the
bridge. A sleek, dangerous-looking submarine passed us –
cold and efficient and deadly. Planes passed overhead, one
with four motors. We gazed at all the changes at the Presidio
and the marina and San Francisco skyline. Ahead looking
cruelly bleak Alcatraz loomed up. The G.I.s began to yell to
the Dutch officers, kidding them that the crow's nest was
going to hit the bridge and they'd better lower it quick. We
stood watching it, breathless, hunched down into our
collars, hands pulled up into the sleeves of field jackets
which felt very good indeed over WAC suits. Nearer, nearer
– a roar burst from 1,500 throats as we sailed under the
beautiful bridge which was shining under early sun. We will
never forget that cheer and the grinning Sergeant beside us
who said hoarsely, 'I been waitin' tree years for dis!' We were
home – all the foxholes far behind! Here was what the
fellows had fought for. They were going to step onto that
shore again about which they had thought in steaming
jungles or on tortured beachheads. They don't know it but
they will soon find out that somehow they have changed
and are different. Landing will be heaven, but unsettling too.
With us, they are between two worlds.

The CIC presented a long questionnaire which Jerry filled
out. We were processed again by the CIC, given our landing
slip, ration books and home mail! We have everything but
the Diary!

We watch Buster and Gadget and other G.I. friends troop

off the ship, gear on their shoulders, as the band plays down below on the dock. The officers all cheer the band. No one else can be seen on the dock . . .

We land at the Cartwright Hotel and Jerry goes off in the same station wagon to the Red Cross Center to arrange for cash orders for clothes, continental passage etc. June and Bedie take their long-promised hot bath, sitting for hours in the tub, soaking the whole room with the shower. We have a suite, two rooms with connecting bath, three closets. My bath follows theirs, then we go downstairs to sit looking out the big wide windows, watching the people and the passing traffic. There are so many shining cars, sliding smoothly. We are homesick, uprooted, in a town of strange faces. And so we start to crab. We criticize and make fun of the hats which are crazier, wilder than ever. I'll be damned if I will wear one or buy one. June asks, 'Are all people in America rich, Mama?' Bedie says, 'They look as though they were all going to a wedding!' It is spring hats with flowers and pastel shades that look so gay. The hairdo is long bob curled under. Everyone seems to have permanent waves and everyone slathers on lipstick and rouge. There is a distinct undercurrent of sadness and longing in America. Many homes have heartbreaking losses, and every week ships sail overseas loaded with men.

Natalie Crouter and her family had finally arrived back in the United States, an experience which they found more than a little surreal. However, Natalie had been relieved of three years' work – her precious diary. This was not a small thing: running to some 5,000 typescript pages, it had recorded all aspects of both family and camp life, from the monotonous daily diet and petty arguments over personal space to relations with the Japanese. After three years of campaigning, the diary was eventually returned to her. Natalie Crouter attended a major camp reunion in 1977; however, her husband Jerry died in 1951, his health damaged by his time in captivity. SEE ALSO PP. 542–3, 727–8.

Friday 27 April 1945

Charles Ritchie, a Canadian diplomat, arrives at the
United Nations conference at San Francisco

The Bay is a beautiful background, the sun shines
perpetually, the streets are thronged, there are American
sailors everywhere with their girls and this somehow adds
to the musical comedy atmosphere. You expect them at any
moment to break into song and dance, and the illusion is
heightened because every shop and café wafts light music
from thousands of radios. Colours too are of circus bright-
ness, the flamboyant advertisements, the flags of all the
Conference nations, the brilliant yellow taxis. This seems a
technicolor world glossy with cheerful self-assurance. The
people are full of curiosity about the Conference delegates.
They crowd around them like the friendly, innocent Indians
who crowded around the Spanish adventurers when they
came to America and gaped at their armour and took their
strings of coloured beads for real. The delegates are less
picturesque than they should be to justify so much curiosity.
There are the inevitable Arabs and some Indians in turbans
who are worth the price of admission, and the Saudi Arabian
prince who gleams like Valentino, but in general the
delegates are just so many men in business suits with
circular Conference pins in their buttonholes making them
look as if they were here for the Elks' Convention. The
exceptions are the Russians – they have stolen the show.
People are impressed, excited, mystified and nervous about
the Russians. Groups of wooden-looking peasant Soviet
officers sit isolated (by their own choice) at restaurant tables
and are stared at as if they were wild animals. They are
painfully self-conscious, quiet, dignified – determined not to
take a step which might make people laugh at the beautiful
Soviet Union. The crowds throng outside the hotel to see
Molotov, that square-head is much more of a sight than
Eden. He is power. When he came into the initial plenary
session he was followed by a half-a-dozen husky gorillas

from NKVD. The town is full of stories about the Russians –
that they have a warship laden with caviare in the harbour,
etc, etc.

*The main task of the San Francisco conference was to negotiate the
charter of the new United Nations organization. Although the gathering
was impressive, with literally thousands of diplomats and reporters
installed in the various hotels, there was also a slight air of cynicism.
More than a few of those in attendance had been present at the found-
ing of the League of Nations over twenty years before. Everyone
remarked that they missed the guiding hand of Roosevelt, who had died
two weeks before. President Harry S. Truman had decided not to attend
and his Secretary of State, Edward Stettinius, was the master of
ceremonies. The challenge for the United States was to win over the
Russian delegation and to persuade them to accept a system of voting
that would underpin the formation of a security council.*

*After the war, Charles Ritchie would continue to serve as a Canadian
diplomat and would become Canadian ambassador to the United States
in the 1960s. SEE ALSO PP. 160–2.*

Saturday 28 – Sunday 29 April 1945

Wing Commander 'Bill' Hudson, POW, finds that the
Japanese guards have left Rangoon gaol, leaving a polite
note on the gate

The incredible Japs kept up their pretence to the last. Tenko
was as ever – the same old routine – except that the sgt was
a stranger and looked more like a soldier than our other
custodians. He had several hand grenades stuck in his
belt.

I complained that the food and bingo buckets had not
arrived. The interpreter told the Japs and suggested he could
fetch them now. The sgt said 'Tomorrow'.

We had a church service near the water trough and I went
up to sleep quite early. I remember hearing a commotion
down near the main gate but did not bother to investigate.

'Shoto' was accentuated by the Japs now that I come

to think about it. And this was the first time for days that they had worried to tell us to sleep and keep quiet.

I lay on my bag talking for half an hour when I saw a reflection of a fire. I walked to the balcony to see a smallish fire just outside the gaol near the main gate. The Jap section of the gaol was suspiciously quiet. I had remembered the truck moving off. Some intuition, or was it the extraordinary stillness, told me that something strange was in the air.

I went to the front balcony and could not find a guard. I waited for ten minutes but no guard. This was extraordinary . . .

Two notes, or letters, neatly written in English, were left behind by our former hosts.

One read:

Rangoon
29 April, 1945

Gentlemen,

Bravely you have come here opening prison gate. We have gone keeping your prisoner safely with Nipponese knightship. Afterwards we may meet again at the front somewhere. Then let us fight bravely each other. (We had kept the gate's keys in the gate room.).

Nipponese Army

The other I found at the main gate of the gaol:

Rangoon
29 April, 1945

To the whole captured persons of Rangoon Jail. According to the Nippon military order, we hereby give you liberty and admit to leave this place at your own will. Regarding food and other materials kept in the compound, we give you permission to consume them, as far as your necessity is concerned.

We hope that we shall have an opportunity to meet you again at battlefield of somewhere.

We shall continue our war effort eternally in order to get the emancipation of all Asiatic Races.

Haruo Ito
Chief Officer of Rangoon Branch Jail

In April 1945 the Japanese forces defending Rangoon suddenly decided upon a 'moonlight flit'. Although ordered to defend Rangoon to the last, they decided to make a run for it and, remarkably, they did so on the date of the Emperor's birthday. Anxious to avoid being cut off from their supply routes by a large British amphibious operation, they withdrew three days before the British troops entered the centre of Rangoon. Allied POWs in Rangoon gaol awoke to find their hosts had fled. The POWs then set about trying to inform the advancing troops that the enemy had disappeared. On the roof of Rangoon gaol they painted messages in large white letters – 'Japs Gone' and 'Extract Digit' – but in vain. (See Plate 15.)

The prisoners feared being attacked by any remnants of the escaping Japanese army, or the local Burmese nationalists, who had supported the Japanese. Lionel Hudson was a senior officer in the gaol and was confronted with the issue of what to do during the interregnum. They disarmed Indian and Burmese collaborators and fortified the gaol to await their liberation.

In the last phase of the war the prisoners did better than their captors. Ito and his sixty men were the very last Japanese troops to leave Rangoon, but only seventeen would survive the desperate retreat through the jungle to Moulemein near the Thai border. Lionel Hudson survived to meet his captor, Haruo Ito, at a reunion in a Toyko hotel some forty years later. SEE ALSO PP. 654–7, 707–9.

MAY 1945

T HE WEIGHT OF AIR operations against Japanese cities continued to increase, with regular raids of approximately 500
aircraft against cities including Nagoya, Otaka and Toyko. The
14th Air Force commanded by Chennault was also delivering a
fearful pounding to Japanese positions along the coast of mainland China.

The fiercest fighting during May occurred on the island of
Okinawa. Here the Japanese decided to launch a counter-
offensive which, although vigorous, did not break through
American defences. Intense artillery duels occurred as the
Japanese began to use their well-protected heavy guns in
support of attacks. The aircraft carriers *Bunker Hill*, *Enterprise*,
Victorious and *Formidable* all suffered hits and several destroyers
were sunk as the Japanese launched another 500 kamikaze
attacks. So severe was the damage to the escort carrier *Sangamon
Bay* that she had to be scuttled. American forces launched a new
offensive on 11 May, but progress was slow and there was no
breakthrough until the 21st, when Japanese forces began to pull
out of the Shuri Line towards another line of pre-prepared
positions.

Across south-east Asia the Allied offensive was slowed by
the onset of the monsoon season; nevertheless, the British
launched a large amphibious operation codenamed Dracula to
capture Rangoon. In the event little resistance was offered and
the 26th Indian Division occupied the city with few incidents.
Most Japanese troops had already fled into Thailand. By the
second week of May British forces in Burma were largely
mopping up and preparing for a planned assault on Malaya,
codenamed Zipper and scheduled for the autumn of 1945. An
Australian brigade of nearly 20,000 men arrived in Borneo to
find little Japanese opposition and began to establish control.

In America President Harry S. Truman was gradually establishing his new administration. Truman promised the American
people that he would continue with his predecessor's policies in

the realm of international affairs; the problem was that Roosevelt had told Truman almost nothing about what these policies were. Roosevelt had been immensely secretive even with his inner circle, and so Truman knew nothing about the big secrets of the war, including the reading of German and Japanese codes. He had also been unaware of the Manhattan Project, which was on the verge of producing the world's first atomic bomb. Work on this weapon was now at an advanced stage and efforts were increasingly focused on producing two operational weapons, codenamed Fat Man and Little Boy. The locations to be attacked were not yet decided, and on 11 May 1945 the Target Committee met at Los Alamos for discussions. At least six possible targets were reviewed, including Kyoto, Hiroshima, Yokohama, the Kokura arsenal, Niigata and the emperor's palace.

In Europe, Admiral Dönitz succeeded Adolf Hitler as Führer and met with Montgomery at Lüneburg Heath on 3–4 May to agree a surrender of German forces. April and May were months of liberation for many POWs and internees in both Europe and Asia. In Europe almost all internees and prisoners had been liberated by the end of May. British and Norwegian troops landed in Norway on 8 May, and one of the last territories to be freed was the Channel Islands, on 12 May.

Across Asia, large numbers of POWs and internees were being rescued from locations in Burma and the Philippines. The appalling treatment dealt out by the Japanese was becoming increasingly clear, and a number of secret service missions were launched in an attempt to render assistance. The secret services, and especially SOE, would work with the local resistance to smuggle more food into POW camps and assemble rescue teams to move in on the camps the moment war was over. The intention was to prevent massacres – an outcome that was greatly feared, but which rarely materialized.

Tuesday 1 May 1945

Peter Pinney's Australian commando unit comes upon a
secret trail in the jungle on Bougainville

Sometimes, slipping quietly through the scrub, a patrol will
come across a secret trail leading to a number of Jap huts.
Four Section followed such a trail to several huts hard by
gardens near Commando Road, and studied the layout as an
estimated dozen or so happy Nipponese settled down for
the night. There were pigs and chickens, and a dog. Late at
night, when the moon was up and the livestock were asleep,
the section started moving in – slow, silent.

Everyone was in position at dawn. The cook, who had to
prepare breakfast before daylight in case one of our planes
saw his smoke, decided to use the toilet. He ankled over to
the House Pek-pek, only a few paces from several of our
men. He was sitting there when Buster Luke, stretching himself to ward off sudden cramp, disturbed a spare Bren
magazine he had propped against some weeds, and it fell
over.

It was only a small metallic sound: but it scared the
hackles out of that squatting Jap. He must have known at
once what it signified. He half-rose, tugging at his trousers,
gazing anxiously about. In the half-light he could see the
glint of guns.

There was no time to pull his tweeds up. He must have
known he was already dead. He leapt from the loo at a
galloping hop, clutching at his trousers, hopelessly hobbled,
fell over and rose again and stumbled off like a Sunday-
dinner chook without its head. For the first couple of
seconds he was so terrified he could find no words – but
abruptly he's yelling bloody murder. Hysterical. Knowing
that he'll never make it, that he's doomed, that his life has
reached its end.

Cowell wanted to abort the ambush: he was almost
equally terrified, and later claimed the element of surprise
had been lost. There was no one in the world more surprised

at that moment than eleven Japs waking in those huts. But fortunately Cowell was too far back to have much influence on events, and apparently too scared to blow his whistle. Everyone opened up.

Even as they raked the huts with gunfire, Japs were tumbling out and jumping into foxholes. It turned out there were rather more than a dozen. Fowls climbed vertically in the air ratcheting their panic to the dawn, Japs screamed and gabbled amid a hail of bullets, and the dog shrieked off due north. When the first magazines were expended a few grenades livened things up. Once, during a lull, the complacent mutter of Russian George's Sten gun was heard, and half the section burst out laughing. It sounded so much like an ineffectual toy. And then it jammed.

George was sitting up and now began bashing his gun against a tree. He was furious. The cartridge would not eject. Slugs were zipping all around him.

Bash.

'You bastard!'

Bash.

'You bloody bastard!'

Bash.

A bullet snicked his sleeve. Another touched his beret. He turned around and snarled at the Owen gunner behind him.

'Hit the dirt, Russia,' shouted Norman. 'Them's Jap slugs, not mine!'

Another Sten had five stoppages, finally jammed with a slug lodged in its barrel. Two Owen guns jammed. The remaining Japs were over their shock, and raking the prone section with more accurate fire, when the whistle sounded.

Cowell was even further back than before. The section threw a few more bombs and withdrew. They could only claim six certainties: but a later patrol counted eighteen bodies.

Four automatics had jammed. For lack of anything better, is it any wonder some of us prefer the reliable old Lee Enfield rifle?

By May 1945 Japanese units on Bougainville had virtually ceased to receive meaningful supplies and many soldiers were living off the land, cultivating small patches of ground in the jungle, keeping a few chickens and supplementing their produce with supplies bought or commandeered from the local population. Although this rendered the enemy weak as a fighting force, it also meant they were highly dispersed. Pinney's war became a game of 'hunt the two-toed slipper', sneaking along trails in the hope of glimpsing one or two of the enemy. This form of conflict prefigured future wars in Malaya in the 1950s and Vietnam in the 1960s.

Peter Pinney himself would survive the war and made it home to Australia early by stowing away on a bomber. After fifteen years of travelling the world he turned to cray fishing in the Torres Strait. SEE ALSO PP. 379–81, 670–1.

Thursday 3 – Saturday 5 May 1945

Fumiko Amano, a fourteen-year-old girl in Hiroshima, gives away her tangerines at the railway station

3 May
Clear skies.

Got up at 6:05. The air-raid siren sounded this morning so I ran to catch the train at 7:05.

When I met Ohata-san she asked, 'Won't you come play with me when your stomach gets better?'

I was a little surprised. I didn't know how to answer her. 'Yes. I'll go when I get better,' I answered. Her attitude changes so often. But I don't think she could ever be a close friend again. I know the way she is down in her heart, that's why.

10:40. Took my weight. I lost 2 kilograms. Now I weigh 36 kilograms. It bothers and worries me when they tell me to rest. Tanaka-san lost 6 kilograms and now weighs 30 kilograms.

I'll go get some medicine this afternoon. Nomura-san gave me some dahlias. Tanaka-san lent me a book, *Cloudy then Clear Skies*.

4 May

Clear skies.

Got up at 6:10. A monotonous day. I was tired and my back hurt so I didn't operate the machine in the morning. I finally got on the machine in the afternoon.

Everyone received rations of two summer tangerines during our three o'clock break. On my way home, a train full of sailors on leave arrived at Mukainada Station. I thought I'd offer them my two tangerines and approached them. But when I got near them they started shouting and calling out, 'Give them to me! Give them to me!' I only had two tangerines and didn't know what to do.

My face turned red and I gave them away. I'm really sorry for the ones who didn't get anything. But I did the right thing. One can only pray that they are fighting hard at the front.

5 May

Clear.

Got up at 6:05. I was very weak when I got up. Then, as I started walking around, I grew more tense. The air-raid sirens go off every morning now. I worked at the machine all day.

A transfer student from Niigata Prefecture named Hirata Mitsuko came today. We talked about all sorts of things. She spoke so beautifully it made me embarrassed. Hirata-san told me that her father died in Tientsin. I'll try to be her friend.

We had an air-raid warning this morning. It seems that there were about 20 planes. I took shelter in a cave on the mountain. It was unbearable. I felt so miserable not being able to move. There was another air-raid in the afternoon.

Fumiko's diary records continual illness and stomach pains by May 1945 due to a near-starvation diet. Only on hearing that Germany had surrendered did she feel her first doubts about the course of the war, realizing that Russia was now free to join the war against Japan. This underlines the extent to which the Japanese domestic population had been denied reliable information about the progress of the war. Fumiko did learn, however, that Joseph Goebbels had committed suicide and

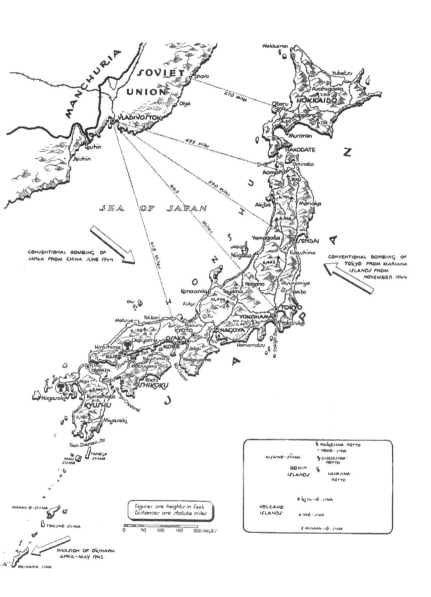

The Advance on Japan, 1945

noted in her diary that she was pleased that he had taken the honourable course rather than surrendering. SEE ALSO PP. *699–701, 774–6.*

Monday 7 May 1945

Admiral Matome Ugaki watches the failure of a 'special attack' against the American fleet at Okinawa

Fair, later cloudy. Third *Tan* Operation. At 0410 I left the office and went to the airfield together with Commander in Chief Teraoka to say farewell to the members of the Fourth *Mitate* Unit of the kamikaze special attack force. In the eastern sky dawn was breaking. Lieutenant Katsumi Noguchi, its commander, and all other members of the unit were picked up from the Third Air Fleet, so I let the Third Air Fleet mostly take care of the third *Tan* Operation.

As in the past, departure was delayed, and takeoff was finished at 0645. One of them crashed on the ground right after takeoff. Out of twenty-four *Gingas* which had been prepared, twenty-one planes took to the air, thus ominously casting a dark cloud over the outcome of the operation.

A weather observation flying boat reported a squall area extending for scores of miles south of Okinotorishima, but failed to make a preattack reconnaissance of Ulithi and also a weather observation. Planes that put about from the way due to engine troubles gradually increased, and those still flying toward the destination at last were reduced to only nine. Though the scheduled time of 'charge in' set as 1530 to 1600 passed, no news came in, and no change was observed in enemy radio activities. As sunset time at Ulithi was 1754 and they still had some time to fly, I suppressed my impatience to wait for further news when the report of the *Gingas*'s return to the base came in. And, alas, they were reduced to six now.

A great many clouds hovered near Okinotorishima. Though the lead land-based bomber managed to find the island after combing through thick clouds, the attack force failed to follow it. As those which followed the commander's plane were reduced to only four, and in addition met enemy planes on the way two or three times, he gave up the attack and returned to base.

Much fuss and little result! It only ended in another case of reducing our own strength by our own hands. Nothing but a complete failure! The *Gingas* have a long radius of action, but their 'Homare'-type engines have many defects. In the previous attempt, one-third of the participating *Gingas* were forced to drop out, while in this attempt more than that dropped out.

Kamikaze attacks against the Allied fleet off Okinawa were losing momentum in May 1945. This was in part because of the poor condition of the remaining stocks of aircraft, but may also have been because the hearts of some of the pilots were not in it. By contrast, Admiral Ugaki was an officer of 'indomitable spirit'. On 15 August 1945 – a full week after the atomic attacks on Hiroshima and Nagasaki – it became clear to him that Japan was surrendering. However, Ugaki believed that Japan should 'fight to the last moment'. Not yet having received the formal written order from his superiors to cease fire, he would decide to lead a last kamikaze attack on American naval forces. Taking with him a short sword given to him by Admiral Yamamoto, he asked for volunteers to accompany him. His attack group would take off at 19.24 on 15 August, but after that nothing was heard of them. It is presumed that in the dwindling light they failed to find their target and came down in the sea. SEE ALSO PP. 105–7, 394–5, 632–3.

Sunday 27 – Thursday 31 May 1945

Joseph McNamara, on the destroyer USS *Anthony*, comes under kamikaze attack off the island of Okinawa

Joseph McNamara and his ship saw an extraordinary amount of action during the Pacific war, having fought at Bougainville in 1943, then at Emirau, Saipan, Guam and Tinian in 1944, to mention only a few engagements. Joseph McNamara's stream-of-consciousness diary captures the sense of peril induced by a kamikaze attack.

General Hodges and the American 1st Army is on its way from Europe to the Pacific.

27 May

A day of horror – Unbelieveable. The 'Braine' #630 just off to starboard is hit by two suicide planes. One on #2 gun, the other on the afterstack. One flaming comes at us only to miss by inches going over the #5 gun.

We shot down two. We take the 'Braine' under tow at 0930, death toll unknown.

Our ship has all compartments full of badly wounded men. Some have already died, others will soon go, under morphine shots – they look yellow and half dead already.

The injuries are beyond belief – eyes burned – both legs, both arms broken – burned all clothes off others beyond belief. The ship itself is almost a total wreck.

One Jap hit the water so close to us his body was thrown up on the forward torpedo tubes. The men found him, covered with rag dolls, charms, etc. He was immediately pitched into the water – sharks in schools tore him to pieces. They hang around us.

I feel sick and my mind is dazed. These Japanese men in planes *cannot be stopped by destroyer fire*. All flaming – one jet went on to hit the Braine. We will take the men to the hospital ship.

By 1800 – three men have died aboard, many others in a bad way. We proceed at 30 knots to the hospital ship in the southern anchorage. On arrival they will be transferred to landing barge then to the hospital.

At anchorage. Men going off. General quarters sounds – secured one hour later. They cut off one mans leg at the knee and one man lost both arms at the elbow. Used 28 units of blood plasma. The Doc Elder, Evans George, aid surgeon aided by deck hands and many others do great work. Several of the men boarded the 'Braine' and moved the hoses to extinguish the fires.

28 May

General quarters – Several times – seven during the night. Planes.

At 0530 again as I go down portside, Jap plane burst into flames just off portside.

0930 – firing just a few hundred yards away with our fighters close to the water because of rain and fog. The ship shot down 2 Japs almost at our bow.

29 May

We go up to Kerma Rhetta for repairs to radar damaged by Jap plane exploding as it passed by on plunge, also repairs to up-risers in aft boiler space. We will spend five days alongside the Hamel.

The #638 under tow by two tugs goes by. She is almost blown in two at gun #4. Braine killed 90 men. Many others injured for life.

The bay is full of ships with holes in sides, guns blown off, burned and broken. The Jap suicide plane is the greatest weapon ever devised by the enemy against our Navy.

The other side of this repair ship is #458 with only 75 men survivors blown apart from fantail to bridge. All engineering spaces blown up all hands killed. The #636 DE lays head down off to port – 29 damaged ships now in harbor.

30–31 May

General quarters – average every 6 hours. One ship here shot down plane with single salvo.

We are to paint up six new Jap kills [symbols of aircraft shot down, painted on the ship's superstructure] making 17 in all. The Okinawa isle had 35 raids in 24 hours.

On 'San Mateo' ship hit by two suicide planes, 4 men were trapped two days in the number 4 magazine, the aft component being under water. Rescued when compartment was pumped out – okay.

Here is the PBY and PBM base – three floating dry docks with 3 DD's in them.

The time ravaged rocks that surround us towering hundreds of feet in the sky are very beautiful. Clouds surmount their tops, the sides even terraced completely, the gardens being bright green with the natural surrounding browns.

The Anthony was later awarded a unit commendation for its extra-ordinary bravery in the face of persistent kamikaze attack at Okinawa. Joseph McNamara survived the war and was discharged from the navy in November 1945. Only on his arrival home did he learn of the death of his brother Robert, aged nineteen, on 27 September 1945 as the result of a routine flying accident in a C-47 transport plane in China. In September 1978, at the age of sixty-seven, Joseph McNamara typed out his diary and dedicated it to his brother, Lieutenant Robert J. McNamara. SEE ALSO PP. 471–4.

JUNE 1945

DURING JUNE the Okinawa campaign drew to a close. In addition to the punishment inflicted by kamikaze attacks, a large typhoon affected most of the Allied fleet to some degree. By 10 June most of the fighting was concentrated on the Oruku peninsula and a few days later many Japanese soldiers began to commit suicide, believing the end was near. On 21 June General Ushijama's headquarters was over-run and his body was found nearby. A day later all resistance on Okinawa ceased. The campaign had cost the Allies over 12,000 lives. Some 160,000 Japanese had been killed, of whom 40,000 were civilians. Over 10,000 Japanese prisoners were taken, a sign that morale was collapsing.

In mid-June Harry S. Truman approved the planning of an operation against the nearby Japanese island of Kyushu which would involve 160,000 troops – of which a third were expected to be casualties. The US joint chiefs of staff were anxious about the strain on American forces and hesitated to launch this operation, knowing that there were likely to be alternatives. By the end of the month scientists at Los Alamos were already beginning to prepare for the test of the first atomic bomb, and so an inner circle of military planners were now working on future conventional operations that they hoped would not have to be launched. However, outside Washington few were aware of the bomb's existence.

Elsewhere in the Pacific the British carrier *Indomitable* joined in an attack on the vast Japanese fleet base at Truk. This was a substantial garrison with fortified emplacements, but it had long been cut off and was now weakened by lack of supplies. A similar attack occurred at Wake Island. Substantial fighting continued on the Philippines, on the island of Luzon, until 28 June. At this point the Philippines campaign was declared over, although in practice mopping-up operations were still under way, jointly conducted by Filipino and American units together with irregular guerrilla forces.

In Europe the war was over. On Tuesday 5 June the four Allied occupying powers signed a declaration of the defeat of Germany which divided the country into four zones. For the time being, there was no serious separation of these areas and it was possible for both soldiers and civilians to cross unimpeded from one zone to another. Accordingly, people continued to pour westwards out of the Soviet area. The sixth of June, the anniversary of the Normandy landings the previous year, was decreed a commemorative holiday for troops in Europe by Eisenhower. The cost of victory in western Europe had been high, with approximately 800,000 casualties. It was only now that the full extent of Hitler's crimes was becoming apparent, and those who lived near concentration camps were forced to view evidence of these grim activities. Orders were given for films to be made of the concentration camps and shown to all German POWs. On 8 June Eisenhower's headquarters publicized the details of the German plans to exterminate all Jews in Europe by the summer of 1946. All over Europe, survivors of the Holocaust were attempting to contact family members and were themselves beginning to realize the extent of the devastation wrought on Jewish communities across the continent.

During June, Britain's coalition government was virtually suspended while the two parties campaigned in a general election. Even front-line troops were balloted in one of the most difficult but successful polling operations ever conducted. On Monday 18 June British demobilization of the armed forces began. The British 2nd Army in Germany was to be disbanded and sent back to Britain.

Preparations for war crimes trials were already under way in Europe, and also in some locations in the Far East, including the

Philippines. In London, William Joyce, known as Lord Haw Haw, was put on trial for having broadcast Nazi propaganda to Britain throughout the war. He was eventually convicted and executed. John Amery, son of the Cabinet minister Leo Amery, was also hanged in Wandsworth prison for treachery. P. G. Wodehouse, who had undertaken radio broadcasts to America for the Germans, escaped prosecution by not returning to Britain. His crimes were considered to be of a lesser order, although MI5 files released in 1999 would reveal that he had been paid the equivalent of £4,000 a month at 2005 prices by the Nazis for his radio work. Some leading Nazis, including Himmler and Goebbels, had already committed suicide, but others, including Goering, were in custody and undergoing interrogation. Across Asia, the hunt was already on for some of the more notorious figures who had been responsible for atrocities against POWs.

On 23 June the constitution of the United Nations was approved, marking the achievement of Roosevelt's most substantial wartime ambition.

Friday 1 – Saturday 16 June 1945

Hilda Bates records the life of children in Kuching internee camp in Borneo

1 June

We are now undergoing a reign of terror due to an indiscretion on the part of one of the Dutch girls, and because of this the Tommies are being hounded and beaten up unmercifully. Yesterday a Punjabi soldier was hung from a tree by his arms – and beaten, and when a Dutch soldier tried to interfere, he was immediately knocked down and stamped on by the Guards.

This was witnessed by his son and daughter – aged 10 and 12. When his wife made a protest to the Japanese Commandant, he, as one would expect, said he had no knowledge of the incidents.

Lately I have been acting foster mother again to two small

boys, whose mother has lost control of her nerves and temper. They lived in a constant state of fear and apprehension, and it took a whole week before they could summon up enough courage to speak to me, or answer without flinching. Sometimes they would tell lies if they thought I would prefer to hear such, – rather than the truth. It really is pathetic how very little these children know of the outside world – having been imprisoned for most of their short lives. On one occasion I remarked to one small boy, 'Don't rush so; You are not catching a train,' to which the child replied 'How *do* you catch a train?'

16 June

The reign of terror is abating, but has left many marks. One male internee was paralysed for a week following Japanese brutality, simply because he had not made his bow in what the Japs considered a proper manner. Also, the husband of one of our women in the camp, – is very ill, and we are all very distressed for this wife, who is a real Londoner, and has a heart of gold. Mr. & Mrs. Bidmead came to Borneo, together with their youngest son, as they had had such a bad time during the air raids, when they were in Epping, and Mr Bidmead thought that life for them would be safer and most restful if they joined him for his last tour. Now unfortunately, the boy too, has been admitted to the male camp hospital suffering with acute dysentery.

More excitement followed when a four-year-old boy swallowed a piece of barbed wire. After much persuasion, the Japs allowed him to be taken to the civilian hospital in Kuching. There he was X-rayed, which showed the wire to be well down in the colon and he was then given large amounts of sweet potatoes in order to help things forward, and sure enough the next day, the offending wire made its appearance!

The child thoroughly enjoyed being able to eat so much more than he was usually allowed, and his young brother is now wondering what *he* can do to get so much extra food and attention!

Hilda Bates had been a district nurse in Borneo before the war and continued her medical duties while interned at the camp at Kuching. The camp was actually called Batu Lintang POW Camp, although it also held civilian internees, and was located in the southern part of the town of Kuching in the western part of Borneo. Thousands of children spent the war in internment as enemy civilians in locations including Singapore, the Philippines, Java and Hong Kong. SEE ALSO PP. *684–5, 800–1, 812–13, 834.*

Sunday 3 June 1945

Masako Nojiri, a novelist in Kawasaki, encounters American propaganda leaflets showing President Harry S. Truman

Masako Nojiri was a well-known novelist and writer working near Kawasaki, and was increasingly involved in local information work in factories during 1945.

At 10:00 I went to Akiha factory in Kawasaki by train as to give a speech of comfort to the workers there. Although everything in the factory had been burned, a test for the re-production was finally possible this morning. Manufacture restarted there in accordance with orders from the army command. Despite the ruins, a stage was established and there was an audience of about 200. When Mr. Fuku and I were returning in the train, we found that it was very crowded with people who had been burned seriously. I felt relieved upon arriving at Kamakura finally. Mr. Kameda came and showed me the propaganda papers that had been distributed from the enemy plane. There was a photo of Truman with a message saying that the 'Japanese military authorities and the false Japanese military statesmen are the real enemy of the world and that America would never enslave the Japanese'.

Mr. Kadota came. It seemed that there was a great sense of instability and fear in the local population. Moreover, there were growing rumours that Yokosuka and Kamakura would

be bombed on June 3 or 6 . . . it was 2:00 in the morning
before I could finally go to bed. I couldn't sleep until 3:00 am.
SEE ALSO P. 792–3.

Friday 15 June 1945

General 'Hap' Arnold, commander of the US Army Air Force, visits the islands of Tinian and Iwo Jima, and receives a cable from General George Marshall

Up at 7:15, first anniversary of 20th Air Force and first
mission over Japan . . . Took off for Tinian 10:30 . . . Tinian is
just one large airport; runways 8,500 feet long, 4 of them, all
usable, in between are sugar-cane fields . . .

At lunch a cable was received, to me from Marshall,
stating that there would be meeting with the President and
the JCS [US Joint Chiefs of Staff] to discuss 'can we win the
war by bombing?' I am sending LeMay back with all
the information he has . . .

Took off for Iwo Jima at 2:25, distance 745 miles. Rested;
arrived at Iwo Jima at 5:40, circled until 6:00, landed 6:00.
Iwo Jima an island 5 miles long, 2 miles wide at widest part,
volcanic, now leveled off for aviation purposes with landing
strips about 500 feet above sea level. Fifty miles to north and
50 miles to south, two lone peaks stick out of water about
3,000 feet. Steam comes up through the runways. Iwo has an
extinct, not too extinct, volcano on the northeast end.
Sulphur and fumes come out of crater floor. A high hill, 2,000
feet, is located between crater and rest of island. Soil is
volcanic, black. About 1,200 Japs lived there normally, raising sugarcane, harvesting sulphur and a plant from which
they extract juice to make vanilla. Our Marines bumped into
about 2,000 Japs with 3 Divisions and [we] lost 3,000 men
killed. There are still Japs on Iwo in numbers up to 200 in
caves, hiding in debris. Every once in a while they come out
and get killed usually, but occasionally surrender. Last night
3 were killed.

Some time before, a few days ago, 6 came out and

prepared to fight but seeing some of our Negroes (3) were so surprised, as they had never seen any before they surrendered. The Negroes searched the Japs again and again, found nothing but their pistols, took them. Then, not knowing what to do, took the Japs to the Negroes' tent to feed them. There was nothing but canned goods. The Negroes tried to open the cans with a pocketknife but with no luck. After many failures, one Jap went deep inside his trousers and pulled out a knife a foot long and handed it to a group of 3 badly scared Negroes. The cans were then opened, the Japs fed and put in the compound.

We have made 3 landing fields on Iwo, we use them for 3 groups of fighters and to save crippled B-29s. So far 1,299 crippled planes or planes out of gas have landed here. Of the 528 B-29s that went over to bomb Osaka today, 43 had to land at Iwo . . .

American military aviation was still 'owned' by the army and the navy, and would not form a separate third service until 1948. Nevertheless, the importance of air power continued to increase during the war, and this mode of warfare was now looked to as the expedient means of ending the conflict with Japan. Had the atomic weapons that were being readied for testing at Los Alamos proved unworkable, then intensified conventional bombing of cities might well have been the route forward after Okinawa. Although serious fighting had finished on Iwo Jima during March, remarkably a few Japanese were still being flushed out of underground caves in June.

Hap Arnold retired from the US Army Air Force in 1946. He died on 15 January 1950. SEE ALSO PP. 317–18, 367–8.

Saturday 16 June 1945

Helmut Hörner, a German POW, goes on strike and watches a film in Colorado

Helmut Hörner was an ordinary private in the Wehrmacht. He had fought on the Eastern Front and then in France during 1944. Wounded several times, he was captured in 1944 and incarcerated by the French, at whose hands he endured unpleasant treatment. He was later handed over to the Americans and moved by ship to the United States, where he spent over a year working on farms. He began work on sugar beet in the midwest and eventually moved on to harvesting peaches in New Jersey. In June 1945 he was working at Camp Greeley in Colorado, where the prisoners decided to go on strike for better food.

The pressure on the farmers has worked wonders. Not that we have had a great feast, but at least a minimum for existence is assured. But in return, the quotas are raised, something that cautious people could see coming. The incentive to return earlier to camp resulted in a number of groups returning to camp by 3.00 p.m. The Austrians, who normally were quite lazy, are especially industrious. No wonder then that the Americans with their keen sense of business, reach such conclusions.

In the meantime, the newspapers have poisoned the whole atmosphere with their reports of the German concentration camps, about whose existence we had no idea. We knew that Hitler locked up those who spoke against him, but the gassing and complete destruction of the Jewish people in the lands controlled by the Third Reich was not known to anyone among us. But now we have to bear the consequences of the inhumane crimes, even though it surpasses our understanding to believe that these atrocities happened.

To help us understand, today we do not go to work, but must view a film that was made by the Allies as they liberated the German concentration camps. If one had been able to film the rage of the plague or cholera in the dark Middle Ages, then every mortal person on this earth would be inclined to doubt the reality of what we saw and pass it off as hate propaganda. Some among us maintain that they saw such burned corpses in Germany after the attacks with phosphorus bombs. Also the Polish officers that Germans found in Katyn are supposed to have looked like that.

Personally, however, I distance myself as a German and a soldier from now on through all eternity from this Thousand-year Reich with all of its lies, inhumanity, and accomplices who knowingly carried out and covered up these beastlike atrocities. But as an individual, I am ashamed to my bones to be a human being.

Approximately half a million German POWs, and a smaller number of Italian POWs, were confined in the United States during the Second World War. Most of them were employed as farm labour in 511 camps scattered across the more agricultural states of America. Towards the end of the war prisoners became harder to manage and would often escape, since security was not very tight. They would often go on strike for improved conditions, as Helmut Hörner's camp did (successfully) in June 1945 or refuse to clean their quarters. American guards preferred hard-core Nazis to anti-Nazis, as they were more disciplined and easier to manage. After the war Hörner travelled to Britain and then in 1948 returned to Germany, where he worked as a dental technician. He died in 1992.

Monday 18 June 1945

In Washington DC, Fleet Admiral William Leahy listens to plans for further operations against the Japanese islands

William D. Leahy was born in Hampton, Iowa on 6 May 1875. He graduated from the US Naval Academy in 1897 and was assigned as a young officer to the battleship USS Oregon. *During the First World War he commanded a troop transport and served as Director of Gunnery Exercises. He was Chief of the Bureau of Navigation from 1933 until 1935, and in 1937 became Chief of Naval Operations. Retiring in 1939, he was recalled to active duty in June 1942 as Chief of Staff to President Roosevelt as the Commander-in-Chief and became a member of the US joint chiefs of staff.*

General of the Army, D. D. Eisenhower, arrived in Washington from Europe and led a parade from Army Headquarters to the Capitol Building. The streets were crowded by a larger number of spectators than has been seen before by anybody now in Washington.

In the Chamber of the House of Representatives, before a joint session of the House and Senate, General Eisenhower made a very well prepared address which was not delivered with particular skill. The galleries were crowded with visitors and on the floor of the Chamber seats were provided for the Supreme Court, Cabinet Officers, Ministers, and Ambassadors from foreign countries, and the American Chiefs of Staff.

Immediately following General Eisenhower's address we proceeded to the Statler Hotel and participated in a luncheon for 1,000 guests given by the City of Washington in honor of the General . . .

From 3:30 to 5:00 PM. the President conferred with the Joint Chiefs of Staff, the Secretary of War, the Secretary of the Navy; and Assistant Secretary of War McCloy, in regard to the necessity and the practicability of an invasion of Japan. General Marshall and Admiral King both strongly advocated an invasion of Kyushu at the earliest practicable date.

General Marshall is of the opinion that such an effort will not cost us in casualties more than 63,000 of the 190,000 combatant troops estimated as necessary for the operation.

The President approved the Kyushu operation and withheld for later consideration the general occupation of Japan. The Army seems determined to occupy and govern Japan by military government as is being done in Germany. I am unable to see any justification from a national defense point of view for a prolonged occupation of Japan. The cost of such an occupation will be enormous in both lives and treasure.

It is my opinion at the present time that a surrender of Japan can be arranged with terms that can be accepted by Japan and that will make fully satisfactory provision for America's defense against future trans-Pacific aggression.

Dined with the President at a dinner given in honor of General Eisenhower to a large number of military and political officers.

For the first time in my experience cocktails were served to the guests in the East Room of the White House. A number of enlisted men, brought by General Eisenhower from Europe, attended the dinner which was served on small tables filling the State Dining Room.

By late June 1945 an anxious debate was developing in Washington over the next steps to be taken against Japan. The invasion of Okinawa had been successful but costly, and constituted an operation of the sort that no-one wished to repeat. Kamikaze attacks – especially by suicide boats – emphasized the fact that it would be quite possible to lose a number of major ships against even a weakened enemy. To a degree the issues were psychological. With the war in Europe won and Japan obviously in decline, there was less determination to win at any cost and some, like Leahy, wondered what deal might be done to cut the war short.

Fleet Admiral William D. Leahy would continue to serve in various advisory capacities until his death in 1959.

Friday 22 June 1945

Charles Sulzberger reads the secret text of Hermann Goering's interrogation

Charles Sulzberger was born in 1912 and became one of America's leading foreign correspondents. His task at this time was to follow Eisenhower and his headquarters around the Mediterranean. He became close friends with many of the leading figures on whom he commented in his writings and often received privileged information. Now, with the arrest of Axis leaders beginning in the countries of Europe and Asia, there seemed the tantalizing prospect of learning something of how the other side had viewed the war.

Through General Ted Curtis, Air Chief of Staff in Europe, I have been shown some of the Allied interrogations. Goering was interrogated by Warburg, German Jew, now American officer. He had met Goering long before the war in Sweden, at various parties. Goering never recognised his interrogator but was puzzled by his exquisite German and his intimate knowledge of Goering's Swedish movements.

Goering told us that Hitler always hoped he could come to terms with Britain until Churchill became the Prime Minister. At various times Hitler considered invading Iceland, Greenland, Gibraltar, Malta, the Azores. In early 1945 Hitler planned to renounce the Geneva Conventions and thus end desertions by depriving deserters of legal protection, giving himself a free hand against Allied prisoners, starting a barter exchange for human lives.

Goering planned a Luftwaffe surprise attack on the British fleet in Scapa Flow in 1939 but Hitler cancelled it. Goering then hoped to move through Spain and grab Gibraltar, then seek a negotiated peace in 1941 before the war with Russia. He said: 'I knew we could defeat the Russian army. But how were we ever to make peace with them? After all, we couldn't march to Vladivostok.'

In March, 1945, Goering planned a mass bombardment of all Soviet electric power stations under the code name 'Eisenhower'. Hitler over-ruled this to attack the Oder River bridges.

Goering concluded that air forces alone can't bring a great nation to its knees because an air force 'cannot occupy'. He said his greatest Luftwaffe losses started when Hitler ordered his bombers to transport supplies to Paulus at Stalingrad. 'There dies the core of the German bomber fleet,' he said.

The interrogations of senior Nazi officials and the subsequent testimony offered at the Nuremberg trials were a matter of endless fascination for everyone who had participated in the war. Although selected reporters like Sulzberger had sat at the side of Eisenhower, Churchill and Macmillan for much of the last three years, none of them really knew what had made the Third Reich tick. Goering's answers were bombastic and self-vindicating; nevertheless, they shed light upon the internecine warfare within Hitler's inner circle and also upon Hitler's increasing determination to control even the fine detail of military decision-making. Like so many journalists, Sulzberger used his diary to record matters that would not make it into newsprint. Later, he agonized over publishing the contents of his diary, but eventually concluded that if famous politicians could publish their recollections, 'why not a modest newspaperman?'

After the war Charles Sulzberger became the chief foreign affairs correspondent of the New York Times. *He died on 20 September 1993.*

JULY 1945

ON 10 JULY the Allies mounted the first air raid on Tokyo that involved more than 1,000 aircraft. Meanwhile, because of the successful operations against Japanese naval and air power, Allied battleships were able to shell Tokyo with relative impunity, focusing on the area around Hitachi to the north-east of the city. Japanese aircraft occasionally attempted attacks against the US navy, but these were now sporadic.

One of the most elaborate weapons projects of the Second World War – the atomic bomb – was now coming to fruition. Like wartime codebreaking, it had involved tens of thousands of people all working in the greatest secrecy. The bomb was tested in the desert of New Mexico in mid-July, just before the Potsdam Conference at which the three main Allied leaders met to continue finalizing the major peace settlements. Some have suggested that Truman hoped that the new weapon would give him greater influence in dealing with Stalin in the post-war period, and there is no doubt that Churchill was of this view. Churchill was anxious to know the result of the new Mexico test and asked Truman to cable him letting him know if the test was a 'plop or a flop'. He received the reply 'it's a plop'.

On 21 July Churchill and Truman agreed to drop the atomic bomb on Japan if it did not accede to proposals to surrender first. A few days later, when they told Stalin about the new weapon, he barely reacted, being well aware of its existence already as the result of extensive Soviet espionage in the west. At the end of July the Japanese rejected Allied overtures designed to secure complete capitulation, and held out for a qualified and conditional surrender. Although Tokyo had been busy exploring peace terms through diplomats in Moscow, Japanese hopes of a generous settlement were bizarrely out of touch with reality. Revelatory material released in 2002 shows that the Allies were intimately aware of this diplomatic activity through the medium of signals intelligence and saw clearly that Japan was still hoping, rather improbably, to bargain rather than to surrender. Japanese diplomats who were secretly attempting to pursue these options had not informed the Japanese military, who they knew would not accept the idea of surrender.

Some of the conversations about the use of the bomb had occurred when the 'Big Three' met at Potsdam. This meeting began on 17 July with Truman, Stalin and Churchill present; however, Churchill was replaced part-way through the conference by Clement Attlee when the result of the British general election became known. The Allied leaders agreed at Potsdam that Germany should be disarmed and demilitarized, that denazification would begin and that a major trial of war criminals would be set up.

Polling day in the British general election was 5 July. Churchill had appealed to the Labour Party to maintain the coalition until the end of the war against Japan, but Attlee would not agree. Because of the balloting of troops, including those in the front line in Asia, it was three weeks before the results were available. Attlee's Labour Party won a landslide majority and replaced the coalition War Cabinet under Winston Churchill with a new Labour government. Attlee's views on world affairs were those of a liberal internationalist; they were also notably anti-colonial, and therefore similar in tone to those of the late Franklin D. Roosevelt. However, the views of his Foreign Secretary, Ernest Bevin, were more traditional and in part reflected extensive discussions with Anthony Eden during the handover of business. Behind the scenes heated arguments developed between the military and the new Cabinet over the speed and extent of demobilization. Clement Attlee's new administration was keen to concentrate on post-war tasks, but the services wished to retain strength in order to deter the Russians in Europe and the Middle East. Even without the onset of the Cold War, post-war administrative tasks in locations as diverse as Austria and Indonesia would keep many in service until late 1946.

Large numbers of displaced people in Europe and Asia now awaited repatriation. Many of these were forced labourers taken from Russia or eastern Europe by the Germans. Eisenhower's headquarters in Europe calculated that there might be two and a half million awaiting resettlement. In many cases the repatriation of these people to the east was not voluntary; how-ever, they were claimed by Moscow under the terms of the Yalta settlement. In late July Eisenhower's headquarters began to lift some of the restrictions on fraternization between Allied soldiers and German civilians, recognizing that in practice this was already happening.

By the end of July war crimes inquiries were well under way throughout Europe and Asia, and both are covered in this volume. The French were busy with their internal collaboration trials, which had already resulted in 1,629 sentences of death, 757 of hard labour for life, 5,328 of other hard labour and 1,136 of solitary confinement, as well as 11,073 other prison sentences. On the last day of July Pierre Laval, the collabor-ationist prime minister of Vichy France, was captured by American forces in Austria and was handed over to the French. He was tried, and then executed on 15 October 1945.

Friday 6 July 1945

Claude Mauriac, in de Gaulle's private office, reflects on the public execution of French collaborators

Claude Mauriac had been a resistance worker and had been pressed into service as a civil servant after the liberation of Paris in September 1944.

In all this morning's papers, from ten different angles, the poor shaven skull and the bewildered eyes of Jean Luchaire, brought back yesterday to Paris, leapt out at one. And though, of course, I would not dream of casting doubt on his guilt, which is a serious matter, any man, however grave his crimes, is purged in a way of his sins once he falls into the hands of his enemies. Moreover, he will not escape the punishment, which pays once and for all, according to the well-known cliché, a debt worked out in advance. And Jean Luchaire, with his air of a cornered beast is pitiable because of his total solitude and defeat. The cries of vengeance, the sneers and abuse hurled at him, are painful to hear. Despicable journalists dare to write that he 'struts' and 'swaggers', and, much he appears to, the poor devil, who has nothing ahead of him before the inevitable firing squad but a calvary of taunts and abandonment.

In connection with this I must mention the shamelessness of those photographs which affront our instinctive good taste. I am not referring to the German charnel houses since, perhaps, it is necessary for us to have exact knowledge of the appalling lengths to which that nation was prepared to go. I was thinking much more of photographs like those which showed us the fascist Starace as he received his sentence. Surrounded by a dozen faces, radiating a small malignant joy, his own face, the detachment of which seems to mark the only human being among all those puppets, has an out-of-this-world serenity. I imagine that the public, like the journalists, did not realise what was appalling about that contrast between the hatred and the serenity; that the serenity had nothing serene or happy about it, but was born of despair so deep that the man experiencing it was unable to display anything but a sad irony. But if it was shameful that the publication of such a photograph (in *Action*) could pass unnoticed, the abomination of one published by *Le Monde Illustré* is so flagrant that it has been openly discussed. It shows the same traitor Starace not facing death as, like traitors, he is compelled to turn his back to the firing squad, but he is on the very brink of death. And from the thousand shades of expression, which an evil and curious joy plants on the faces of the spectators, emerges his own face, about which I prefer to say nothing. I believe the crimes of this man to have been many and his death to have been justifiable. But, once again, that is not the point. There is, in all that, the absence of the elementary pity, which the sight of death demands, if we are not to compromise our dignity and, in a certain sense too, just as important, our security. To sum up, no one who has seen those faces of which I have written, will ever be able to feel quite at ease again anywhere on this planet, or elsewhere.

Claude Mauriac, who served in de Gaulle's Cabinet Office, had worked with his father to try to secure reduced sentences for some French fascists. He felt qualms of conscience as 'an accessory to the injustices of the present Justice'. Penalties were being negotiated over by political factions and he noted that death was being 'dealt out to small fry while those really guilty get away with minor penalties'. Lawyers and judges who knew the system, he complained, were getting off with minor sentences, while naïve intellectuals like Robert Brasillach, who had written for fascist magazines, were being shot out of hand. More broadly, he was alarmed by the visible and open pleasure that the French public derived from visiting punishment upon collaborators. He feared that the French public was being corrupted by the enjoyment of cruelty.

Saturday 7 – Monday 23 July 1945

Eddie Stanton, Australian army police liaison officer, reflects on Australian and American behaviour at Milne Bay in Papua New Guinea

By early 1945 Eddie Stanton had been promoted to Lieutenant and was back at Milne Bay, continuing to work with local police units. He was presiding over the closing down of bases and airfields as front-line units were moved on closer to Japan.

7 July
Showery
Courier departs from Lae.

Have received an order to establish a Police Post on the main road leading to the native villages. Australians & Americans continually drive out to the native habitations to try and secure a woman. The money they offer soon gets results. I wonder if the wives & girlfriends of these white men would raise an eyebrow, if they knew their 'loved' ones were sleeping with native women. I feel sure that, even if there were white women up here, there would be a fair percentage of white gents desirous of seeking the company of native females. The reason is, I think, that the white can indulge in many types of eroticism that would not be acceptable to a white woman. The passion of man reveals itself in many ways. The native woman is uncomplaining. It is a shame that some people exert so little control over their genitalia. I mightn't have to build the camp then . . .

23 July

. . . We receive a report today that an American soldier paid a native woman 1 carton of cigarettes to take off her grass skirt while he photographed her genitalia. This fellow will now print hundreds of this negative & sell them at 10/- each to his fellow soldiers. And we hear missionaries say it's about time we raised the natives' culture to our level.

There was plenty of work to do, including investigating some recent murders of policemen by locals. Nevertheless, Stanton confessed himself bored – 'I crave action' – and wanted to transfer out. Meanwhile, he found himself trapped between the soldiers, whom he regarded as depraved or lustful, and religious figures who were arriving under the auspices of the civilian administration to do 'good work', and who repelled him equally: he noted that two female missionaries had just arrived from Port Moresby, both 'mad with zeal'.

Eddie Stanton remained on duty in New Guinea after the end of the war and was not discharged by the Australian army until August 1946. Thereafter he returned to Sydney and began a university degree. SEE ALSO PP. *286–8, 377–9, 533–4.*

Monday 16 – Tuesday 17 July 1945

Sir Alexander Cadogan, a senior British diplomat at the Potsdam Conference near Berlin, visits Hitler's study in the Chancellery

Amongst other things we went to Hitler's Chancellery. At the main entrance there was a pile of rubble out of which were sticking medal ribbons, and occasionally decorations. I picked up a ribbon and some people found Iron Crosses. I failed in that. But I gave 3 cigarettes to a Russian sentry who then pulled out from behind a door an old felt boot. I told him I didn't want boots, but he signed me to look inside and it was full of Iron Crosses! So I took one. We went into

Hitler's study. It had been pretty badly damaged. There was the undercarriage of his enormous desk, with, alongside it, its marble top. (I've got a bit of that as a paper-weight!) In the banqueting hall a Russian sergeant climbed into the crystal chandelier (astonishingly still intact) and wrenched off a little crystal rosette for me! . . . Anthony [Eden] arrived about 4 and I sat in his garden and reported to him on my talks with the Americans . . .

P.M. arrived about 7 and A.[nthony Eden] and I walked through the gate into his garden and found him and Mary [Churchill] and Monty there . . .

We are now off – P.M. A. and I to see Berlin. I don't necessarily want to see it again, but I want to hear the P.M.s comments on Hitler's study! . . .

We were shown the room in which, according to one story, Hitler died. Next door was another room said to have been Eva Braun's. On one table there was still a vase with a branch in it which had evidently been a spray of blossom.

At the exit from the dug-out there is a shallow crater where Hitler and Eva Braun were said to have been originally buried, and afterwards dug up and burnt. This is according to another story, of which there are many, but nobody knows the truth . . .

In mid-July Churchill, Roosevelt and Stalin gathered in Berlin, together with their staffs, for the Potsdam Conference. Almost all took the opportunity to indulge in bunker tourism, visiting Hitler's underground complex at the Chancellery. Hitler and his mistress, Eva Braun, had married on 30 April 1945 before killing themselves. Subsequently, his assistants used about 200 litres of petrol to burn the bodies. Soviet military doctors identified the presumed corpses and moved them to several locations before transporting them to Moscow. It appears that the NKVD obliterated most of what remained of the bodies for fear that fanatics would seek relics of the dictator. Within a week of the Allied parties' arrival there was little left of Hitler's office as parties from the Potsdam Conference toured the site and removed anything portable.

Cadogan became British ambassador to the United Nations in 1946.
SEE ALSO PP. 55–6.

Monday 16 – Wednesday 25 July 1945

Harry S. Truman arrives in Potsdam and discusses the atomic bomb

Harry S. Truman was born in Lamar, Missouri in 1884. He grew up in Independence and farmed for over a decade before going to fight in France during the First World War as a captain in the artillery. On his return he opened a haberdashery in Kansas and eventually went into politics. For much of the Second World War he headed the Senate war investigating committee that probed issues of waste and corruption. In the election of 1944 Roosevelt chose Truman as his running mate for vice-president, replacing the previous incumbent, Henry Wallace. Assuming the presidency in April 1945 on Roosevelt's death, Truman knew far less about world affairs than the other statesmen arriving at Potsdam. He was also unique among them in keeping a diary.

Harry S. Truman

16 July

At 3:30 p.m. Mr. Secretary Byrnes, Admiral (5-star) Leahy and I left in an open car for Berlin, followed by my two aides and various and sundry secret service and military guards, and preceded by a two-star general in a closed car with a couple of plain-clothes men to fool 'em if they wanted to do any target practice of consequence on the president. They didn't.

We reviewed the Second Armored Division and tied a citation on the guidon of Company E, 17th Armored Engineer Battalion. General Collier, who seemed to know his stuff, put us in a reconnaissance car built with side seats and no top, just like a hoodlum wagon minus the top on a fire truck, with seats and no hose, and we drove slowly down a mile and a half of good soldiers and some millions of dollars' worth of equipment – which had amply paid its way to Berlin.

Then we went on to Berlin and saw absolute ruin. Hitler's folly. He overreached himself by trying to take in too much territory. He had no morals and his people backed him up. Never did I see a more sorrowful sight, nor witness retribution to the nth degree.

The most sorrowful part of the situation is the deluded Hitlerian populace. Of course Russians have kidnapped the able-bodied and I suppose have made involuntary workmen of them. They have also looted every house left standing and have sent the loot to Russia. But Hitler did the same thing to them.

It is the Golden Rule in reverse – and it is not an uplifting sight. What a pity that the human animal is not able to put his moral thinking into practice. We saw old men, old women, young women, children from tots to teens carrying packs, pushing carts, pulling carts, evidently ejected by the conquerors and carrying what they could of their belongings to nowhere in particular.

I thought of Carthage, Baalbek, Jerusalem, Rome, Atlantis, Peking, Babylon, Nineveh, Scipio, Ramses II, Titus, Herman, Sherman, Genghis Khan, Alexander, Darius the Great – but Hitler only destroyed Stalingrad – and Berlin. I hope for some sort of peace, but I fear that machines are ahead of morals by some centuries and when morals catch up perhaps there'll be no reason for any of it.

I hope not. But we are only termites on a planet and maybe when we bore too deeply into the planet there'll be a reckoning. Who knows?

17 July

Just spent a couple of hours with Stalin. Joe Davies called on Maisky and made the date last night for noon today. Promptly at a few minutes before twelve I looked up from my desk and there stood Stalin in the doorway. I got to my feet and advanced to meet him. He put out his hand and smiled. I did the same, we shook, I greeted Molotov and the interpreter and we sat down.

After the usual polite remarks we got down to business. I told Stalin that I am no diplomat but usually said yes and no to questions after hearing all the argument. It pleased him. I asked him if he had the agenda for the meeting. He said he had and that he had some more questions to present. I told him to fire away. He did and it is dynamite – but I have some dynamite too which I am not exploding now. He wants to fire Franco, to which I wouldn't object and divide up the Italian colonies and other mandates, some no doubt that the British have. Then he got on the Chinese situation told us what agreements had been reached and what was in abeyance. Most of the big points are settled. He'll be in the Jap war on August 15. Fini Japs when that comes about.

We had lunch, talked socially, put on a real show, drinking toasts to everyone. Then had pictures made in the backyard.

I can deal with Stalin. He is honest, but smart as hell.

18 July

Ate breakfast with nephew Harry, a sergeant in the field artillery. He is a good soldier and a nice boy. They took him off *Queen Elizabeth* at Glasgow and flew him here. Sending him home Friday. When to lunch with P.M. at 1:30, walked around to British headquarters. Met at the gate by Mr. Churchill. Guards of honor drawn up. Fine body of men – Scottish Guards. Band played 'Star-Spangled Banner.' Inspected guard and went in for lunch. P.M. and I ate alone.

Discussed Manhattan (it is a success). Decided to tell Stalin about it. Stalin had told P.M. of telegram from Jap emperor asking for peace. Stalin also read his answer to me. It was satisfactory. Believe Japs will fold up before Russia comes in. I am sure they will when Manhattan appears over their homeland. I shall inform Stalin about it at an opportune time.

Stalin's luncheon was a most satisfactory meeting. I invited him to come to the U.S. Told him I'd send the battleship Missouri for him if he'd come. He said he wanted to cooperate with the U.S. in peace as we had cooperated in war, but it would be harder. Said he was grossly misunderstood in the U.S. and I was misunderstood in Russia. I told him that we each could help to remedy that situation in our home countries and that I intended to do my part at home. He gave me a most cordial smile and said he would do as much in Russia.

We then went to the conference and it was my job to present the ministers' proposed agenda. There were three proposals, and I banged them through in short order, much to the surprise of Mr. Churchill. Stalin was very much pleased. Churchill was too, after he had recovered. I'm not going to stay around this terrible place all summer just to listen to speeches. I'll go home to the senate for that . . .

25 July

We met at 11:00 a.m. today. That is, Stalin, Churchill and the U.S. president. But I had a most important session with Lord Mountbatten and General Marshall before that. We have discovered the most terrible bomb in the history of the world. It may be the fire destruction prophesied in the Euphrates Valley era, after Noah and his fabulous ark. Anyway, we think we have found the way to cause a disintegration of the atom. An experiment in the New Mexico desert was startling – to put it mildly. Thirteen pounds of the explosive caused a crater six feet deep and twelve hundred feet in diameter, knocked over a steel tower a half mile away, and knocked men down ten thousand yards away. The explosion was visible for more than two hundred miles and audible for forty miles and more.

This weapon is to be used against Japan between now and August 10. I have told the secretary of war, Mr. Stimson, to use it so that military objectives and soldiers and sailors are the target and not women and children. Even if Japs are savages, ruthless, merciless and fanatic, we as the leader of the world for the common welfare cannot drop this terrible bomb on the old capital or the new. He and I are in accord. The target will be a purely military one and we will issue a warning statement asking the Japs to surrender and save lives. I'm sure they will not do that, but we will have given them the chance. It is certainly a good thing for the world that Hitler's crowd or Stalin's did not discover this atomic bomb. It seems to be the most terrible thing ever discovered, but it can be made the most useful.

Harry S. Truman was a prolific but erratic diarist, sometimes writing little, at other times jotting down his thoughts at great length in diary books and journals and on odd scraps of paper. The material was haphazardly recorded – so much so that in 2003, a further volume of his diary that had been overlooked for years was discovered in the Truman Library. He had chosen to pen this volume in a real estate ledger.

Truman's diary for July 1945 emphasizes the desire to use the atomic bomb to hit military targets in Japan rather than civilian centres. However, this entry is misleading. There was also a desire to derive scientific data from an attack that would be an experiment as well as a military operation. This required the choice of targets that had hitherto been left unscathed, so that the impact of the atomic bombs could be measured accurately – which ruled out any significant military installations that had already been bombed by July 1945. A number of targets were discussed; Hiroshima and Nagasaki were eventually chosen largely because hitherto, having only limited military targets, they had suffered relatively little damage.

Wednesday 18 – Saturday 21 July 1945

Ichiro Hatano, a teenage Japanese boy living near Okatani in Japan, worries about the American leaflets predicting 'a catastrophe'

Ichiro Hatano's mother, Isoko Hatano, was head of the Educational Advisory Centre at Bunridai University and was often busy. To avoid the increasing bombing they had taken lodgings at Aoyanagi. Particularly if his mother was away, Ichiro would write in his diary, always dutifully recording something every day. He was in the third year of his junior school and there too, his form master urged all the children to keep diaries.

18 July

Kinji said to me today: 'Japan is soon going to be reduced to ashes.' It's not true, is it? It was at school that he heard this catastrophe predicted, by his teacher, Mr Yamamoto: but it's a lie. Japan is small but it would be impossible to reduce it to ashes, however many bombs were dropped on it. I advised Kinji not to talk nonsense but he said, completely wrapped up in his thoughts: 'As time goes on, so total destruction becomes more and more possible.' I don't like it when Kinji takes up these attitudes; either he thinks everybody else is balmy, or else he is living in another world. I asked him if he had told you what he had told me. He said, 'No. My teacher said I was not to frighten her.' So you probably don't know anything about it, Mother; but is it right for a teacher to tell his pupils things that they are not to repeat to their mothers, and anyway where does he get his information from?

He seems to like Kinji, but a master should not scare the children. Personally, I don't believe in his predictions, and yet they worry me. I wonder what you will think, Mother. You work very hard every day and I would not like to worry you, but you must be warned in advance, mustn't you?

20 July

. . . Is there any truth in this story about the leaflets dropped on Osaka?

Today, just as I was beginning to talk to you about them, our neighbour came in and you said how dangerous it was to gossip carelessly.

You're right: lots of people have been arrested recently for careless talk. So I held my tongue, but Oyama told me that he had seen some leaflets come down and I believe him, because he never tells lies. It must have been an enemy aeroplane which dropped them.

21 July

At school I saw some of the leaflets that fell at Okatani; in them it said, in good Japanese: 'Japan is a beautiful country covered with flowers but after March it will be only a pile of ashes.'

Apparently there are other leaflets advising the population to leave, so as to escape a future air-raid, but those have not got around. At school everybody was talking about it, particularly the boys who come from Okatani.

I hurried home and there found the family and neighbours exchanging news; apparently leaflets were dropped on the surrounding hills as well as Okatani.

Yuzo was sorry he had not been able to get one; he seems to think these leaflets are just the same as the advertisement hand-outs they give you in the street in Tokyo.

Yuzo also said: 'The latest leaflets hurt your hands if you touch them!' He maintains you told him this, Mother, but I doubt it; even if you said so, it must have been to discourage Yuzo and his friends from trying to get hold of them.

The country women hereabouts are as terrified of the leaflets as if they were bad spells; they say that they not only rot the hands that touch them but blind the eyes that read them.

Ichiro was extremely anxious about the war. It was already clear to him that things were not going well. In addition, his mother and father had been marked out by the authorities as intellectuals and liberals, and their house had been visited by the secret police during early 1945. In both the European war and the Asia–Pacific war there had been great anxiety about things dropped from aircraft. The leaflets seen by Ichiro and his friends were warning messages asserting that if Japan did not surrender the bombing would intensify. They were dropped both before and after the atomic attacks, but their significance was not always clear to those who read them. SEE ALSO P. 794–5.

Tuesday 24 July 1945

Admiral Lord Louis Mountbatten arrives at Potsdam and is twice told about the new atomic bomb

Mountbatten had become Supreme Allied Commander in south-east Asia in late 1943 and had presided over the war in Burma. He flew to Germany at the end of the European war to participate in the Potsdam Conference, attended by Churchill, Truman and Stalin. While they were there Truman received news of the successful test of the first atomic bomb in the New Mexico desert, changing the future outlook considerably.

I can never describe the friendliness of the reception I had from the American Chiefs of Staff. Hard-boiled old Fleet Admiral King took my hand in both his hands and shook it a dozen times with great warmth. Bill Somervell seemed even more pleased to see me.

General Marshall and General Arnold invited me to come back and have a drink with them. Then Marshall swore me to secrecy and said he would reveal to me the greatest secret of the war. It appeared that the team of British and American scientists who had been working on the release of atomic energy had at last succeeded in utilizing the release of energy from the fission of element 235, an isotope of uranium, and that when this had been applied in a bomb the results had been quite shattering. An experimental bomb exploded in New Mexico and had had unbelievable results. The steel girder structure half a mile away had either melted or been vaporised; there was nothing left of it. It was estimated that all human beings within a radius of two or three miles would be killed, and those beyond this radius for a mile or two, would be so burned as to be unlikely to recover.

Marshall told me they now had an atomic bomb on the way over to Okinawa, ready for release round about 5th August.

I said: 'This will surely mean the end of the war within the next few days, or anyway within the next few weeks?'

Marshall and Arnold both agreed that this was so, and that they couldn't possibly visualize the war going on beyond the end of 1945 in any case.

I then asked them why the meeting of the Combined Chiefs of Staff that afternoon had given the official date of the end of the war as the 15th November 1946; and they pointed out that on account of secrecy the planners had to work without knowledge of the bomb's existence, and that this was a fair estimate of how long it might have taken if there had been no bomb.

Finally General Marshall reminded me of my promise not to tell a living soul – not even the Prime Minister, with whom General Marshall knew I was dining that night . . .

At 2030 I dined alone with the Prime Minister in his house . . . After dinner we moved into the study, and the Prime Minister closed the doors. After looking around in a conspiratorial manner, he said: 'I have a great secret to tell you' – and proceeded to tell me the story of the atomic bomb.

Ten days after the start of the Potsdam Conference, the British election result was announced. Counting had taken some time because of the need to take in votes from those still on active service. Churchill was replaced as Prime Minister by Clement Attlee, who now flew out to join the proceedings at Potsdam.

In the first days of August 1945 Mountbatten was busy meeting with numerous staff officers in London, finding himself in the surreal position of planning future operations against Japan in a war which he knew privately was about to end. SEE ALSO PP. 462–5, 671–2.

AUGUST 1945

O N 6 AUGUST an atomic bomb devastated Hiroshima, destroying some 60 per cent of the city. On 9 August a second atomic bomb was dropped on the city of Nagasaki. About 80,000 people were killed in the first attack and about half that number in the second. This onslaught was accompanied by many severe conventional attacks, the last of which was a heavy raid against Kumagaya on the night of 14 August. On 10 August the Japanese proposed to surrender on condition that they could retain the emperor, but received the reply that only unconditional surrender was acceptable.

The deep Allied commitment to unconditional surrender had come about partly because of an appreciation that this was an ideological war. Both London and Washington wished to see complete surrender followed by occupation so that they could institute denazification programmes in Germany and similar programmes in Japan to cleanse the minds of the Japanese people of the cult of militarism. In short, they believed that avoiding future war required some remodelling of these societies, of a kind that could be achieved only by a prolonged period of administration – a view quite different from previous approaches to war termination.

The idea of unconditional surrender also reflected mutual Allied distrust earlier in the war. The Soviet Union in particular feared a partial peace, which might have delivered an agreement with Germany in the west that allowed it to keeping fighting on the Eastern Front. The delays over the launching of D-Day had reinforced Soviet fears that they might be left to deal with Germany largely alone. Only after convincing reassurance had been afforded did Stalin promise to enter the war against Japan as soon as possible. Unconditional surrender was forthcoming on 15 August and 'Victory Japan Day' or 'VJ-Day' was declared. The Japanese Emperor gave a radio broadcast informing his people that they must now 'bear the unbearable'. The Emperor had hitherto been a remote figure and had never used the radio before; this was the first time that most Japanese had heard his voice. In the event the Japanese were allowed to retain the imperial household.

Intense secrecy had surrounded the development of the bomb. Many wartime figures, even senior generals and diplomats, had not been told, and to them this sudden end to the war came as a major surprise. Many had expected to be fighting until the summer of 1946. In reality, scientists and engineers had quietly been busy transforming war in a manner that was unprecedented. In a thousand laboratories and factories across the globe they had been working away on other horrors of the industrial age, and by 1945 they had produced the nerve gas sarin and deadly weaponized germs such as brucella. These unpleasant weapons could now be delivered, if necessary, by new ballistic rockets such as the V-2 against which there was no defence. Some scientists had suggested that these weapons might be put under international control. However, as early as August 1945 most of them recognized that the new weapons brought with them the concept of deterrence, which would dictate a system of international restraint dependent on the creation of fear.

Stalin had hung back from involvement in the Pacific. The Soviet Union having suffered the vast majority of the casualties against Germany, he was content to see the Americans and the British do the lion's share of fighting in the war in Asia and the Pacific against Japan. However, when the prospect of Japanese surrender loomed after the attack on Hiroshima, Moscow declared war on Japan on 8 August, seizing the opportunity to grab some of the northern Japanese islands and territory in Manchuria. These acquisitions had been discussed at the recent conferences at Yalta and Potsdam, but Stalin clearly thought that possession was nine-tenths of the law.

Nationalists in Indonesia also saw a window of opportunity. On 17 August the Republic of Indonesia was declared and it was announced that Dutch colonial rule was over. The British occupying forces would not arrive until the end of September, by which time relations between the Indonesians and the former Dutch internees, whom they viewed with hostility as a potential revived colonial administration, had deteriorated.

During August, President Truman announced that Lend–Lease operations designed to support the Allies would cease at the end of the month. The desire to halt this programme was understandable, as it had already cost the United States a total of $48.5 billion. However, the abrupt nature of the American decision had very serious economic effects on a number of ailing Allied economies which relied heavily on this support. London immediately sought a loan from the United States. Britain's parlous economic situation was reflected in a food ration allocation that declined rather than improved after the end of the war.

At the end of August the final list of major Nazi war criminals to be tried at Nuremberg was drawn up by a Four Power Commission of Prosecutors in London. This list included Hermann Goering, Rudolf Hess, Joachim von Ribbentrop, Dr Ley, Alfred Rosenberg, Dr Hans Frank, Julius Streicher, General Keitel, Dr Funk, von Shirach, Dr Schacht, Fritz Sauckel, Professor Albert Speer, Martin Bormann, Fritz von Papen, General Jodl, Albert Krupp, Admiral Raeder, Admiral Dönitz, Baron von Neurath, Artur von Seyss-Inquart and Otto Frische. Other countries continued their own local tribunals; on Monday 6 August the Belgians announced that 2,117 collaborators, out of some 16,000 who had been found guilty of working with the enemy, had already been sentenced to death. In the Philippines a war crimes tribunal was already under way. Meanwhile, across the rest of Asia, August would trigger a search for Japanese war criminals, especially the more odious figures from the camps, and the list of wanted persons was already long.

Monday 6 August 1945

Fumiko Amano, a teenage girl working in a factory on the outskirts of Hiroshima, sees a sudden flash

Got up at 6:55. The train was late and I arrived at the factory a little late. I was changing into my exercise uniform when a flash and strong ray of light entered the building from the west and lit up the whole workplace and the machines. I thought there must have been an electrical short. Everyone glanced toward the middle of the factory. Then . . . ! A huge bomb exploded and the winds from the explosion blew off all of the roofs from the houses facing the center of Hiroshima. The dust and dirt was caught up in the winds from the explosion and we were surrounded in darkness.

A pillar of fire rose up over Hiroshima and the cloud from the explosion kept rising and rising.

I got together my things and ran with everyone else to the bomb shelter. Rumors were spreading about just what kind of bomb this was. It could do all this in just a second's time.

The injured were being transported out from the factory. Our teacher had his arms and legs wrapped in bandages. It looks like Maruoka-san and Shakuta-san were badly injured.

I wanted to go back as soon as I could and check on Mother and Father in the city but spent the whole day near the main building and the bomb shelter. I'm impatient.

The sky over Hiroshima is burning bright red. We spotted many planes over the city today. How resentful I felt. There was a rumor that the middle of Minami-machi was destroyed and Nishiyama-san was very worried. Nishiyama-san's house was in Minami-machi.

Truck after truck passed by the factory gate carrying the injured. I looked to see if I knew any of the injured passing by. Nakamoto-san's little brother injured his eye and was being carried off. Nakamoto-san was crying. There weren't any words to console her. I was worried about Mother and Father and Older Brother.

This is the end of my factory diary . . .

Fumiko Amano returned quickly to her house, which was somewhat closer to the centre of the city, and found that it had been destroyed. She later recalled that the 'fire had incinerated everything so neatly'. When she reached home she was met by a scene of devastation. First of all a 'sooty face' appeared from a nearby air-raid shelter, which proved to be the girl next door. Although the street contained a number of corpses, her neighbours brought good news. Remarkably, her mother, father and elder brother, Hideso, had survived. However, her brother was badly injured because at the time of the blast, 8.15 in the morning, he had just wandered out onto the veranda. The black trousers he was wearing were burned off his legs, leaving terrible injuries that looked like molten lava.

Hideso died of his injuries on 19 August. Fumiko Amano first published her diary in Japanese in 1992. SEE ALSO PP. 699–701, 737–40.

Sir Cuthbert Headlam MP hears the first news of Hiroshima and reflects on science and war

Sir Cuthbert Headlam was born in 1876. He was a long-serving Conservative MP, sitting in the House of Commons intermittently from 1924 to 1951, and a major figure in the party organization in the north-east of England.

The news tonight is that some new and fearful form of bomb – something to do with the 'splitting of the atom' (God help us) – has been dropped in Japan – the havoc so fearful that no one can tell how much damage has been done. It is a ghastly discovery on which our scientists and the Americans have been at work for some years: the Germans were also busy on the same thing and we apparently won the race by a short head – and so, according to Winston, won the war instead of losing it. It seems that this wretched bomb is so devastating in its effect that it wipes out a whole town at one blow – if this is really the case, it means either the end of war or the end of civilization. Apparently its discovery – the discovery of the bomb – has cost 500 million pounds – it is all beyond my comprehension and makes one hate 'Science' more than ever . . .

When the weapons programme codenamed the Manhattan Project was initiated in 1942 in the United States under Brigadier-General Leslie Groves, there was already anxiety that the enemy might be working along the same lines. British, American and Canadian scientists worked together in the hope of producing an atomic weapon faster than the Nazis. There was real concern lest the Axis achieve the bomb first, and Germany's efforts in the atomic field were repeatedly attacked and disrupted. During the war highly secret espionage aircraft had flown over Germany, sampling the air for traces of uranium and plutonium gas, attempting to assess how far the Germans had progressed with their own atomic bomb project. Churchill's summary was not entirely accurate, for when Allied military scientists entered Germany in May 1945 they discovered that the Germans were some years behind the Allies.

Monday 6 – Wednesday 8 August 1945

John J. Maginnis, a US civil affairs officer, battles with the Soviet intelligence service in Berlin

John J. Maginnis was a US army officer who had trained in the Civil Affairs Training School in Pittsburgh in 1943. He had then accompanied the US army during the invasion of France and had worked as a liaison officer with the French resistance. By August 1945 he was helping to administer occupied Berlin, a city divided into British, American, French and Soviet sectors. His diary underlines how quickly the Second World War was becoming a Cold War, against the background of the explosion of the first atomic bomb.

6 August

Staff meeting at 0930 hours, Kommandatura [Berlin Military Government] meeting at 1030, and A1A1 meeting at 1300.

We had some luck with the Russian abductors last night. Lieutenant Colonel Stahl, VBK [Verwaltungsbezirk: city borough] CO in Steglitz, informed me yesterday that a car carrying several civilians was seen driving around a location where there had been a snatching a few days earlier. He thought they looked suspicious, and I told him to lay a trap. He called me first thing this morning to report that, sure enough, they had come back at night to make a snatch, he had captured them, and was holding them in the jail. They said they were only Russian soldiers, although out of uniform, but we felt certain that they were from the NKVD. I told him that under no circumstances were they to be released. As far as we were concerned, we had picked up four civilians. If they had been in uniform we would have been forced, according to agreement, to return them to Russian MPs at one of the exchange points. After the deputy commanders' Kommandatura meeting, I told Colonel

Howley about it. He was intrigued, saying that we would sit tight and see what happened. Later in the day a Russian captain appeared and asked for the return of the men we were holding. We were holding no Russian military personnel, we said, adding that according to agreement we always promptly returned all Russian soldiers picked up in our sector.

7 August

Routine. Very busy.

We had word today that an atomic bomb had been dropped on Japan, causing great destruction. Everyone was puzzled. What was an atomic bomb?

The NKVD incident in Steglitz was becoming more interesting. A Russian major showed up with a demand that we release the would-be abductors. The Russian spy system must have been good for he designated the jail they were in, and even the cells. Our answer was the same – we had no Russian soldiers in jail. By now we realized that they were secret police and had learned that one of them was a top NKVD officer. This accounted for Soviet anxiety to get them back. I suggested to Colonel Howley that we might ship them out of Berlin to the US zone, conveniently lose them there, and let the Russian Berlin command sweat the whole thing out; such action, I ventured, might discourage the snatching business. He thought this would be too risky, but from the gleam in his eye I knew that the idea appealed to him.

8 August

Routine. Worked late.

The top blew off the NKVD detention in Steglitz, and I was lucky not to have been burned by it. A Russian colonel arrived this morning to demand the release of the NKVD personnel. We still insisted that we knew nothing about it. Late this afternoon, however, I had a call from General Parks. It seemed that General Garbatov had just called him about the matter. General Parks asked: 'We're not holding any Russian soldiers here in jail, are we?'

I replied, 'Well, sir, yes and no.'

'Maginnis,' he said, 'you'd better get over here pronto and tell me about this,' which I did. He told me pointedly that he did not like what we had been doing, but he felt better about it when he realized that the Russians in question had been NKVD police in civilian clothes bent on a snatching mission. We then discussed the implications of the situation, and General Parks said that I was to release the Russians but not until he told me to. 'I have a few questions to put to General Gabatov first,' he said rather smugly. He certainly did not compliment me for this operation, but it was plain to see that he was not displeased. For my part, I was pleased to have been able to give the Russians a little of their own medicine.

French troops moved into Berlin today. I was successful today, finally, in drawing mosquito netting for my bed. Now I could sleep with the windows open.

Captain Maginnis's boss, General Floyd Lavinius Parks, had led the first US troops into Berlin in May 1945. In his capacity as first head of the Kommandatura in Berlin, Parks effectively played the role of the city's first post-war mayor. Thereafter, he was the commander of the US occupation zone in Berlin from August to October 1945. His duties in Berlin during the summer of 1945 had included setting up the arrangements for the Potsdam Conference. As a member of the Kommandatura, he chaired meetings of the American, Soviet, British and French occupation commanders. He was a tough customer, having previously served with the 1st Allied Airborne Army, parachuting into the Low Countries and then behind the German forces trying to prevent US troops from crossing the Rhine. One of the issues that he had to deal with in Berlin was 'body-snatching' by the NKVD or Soviet intelligence service – mostly of German experts in rocket science, atomic energy and intelligence, but also Russian deserters and anti-communists. The four Allies occupying the city had access to all sectors of Berlin and their secret services were actively hunting for German war criminals, spies and scientists who had worked on Hitler's top secret weapons programmes. Overnight, John Maginnis had found himself catapulted out of the Second World War and into the murky territory of agents and rackets portrayed in the 1949 film The Third Man.

Tuesday 7 August 1945

The Viceroy, Lord Wavell, in Delhi reflects on news of the atomic bomb

The avuncular Lord Wavell, formerly British commander in the Middle East, had become Viceroy of India in the summer of 1943, presiding over a turbulent country which was agitating for independence while at the same time providing the rear area for the war in Burma.

So the atomic bomb has come, a surprise to me, though I think I have known or suspected the majority of war secrets. I knew vaguely that they were working at it, but had no idea it was near going into use. The correspondence there has been about Travancore mineral salts (Monasite, etc.) is connected with it, I fancy. A very dangerous scientific development, since I doubt whether man has yet the wisdom to use it wisely. It may end war or it may end civilisation. It is not a weapon that any thinking man would willingly put into the hands of the present-day world. It has shown it cannot be trusted with a box of matches, is it reasonable to think it can play with a Mills grenade and not pull the pin out?

During the war secret missions of atomic scientists, sometimes disguised as archaeologists, had been sent all over the world, including to Travancore in India, in an attempt by Britain and the United States to monopolize the sources of various radioactive elements, including uranium and thorium. Wavell was not alone in feeling that the atomic bomb offered the prospect of either utopia or oblivion, and that the latter was more likely. Wavell noted in his diary the next day that one of the first 'horrors of peace' was being compelled to write a text for his 'victory broadcast'. In practice his attention was largely focused on the issue of the transfer of power to the Indian nationalists, a process that would eventually be completed by Mountbatten, who succeeded him in March 1947 and became the last Viceroy.

George Bilaikin meets Harry S. Truman in the White House as the President returns from the Potsdam Conference

For most of the war George Bilaikin had been the diplomatic corres-
pondent for Allied newspapers in London; he now worked for the Daily
Mail. *He was forty-two years old and, having been in the job for many*
years, enjoyed excellent contacts.

The president stepped out, looking fit and somewhat tanned
from the ship voyage. He shook hands with Matt, myself,
and Bill and seemed delighted to be back and glad to see us.
Then he went into the reception room and greeted the others
waiting there.

None of the other members of the president's party came
to the White House but instead went directly to their homes.

After a few moments chatting in the reception room the
president suggested we all go upstairs and have a drink, so
we went to his study on the residence floor.

Almost at once after entering the room the president
walked over to the piano and sat down. He played a few
bars and then got up and put in a telephone call to Mrs
Truman in Independence. His call went through in a few
moments, and he spoke briefly with her. After he talked with
her he told us Mrs Truman would leave tomorrow to return
to Washington Friday.

He ordered drinks and we all sat down, and for about a
half hour the president talked and answered questions about
the Potsdam Conference and particularly about the
personalities of the conference – Stalin, Churchill, and Attlee,
especially.

The greatest interest was evident concerning Stalin and
the president was asked various questions about the Russian
leader. The president seemed to have been favourably
impressed with him and to like him.

Stalin was one, he said, who if he said something one time
would say the same thing the next time; in other words he
could be depended upon. He did not feel the same way
about Molotov, foreign minister, or Vishinsky, although he

said Secretary of State Byrnes got on well with Molotov. The president felt the others were not as dependable, although he seemed to feel this might be due in part to their having to get Stalin's word before committing themselves . . .

In response to someone's question about the defeat of Churchill's forces in the British election, the president said that Churchill did not expect it; that when he left Potsdam to go back to Britain for the determination of the result on July 26 he was entirely confident.

The election, the president said, set the conference back about three days because of the absence of the prime minister, but with the return of Attlee it resumed without real interruption. Of Attlee he did not express a pronounced opinion although he seemed to like him well enough. Of Bevin, however, he spoke frankly. Bevin he compared with John L. Lewis but said the Britisher was crude and uncouth. Stalin and Molotov, the president said, might be rough men, but they knew the common courtesies, but Bevin he said was entirely lacking in all of them – a 'boor,' the president said.

President Harry S. Truman had just returned from Potsdam and had agreed to have informal drinks with the press corps at the White House to discuss his impressions. Truman was renowned for 'straight talking' and let fly with his personal impressions of both the Russian and British delegations, including Clement Attlee's new Cabinet colleagues. Truman singled out Ernest Bevin, the new Foreign Secretary, for unfavourable comment. Truman was fairly confident that his more astringent comments would not be reported in the press, but Bilaikin did not hesitate to record them in his diary.

The day after his interview at the White House, Bilaikin set out on an investigation of conditions in newly occupied Europe and reported from Paris, Berlin, Prague and Belgrade.

Dr Michihiko Hachiya speaks to his neighbours about the Hiroshima blast

Michihiko Hachiya was the director of the Communications Hospital (Teishin Byoin) in Hiroshima. He had not kept a wartime diary, but began one following the atomic attack and maintained it for two months, recording all that he saw of the aftermath.

I neither saw nor heard Mr Katsutani when he came in. It was not until I heard someone sobbing that my attention was attracted, and I recognised my old friend. I had known Mr Katsutani for many years and knew him to be an emotional person, but even so, to see him break down brought tears to my eyes. He had come all the way from Jigozen to look for me, and now that he had found me, emotion overcame him . . .

Mr Katsutani paused for a moment to catch his breath and went on: 'I *really* walked along the railroad tracks to get here, but even they were littered with electric wires and broken railway cars, and the dead and wounded lay everywhere. When I reached the bridge, I saw a dreadful thing. It was unbelievable. There was a man, stone dead, sitting on his bicycle as it leaned against the bridge railing. It is hard to believe that such a thing could happen!'

He repeated himself two or three times as if to convince himself that what he said was true and then continued: 'It seems that most of the dead people were either on the bridge or beneath it. You could tell that many had gone down to the river to get a drink of water and had died where they lay. I saw a few live people still in the water, knocking against the dead as they floated down the river. There must have been hundreds and thousands who fled to the river to escape the fire and then drowned.

'The sight of the soldiers, though, was more dreadful than the dead people floating down the river. I came onto I don't know how many, burned from the hips up; and where the skin had peeled, their flesh was wet and mushy. They must have been wearing their military caps because the black hair on top of their heads was not burned. It made them look like they were wearing black lacquer bowls. 'And they had no faces! Their eyes, noses and mouths had been burned away, and it looked like their ears had melted off. It was hard to tell front from back. One soldier, whose features had been destroyed and was left with his white teeth sticking out, asked me for some water, but I didn't have any. I clasped my hands and prayed for him. He didn't say anything more. His plea for water must have been his last words. The way they were burned, I wonder if they didn't have their coats off when the bomb exploded.'

See also pp. 791–2, 798–9.

'Dusty' Rhoades, a US army pilot, talks to General Douglas MacArthur about the meaning of the atomic bomb

Manila, P.I., Aug. 7, 1945   2100
Now that it has happened, we can speculate a bit about the atomic bomb, and its impact not only upon the physical world but also upon the social world. This project has been the most carefully guarded secret of the war, but now that the first one of them has been loosed, many details have been released to the public. Even I did not know just what to expect, but I knew that some project of the greatest importance was to be tried on Japan during the first week of August.

After the release of the publicity on the bomb, I was fortunate to be able to discuss some of its aspects with Dr. Compton and Dr. Moreland ... We now have three of the units available, and the production rate of three per month. Unless Japan capitulates, we apparently will systematically depopulate the entire nation. It seems barbaric, but it spares American lives. I now believe the war will end not later than August 31 ...

The physical effects of the bomb are practically predictable, but its impact upon the social structure of the world is at present imponderable. Man at last has a weapon with which he can quickly and totally destroy himself. This immediately means that mankind will have to develop a method of living together in peace. This in turn means that a workable world-state is a must on the agenda of society, and I'm afraid we haven't yet reached the state where all races and nationalities can live together without quarreling. It is useless to argue that we can, when even we in America are unable to find a solution to the Negro problem. To introduce the Chinese, Japanese, Indians, British, Russians, etc., into a world-state overnight and expect harmony therefrom is ridiculous. Yet man can never survive another war with such weapons. Perhaps it were better had we never developed this monster.

General MacArthur definitely is appalled and depressed by this Frankenstein monster. I had a long talk with him today, necessitated by the impending trip to Okinawa. He wants time to think this thing out, so he has postponed the trip to some future date to be decided later. He wants to remain in immediate contact with the communications network in order to be ready for any duties assigned him when the Japanese are ready to surrender.

Although 'Dusty' Rhoades was a humble major in the army air force, his position as Douglas MacArthur's personal pilot brought him into contact with many interesting people. Two of these were Dr Karyl Taylor Compton and Dr Edward Moreland, defence scientists from MIT who had been sent out from the United States to investigate the effects of the nuclear attacks on Hiroshima and Nagasaki. Although the use of atomic bombs was intended to end the war, the event also served as a vast laboratory for a new kind of weapon, and scientists wished to gather as much information as possible. They discussed the problems of controlling atomic energy. Humankind's political development seemed out of step with technological development and few could see how disaster might be avoided in the long term, other than through world government. Although MacArthur was initially unenthusiastic about this new weapon, by November 1945, as we shall see, his attitude would have changed.

After the war 'Dusty' Rhoades returned to the United States and resumed his pre-war career in commercial aviation. In 1971 he retired as Vice-President of Engineering at United Airlines. SEE ALSO PP. 514–16, 628–9.

Wednesday 8 – Tuesday 14 August 1945

Lord Halifax, British ambassador in Washington, ponders the biggest test of human sanity and character

Lord Halifax was one of an inner circle in Washington who had been aware of the development of the atomic bomb and had taken the opportunity to discuss the options for deployment with Henry Stimson, Secretary of War.

The news about the atomic bomb is filling all the papers and occupying all men's minds. It surely is the biggest revolution in material human history that there has ever been and accounts that began to come through of its effects are overwhelming in the imagination. When I was in America I asked Stimson whether they had ever considered, when they got the secret, telling the Japs and giving them a 48 hour chance to pull out; they said they had considered it very carefully but had come to the conclusion that the world would never believe in the terrible power of the new discovery merely on hearsay report of what this power was estimated to be, and that practical demonstration was the only means by which the necessity of future control could be driven into the world's thinking. I think this is a good argument and in the long view is right . . .

At lunchtime came news of the Jap surrender. How all the Axis powers have followed a single pattern: treachery; gangster methods; startling successes; gross miscalculations; utter and tragic failures. They certainly have deserved all they have had – and it is a startling demonstration of the atomic power. How will the world deal with this? Co-operation or competition? Salvation or suicide? It is going to be the biggest test of human sanity and character that there has ever been.

Halifax returned briefly to Britain for discussions at the Foreign Office in August 1945 and continued as ambassador to the United States until May 1946. He died at Garroby Hall in 1959. SEE ALSO PP. 220–1.

Friday 10 August 1945

Henry L. Stimson, Secretary for War, discusses surrender terms for Japan at the White House

Henry Stimson was one of Roosevelt's longest-serving Cabinet members. During the second week of August he was intimately involved in discussions over the precise surrender terms to be extended to Japan. As his diary demonstrates, Japanese attitudes at this stage were gauged not so much by talking to Tokyo as by intercepting Japanese communications.

Today was momentous. We had all packed up and the car was waiting to take us to the airport where we were headed for our vacation when word came from Colonel McCarthy at the [War] Department that the Japanese had made an offer to surrender. Furthermore they had announced it in the clear. That busted our holiday for the present and I raced down to the office, getting there before half past eight. There I read the messages. Japan accepted the Potsdam list of terms put out by the President 'with the understanding that the said declaration does not comprise any demand which prejudices the prerogatives of his majesty as a sovereign ruler'. It is curious that this was the very single point that I feared would make trouble. When the Potsdam conditions were drawn and left my office where they originated, they contained a provision which permitted the continuance of the dynasty with certain conditions. The President and [Jimmy] Byrnes struck that out. They were not obdurate on it but thought they could arrange it in the necessary secret negotiations which would take place after any armistice. There has been a good deal of uninformed agitation against the Emperor in this country mostly by people who know no more about Japan than has been given them by Gilbert and Sullivan's 'Mikado', and I found today that curiously enough it had gotten deeply embedded in the minds of influential people in the State Department. Harry Hopkins is a strong anti-Emperor man in spite of his usual good sense and so are Archibald MacLeish and Dean

Acheson – three very extraordinary men to take such a position.

As soon as I got to the [War] Department I called up Connolly at the White House and notified him that I was not going away and would be standing by if he wanted me. Not more than ten minutes afterwards they called back to say that the President would like me to come right over, so I hurried around there and joined in the conference consisting of the President, Byrnes, Forrestal, Admiral Leahy, and the President's aides. Byrnes was troubled and anxious to find out whether we could accept this in the light of some of the public statements [on 'unconditional' surrender] by Roosevelt and Truman. Of course during three years of a bitter war there have been bitter statements made about the Emperor. Now they come to plague us. Admiral Leahy took a good plain horse-sense position that the question of the Emperor was a minor matter compared with delaying a victory in the war which was now in our hands.

The President then asked me what my opinion was and I told him that I thought that even if the question hadn't been raised by the Japanese we would have to continue the Emperor ourselves under our command and supervision in order to get into surrender the many scattered armies of the Japanese who would own no other authority and that something like this use of the Emperor must be made in order to save us from a score of bloody Iwo Jimas and Okinawas all over China and New Netherlands. He was the only source of authority in Japan under the Japanese theory of the State. I also suggested that something like an armistice over the settlement of the question was inevitable and that it would be a humane thing and the thing that might effect the settlement if we stopped the bombing during that time – stopped it immediately. My last suggestion was rejected on the ground that it couldn't be done at once because we had not yet received in official form the Japanese surrender, having nothing but the interception to give it to us, and that so far as we were concerned the war was still going on ... When we adjourned Byrnes and I went into another room to discuss the form of the paper ... By this time the news was out and the howling mob was in front of the White House, access to which by the public was blockaded on Pennsylvania Avenue . . .

After a fifteen or twenty minutes delay, which is unusual in this Administration, the President and Byrnes came in from a conference which had been going on in the other room and the President announced to the Cabinet that we had received official notice from Japan through the intermediary, Sweden, and that Byrnes had drawn a reply to it of which they thought they could get an acceptance from Great Britain, China, and perhaps Russia, with all of whom they were communicating. The paper was in the exact form that Byrnes had read me over the telephone and which I told him I approved.

This has been a pretty heavy day.

There has been a great deal of debate about the motivation underpinning the use of atomic weapons. In fact, few perceived that there was much of a decision to take. After five years of brutal and brutalizing war, it was inconceivable that such a weapon would not be used once it became available. In other words, few realized that a great decision had been taken. Stimson now wanted to settle the war with Japan quickly to prevent the Russians from seizing too much territory in Asia, and the issue of the Emperor was an impediment. The White House gradually concluded that the American forces would need the imperial house to help maintain order and counter any tendency for Japan to move towards communism. By Tuesday 14 August a peace agreement had been secured using a formula whereby the Emperor was placed under direct authority of the US military. SEE ALSO PP. 119–21, 809–10.

Night of Monday 13 August 1945

Frances Partridge, writer, pacifist and member of the Bloomsbury Group, greets a rumour of peace

Frances Partridge was born in 1900 and lived and worked among the writers and artists who would become known as the Bloomsbury Group. In common with many of them, she was an ardent pacifist and socialist. She spent much of the war in Wiltshire with her husband Ralph and son

Burgo at their house, Ham Spray. They were now on a family holiday at St Helen's in Cornwall.

Nance brought a rumour that Japan had asked for peace, and we are all waiting expectantly for V.J. Day to be announced.

Ralph and I were in bed and nearly asleep when a strange cacophony penetrated our consciousness: the church bells began tolling, and a cracked trumpet hooted out military refrains. Next began the sound of young voices singing, feet marching, cheering and beating on tins.

We woke up completely. Ralph said: 'It can only mean one thing. Peace.'

The contrast between the long tedious frightfulness just ended and the pitiful desire of puny human beings to make *some* sort of noise at all was more than I could manage to swallow, and I lay saying bitter things about them, while Ralph rightly laughed at me for not appreciating the greatness of the occasion. The procession clanked off along the pier; then the momentary quiet was shattered by the hooter of the *Scillonian* lying in the harbour, which gave tongue again and again like the last trump. Shouts; more trumpets, rockets and then maroons going off with a deafening whoosh followed by an echo like a whole town collapsing. Silence once more. The sound of a solitary tin being kicked along the street woke Burgo, who came and snuggled into bed with us. 'The whole world is now at PEACE!' we said to each other.

Ralph Partridge was amused at his wife's reaction because of her long-standing and ardent commitment to peace. Two days later, on the evening of 15 August, the family would watch torchlight processions at Penninis – 'like a pagan festival' – held to celebrate VJ-Day. They would return to Ham Spray on 23 August to be greeted by the unwelcome news that the clothes ration had been reduced. The RMS Scillonian *was an ancient passenger boat that had long carried passengers between Cornwall and the Scilly Isles. SEE ALSO PP. 811–12.*

Wednesday 15 August 1945: VJ-Day

Dr Michihiko Hachiya in Hiroshima reflects on the meaning of surrender

On 14 August the Japanese Emperor had recorded a speech announcing the Japanese surrender and telling his people that they must 'bear the unbearable'. Despite attempts to steal the recorded speech it was broadcast on 15 August – VJ-Day – bringing the war against Japan to an end.

The one word – surrender – had produced a greater shock than the bombing of our city. The more I thought, the more wretched and miserable I became.

But the order to surrender was the Emperor's order and to this we could not object. His injunction to bear the unbearable could mean but one thing. As a nation we must be patient. I repeated his words again and again to myself, but no matter how hard I tried, I could not rid my mind of despair. Finally, I found myself thinking of something else.

When war was declared four years ago, no one was unhappy about the consequences, but no one then had thought of this day. Why had the Emperor not been requested to speak then? He was not requested because Tojo was the only actor on the stage and did what he pleased. I can still hear his high-pitched voice ringing in my ears.

To myself, I began denouncing the army: 'What do you fellows think about the Emperor? You started the war at your pleasure. When the outlook was good, you behaved with importance; but when you began to lose, you tried to conceal your losses, and when you could move no more, you turned to the Emperor! Can you people call yourselves soldiers? You have no choice but to commit *harakiri* and die!'

As if echoing my thoughts, someone shouted: 'General Tojo, you great, thick-headed fool; cut your stomach and die!'

Goaded by the tumult in my mind and the general excitement, I thought I must flee and had reached the back gate of the Bureau when I was stopped by a voice that exclaimed: 'Doctor, what's the matter?'

This question brought me to my senses and I became ashamed that I had been on the verge of fleeing. I returned to the Bureau and my patients.

Only the voice of the Emperor, speaking on the radio for the first time, could ensure that the Japanese population would lay down their arms. Some wondered why he had not spoken earlier. For more than a decade there had been an assumption that Japan had become a victim not only of militarism but also of fascism. However, Japan's story of expansion and conquest was much more complex and was not characterized by a single figure with a clear vision; indeed, Japan's conquests had been marked by hesitation and uncertainty. Remarkably, in both the east and the west, leaders and populations alike mostly blamed General Tojo Hideki, rather than the Emperor, for Japan's excesses. The Emperor was rehabilitated after the war while Tojo went on to stand trial as a war criminal. SEE ALSO PP. 783–4, 798–9.

Masako Nojiri, a Japanese novelist at Kawasaki, listens to the Emperor's broadcast

In the morning, there was an announcement that His Majesty would make a personal broadcast at noon. After I wrote a message to the publishers twice, I entrusted Mr. Natsume who took it to Tokyo. As the 'Kimigayo' (the national anthem) was being played in the background, His Majesty, the Japanese Emperor officially announced through an Imperial mandate broadcast that he agreed and accepted the Potsdam Proposal and all conditions from the Cairo Meeting. That means: Taiwan, Manchuria and Korea were not to be Japanese occupied territories anymore and there would be an occupation of Japan. Although I have prepared for this in my heart, it is difficult to accept that this moment has actually come. It seemed to be an entirely unexpected event to all people throughout the world. In the afternoon I wrote a comment for the Third Company Confederation which Mr. Higashi Okayama requested. Although I never became upset, I was very exhausted and I postponed my writing as my ideas could not come out.

Sinozaki, from the tofu store came to me in the evening and told me that many people expected quite the opposite, they had expected 'good' news from the Emperor. As a result, they were shocked and disappointed with the Emperor's broadcast.

Masako Nojiri typifies the extent to which Japanese civilians were unprepared for surrender. Having been at war since 1937, they were used to a society of deprivation and 'war mobilization'. Although conditions had worsened markedly, they had been given only limited information about the defeats experienced by Japanese forces. The most that the population had expected was some kind of armistice; certainly not complete surrender. SEE ALSO P. 748–9.

Commander Hugh Mulleneux of the Royal Navy, with the British Pacific Fleet off Japan, watches the last diehards launch their attacks

Hugh Mulleneux had joined the Royal Navy in 1931 and served on a number of ships, including HMS Renown, *during the 1930s. During the Normandy landings in 1944 he had been a staff officer in Combined Operations Command. By 1945 he was serving with the British Pacific Fleet off the coast of Japan.*

VJ-Day. Air strikes started off as scheduled at about 0400 but were called off later and things looked hopeful. [The British aircraft carrier] 'Indefatigable' lost one Seafire – a tragic loss on such a day and one hopes the pilot is safe. At 0800 we had great news from the broadcast speech of President Truman and the Prime Minister although we didn't hear either of the speeches themselves. At 1120 we got the official signal to 'Cease Hostilities against Japan' which was made by flags and practically amounted to 'dressing ship'.

The Captain broadcast that the signal [*ship*] was flying orders as to cease hostilities against Japan – and I duly flocked up, like a school-boy, to the bridge to see the signal flying. As I arrived on the bridge there was a noise of machine gun fire which might be a fin-de-joie – but not a bit of it, it came from fighters overhead and was clearly followed by a Jap plane descending in flames – also a bomb which nearly hit 'Indefatigable'. There upon an order to Repel Aircraft status and [I] stayed there until about 1400! Admiral Halsey broadcast to the fleet at 1300 – a very good little speech. He also made a classic signal ordering 'All hands' – even the US Tank Corps – to 'Splice the Mainbrace' – which in fact applied to 14 British ships!

It is still hard to believe that it is really true. We have so much to thank God for, and now may He help us win the peace.

The British carrier HMS Indefatigable *and her complement of Seafires – Spitfires adapted for use on aircraft carriers – took part in air strikes against the Japanese home islands during late July and early August 1945, operating with the American 3rd Fleet. Her aircraft flew what was officially the last sortie of the war on 15 August 1945, in which her Seafires shot down eight enemy aircraft. She would join the Japanese surrender ceremony in Tokyo Bay on 3 September 1945, and then spent much of late 1945 ferrying Allied POWs to Australia.*

After the war Mulleneux served in the Gunnery and Anti-Aircraft Warfare Division of the Admiralty in the late 1940s and returned to sea with HMS Hornet *during the early 1950s before retiring in 1954.*

***

Ichiro Hatano, a teenage boy at Okatani in Japan, hears the news that the war is over

It's amazing, unbelievable! Yesterday, during the evening, my uncle arrived from Tokyo to tell us that the war is over. Nobody believed him at first; the conflict had seemed to be interminable. But it is true. Suddenly, all in a moment, the war is over.

It was the Emperor's decision; how great is His wisdom! Once again I marvel at His strength and His benevolence towards His people.

The war is over. Yet, despite my feeling of relief, I cannot welcome the news wholeheartedly. I hate the idea of our unconditional surrender; to my mind death would have been preferable.

On the one hand, I feel as though a window on one side of my heart were opening and letting in a breath of fresh air; on the other, I am despondent. What a contrast! Yesterday I was too happy to thank my uncle for coming to tell us the news, and today I can hardly bear to think of it.

What is going to be the outcome of it all? Will there really be peace and shall we be able to stay quietly at home with Mother? There is a rumour that, since Japan has lost, all the young men will be drafted into agriculture and all the girls will be sold to the enemy as prostitutes. I feel so bewildered that I cannot judge how much truth there is in all this gossip.

The only thing that is clear to me is that the war has ended before we are all dead and that we are going back to the house at Suwa, where we shall have a little more freedom than we do here. The house is not larger, but you can talk without the neighbours hearing everything you say; we shan't be for ever pestered by the horrible old woman here, who is always spying on us and scolding us; and Mother will have less to put up with. I shall suggest to her straight away that we take up our correspondence again; I get more interest and enjoyment from it than from a diary written for my eyes alone.

So I'll say good-bye to this diary today, although I think it is worth keeping carefully.

Ichiro's diary shows how hard it was for Japanese people even to find out about the impact of the atomic bombs. The radio had initially given his family the impression that the bomb damage at Hiroshima was 'very localized', but they learned a different story from friends. Ichiro was inclined to disbelieve initial reports, but by 9 August the truth had become obvious and he recorded: 'They say it is like hell there.' No-one knew what would happen next. His father's friend had advised him to buy a house in Tokyo as at present they were 'so cheap'. However, they thought it likely that Tokyo would also be a target for atomic bombing.

Later in 1945 Ichiro returned to Tokyo and eventually attended university there. SEE ALSO PP. 768–70.

H. L. Mencken, editorial writer for the *Baltimore Evening Sun*, watches 'morons' celebrating VJ-Day in Baltimore

When the end of the war was announced last night I was in my office, working on my record of my magazine days. My first news of it came with the blowing of factory whistles and ringing of church bells. Even the nuns of the House of [the] Good Shepherd clanged their bell, though only briefly. This was at 7.05 p.m. The uproar went on intermittently for two hours, with morons dashing by in their automobiles, blowing their horns. At 8.50 I went to Baltimore and Gilmor streets to mail letters. A few dozen of the neighborhood oakies, lintheads and other such vermin were gathered there in ragged groups, but they were making no noise. At 9.10 the celebration in West Baltimore ceased abruptly, and after that there was only an occasional toot of an automobile horn. I heard a couple of shots about midnight: they seemed to come from the linthead barracks in the 1500 block of Baltimore street.

The *Sun* of this morning reports that the crowd in Baltimore street, from Eutaw to the Fallsway, ran to 200,000. For 200,000 read 50,000: such estimates are always grossly exaggerated, especially when made by the police. In my reportorial days I often counted a crowd, and then asked the cops to estimate it. They always at least doubled it, and usually tripled or quadrupled it. Any number above 1,000 staggers a policeman.

The American people will now begin paying for their folly. The bills will keep on coming in for 50 years.

Henry Mencken had never been a fan of the war and had supported the isolationist cause prior to Pearl Harbor. Thereafter, he pondered the cost of the war to the American taxpayer. His sentiments were shared by many others and there was huge resentment at the cost of keeping soldiers overseas once the conflict had ended. There was little tolerance for the sorts of task of post-war occupation, administration and re-habilitation that MacArthur was beginning in his new role of Supreme Commander Allied Powers in Japan. Accordingly, many

of the American armed forces were demobilized remarkably quickly.
Henry Mencken suffered a cerebral thrombosis in 1948 from which he
never fully recovered, and died on 29 January 1956. SEE ALSO PP. 392–3.

Wednesday 15 – Friday 31 August 1945

Evelyn Waugh is demobilized and spends time with his son Auberon after VJ-Day

Evelyn Waugh was a talented novelist but a less than talented soldier.
In spite of this he had served in the Commandos, the Special Operations
Executive and finally the Special Air Service. For a while the Special Air
Service had sought action in the war against Japan, but when this bid
for further glory failed Waugh was demobilized and found himself
pressed reluctantly into the company of his family.

15 August, Ickleford, Hitchin
Peace declared. Public holiday. Remained more or less drunk
all day. Collected the boy Auberon at the Eldons and drove
him to Ickleford. He behaved very politely.

16 August
Another public holiday. Hangover, Winston [Churchill, the
Prime Minister's grandson] a boisterous boy with head too
big for his body. Randolph [Churchill] made a bonfire and
Auberon fell into it. American came to luncheon and signed
R.[andolph] up for highly profitable daily column. Some
village sports and damp bonfire and floodlit green.

31 August, Hyde Park Hotel
The boy Auberon stayed a week at Ickleford and won golden
opinions on all sides, even mine, so that I was encouraged to
have him for a few days in London and show him some
sights.
    On the day we returned, Wednesday, I took him to the
Zoo, which was crowded with the lower classes and
practically devoid of animals except rabbits and guinea pigs.
On Friday I devoted the day to him, hiring a car to fetch him

from Highgate and to return him there. I wore myself out for his amusement, taking him up the dome of St Paul's, buying him three-cornered postage stamps and austerity toys, showing him London from the top of the hotel, taking him to tea with Maimie, who gave him a sovereign and a box of variegated matches. Finally when I took him back to Highgate my mother said, 'Have you had a lovely day?' 'A bit dull.' So I felt absolved from paying further attention to him and sent him back to Pixton in Gabriel's charge on Monday. I have resumed the normal life of Hyde Park Hotel, White's, Nancy's shop, the Beefsteak.

The end of the war had little impact on Evelyn Waugh's well-established priorities, which were writing, socializing with the upper echelons, Roman Catholicism and drinking. Waugh continued to spend considerable time with his wartime special operations comrade Randolph Churchill, the wartime Prime Minister's son, whom he had accompanied on a mission to Yugoslavia. Waugh enjoyed a curious love–hate relationship with Randolph Churchill and a distant relationship with his own son Auberon. As his diary chronicles, he conspired to avoid spending time in the company of his family at Ickleford, near Hitchin; nevertheless he had managed to father five children by 1946. Although Waugh's diary chronicles his socializing, his writing goes almost unrecorded. However, he produced no fewer than three novels during wartime as a serving army officer.

Saturday 18 August 1945

Dr Michihiko Hachiya in Hiroshima talks to Mr Hirohata and observes the after-effects of radiation from the bomb

Downstairs I ran into Mr Hirohata sitting on a bench and sat down beside him. Mr. Hirohata had been employed in the Telephone Bureau and was at work in the building when the explosion occurred. Despite the fact that he was less than four hundred meters from the hypocenter, Mr. Hirohata escaped injury.

'How did you avoid injury when nearly everyone around you was killed or hurt?' I asked.

'The thick concrete wall of the building protected me,' answered Mr Hirohata, 'but people standing near the windows were killed instantly or died later from burns or cuts. The night shift was just leaving and the day shift coming on when the explosion occurred. Forty or more were killed near the entrance. About fifteen employees in the construction department, stripped to the waist, were outside taking gymnastics. They died instantly.

'Doctor, a human being who has been roasted becomes quite small, doesn't he? Those people all looked like little boys after the explosion. Is there any reason why my hair should be falling out and I feel so weak? I'm worried, doctor, because I have been told that I would die and this had already happened to some people I know who didn't seem to be hurt at all by the *pika* [bomb].'

'Mr Hirohata, I don't believe you need to worry about yourself,' I answered, trying to be reassuring. 'Like so many others, you've been through a dreadful experience, and on top of that have tried to work night and day here at the Bureau. What else could one expect? You must go home, stay absolutely quiet in bed, and get all the good nourishing food you can.'

There was something about this poor old man, the way he sat, his manner of speech, and color of his skin, that told me he was going to die. But what could one do?

The girl students came to help this morning and under the supervision of the nurses thoroughly cleaned the wards. Everything became neat and tidy.

Outside, a gentle rain was falling.

Residents of Hiroshima were astonished to find that their survival was sometimes determined by exactly where they had been standing at the time of the blast or even what they were wearing. Some were sheltered from the effects by walls near which they happened to be walking. Others found that their white clothing protected them from the flash while people nearby wearing black clothes were badly affected. Although Dr Hachiya recorded the after-effects of Hiroshima for only two months, they would continue for many years. The short-term effects were mostly flash burns and radiation sickness; longer-term effects included a range of tumours of the thyroid, breast, lung and salivary glands, leukaemia and birth defects. Casualties from the bomb stretched over some decades.

Michihiko Hachiya's Hiroshima diary first circulated among Japanese and American medics studying the effects of the blast and radiation. Warner Wells, a surgeon from the University of North Carolina, had noticed the work in an obscure medical journal of the Communications Ministry, for which Hachiya had worked in Hiroshima, and arranged for the work's translation. When it was published in the United States, in 1955, it received critical acclaim and was translated into more than a dozen languages. Hachiya accepted only a small sum for his work, which he put into an educational fund for children orphaned by the atomic bomb. SEE ALSO PP. 783–4, 791–2.

Thursday 23 – Thursday 30 August 1945

Hilda Bates, in Kuching internee camp in Borneo, enjoys a supply of fashion books

23 August

Still in ignorance of what is going on in the outside world, the Japs persist in saying that the war is *not* over. Nevertheless, they are furnishing the soldiers sick bay with bed chairs, and mosquito nets, and substantial amounts of medicine are being issued. Significant in itself, is the fact that the soldiers death list has fallen from ten to fifteen daily, to three or four.

26 August

The Japanese Commandant has stated his wish to speak to all the women in the chapel. We duly gathered there, where-upon he said he had good news for us, and solemnly read one of the pamphlets which we of course had seen long before! He then went on to say that owing to the wicked bombing by the Americans the Japanese had asked for peace, in order to save the lives of millions of Japanese women and children, but the Jap army wished to fight on. He was cut off from Tokyo and had received no orders, and we were to carry on as usual. Any unattached women with a friend in the men's camp, would now be allowed to visit him for half an hour.

27 August

To-day seven planes came over, just skimming the roofs of our huts, dropping more pamphlets, tooth brushes and powder, which were much appreciated after years of cleaning teeth with soot or twigs. The soldiers received shorts, hoes, and blankets with instructions not to appear naked in future!

30 August

At 11.30 a.m. today [a] sea-plane dropped twenty parachutes with packages attached. One fell outside our hut and was labelled 'bread.' Others contained flour, tinned rabbit, and other meat.

The goods were collected by the Japs under the supervision of Australian Officers who distributed them to the groups of internees. All sorts of what we had thought of as luxuries arrived; such as sugar, sweets, milk, bundles of clothing, and even fashion books!

Japanese treatment of POWs and internees improved markedly in many areas during July and August 1945, reflecting a recognition by some camp commanders that the war was drawing to an end and they might be called to account. In some locations, especially in Thailand, the Allies had even infiltrated secret service personnel close to camps to help smuggle in vital supplies to help prolong the lives of the prisoners, whose health was now very precarious. Bates was fortunate, for Borneo was the site of several massacres during 1945 in which approximately 600 POWs and a similar number of civilians died as guards vented their frustrations about the way the war was going. SEE ALSO PP. 684–5, 746–8, 812–13, 834.

Saturday 25 August – Wednesday 5 September 1945

Tom Forsyth, a Canadian POW, is liberated from Camp Niigata 5B in Japan

At 20 to nine on Aug 25th, 1945 a flight of American planes flew over our camp, circled, wheeled, dived and rolled, eleven Sikorsky's and one Grumman fighter. We all crowded in the square and waved our hands and yelled our heads off. It was a time of great rejoicing, we felt we were almost free.

This afternoon two different flights came over, dropped some toilet articles, cigarettes, chocolates, books, magazines, etc. Thereafter, every second or third day the B-29s began to come over and opening their bomb bays would vomit forth 40 gal steel drums full of food supplies. Sometimes they would be in twos, the bottoms welded together. Too often they broke away from the parachutes and dropped like a stone and when they hit the ground they crumpled like paper. It was maddening to see tomato juice sprayed on the ground. At times the dropping supplies were actually dangerous. A Japanese woman 200 yards outside the camp was struck by a case of canned peaches. Sgt Neal said it was the best thing that ever hit her, but it killed the poor woman. One of our men saw a drum dropping through the treetops, he leaped right out of his wooden sandals and ran. When he went back to look for his sandals they were beneath the drum!

Several bales crashed through the roofs of our huts. One pilot dropped a bale right through the middle of the big P.O.W. sign, others dropped their loads as far away as half a mile from camp. We had to form a picket line around the outskirts of the area to keep the Japanese civilians away. Most planes flew too low and did not give the chutes a chance to open, but the ones who flew high and judged accurately provided a wonderful spectacle for us when the chutes opened and drifted down they were a beautiful sight. They were white, blue, orange and green. They were fascinating to watch for they brought food, and food meant life.

When the first planes came over Major Fellowes persuaded the Japanese interpreter to go with him to Tokyo and make arrangements for our camp to be evacuated. We really gorged on the supplies dropped to us and the American rations to carry with us on our train trip. We left 5B forever on the night of Sept. 5th. When we left our camp the guards were still armed and the nearest Americans were many, many miles away. We rode in trucks to a lonely part of the railroad far from any station, and still a small curious crowd collected out of nowhere.

In August 1945 a vast operation was mounted by the Allies to try to reach POWs with supplies and medical aid with all possible speed. The intelligence services had been ordered to turn their attention to tracking down POW camps and even making contact before the surrender to ensure rapid recovery. By the end of the war the appalling treatment of POWs was well known and the race was on to save as many as possible. Sadly some died from their maltreatment while awaiting liberation or shortly afterwards.

Tom Forsyth survived to be liberated from Camp Niigata 5B and returned to Canada on 2 October 1945. Three weeks later he received a parcel from his parents which had been sent to him in 1941; it had clearly got as far as Japan, as it had Japanese characters stamped on it. In the 1990s Tom Forsyth was living at Ferne Middleton in Ontario. SEE ALSO PP. *180–1, 433–4, 501–2.*

SEPTEMBER 1945

ON 2 SEPTEMBER the American battleship *Missouri* provided a memorable venue for the signing of the surrender treaty with Japan. General Douglas MacArthur accepted the surrender, while Admirals Nimitz and Fraser signed for the United States and Britain respectively. Japan was represented by General Yoshijiro Umezu, Chief of the Army General Staff, at the head of a large delegation of diplomats and officers. Two days later, having heard about the surrender ceremony, Japanese forces on Wake Island finally laid down their arms. On 7 September the Japanese garrison on the Ryukyus Islands surrendered at Kadina air base. Elsewhere, small numbers of Japanese forces, cut off from their lines of communications, fought on. On 5 September American troops in Tokyo arrested Iva Togo Aquino, a Japanese American suspected of being 'Tokyo Rose', the wartime radio propagandist. Three days later General Tojo, who was already in Allied custody, attempted suicide in order to avoid trial. He was unsuccessful and instead spent some time in hospital.

In September 1945 Mountbatten completed the surrender ceremony of the Japanese forces in Malaya. Keen to include all involved in the fighting, he invited the guerrillas of the Malayan Communist Party to participate. This parade was widely photographed. Within two years these victory photographs would become a key source in tracking down the guerrillas after they broke with the government and triggered the Malaya Emergency, which ran from 1948 until 1960. The British would hold Malaya until 1958.

Elsewhere the end of the war had prompted calls for imperial retreat. On 20 September Mahatma Gandhi and Jawaharlal Nehru demanded that British troops leave India at once. However, they were now pushing at an open door, since Clement Attlee, the new British Prime Minister, was no less averse to the concept of empire than Gandhi. Across south Asia, a speedy process would see the creation of the independent states of India, Pakistan, Burma and Ceylon within three years of the end of the war.

On 2 September Ho Chi Minh declared the independence of Vietnam in his new capital of Hanoi – to the alarm of the French, who wished to recover their colony. Indeed, Free French forces in the Far East had been blind to almost any cause other than resuming control of French Indochina by any means possible. Allied officers arrived in Hanoi to find that Ho Chi Minh had set up a provisional independent government there. However, further south, the French were already gaining control of Saigon, assisted by British troops and some rearmed Japanese forces. On 26 September Colonel Peter Dewey, a member of the Office of Strategic Services – forerunner of the CIA – was shot and killed by the Vietminh in Saigon. He was later gazetted the first American casualty in Vietnam.

On 11 September the Council of [Allied] Foreign Ministers met for the first time. This council was intended to function as the 'engine-room' of a process that sought to resolve the remaining disagreements over the post-war settlements. However, the foreign ministers, including Truman's new appointee, Jimmy Byrnes, proved unable to agree on the peace treaties with Bulgaria, Hungary, Italy or Romania because of arguments with the Soviet Union over free elections in eastern Europe. Tempers frayed, and the meeting eventually broke up over the issue of Chinese and French participation in the negotiations. The collapse of this conference revealed a growing rift between east and west which would soon be referred to as the Cold War.

Throughout September the national processes for dealing with traitors continued. Vidkun Quisling, the Norwegian Nazi leader, was sentenced to death in Oslo. In the Far East, the process was divided between the major war crimes trials of figures such as Tojo in Tokyo, which would take a period of some four years, and minor trials of middle-ranking officers and guards in locations such as Manila and Singapore. Britain's gathering of evidence for war crimes trials had already begun in Singapore, where statements were collected from former POWs, most of which related to war crimes against the POWs themselves. A total of 35,963 such statements were taken. Efforts were also being made to collect information from local people who were victims of Japanese crimes and who could act as witnesses.

Saturday 1 September 1945

General Joseph Stilwell talks with the deputy chief of the Manhattan Project and then visits the ruined city of Yokohama

In October 1944 Stilwell had been recalled from China to the United States and replaced by General Albert Wedemeyer. He had gone on to be Chief of Army Ground Forces and commanded the US 10th Army on Okinawa after the death of General Buckner in June 1945. By September he had time to talk to a range of interesting people in Tokyo, including Brigadier-General Thomas F. Farrell, who was deputy to Leslie Groves, head of the Manhattan Project, and was representing him in field operations in the Pacific.

Eight-thirty: weather very dirty. Farrell says the atomic scientists are a bunch of temperamental bugs. Screw each other's wives. Squabble. Rush off on tangents. Have to be herded and pushed around to keep their noses on the job. Only war could get them together. He says they are capable of solving *any* problem whatsoever. Oppenheimer the keenest brain. Many Jews among them. The Limmie Anderson [Sir John Anderson] violated the agreement, and gave Joliott's associates unauthorized information. Joliott [Joliot: leading French nuclear scientist and communist] wild because French not included. Threatened to tell the Russians. U.S. is stockpiling materials and will strip the Belgian Congo of raw stuff as quickly as possible. We control secrets of manufacture. Bomb arrived by 4 barometric devices and detonated by proximity fuses. Force of explosion is measured by blast instruments on parachutes dropped by accompanying planes. Light of explosion = 1000 suns . . .

At 1:15, rode through town, up the bluff to race-course and CP, Eleventh Airborne. Back and all through town to Kawasaki. The place is *ruined*. Completely gutted. Soul-satisfying sight. Only the stone, brick and concrete buildings remain standing. Safes standing where the stores burned down around them. Shanties dot the rusty landscape. Almost impossible to locate anything. Main routes remain, but business is 100% dead. Naturally the place looked dead when we came in. It is whatakick to stare at the arrogant, ugly brown-faced, buck-toothed, bowlegged bastards, and realize where this puts them. Many newly demobilized soldiers around. Most police salute. People generally apathetic. We gloated over the destruction and came in at 3:00 feeling fine. Rain continues.

Brigadier-General Farrell had been asked to oversee the scientific and medical investigations into the effects of the Hiroshima and Nagasaki explosions. He was also arranging a more secret programme to assess how far the Japanese had progressed with their own nuclear programme. Stilwell's visit to Yokohama, a city devastated by conventional bombing with B-29s, reminds us that more people died in some of these conventional attacks than in the atomic attacks at Hiroshima and Nagasaki.

General Joe Stilwell would continue his inimitable and pugnacious diary beyond the end of the war in Asia and the Pacific. He died after an operation on 12 October 1946 at the age of sixty-three. SEE ALSO PP. 357–9, 421–2, 615–16.

Sunday 2 September 1945

Don McLaren, an Australian POW in Japan, enjoys an emergency food drop

Don McLaren had been taken prisoner in Singapore in 1942 and in 1943 had been put to work on the Thai–Burma railway, assisting in the construction of the famous 'Pack of Cards' bridge. In contrast to the many POWs who were returned to Changi after the completion of the railway, Don McLaren was moved to Japan, where he had been used for forced labour. By early September McLaren and his fellow POWs were regularly wandering around the camp, exploring the nearby countryside and buying fresh vegetables, but they were still awaiting recovery and were dependent on air drops for supplies.

We did have one problem now with the food coming out in parachutes. It was dropping at times a mile or more from the camp, and if we were not quick it would be gone. One box that was dropped contained underwear, typical army issue, sleeveless singlets and long legged cotton underpants. I got hold of a pair of underpants, cut the legs off, and so I had a pair of shorts, however no pocket. I have been doing some trading and have the tidy sum of 130 yen saved up, so I must have a pocket.

When I first joined the army in 1940, I was issued with the usual 'housewife', (it's a little kit with needles, cotton and bits of wool). I have always kept it and often used it, so now I have made a very neat fob pocket to store my wealth.

I was showing the boys my new shorts and the fob pocket loaded with yen when the call went up, 'Aircraft approaching' and yes, sure enough, a B29 is coming in, bomb doors open and out comes the parachutes.

It was great to watch, but we had so much food, we didn't need any for days. One parachute failed to open. It had a round thing dangling from it and the object was coming straight at me. I know enough about falling objects that you never turn and run, make sure nothing is behind you, walk backwards until you know you are no longer in the line of fall. I could tell after several paces this object will not hit me, so I stopped. Bang, this drum hit the ground with a terrible force. It burst open and all I could see for a few seconds was a sheet of green. Next thing, splat, the green stuff was liquid pea soup. I was covered in it. I could hear men in hysterics. I couldn't see a bloody thing. I kept saying 'get me some water, get some water!' I eventually cleared my eyes and scraped it off my torso, but you should have seen my fob pocket, it was full of pea soup and all my yen was covered in soup.

On 10 September Don McLaren would be recovered by American forces who took him by truck to a nearby air base. He would then be flown by DC-3 over Nagasaki – 'the devastation was unbelievable' – to Okinawa. From there he would be flown to Manila and be placed on a hospital ship to take him home to Australia, via New Zealand. Numerous national groups had been taken to Japan for use as slave labour, and McLaren found that he was sharing part of the journey with Javanese prisoners who were also going home. SEE ALSO PP. 238–9, 387–8, 821–2.

Tuesday 4 – Wednesday 5 September 1945

Henry L. Stimson, Secretary of War, discusses future control of the atomic bomb with Byrnes and Truman

Henry Stimson formally tendered his resignation to Harry S. Truman on 4 September 1945, largely on grounds of ill health. His major project in his last days of office had been an attempt to work out a framework for the control of atomic power.

4 September

At the Pentagon I tried to arrange my duties so far as possible so as to confine them to getting off [retiring] . . . But it is dreadfully hard to pull free from the entanglements of such a position as I am in.

Then I found there was an invitation to go to the White House for their first luncheon Cabinet meeting.

At the talk afterwards with Byrnes I took up the question which I had been working at with McCloy up in St. Hubert's, namely how to handle Russia with the big bomb. I found that Byrnes was very much against any attempt to cooperate with Russia. His mind is full of his problems with the coming meeting of the foreign ministers and he looks to having the presence of the bomb in his pocket, so to speak, as a great weapon to get through the thing he has. He also told me of a number of acts of perfidy, so to speak, of Stalin which they had encountered at Potsdam and felt in the light of those that we could not rely upon anything in the way of promises from them. I told him our views as contained in the memorandum, the latest copy of which I had taken over there but which I did not take into the meeting. Then we parted and he started off for his mission abroad . . .

5 September

The President said he was very sorry to have me go. He would have been glad to have me stay through his term but he recognized that I had necessary reasons for going. He told me that I should make up my mind when it would be most convenient to me and let him know and that it would take effect then ... We also arranged that he is to let me know when I could have a longer interview with him than was possible this morning in order to cover a number of things on which I am preparing to leave with him my final views. The chief of these I said was the subject of our relations with Russia in regard to the atomic bomb, and I described the talk that I had had with Byrnes and told him what our differences were. I told him that both my plan and Byrnes' plan contained chances which I outlined, and I said that I thought that in my method there was less danger than in his and also we would be on the right path towards world establishment of an international world, while on his plan we would be on the wrong path in that respect and would be tending to revert to power politics.

Stimson had seen value in using the atomic bomb against Japan partly because it would underline American power in dealing with the Soviet Union. He had also been keen to close down any opportunities for Soviet land-grabbing in Asia. Nevertheless, looking to the long term he could see that the west could not keep the bomb secret for long and advocated international control, perhaps by the United Nations or some other world body. This approach was not adopted and instead Truman was soon referring to the atomic bomb as America's 'sacred trust'. Stimson was right, for while many predicted that the Soviet Union would not acquire the bomb until the mid-1950s, in fact Moscow tested its first atomic weapon in August 1949.

Stimson retired after the war and died in New York on 20 October 1950. SEE ALSO PP. 119–21, 787–9.

Wednesday 5 September 1945

Frances Partridge reckons with the reality of atomic
warfare and a world of fear

The Times this morning had a correspondent's account of the
effects of the atomic bomb. They are beyond words horrible
and sickening to the heart. Now, days and weeks after the
explosion, people unhurt at the time are falling ill and dying;
even the doctors who came to take care of the wounded are
succumbing. The symptoms are terrible – the skin becomes
patched with blue, there is bleeding from nose and mouth,
and when inoculations are given the flesh rots away from the
needle. Death always follows. I thought with despair of poor
Burgo, now so full of zest for life and unaware of its horrors.
My own instincts lead me to love life, but as I read on, a
desire welled up inside me to be dead and out of this hateful, revolting, mad world. Ralph and I talk and talk about it,
and the conviction is growing in my mind that this is the *end*
of the world and civilization we have known and enjoyed.
Either by accident or design, how can it possibly be that
someone will not destroy the earth? Any power wishing for
world domination can get it in a single night by blotting out
all its rivals, without any declaration of war, and Fear, that
most potent force, will reign supreme. I see the earth
reduced to a few meteorites and moons circling round in
empty space. Nobody can deny all this if you put it to them,
but human beings are too emotionally drained to react as
violently as one might expect. It's as if exhausted humanity
had sunk back into inarticulacy.

*The speed with which the public appreciated the extent to which atomic
warfare had changed the nature of the world was remarkable. Within
days, complex debates about international control, disarmament and
deterrence had sprung up in the broadsheet press. Few were optimistic
about the possibility of avoiding further instances of atomic bombing
over time. However, at this stage the full scope of the dangers presented
by such weapons, especially long-term problems associated with*

radiation, were not widely understood, even by the scientists who had developed the weapons. Statesmen quickly equated atomic bombs with great power status, and even the new Labour government couldn't resist this association. Debating the issue of whether Britain should acquire nuclear weapons in October 1946, Ernest Bevin, the Foreign Secretary, would insist: 'We have got to have this thing over here whatever it costs . . . we've got to have the bloody Union Jack on top of it.'

Frances Partridge continued to live at Ham Spray with her husband and fellow pacifist Ralph until he died in 1960. She told the story of her circle of friends, the Bloomsbury set, in seven volumes of diaries and memoirs which she began to publish at the age of seventy-eight. She died at her Belgravia home in February 2004 at the age of 103. SEE ALSO P. 789–90.

Saturday 15 September 1945

Hilda Bates hears of Japanese plans for the civilian internees in Kuching camp in Borneo

Yesterday I went to a luncheon party given by Australian officers, together with other internees, and we were driven there in a truck thoughtfully provided with a long settee so that we could sit comfortably, instead of having to crouch on the floor, Nip fashion!

We visited the wharf, and it was so good to see shi[ps] flying British and American ensigns. The officers brought us back to the billets, and stayed with us until 6 p.m.

The Australians in charge of the evacuation take little rest; Nothing seems too good for us, or is too much trouble to carry out.

There was still many very sick soldiers now in Kuching Hospital – which has been entirely re-equipped. It is grand to note their improvement in health, – many having put on a stone in weight within a few days.

Our late Japanese Commandant [Lieutenant Colonel Suga] yesterday committed hari-kiri after being interrogated by the Australians. His method was to plunge a blunt knife into his belly with the assistance of his batman. The second-in-command [Captain Nagata] also tried to do this, but without success. Then the Jap doctor [Lieutenant Yamamoto] attempted to cut his throat by rubbing it on barbed wire, but was told to desist by an Australian, who remarked 'That's enough, my lad; You can have another shot to-morrow!'

Official orders to the Commandant from Japanese High Command [dated 17 August] have been found in his quarters to this effect:-

1. All prisoners of war and male internees to be marched to a camp at milestone 21, – and bayonetted there.
2. All sick unable to walk to be treated similarly in the Square at Kuching.
3. All women and children to be burnt in their barracks.

These orders did not endear the Japanese to the Australians and we were thankful that we had not known of them earlier. It seemed that we had only forty-eight hours to live, – before the actual capitulation.

Although Colonel Suga Tatsuji had not had time to carry out the last fateful order, his staff had destroyed most of the camp records before the arrival of the Australian forces, making it impossible to trace many individuals. Had he not committed suicide, Suga would almost certainly have been tried for other crimes committed during the war. Many atrocities had been committed against POWs in Borneo and accordingly Suga's superior, General Doihara Kenji, was hanged for his crimes in 1948. SEE ALSO PP. 684–5, 746–8, 800–1, 834.

Sunday 16 September 1945

Stephen Spender, writer and expert on German culture, and his driver discuss fraternization with the Germans

By August 1945, the writer Stephen Spender had joined a small team of specialists who were looking at the problem of recreating the German educational system from the bottom up. They were part of a larger programme of 'denazification' and their task was to visit universities and libraries, eliminating any traces of influence left by the Third Reich.

Met my driver at breakfast and walked with him to the garage outside Bonn where the Humber is being repaired. I talked quite a lot to him because I worry about him having nothing to do. He said he was getting very browned off as all he had to do now every day was go to the garage and watch them at work on the car. He said they had tested every part of it and replaced all those that seemed deficient. Theoretically the car ought to be in perfect running order, but in fact it went on behaving exactly as it had done a week ago. He said he thought the trouble must be the carburettor, which cannot be replaced.

He told me that he had quite a time in the evenings and that now he had a nice girl, aged 18. I asked: 'Do you take precautions so that you won't get her into trouble?' He looked astonished and answered: 'I never touch her, I wouldn't think of doing so, that wouldn't be any pleasure for me nor for her, sir.' I was rather dazed by this reply. He told me that he thought it would be very wrong, in times like these, to leave a girl with a baby. He said, 'It makes me very angry, sir, sometimes to read in newspapers and see what they imagine our fellows do when they fraternize out here. As a matter of fact, very few do what they think at all. I myself wouldn't dream of it. Yet even my girl at home thinks the same thing.'

He told me that one night he and another chap had gone to a fair with their girls and that on their way back they ran into some Germans who were attacking some other German girls who had been fraternizing with our men. So they had a free fight with the Germans and saw their girls home as well as their own girls.

In 1945 women in areas of Germany that had been occupied by the British and Americans often faced violence from German men who resented relationships between their countrywomen and occupation troops. 'Fraternization' was accelerated by the relative affluence of occupying troops and the destitution of local women. Initially, all social contact between Allied soldiers and local civilians was forbidden, but

these restrictions were gradually lifted. The decorous pattern of
behaviour professed by Stephen Spender's driver was not followed by all
Allied soldiers and it was common for troops to use ample supplies of
food and cigarettes to buy the favours of local women.

After the war, Stephen Spender would be an active commentator on
culture and the arts; he spent some of his time working for the CIA-
sponsored Congress for Cultural Freedom.

Thursday 20 September 1945

Peggy Wightman, a Wren signaller serving at the naval headquarters on Ceylon, assists with British POWs returning from the camps in Thailand

I am exhausted now from a very worthwhile day. I have
been with the prisoners; we had to be at the Officers' Club to
meet them when they came ashore. I can't begin to tell you
how dreadful it is. When they first come in they are all so
dazed and nervous, three very ill looking naval officers came
in first and they were rather overcome by everything. The
Club, run by the NAAFI, had put up a wonderful show; it is
closed except to the repatriated prisoners and their friends,
everything is free, and they are showered with chocolates
and cigarettes and provided with a lovely lunch. Actually
another officer and I brought two naval commanders up to
our Mess for lunch, they were so grateful it was pathetic,
they looked like very old men and yet they can't have been
more than in their early forties. They all want to talk about
the camp, although they also asked thousands of questions.
They had kept up with the news remarkably well but four
years is a long time so some of the things they asked us
about seemed very odd.

They were terribly hopeful and talked as though everything would be as they left it at home. They said their last
letters were two years old, it worried us that they seemed to
think their wives and girl friends would be just where they
had been in October 1943. I only hope they will be able to
find them. One man didn't know where his wife was; three

years ago she was in South Africa and he had hoped to find a cable at the bank but there was nothing for him, however he was sure he would find a letter waiting for him when he got back on board.

We had transport and took them all around the town, they wanted to shop and buy presents to take home. One wanted to know how to buy a lipstick, he said he had almost forgotten the taste of it but thought it wouldn't be long before he found out.

By September large numbers of liberated British POWs passed through Ceylon, where they berthed for two or three days at a time, on ships moving them from Burma and Thailand back to Britain. Many of them were in a very poor state of health and their stories shocked the service personnel on Ceylon who offered them assistance.

Peggy Wightman survived the war and continued to serve on Ceylon at Trincomalee during 1946. She returned to England in late 1946 and served for two years at naval shore stations, eventually living at Petersfield in Hampshire. She met her husband, Barry Kent, also a signaller, during her naval service. Her diaries and letters lay undiscovered in the attic until found there by her husband in 1993. SEE ALSO PP. 675–7.

OCTOBER – DECEMBER 1945

DURING OCTOBER reinforcements began to arrive in south-east Asia to assist Admiral Mountbatten in maintaining control of an expanded command area. At the end of the war his area of responsibility had been increased to incorporate French Indochina and the Netherlands East Indies. The British, French and Dutch refused to accept declarations of independence by Indonesia and Vietnam, and in Indochina, General Douglas Gracey and the 20th Indian Division had found themselves in the awkward position of handing over power to a hated French administration which was gradually returning. The British kept order, but the scale of the task meant rearming surrendered

Japanese prisoners. Vietminh insurgents attempting to prevent the return of the French were met by force from curious mixed parties consisting of British troops, Gurkhas, rearmed Japanese and French Foreign Legionnaires, some of whom had been serving in the German army only months before. In the Netherlands East Indies, Britain's General Christison also rearmed Japanese troops in the effort to maintain order in a dangerous situation where Dutch colonialists and Indonesian nationalists alike were spoiling for a fight.

Ambassador Patrick J. Hurley, America's representative in China, had continued to pursue a hard line in support of the Chiang Kai-shek nationalist regime, and had busied himself in purging the American embassy of anyone who had sought a compromise with the communists. He made his preferences clear by regularly referring to the communist leader as 'Moose Dung'. Hurley's policy was bolstered by the arrival of significant numbers of US Marines, fresh from conflict in the Pacific. Officially they were there to disarm the Japanese, but in reality they offered support to Chiang's forces and offset the growing Soviet presence in Manchuria.

Also during October, the US commander General George S. Patton – always something of a firebrand – was removed from his post for making press comments that were supposedly sympathetic to former Nazis. (The Nazi Party had been outlawed in Germany by this time.) His misfortunes were further compounded by a serious car crash, in which he received injuries as a result of which he would die in late December.

In a climate of intensifying friction with the Soviet Union, western military planners were anxious to learn what they could from the Germans about how to fight the Russians. Nevertheless, some semblance of Allied solidarity was maintained by the war crimes trials now under way. On 18 October the first session of the International Military War Crimes Tribunal at Nuremberg began proceedings against twenty-one senior figures of the Nazi state. All pleaded innocent. The following day indictments were issued against the most prominent figures involved in the war. A week later one of the defendants, Robert Ley, former chief of the German Labour Front, committed suicide. On 25 October the UN Charter was ratified by its major signatories and came into force.

By the middle of November the Chinese civil war was intensifying, with a struggle developing for the part of Manchuria that Soviet forces had not yet occupied. Nationalist troops had attempted to begin an offensive into south-west Manchuria through the Liaodong Peninsula, but found their way blocked by the occupying Soviet force, which was busy disarming the Japanese. Instead the nationalist forces landed in Chinwangtao, in an area held by the US marines, and attacked across the Great Wall of China. By late November they had reached Chinchow. While the nationalists moved into areas not under Russian control, the new communist Chinese 4th Army avoided areas under the control of recently arrived units of US marines and so occupied most of Shantung province. Here, amid immense confusion, the remnants of the Second World War overlapped with an emerging Cold War.

In south-east Asia, Mountbatten was increasingly perturbed by political problems within his greatly expanded command area. Relative stability prevailed in Malaya and Burma. In Thailand, the British declared themselves to be occupying an enemy country and sought a harsh peace. In the Netherlands East Indies, fighting between recently arrived British troops and the local nationalists who had recently declared an independent Indonesia was increasing and a senior British officer, Brigadier Mallaby, had been killed in the fighting. The British finally decided that they had little option other than force and swiftly landed 24,000 troops of the 5th Division, along with 24 Sherman tanks. After an ultimatum was ignored, considerable fighting ensued. Only in late November did the British have enough troops to begin to control important flashpoints and centres of resistance such as Surabaya and Semarang.

In Germany, administrators of the occupying powers were struggling with different types of problem. Large numbers of displaced people, together with a shortage of fuel, food and housing, presented an impending humanitarian crisis on a massive scale. Meanwhile, the military were confronted with the sizeable task of building a denazified infrastructure, which involved intervening in many aspects of civilian life. Typically, the revival of German civilian radio required the appointment of music control officers who would watch out for the playing of military marches and other types of 'inflammatory' music. Local concert programmes had to be scrutinized to remove works appropriated by the Nazis, such as Siegfried's funeral march from Wagner's *Götterdämmerung* and the slow movements of Beethoven's Third and Seventh Symphonies. They were ordered to be particularly vigilant against the playing of Beethoven's 'Eroica' on Hitler's birthday.

On 5 December Patrick J. Hurley resigned his ambassadorship in China, having failed to negotiate a peace between the rival claimants to government. In fact, he had never sought a settlement on terms other than dominance for Chiang Kai-shek. A master at blaming others, he claimed his failure was attributable to pro-communist American Foreign Service officers. Few diplomats stationed in China at the time could foresee the dire consequences of these cavalier charges. By the early 1950s, all those who had genuinely sought a settlement in China would be hounded out of government by Senator Joseph McCarthy. On 14 December General of the Army George C. Marshall arrived in China as the personal representative of President Harry S. Truman. Like Hurley, he was assigned the task of mediating in the dispute between the communists and the nationalists. Although his efforts were genuine, they were no less futile. As the communist delegation emerged from a plane at an airport near Chungking, they were beaten by nationalist soldiers and had to be rescued by American diplomats. This blatant hostility pointed the way to China's turbulent future.

During December almost 100 German industrialists who had been close to Hitler were arrested. Many SS personnel, convicted of atrocities at Belsen and other concentration camps, were hanged. However, it became clear that minor war crimes were so widespread as to be almost innumerable. The occupying authorities became perplexed about how to deal with the ensuing issues of justice without incarcerating a very large number of people for some decades. Subsequently some of the sentences distributed appeared increasingly light.

Admiral Mountbatten, now established in his new headquarters at Singapore, was anxious to begin war crimes trials relating to the Asia–Pacific conflict as soon as possible. However, he had to wait for London to finalize the proper procedure for the trials of Japanese suspects, which did not happen until 12 October. At this point the Attorney-General, Hartley

Shawcross, opted to delegate most decisions, including those about whose crimes would warrant the death sentence, to a local judge advocate-general organization in Singapore. This allowed the first British trials to begin in January 1946, while proceedings in Tokyo would not begin until six months later. Even so, the trials in Singapore would proceed more slowly than many had hoped. In May 1946 there would still be nearly 9,000 suspects under arrest awaiting trial. Ultimately, as in Germany, the authorities would have to accept that the scale of the task was beyond completion, and fewer than a thousand were eventually prosecuted. Of those, 919 suspects would be brought before the court, and 220 death sentences carried out. In Tokyo, where the twenty-five 'top' war criminals of the conflict in Asia and the Pacific would be tried, seven would eventually face a death sentence, including General Tojo Hideki. By October 1949 all war crimes proceedings would be terminated.

The remnants of Europe and Asia now crawled towards a semblance of peace. Despite the creation of the new United Nations organization, trust was already in short supply. British and American leaders had not forgotten that the Soviet Union had been an ally of their main enemy in Europe for the first two years of the war and that it still hoped to hang on to most of the gains it had made during its period of collaboration with Hitler. The Soviet Union had also respected its neutrality pact with the Allies' other main enemy, Japan, until after the close of the war with Germany. Conversely, Moscow firmly believed that the west had stood back deliberately and waited for Soviet troops to wear Germany down, at enormous cost in Russian lives, before embarking on a short campaign in the west beginning with D-Day in June 1944. On the ground, friction was already developing among the four occupying powers of conquered Germany, and in the rubble of Berlin the contest of Cold War espionage had already begun in earnest.

On 22 December 1945 the veteran American correspondent Charles Sulzberger, on a visit to London, was invited to dinner there by the American diplomat Adlai Stevenson and his wife. Among the other guests was a Soviet diplomat, Andrei Gromyko. Both Stevenson and Gromyko would eventually play important roles in the emerging Cold War, notably during the Cuban Missile Crisis of 1962. On this occasion the dinner-table talk was about where to build the permanent headquarters of the UN. Churchill had apparently already suggested either Geneva or Marrakesh, the latter being a location he had come to love as a result of his wartime visits. Sulzberger interjected at this point and suggested that central Berlin should be kept in its current state of devastation and used as the seat for the UN headquarters building. A surprised Gromyko asked why. 'Because', Sulzberger responded, 'it is the best example of what happens without international order. You should build a round tower as a headquarters and each floor should have a wide balcony all around it. Then, if there is any disagreement, the statesmen can adjourn their talks and go out and see what happens when statesmen disagree.' Adlai Stevenson apparently smiled, while Andrei Gromyko grunted. Sulzberger noted in his diary: 'No one thought I was serious. But I was.'

Monday 8 October 1945

Don McLaren, a liberated POW, stops off in Wellington and visits a cake shop on the long journey home to Australia

I went ashore and saw these beautiful cream cakes in a shop window. I went inside and asked the lady, 'How much are those cream cakes?' She told me, 'Four and eleven pence.' I pulled out my yen. That was all the money I had.

I told her, 'I'll give you 100 yen, that will be a lot more than four and eleven pence.' She looked at me as though I had the plague. I said, 'I really want that cream cake.' Again the plague stare. A police officer was in the shop and he heard me say, 'I really want that cream cake.' He saw my 100 yen and asked me, 'Where are you from?' I told him that I'm off the hospital ship and I've just come from Japan.

I don't know why, I'm a grown man, but I started to cry. The woman started howling, it was very embarrassing. The police officer paid for the cake and I made him take the 100 yen. I went back to the ship with my cake and I shared it. We thought, how wonderful, cakes and cups of tea.

Lucky for us Aussies, a ship tied up near our hospital ship and was sailing to Sydney the next day. The ship's name was 'Tijitjalenka' and was due in Sydney on Friday, October 12. We made some wild statements to the Red Cross clown that we wanted to go on that ship. After several hours of typical red tape, we were informed we would indeed be going on that ship. We were so excited, our school boy stuff came out and we started to talk to the clown. (It took me years and years to accept the Red Cross.) More on that later.

The journey across the Tasman was extremely rough and not one of us was sea sick. On our last morning at sea, every ex-prisoner of war was up on deck peering over the bow, just waiting to see Australia. It wasn't long after we could all see Australia.

I'm not ashamed of it, we were all crying . . .

Don McLaren noted that at this point he did not know how very few of his original unit had survived. He observed that had he realized how many would not see Australia again he would have been yet more emotional. Many of those who did survive suffered from what we now term 'post-traumatic stress' and had difficulty readjusting to civilian life. Don tried returning to his old job at Amber & Sons, but could not settle down to a conventional routine. Instead, he joined a friend and fellow ex-serviceman in a trapping business which allowed them both to live an open-air existence. Eventually he returned to the furniture business in Adelaide, married and had two daughters. He obtained his pilot's licence in 1970 and was still flying in 1992 at seventy years of age. SEE ALSO PP. 238–9, 387–8, 807–9.

Monday 29 October 1945

Gustave Gilbert, Nuremberg psychologist, takes the opportunity to speak with Hermann Goering in his cell

Gustave Gilbert had arrived at Nuremberg on 23 October 1945, the day that the International Military Tribunal received the indictment against twenty-three Nazi war criminals. He had spent the war as a German-speaking intelligence officer. He was also a trained psychologist and now

served in that role and also as interpreter and liaison man for the
prison commandant, Colonel B. C. Andrus. As a psychologist, Gilbert
expressed a personal interest in 'what made human beings join the Nazi
movement and do the things they did', and – being a fluent German
speaker – he tried to engage his charges in 'normal' conversations, rather
than interrogations, hoping that this might throw some light on these
questions.

(After commenting on Robert Ley's suicide) [Goering said]
'. . . I hope Ribbentrop doesn't break down. I'm not afraid of
the soldiers; they'll behave themselves. But Hess – he's
insane. He's been insane for a long time. We knew it when he
flew to England. Do you think Hitler would have sent the
third man in the Reich on such a lone mission to England
without the slightest preparation? Hitler really blew up
when he found out. Do you think it was a pleasure for us to
have to state publicly that one of our leading figures was
crazy? If he had really wanted to deal with the British, there
were reliable para-diplomatic channels through neutral
countries. My own connections with England were such that
I could have arranged it within 48 hours. No, Hess took off
without a word, without papers, without anything. Just left
a crazy note behind.'

In discussing Hitler, I remarked: 'The people now say that
it's too bad that the assassination attempt on July 20th last
year didn't succeed. They seem pretty disillusioned about
the Nazi leadership'.

This reference to the German people really irritated him.
[Goering replied,] 'Never mind what the people say now!
This is the one thing that doesn't interest me a damn bit! I
know what they said before! I know how they cheered and
praised us when things were going well. I know too much
about people!'

Despite spending a full year with many of the Nuremberg prisoners,
Gilbert judged his efforts to be disappointing and inconclusive. The 'little
men' merely asserted their lack of responsibility and their need to follow
orders; the 'big men' were obsessed with personal jealousies and mutual
recriminations. Nevertheless, Hermann Goering's comments on Hess
were not without an element of truth. Goering and others certainly had

established channels through which they could, and did, contact senior British representatives during 1940 and 1941.

Goering had not been in good health when first captured by the Allies, having become addicted to paracodeine. He had two suitcases of the drug in his possession when he was arrested; however, he was gradually weaned off it during the course of his captivity by the Nuremberg medics. He was sentenced to death in 1946 but escaped execution by committing suicide.

Wednesday 31 October 1945

William Shirer, veteran CBS reporter, watches the Russians in occupied Berlin

William Shirer's Berlin Diary, *his account of time spent with Hitler and his circle during 1939 and 1940, had been one of the bestselling non-fiction books in the United States during 1941 and 1942. It almost certainly inspired some of the other diarists in this collection, such as Cecil Brown, to emulation. In the autumn of 1945 Shirer was sent back to the city he knew so well to report on the transformation that had been wrought.*

With difficulty we made our way through blocks of rubble to the Alexanderplatz. For the first time we began to see numbers of Russian soldiers, for we were now in the Soviet sector, having passed through the British sector in the Kurfürstendamm and Tiergarten areas. Most of the Russian troops appeared poorly clad, their uniforms dirty and shoddy. Perhaps that was because they had done so much magnificent fighting in them. About one Russian in four, officer or man, carried a slung carbine. Almost all of them carted ordinary civilian suitcases, looted no doubt from Germans, and filled, no doubt, with black-market purchases. The Russians, Howard said, had recently received two or three years' back pay in paper marks, and our GI's had not been slow to take advantage of it. Our troops had had cigarettes and cheap watches shipped posthaste from home, and here in the Alexanderplatz or in the Tiergarten they disposed of them at fantastic prices to the Russian comrades. 'Mickey Mouse' watches – whatever they are – fetched ten thousand marks a piece, Howard said, which a GI could convert into one thousand American dollars and send home. Now, however, the army was stepping in to stop the racket, and the Russians were also beginning to co-operate. Both commands were checking up not only on their own troops but on Germans who were palming off a weird assortment of knick-knacks on the property-hungry Red Army men.

Indeed, hardly had we entered the square and paused to see the sinister Gestapo jail and headquarters, which had been nicely smashed, before a large squad of Russian military police began rounding up a hundred or so black-market operators, about a third of whom were Soviet soldiers and the rest German civilians.

One little incident followed that I did not much like. The Russians, as every American soldier here knows, do not let you take photographs in their sector without a special permit. But an American lieutenant colonel was blandly photographing the round-up of the black-marketeers by the Russian MP's. Two Russian guards immediately grabbed him and proceeded to march him off to the hoosegow. He was a rather elderly fellow and evidently not a combat officer; but he grew combative enough with the Russians. What I did not like was that the German civilians on the platz gathered around with obvious glee to see the spectacle of a couple of Russian soldiers arresting an American colonel. A Russian officer intervened and appeared to explain in Russian that if the colonel would give up his film he would be freed. But either the American did not understand or he did not want to part with his film. So off to the jug he was marched while the Germans guffawed. Perhaps, I thought, they saw their first glimmer of hope in this little incident. In the end – *Ja?* – the Russians and Americans would never understand each other and never get along. If so, that was a German's chance.

William Shirer was not wrong to assert that Berliners saw opportunity in inter-Allied competition. The major source of employment after the war for Berliners was the black market; once that dried up, its place was taken by Cold War spying. This murky business employed vast numbers of Berliners in the late 1940s, often on a piecemeal basis.

A tireless critic of all oppression, Shirer would champion the rights of writers during the McCarthy period in America and was himself blacklisted. Despite his remarkable track record he found himself unemployable. He died in Berkshire Hills, Massachusetts, in 1993.

Thursday 8 – Monday 12 November 1945

Signalman John Edward Jowers, British army, enjoys some shopping in occupied Bangkok

John Edward Jowers was born in 1922 and had begun work as a Post Office messenger at the age of fourteen. A year later he joined the Young Communist League. Shortly before the outbreak of the war in Asia and the Pacific he was working as a telegraphist in the City of London. He was called up in 1942 and was eventually attached to an air formation signals unit designed to facilitate Army–RAF co-operation. After serving in India and Burma during the war he became part of the British force occupying Thailand.

8 November

We had this afternoon off in lieu of yesterday, and I went into Bangkok again.

The Red Cross was closed today, so we first went to the photo shop to pick up some prints, and then Ken Lloyd and I went down to a bookshop I'd noticed to see if we could get a Siamese grammar. As luck would have it, he had a single copy of a Siamese language text-book there which answered my requirements, so I snapped it up right away.

After a dinner at the Chainarong, we made our way in the truck to the Odeon, in the New Road. We had some trouble at first in the parking of the truck, pilfering is rife around there, the usual stunts of siphoning out petrol and stealing things being carried to the extent of stealing the tyres off a stand truck!!

However, we finally managed to get it looked after by

some Punjabis, though not until Grem had lost a leather driving jacket.

Len Grubb maintained his reputation by suddenly appearing with a Thai girl on his arm, and disappeared inside.

It wasn't too bad a programme, George Formby in *He Snoops to Conquer*, quite a good film by usual Formby standards, and Brian Donlevy and Akim Tamiroff in *The Great McGinty*, one of Preston Sturges' films. For some reason it had French subtitles on it.

10 November

Yesterday, Collins took over command of the Section, and Jones left by plane for Saigon. He departed without saying cheerio, and with no parting regrets.

Today, the most cheering thing that happened to me was a letter from Irene. No wonder I've not heard from her for so long – she hasn't written! However, I was so thankful to hear that she hadn't thrown me over that I forgave her on the spot. I wrote a long letter to her tonight, enclosing snippets of the material I've bought her.

11 November

More *dhobi* again this morning, and Bangkok again this afternoon. Only four of us went in, and after doing business at the photographers, some refreshment at the Red Cross, and dinner at the Chainarong, we hailed tongas and set off for the Odeon.

On arrival we were disappointed to find that the change of programme didn't come until tomorrow, so were at a loss as to what to do. Len Manwaring and Grem went along to a Siamese place, the Capitol, so Len Grubb and I, after walking around for a while, walked slowly back to the Monument to Democracy.

We were accosted several times on the way by women 'on the game', and also passed an opium-den. It was exactly as depicted in books such as Sax Rohmer writes.

As I looked in through a long, narrow grill-window affair which faced right on to the street, I could see the interior, a long cellar-like place, with shelves around the walls on which were sprawled numerous reclining men, sucking away on their opium-pipes. More were huddled up on the floor and in the corners.

We went into a bar on Rajadamnern Avenue and had some cold drinks, and later on met the others in the Chainarong. Altogether it was a most disappointing evening, and I doubt if I shall go in on a Sunday again.

12 November

It has been rather wet today, and consequently it has been much cooler than normal. Although we have sprayed our billets out with what passes as D.D.T. several times, it still hasn't made any appreciable difference to the mosquitoes.

My money has been getting extremely low recently, and so tonight I went out to do a deal with cigarettes. I finally contacted a Siamese Air Force chap, and sold him 10 tins of State Express and 26 packets of Players for 570 ticals. This is equivalent to £9.10s.0d, and even at current English prices renders a profit of £5.

In fact, since I've been here I've got myself a pair of shoes, Irene two pairs of shoes and six dress lengths of silk, been in to Bangkok half-a-dozen times, paid for numerous meals and cold drinks in restaurants, bought photographs and Siamese language books, and now have Tcs.110 more than what I started with!!! This place is certainly the gen!!

Today I sewed up my first parcel to Irene, and as soon as I get all the necessary postal information I shall send it off.

With rationing intensifying in Britain, among the main preoccupations of soldiers abroad immediately after the war were bartering and shopping. In late November John Jowers was delighted to find that he could buy almost unlimited amounts of silk and shoes in Bangkok to send home to Irene. Silk was an almost unobtainable commodity in Britain; by December he would have sent no less than 68 yards of the fabric home. Energetic black-market currency dealing at every location had ensured that he was showing a profit and so his purchases had cost him nothing. He also noted wistfully that he was now allowing 'this diary to slide', because with the passing of active service 'there isn't a great deal of interest to record'. He returned to Britain in 1946.

Sunday 18 – Friday 30 November 1945

William MacMahon Ball, a junior Australian diplomat, is the man on the spot during fighting at Batavia in the Netherlands East Indies

William MacMahon Ball was a brilliant student who graduated from Melbourne University in 1923 and then lectured in psychology, logic and ethics. He took up a Rockefeller Fellowship in political science in 1929, and a Carnegie Travelling Fellowship took him to Europe and the USA in 1938–9. By 1940 he was Controller of Short Wave Broadcasts for the Australian government. From 1945 he was seconded to a series of diplomatic posts. In April 1945 he advised the Australian delegation to the San Francisco United Nations conference. By November he was Australian representative in the Netherlands East Indies during the burgeoning struggle for independence.

William MacMahon Ball

18 November

To de Galeries at 9 a.m. to go through signals with Coombe. Picked up statement about economic conditions here from Hunt. But already we had noticed that things were much livelier than usual. Some street battles went on in our back-street. Then we ran into a little ambuscade five doors from here, while driving down to G.H.Q. I pulled up the car and we waited for a moment, but as the road seemed to be in direct line of fire between Indian soldiers leaping around excitedly with their tommy-guns and the house from which Indonesians were sniping, we decided to accept the example of some Dutch officers and returned to take another road. There was intermittent firing throughout the morning and there were a good many road-blocks. The correspondents at the Press Camp were not able to get into town, much to their annoyance. Van Oyen and van der Plas were both shot at last night, but not hit.

Major Livingstone, in calling this afternoon, mentioned nonchalantly that he had just seen two Dutchmen shot while he was driving to our mess.

Later in the morning had a short chat with Dening. This I reported to Canberra and I also gave the Sjahrir version of last night's meeting which I got from one of my reliable sources.

This afternoon Walsh called and stayed for two hours. From an intellectual viewpoint it was a terribly tedious talk. But I did my best to implant firmly in his mind my ideas of this situation. I do not think he was impressed.

Spent the evening at home writing, with a bit of talk.

The missing signals from Canberra are beginning to roll in. And Canberra asks blithely for factual statements of prospects of success in negotiations between Dutch and Indonesians. I begin to understand for the first time what it feels like to be 'the man on the spot'; as though facts distinct from opinions, instructions, interpretations and predictions were not the very things that are impossible to find in Batavia. It is strange living in this marble palace with a front verandah at least twice the size of any house I've lived in, and with splendid meals expertly cooked, but with no pillow, no bedding, very few electric globes, taps that often don't run and sewers that often don't work. It is just part of what Joe calls the burlesque of life here: like this morning, when guns were firing in the front and back streets, and yet the girls in their summer dresses were strolling with their boy friends and thinking only of the lovely time they were going to have together. The coolies in the Plein opposite went on working and the squirrels went on munching in the tamarind trees. I never realised before that peace and violence could mate so easily.

30 November

En route to Singapore by air. Left Batavia airstrip at 8 a.m. on a wretched trip by Dakota to Singapore. From Batavia to Palembang we had companionship of a little girl, who looked about 6 but said she was 9. She was travelling quite unescorted and quite unperturbed. She seemed to take quite for granted that she should stroll out to the air strip and climb on to the Dakota with a lot of men. She had been interned for three years and her mother had died in the camp. She was going to join her father in Palembang. She hadn't seen him for 3 years and he did not know that she was coming. She seemed to regard all this as perfectly normal. Nevertheless, I was relieved to see that the R.A.F. blokes at Palembang immediately took a fatherly interest in her until her father arrived. I was very jealous of Joe because he was able to talk in Dutch.

My immediate neighbour in the Dakota was the former Jap. Commandant of Tjideng Camp, notorious for his harshness to the women. He was a very dignified Japanese on this journey, quite impassive. It must have been a dreadful journey for him. He was wearing very heavy handcuffs which pressed deep ridges in his wrists and chained by the handcuffs to the iron seat. He was left there chained, unable to make any but the smallest movement and having to sit turned to the side on which he was chained, from 8 a.m. when we took off until 5 when we landed at Singapore. He was left chained during our two stops at Palembang and Padang, when the heat inside the plane was unbearable. He was given neither food nor drink.

When we arrived at Singapore he was ordered brusquely to carry several heavy suitcases and load them on a truck. This caused some amusement to bystanders since he found it very awkward dealing with these suitcases in his handcuffs. The whole incident disgusted me. By all means try him and shoot him promptly. But this kind of petty spleen vengeance suggests that we have in ourselves the same brutish impulses that we so deplore in the Japs. I think it is quite wrong to put ex-P.O.W.'s and internees in charge of the Japanese war criminals. They should be called as witnesses but not given any executive authority.

William MacMahon Ball was witnessing a bitter independence struggle that would continue until 1948, when the state of Indonesia was declared. On 30 November Ball left Batavia (Jakarta) for Singapore in the company of the camp commandant from Tjideng, Captain Kenitji Sone, who was notorious for his brutality towards Dutch women and children. In 1945 Japanese war crimes suspects en route to captivity and trial were often treated badly by their captives. Some would be executed by hanging at Singapore in 1946.

Ball would later become Australian minister to Japan, and eventually would take up the Foundation Chair in Political Science at Melbourne University.

Sunday 18 – Wednesday 21 November 1945

Field Marshal Lord Alanbrooke visits Douglas MacArthur in Tokyo and talks about the 'Russian problem' in Europe and in Asia

The end of the Second World War had left the British and American military with many substantial administrative tasks, ranging from occupying enemy countries to rehabilitation and relief. This was true not only in Germany and Japan, but also in Mountbatten's recently expanded area of control in south-east Asia. In October and November 1945 Alanbrooke, Chief of the Imperial General Staff, embarked on a world tour to survey some of these extensive responsibilities. By late November he had reached Tokyo and here met with MacArthur, who was now in charge of occupied Japan.

18 November
MacArthur most interesting in connection with the Russians. According to him they were at present intent on converting Manchuria and China if possible into Communist states with

some allegiance to the Soviet Union, as has already been done in Mongolia.

He felt certain they would also attempt to convert Japan into a similar subject country, so as to be able to use the Japanese manpower at a later date for operations in the Pacific.

He considered them a greater menace than the Nazis had ever been, complete barbarians, as exemplified by one commander [in Manchuria] who had issued orders that every woman between the age of 16 and 60 was to be raped twice by Russian soldiery as an example of the superiority of the Russian race!

MacArthur considers that they should be met by force if necessary and not by conciliatory methods which were only interpreted as weakness by the Russians – He is not at all happy about the situation, his own force is only about 1/3 of its organised strength whilst there is no diminution in the Russian force . . .

21 November

I told him that I had been interested to find the same lack of co-operation on the part of the Russians on this Eastern Theatre as existed in the Western one. This started him off on the question of the threat of Russia to the future peace of the world. In his opinion we should prepare for trouble, and assemble at least 1000 atomic bombs in England and in the States. We must then prepare a safe aerodrome by tunnelling into the side of a mountain so that we shall be able to go on operating from England even when attacked. In the Pacific with the new super bomber which is now on the slips in America, we shall be able to attack Russia from America after refuelling at OKINAWA. With such a combined attack from East and West Russia could be brought to her senses if she started giving trouble. But we must prepare at once.

The military strategists of Britain, America and the Soviet Union marched out of the Second World War and into the Cold War without breaking step. As early as 1944 British contingency planners had begun to discuss the possible need to rearm Germany to counter Russia. London was quick to appreciate the impact of new weapons and methods of war on the international system. Sir Henry Tizard, a leading defence scientist, prepared two insightful reports at the end of the war which already pointed towards a strategy of deterrence. By November 1945 the RAF had already drawn up its first target maps for an attack on Russian cities. Alanbrooke, however, would not be troubled by these issues for much longer: in 1946 he handed over the role of CIGS to Bernard Montgomery. Thereafter, he devoted a happy retirement to his passion for ornithology. SEE ALSO PP. 516.

Saturday 24 – Wednesday 28 November 1945

Hilda Bates arrives home in Britain after five years at Kuching internee camp in Serawak, north-west Borneo

24 November

Last night we sighted the coast of England, and this morning docked at Southampton, where we were greeted by the Mayor, together with brass bands and cheering crowds, though most of us had to spend another night on board.

28 November

Here I am, actually sitting in my sister Nora's flat, – by the fire, consuming chocolate which was given us on the train to London. Nora, Philippa, and the Coe family were all at the London terminus to meet me, and I was driven to the flat by the Red Cross. This flat is situated in the middle of Grays Inn, so peaceful, overlooking lawns on both sides.

Poor old London! Such a different town from the one I used to know, and all the people look so tired and wan.

Sometimes I wake in the night, and wonder whether the three and a half year nightmare is *really* over. Then I think: – What of the future? It certainly does not look like a world of peace and plenty. I realise that at home they have had their own particular Hell. One can only hope that *whatever* happens, we shall have *PEACE*.

SEE ALSO PP. 684–5, 746–8, 800–1, 812–13.

SOURCE NOTES

1939

Epigraph: W. Storrs Lee (ed.), *Partridge in a Swamp: The Journals of Viola C. White, 1918–1941* (Taftsville, Vt.: Countryman Press, 1979), pp. 254–5.

Early Jan. 1941: Silvia Baker, *Alone and Loitering: Pages from an Artist's Travel-Diary, 1938–1944* (The Travel Book Club, 1947), pp. 75–9.

10–11 Jan. 1941: John Colville, *The Fringes of Power* (Hodder & Stoughton, 1985), pp. 331–2.

27 Jan. 1941: Samuel Grafton, *An American Diary* (New York: Doubleday, Doran & Co., 1943), pp. 86–7.

5–7 Feb. 1941: Ben Pimlott (ed.), *The Second World War Diaries of Hugh Dalton, 1940–45* (Cape, 1986), pp. 152–4.

6–15 Feb. 1941: David Dilks (ed.), *The Diaries of Sir Alexander Cadogan, 1938–1945* (Cassell, 1971), pp. 353–5.

9 Feb. 1941: Otto D. Tolischus, *Tokyo Record* (New York: Reynal & Hitchcock, 1943), pp. 7–8.

6–25 Feb. 1941: John Ferris, 'From Broadway House to Bletchley Park: The Diary of Captain Malcolm Kennedy, 1934–46', *Intelligence and National Security*, vol. 4, no. 3 (July 1989), p. 438.

9–25 Mar. 1941: Lee (ed.), *Partridge in a Swamp*, pp. 240–1.

15 Mar. 1941: Guy Heriot, *Changi Interlude: Leaves from the Diary of a Third Class Internee* (Lewes: W. E. Baxter, 1946), pp. 8–9.

17–18 Mar. 1941: Fred Taylor (ed.), *The Goebbels Diaries, 1939–1941* (Hamish Hamilton, 1982), pp. 269–72.

22 Apr. 1941: Tolischus, *Tokyo Record*, pp. 105–6.

28 Apr. 1941: Grafton, *American Diary*, p. 104.

7 May 1941: Alan Bishop and Y. Aleksandra Bennett (eds), *Vera Brittain, Diary 1939–1945: Wartime Chronicle* (Victor Gollancz, 1989), pp. 86–7.

4 June 1941: James Leutze (ed.), *The London Observer: The Journal of General Raymond E. Lee, 1940–1941* (Hutchinson, 1971), pp. 303–4.

6–21 June 1941: Koichi Kido, *The Diary of Marquis Kido, 1931–45: Selected Translations into English* (Frederick, Md.: University Publications of America, 1984), pp. 279–80, 283–4.

21–22 June 1941: Colville, *Fringes of Power*, pp. 404–5.

25–27 June 1941: Tolischus, *Tokyo Record*, pp. 141–2.

30 July – 2 Aug. 1941: Cecil Brown, *Suez to Singapore* (New York: Halcyon House, 1942), pp. 124–7.

2 Aug. 1941: Kido, *Diary of Marquis Kido*, p. 298.

8 Aug. 1941: J. Barnes and D. Nicholson (eds.) *The Empire at Bay: The Leo Amery Diaries 1929–1945* (Hutchinson, 1988), pp. 700–1.

14–17 Aug. 1941: Tolischus, *Tokyo Record*, pp. 226–7.

26 Aug. 1941: Pimlott (ed.), *Diaries of Hugh Dalton*, pp. 274–5.

28 Aug. 1941: Brown, *Suez to Singapore*, pp. 124–7.

2–16 Sept. 1941: Charles Stuart (ed.), *The Reith Diaries* (Collins, 1975), pp. 280–1.

11 Sept. 1941: Charles A. Lindbergh, *The Wartime Journals of Charles A. Lindbergh* (New York: Harcourt Brace Jovanovich, 1970), pp. 536–7.

6–7 Oct. 1941: Gwendolyn Mildo Hall (ed.), *Love, War, and the 96th Engineers (Colored): The World War II New Guinea Diaries of Captain Hyman Samuelson* (Urbana and Chicago: University of Illinois Press, 2001), p. 12.

16 Oct. 1941: Admiral Matome Ugaki, *Fading Victory: The Diary of Admiral Matome Ugaki* (Pittsburgh: University of Pittsburgh Press, 1991), pp. 8–9.

16–17 Oct. 1941: Diary of Oliver Harvey, MSS 56398, British Museum.

29 Oct. – 6 Nov. 1941: Lee (ed.), *Partridge in a Swamp*, pp. 250–1.

17 Nov. 1941: Leutze (ed.), *London Observer*, pp. 452–3.

22–28 Nov. 1941: Jack K. Woodward, *Three Times Lucky* (Brisbane: Boolarong Publications, 1991), pp. 47–9.

23–30 Nov. 1941: Lewis H. Brereton, *The Brereton Diaries: The War in the Air in the Pacific, Middle East and Europe, 3 October 1941 – 8 May 1941* (New York: William Morrow, 1946), pp. 30–3.

25–27 Nov. 1941: Diary of Henry L. Stimson, Yale University Library.

26 Nov. – 5 Dec. 1941: Georges 'Blacky' Verreault, *Diary of a Prisoner of War in Japan, 1941–1945* (Quebec: Vero, 1996), pp. 34–5.

29 Nov. 1941: Kido, *Diary of Marquis Kido*, pp. 320–1.

3–10 Dec. 1941: Diary of Kawamura Saburo, WO 325/1, PRO.

6–10 Dec. 1941: Ferris, 'From Broadway House', pp. 439–40.

7 Dec. 1941: Diary of Ginger Leonard, with thanks to B. Z. Leonard.

——Diary of Helen Clarke Grimes, Rhode Island Historical Society

Library, Providence. More of Helen Grimes's diary may be read at Jane Lancaster's site at www.quahog.org/factsfolklore/index.php?id=98.

7–10 Dec. 1941: Diary of Richard F. Tamabayashi, 'Boy Scouts, My Diary', 7–15 December 1941, File 50, Hawaii War Record Depository, Thomas Hale Hamilton Library, University of Hawaii at Manoa.

——Diary of Reginald Carter, MSS Eur D975, India Office Collections, British Library.

8 Dec. 1941: Shu Xiangcheng, diary, special collections, Hong Kong University Library.

8–16 Dec. 1941: Martin Ogle, diary, Mss.Ind.Ocn.S173, Rhodes House, Oxford.

9–14 Dec. 1941: Anne Morrow Lindbergh, *War Within and Without: Diaries and Letters, Nineteen Thirty-Nine to Nineteen Forty-Four* (New York: Harcourt Brace Jovanovich, 1980), pp. 242–3.

10 Dec. 1941: Brown, *Suez to Singapore*, pp. 326–9.

13 Dec. 1941: Diary of John Kennedy, 4/2/3, John Kennedy papers, Liddell Hart Centre for Military Archives, King's College, London.

14 Dec. 1941: Mollie Panter–Downes, *London War Notes, 1939–1945* (New York: Farrar, Straus & Giroux, 1971), pp. 185–7.

Mid-Dec. 1941: Charles Ritchie, *The Siren Years: Undiplomatic Diaries, 1937–1945* (Toronto: Macmillan, 1974), p. 128.

15–24 Dec. 1941: Juan Labrador, *A Diary of the Japanese Occupation: December 7, 1941 – May 7, 1945* (Manila: Santo Tomas University Press, 1989), pp. 18–23.

19–22 Dec. 1941: Verreault, *Diary of a Prisoner of War*, pp. 40–2.

23 Dec. 1941: Diary of Robert T. Smith, reproduced with the kind permission of Brad Smith. These diaries may be read at home.att.net/~ww2aircraft/RTSmith2.html.

25–26 Dec. 1941: Diary of J. A. Roxburgh, PR84/117, Australian War Memorial.

1942

Epigraph: Don McLaren, *Mates in Hell: SX8918 The Secret Diary of Don McLaren, Prisoner of the Japanese, Changi, Burma Railway, Japan, 1942–1945* (Henley Beach: Seaview Press, 1998), p. 19.

1 Jan. 1942: Sheila Allan, *Diary of a Girl in Changi* (Roseville, NSW: Kangaroo, 1994), p. 20.

2–13 January 1942: Fred Mathieson, *Motor Transport at War: The Diary of NX 18655 Dvr. Mathieson, F.G., 1940–45 Ex 2nd Division AASC* (privately published, 1992), pp. 104–7.

4–5 Jan. 1942, Richard C. Malonnee, 'The Withdrawal to Bataan Diary', US Army Military History Institute.

——Diary of Tom Forsyth, MG 30 File E181, National Archives of Canada.

10 Jan. 1942: Diary of Hilda Lacey, Mss.Ind.Ocn.R8, Rhodes House, Oxford.

12 Jan. 1942: Diary of James Roxburgh.

18 Jan. 1942: Brown, *Suez to Singapore*, pp. 422–3.

19 Jan. 1942: Allan, *Diary of a Girl in Changi*, pp. 24–5.

24 Jan. 1942: Alice Y. Lan and Betty M. Hu, *We Flee From Hong Kong* (Toronto: Evangelical Publishers, 1944), pp. 50–1.

2–10 Feb. 1942: Diary of Hilda Lacey.

7–8 Feb. 1942: Clyde J. Berwick, *The War Diary of Clyde J. Berwick* (privately published, 1994), pp. 12–15.

12 Feb. 1942: Goh Eck Kheng (ed.), *Life and Death in Changi: The War and Internment Diary of Thomas Kitching* (Singapore: Landmark Books, 2002),
pp. 57–8.

13 Feb. 1942: Brian Bond (ed.), *The Diaries of Lt-General Sir Henry Pownall*, vol. 2: *1940–1944* (London: Leo Cooper, 1974), p. 85.

13 Feb. – 5 Mar. 1942: Colin Inglis, *Singapore to Colombo: The Diary of C. W. A. Inglis, Indian Engineers* (privately published, 1945),
pp. 12–14, 16–18.

14 Feb. 1942: Diary of Joseph Hodder, MSS.Ind.Ocn. S52, Rhodes House,
Oxford.

——Diary of Len Baynes, 010 Army, Liddle Collection, Brotherton Library, University of Leeds.

15 Feb. 1942: Allan, *Diary of a Girl in Changi*, pp. 30–1.

15–16 Feb. 1942: Stan Arneil, *One Man's War* (Melbourne: Alternative Publishing Co–operative, 1980), pp. 9–10.

22–23 Feb. 1942: Diary of Reginald Carter.

1–3 Mar. 1942: Mathieson, *Motor Transport at War*, pp. 120–1.

6–11 Mar. 1942: Bishop and Bennett (eds), *Vera Brittain, Diary*,
pp. 132–4.

8 Mar. 1942: Diary of Hilda Lacey.

8–12 Mar. 1942: Diary of the Earl of Halifax, Borthwick Institute, York.

9–12 Mar. 1942: Tom Fagan, diary, PR 87/230, 0149/0032/0044, Australian War Memorial.

9 Mar. – 18 Apr. 1942: William Wilkie (ed.), *All of 28. And More: The Diary of Edgar Wilkie* (privately published, 1987), pp. 62–4, 66–8.

12 Mar. 1942: R. M. Smith with P. D. Smith, *With Chennault in China: A Flying Tiger's Diary* (Blue Ridge Summit, Pa.: Tab Books, 1984), pp. 70–1.

——Labrador, *Diary of the Japanese Occupation*, pp. 75–7.

16 Mar. 1942: F. Bloom, *Dear Philip: A Diary of Captivity, Changi 1942–45* (Bodley Head, 1980), pp. 22–4.

1–9 Apr. 1942: Diary of Kawamura Saburo.

5 Apr. 1942: McLaren, *Mates in Hell*, p. 20.

11 Apr. 1942: R. Renton Hind, *Spirits Unbroken: The Story of Three Years in a Civilian Internment Camp under the Japanese, at Baguio and at old Bilbid Prison in the Philippines, from December 1941 to February 1945* (San Francisco: John Howell, 1946), pp. 44–6.

12 Apr. 1942: Keith A. Barlow (ed.), *Bunker's War: The World War II Diary of Col. Paul D. Bunker* (Novato, Calif.: Presidio, 1996), pp. 128–9.

13–30 Apr. 1942: Anonymous pocket diary of a Japanese soldier, captured at Guadalcanal 1943, translated by the Combat Intelligence Center South Pacific Force, Item #1328 (S–1117), 5 May 1944, E18888.1328, Box 9, Records of Japanese Navy and Related Documents, NORPAC and SORPAC translations, US Naval Historical Center, Navy Yard, Washington DC.

14–20 Apr. 1942: Brereton, *Brereton Diaries*, pp. 118–19.

18 Apr. 1942: Robert J. Casey, *Torpedo Junction: With the Pacific Fleet from Pearl Harbor to Midway* (New York: Bobbs-Merrill, 1942), pp. 307–8.

27 Apr. 1942: Angela Bolton, *The Maturing Sun: An Army Nurse in India, 1942–1945* (Headline, 1988), pp. 53–4.

4 May 1942: Charles R. Bond, Jr and Terry Anderson (eds), *A Flying Tiger's Diary*, Centennial Series of the Association of Former Students, Texas A&M University, no. 15 (College Station, Tex.: Texas A&M University Press, 1993), pp. 164–5.

——Diary of Lt Miyoshi, translated by American Military Intelligence, WO 208/1503, PRO.

Early May 1942: Don Peacock, *The Emperor's Guest: The Diary of a British Prisoner-of-War of the Japanese in Indonesia* (Cambridge: Oleander Press, 1989), pp. 26–9.

12 May 1942: Claire Gorfinkel (ed.), *The Evacuation Diary of Hatsuye Egami* (Pasadena, Calif.: Intentional Productions, 1995), pp. 19–21, 24–5.

17–18 May 1942: Smith with Smith, *With Chennault in China*, pp. 88–9.

24 May 1942: Barlow (ed.), *Bunker's War*, pp. 168–9.

Late May 1942: Rena Krasno, *Strangers Always: A Jewish Family in Wartime Shanghai* (Berkeley, Calif.: Pacific View Press, 1992), pp. 21, 23–4.

1 June 1942: Gabrielle Chan (ed.), *War on Our Doorstep: Diaries of Australians at the Frontline in 1942* (South Yarra: Hardy Grant Books, 2003), pp. 119–20.

4 June 1942: Casey, *Torpedo Junction*, pp. 379–80.

17 June 1942: Carol M. Petillo (ed.), *The Ordeal of Elizabeth Vaughan: A Wartime Diary of the Philippines* (Athens, Ga.: University of Georgia Press, 1985), p. 101.

18–22 June 1942: Hall (ed.), *Love, War, and the 96th Engineers*, pp. 61–2.

9 July 1942: Hank Nelson (ed.), *The War Diaries of Eddie Allan Stanton: Papua 1942–45, New Guinea 1945–46* (Sydney: Allen & Unwin, 1996), pp. 42–3.

12–13 July 1942: Diary of James Armstrong, P89/165, Australian War Memorial.

Mid-July 1942: Bolton, *Maturing Sun*, pp. 85–6.

23 July 1942: Lan and Hu, *We Flee From Hong Kong*, pp. 85–6.

28 July 1942: Jean Larteguy (ed.), *The Sun Goes Down: Last Letters from Japanese Suicide-Pilots and Soldiers* (New English Library, 1973), pp. 32–3.

31 July 1942: Richard Tregaskis, *Guadalcanal Diary* (New York: Random House, 1943), p. 15.

7 Aug. 1942: Tregaskis, *Guadalcanal Diary*, pp. 41–2.

9–15 Aug. 1942: Diary of Oliver Harvey.

12 Aug. 1942: Barnes and Nicholson (eds), *Empire at Bay*, p. 826.

Mid-Aug. 1942: Ursula Bacon, *Shanghai Diary: A Young Girl's Journey from Hitler's Hate to War-Torn China* (Milwaukie, Oreg.: Milestone Books, 2002), pp. 118–20.

28 Aug. 1942: Diary of Lt Kiyoshi Yamamoto, 422/8/43, Australian War Memorial.

30 Aug. 1942: Peter Vladimirov, *The Vladimirov Diaries – Yenan, China: 1942–1945* (New York: Doubleday, 1975), pp. 53–4.

14 Sept. 1942: Tregaskis, *Guadalcanal Diary*, pp. 231–2.

16 Sept. 1942: Barlow (ed.), *Bunker's War*, pp. 238–9.

17–19 Sept. 1942: A. B. Feuer (ed.), *Bilbid Diary: The Secret Notebooks of Commander Thomas Hayes, POW, the Philippines, 1942–45* (Hampden, Conn.: Archon, 1987), pp. 91–4.

23–25 Sept. 1942: George Turnbull Dick (ed.), *The 1942–1943 Diary of A Corporal Fitter IIE of No. 30 Beaufighter Squadron in New Guinea* (Glenbrook: Adam Press, 1995), pp. 8–9.

24 Sept. 1942: John W. Huston (ed.), *American Airpower Comes of Age: General Henry H. 'Hap' Arnold's World War II Diaries*, vol. 1 (Maxwell, Ala.: Air University Press, 2002), pp. 390, 401.

28 Sept. 1942: C. Mendenhall, *Submarine Diary: The Silent Stalking of Japan* (Chapel Hill, NC: Algonquin, 1991), pp. 102–5.

Late Sept. 1942: Vladimirov, *Vladimirov Diaries*, pp. 64–7.

8–9 Oct. 1942: Diary of Lt Tadayoshi Matsumoto, captured at Guadalcanal early 1943, translated by the Combat Intelligence Center South Pacific Force, Item #1322, Box 9, Records of Japanese Navy and Related Documents, NORPAC and SORPAC translations, US Naval Historical Center, Navy Yard, Washington DC.

9 Oct. 1942: Barlow (ed.), *Bunker's War*, pp. 250–1.

20 Oct. 1942: John Nevell, *From the Bush to Changi and Back: Personal War Diary 1941–1945* (Buccan, Qld: M. M. Nevell, 1998), pp. 36–7.

24–28 Oct. 1942: Diary of William M. Leaney, 84/45/1, Imperial War Museum.

Early Nov. 1942: H. F. O'B. Traill, *Some Shape of Beauty* (Kuala Lumpur: Incorporated Society of Planters, 1986), pp. 20–4.

14 Nov. 1942: A. Lindbergh, *War Within and Without*, pp. 304–5.

19 Nov. 1942: Hall (ed.), *Love, War, and the 96th Engineers*, pp. 130–1.

20 Nov. 1942: Petillo (ed.), *Ordeal of Elizabeth Vaughan*, p. 159.

23 Nov. 1942: Ronnie Day (ed.), *Mack Morriss: South Pacific Diary 1942–1943* (Lexington, Ky.: University Press of Kentucky, 1996), pp. 26–7.

8–10 Dec. 1942: Diary of William M. Leaney.

14–16 Dec. 1942: Dick (ed.), *Diary of a Corporal Fitter*, pp. 25–6.

Mid-Dec. 1942: Hind, *Spirits Unbroken*, pp. 79–80.

21 Dec. 1942: David E. Lilienthal, *The Journal of David E. Lilienthal*, vol. 1: *The TVA Years, 1939–1945* (New York: Harper & Row, 1964), pp. 576–7.

26–30 Dec. 1942: F. Bloom, *Dear Philip: A Diary of Captivity, Changi 1942–45* (Bodley Head, 1980), p. 89.

29 Dec. 1942: Nevell, *From the Bush*, pp. 40–1.

1943

Epigraph: Peter Pinney, *The Barbarians: A Soldier's New Guinea Diary* (St Lucia: University of Queensland Press, 1988), pp. 70–1.

7–8 Jan. 1943: Theodore H. White (ed.), *The Stilwell Papers: Joseph W. Stilwell* (Macdonald, 1949), pp. 178–9.

Mid-Jan. 1943: Bacon, *Shanghai Diary*, pp. 132–3.

16 Jan. 1943: Diary of E. V. Bowra, P/230-231, Imperial War Museum.

18 Jan. 1943: Day (ed.), *Mack Morriss*, pp. 88–9.

——Charles Huxtable, *From the Somme to Singapore: A Medical Officer in Two World Wars* (Kenthurst, NSW: Kangaroo Press, 1987), p. 109.

4–5 Feb. 1943: Huston (ed.), *American Airpower Comes of Age*, vol. 1, p. 487.

Early Feb. 1943: Peacock, *Emperor's Guest*, pp. 64–7.

14 Feb. 1943: Petillo (ed.), *Ordeal of Elizabeth Vaughan*, pp. 188–9.

19–21 Feb. 1943: Day (ed.), *Mack Morriss*, pp. 101–2.

25 Feb. 1943: Oleta Stewart Toliver (ed.), *An Artist at War: The Journal of John Gaitha Browning* (Denton, Tex.: University of North Texas Press, 1994), p. 9.

21–23 Mar. 1943: Nelson (ed.), *War Diaries of Eddie Allan Stanton*, pp. 131–2.

23 Mar. 1943: Pinney, *Barbarians*, pp. 68–70.

23 Mar. – 17 Apr. 1943: M. R. R. Foord, *The Fortunate Soldier: With the New Zealand Army on Tongatabu, 1943* (privately published, 1996), pp. 79–81.

26 Mar. – 5 Apr. 1943: Judy and Stuart Dewey (eds), *POW Sketchbook: A Story of Survival* (Cholsey: Pie Powder Press, 1985), pp. 28–9.

1 Apr. 1943: McLaren, *Mates in Hell*, pp. 47–8.

11 Apr. 1943: Diary of Tamura Yoshikazu, quoted in Keiko Tamura,

'A Japanese Soldier's Experience of War', Australia–Japan Research Project, 2001 at ajrp.awm.gov.au/ajrp/ajrp2.nsf/.

15 Apr. 1943: Augusta H. Clawson, *Shipyard Diary of a Woman Welder* (New York: Penguin, 1944), pp. 39–42.

——Charles A. Fecher (ed.), *The Diary of H. L. Mencken* (New York: Knopf, 1989), pp. 246–7.

18 Apr. 1943 (entry written 18 Apr. 1944): Ugaki, *Fading Victory*, pp. 354–5.

—— Day (ed.), *Mack Morriss*, pp. 88–9.

4 May 1943: Diary of Tamura Yoshikazu, quoted in Keiko Tamura, 'A Japanese Soldier's Experience of War'.

——Clawson, *Shipyard Diary*, pp. 119–20.

7 May 1943: Petillo (ed.), *Ordeal of Elizabeth Vaughan*, pp. 188–9.

23 May 1943: F. Bloom, *Dear Philip*, pp. 106–7.

1 June 1943: S. L. Faulk (ed.), *Foo: A Japanese-American Prisoner of the Rising Sun – The Secret Prison Diary of Frank 'Foo' Fujita* (Denton, Tex.: University of North Texas Press, 1993), pp. 155–6.

Mid-June 1943: Traill, *Some Shape of Beauty*, pp. 56–9.

19 June – 26 Jul. 1943: Larteguy (ed.), *The Sun Goes Down*, pp. 49–52.

10–24 July 1943: Robert T. Boody, *Food-Bomber Pilot: China–Burma–India* (privately published, 1989), pp. 17–18.

10 July 1943: Petillo (ed.), *Ordeal of Elizabeth Vaughan*, pp. 233–4.

Mid-July 1943: Krasno, *Strangers Always*, pp. 73–4.

12 July 1943: White (ed.), *The Stilwell Papers*, pp. 204–5.

16 July 1943: D. Clayton James (ed.), *South to Bataan, North to Mudken: The Prison Diary of Brigadier General W. E. Brougher* (Athens, Ga.: University of Georgia Press, 1971), pp. 81–2.

3 Aug. 1943: Diary of Tadashi Higa, captured at Baanga Island, New Georgia, 20 Aug. 1943, translated by the Combat Intelligence Center South Pacific Force, Item #1340 (S-5059), 20 May 1944, Box 9, Records of Japanese Navy and Related Documents, NORPAC and SORPAC translations, US Naval Historical Center, Navy Yard, Washington DC.

6–26 Aug. 1943: Dewey and Dewey (eds), *POW Sketchbook*, pp. 36–7.

11–24 Aug. 1943: Barnes and Nicholson (eds), *Empire at Bay*, pp. 934–7.

14–15 Aug. 1943: Diary of Tom Forsyth.

16 Aug. 1943: Fred C. Robbins, *Overseas Diary: India and Burma, World War II* (Gainesville, Mich.: Rumaro Press, 1990), pp. 12–13.

——Brian Gomme, *A Gunner's Eye View: A Wartime Diary of Active*

Service in New Guinea (This is the only day-to-day record of events as they happened at Salamaua) (privately published, 1997), pp. 52–3.

3 Sept. 1943: Gomme, Gunner's Eye View, pp. 62–4.

20 Sept. 1943: Leslie G. Hall, The Blue Haze: Incorporating the History of 'A' Force Groups 3 & 5 Burma–Thai Railway 1942–1943 (Kenthurst, NSW: Kangaroo Press, 1996), pp. 230–1.

20–23 Sept. 1943: Marcial P. Lichauco, 'Dear Mother Putnam': A Diary of the War in the Philippines (Washington DC: privately published, 1949), pp. 120–3.

21–22 Sept. 1943: Andy Fletcher, NX 20365 (Walcha, NSW: privately published, 1980), pp. 108–10.

22 Sept. 1943: Vladimirov, Vladimirov Diaries, pp. 153–4.

22–25 Sept. 1943: James Clayton (ed.), South to Bataan, pp. 91–2.

1 Oct. 1943: Labrador, Diary of the Japanese Occupation, p. 173.

8 Oct. 1943: Kido, Diary of Marquis Kido, pp. 370–1.

10–11 Oct. 1943: Allan, Diary of a Girl in Changi, pp. 74–5.

14 Oct. 1943: L. de Asis, From Bataan to Tokyo: Diary of a Filipino Student in Wartime Japan, 1943–1944 (Center for East Asian Studies, University of Kansas, 1979), pp. 60–1.

15 Oct. 1943: Philip Ziegler (ed.), Personal Diary of Admiral the Lord Louis Mountbatten (London: Collins, 1988), pp. 8–9.

20–28 Oct. 1943: Robbins, Overseas Diary, pp. 84–5.

23 Oct. 1943: Bolton, Maturing Sun, pp. 113–14.

25–29 Oct. 1943: Diary of Lt-Col. Arthur Milner, ADM1/19931, PRO.

1–8 Nov. 1943: Joseph McNamara, Tin Can Duty in the Pacific 1943–1944–1945 (privately published, 1980), pp. 29–30.

5 Nov. 1943: Diary of Tom Fagan.

10 Nov. 1943: James J. Fahey, Pacific War Diary, 1942–5 (New York: Houghton Mifflin, 1963), p. 75.

27 Nov. 1943: David Zellmer, The Spectator: A World War II Bomber Pilot's Journal of the Artist as a Warrior (Westport, Conn.: Praeger, 1999), pp. 19–20.

5 Dec. 1943: de Asis, From Bataan to Tokyo, pp. 91–2.

9 Dec. 1943: Diary of Adm. James Somerville, Churchill Archives Centre, Churchill College, Cambridge.

10 Dec. 1943: Diary of Tom Fagan.

14–15 Dec. 1943: S. M. Kahn, Between Tedium and Terror: A Soldier's World War II Diary, 1943–45 (Urbana and Chicago: University of Illinois Press, 1993), pp. 34–6.

16–24 Dec. 1943: Berwick, *War Diary*, pp. 82–3.

17 Dec. 1943: Gomme, *Gunner's Eye View*, pp. 88–9.

25 Dec. 1943: Adrian Wood (ed.), *If This Should Be Farewell: A Family Separated by War – The Journal and Letters of Ernest and Mary Hodgkin, 1942–45* (Fremantle: Fremantle Arts Centre Press, 2003), pp. 146–9.

Late Dec. 1943: Krasno, *Strangers Always*, pp. 93–4.

1944

Epigraph: Diary of Hilda Bates, 91/35/1, Imperial War Museum.

1–17 Jan. 1944: Mathieson, *Motor Transport at War*, p. 171.

12 Jan. 1944: Nevell, *From the Bush*, pp. 101–2.

20 Jan. 1944: Diary of Tom Forsyth.

21–24 Jan. 1944: Hiromitsu Iwamoto (ed.), *The Naval Land Unit that Vanished in the Jungle by Tetsuo Watanabe* (Palmerston, ACT: Tabletop Press, 1995), pp. 34–5.

26 Jan. 1944: Toliver, *Artist at War*, pp. 170–1.

29 Jan. 1944: Kahn, *Between Tedium and Terror*, pp. 56–7.

6 Feb. 1944: Larteguy (ed.), *The Sun Goes Down*, pp. 76–7.

14 Feb. 1944: Weldon E. (Dusty) Rhoades, *Flying MacArthur to Victory* (College Station, Tex.: Texas A&M Press, 1987), pp. 184–5.

——Alex Danchev and D. Todman (eds), *War Diaries 1939–1945: Field Marshal Lord Alanbrooke* (Weidenfeld & Nicolson, 2001), p. 521.

19 Feb. 1944: Brian Bond (ed.), *Diaries of Lt-General Sir Henry Pownall*, p. 142.

23–24 Feb. 1944: M. Heijmans-van Bruggen (ed.), *De Japanse bezetting in dagboeken, Tjimahi 4* (Amsterdam: NIOD, 2002), p. 348.

Late Feb. 1944: Richard Buckle (ed.), *Self-Portrait with Friends: The Selected Diaries of Cecil Beaton, 1926–1974* (Weidenfeld & Nicolson, 1979), pp. 122–3.

27–28 Feb. 1944: Diary of Lt H. F. Hooper, 95/5/1, Imperial War Museum.

3–13 Mar. 1944: Eric Murrell, *For Your Tomorrow: A Cipher-Sergeant's Diary, 1941–1945* (Plush: Plush Publishing, 1999), pp. 146–7, 150–1.

8 Mar. 1944: Jesse Henry Gardner, *Beachheads and Black Widows: A*

South Pacific Diary (privately published, 1995), pp. 39–42.

14–16 Mar. 1944: E. Soviak (ed.), *A Diary of Darkness: The Wartime Diary of Kiyosawa Kiyoshi* (Princeton: Princeton University Press, 1999), pp. 155–8.

23–25 Mar. 1944: Nelson (ed.), *War Diaries of Eddie Allan Stanton*, p. 219.

3 Apr. 1944: Wood (ed.), *If This Should Be Farewell*, pp. 161–2.

5 Apr. 1944: Boody, *Food-Bomber Pilot*, pp. 44–5.

5–6 Apr. 1944: Diary of Lt Hubert Hooper.

9 Apr. 1944: Buckle (ed.), *Self-Portrait with Friends*, p. 129.

10–14 Apr. 1944: Lynn Z. Bloom (ed.), *Natalie Crouter, Forbidden Diary: A Record of Wartime Internment, 1941–45* (New York: Burt Franklin, 1980), pp. 323–5.

15 Apr. 1944: T. M. Campbell and G. C. Herring (eds), *The Diaries of Edward R. Stettinius, Jr. 1943–1946* (New York: New Viewpoints, 1975), pp. 52–3.

18–19 Apr. 1944: T. E. Dorman, *The Green War* (privately published, 1977), pp. 30–1.

20 Apr. 1944: Arthur Gately, *A Call to Arms: War Service with the RAAF 1942–1946, Diary Notes and Memoirs of Arthur Gately* (Fairbairn: Aerospace Centre, 2003), pp. 57–8.

23–28 Apr. 1944: Iwamoto (ed.), *Naval Land Unit that Vanished*, pp. 53–6.

23–29 Apr. 1944: Alf Simpson, *Bless 'em All: Pages from the Diary of an Official War Artist* (London: ISO Publications, 1990), pp. 115–18.

29 Apr. – 4 May 1944: Peacock, *Emperor's Guest*, pp. 127–9.

Early May 1944: Buckle (ed.), *Self-Portrait with Friends*, pp. 138–9.

6 May 1944: Labrador, *Diary of the Japanese Occupation*, p. 196.

13–31 May 1944: T. P. M. Lewis, *Changi – The Lost Years: A Malayan Diary 1941–1945* (Kuala Lumpur: Malayan Historical Society, 1984), pp. 220–2.

1 June 1944: Mendenhall, *Submarine Diary*, pp. 175–6.

5 June 1944: Dorman, *Green War*, pp. 40–2.

26 June 1944: C. Lindbergh, *Wartime Journals*, pp. 856–7.

27 June 1944: Vladimirov, *Vladimirov Diaries*, pp. 225–6.

28 June 1944: Diary of Taiso Nishikawa, translated by British Military Intelligence, WO 208/1503, PRO.

2 July 1944: Henry Kasper, *Merchant Marine War Diary (1944): Saipan – Pelelieu* (New York: Vantage Press, 1990), pp. 70–2.

6–7 July 1944: Diary of Taro Kawaguchi, Nakahara Unit of Homare

Unit 11943 (43rd Div. Hospital Unit), in the private possession of Master Sergeant J. William Winter.

13 July 1944: Kido, *Diary of Marquis Kido*, pp. 387–8.

15–20 July 1944: Allan, *Diary of a Girl in Changi*, p. 116.

16–20 July 1944: Soviak (ed.), *Diary of Darkness*, pp. 224–5.

18 July 1944: Campbell and Herring (eds), *Diaries of Edward R. Stettinius*, pp. 92–3.

21 July 1944: Verreault, *Diary of a Prisoner of War*, pp. 126–7.

——Oscar W. Conner, *Except These Days Were Shortened: A Wartime Diary of the South Pacific W.W. II – 1944–45* (Jackson, Mich.: Nature Book Publishing, 1982), pp. 78–9, 82–3.

28 July 1944: C. Lindbergh, *Wartime Journals*, pp. 888–9.

3 Aug. 1944: Robbins, *Overseas Diary*, pp. 130–1.

3–4 Aug. 1944: Pimlott (ed.), *Diaries of Hugh Dalton*, pp. 777–8.

21 Aug. 1944: Toliver, *Artist at War*, pp. 233–4.

28 Aug. 1944: Gately, *Call to Arms*, p. 89.

1–7 Sept. 1944: Lewis, *Changi*, p. 232.

9 Sept. 1944: C. Lindbergh, *Wartime Journals*, pp. 918–19.

11–20 Sept. 1944: Diary of Lt Okuma, translated by Australian Military Intelligence, WO 208/1503, PRO.

19 Sept. 1944: White (ed.), *Stilwell Papers*, p. 305.

21 Sept. 1944: Lichauco, 'Dear Mother Putnam', pp. 179–80.

27–28 Sept. 1944: A. B. Feuer (ed.), *General Chennault's Secret Weapon – the B-24 in China: Based on the Diary and Notes of Captain Elmer E. Haynes* (Westport, Conn.: Praeger, 1992), pp. 49–51.

3 Oct. 1944: Toliver, *Artist at War*, p. 241.

6–7 Oct. 1944: Kasper, *Merchant Marine*, pp. 121, 126.

8 Oct. 1944: A. Lindbergh, *War Within and Without*, pp. 443–4.

14–21 Oct. 1944: Diary of Yashio Shioya, translated by British Military Intelligence, WO 208/1503, PRO.

20–21 Oct. 1944: Rhoades, *Flying MacArthur to Victory*, pp. 297–8, 301.

20 Oct. – 6 Nov. 1944: Lichauco, 'Dear Mother Putnam', pp. 188–9.

23 Oct. 1944: Ugaki, *Fading Victory*, pp. 487–8.

Early Nov. 1944: Amanda Smith (ed.), *Hostage to Fortune: The Letters of Joseph P. Kennedy* (New York: Viking Penguin, 2001), pp. 611–12.

6 Nov. 1944: Barnes and Nicholson (eds), *Empire at Bay*, pp. 1018–19.

7 Nov. 1944: Faulk (ed.), *Foo*, pp. 244–5.

15 Nov. 1944: Larteguy (ed.), *The Sun Goes Down*, pp. 86–7.

26 Nov. 1944: Conner, *Except These Days Were Shortened*, pp. 214–15.

27 Nov. 1944: Chester W. Marshall, *Final Assault on the Rising Sun: Combat Diaries of B-29 Air Crews over Japan* (North Branch, Minn.: Speciality Press, 1995), pp. 58–9.

1–2 Dec. 1944: Alan J. Brundrett, *Two Years in Ceylon: The Diary of a Naval Secretariat Member, 1944–6* (Lewes: Book Guild, 1996), pp. 315–17.

5 Dec. 1944: J. Roose-Evans (ed.), *Joyce Grenfell. The Time of My Life: Entertaining the Troops – Her Wartime Journals* (Hodder & Stoughton, 1989), pp. 196–7.

16 Dec. 1944: John Ciardi, *Saipan: The War Diary of John Ciardi* (Fayetteville: University of Arkansas Press, 1988), pp. 58–61.

19 Dec. 1944: Lionel Hudson, *Rats of Rangoon: The Inside Story of the 'Fiasco' that Took Place at the End of the War in Burma* (Leo Cooper, 1987), pp. 5–6.

——Feuer (ed.), *Bilbid Diary*, pp. 219–21.

22–26 Dec. 1944: H. A. Hurst, *The War Time Diary of H. A. Hurst: RAAF A30542 from January 1944 to January 1945* (privately published, July 1997), pp. 31–3.

27 Dec. 1944: Robert Payne, *China Awake* (Binghampton, NY: Vail-Ballou Press, 1947), pp. 13–14.

Late Dec. 1944: Krasno, *Strangers Always*, pp. 151–2.

1945

Epigraph: D. Piper, *I Am Well, Who Are You? Writing of a Japanese Prisoner of War* (Exeter: Brightsea, 1998), p. 91.

6 Jan. 1945: Peter Pinney, *The Glass Cannon: A Bougainville Diary 1944–45* (St Lucia: University of Queensland Press, 1990), pp. 54–5.

13 Jan 1945: Ziegler (ed.), *Personal Diary of Mountbatten*, pp. 168–9.

15–16 Jan. 1945: George Wright-Nooth, *Prisoner of the Turnip Heads: The Fall of Hong Kong and Imprisonment by the Japanese* (Cassell, 1994), pp. 236–7.

25 Jan. 1945: Diary of Lt Peggy Wightman, 97/34/1, Imperial War Museum.

——Roose-Evans (ed.), *Joyce Grenfell*, pp. 240–1.

28 Jan. 1945: Heijmans-van Bruggen (ed.), *De Japanse bezetting in dagboeken, Tjimahi 4*, pp. 353–4.

31 Jan. – 1 Feb. 1945: Stephen J. Lofgren, 'Diary of First Lieutenant Sugihara Kinryu: Iwo Jima, January–February 1945', *Journal of Military History*, vol. 59, no. 1 (Jan. 1995), pp. 112–13.

14 Feb. 1945: Diary of Hilda Bates.

16 Feb. 1945: Ciardi, *Saipan*, p. 100.

17 Feb. 1945: Lofgren, 'Diary of First Lieutenant Sugihara Kinryu', pp. 122–3.

18 Feb. 1945: Labrador, *Diary of the Japanese Occupation*, pp. 268–70.

19 Feb. 1945: Marshall, *Final Assault on the Rising Sun*, p. 91.

20 Feb. 1945: Kahn, *Between Tedium and Terror*, pp. 238–40.

23 Feb. 1945: Diary of G. J. Green, 02/52/1, Imperial War Museum.

28 Feb. 1945: Diary of James Somerville.

3–5 Mar. 1945: Fumiko Amano, *Fumiko's Diary* (Las Vegas: Martin's Press, 1995), pp. 2–3.

7 Mar. 1945: Fahey, *Pacific War Diary*, pp. 296–7.

12–20 Mar. 1945: Diary of Lt-Col. R. A. G. Nicholson, 115th Field Regiment, Royal Artillery, CAB 106/159, PRO.

13–16 Mar. 1945: Diary of Captain Koyanango of the Japanese 3rd Air Fleet HQ, preserved in the papers of Vincent A. Kimberlin, US Army Military History Institute, Carlisle Barracks, Pennsylvania.

18 Mar. 1945: Hudson, *Rats of Rangoon*, pp. 92–4.

20 Mar. – 10 May 1945: Diary of Les Vancura, Navy 052, Liddle Collection, Brotherton Library, University of Leeds.

23 Mar. 1945: Bloom (ed.), *Natalie Crouter*, pp. 504–5.

26 Mar. 1945: J. Bryan III, *Aircraft Carrier* (New York: Ballantine, 1954), p. 92.

27 Mar. 1945: Diary of Fukuzo Obara, US Army Military History Institute, Carlisle Barracks, Pennsylvania.

1–3 Apr. 1945: David Vining (ed.), *American Diaries of World War II* (New York: Pepys Press, 1982), p. 249.

7 Apr. 1945: R. H. Minear (ed.), *Yoshida Mitsuru: Requiem for Battleship Yamato* (Seattle: University of Washington Press, 1985), pp. 112–15. (None of Yoshida's personal effects survived the sinking of the *Yamato*; however, he wrote this account after he had been rescued.)

13–14 Apr. 1945: Mary Williamson (ed.), *The Diary of a Virginia Gentlewoman 1943–1947: Laura Crabill Evans (Mrs. Lemuel) of Shenandoah County, Virginia* (2000), pp. 83–4.

20–24 Apr. 1945: Larteguy (ed.), *The Sun Goes Down*, pp. 104–5.

21 Apr. 1945: Bloom (ed.), *Natalie Crouter*, pp. 504–5.

27 Apr. 1945: Ritchie, *Siren Years*, p. 188.

28–29 Apr. 1945: Hudson, *Rats of Rangoon*, pp. 162–4.

1 May 1945: Pinney, *Glass Cannon*, pp. 174–5.

3–5 May 1945: Amano, *Fumiko's Diary*, pp. 40–1.

7 May 1945: Ugaki, *Fading Victory*, pp. 606–7.

27–31 May 1945: J. McNamara, *Tin Can Duty*, pp. 107–11.

1–16 June 1945: Diary of Hilda Bates.

3 June 1945: Masako Nojiri, *Diary of Masako Nojiri in a Defeated War* (Tokyo: Grass Thinking Society, 1995), p. 232 [in Japanese].

15 June 1945: John W. Huston (ed.), *American Airpower Comes of Age: General Henry H. 'Hap' Arnold's World War II Diaries*, vol. 2 (Maxwell Ala.: Air University Press, 2002), pp. 330–1.

16 June 1945: A. K. Powell (trans. and ed.), *A German Odyssey: The Journal of a German Prisoner of War* (Golden, Colo.: Fulcrum, 1991), pp. 299–300.

18 June 1945: Diary of Fleet Admiral William D. Leahy, microfilm, William D. Leahy Papers, Library of Congress, Manuscript Division.

22 June 1945: C. S. Sulzberger, *A Long Row of Candles: Memoirs and Diaries 1934–54* (Macdonald, 1969), pp. 256–7.

6 July 1945: Claude Mauriac, *The Other de Gaulle: Diaries 1944–1954* (Angus & Robertson, 1973), pp. 118–19 [first publ. Paris: Librairie Hachette, 1970].

7–23 July 1945: Nelson (ed.), *War Diaries of Eddie Allan Stanton*, pp. 291–2.

16–17 July 1945: Dilks (ed.), *Diaries of Sir Alexander Cadogan*, pp. 638–9.

16–25 July 1945: Diary of Harry S. Truman, July 17, box 333, President's secretary's files; diary, July 16, box 322, President's secretary's files, Harry S. Truman Library, Independence, Missouri.

18–21 July 1945: Isoko and Ichiro Hatano, *Mother and Son: A Japanese Correspondence* (Chatto & Windus, 1962), pp. 96–8.

24 July 1945: Ziegler (ed.), *Personal Diary of Mountbatten*, pp. 228–9.

6 Aug. 1945: Amano, *Fumiko's Diary*, pp. 91–2.

——S. Ball, *Parliament and Politics in the Age of Churchill and Attlee: The Headlam Diaries 1935–1951* (Cambridge: Cambridge University Press, 1999), p. 473.

6–8 Aug. 1945: R. A. Hart (ed.), *Military Government Journal*,

Normandy to Berlin: Major General John J. Maginnis (Cambridge, Mass: University of Massachusetts Press, 1971), pp. 281–2.

7 Aug. 1945: Penderal Moon (ed.), *Wavell: The Viceroy's Journal* (Oxford: Oxford University Press, 1973), p. 162.

——George Bilaikin, *Second Diary of a Diplomatic Correspondent* (Samson, Low, Marston, 1947), pp. 161–2.

——Michihiko Hachiya, *Hiroshima Diary: The Journal of a Japanese Physician, August 6 – September 30, 1945* (Chapel Hill, NC: North Carolina Press, 1955), pp. 15–16.

——Rhoades, *Flying MacArthur to Victory*, pp. 428–9.

8–14 Aug. 1945: Diary of the Earl of Halifax.

10 Aug. 1945: Diary of Henry Stimson, Yale University Library.

13 Aug. 1945: Frances Partridge, *Everything to Lose: Diaries, May 1945–December 1960* (Phoenix, 1985), p. 25.

15 Aug. 1945: Hachiya, *Hiroshima Diary*, pp. 82–3.

——Nojiri, *Diary of Masako Nojiri*, p. 308.

——Diary of Commander Hugh Mulleneux, GB99, Liddell Hart Centre for Military Archives, King's College, London.

——Hatano and Hatano, *Mother and Son*, pp. 107–8.

——Fecher (ed.), *Diary of H. L. Mencken*, pp. 246–7.

15–31 Aug. 1945: Michael Davie (ed.), *The Diaries of Evelyn Waugh* (London: Penguin, 1984), pp. 632–3.

18 Aug. 1945: Hachiya, *Hiroshima Diary*, pp. 92–3.

23–30 Aug. 1945: Diary of Hilda Bates.

25 Aug. 1945 – 5 Sept. 1945: Diary of Tom Forsyth.

1 Sept. 1945: Nicolas Sarantakes (ed.), *Seven Stars: The Okinawa Battle Diaries of Simon Bolivar Buckner Jr., and Joseph Stilwell* (College Station, Tex.: Texas A&M University Press, 2004), pp. 110–11.

2 Sept. 1945: McLaren, *Mates in Hell*, pp. 98–9.

4–5 Sept. 1945: Diary of Henry Stimson.

5 Sept. 1945: Partridge, *Everything to Lose*, p. 26.

15 Sept. 1945: Diary of Hilda Bates.

16 Sept. 1945: John Goldsmith (ed.), *Spender: Journals 1939–1983* (Faber, 1985) pp. 78–9.

20 Sept. 1945: Diary of Peggy Wightman.

8 Oct. 1945: McLaren, *Mates in Hell*, p. 105.

29 Oct. 1945: G. M. Gilbert, *Nuremberg Diary* (Eyre & Spottiswoode, 1948), pp. 12–13.

31 Oct. 1945: William Shirer, *End of a Berlin Diary* (Hamish Hamilton, 1947), pp. 142–3.

8–12 Nov. 1945: J. E. Jowers, *Getting My Knees Brown: The War Diary of 14239274 Signalman John Edward Jowers, 1st January 1943 – 28th April 1946, While Serving in India, Burma and Thailand with 228 Indian Wing Signal Section, 6 Indian Air Formation Signals* (privately published, 1977), pp. 142–3.

18–30 Nov. 1945: Alan Rix (ed.), *Intermittent Diplomat: The Japan and Batavia Diaries of W. MacMahon Ball* (Melbourne: Melbourne University Press, 1988), pp. 244–7.

18–21 Nov. 1945: Diary of Lord Alanbrooke, Liddell Hart Centre for Military Archives, King's College, London.

24–28 Nov. 1945: Diary of Hilda Bates.

REFERENCES

The main research for this project was conducted in the following locations. Some of the published material is long out of print and most of this was consulted in the Library of Congress and the British Library of Political and Economic Science. Where material is unpublished, full archival locations are given in the references.

Auckland Public Library
Auckland University Library
Australian War Memorial, Canberra
Birmingham University Library, Special Collections
Bodleian Library, University of Oxford
Bollings Air Force Base, Washington DC
Borthwick Institute, York
British Library, London
British Library of Political and Economic Science, London
Brotherton Library Special Collections, University of Leeds
Canadian National Archives, Ottawa
Churchill Archives Centre, Churchill College, Cambridge
Dwight D. Eisenhower Library, Abilene, Kansas
Franklin D. Roosevelt Library, Hyde Park, New York
Hallward Library, University of Nottingham
Harry S. Truman Library, Independence, Missouri
Hong Kong University Library, Special Collections
Imperial War Museum, London
India Office Library and Records, Oriental Collections, British
    Library
International Museum of Social History, Amsterdam
John F. Kennedy Library, Boston
Lauinger Library, Georgetown University, Washington DC
Library of Congress, Washington DC
Liddell Hart Centre for Military Archives, King's College, London
MacArthur Memorial, Norfolk, Virginia
National Archives of Australia, Canberra
National Army Museum, London
National Cryptologic Museum, Fort Meade, Maryland
National Library of Australia, Canberra

Public Record Office (PRO), Kew, London
Rhode Island Historical Society Library
Rhodes House, Bodleian Library of Commonwealth and African
    Studies, Oxford
US Army Military History Institute, Carlisle Barracks, Pennsylvania
US National Archives, Washington DC
US Naval Operational Archives Branch, Navy Yard, Washington DC
    Yale University Library

Unpublished sources

Armstrong, James, diary, P89/165, Australian War Memorial
Bates, Hilda, diary, 91/35/1, Imperial War Museum
Baynes, Len, diary, 010 Army, Liddle Collection, Brotherton Library,
    University of Leeds
Bowra, Brigadier E. V., diary, P/230-231, Imperial War Museum
Brooke, Field Marshal Sir Alan, Chief of the Imperial General Staff,
    Liddell Hart Centre for Military Archives, King's College,
    London
Brown, Gunner Stephen, diary, PR 91/061, Australian War
    Memorial
Cadogan, Sir Alexander, diary, A/CAD, Churchill Archives Centre
Carter, Reginald, diary, MSS Eur D975, India Office Collections,
    British Library
Fagan, Tom, diary, PR 87/230, 0149/0032/0044, Australian War
    Memorial
Forsyth, Tom, diary, MG 30 File E181, Canadian National Archives
Green, G. J., diary, 02/52/1, Imperial War Museum
Grimes, H. C., diary, Rhode Island Historical Society Library,
    Providence
Halifax, Earl of, diary, Borthwick Institute, York
Harvey, Oliver, diary, MSS 56398, British Museum
Higa, Pte Tadashi, diary, captured at Baanga Island, New Georgia,
    20 Aug. 1943, translated by the Combat Intelligence Center South
    Pacific Force, Item #1340 (S-5059), 20 May 1944, Box 9, Records of
    Japanese Navy and Related Documents, NORPAC and SORPAC
    translations, US Naval Historical Center, Navy Yard, Washington
    DC
Hodder, Joseph, diary, MSS Ind. Ocn.S52, Rhodes House, Oxford

Hooper, Lt Hubert F., diary, 95/5/1, Imperial War Museum

Kawaguchi, Taro, diary, Nakahara Unit of Homare Unit 11943 (43rd Div. Hospital Unit), in the private possession of Master Sgt J. William Winter, who found it at Saipan

Kennedy, John, diary, 4/2/3, John Kennedy papers, Liddell Hart Centre for Military Archives, King's College, London

Koyanango, Capt., diary, Japanese 3rd Air Fleet HQ, preserved in the papers of Vincent A. Kimberlin, US Army Military History Institute

Lacey, Hilda, diary, Mss.Ind.Ocn.R8, Rhodes House, Oxford

Leahy, Fleet Admiral William D., diary, microfilm, William D. Leahy Papers, Library of Congress, Manuscript Division

Leaney, William M., diary, 84/45/1, Imperial War Museum

Leonard, Ginger, diary, with thanks to B. Z. Leonard, www.gingers-diary.com/index.html

Lewis, Thomas Price, 'Notes on war experiences before Entering Changi Jail', Mss.Ind.Ocn.S289(i), Rhodes House, Oxford

Lindbergh, Charles, papers and photographic collection, Yale University Library

Malonnee, Richard, 'The Withdrawal to Bataan Diary', US Army Military History Institute

Matsumoto, Tadayoshi, 2nd Lt, diary, captured at Guadalcanal early 1943, translated by the Combat Intelligence Center South Pacific Force, Item #1322, Box 9, Records of Japanese Navy and Related Documents, NORPAC and SORPAC translations, US Naval Historical Center, Navy Yard, Washington DC

Milner, Lt-Col. Arthur, diary, ADM1/19931, PRO

Miyoshi, Lt diary, translated by American Military Intelligence, WO 208/1503, PRO

Mulleneux, Cmdr Hugh, diary, GB99, Liddell Hart Centre for Military Archives, King's College, London

Nicholson, Lt-Col. R. A. G., diary, 115th Field Regiment, Royal Artillery, CAB 106/159, PRO

Nishikawa, 2nd Lt Taiso, diary, translated by British Military Intelligence, WO 208/1503, PRO

Obara, 2nd Lt Fukuzo, diary, US Army Military History Institute

Ogle, Martin, diary, Mss.Ind.Ocn.S173, Rhodes House, Oxford

Okuma, Lt, diary, translated by Australian Military Intelligence, WO 208/1503, PRO

Roxburgh, Sgt J. A., diary, PR84/117, Australian War Memorial

Saburo, General Kawamura, diary, WO 325/1 & 2, PRO

Shioya, Yashio, diary, translated by British Military Intelligence, WO 208/1503, PRO

Shu Xiangcheng, diary, special collections, Hong Kong University Library

Smith, Robert T., diary, reproduced with the kind permission of Brad Smith. These diaries may be read at home.att.net/~ww2aircraft/RTSmith2.html

Somerville, Adm. James, diary, Churchill Archives Centre, Churchill College, Cambridge

Stimson, Henry L., diary, Yale University Library

Tamabayashi, R. F., diary, 'Boy Scouts, My Diary', 7–15 December 1941, File 50, Hawaii War Record Depository, Thomas Hale Hamilton Library, University of Hawaii at Manoa

Truman, Harry S., diary, Harry S. Truman Library, Independence, Missouri

Vancura, Les, diary, Navy 052, Liddle Collection, Brotherton Library, University of Leeds

Wightman, Lt Peggy, diary, 97/34/1, Imperial War Museum

Yamamoto, Kiyoshi, diary, 422/8/43, Australian War Memorial

Japanese sergeant's diary, captured at Guadalcanal, 18 Jan. 1943, translated by the Combat Intelligence Center South Pacific Force, Item #1195 (S-1444), 28 March 1944, Box 8, Records of Japanese Navy and Related Documents, NORPAC and SORPAC translations, US Naval Historical Center, Navy Yard, Washington DC

Anonymous pocket diary of a Japanese soldier, captured at Guadalcanal 1943, translated by the Combat Intelligence Center South Pacific Force, Item #1328 (S-1117), 5 May 1944, E18888.1328, Box 9, Records of Japanese Navy and Related Documents, NORPAC and SORPAC translations, US Naval Historical Center, Navy Yard, Washington DC

Published sources

Unless otherwise stated the place of publication is London.

Allan, S., *Diary of a Girl in Changi* (Roseville, NSW: Kangaroo Press, 1994)

Amano, F., *Fumiko's Diary* (Las Vegas: Martin's Press, 1995)

Arneil, S., *One Man's War* (Melbourne: Alternative Publishing Co-operative, 1980)

Bacon, U., *Shanghai Diary: A Young Girl's Journey from Hitler's Hate to War-Torn China* (Milwaukie, Oreg.: Milestone Books, 2002)

Baker, S., *Alone and Loitering: Pages from an Artist's Travel-Diary, 1938–1944* (The Travel Book Club, 1947)

Ball, S., *Parliament and Politics in the Age of Churchill and Attlee: The Headlam Diaries 1935–1951* (Cambridge: Cambridge University Press, 1999)

Barlow, K. A., (ed.), *Bunker's War: The World War II Diary of Col. Paul D. Bunker* (Novato, Calif.: Presidio, 1996)

Barnes, J. and Nicholson, D. (eds), *The Empire at Bay: The Leo Amery Diaries 1929–1945* (Hutchinson, 1988)

Bassett, John T., *War Journal of an Innocent Soldier* (Hamden, Conn.: Archon, 1989)

Baume, E., *I've Lived Another Year: A Journalist's Diary of the Year 1941* (Harrap, 1942)

Berwick, C. J., *The War Diary of Clyde J. Berwick* (privately published, 1994)

Bilaikin, G., *Second Diary of a Diplomatic Correspondent* (Samson, Low, Marston, 1947)

Bishop, A. and Bennett, Y. A. (eds), *Vera Brittain, Diary 1939–1945: Wartime Chronicle* (Victor Gollancz, 1989)

Bloom, F., *Dear Philip: A Diary of Captivity, Changi 1942–45* (Bodley Head, 1980)

Bloom, L. Z. (ed.), *Natalie Crouter, Forbidden Diary: A Record of Wartime Internment, 1941–45* (New York: Burt Franklin, 1980)

Bolton, A., *The Maturing Sun: An Army Nurse in India, 1942–1945* (Headline, 1988)

Bond, B. (ed.), *The Diaries of Lt-General Sir Henry Pownall*, vol. 2: *1940–1944* (Leo Cooper, 1974)

Bond, C. R., Jr and Anderson, T. (eds), *A Flying Tiger's Diary*, Centennial Series of the Association of Former Students, Texas A&M University, no. 15 (College Station, Tex.: Texas A&M University Press, 1993)

Boody, R. T., *Food-Bomber Pilot: China–Burma–India* (privately published, 1989)

Brereton, L. H., *The Brereton Diaries: The War in the Air in the Pacific,*

Middle East and Europe, 3 October 1941 – 8 May 1945 (New York: William Morrow, 1946)

Brown, C., *Suez to Singapore* (New York: Halcyon House, 1942)

Brundrett, Alan J., *Two Years in Ceylon: The Diary of a Naval Secretariat Member, 1944–6* (Lewes: Book Guild, 1996)

Bryan, J., III, *Aircraft Carrier* (New York: Ballantine, 1954)

Buckle, R. (ed.), *Self-Portrait with Friends: The Selected Diaries of Cecil Beaton, 1926–1974* (Weidenfeld & Nicolson, 1979)

Campbell, T. M. and Herring, G. C. (eds), *The Diaries of Edward R. Stettinius, Jr. 1943–1946* (New York: New Viewpoints, 1975)

Casey, R. J., *Torpedo Junction: With the Pacific Fleet from Pearl Harbor to Midway* (New York: Bobbs-Merrill, 1942)

Chan, G. (ed.), *War on Our Doorstep; Diaries of Australians at the Frontline in 1942* (South Yarra: Hardy Grant Books, 2003)

Ciardi, J., *Saipan: The War Diary of John Ciardi* (Fayetteville: University of Arkansas Press, 1988)

Clawson, A. H., *Shipyard Diary of a Woman Welder* (New York: Penguin, 1944)

Clayton, James D. (ed.), *South to Bataan, North to Mudken: The Prison Diary of Brigadier General W. E. Brougher* (Athens, Ga.: University of Georgia Press, 1971)

Colville, J., *The Fringes of Power* (Hodder & Stoughton, 1985)

Conner, O. W., *Except These Days Were Shortened: A Wartime Diary of the South Pacific W.W. II – 1944–45* (Jackson, Mich.: Nature Book Publishing, 1982)

Crouter, N., *Forbidden Diary: A Record of Wartime Internment, 1941–45* (New York: Burt Franklin, 1980)

Danchev, A. and Todman, D. (eds), *War Diaries 1939–1945: Field Marshal Lord Alanbrooke* (Weidenfeld & Nicolson, 2001)

Davie, M. (ed.), *The Diaries of Evelyn Waugh* (Weidenfeld & Nicolson, 1976)

Day, R. (ed.), *Mack Morriss: South Pacific Diary 1942–1943* (Lexington, Ky.: University Press of Kentucky, 1996)

de Asis, L., *From Bataan to Tokyo: Diary of a Filipino Student in Wartime Japan, 1943–1944* (Center for East Asian Studies, University of Kansas, 1979)

Dewey, J. and S. (eds), *POW Sketchbook: A Story of Survival* (Cholsey: Pie Powder Press, 1985)

Dick, G. T. (ed.), *The 1942–1943 Diary of a Corporal Fitter IIE of No. 30*

Beaufighter Squadron in New Guinea (Glenbrook: Adam Press, 1995)

Dilks, D. (ed.), *The Diaries of Sir Alexander Cadogan, 1938–1945* (Cassell, 1971)

Dorman, T. E., *The Green War* (privately published, 1977)

Fahey, J. J., *Pacific War Diary, 1942–5* (New York: Houghton Mifflin, 1963)

Faulk, S. L. (ed.), *Foo: A Japanese-American Prisoner of the Rising Sun – The Secret Prison Diary of Frank 'Foo' Fujita* (Denton, Tex.: University of North Texas Press, 1993)

Fecher, Charles A. (ed.), *The Diary of H. L. Mencken* (New York: Knopf, 1989)

Ferris, J., 'From Broadway House to Bletchley Park: The Diary of Captain Malcolm Kennedy, 1934–46', *Intelligence and National Security*, vol. 4, no. 3 (July 1989), pp. 421–50.

Feuer, A. B., (ed.), *Bilbid Diary: The Secret Notebooks of Commander Thomas Hayes, POW, the Philippines, 1942–45* (Hampden, Conn.: Archon, 1987)

——(ed.), *General Chennault's Secret Weapon – The B-24 in China: Based on the Diary and Notes of Captain Elmer E. Haynes* (Westport, Conn.: Praeger, 1992)

Fletcher, A., *NX 20365* (Walcha, NSW: privately published, 1980)

Foord, M. R. R., *The Fortunate Soldier: With the New Zealand Army on Tongatabu, 1943* (privately published, 1996)

Gardner, J. H., *Beachheads and Black Widows: A South Pacific Diary* (privately published, 1995)

Gately, A., *A Call to Arms: War Service with the RAAF 1942–1946, Diary Notes and Memoirs of Arthur Gately* (Fairbairn: Aerospace Centre, 2003)

Gayn, M., *Japan Diary* (New York: William Sloane, 1948)

Gilbert, G. M., *Nuremberg Diary* (Eyre & Spottiswoode, 1948)

Giles, J. H. (ed.), *The GI Journal of Sergeant Giles* (Boston: Houghton Mifflin, 1965)

Gillin, D. G. and Myers, R. H. (eds), *Last Chance in Manchuria: The Diary of Chang Kia-Ngau* (Stanford, Calif.: Hoover Institution Press, 1989)

Goldsmith, J. (ed.), *Spender: Journals 1939–1983* (Faber, 1985)

Gomme, B., *A Gunner's Eye View: A Wartime Diary of Active Service in New Guinea (This is the only day-to-day record of events as they happened at Salamaua)* (privately published, 1997)

Gorfinkel, C. (ed.), *The Evacuation Diary of Hatsuye Egami* (Pasadena, Calif.: Intentional Productions, 1995)

Grafton, Samuel, *An American Diary* (New York: Doubleday, Doran & Co., 1943)

Hachiya, M., *Hiroshima Diary: The Journal of a Japanese Physician, August 6 – September 30, 1945* (Chapel Hill: University of North Carolina Press, 1955)

Hall, G. M. (ed.), *Love, War, and the 96th Engineers (Colored): The World War II New Guinea Diaries of Captain Hyman Samuelson* (Urbana and Chicago: University of Illinois Press, 2001)

Hall, Leslie G., *The Blue Haze: Incorporating the History of 'A' Force Groups 3 & 5 Burma–Thai Railway 1942–1943* (Kenthurst, NSW: Kangaroo Press, 1996)

Hamid, E. (ed.), *Behind the Fence, Life as a POW in Japan: The Diaries of Les Chater* (St Catherine's, Ontario: Vanwell, 2001)

Hart, R. A. (ed.), *Military Government Journal, Normandy to Berlin: Major General John J. Maginnis* (Amherst: University of Massachusetts Press, 1971)

Harvey, J. (ed.), *The War Diaries of Oliver Harvey, 1941–1945* (Collins, 1978)

Hatano, I. and I., *Mother and Son: A Japanese Correspondence* (Chatto & Windus, 1962)

Heijmans-van Bruggen, M. (ed.), *De Japanse bezetting in dagboeken, Tjimahi 4* (Amsterdam: NIOD, 2002)

Heriot, G., *Changi Interlude: Leaves from the diary of a Third Class Internee* (Lewes: W. E. Baxter, 1946)

Hind, R. R., *Spirits Unbroken: The Story of Three Years in a Civilian Internment Camp under the Japanese, at Baguio and at Old Bilbid Prison in the Philippines, from December 1941 to February 1945* (San Francisco: John Howell, 1946)

Hudson, L., *Rats of Rangoon: The Inside Story of the 'Fiasco' that Took Place at the End of the War in Burma* (Leo Cooper, 1987)

Hurst, H. A., *The War Time Diary of H. A. Hurst: RAAF A30542 from January 1944 to January 1945* (privately published, July 1997)

Huston, J. W. (ed.), *American Airpower Comes of Age: General Henry H. 'Hap' Arnold's World War II Diaries*, vol. 1 (Maxwell, Ala.: Air University Press, 2002)

——(ed.), *American Airpower Comes of Age: General Henry H. 'Hap' Arnold's World War II Diaries*, vol. 2 (Maxwell, Ala.: Air University Press, 2002)

Huxtable, C., *From the Somme to Singapore: A Medical Officer in Two World Wars* (Kenthurst, NSW: Kangaroo Press, 1987)

Inglis, C. W. A., *Singapore to Colombo: The Diary of C. W. A. Inglis, Indian Engineers* (privately published, 1945)

Israel, F. L. (ed.), *The War Diary of Breckinridge Long: Selections from the Years 1939–1944* (Lincoln: University of Nebraska Press, 1966)

Iwamoto, H. (ed.), *The Naval Land Unit that Vanished in the Jungle by Tetsuo Watanabe* (Palmerston, ACT: Tabletop Press, 1995)

Jowers, J. E., *Getting My Knees Brown: The War Diary of 14239274 Signalman John Edward Jowers, 1st January 1943 – 28th April 1946, While Serving in India, Burma & Thailand with 228 Indian Wing Signal Section, 6 Indian Air Formation Signals* (privately published, 1977)

Kahn, S. M., *Between Tedium and Terror: A Soldier's World War II Diary, 1943–45* (Urbana and Chicago: University of Illinois Press, 1993)

Kasper, H., *Merchant Marine War Diary (1944): Saipan–Pelelieu* (New York: Vantage Press, 1990)

Kheng, G. E. (ed.), *Life and Death in Changi: The War and Internment Diary of Thomas Kitching* (Singapore: Landmark Books, 2002)

Kido, Koichi, *The Diary of Marquis Kido, 1931–45: Selected Translations into English* (Frederick, Md.: University Publications of America, 1984)

Kike Wadatsumi no Koe, *Listen to the Voices from the Sea* (Scranton: Scranton University Press, 2000)

Krasno, R., *Strangers Always: A Jewish Family in Wartime Shanghai* (Berkeley, Calif.: Pacific View Press, 1992)

Labrador, J., *A Diary of the Japanese Occupation: December 7, 1941 – May 7, 1945* (Manila: Santo Tomas University Press, 1989)

Lan, A. Y. and Hu, B. M., *We Flee From Hong Kong* (Toronto: Evangelical Publishers, 1944)

Larteguy, J. (ed.), *The Sun Goes Down: Last Letters from Japanese Suicide-Pilots and Soldiers* (New English Library, 1973)

Lawrence, D., *Diary of a Washington Correspondent* (New York: H. C. Kinsey & Co., 1942)

Lee, W. S. (ed.), *Partridge in a Swamp: The Journals of Viola C. White, 1918–1941* (Taftsville, Vt.: Countryman Press, 1979)

Leutze, J. (ed.), *The London Observer: The Journal of General Raymond E. Lee, 1940–1941* (Hutchinson, 1971)

Lewis, J. E. (ed.), *The Mammoth Book of War Diaries and Letters* (New York: Carroll & Graf, 1998)

Lewis, T. P. M., *Changi – the Lost Years: A Malayan Diary 1941–1945* (Kuala Lumpur: Malayan Historical Society, 1984)

Lichauco, M. P., *'Dear Mother Putnam': A Diary of the War in the Philippines* (Washington DC: privately published, 1949)

Lilienthal, D. E., *The Journal of David E. Lilienthal*, vol. 1: *The TVA Years, 1939–1945* (New York: Harper & Row, 1964)

Lindbergh, A. M., *War Within and Without: Diaries and Letters, Nineteen Thirty-Nine to Nineteen Forty-Four* (New York: Harcourt Brace Jovanovich, 1980)

Lindbergh, C. A., *The Wartime Journals of Charles A. Lindbergh* (New York: Harcourt Brace Jovanovich, 1970)

Lofgren, S. J., 'Diary of First Lieutenant Sugihara Kinryu: Iwo Jima, January–February 1945', *Journal of Military History*, vol. 59, no. 1 (Jan. 1995), pp. 97–133.

McLaren, D., *Mates in Hell: SX8918 The Secret Diary of Don McLaren, Prisoner of the Japanese, Changi, Burma Railway, Japan, 1942–1945* (Henley Beach: Seaview Press, 1998)

McNamara, J., *Tin Can Duty in the Pacific 1943–1944–1945* (privately published, 1980)

Marshall, C. W., *Final Assault on the Rising Sun: Combat Diaries of B-29 Air Crews over Japan* (North Branch, Minn.: Speciality Press, 1995)

Mathieson, F., *Motor Transport at War: The Diary of NX 18655 Dvr. Mathieson, F.G. 1940–45 Ex 2nd Division AASC* (privately published, 1992)

Mauriac, Claude, *The Other de Gaulle: Diaries 1944–1954* (Angus & Robertson, 1973) [first publ. Paris: Librairie Hachette, 1970]

Melby, J. F., *The Mandate of Heaven: Record of a Civil War, China 1945–49* (Toronto: Toronto University Press, 1968)

Mendenhall, C., *Submarine Diary: The Silent Stalking of Japan* (Chapel Hill, NC: Algonquin, 1991)

Miller, R., *Nothing Less than Victory* (New York: Morrow, 1993)

Minear, R. H. (ed.), *Yoshida Mitsuru: Requiem for Battleship Yamato* (Seattle: University of Washington Press, 1985)

Moon, Penderal (ed.), *Wavell: The Viceroy's Journal* (Oxford: Oxford University Press, 1973)

Murrell, E., *For Your Tomorrow: A Cipher-Sergeant's Diary, 1941–1945* (Plush: Plush Publishing, 1999)

Nelson, H. (ed.), *The War Diaries of Eddie Allan Stanton: Papua 1942–45, New Guinea 1945–46* (Sydney: Allen & Unwin, 1996)

Nevell, J., *From the Bush to Changi and Back: Personal War Diary 1941–1945* (Buccan, Qld: M. M. Nevell, 1998)

Nojiri, M., *Diary of Masako Nojiri in a Defeated War* (Tokyo: Grass Thinking Society, 1995) [in Japanese]

Panter-Downes, M., *London War Notes, 1939–1945* (New York: Farrar, Straus & Giroux, 1971)

Partridge, F., *Everything to Lose: Diaries, May 1945–December 1960* (Phoenix, 1985)

Payne, R., *China Awake* (Binghampton, NY: Vail-Ballou Press, 1947)

Peacock, D., *The Emperor's Guest: The Diary of a British Prisoner-of-War of the Japanese in Indonesia* (Cambridge: Oleander Press, 1989)

Petillo, C. M. (ed.), *The Ordeal of Elizabeth Vaughan: A Wartime Diary of the Philippines* (Athens, Ga.: University of Georgia Press, 1985)

Pimlott, B. (ed.), *The Second World War Diaries of Hugh Dalton, 1940–45*
(Cape, 1986)

Pinney, P., *The Barbarians: A Soldier's New Guinea Diary* (St Lucia: University of Queensland Press, 1988)

——*The Glass Cannon: A Bougainville Diary 1944–45* (St Lucia: University of Queensland Press, 1990)

——*The Devil's Garden: Solomon Islands War Diary, 1945* (St Lucia: University of Queensland Press, 1992)

Piper, D., *I Am Well, Who Are You? Writing of a Japanese Prisoner of War* (Exeter: Brightsea, 1998)

Powell, A. K. (trans. and ed.), *A German Odyssey: The Journal of a German Prisoner of War* (Golden, Colo.: Fulcrum, 1991)

Reckitt, B. N., *Diary of Military Government in Germany 1945* (Ilfracombe: Stockwell, 1989)

Rhoades, W. E., *Flying MacArthur to Victory* (College Station, Tex.: Texas A&M Press, 1987)

Ritchie, C., *The Siren Years: Undiplomatic Diaries, 1937–1945* (Toronto: Macmillan, 1974)

Rix, A. (ed.), *Intermittent Diplomat: The Japan and Batavia Diaries of W. MacMahon Ball* (Melbourne: Melbourne University Press, 1988)

Robbins, F. C., *Overseas Diary: India and Burma, World War II* (Gainesville, Mich.: Rumaro Press, 1990)

Roose-Evans, J. (ed.), *Joyce Grenfell. The Time of My Life: Entertaining the Troops – Her Wartime Journals* (Hodder & Stoughton, 1989)

Sarantakes, N. (ed.), *Seven Stars: The Okinawa Battle Diaries of Simon Bolivar Buckner Jr., and Joseph Stilwell* (College Station, Tex.: Texas A&M University Press, 2004)

Shirer, William, *End of a Berlin Diary* (Hamish Hamilton, 1947)

Simpson, A., *Bless 'em All: Pages from the Diary of an Official War Artist* (London: ISO Publications, 1990)

Smith, Amanda (ed.), *Hostage to Fortune: The Letters of Joseph P. Kennedy* (New York: Viking Penguin, 2001)

Smith, R. M. with Smith, P. D., *With Chennault in China: A Flying Tiger's Diary* (Blue Ridge Summit, Pa.: Tab Books, 1984)

Soviak, E. (ed.), *A Diary of Darkness: The Wartime Diary of Kiyosawa Kiyoshi* (Princeton: Princeton University Press, 1999)

Stuart, C. (ed.), *The Reith Diaries* (Collins, 1975)

Sulzberger, C. S., *A Long Row of Candles: Memoirs and Diaries 1934–54* (Macdonald, 1969)

Tamura, K., 'A Japanese Soldier's Experience of War', Australia-Japan Research Project, 2001 at ajrp.awm.gov.au/ajrp/ajrp2.nsf/.

Taylor, F. (ed.), *The Goebbels Diaries, 1939–1941* (Hamish Hamilton, 1982)

Tolischus, O. D., *Tokyo Record* (New York: Reynal & Hitchcock, 1943)

Toliver, O. S., *An Artist at War: The Journal of John Gaitha Browning* (Denton, Tex.: University of North Texas Press, 1994)

Traill, H. F. O'B., *Some Shape of Beauty* (Kuala Lumpur: Incorporated Society of Planters, 1986)

Tregaskis, R., *Guadalcanal Diary* (New York: Random House, 1943)

Trevor-Roper, Hugh (ed.), *The Goebbels Diaries: The Last Days* (Secker & Warburg, 1977)

Ugaki, Admiral Matome, *Fading Victory: The Diary of Admiral Matome Ugaki* (Pittsburgh: University of Pittsburgh Press, 1991)

Verreault, G., *Diary of a Prisoner of War in Japan, 1941–1945* (Quebec: Vero, 1996)

Vining, D. (ed.), *American Diaries of World War II* (New York: Pepys Press, 1982)

Vladimirov, P., *The Vladimirov Diaries – Yenan, China: 1942–1945* (New York: Doubleday, 1975)

Welch, John F. (ed.), *Dead Engine Kids: World War II Diary of John J. Briol, B-17 Ball Turret Gunner* (Silver Wings Aviation, 1993)

White, T. H. (ed.), *The Stilwell Papers: Joseph W. Stilwell* (Macdonald, 1949)

Wilkie, William (ed.), *All of 28. And More: The Diary of Edgar Wilkie* (privately published, 1987)

Williamson, M. (ed.), *The Diary of a Virginia Gentlewoman 1943–1947: Laura Crabill Evans (Mrs. Lemuel) of Shenandoah County, Virginia* (privately published, 2000)

Wood, A. (ed.), *If This Should Be Farewell: A Family Separated by War – The Journal and Letters of Ernest and Mary Hodgkin, 1942–45* (Fremantle: Fremantle Arts Centre Press, 2003)

Woodward, J. K., *Three Times Lucky* (Brisbane: Boolarong Publications, 1991)

Wright-Nooth, G., *Prisoner of the Turnip Heads: The Fall of Hong Kong and Imprisonment by the Japanese* (Cassell, 1994)

Zellmer, D., *The Spectator: A World War II Bomber Pilot's Journal of the Artist as a Warrior* (Westport, Conn.: Praeger, 1999)

Ziegler, P. (ed.), *Personal Diary of Admiral the Lord Louis Mountbatten* (London: Collins, 1988)

ACKNOWLEDGEMENT OF PERMISSIONS

The author has endeavoured to identify the current copyright owners of the selections in this book and to obtain permission to include them, whenever necessary. In the event of an error or omission in any acknowledgement, please contact the author through the publisher and, if appropriate, an acknowledgement will be made in future reprints.

Permission for the use of material reproduced in this book was kindly granted by the following archives and individuals with regard to unpublished sources.

From the James Armstrong diary, with the permission of the Australian War Memorial. From the Hilda Bates diary, with the permission of the trustees of the Imperial War Museum. From the Len Baynes diary, with the permission of the Liddle Collection, Brotherton Library, University of Leeds. From the Brigadier E. V. Bowra diary, with the permission of the trustees of the Imperial War Museum. From the Field Marshal Sir Alan Brooke diary, with the permission of the trustees of the Liddell Hart Centre, King's College, London. From the Alexander Cadogan diary, with the permission of the Churchill Archives Centre, Churchill College, Cambridge. From the Reginald Carter diary, with the permission of the British Library. From the Tom Fagan diary, with the permission of the Australian War Memorial. From the Tom Forsyth diary, with the permission of National Archives of Canada. From the G. J. Green diary, with the permission of the trustees of the Imperial War Museum. From the Helen Grimes diary, with the permission of Rhode Island Historical Society Library, Providence. From the Earl of Halifax diary, with the permission of the Borthwick Institute, York. From the Oliver Harvey diary, with the permission of the British Library. From the Tadashi Higa diary, with the permission of the US Naval Historical Center, Navy Yard, Washington DC. From the Joseph Hodder diary, with the permission of Rhodes House, Bodleian Library of Commonwealth and African Studies, University of Oxford. From the Hubert Hooper diary, with the permission of the trustees of the Imperial War Museum. From the Taro Kawaguchi diary, with the permission of Master Sergeant J. William Winter. From the John Kennedy diary, with the permission of the trustees of the Liddell Hart Centre for

Military Archives, King's College, London. From the Captain Koyanango diary, with the permission of the US Army Military History Institute, Carlisle Barracks, Pennsylvania. From the Hilda Lacey diary, with the permission of Rhodes House, Bodleian Library of Commonwealth and African Studies, University of Oxford. From the Fleet Admiral William D. Leahy diary, with the permission of the Library of Congress, Manuscript Division. From the William Leaney diary, with the permission of the trustees of the Imperial War Museum. From the diary of 'Ginger' Leonard, with the permission of B. Z. Leonard. From the Thomas Price Lewis diary, with the permission of Rhodes House, Bodleian Library of Commonwealth and African Studies, University of Oxford. From the Tadayoshi Matsumoto diary, with the permission of the US Naval Historical Center, Navy Yard, Washington DC. From the Commander Hugh Mulleneux diary, with the permission of the trustees of the Liddell Hart Centre for Military Archives, King's College, London. From the Fukuzo Obara diary, with the permission of the US Army Military History Institute, Carlisle Barracks, Pennsylvania. From the Martin Ogle diary, with the permission of Rhodes House, Bodleian Library of Commonwealth and African Studies, University of Oxford. From the J. A. Roxburgh diary, with the permission of the Australian War Memorial. From the Shu Xiangcheng diary, with the permission of Hong Kong University Library. From the Admiral James Somerville diary, with the permission of the trustees of the Churchill Archives Centre, Churchill College, Cambridge. From the Henry L. Stimson diary, with the permission of Yale University Library. From the Richard F. Tamabayashi diary, with the permission of the Hawaii War Record Depository, Thomas Hale Hamilton Library, University of Hawaii at Manoa. From the Les Vancura diary, with the permission of the Liddle Collection, Brotherton Library, University of Leeds. From the F. Watt diary, with the permission of the trustees of the Imperial War Museum. From the Peggy Wightman diary, with the permission of the trustees of the Imperial War Museum. From the Kiyoshi Yamamoto diary, with the permission of the Australian War Memorial. From the anonymous Japanese sergeant's diary captured at Guadalcanal, 18 Jan. 1943, with the permission of the US Naval Historical Center, Navy Yard, Washington DC. From the anonymous pocket diary of a Japanese soldier captured at Guadalcanal 1943, with the permission of the US Naval Historical Center, Navy Yard, Washington DC.

*

Various estates and publishers have kindly granted permission to reproduce extracts from the following copyright works.

From *Diary of a Girl in Changi*, copyright Sheila Allan 1994, reprinted by permission of the publishers, Kangaroo Press. From *Fumiko's Diary*, copyright Fumiko Amano 1995, reprinted by permission of the publishers, Martin's Press. From *One Man's War*, copyright Stan Arneil 1980, reprinted by permission of the publishers, Alternative Publishing Co-operative. From *Shanghai Diary: A Young Girl's Journey from Hitler's Hate to War-Torn China*, copyright Ursula Bacon 2002, reprinted by permission of the publishers, Milestone Books. From *Alone and Loitering: Pages from an Artist's Travel-Diary, 1938–1934*, copyright Sylvia Baker 1947, reprinted by permission of the publishers, The Travel Book Club. From *Bunker's War: The World War II Diary of Col. Paul D. Bunker*, copyright K. A. Barlow 1996, reprinted by permission of the publishers, Presidio. From *The Empire at Bay: The Leo Amery Diaries 1929–1945*, copyright J. Barnes and D. Nicholson 1988, reprinted by permission of the publishers, Hutchinson. From *The War Diary of Clyde J. Berwick*, copyright Clyde Berwick 1994, privately published. From *Second Diary of a Diplomatic Correspondent*, copyright George Bilaikin 1947, reprinted by permission of the publishers, Samson, Low, Marston. From *Vera Brittain, Diary 1939–1945: Wartime Chronicle*, copyright A. Bishop and Y. A. Bennett 1989, reprinted by permission of the publishers, Victor Gollancz. From *Dear Philip: A Diary of Captivity, Changi 1942–45*, copyright Freddy Bloom 1980, reprinted by permission of the publishers, Bodley Head. From *Natalie Crouter, Forbidden Diary: A Record of Wartime Internment, 1941–45*, copyright L. Z. Bloom 1980, reprinted by permission of the publishers, Burt Franklin. From *The Maturing Sun: An Army Nurse in India, 1942–1945*, copyright Angela Bolton 1988, reprinted by permission of the publishers, Headline. From *The Diaries of Lt-General Sir Henry Pownall*, vol. 2: *1940–1944*, copyright B. Bond 1974, reprinted by permission of the publishers, Leo Cooper. From *A Flying Tiger's Diary*, copyright C. R. Bond, Jr and Terry Anderson 1993, reprinted by permission of the publishers, Centennial Series of the Association of Former Students, Texas A&M University. From *Food-Bomber Pilot: China–Burma–India*, copyright Robert T. Boody 1989, privately published. From *The Brereton Diaries: The War in the Air in the Pacific, Middle East and Europe, 3 October 1941 – 8 May 1945*, copyright L. H. Brereton 1946, reprinted by permission of the publishers, William Morrow. From *Suez to Singapore*, copyright Cecil Brown 1942, reprinted by permission of the publishers, Halcyon House. From *Two Years in Ceylon: The Diary of a Naval Secretariat Member, 1944–6*, copyright Alan Brundrett 1996, reprinted by permission of the publishers, The Book Guild. From *Self-Portrait with Friends: The Selected Diaries of Cecil Beaton, 1926–1974*, copyright R. Buckle 1979, reprinted by permission of the publishers, Weidenfeld & Nicolson. From *The Diaries of Edward R. Stettinius, Jr. 1943–1946*, copyright T. M. Campbell and G. C. Herring 1975, reprinted by permission of the publishers, New Viewpoints. From *Torpedo Junction: With the Pacific Fleet from Pearl Harbor to Midway*, copyright R. J. Casey 1942, reprinted by permission of the publishers, Bobbs-Merrill. From *War on Our Doorstep: Diaries of Australians at the Frontline in 1942*, copyright G. Chan 2003, reprinted by permission of the publishers, Hardy Grant Books. From *Saipan: The War Diary of John Ciardi*, copyright J. Ciardi 1988, reprinted by permission of the publishers, University of Arkansas Press. From *Shipyard Diary of a Woman Welder*, copyright A. H. Clawson 1944, reprinted by permission of the publishers, Penguin. From *South to Bataan, North to Mudken: The Prison Diary of Brigadier General W. E. Brougher*, copyright James Clayton 1971, reprinted by permission of the publishers, University of Georgia Press. From *The Fringes of Power*, copyright John Colville 1985, reprinted by permission of the publishers, Hodder & Stoughton. From *Except These Days Were Shortened: A Wartime Diary of the South Pacific W.W. II – 1944–45*, copyright Oscar Conner 1982, reprinted by permission of the publishers, Nature Book Publishing. From *War Diaries 1939–1945: Field Marshal Lord Alanbrooke*, copyright A. Danchev and D. Todman 2001, reprinted by permission of the publishers, Weidenfeld & Nicolson. From *The Diaries of Evelyn Waugh*, copyright M. Davie 1976, reprinted by permission of the publishers, Weidenfeld & Nicolson. From *Mack Morriss: South Pacific Diary 1942–1943*, copyright R. Day 1996, reprinted by permission of the publishers, University Press of Kentucky. From *From Bataan to Tokyo: Diary of a Filipino Student in Wartime Japan, 1943–1944*, copyright L. de Asis 1979, reprinted by perission of the publishers, University of Kansas. From *POW Sketchbook: A Story of Survival*, copyright J. and S. Dewey 1985, reprinted by permission of the publishers, The Pie Powder Press. From *The 1942–1943 Diary of a Corporal Fitter IIE of No. 30 Beaufighter Squadron in New Guinea*, copyright G. T. Dick 1955, reprinted by permission of the publishers, Adam Press. From *The Diaries of Sir Alexander Cadogan, 1938–1945*, copyright David Dilks 1971, reprinted by permission of the publishers, Cassell. From *The Green War*, copyright T. E. Dorman 1977, privately published. From *Pacific War Diary, 1942–5*, copyright J. J. Fahey 1963, reprinted by permission of the publishers, Houghton Mifflin. From *Foo: A Japanese-American Prisoner of the Rising Sun – The Secret Prison Diary of Frank 'Foo' Fujita*, copyright S. L. Faulk 1993, reprinted by permission of the publishers, University of North Texas Press. From *The Diary of H. L. Mencken*, copyright Charles A. Fecher 1989, reprinted by permission of the publishers, Alfred A. Knopf. From 'From Broadway House to Bletchley Park: The Diary of Captain Malcolm Kennedy, 1934–46', copyright John Ferris 1989, reprinted by permission of the publishers, Frank Cass. From *Bilbid Diary: The Secret Notebooks of Commander Thomas Hayes, POW, the Philippines, 1942–45*, copyright A. B. Feuer 1987, reprinted by permission of the publishers, Archon Books. From *NX 20365*, copyright Andy Fletcher 1980, privately published. From *The Fortunate Soldier: With the New Zealand Army on Tongatabu, 1943*, copyright M. R. R. Foord 1996, privately published. From *Beachheads and Black Widows: A South Pacific Diary*, copyright J. H. Gardner 1995, privately published. From *A Call to Arms: War Service with the RAAF 1942–1946, Diary Notes and Memoirs of Arthur Gately*, copyright Arthur Gately 2003, reprinted by permission of the publishers, Fairbairn Aerospace Centre. From *The GI Journal of Sergeant Giles*, copyright J. H. Giles 1965, reprinted by permission of the publishers, Houghton Mifflin. From *Spender: Journals 1939–1983*, copyright J. Goldsmith 1985, reprinted by permission of the publishers, Faber & Faber. From *A Gunner's Eye View: A Wartime Diary of Active Service in New Guinea*, copyright Brian Gomme 1997, privately published. From *The Evacuation Diary of Hatsuye Egami*, copyright C. Gorfinkel 1995, reprinted by permission of the publishers, Intentional Productions. From *Hiroshima Diary: The Journal of a Japanese Physician, August 6 – September 30, 1945*, copyright M. Hachiya 1955, reprinted by permission of the publishers, University of North Carolina Press. From *Love, War, and the 96th Engineers (Colored): The World War II New Guinea Diaries of Captain Hyman Samuelson*, copyright G. M. Hall 2001, reprinted by permission of the publishers, University of Illinois Press. From *Behind the Fence, Life as a POW in Japan: The Diaries of Les Chater*, copyright E. Hamid 2001, reprinted by permission of the publishers, Vanwell Publishing. From *Military Government Journal, Normandy to*

Berlin: Major General John J. Maginnis, copyright R. A. Hart 1971, reprinted by permission of the publishers, University of Massachusetts Press. From *Mother and Son: A Japanese Correspondence*, copyright Ichiko Hatano 1962, reprinted by permission of the publishers, Chatto & Windus. From *Changi Interlude: Leaves from the Diary of a Third Class Internee*, copyright Guy Heriot 1946, reprinted by permission of the publishers, W. E. Baxter. From *Spirits Unbroken: The Story of Three Years in a Civilian Internment Camp under the Japanese, at Baguio and at Old Bilbid Prison in the Philippines, from December 1941 to February 1945*, copyright R. R. Hind 1946, reprinted by permission of the publishers, John Howell. From *Rats of Rangoon: The Inside Story of the 'Fiasco' that Took Place at the End of the War in Burma*, copyright Lionel Hudson 1987, reprinted by permission of the publishers, Leo Cooper. From *The War Time Diary of H. A. Hurst: RAAF A30542 from January 1944 to January 1945*, copyright H. A. Hurst 1997, privately published. From *American Airpower Comes of Age: General Henry H. 'Hap' Arnold's World War II Diaries*, vols 1 and 2, copyright J. W. Huston 2002, reprinted by permission of the publishers, Air University Press. From *From the Somme to Singapore: A Medical Officer in Two World Wars*, copyright Charles Huxtable 1987, reprinted by permission of the publishers, Kangaroo Press. From *Singapore to Colombo: The Diary of C. W. A. Inglis, Indian Engineers*, copyright C. W. Inglis 1945, privately published. From *The War Diary of Breckinridge Long: Selections from the Years 1939–1944*, copyright F. L. Israel 1966, reprinted by permission of the publishers, University of Nebraska Press. From *The Naval Land Unit that Vanished in the Jungle by Tetsuo Watanabe*, copyright H. Iwamoto 1995, reprinted by permission of the publishers, Tabletop Press. From *Getting My Knees Brown: The War Diary of 14239274 Signalman John Edward Jowers, 1st January 1943 – 28th April 1946, While Serving in India, Burma & Thailand with 228 Indian Wing Signal Section, 6 Indian Air Formation Signals*, copyright J. E. Jowers 1977, privately published. From *Merchant Marine War Diary (1944): Saipan–Pelelieu*, copyright Henry Kasper 1990, reprinted by permission of the publishers, Vantage Press. From *Life and Death in Changi: The War and Internment Diary of Thomas Kitching*, copyright G. E. Kheng 2002, reprinted by permission of the publishers, Landmark Books. From *The Diary of Marquis Kido, 1931–45: Selected Translations into English*, copyright Koichi Kido 1984, reprinted by permission of the publishers, University Publications of America. From *Strangers Always: A Jewish Family in Wartime Shanghai*, copyright

Rena Krasno 1992, reprinted by permission of the publishers, Pacific View Press. From *A Diary of the Japanese Occupation: December 7, 1941 – May 7, 1945*, copyright Juan Labrador 1989, reprinted by permission of the publishers, Santo Tomas University Press. From *We Flee From Hong Kong*, copyright Alice Lan and Betty Hu 1944, reprinted by permission of the publishers, Evangelical Publishers. From *The Sun Goes Down: Last Letters from Japanese Suicide-Pilots and Soldiers*, copyright J. Larteguy 1973, reprinted by permission of the publishers, New English Library. From *Diary of a Washington Correspondent*, copyright David Lawrence 1942, reprinted by permission of the publishers, H. C. Kinsey & Co. From *Partridge in a Swamp: The Journals of Viola C. White 1918–1941*, copyright W. S. Lee 1979, reprinted by permission of the publishers, The Countryman Press. From *The London Observer: The Journal of General Raymond E. Lee 1940–1941*, copyright James Leutze 1971, reprinted by permission of the publishers, Hutchinson. From *The Mammoth Book of War Diaries and Letters*, copyright J. E. Lewis 1998, reprinted by permission of the publishers, Carroll & Graf. From *Changi – the Lost Years: A Malayan Diary 1941–1945*, copyright Thomas Price Lewis 1984, reprinted by permission of the publishers, Malayan Historical Society. From *'Dear Mother Putnam': A Diary of the War in the Philippines*, copyright Marcel Lichauco 1949, privately published. From *The Journal of David E. Lilienthal*, vol. 1: *The TVA Years, 1939–1945*, copyright David Lilienthal 1964, reprinted by permission of the publishers, Harper & Row. From *War Within and Without: Diaries and Letters, Nineteen Thirty-Nine to Nineteen Forty-Four*, copyright Anne Morrow Lindbergh 1980, reprinted by permission of the publishers, Harcourt Brace Jovanovich. From *The Wartime Journals of Charles A. Lindbergh*, copyright Charles Lindbergh 1970, reprinted by permission of the publishers, Harcourt Brace Jovanovich. From 'Diary of First Lieutenant Sugihara Kinryu: Iwo Jima, January–February 1945', copyright S. J. Lofgren 1995, reprinted by permission of the publishers, *The Journal of Military History*. From *Mates in Hell: SX8918 The Secret Diary of Don McLaren, Prisoner of the Japanese, Changi, Burma Railway, Japan 1942–1945*, copyright Don McLaren 1998, reprinted by permission of the publishers, Seaview Press. From *Tin Can Duty in the Pacific 1943–1944–1945*, copyright J. McNamara 1980, privately published. From *Final Assault on the Rising Sun: Combat Diaries of B-29 Air Crews over Japan*, copyright Chester W. Marshall 1995, reprinted by permission of the publishers, Speciality Press. From *Motor Transport at War: The Diary of NX 18655 Dvr.*

Mathieson, F.G. 1940–45 Ex 2nd Division AASC, copyright Fred Mathieson 1992, privately published. From *Submarine Diary: The Silent Stalking of Japan*, copyright Corwin Mendenhall 1991, reprinted by permission of the publishers, Algonquin Books. From *Nothing Less than Victory*, copyright R. Miller 1993, reprinted by permission of the publishers, Morrow. From *Yoshida Mitsuru: Requiem for Battleship Yamato*, copyright R. H. Minear 1985, reprinted by permission of the publishers, University of Washington Press. From *For Your Tomorrow: A Cipher-Sergeant's Diary, 1941–1945*, copyright Eric Murrell 1999, reprinted by permission of the publishers, Plush Publishing. From *The War Diaries of Eddie Allan Stanton: Papua 1942–45, New Guinea 1945–46*, copyright Hank Nelson 1996, reprinted by permission of the publishers, Allen & Unwin. From *From the Bush to Changi and Back: Personal War Diary 1941–1945*, copyright J. Nevell 1998, privately published. From *Diary of Masako Nojiri in a Defeated War*, copyright Masako Nojiri 1995, reprinted by permission of the publishers, Grass Thinking Society. From *London War Notes, 1939–1945*, copyright Mollie Panter-Downes 1971, reprinted by permission of the publishers, Farrar, Straus & Giroux. From *Everything to Lose: Diaries, May 1945 – December 1960*, copyright F. Partridge 1985, reprinted by permission of the publishers, Phoenix. From *China Awake*, copyright Robert Payne 1947, reprinted by permission of the publishers, Vail-Ballou Press. From *The Emperor's Guest: The Diary of a British Prisoner-of-War of the Japanese in Indonesia*, copyright Don Peacock 1989, reprinted by permission of the publishers, Oleander Press. From *The Ordeal of Elizabeth Vaughan: A Wartime Diary of the Philippines*, copyright C. M. Petillo 1985, reprinted by permission of the publishers, University of Georgia Press. From *The Second World War Diaries of Hugh Dalton, 1940–45*, copyright Ben Pimlott 1986, reprinted by permission of the publishers, Jonathan Cape. From *The Barbarians: A Soldier's New Guinea Diary*, copyright Peter Pinney 1988, reprinted by permission of the publishers, University of Queensland Press. From *The Glass Cannon: A Bougainville Diary 1944–45*, copyright Peter Pinney 1990, reprinted by permission of the publishers, University of Queensland Press. From *The Devil's Garden: Solomon Islands War Diary, 1945*, copyright Peter Pinney 1992, reprinted by permission of the publishers, University of Queensland Press. From *I Am Well, Who Are You? Writing of a Japanese Prisoner of War*, copyright D. Piper 1998, reprinted by permission of the publishers, Brightsea Press. From *Diary of Military Government in Germany 1945*, copyright

B. N. Reckitt 1989, reprinted by permission of the publishers, Stockwell. From *Flying MacArthur to Victory*, copyright W. E. Rhoades 1987, reprinted by permission of the publishers, Texas A&M Press. From *The Siren Years: Undiplomatic Diaries, 1937–1945*, copyright Charles Ritchie 1974, reprinted by permission of the publishers, Macmillan. From *Intermittent Diplomat: The Japan and Batavia Diaries of W. MacMahon Ball*, copyright A. Rix 1988, reprinted by permission of the publishers, Melbourne University Press. From *Overseas Diary: India and Burma, World War II*, copyright F. C. Robbins 1990, reprinted by permission of the publishers, Rumaro Press. From *Joyce Grenfell. The Time of My Life: Entertaining the Troops – Her Wartime Journals*, copyright J. Roose-Evans 1989, reprinted by permission of the publishers, Hodder & Stoughton. From *Seven Stars: The Okinawa Battle Diaries of Simon Bolivar Buckner Jr., and Joseph Stilwell*, copyright N. Sarantakes 2004, reprinted by permission of the publishers, Texas A&M University Press. From *Bless 'em All: Pages from the Diary of an Official War Artist*, copyright Alf Simpson 1990, reprinted by permission of the publishers, ISO Publications. From *Hostage to Fortune: The Letters of Joseph P. Kennedy*, copyright Amanda Smith 2001, reprinted by permission of the publishers, Viking Penguin. From *With Chennault in China: A Flying Tiger's Diary*, copyright Robert Moody Smith 1984, reprinted by permission of the publishers, Tab Books Inc. From *A Diary of Darkness: The Wartime Diary of Kiyosawa Kiyoshi*, copyright E. Soviak 1999, reprinted by permission of the publishers, Princeton University Press. From *The Reith Diaries*, copyright C. Stuart 1975, reprinted by permission of the publishers, Collins. From 'A Japanese Soldier's Experience of War', copyright K. Tamura 2001, reprinted by permission of the Australia–Japan Research Project, Australian War Memorial. From *The Goebbels Diaries, 1939–1941*, copyright F. Taylor 1982, reprinted by permission of the publishers, Hamish Hamilton. From *Tokyo Record*, copyright Otto Tolischus 1943, reprinted by permission of the publishers, Reynal & Hitchcock. From *An Artist at War: The Journal of John Gaitha Browning*, copyright O. S. Toliver 1994, reprinted by permission of the publishers, University of North Texas Press. From *Some Shape of Beauty*, copyright Henry F. O'B. Traill 1986, reprinted by permission of the publishers, The Incorporated Society of Planters. From *Guadalcanal Diary*, copyright Richard Tregaskis 1943, reprinted by permission of the publishers, Random House. From *Fading Victory: The Diary of Admiral Matome Ugaki*, copyright Matome Ugaki 1991, reprinted by permission of the publishers, University of Pittsburgh Press. From *Diary of a Prisoner of War in Japan, 1941–1945*, copyright Georges Verreault 1996, reprinted by permission of the publishers, Vero. From *American Diaries of World War II*, copyright D. Vining 1982, reprinted by permission of the publishers, The Pepys Press. From *The Vladimirov Diaries – Yenan, China: 1942–1945*, copyright P. Vladimirov 1975, reprinted by permission of the publishers, Doubleday. From *Dead Engine Kids: World War II Diary of John J. Briol, B-17 Ball Turret Gunner*, copyright John F. Welch 1993, reprinted by permission of the publishers, Silver Wings Aviation. From *The Stilwell Papers: Joseph W. Stilwell*, copyright Theodore White 1949, reprinted by permission of the publishers, Macdonald. From *All of 28. And More: The Diary of Edgar Wilkie*, copyright William Wilkie 1987, privately published. From *The Diary of a Virginia Gentlewoman 1943–1947: Laura Crabill Evans*, copyright M. Williamson 2000, privately published. From *If This Should Be Farewell: A Family Separated by War – The Journal and Letters of Ernest and Mary Hodgkin, 1942–45*, copyright Adrian Wood 2003, reprinted by permission of the publishers, Fremantle Arts Centre Press. From *Three Times Lucky*, copyright J. K. Woodward 1991, reprinted by permission of the publishers, Boolarong Publications. From *Prisoner of the Turnip Heads: The Fall of Hong Kong and Imprisonment by the Japanese*, copyright G. Wright-Nooth 1994, reprinted by permission of the publishers, Cassell. From *The Spectator: A World War II Bomber Pilot's Journal of the Artist as a Warrior*, copyright David Zellmer 1999, reprinted by permission of the publishers, Praeger. From *Personal Diary of Admiral the Lord Louis Mountbatten*, copyright Philip Ziegler 1988, reprinted by permission of the publishers, Collins.

ILLUSTRATION CREDITS

The author and publishers would like to thank the following for permission to reproduce illustrations, including the Australian War Memorial, Canberra (AWM), the Imperial War Museum, London (IWM) and the United States National Archives (USNA).

In-text illustrations: p. 72: Vera Brittain, 1936, by Howard Coster, National Portrait Gallery, London; p. 87: Leo Amery, Imperial War Museum NA18546; p. 97: Sir John Reith, newly appointed Minister of Information, 30 January 1940, © Bettmann/CORBIS; p. 103: Hyman Samuelson, courtesy of Illinois University Press; p. 108: Oliver Harvey, Camera Press/David Gurney; p. 117: Colonel Lewis Brereton, AWM MED0878; p. 119: Henry L. Stimson, USNA ARC Identifier 199142; p. 150: Anne Lindbergh, 3193, courtesy of Yale University Library; p. 190: Alice Lan and Betty Hu, courtesy of the Bethel Mission; p. 200: Sir Henry Pownall, IWM IB 1100C; p. 222: Tom Fagan, AWM 122088; p. 305: Mao Tse-tung, USNA ARC Identifier 196235; p. 320: Corwin Mendenhall, courtesy of the US Navy; p. 330: William Leaney, courtesy of the IWM Department of Documents; p. 359: Joseph Stilwell, AWM 012495; p. 392: Henry L. Mencken,- courtesy of the Enoch Pratt Free Library, Baltimore; p. 421: Joseph Stilwell with Chiang Kai-shek and Mme Chiang, USNA, ARC Identifier 531135; p. 449: Andy Fletcher, AWM 108315; p. 463: Admiral Lord Louis Mountbatten, IWM IB 120; p. 514: 'Dusty' Rhoades, AWM 015199; p. 521: Cecil Beaton, IWM IB 4287C; p. 530: Jesse Gardner, courtesy of Jesse Gardner; p. 544: Edward Stettinius, Alexander Cadogan and Averell Harriman, USNA ARC Identifier 195331; p. 562: Gordon Grimsdale with Claire Chennault, IWM IB 1100C; p. 598: Charles MacDonald and Charles Lindbergh, 5108, courtesy of Yale University Library; p. 656: Lionel Hudson, AWM SEA0241; p. 660: Harry Hurst, AWM P01590.001; p. 684: Hilda Bates, IWM Department of Documents; p. 696: Sir James Somerville, USNA 111-SC-231780; p. 763: Harry Truman, 28 April 1945, Bettmann/CORBIS; p. 829: William MacMahon Ball, AWM 003532.

Plate section: p. 1: above, AWM P02223.001; below, USNA 080-G-19948; p. 2: above, AWM 127893; below, AWM 011529/15; p. 3: above, IWM IND 875; below, USNA 208-AA12X-21; p. 4: above, USNA 111-

SC-197901; below, USNA 210-G-3C-310; p. 5: AWM P00455.005; p. 6: above, AWM 026018; below, AWM 030375/03; p. 7: above, AWM 014235; below, IWM IND 2084; p. 8: above, AWM 127638; middle, AWM P00406.034; below, AWM 120517; p. 9: above, IWM IB 2904C; below, AWM 072837; p. 10: IWM IND 4652; p. 11: above, USNA II-SC-317845; below, USNA ARC Identifier 520756; p. 12: above, USNA ARC Identifier 513218; side, USNA 0333 TR 11 947; below, AWM P02018.393; p. 13: above, USNA ARC Identifier 520868; below, AWM P01234.010; p. 14: USNA 080-G-490320; p. 15: above right, IWM IND 4845; below right, AWM P02491.065; left, IWM IND 4772; p. 16: above, USNA 080-G-490444; below, AWM P02310.007.

Material for the inside covers was kindly provided by the Public Record Office, and taken from the diaries of William J. Leaney and Lieutenant Hubert Hooper, which are lodged in the Imperial War Museum.

INDEX

Saving Your Diaries from the Dustbin of History

Every day new and exciting materials concerning the Second World War come to light. Sometimes these are found by relatives and, happily, they become treasured family possessions. However, it is not unusual for them to be found in old chests of drawers by house-clearers and then thrown away. Even when their historical value is recognized by relatives or friends, there is often puzzlement about what to do with the material. Giving or lending diaries to an established archive, or making a photocopy available, ensures the long-term professional preservation of the information. It also ensures the material is accessible to historians who are writing books about the war. In turn, this means that the author of the diary is able to make a wider contribution to the history of the period that they so painstakingly recorded, or even perhaps to find their own 'place in history'.

Over the years I have given material I have come across to the Liddell Hart Centre for Military Archives at King's College, London. The best locations to deposit war diaries are centres that specialize in the history of warfare, and there are many choices. Some of the most important ones are the following:

- The Australian War Memorial, GPO Box 345, Canberra ACT 2601, Australia, tel. +61 (02) 6243 4315, fax +61 (02) 6243 4545 www.awm.gov.au/index.asp
- Churchill Archives Centre, Churchill College, University of Cambridge, Cambridge CB3 0DS, tel. 01223 336087, fax 01223 336135
  www.chu.cam.ac.uk/archives/home.shtml
- Imperial War Museum, Department of Documents, Lambeth Road, London SE1 6HZ, tel. 020 7416 5000, fax 020 7416 5374 www.iwm.org.uk/corporate/contact.htm
- Liddell Hart Centre for Military Archives, King's College, The Strand, London WC2R 2LS, tel.: 020 7848 2187 or 020 7848 2015, fax 020 7848 2760 www.kcl.ac.uk/lhcma/home.htm

There are also many specialist museums and archives dealing with particular branches of the services, corps or regiments. Wherever you live there will also be a specialist archive or a major library near you. In many cases this will be the local county archive or the 'special collections' section of the library of a nearby university. Many universities have units that deal with particular types of records. For example, the University of Sussex looks after the superb Mass-Observation Archive, while the University of Warwick hosts the Modern Records Centre.

Few war records are worthless, and our view of what is important is always changing. At one time the main interest was the papers of generals and admirals; now the lives of ambulance drivers, munitions workers and children are considered no less fascinating. We cannot know which aspects of history future generations will wish to explore. However, we can take the trouble to preserve our family materials and offer our successors the richest opportunities for exploring every aspect of the past. Those who took the trouble to keep their diaries from a 'faraway war' deserve nothing less.